Ultra-High Field Neuro MRI

Advances in Magnetic Resonance Technology and Applications Series

Series Editors

In-Young Choi, PhD
Department of Neurology, Department of Radiology, Department of Molecular & Integrative Physiology, Hoglund Biomedical Imaging Center, University of Kansas Medical Center, Kansas City, KS, United States

Peter Jezzard, PhD
Wellcome Centre for Integrative Neuroimaging, Nuffield Department of Clinical Neurosciences University of Oxford, Oxford, United Kingdom

Brian Hargreaves, PhD
Department of Radiology, Department of Electrical Engineering, Department of Bioengineering Stanford University, Stanford, CA, United States

Greg Zaharchuk, MD, PhD
Department of Radiology, Stanford University, Stanford, CA, United States

Titles published:

Volume 1 – Quantitative Magnetic Resonance Imaging – Edited by Nicole Seiberlich and Vikas Gulani

Volume 2 – Handbook of Pediatric Brain Imaging – Edited by Hao Huang and Timothy Roberts

Volume 3 – Hyperpolarized Carbon-13 Magnetic Resonance Imaging and Spectroscopy – Edited by Peder Larson

Volume 4 – Advanced Neuro MR Techniques and Applications – Edited by In-Young Choi and Peter Jezzard

Volume 5 – Breast MRI – Edited by Katja Pinker, Ritse Mann and Savannah Partridge

Volume 6 – Motion Correction in MR – Edited by André Van Der Kouwe and Jalal B. Andre

Volume 7 – Magnetic Resonance Image Reconstruction – Edited by Mehmet Akçakaya, Mariya Doneva and Claudia Prieto

Volume 8 – MR Linac Radiotherapy – Edited by Enis Ozyar, Cem Onal and Sara L. Hackett

Volume 9 – Imaging Neuroinflammation – Edited by Cornelia Laule and John D. Port

Visit the Series webpage at https://www.elsevier.com/books/book-series/advances-in-magnetic-resonance-technology-and-applications

Advances in Magnetic Resonance Technology and Applications

Volume 10

Ultra-High Field Neuro MRI

Edited by

Karin Markenroth Bloch
Lund University BioImaging Center, Lund University, Lund, Sweden

Maxime Guye
Centre for Magnetic Resonance in Biology and Medicine, Aix-Marseille University, Marseille, France

Benedikt A. Poser
Faculty of Psychology and Neuroscience, Maastricht University, Maastricht, The Netherlands

ACADEMIC PRESS

An imprint of Elsevier

ELSEVIER

Academic Press is an imprint of Elsevier
50 Hampshire Street, 5th Floor, Cambridge, MA 02139, United States
525 B Street, Suite 1650, San Diego, CA 92101, United States
The Boulevard, Langford Lane, Kidlington, Oxford OX5 1GB, United Kingdom
125 London Wall, London, EC2Y 5AS, United Kingdom

Notices

Knowledge and best practice in this field are constantly changing. As new research and experience broaden our understanding, changes in research methods, professional practices, or medical treatment may become necessary.

Practitioners and researchers must always rely on their own experience and knowledge in evaluating and using any information, methods, compounds, or experiments described herein. In using such information or methods they should be mindful of their own safety and the safety of others, including parties for whom they have a professional responsibility.

To the fullest extent of the law, neither the Publisher nor the authors, contributors, or editors, assume any liability for any injury and/or damage to persons or property as a matter of products liability, negligence or otherwise, or from any use or operation of any methods, products, instructions, or ideas contained in the material herein.

ISBN: 978-0-323-99898-7
ISSN: 2666-9099

For information on all Academic Press publications visit
our website at https://www.elsevier.com/books-and-journals

Original cover art by Emilia Bloch, all rights reserved ©
The MR images are reproduced from chapters 1, 11, 12 and 13 with the authors' consent.

Publisher: Mara E. Conner
Acquisitions Editor: Tim Pitts
Developmental Editor: Emily Thomson
Production Project Manager: Surya Narayanan Jayachandran
Cover Designer: Vicky Pearson Esser

Typeset by STRAIVE, India

Working together
to grow libraries in
developing countries

www.elsevier.com • www.bookaid.org

Contents

v

List of contributors

Nicolas S. Arango
Department of Electrical Engineering, Massachusetts Institute of Technology, Cambridge, MA, United States

David Berron
German Center for Neurodegenerative Diseases, Magdeburg, Germany

Matthew J. Betts
Institute of Cognitive Neurology and Dementia Research, Otto-von-Guericke University Magdeburg; German Center for Neurodegenerative Diseases (DZNE); Center for Behavioral Brain Sciences, University of Magdeburg, Magdeburg, Germany

Berkin Bilgic
Athinoula A. Martinos Center for Biomedical Imaging, Charlestown; Department of Radiology, Harvard Medical School, Boston, MA, United States

Isabella M. Björkman-Burtscher
Department of Radiology, Institute of Clinical Sciences, Sahlgrenska Academy, University of Gothenburg; Department of Radiology, Sahlgrenska University Hospital, Gothenburg, Sweden

Vincent Oltman Boer
Center for Functional and Diagnostic Imaging and Research, Danish Research Centre for Magnetic Resonance, Copenhagen University Hospital—Hvidovre and Amager, Hvidovre, Denmark

Saskia Bollmann
School of Information Technology and Electrical Engineering, Faculty of Engineering, Architecture and Information Technology, The University of Queensland, Brisbane, QLD, Australia

Nicolas Boulant
University of Paris-Saclay, CEA, CNRS, BAOBAB, NeuroSpin, Gif sur Yvette, France

Richard Bowtell
Sir Peter Mansfield Imaging Centre, School of Physics and Astronomy, University of Nottingham, Nottingham, United Kingdom

Henry Braun
Center for Magnetic Resonance Research/Radiology, University of Minnesota, Minneapolis, MN, United States

Jonathan C.W. Brooks
Wellcome Wolfson Brain Imaging Centre, University of East Anglia, Norwich, United Kingdom

Matthan W.A. Caan
Department of Biomedical Engineering and Physics, Amsterdam UMC, Location AMC, Amsterdam, The Netherlands

Virginie Callot
Aix-Marseille University, CNRS, CRMBM; APHM, Hôpital Universitaire Timone, CEMEREM, Marseille, France

Kimberly L. Chan
Advanced Imaging Research Center, University of Texas Southwestern Medical Center, Dallas, TX, United States

Stuart Clare
Nuffield Department of Clinical Neurosciences; Wellcome Centre for Integrative Neuroimaging, University of Oxford, Oxford, United Kingdom

Jérémie D. Clément
System Technologies, Siemens Healthcare GmbH, Erlangen, Germany

Anna J.E. Combes
Vanderbilt University Institute of Imaging Science; Department of Radiology and Radiological Sciences, Vanderbilt University Medical Center, Nashville, TN, United States

Mirco Cosottini
Department of Translational Research and New Technologies in Medicine and Surgery, University of Pisa, Pisa, Italy

Tolga Cukur
Department of Electrical and Electronics Engineering; National Magnetic Resonance Research Center (UMRAM), Bilkent University, Ankara, Turkey

Andreas Deistung
Erwin L. Hahn Institute for Magnetic Resonance Imaging, University of Duisburg-Essen, Duisburg; University Clinic and Outpatient Clinic for Radiology, University Hospital Halle (Saale), Halle (Saale), Germany

Aurélien Destruel
Aix-Marseille University CNRS, CRMBM; APHM, Hôpital Universitaire Timone, CEMEREM, Marseille, France

Graziella Donatelli
Department of Diagnostics and Imaging, Azienda Ospedaliero Universitaria Pisana; Imago7 Research Foundation, Pisa, Italy

Serge O. Dumoulin
Spinoza Centre for Neuroimaging; Computational Cognitive Neuroscience and Neuroimaging, Netherlands Institute for Neuroscience; Experimental and Applied Psychology, Vrije Universiteit Amsterdam, Amsterdam; Experimental Psychology, Utrecht University, Utrecht, The Netherlands

Emrah Düzel
Institute of Cognitive Neurology and Dementia Research, Otto-von-Guericke University Magdeburg; German Center for Neurodegenerative Diseases (DZNE); Center for Behavioral Brain Sciences, University of Magdeburg, Magdeburg, Germany; Institute of Cognitive Neuroscience, University College London, London, United Kingdom

Jozien Goense
Department of Psychology, University of Illinois Urbana-Champaign, Champaign; Department of Bioengineering; Beckman Institute for Advance Science and Technology; Neuroscience Program, University of Illinois Urbana-Champaign, Urbana, IL, United States

Xenia Grande
Institute of Cognitive Neurology and Dementia Research, Otto von Guericke University; German Center for Neurodegenerative Diseases, Magdeburg, Germany

Vincent Gras
University of Paris-Saclay, CEA, CNRS, BAOBAB, NeuroSpin, Gif sur Yvette, France

Dorothea Hämmerer
Institute of Cognitive Neurology and Dementia Research, Otto-von-Guericke University Magdeburg; German Center for Neurodegenerative Diseases (DZNE); Center for Behavioral Brain Sciences, University of Magdeburg, Magdeburg, Germany; Institute of Cognitive Neuroscience, University College London, London, United Kingdom

Gilbert Hangel
Department of Neurosurgery; High Field MR Centre, Medical University of Vienna, Vienna, Austria

Boel Hansson
Department of Medical Imaging and Physiology, Skane University Hospital, Lund, Sweden

Noam Harel
Center for Magnetic Resonance Research/Radiology, University of Minnesota, Minneapolis, MN, United States

Olivia K. Harrison
Department of Psychology, University of Otago, Dunedin, New Zealand; Translational Neuromodeling Unit, Institute for Biomedical Engineering, University of Zurich and ETH Zurich, Zurich, Switzerland; Nuffield Department of Clinical Neurosciences, University of Oxford, Oxford, United Kingdom

Anke Henning
Advanced Imaging Research Center, University of Texas Southwestern Medical Center, Dallas, TX, United States; Max Planck Institute for Biological Cybernetics, Tübingen, Germany

Tom Hilbert
Advanced Clinical Imaging Technology, Siemens Healthcare AG; Department of Radiology, Lausanne University Hospital and University of Lausanne; LTS5, EPFL, The Swiss Federal Institute of Technology in Lausanne, Lausanne, Switzerland

Laurentius Huber
Maastricht Brain Imaging Centre, Faculty of Psychology and Neuroscience, Maastricht University, Maastricht, Netherlands; Functional Magnetic Resonance Imaging Facility, National Institute of Mental Health, National Institutes of Health, Bethesda, MD, United States

Özlem Ipek
School of Biomedical Engineering and Imaging Sciences, King's College London, London, United Kingdom

Kesavi Kanagasabai
Department of Medical Biophysics, Western University, London, ON, Canada

Lars Kasper
Techna Institute to Krembil Brain Institute, University Health Network Toronto, Toronto, ON, Canada

Evgeniya Kirilina
Department of Neurophysics, Max Planck Institute for Human Cognitive and Brain Sciences, Leipzig, Germany

Tomas Knapen
Spinoza Centre for Neuroimaging; Computational Cognitive Neuroscience and Neuroimaging, Netherlands Institute for Neuroscience; Experimental and Applied Psychology, Vrije Universiteit Amsterdam, Amsterdam, The Netherlands

Oliver Kraff
University Duisburg-Essen, Erwin L. Hahn Institute for MRI, Essen, Germany

Mark E. Ladd
Erwin L. Hahn Institute for MRI, University Duisburg-Essen, Essen; Medical Physics in Radiology, German Cancer Research Center (DKFZ); Faculty of Medicine; Faculty of Physics and Astronomy, Heidelberg University, Heidelberg, Germany

Katie M. Lavigne
Douglas Mental Health University Institute; Department of Psychiatry; Montreal Neurological Institute-Hospital, McGill University, Montreal, QC, Canada

Stéphane Lehéricy
Paris Brain Institute Center for NeuroImaging Research—CENIR; Sorbonne University, UMR S 1127, CNRS UMR 7225, ICM Team Movement, Investigations and Therapeutics (MOVIT); Neuroradiology Department, Pitie-Salpetriere hospital, Assistance Publique—Hôpitaux de Paris, Paris, France

Caterina Mainero
Athinoula A. Martinos Center for Biomedical Imaging, Department of Radiology, Massachusetts General Hospital; Harvard Medical School, Boston, MA, United States

Shaihan J. Malik
School of Biomedical Engineering and Imaging Sciences, King's College London, London, United Kingdom

José P. Marques
Radboud University, Donders Institute for Brain, Cognition and Behaviour, Centre for Cognitive Neuroimaging, Nijmegen, The Netherlands

Angelika Mennecke
Institute of Neuroradiology, Universitätsklinikum Erlangen, Friedrich-Alexander-Universität Erlangen-Nürnberg, Erlangen, Germany

Mahmud Mossa-Basha
Department of Radiology, University of Washington, Seattle, United States

Armin N. Nagel
Institute of Radiology, Friedrich-Alexander-Universität Erlangen-Nürnberg (FAU), University Hospital Erlangen, Erlangen; Division of Medical Physics in Radiology, German Cancer Research Center (DKFZ), Heidelberg, Germany

Aart J. Nederveen
Department of Radiology and Nuclear Medicine, Amsterdam UMC, Location AMC, Amsterdam, The Netherlands

Christian Neelsen
Division of Radiology, German Cancer Research Center (DKFZ), Heidelberg; Department of Radiology, Charité-Universitätsmedizin, Berlin, Germany

Markus Nilsson
Diagnostic Radiology, Department of Clinical Sciences Lund, Lund University, Lund, Sweden

David G. Norris
Donders Institute for Brain, Cognition and Behaviour, Radboud University Nijmegen, Nijmegen, The Netherlands; Erwin L. Hahn Institute for MRI, University Duisburg-Essen, Essen, Germany

Nils Nothnagel
School of Psychology and Neuroscience, University of Glasgow, Glasgow, United Kingdom

Stephan Orzada
German Cancer Research Center (DKFZ), Medical Physics in Radiology (E020), Heidelberg, Germany

Daniel Paech
Division of Radiology, German Cancer Research Center (DKFZ), Heidelberg; Clinic for Neuroradiology, University Hospital Bonn, Bonn, Germany

Lena Palaniyappan
Douglas Mental Health University Institute, Montreal, QC; Robarts Research Institute; Department of Medical Biophysics, Western University, London, ON; Department of Psychiatry, McGill University, Montreal, QC, Canada

Tara Palnitkar
Center for Magnetic Resonance Research/Radiology, University of Minnesota, Minneapolis, MN, United States

Rémi Patriat
Center for Magnetic Resonance Research/Radiology, University of Minnesota, Minneapolis, MN, United States

Valentina Perosa
German Center for Neurodegenerative Diseases (DZNE), Magdeburg, Germany; J. Philip Kistler Stroke Research Center, Department of Neurology, Massachusetts General Hospital, Harvard Medical School, Boston, MA, United States

Kerrin Pine
Department of Neurophysics, Max Planck Institute for Human Cognitive and Brain Sciences, Leipzig, Germany

Bruno Pinho-Meneses
Siemens Healthineers, MR Magnet Technology, Eynsham, Oxon, United Kingdom

Jonathan R. Polimeni
Athinoula A. Martinos Center for Biomedical Imaging, Massachusetts General Hospital, Charlestown; Department of Radiology, Harvard Medical School, Boston; Division of Health Sciences and Technology, Massachusetts Institute of Technology, Cambridge, MA, United States

Nikos Priovoulos
Spinoza Centre for Neuroimaging, Royal Netherlands Academy of Arts and Sciences (KNAW); Department of Biomedical Engineering and Physics, Amsterdam UMC, Amsterdam, Netherlands

Martin Reuter
Athinoula A. Martinos Center for Biomedical Imaging, Massachusetts General Hospital, Charlestown; Department of Radiology, Harvard Medical School, Boston, MA, United States; German Center for Neurodegenerative Diseases (DZNE), Bonn, Germany

Simon Daniel Robinson
High Field MR Centre, Department of Biomedical Imaging and Image-Guided Therapy, Medical University of Vienna, Vienna; Department of Neurology, Medical University of Graz, Graz, Austria; Centre of Advanced Imaging, University of Queensland, Brisbane, QLD, Australia

William D. Rooney
Advanced Imaging Research Center, Oregon Health and Science University, Portland, OR, United States

Karl Rössler
Department of Neurosurgery, Medical University of Vienna, Vienna, Austria

Loreen Ruhm
Advanced Imaging Research Center, University of Texas Southwestern Medical Center, Dallas, TX, United States; Max Planck Institute for Biological Cybernetics, Tübingen, Germany

Bobby A. Runderkamp
Department of Radiology and Nuclear Medicine, Amsterdam UMC, Location AMC, Amsterdam, The Netherlands

Ferdinand Schweser
Buffalo Neuroimaging Analysis Center, Department of Neurology, Jacobs School of Medicine and Biomedical Sciences; Center for Biomedical Imaging, Clinical and Translational Science Institute, University at Buffalo, The State University of New York, New York, NY, United States

Xingfeng Shao
Laboratory of FMRI Technology (LOFT), USC Mark & Mary Stevens Neuroimaging and Informatics Institute, Keck School of Medicine, University of Southern California, Los Angeles, CA, United States

Seth A. Smith
Vanderbilt University Institute of Imaging Science; Department of Radiology and Radiological Sciences, Vanderbilt University Medical Center, Nashville, TN, United States

Oren Solomona
Center for Magnetic Resonance Research/Radiology, University of Minnesota, Minneapolis, MN, United States

Jason P. Stockmann
A. A. Martinos Center for Biomedical Imaging, Massachusetts General Hospital, Charlestown; Harvard Medical School, Boston, MA, United States

Dagmar Timmann
Department of Neurology and Center for Translational Neuro- and Behavioral Sciences (C-TNBS), Essen University Hospital; Erwin L. Hahn Institute for Magnetic Resonance Imaging, University of Duisburg-Essen, Duisburg, Germany

Michela Tosetti
Laboratory of Medical Physics and Magnetic Resonance, IRCCS Stella Maris, Pisa, Italy

Siegfried Trattnig
High Field MR Centre, Medical University of Vienna, Vienna, Austria

Constantina A. Treaba
Athinoula A. Martinos Center for Biomedical Imaging, Department of Radiology, Massachusetts General Hospital; Harvard Medical School, Boston, MA, United States

Kamil Ugurbil
Center for Magnetic Resonance Research (CMRR); Departments of Radiology, Neurosciences and Medicine, University of Minnesota, Minneapolis, MN, United States

Kâmil Uludağ
Techna Institute to Krembil Brain Institute, University Health Network Toronto; Department of Medical Biophysics, University of Toronto, Toronto, ON, Canada; Center for Neuroscience Imaging Research, Institute for Basic Science & Department of Biomedical Engineering, Sungkyunkwan University, Suwon, Republic of Korea

Anja Gwendolyn van der Kolk
Department of Medical Imaging, Radboudumc Nijmegen, Nijmegen, The Netherlands

Wietske van der Zwaag
Spinoza Centre for Neuroimaging, Royal Netherlands Academy of Arts and Sciences (KNAW); Computational Cognitive Neuroscience and Neuroimaging, Netherlands Institute for Neuroscience, KNAW, Amsterdam, Netherlands

Luca Vizioli
Center for Magnetic Resonance Research (CMRR), University of Minnesota, Minneapolis, MN, United States

Danny J.J. Wang
Laboratory of FMRI Technology (LOFT), USC Mark & Mary Stevens Neuroimaging and Informatics Institute, Keck School of Medicine, University of Southern California, Los Angeles, CA, United States

Andrew Webb
C.J. Gorter Center for MRI, Department of Radiology, Leiden University Medical Center, Leiden, The Netherlands

Christopher Wiggins
Institute of Neuroscience and Medicine Imaging Core Facility, INM-ICF, Forschungszentrum Jülich, Jülich, Germany

Laura Wisse
Institute for Clinical Sciences Lund, Lund University, Lund, Sweden

Xiaoping Wu
Center for Magnetic Resonance Research, Radiology, Medical School, University of Minnesota, Minneapolis, MN, United States

Essa Yacoub
Center for Magnetic Resonance Research (CMRR), University of Minnesota, Minneapolis, MN, United States

Wafaa Zaaraoui
CRMBM, CNRS, Aix-Marseille Université, Marseille, France

Moritz Zaiss
Institute of Neuroradiology, Universitätsklinikum Erlangen, Friedrich-Alexander-Universität Erlangen-Nürnberg; Magnetic Resonance Center, Max-Planck-Institute for Biological Cybernetics, Tübingen; Department Artificial Intelligence in Biomedical Engineering, Friedrich-Alexander-Universität Erlangen-Nürnberg, Erlangen, Germany

Zihao Zhang
State Key Laboratory of Brain and Cognitive Science, Institute of Biophysics, Chinese Academy of Sciences, Beijing; Institute of Artificial Intelligence, Hefei Comprehensive National Science Center, Hefei, China

Chengcheng Zhu
Department of Radiology, University of Washington, Seattle, United States

Editor's biographies

Karin Markenroth Bloch leads the Swedish National 7T facility at Lund University, Lund, Sweden. She obtained a PhD in Nuclear Physics from Chalmers University of Technology, after which she started her career in MRI at DRCMR, Copenhagen, at one of the first Nordic 3T scanners in clinical use. These early experiences stimulated her interest in leveraging the potential of high field strength in clinical applications as much as research and neuroscience. Following a career in Philips as a clinical scientist, Dr. Markenroth Bloch returned to academia to help start up and, since 2016, head the Swedish National 7T facility. In this role, her ambition is to make 7T MR broadly accessible to users in a range of applications. Her personal research interests are in methods for velocity-encoded phase-contrast MRI, and their use in studying the flow of blood and CSF in the brain. Dr. Markenroth Bloch is engaged in several international and local MRI communities, and in public outreach and popular science initiatives. She has been involved in the International Society for Magnetic Resonance in Medicine (ISMRM) in a range of capacities, including as a member of the Board of Trustees, the ISMRM High Field Study Group committee, and the ISMRM and European Society for Magnetic Resonance in Medicine and Biology (ESMRMB) program committees.

Maxime Guye, MD, PhD, is a neurologist; Professor of Biophysics at the School of Medicine, Aix-Marseille University (AMU), Marseille, France; and hospital doctor in the Department of Medical Imaging and the Department of Clinical Neuroscience at Marseille University Hospital. He heads the clinical site of the Centre for Magnetic Resonance in Biology and Medicine (CRMBM), jointly operated by AMU, the French National Centre for Scientific Research (CNRS), and the University Hospital System. After a fellowship in the UCL Epilepsy Imaging Group (London, United Kingdom), he started his research on epilepsy imaging using multimodal MRI and electrophysiology in Marseille in 2002. Since 2014, he leads the 7T MRI facility in Marseille and is particularly involved in clinical research and applications of 7T MRI in neurological diseases. He is actively involved in the MRI community at the national and international level. He was elected to the ISMRM High Field Study Group committee and was a member of the ISMRM program committee. He has been President of the French Society for Magnetic Resonance in Biology & Medicine and member of the scientific committee of the French Society of Radiology.

Benedikt A. Poser is Professor of MR Methods for Neuroscience at Maastricht University, Maastricht, Netherlands. He has a background in Physics and Business Management and obtained a PhD in MR Physics from Radboud University, Nijmegen, Netherlands, in 2009. He gained early experience with ultra-high field (UHF) MRI and its adoption for functional imaging at the Erwin L. Hahn Institute in Essen, Germany, on one of the first human 7T systems in Europe. Following a fellowship at the University of Hawaii, Honolulu, HI, United States, he returned to Europe in 2013 for a faculty appointment at Maastricht University, where he leads the MR Methods group, and since 2020 holds a Chair in the Cognitive Neuroscience Department. The central focus of his work has been the development of acquisition strategies for functional and structural MRI at UHF, and bringing parallel-transmit technologies to neuroscientific application at 7T and 9.4T. Benedikt Poser is an active member of the MRI community, with engagement in several roles in the European and International societies. Among other functions, he served on the ISMRM and ESMRMB program committees, and as President of the ESMRMB. Together with the coeditors of this book, he also enjoyed a fruitful and rewarding time on the ISMRM High Field Study Group committee.

Foreword

Kamil Ugurbil

Center for Magnetic Resonance Research (CMRR), University of Minnesota, Minneapolis, MN, United States
Departments of Radiology, Neurosciences and Medicine, University of Minnesota, Minneapolis, MN, United States

In the foreword to another book dedicated to ultra-high field (UHF) magnetic resonance in 2005, Paul Lauterbur, who received the Nobel Prize for the invention of magnetic resonance imaging in 2003, wrote: "Experts who had said, and even written, that frequencies above 10 MHz would never be practical watched in amazement as scientists and engineers pushed instrument performances to ever-higher levels at ever-increasing magnetic field strengths." In my opinion, this is an incisive summary of the history of UHF ($\geq$7 tesla) magnetic resonance. Paul, who was in fact one of the "experts" who predicted the impracticality of frequencies above 10 MHz, would be even more amazed if he had seen what has been achieved at 7T today as documented by all the chapters in this book. The prediction about the 10 MHz limit was disproven early in the development of MRI when 1.5T was introduced as the "high field" clinical scanner. Industry must have expected further automatic improvements with even higher magnetic fields since they subsequently launched initiatives to develop 4T scanners. But at 4T, they encountered for the first time the dilemma of radiofrequency (RF) inhomogeneity that preoccupied early years of human UHF imaging. In response, they abandoned the 4T effort and found academic homes for their prototype instruments. Yet, today, our repertoire of human imaging at 7T is vast, thanks to advanced technologies that sprung into existence as human ingenuity was brought to bear on the significant challenges posed by UHF. Using technologies such as parallel transmission, we can obtain anatomic images of diagnostic quality in the brain, extremities, and organ systems of the torso, a feat that was initially thought to be impossible. In general, UHF images have a much increased signal-to-noise ratio (SNR), which can be traded in for higher resolutions, contrast, and/or speed. For some clinical applications, important advantages have been demonstrated and are being exploited. However, we still need to make the case for the wider relevance of UHF gains in clinical practice. After all, any increase in SNR will not make a difference as long as there is enough to make a diagnosis: for example, a 2 cm diameter tumor in the brain can be detected just fine at 0.5T. However, one can hardly claim that current MRI capabilities are sufficient for all clinical problems we face. Thus, with a lot of technological advances that are now part of its repertoire, we must focus on exploiting the UHF gains to push the boundaries of biomedical research and clinical applications in order to make an impact. This will inevitably happen, but we will also be challenged by the increasing capabilities of MRI at lower magnetic fields, which are benefitting tremendously from the recently flourishing activities and advances in image reconstruction.

There is of course one area where UHF needs no further justification, namely functional magnetic resonance imaging (fMRI) of the brain. When fMRI came into existence, the field of cognitive neuroscience embraced it with great enthusiasm and started using it essentially for performing functional cartography with a few millimeters resolution. However, functional cartography, while useful and informative, does not provide a mechanistic link between neuronal activity and behavior or perception. Clearly, pursuing fMRI resolutions of single or a small cluster of cells to capture neural processes as in electrophysiological or optical recordings was unrealistic. However, mesoscopic scale organizations, exemplified by the canonical ensemble of orientation-tuned neurons in the primary visual cortex, so-called orientation columns, were an interesting target. Whether fMRI can reach that critical scale is a question of neurovascular coupling as well as of sensitivity (i.e., SNR and contrast-to-noise ratio). Answering this question became the single most important driving force for the development of tools in my group and led to the introduction of human 7T at our institute. The first fMRI papers were published in 1992, and in 1995 we were discussing a 9.4T horizontal bore animal magnet and 7T human magnet with Magnex. The former was used in numerous animal model experiments, providing an affirmative answer on neurovascular coupling and demonstrated the capabilities of fMRI; whether based on per-fusion or versions of blood oxygenation level dependent (BOLD) contrast, we were able to obtain func-tional maps at this mesoscopic scale, both across cortical layers and tangent to the cortex. Ultimately, 7T gave us the first human images of orientation domains, together with ocular dominance columns. Functional imaging at this resolution is now a burgeoning activity enabling for the first time human neuroscience at the mesoscopic spatial scale.

fMRI, especially of limited regions in the brain such as the visual cortex, was in some ways the perfect first UHF application because it avoided the complications of imaging at such high magnetic fields. fMRI relies on alterations in image intensity in a time series, and, as such, is not impacted by spatial signal intensity nonuniformities as long as there is sufficient SNR. In addition, targeting a lim-ited area avoids many of the challenges of UHF that affect whole-brain imaging. Similarly, single voxel spectroscopy with high chemical shift resolution, avidly pursued by our group at 7T, avoided the chal-lenges associated with UHF. Of course, having found a limited utility for 7T did not deter us and others from expanding the use of this platform. It was 7T work that enabled the field to develop an under-standing of the physics involved in imaging the human body at high RF frequencies. Thanks to this work, we now know that beyond $\sim$1.5T the physics of imaging the human body increasingly deviates from the near-field approximation as the RF wavelength becomes smaller than the object to be imaged. This puts us in the traveling wave regime and explains accurately the dilemma of signal inhomogeneity first faced at 4T. Thanks to 7T, we now have technologies to generate uniform excitation and reduce RF power deposition, enabling a vast array of biomedical applications reviewed in this book. Because of these technologies we can even think about going to higher magnetic fields, such as 10.5T, which is now a reality that has already produced exciting results, and 11.7T, which is at field waiting to be used in vivo. Even 14T is on the horizon, and we may wonder what MRI at field strengths as high as 20T could reveal about our body and mind in the future. Beyond doubt, these efforts will bring human bio-medical science to the high level of detail and information content demanded by the complexity of the biological systems we seek to understand. In particular, they will assuredly provide significant ad-vances toward meeting the 21st century challenge of understanding the human brain in health and disease.

Benefits of ultra-high field

The way back and ahead: MR physics at ultra-high field

Bobby A. Runderkamp[a], Matthan W.A. Caan[b], Wietske van der Zwaag[c,d], and Aart J. Nederveen[a]

[a]*Department of Radiology and Nuclear Medicine, Amsterdam UMC, Location AMC, Amsterdam, The Netherlands*
[b]*Department of Biomedical Engineering and Physics, Amsterdam UMC, Location AMC, Amsterdam, The Netherlands*
[c]*Spinoza Centre for Neuroimaging, Royal Netherlands Academy of Arts and Sciences (KNAW), Amsterdam, Netherlands*
[d]*Computational Cognitive Neuroscience and Neuroimaging, Netherlands Institute for Neuroscience, KNAW, Amsterdam, Netherlands*

Highlights

- Basic concepts of magnetism needed to understand ultra-high field MRI have been developed by our scientific forebears.
- The advantages of ultra-high field MRI scale supralinearly with field strength.
- The application of state-of-the-art acceleration techniques is key to understanding the advantages of ultra-high field MRI.
- The increase in spectral resolution with increasing field strength adds to the SNR benefit in several applications of ultra-high field MRI.
- RF at ultra-high field poses serious technical limitations to MRI at ultra-high field.

1.1 Ultra-high field in the light of the history of magnetism

What happens when the magnetic field gets stronger? This question has caught the imagination of physicists over the years, most recently in the quest for high-temperature superconductors that can bear magnetic fields much higher than current superconducting magnets. In ancient times, the Greek philosopher Thales of Miletus was already thinking about the attraction between magnets (see Fig. 1.1). Where did this attraction come from? Thales' answer was this: he assumed that each magnet had its own soul that provided the attraction (Yamamoto, 2018, p. 3).

During the scientific revolution in the 17th century, philosophers became interested in the quantitative knowledge that could be obtained through experiments. Therefore, yet another question emerged: how strong is the magnetic force between objects and how does it depend on the distance to the magnet? In the 17th century, Coulomb discovered that the electrical force between two electrical point charges goes by $1/r^2$. For a long time, researchers assumed that this was also the case for the magnetic force. But this assumption turned out to be wrong. In the 18th century, the Dutch scientist Petrus van Musschenbroek performed accurate measurements of the force between magnets (see Fig. 1.1). He found that it could even vary with $1/r^4$ (De Pater, 1979, p. 157), which later on turned out to be true for bar magnets if the distance between the magnets is sufficiently long.

Advances in Magnetic Resonance Technology and Applications. Volume 10. ISSN 2666-9099. https://doi.org/10.1016/B978-0-323-99898-7.00020-1

3

Representatives of the scientific revolution attempted to measure the forces between magnets by two methods. One was straightforward and consisted of measuring the weight that could be carried by the force between magnets. The other was the so-called deflection method, in which an attempt was made to derive the forces from the amount by which fixed magnets were able to change orientation as a function of distance. The latter method proved to be cumbersome, and Van Musschenbroek intuitively stayed away from it (De Pater, 1979, p. 179). Still, this deflection method was used by many of his contemporaries and highlights a basic intuition that has for long accompanied magnetism: not only position matters, but also the orientation of objects.

So traditionally, two riddles captured the minds of the scientists of the past. Where does the invisible, yet so strong, magnetic force come from? And secondly: why and how does that force vary in strength? Our forebears came to realize that magnetic forces and their effects are rarely linear. Changes in magnetic field strength may lead to unexpected results. But how do these historical riddles relate to ultra-high field MRI?

This book explains how MRI can benefit from using ultra-high fields. But how did we get to this point? Of course, the discovery and development of MRI is first and foremost based on the work done by the founding fathers of MRI. An MRI scanner is a device celebrating the great advances of modern physics. Without quantum mechanics and the Maxwell equations, one cannot understand MRI. Yet, the questions that Thales, Van Musschenbroek, and many others in the past were concerned with are still reflected in our current MRI practice. Could it be that our understanding of magnetism in general and MRI in particular was prepared by the earlier insights and that analogies can still be grasped if one considers both the past and the present from an oblique angle? After all, we still wonder what happens to our medical images when the magnetic field gets stronger. We can present equations for the signal-to-noise ratio (SNR) in which the SNR increases supralinearly with the magnetic field strength. But can we configure an exact relationship between image quality and field strength? Similar to what our forebears did in the 17th century, we are doing experiments to find out exactly that.

We now understand that magnetic forces do not originate from souls, but that Thales' intuition of tiny objects was correct. We know that ferromagnetism originates from the magnetic dipole moment of the electrons and can only be understood using insights from quantum mechanics. The magnetic forces caused by the electron spins can be pretty insidious on a macroscopic level, as we come to realize when we stand in front of an MRI scanner holding a pair of scissors. (This experiment should primarily be considered as a thought experiment as it is unsafe to perform in a real magnet.) The scissors are attracted by the MRI scanner, but one will also notice that the scissors want to rotate. This situation bears resemblance with the historic deflection experiments. We can now discriminate between the translational and the rotational force exerted on the scissors. Both forces depend on the strength of the magnetic field, but the rotational force also depends on the angle. If you hold the scissors parallel to the field lines, the rotational force vanishes. At an angle of 45 degrees, the force is at its maximum (Jackson, 2006). The experienced rotational force is proportional to the square of the main magnetic field of the scanner. This is because the torque τ acting on the scissors is equal to the cross product of the induced magnetic moment M in the scissors and the magnetic field vector B_0: $\tau = M \times B_0$. M, in turn, depends linearly on the strength of the magnetic field, leading to the squared relationship between rotational force and field strength.

So far, our forebears would not be surprised about this state-of-the-art deflection experiment that we can do with a modern MRI scanner. They would however be surprised to hear about the microscopic world of spins and electrons, which are key to understanding the MRI signal generation.

In courses introducing magnetic resonance, the basic force that plays a role in the MRI signal generation is the electromotive force that acts on the electrons in the radiofrequency (RF) receive coil. This electromotive force follows from the principle of magnetic induction, which is based on the third Maxwell equation A magnetic flux varying in time causes an electric current to flow in a nearby conductor. The changing magnetic flux is based on the rotational movement of spins in a magnetic field: the well-known precession movement. This microscopic rotation is governed by exactly the same equation as the rotation of the scissors: torque is equal to the cross product of the magnetic moment of the spin and the magnetic field B_0. Unlike the case in which we hold the scissors in front of the MRI machine, we cannot feel the rotational force of the precessing spins, but the electrons in a coil can, indirectly, through the principle of magnetic induction. And, very interestingly, this force is proportional to the square of the magnetic field.

With some imagination, one can see that the old fascination with forces returns in the electromotive force that underlies the principle of MRI. Like our colleagues in the 18th century, we are not quite sure how much better our images become with increasing magnetic field. They were unsure about the forces between magnets, we are uncertain about the forces in our conductors, or more precisely, their reflection in our images: the SNR. The amount of signal in our images is our present-day analogue of the force between objects, both depending supralinearly on the magnetic field.

There is an important difference between us and our predecessors. Unlike Thales and Van Musschenbroek, our fascination is not only aimed at understanding how things work. We also want to turn our understanding into real-life applications. After the scientific revolution, mankind managed to convert the newly gained knowledge and understanding into previously unseen technological advances. According to the famous Dutch historian of science Dijksterhuis, the development of modern technology is rooted in the mechanization of the world picture, which was so successfully developed during the scientific revolution (Dijksterhuis, 1961, p. 3). As heirs of both the scientific and the industrial revolution, we still like to understand magnetism but at the same time, and more importantly, we want to apply it. At this point of our considerations, we are again delighted to find that the effects of magnetic fields are often not linear. Therefore, the next step we make in increasing the magnetic field strength may be a leap, instead of just a small step.

1.2 SNR gain at ultra-high field

This chapter is about this fascination with magnetic fields, which drives MRI scientists around the globe. Currently, there are already over 100 ultra-high field systems installed worldwide (see Fig. 1.2). The vast majority of them are 7T systems and some have already been in use for over a decade. We consequently already have quite some understanding of the benefits brought by the physics of ultra-high field MRI (Burkett et al., 2021; Kraff and Quick, 2017). But at the same time, the field is moving beyond 7T, up to 9.4, 10.5, 11.7, and even 14T, as is planned in the Dutch project DYNAMIC, started in 2023. What more can we achieve when the magnetic fields get stronger?

Those who learned MRI in the past decades, like the authors of this chapter, learned that the SNR in MRI does not scale quadratically with the magnetic field. This is because of the fact that not only the signal increases with the field strength, as explained above, but so does the noise. At the same time,

FIG. 1.1

Founding fathers of our present-day understanding of magnetism: the Greek philosopher Thales of Miletus (c.624/623—c.548/545 BC) and the Dutch scientist Petrus van Musschenbroek (1692–1761), professor in Duisburg, Utrecht, and Leiden.

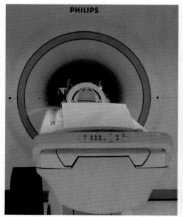
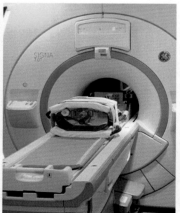
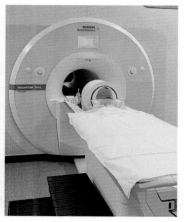

FIG. 1.2

7T MRI systems from three leading vendors: Philips (left, taken by authors), GE (middle, courtesy Dennis Klomp), and Siemens (right, courtesy Knut Nordlid).

the relationship between the noise and B_0 is more complex than we initially thought, as the relative contributions of the coil and the human tissue to the noise term have a different dependency on B_0. This was already stated in an early paper by Hoult and Lauterbur (1979, p. 432): "Sensitivity increases with frequency to the 7/4 power at frequencies below 1 MHz, but only linearly when sample losses are predominant." In addition, measuring SNR at different field strength is not easy to do: we can never measure the SNR with exactly the same hardware. Moreover, the relaxation values differ between field strengths. The most recent papers suggest that if high-end multichannel receive coils are used it is indeed possible to increase the SNR more than linearly. The SNR increase with B_0 was investigated in detail by Pohmann et al. (2016), who found that SNR increases with B_0 to the power of 1.65. This would mean that if one goes from 3 to 7T, the resulting SNR increase would be a factor 4. Improved coil design could even further boost this number. In an attempt to isolate the effect of the main magnetic field on the SNR, Le Ster et al. (2022) presented experimental evidence for an almost quadratic increase with B_0.

1.2.1 How to spend the SNR gain

But how can this extra SNR be spent? Interestingly, in the context of structural imaging, it is rarely advocated to use high field to accelerate imaging. Assuming that the SNR increases by a factor of 4 going from 3 to 7T, in theory, one can scan 16 times faster while keeping the SNR constant. In practice, changes in relaxation times, RF and gradient coil behavior, and the geometry factor penalty are among the factors limiting acceleration.

Shortening the scan time of structural MR images by using ultra-high field does, however, not trigger the imagination of many researchers. Usually, we expect the increase in SNR to be visible in the images and not so much in the scan time.

In general, the increase in SNR is used to increase the spatial resolution in images. For example, in a paper by Lüsebrink et al. (2021), T_1-weighted brain images with ultra-high 0.25^3 mm^3 isotropic resolution were acquired in a total scan time of 8 h in one single volunteer over 8 repetitions. At 3T, the acquisition of images with this SNR would have been virtually impossible.

1.2.2 Scan acceleration at ultra-high field

Due to the increased time required to sample a large matrix, as done in high-resolution imaging, it is often performed in combination with undersampling techniques that allow for high acceleration factors for structural imaging. It is well established at 7T to accelerate via parallel imaging (PI), through GRAPPA or SENSE reconstruction. Chapter 9 describes PI and reconstruction techniques in full detail.

Ideally, acceleration factors should be pushed even further than at 3T. This could be achieved by increasing the number of receive channels. Hendriks et al. (2019) simulated the acceleration that can be obtained by using a 256 channel head coil and found that the acceleration factor could be as high as 24. Interestingly, it was suggested by Wiesinger et al. (2006) that at 7T and higher the geometry factors will stay closer to 1, which would further amplify the benefit of 7T.

Further acceleration through compressed sensing (CS)-based acceleration has also been applied at 7T. In fact, PI and CS are often combined for increased acceleration capability. Through random

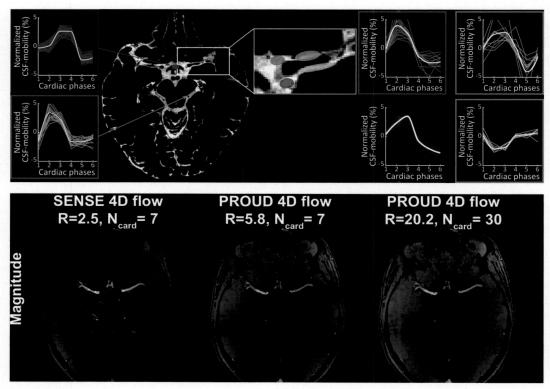

FIG. 1.3

Acceleration factors achieved at ultra-high field MRI using compressed sensing. Top: CSF-mobility in different regions of the brain is visualized (0.45^3 mm³ and 17 times accelerated TSE scans) in large CSF-filled spaces, such as ventricles and subarachnoid liquid around the MCA. Each graph represents one region of interest (ROI); the colored lines represent the signal of each individual voxel within the ROI, and the thick white line is the mean value over voxels. Courtesy Lydiane Hirschler, LUMC, The Netherlands. Bottom: CS acceleration up to 20 times accelerated is shown in magnitude 4D flow scans.

sampling, a sparse data representation and nonlinear reconstruction, the point spread function is only marginally affected, yielding opportunities for high-resolution imaging without intrinsic resolution loss (Lustig et al., 2007).

Meixner et al. (2019) were able to perform 3D MR angiography at 0.31^3 mm³ isotropic resolution in clinically feasible imaging times. Lazarus et al. (2020) applied CS to T_2^*-weighted 3D brain imaging at 7T at 0.6^3 mm³ isotropic resolution, with a reconstruction method that prevented blurring in non-Cartesian sampling.

Another application of CS at 7T is in CSF-mobility measurement with an acceleration factor of 17, in which Hirschler et al. (2020) showed clear cardiac cycle-dependent pulsations in multiple CSF-filled spaces (see Fig. 1.3). A similar strategy was employed by Gottwald et al. (2020) in intracranial 4D flow acquisitions at 7T. With pseudospiral Cartesian undersampling and CS reconstruction with TV regularization in the cardiac dimension, they could achieve a spatiotemporal resolution of [0.5^3 mm^3, 30 ms] in 10 min with an acceleration factor of 20 (see Fig. 1.3).

Recent work has explored further accelerating image acquisition by solving the inverse problem of image reconstruction through the use of neural networks via deep learning. These networks are trained on available reference data and thereby learn a prior that is tailored to imaging data. Using an example of such a network, called the Recurrent Inference Machine, showed that gradient echo imaging at 7T could be accelerated beyond what would be possible through a predefined sparsifying transform in CS (Lønning et al., 2019).

This overview of the contribution of acceleration technology underlines the success of ultra-high field in a distinct manner. We need to apply novel acquisition and reconstruction methods to fully benefit from the advantages of ultra-high field.

1.3 Relaxation time and contrast changes at ultra-high field

The benefit from ultra-high field is not solely determined by SNR, but the signal magnitude is also determined by the relaxation times T_1, T_2, and T_2^*. These are in their turn dependent on the field strength. Consequently, the differences in relaxation times T_1, T_2, and T_2^* of tissue water at different field strengths have a large impact on the obtained images. A useful parameter set for a given sequence at one field strength may not be very efficient, or even completely unusable, at another field strength. Hence, since the advent of human ultra-high field systems, quite some effort has been put into measuring relaxation times at different magnetic field strengths to allow informed parameter optimization. In some cases, a completely different sequence may even be preferred for a certain application when moving between 3 and 7T.

While the longitudinal relaxation time T_1 is longer at higher field, the transverse relaxation time T_2 is relatively constant, and the effective transverse relaxation T_2^* becomes shorter (see Fig. 1.4). The spin-lattice relaxation described by T_1 is less efficient at ultra-high field, as a lower number of protons have the right tumbling frequency to interact with the field. The spin-spin relaxation described by T_2 does not change much with increasing field strength, though it shortens beyond 7T and at longer echo times, due to relaxation through diffusion being more efficient (De Graaf et al., 2006). This is especially true for areas with iron-rich structures. For T_2^*, this diffusion process is even more important, resulting in the shortening of T_2^* with increasing $\boldsymbol{B}_0$.

In human brain tissue, T_1 values of approximately 800 and 1300 ms are found for white and gray matter, respectively, at 3T. At 7T, these values increase to 1100 and 2000 ms (Marques et al., 2010). The T_1 of CSF is long, on the order of several seconds, and does not change much with the applied $\boldsymbol{B}_0$.

The shortening of T_2^* from 66 ms in white matter and 53 ms in gray matter at 3T to 33 ms in white matter and 28 ms in gray matter at 7T is also substantial (Peters et al., 2007). This means that all T_2^*- or BOLD-weighted experiments require a much shorter echo time for maximal contrast. A fortunate side effect is that imaging may become more efficient. As the blood in the veins has an even shorter T_2^*, the identification of veins in T_2^*-weighted data becomes greatly facilitated.

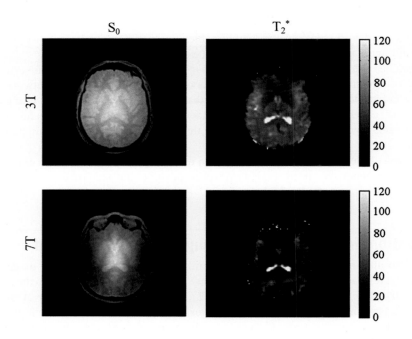

FIG. 1.4

T_2^* maps and S_0 images from (Peters et al., 2007). The 7T T_2^* maps clearly have shorter values in both gray and white matter while T_2^* $_{CSF}$ remains long. The S_0 images clearly display central brightening due to the shorter wavelength at 7T.

In T_2-mapping approaches, the measurement of T_2 is greatly dependent on the sequence used, since the echo spacing and readout module influence the measured T_2. As a result, literature on field strength comparisons is scarce and the theoretical expectation that T_2 at 7T is similar to the T_2 values found at 3T is not experimentally supported (De Graaf et al., 2006).

As the T_1 values become so much longer, a recalibration of all T_1-weighted sequences is required when moving to ultra-high field. Similarly, for those that use an inversion-based fluid or fat-suppression module, the delay times between inversion or suppression pulses and the readout have to be adapted to achieve the correct contrast or suppression.

The T_1 values do not only increase; they are also further apart for tissues such as gray and white matter in the brain, which can be used to obtain increased contrast in T_1-weighted images at ultra-high field. Nevertheless, the concomitant B_1-variations often require an extra acquisition to remove or reduce the added bias field, which leads to somewhat different acquisitions being favored at 7T than at lower field strength (Marques et al., 2010).

The longer T_1 values are also important for scans where a tag is used to map flow or perfusion. In both magnetic resonance angiography (MRA) and arterial spin labeling (ASL)-based perfusion measurements, acquisitions can benefit from the longer presence of the tag in the blood

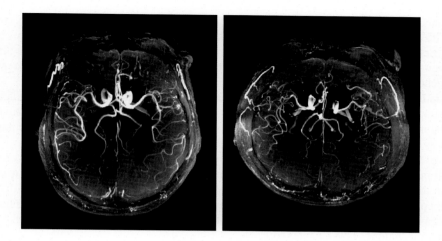

FIG. 1.5

Time-of-flight images in two different subjects depict both small and large vessels. *Figure kindly supplied by Dr. Maarten Bot, Amsterdam UMC.*

(Park et al., 2018). In the case of ASL, these advantages are offset by the disadvantages of an inhomogeneous and often local B_1 transmit field, and the necessity for short echo times due to the shorter T_2^*.

At ultra-high field, the relaxivity of Gadolinium-based contrast agents is diminished, so that also in the case of MRA, a wholly different sequence may be selected when moving from 3 to 7T, such as the time-of-flight images shown in Fig. 1.5.

T_2^*-weighted imaging, such as BOLD-based functional MRI, benefits doubly from ultra-high field because of the increase in SNR and in T_2^* changes (van der Zwaag et al., 2009). Besides a reduction in TE, these acquisitions do not tend to require much adaptation because of the field strength. Improvements in gradient strength, PI performance, and pulse definition have however had a significant impact on acquisition strategies. fMRI at ultra-high field now enables mesoscopic functional imaging at the level of cortical layers and precise mapping of functional neuroanatomy (see Chapter 24).

1.4 Susceptibility

Historically, there has been little awareness of the existence of weak magnetism: dia- and paramagnetism. Interestingly, exactly the effects of dia- and paramagnetism have been proven to be highly valuable for further exploiting the benefit of the SNR gain at 7T and beyond.

When a tissue is placed in a static magnetic field B_0, the induced magnetization vector M is characterized by the magnetic susceptibility. The susceptibility χ describes the magnetic properties of tissue, defined as a proportionality constant of the magnetization within the tissue relative to B_0 with units in ppm. A susceptibility-induced change in the magnetic field yields a frequency shift in Hz proportional to χ, leading to a phase offset that scales with $\boldsymbol{B}_0$. Since the induced frequency shift varies linearly with $\boldsymbol{B}_0$, this adds to the SNR benefit, making the measurement of susceptibility changes at ultra-high field one of the driving forces of improved contrast. At ultra-high field, subtle differences in χ between tissues of 1 ppb are in principle detectable as a phase offset in gradient echo imaging at common echo times (Duyn and Schenck, 2017).

From an historical point of view, one should realize that para- and diamagnetism are again about forces: certain tissues counteract the main magnetic field, and some tissues amplify the main magnetic field. In the macroscopic situation, this would lead to either attraction or repulsion of the magnetized object.

Diamagnetism refers to negative susceptibility resulting from perturbed paired electrons, generating a small but measurable negative change of the magnetization. Water is the dominant diamagnetic material in the brain with a susceptibility of $\chi = -9.05$ ppm. Compared to air with $\chi = 0.37$ ppm, a strong susceptibility effect is seen on air-tissue interfaces, which leads to enlarged field inhomogeneities at ultra-high field. Much effort has gone into mitigating this effect through, e.g., advanced $\boldsymbol{B}_0$-shimming techniques (see Chapter 6).

Materials with unpaired electrons generate a strong positive magnetization and are referred to as paramagnetic or ferromagnetic, with iron in its unbound form having $\chi = 4.92$ ppm. In the human body, iron is bonded, yielding only a weak positive paramagnetism. The susceptibility of hemoglobin in blood changes with the blood oxygenation level. Fully deoxygenated blood has $\chi = -8.0$ ppm, thus being weakly paramagnetic relative to water, while this effect vanishes entirely for fully oxygenated blood.

In the human brain, iron deposition is seen mostly in the dentate nuclei of the cerebellum, basal ganglia, and red nuclei. The susceptibility values of the brain tissues gray matter and white matter are in a small range of −9.2 to −8.8 ppm centered around that of water (Duyn, 2018). The ability of measuring susceptibility with high precision at 7T has enabled quantification of myelin and iron content to understand the development and aging of the human brain, as well as pathological processes, as will be detailed out in the last part of this book.

In practice, each voxel can be understood as a magnetic dipole generating a field extending to its surroundings. The magnetization in a certain voxel is then the superposition of the dipole fields in the vicinity. Quantitative susceptibility mapping (QSM) seeks to locally obtain χ by inverting this process (see Chapter 13).

In addition to a change in phase as outlined above, the magnitude of the magnetization is also affected by susceptibility effects. This is understood by considering microscopic field inhomogeneities, leading to signal dispersion and shorter T_2^* relaxation times. While this effect might partly jeopardize the SNR gained by going to ultra-high field, it leads in practice to a stark increase in contrast. This is exploited in susceptibility weighted imaging (SWI) for various clinical applications, combining the effects of susceptibility on the phase and the magnitude.

One specific property of susceptibility is its dependence on orientation relative to the magnetic field. This is relevant for assessing white matter, which through its anisotropy of myelinated fibers experiences a different χ as a function of its orientation with respect to $\boldsymbol{B}_0$, as can be seen in Fig. 1.6. To model this orientation dependence, a susceptibility tensor can be defined and estimated using tissue measurements under different orientations. The vasculature also shows an orientation dependence. The dipole field of a vessel leads to a macroscopic net phase offset in the proximity of the vessel that depends on the angle between the vessel and the magnetic field, with the offset being

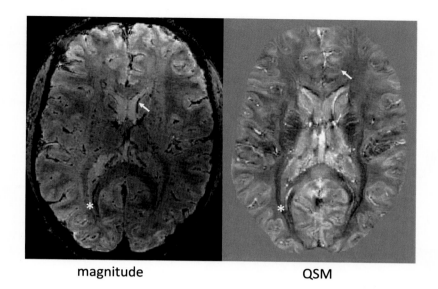

magnitude   QSM

FIG. 1.6

Gradient echo imaging at 7T, showing the magnitude and quantitative susceptibility map (QSM, scaled from −0.15 to 0.15 ppm) of a healthy volunteer. In the magnitude image, void signal in vasculature is seen due to intra-voxel dephasing (arrow). In the QSM image, susceptibility contrast between GM and WM can be appreciated (arrow). Furthermore, susceptibility anisotropy within WM is seen, through an orientation dependence in the splenium of the corpus callosum and the optic radiation (asterisk *). *Data from the Amsterdam Ultra-high field adult lifespan database (AHEAD).*

maximal if this angle is zero. The importance of the angle between microstructures and the main magnetic field reminds us of the situation we encounter when holding a pair of scissors in front of the MRI machine, as referred to in Section 1.1 of this chapter.

1.5 Spectral resolution

Proton magnetic resonance spectroscopy (^{1}H-MRS) allows for the determination of the concentration of brain metabolites, such as N-acetyl-aspartate (NAA), total choline (tCho), and creatine (Cr). The concentrations can be derived from the peak magnitudes in the spectrum. At ultra-high field, the separation between peaks on the frequency axis increases, leading to improved spectral resolution (see Fig. 1.7 and Chapter 26). Although this separation increases only linearly with B_0, it is combined with the supralinear SNR increase. One of the promises of ultra-high field therefore lies in the combination of increased spectral and spatial resolution for the assessment of the concentration of biomolecules in the brain using MRS (Henning, 2018).

Spatially resolved MRS methods often require long scan times and scan acceleration beyond conventional approaches is deemed necessary at ultra-high field. Klauser et al. (2021) managed to apply CS to 3D MR spectroscopic imaging (MRSI). During acquisition, random variable-density

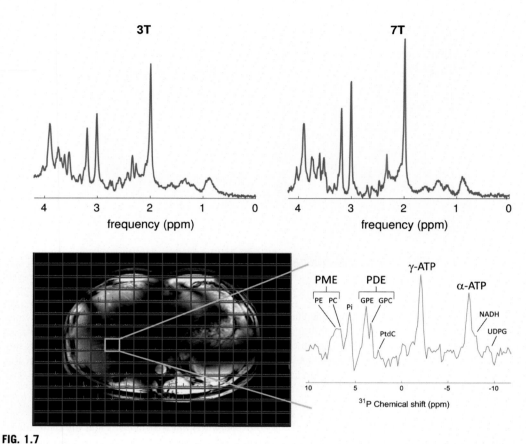

FIG. 1.7

MRS at 7T: top panel shows 3T PRESS spectrum and 7T sLASER spectrum. Peak definition is clearly improved at 7T. Figure kindly supplied by Dr. Anouk Schrantee, Amsterdam UMC. Bottom panel shows a MRSI slab in the liver of a healthy volunteer acquired at 7T with a bore coil for ^{31}P transmission.

undersampling was done in the spatial dimensions. In reconstruction, total generalized variation regularization was employed, imposing sparsity in the first- and second-order spatial derivatives. Moreover, because MRSI data have an explicit time dimension, they show that a denoising effect can be achieved by assuming low-rankness and spatiotemporal separability of the transverse magnetization (see Chapter 26). This way they could achieve 3D maps of multiple metabolites with high sensitivity at 3.3^3 mm^3 resolution in 20 min.

Other nuclei such as ^{23}Na, ^{31}P, ^{13}C offer relevant insights into brain metabolism but attempts at imaging their distributions are traditionally hampered by low SNR (see Chapter 27). Here again, ultra-high field leads to a more than linear increase in SNR and a linear increase in spectral resolution. At the same time, transmit coils used for multi nuclei imaging are often suboptimal. Transmit surface coils yield good SNR in the vicinity of the coil but lower SNR further away. Uniform transmit B_1 would eliminate these problems and would facilitate the use of RF pulses with lower SAR. Fortuitously, the Larmor frequency for ^{31}P at 7T is 121 MHz, very close to ^{1}H Larmor frequency at 3T. In several papers, the use of a multinuclei whole body-sized RF birdcage coil has now been validated (Löring et al., 2016; van Houtum et al., 2019) for use at 7T. Using such a setup, one can establish uniform B_1 similar to the situation for ^{1}H imaging at 3T and the increase in SNR compared with the classical approach using surface coils is substantial (see example in the liver in Fig. 1.7).

Another promising application of ultra-high field is the development of fMRS. Traditionally, a fair amount of signal averaging is used for the acquisition of a single spectrum. At ultra-high field, one can try to choose the number of signal averages such that multiple spectra can be obtained in combination with a task paradigm similar to what is performed in fMRI. The advantage of fMRS is that the neuronal activation upon stimulation can be studied more directly, as opposed to the indirect approach of fMRI, which is based on the blood oxygenation level. An increasing number of papers successfully show dynamic changes of glutamate and lactate detected by fMRS (Bednařík et al., 2015; Mangia et al., 2006).

Magnetization transfer (MT) and chemical exchange saturation transfer (CEST) are used to measure (macro)molecular content in brain tissue. The macromolecular proton pool is characterized by a broad spectrum compared with free water protons. By applying an off-resonance RF pulse, this pool is saturated, which in turn transfers to the free water protons. This results in a decreased free water signal compared with a reference RF excitation, yielding the MT contrast. By adjusting the off-resonance of the RF-pulse, a CEST-spectrum or Z-spectrum can be obtained (van Zijl et al., 2018).

Longer T_1-times allow for longer saturation times and hence sufficient exchange so that the MT contrast increases beyond the conventional gain by going to ultra-high field. Furthermore, higher spectral resolution enables the separation of different macromolecules that would overlap at lower field strength. Myelin mapping and creatine quantification are examples of applications within this context. Practically, sufficient B_1^+-homogeneity (see Chapter 7) must be ensured to avoid a spatially dependent bias in quantification. CEST imaging is another fine example showing the enormous advantage of ultra-high field, way beyond a benefit proportional to the field strength increase (see Chapter 28).

1.6 **RF at ultra-high field**

The advantage of scanning at ultra-high field can be compromised by the increase in RF absorption in tissue compared with 1.5 and 3T. The RF exposure in MRI is limited by the induced heating of the tissue, which can be quantified by the specific absorption rate (SAR). As the SAR goes with the square of the magnetic field strength, this means that sequences requiring high flip angles (FAs) like TSE and FLAIR need to be modified in order to be played out safely. Here, the dependence on the magnetic field strength, contrary to what is the case in general, does not work out in our favor.

One of the main challenges to overcome at ultra-high field is the B_1-inhomogeneity due to the RF wavelength approaching to the size of human body dimensions. The RF wavelength at 7T in biological tissues at the Larmor frequency is approximately 12 cm. This results in complex and nonuniform transmit profiles in human tissues due to the presence of constructive and destructive interferences. In the reconstructed images, this leads to hypointense areas and even complete signal dropouts. Outside the brain, this problem is even more alarming, but also in the temporal lobes and the cerebellum signal dropout poses an important limitation. Multiple solutions to this problem have been proposed, such as using dedicated coil designs, dielectric padding, and adiabatic RF pulses. Constructing a body coil at 7T for ^{1}H signal transmission has so far been proven to be cumbersome (Webb and Van de Moortele, 2016).

Parallel transmission (pTx), in which channels in a transmit coil array can be driven individually, offers much flexibility in achieving more homogeneous excitation in the brain. Static shimming, in which relative phases and amplitudes of transmit channel waveforms are optimized, has shown improvement in FA homogeneity in the brain, which consequently leads to a more homogeneous image. However, using a single static shim for FA homogenization is often insufficient. One cost-effective approach that has been pioneered outside the brain is to combine multiple static shim modes delivering complementary B_1^+ distributions with dropouts in distinct locations: TIAMO (Brunheim et al., 2018).

Even more potential is offered by the increase in degrees of freedom in combining pTx with advanced pulse design, in which a trajectory through excitation k-space is traversed. In this regard, Wu et al. (2014) have used a multispoke pulse design to achieve high FA homogeneity through the largest axial liver section at 7T and this was applied to brain as well (Schmitter et al., 2014). Moving to 3D, Aigner et al. (2022) combined pTx with a kt-points pulse, consisting of multiple nonselective hard pulses, to mitigate FA inhomogeneity across the entire heart at 7T. In the brain, kt-points pulses have been used successfully to homogenize signal excitation including the temporal lobes and the cerebellum (see Fig. 1.8).

This section highlights that contrary to the consideration based on SNR, relaxation rate, susceptibility, and spectroscopy as discussed in the previous sections, RF at ultra-high field poses some serious technical limitations for our MRI at ultra-high field imagination to float freely.

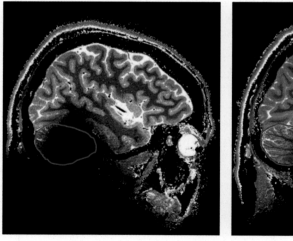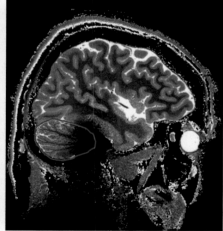

FIG. 1.8

B_1-inhomogeneity at ultra-high field leads to signal loss in areas such as the lower temporal lobes and the cerebellum (outlined in red). On the left, MP2RAGE T_1-map acquired in standard "quadrature" mode. On the right, an MP2RAGE T_1 map of the same subject, now with kt-points pulses for excitation (8Tx).

1.7 **Conclusion**

The history of magnetism has taken an interesting turn in the development of ultra-high field MRI. Observed from an oblique angle, our current fascination with the effects of magnetic fields bears many similarities with the activities and considerations of our scientific forebears. This especially holds for the orientation dependence of magnetic effects, both microscopic and macroscopic, and the nonlinear behavior of the effects of magnetic field strength, either in attractive force or in image quality. The basic concepts needed for understanding ultra-high field MRI have matured over the ages and in this way conquered our scientific hearts and minds.

At the same time, our knowledge of the laws governing microscopic physics has permitted us to make a quantum leap when it comes to understanding magnetism. Consequently, we are tempted to think that we know way more than our scientific forebears. While this is certainly true, we easily forget that another very important difference is that we manage to use our scientific insights to fabricate tools that can change our lives. An ultra-high field MRI scanner is an important example of this insight.

References

Aigner, C.S., Dietrich, S., Schaeffter, T., Schmitter, S., 2022. Calibration-free pTx of the human heart at 7T via 3D universal pulses. Magn. Reson. Med. 87, 70–84.

Bednařík, P., Tkáč, I., Giove, F., et al., 2015. Neurochemical and BOLD responses during neuronal activation measured in the human visual cortex at 7 Tesla. J. Cereb. Blood Flow Metab. 35, 601–610.

Brunheim, S., Gratz, M., Johst, S., et al., 2018. Fast and accurate multi-channel B_1^+ mapping based on the TIAMO technique for 7T UHF body MRI. Magn. Reson. Med. 79, 2652–2664.

Burkett, B.J., Fagan, A.J., Felmlee, J.P., et al., 2021. Clinical 7-T MRI for neuroradiology: strengths, weaknesses, and ongoing challenges. Neuroradiology 63, 167–177.

De Graaf, R.A., Brown, P.B., McIntyre, S., Nixon, T.W., Behar, K.L., Rothman, D.L., 2006. High magnetic field water and metabolite proton T1 and T 2 relaxation in rat brain in vivo. Magn. Reson. Med. 56, 386–394.

De Pater, C., 1979. Petrus van Musschenbroek (1692–1761), een newtoniaans natuuronderzoeker. Drukkerij Elinkwijk BV, Utrecht.

Dijksterhuis, E.J., 1961. The Mechanization of the World Picture. Clarendon Press, Oxford.

Duyn, J.H., 2018. Studying brain microstructure with magnetic susceptibility contrast at high-field. Neuroimage 168, 152–161.

Duyn, J.H., Schenck, J., 2017. Contributions to magnetic susceptibility of brain tissue. NMR Biomed. 30, 1–37.

Gottwald, L.M., Töger, J., Markenroth Bloch, K., et al., 2020. High spatiotemporal resolution 4D flow MRI of intracranial aneurysms at 7T in 10 minutes. Am. J. Neuroradiol. 41, 1201–1208.

Hendriks, A.D., Luijten, P.R., Klomp, D.W.J., Petridou, N., 2019. Potential acceleration performance of a 256-channel whole-brain receive array at 7 T. Magn. Reson. Med. 81, 1659–1670.

Henning, A., 2018. Proton and multinuclear magnetic resonance spectroscopy in the human brain at ultra-high field strength: a review. Neuroimage 168, 181–198.

Hirschler, L., Runderkamp, B.A., Franklin, S.L., et al., 2020. The Driving Force of Glymphatics: Influence of the Cardiac Cycle on CSF-Mobility in Perivascular Spaces in Humans. ISMRM.

Hoult, D.I., Lauterbur, P.C., 1979. The sensitivity of the zeugmatographic experiment involving human samples. J. Magn. Reson. 34, 425–433.

Jackson, D.P., 2006. Dancing paperclips and the geometric influence on magnetization: a surprising result. Am. J. Phys. 74, 272–279.

Klauser, A., Strasser, B., Thapa, B., Lazeyras, F., Andronesi, O., 2021. Achieving high-resolution 1H-MRSI of the human brain with compressed-sensing and low-rank reconstruction at 7 Tesla. J. Magn. Reson. 331, 107048.

Kraff, O., Quick, H.H., 2017. 7T: physics, safety, and potential clinical applications. J. Magn. Reson. Imaging 46, 1573–1589.

Lazarus, C., Weiss, P., El Gueddari, L., et al., 2020. 3D variable-density SPARKLING trajectories for high-resolution T_2*-weighted magnetic resonance imaging. NMR Biomed. 33, 1–12.

Le Ster, C., Grant, A., Van de Moortele, P.-F., et al., 2022. Magnetic field strength dependent SNR gain at the center of a spherical phantom and up to 11.7T. Magn. Reson. Med. 88, 2131–2138.

Lønning, K., Putzky, P., Sonke, J.-J., Reneman, L., Caan, M.W.A., Welling, M., 2019. Recurrent inference machines for reconstructing heterogeneous MRI data. Med. Image Anal. 53, 64–78.

Löring, J., van der Kemp, W.J.M., Almujayyaz, S., van Oorschot, J.W.M., Luijten, P.R., Klomp, D.W.J., 2016. Whole-body radiofrequency coil for 31P MRSI at 7T. NMR Biomed. 29, 709–720.

Lüsebrink, F., Mattern, H., Yakupov, R., et al., 2021. Comprehensive ultrahigh resolution whole brain in vivo MRI dataset as a human phantom. Sci. Data 8, 1–13.

Lustig, M., Donoho, D., Pauly, J.M., 2007. Sparse MRI: the application of compressed sensing for rapid MR imaging. Magn. Reson. Med. 58, 1182–1195.

Mangia, S., Tkáč, I., Gruetter, R., et al., 2006. Sensitivity of single-voxel 1H-MRS in investigating the metabolism of the activated human visual cortex at 7 T. Magn. Reson. Imaging 24, 343–348.

Marques, J.P., Kober, T., Krueger, G., van der Zwaag, W., Van de Moortele, P.F., Gruetter, R., 2010. MP2RAGE, a self bias-field corrected sequence for improved segmentation and T1-mapping at high field. Neuroimage 49, 1271–1281.

Meixner, C.R., Liebig, P., Speier, P., et al., 2019. High resolution time-of-flight MR-angiography at 7 T exploiting VERSE saturation, compressed sensing and segmentation. Magn. Reson. Imaging 63, 193–204.

Park, C.A., Kang, C.K., Kim, Y.B., Cho, Z.H., 2018. Advances in MR angiography with 7T MRI: from microvascular imaging to functional angiography. Neuroimage 168, 269–278.

Peters, A.M., Brookes, M.J., Hoogenraad, F.G., et al., 2007. T_2* measurements in human brain at 1.5, 3 and 7 T. Magn. Reson. Imaging 25, 748–753.

Pohmann, R., Speck, O., Scheffler, K., 2016. Signal-to-noise ratio and MR tissue parameters in human brain imaging at 3, 7, and 9.4 Tesla using current receive coil arrays. Magn. Reson. Med. 75, 801–809.

Schmitter, S., Wu, X., Auerbach, E.J., et al., 2014. Seven-tesla time-of-flight angiography using a 16-channel parallel transmit system with power-constrained 3-dimensional spoke radiofrequency pulse design. Invest. Radiol. 49, 314–325.

van der Zwaag, W., Francis, S., Head, K., et al., 2009. fMRI at 1.5, 3 and 7 T: characterising BOLD signal changes. Neuroimage 47, 1425–1434.

van Houtum, Q., Welting, D., Gosselink, W.J.M., Klomp, D.W.J., Arteaga de Castro, C.S., van der Kemp, W.J.M., 2019. Low SAR 31P (multi-echo) spectroscopic imaging using an integrated whole-body transmit coil at 7T. NMR Biomed. 32, 1–10.

van Zijl, P.C.M., Lam, W.W., Xu, J., Knutsson, L., Stanisz, G.J., 2018. Magnetization transfer contrast and chemical exchange saturation transfer MRI. Features and analysis of the field-dependent saturation spectrum. Neuroimage 168, 222–241.

Webb, A.G., Van de Moortele, P.F., 2016. The technological future of 7 T MRI hardware. NMR Biomed. 29, 1305–1315.

Wiesinger, F., Van de Moortele, P.F., Adriany, G., De Zanche, N., Ugurbil, K., Pruessmann, K.P., 2006. Potential and feasibility of parallel MRI at high field. NMR Biomed. 19, 368–378.

Wu, X., Schmitter, S., Auerbach, E.J., Uğurbil, K., Van de Moortele, P.-F., 2014. Mitigating transmit B 1 inhomogeneity in the liver at 7T using multi-spoke parallel transmit RF pulse design. Quant. Imaging Med. Surg. 4, 4–10.

Yamamoto, Y., 2018. The Pull of History. World Scientific.

Translating UHF advances to lower field strength

Andrew Webb

C.J. Gorter Center for MRI, Department of Radiology, Leiden University Medical Center, Leiden, The Netherlands

Highlights

- Methods designed to mitigate the intrinsic effects of B_0 and B_1 inhomogeneity at UHF have also found applications at 3T.
- Similarly, methods developed at UHF to monitor and correct for motion and motion-induced frequency shifts can also be used to improve image quality at clinical field strengths.
- UHF has also formed a testbed for very high-resolution imaging protocols: those which show promise for specific clinical applications have rapidly been adapted for clinical scanners.

2.1 Introduction

In addition to the numerous intrinsic advantages of UHF MRI, which are outlined in the rest of this book, one of the rationales often put forward for the commercial development of such state-of-the-art technology is the "Formula One" effect. This refers to the concept that technologies developed to deal with the problems encountered at the cutting edge (Formula 1 cars, UHF scanners) eventually find their way into mainstream commercial products (road cars, 3T/1.5T scanners). In practice, the interaction is more complicated, with Formula 1 often taking existing ideas that have not yet found practical applications, adjusting them until they work at the cutting edge, and then reintroducing them to the mainstream markets. So the interaction is bidirectional rather than unidirectional, which is also true for many methods that straddle UHF and clinical field strengths.

The main intrinsic challenges for UHF neuroimaging compared with 3T include:

(i) the intrinsically higher B_0 inhomogeneity from tissue magnetic susceptibility,
(ii) the higher susceptibility to motion/frequency changes caused by motion/breathing, and
(iii) the inhomogeneous transmit field due to constructive and destructive RF interference.

Various approaches have been adopted at 7T to counteract these issues, including advanced multicoil approaches to B_0 shimming, external probes for continuous magnetic field or motion monitoring, and parallel transmit and/or high-permittivity materials. This chapter summarizes the situations in which such approaches have also found applications at 3 and 1.5T: it should be noted that most of these applications are still very much in the developmental stage and have not yet been incorporated into commercial scanners. In addition, a summary of some of the imaging sequences that have an active interplay between UHF and conventional field strengths is included, and finally, a description of one particular clinical application for which the technology developed at UHF was a major impetus for increased growth at lower fields.

2.2 Multicoil approaches for B_0 shimming

The strong variation in magnetic susceptibility both within tissue and at air-tissue interfaces surrounding the brain results in substantial magnetic field distortions inside the brain, especially in the prefrontal cortex and temporal lobes. Conventional shimming approaches to minimize these distortions decompose the magnetic field distortions into a set of spherical harmonic (SH) basis functions. The corresponding correction fields are then calculated, with each SH correction term produced by a dedicated shim coil of appropriate geometry. UHF systems typically have up to third-order shims, with clinical systems having only first or second order. However, the complexity of the magnetic field distortions at UHF cannot be fully corrected by a limited number of lower-order shim coils. The group of Juchem and de Graaf have developed an approach, termed multicoil (MC) (Juchem et al., 2020) at 7T using a large set of circular coils, which has proved to be very successful in terms of reducing the field inhomogeneities within the brain, as shown in Fig. 2.1.

The MC concept has been translated to 3T with the additional feature that the RF coils of the receive array and the MC shim coils can be integrated in a configuration referred to as iPRES (integrated parallel reception, excitation, and shimming) (Darnell et al., 2017; Stockmann et al., 2016). This separated dual functionality is possible since the RF coils operate at hundreds of MHz whereas the shim coil is fed by a DC current. Up to 32 dual coils have been integrated for operation at 3T. Fig. 2.2 shows one example of the circuit layout, physical embodiment, and imaging results obtained using this integrated approach.

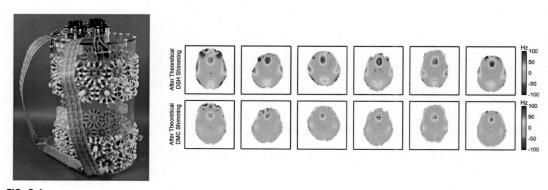

FIG. 2.1

(Left) A coil matrix consisting of four rows of twelve coils (each 100 turns, diameter 47 mm) mounted on the surface of an acrylic structure together with temperature monitoring probes. (Right) Performances of zero through third-order dynamic SH and dynamic MC shimming of the human brain at 7T across six subjects. The residual magnetic field imperfections after dynamic spherical harmonic (DSH) shimming (top row) are reduced with the dynamic multicoil (DMC) shim approach (bottom row). *Figures adapted from Juchem et al. (2011).*

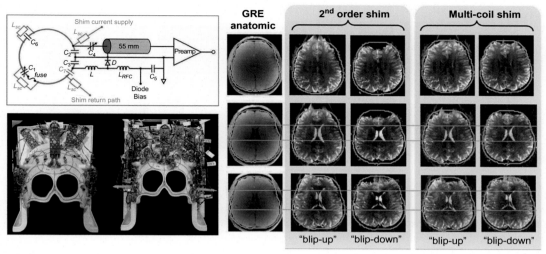

FIG. 2.2

3T (top left) Schematic of a single integrated RF-shim coil element with conventional RF components shown in black, and components in red adding shimming functionality to the coil. (Bottom left) Top half of a 32-channel receive array for 3T coil before and after conversion to a combined RF-shim array. Four toroidal inductive chokes are used on each element to block RF from the shim current path and/or to bridge tuning capacitors. (Right) High-resolution EPI scans show markedly less distortion when MC shims are applied, largely bringing features such as the ventricles back into alignment, as indicated by the orange lines. *Figures adapted from Stockmann et al. (2016).*

2.3 Corrections for motion, B_O-field modulation, and gradient imperfections

Motion remains one of the most problematic issues for MRI at all field strengths, with artifacts typically being greater when the field strength is higher. As demonstrated in early 7T research studies of neurodegenerative disease using elderly subjects, not only is bulk motion a problem, but also erratic breathing patterns and motion of the body in general which produce frequency shifts in the brain (Versluis et al., 2010). A number of different approaches have been developed for correcting the resulting image artifacts, some designed specifically for 7T and others which had originally been shown at lower field strengths. These included the use of navigator-based approaches (Versluis et al., 2012), external field probes (Barmet et al., 2008), and various camera-based devices (Maclaren et al., 2012; Stucht et al., 2015). Related (though simpler) optical technology is now being integrated into clinical systems at 3T, for example, the Philips VitalEye and the Kineticor systems used on Siemens scanners. External field probes have continued to be improved via commercial development, with applications shown in both 7 and 3T neuroimaging, particularly with respect to acquiring high-quality spiral-readout data. Fig. 2.3 shows results at both fields.

(a) (b) (c) (d)

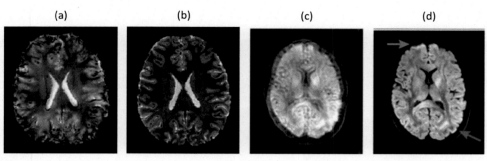

FIG. 2.3

Demonstrations of the use of field-probe corrections on image quality at 7T, (A) and (B), and 3T, (C) and (D). (A) and (B) were acquired using full-density *k*-space sampling with a spiral trajectory, with (A) no corrections and (B) incorporating dynamic field corrections. (C) and (D) are diffusion-weighted images acquired using single-shot spiral trajectories, with no corrections and third-order field evolution corrections, respectively. The arrows highlight blurring artifacts in the frontal (blue) and posterior (red) part of the brain. *Figures adapted from Engel et al. (2018) and Wilm et al. (2017).*

2.4 Development of new materials to tailor the electromagnetic field distribution in vivo

2.4.1 High-permittivity materials

One of the first approaches used to improve the transmit (B_1^+) field homogeneity for neuroimaging at 7T was to insert materials with permittivities equal to, or higher than, those of tissue between the transmit/receive coil and the subject. Originally shown at 7T (Yang et al., 2006) using large water bags, the approach became much more practical with the development of "dielectric pads" (Haines et al., 2010), which incorporated stable suspensions of metal titanates in water (or deuterated water). Numerous applications have been shown using permittivities in the range ~100–400 (van der Jagt et al., 2015; Manoliu et al., 2015; Lemke et al., 2015). Permittivities at the lower end of this range have been used to homogenize the field, in particular by increasing the transmit efficiency in the temporal lobes and cerebellum, while materials with higher permittivities have been used to target the field to specific areas of the head such as the inner ear. Examples are shown in Fig. 2.4.

This approach has also been demonstrated for neuroimaging at 3T, most recently using molded helmets of high-permittivity ceramics (Sica et al., 2020). Fig. 2.5 shows results obtained using this approach.

High-permittivity materials have also been used to enhance image quality at 3T, and even at 1.5T. Since the secondary magnetic fields induced by these materials are inversely proportional to frequency, materials used at 3T must have higher permittivity values than those used for 7T neuroimaging. For example, cardiac imaging using both single-transmit and dual-transmit approaches has been shown to improve in terms of homogeneity of transmit efficiency and image contrast (Brink and Webb, 2014), as well as resulting in reduced SAR, using barium titanate-based pads. Applications to flow imaging in the femoral arteries (Lindley et al., 2015), as well as general abdominal imaging (de Heer et al., 2012), have also been shown to improve using high-permittivity materials. Example images are shown in

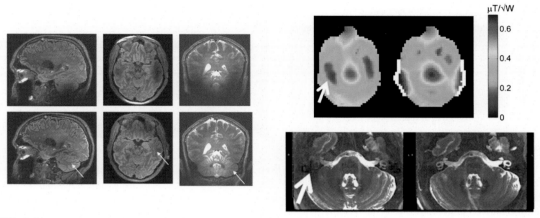

FIG. 2.4

(Left) Illustration of the effect of ~8 mm thick calcium titanate ($\epsilon_r \sim 110$) dielectric pads on 7T neuroimaging. (Right) Localized increase in image intensity in targeted areas of the inner ear using ~1 cm thick barium titanate ($\epsilon_r \sim 300$) dielectric pads. *Figure adapted from van der Jagt et al. (2015).*

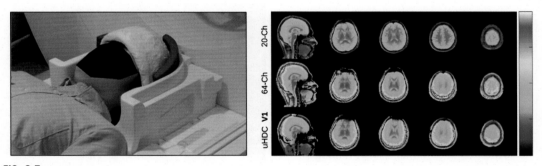

FIG. 2.5

(Left) Photograph of the molded high-permittivity ceramic helmet surrounding the head. (Right) SNR maps from a subject, acquired with a 20-channel receive array head coil (top row), 64-channel receive array head coil (middle row), and 20-channel receive array coil with ceramic helmet (bottom row). The SNR maps were normalized by the corresponding acquired B_1^+ map. *Figures adapted from Sica et al. (2020).*

Fig. 2.6. A number of new solid ceramics have been developed and demonstrated, with values well above 1000 (Rupprecht et al., 2018). There have even been applications shown at 1.5T, using ceramics with permittivities above 3000 (Rupprecht et al., 2018; Zivkovic et al., 2019).

2.4.2 Artificial dielectrics/metasurfaces

One of the disadvantages of the dielectric pad approach is that they can be quite heavy (~kg for body applications), can dry out over time, and also take up space in close-fitting head receive arrays. Artificial dielectrics are thin structures that can potentially mimic the effects of high-permittivity

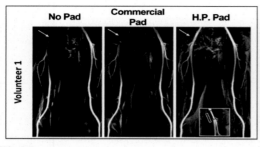
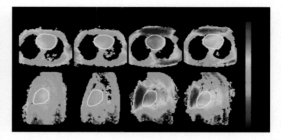

FIG. 2.6

(Left) Representative maximum intensity projections from a volunteer with no dielectric pad in place, a thick commercial aqueous-based pad, and a 2 cm thick barium titanate high-permittivity pad. Compared with baseline and commercial dielectric padding, high-permittivity dielectric padding significantly increased signal around the bifurcation point of the common femoral artery (arrow). (Right) Transverse (top) and sagittal (bottom) maps of the transmit efficiency measured in a volunteer at 3T with the body coil driven in quadrature and dual-transmit mode, with and without dielectric pads present. *(Left) Figure reproduced with permission from Lindley et al. (2015). (Right) Figure adapted from Brink and Webb (2014).*

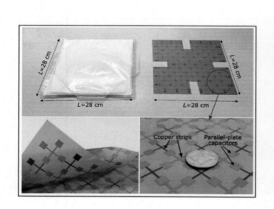
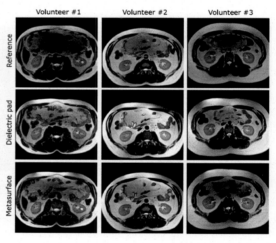

FIG. 2.7

(Left) Photographs of a barium titanate-based dielectric pad ($\epsilon_r \sim 300$) and an artificial dielectric/metasurface etched from a flexible double-sided PCB. (Right) 3T MR images of three healthy volunteers obtained with the body matrix coil used as the receiver. *Figures adapted from Vorobyev et al. (2021).*

materials, but can be constructed from thin conductors on flexible printed circuit boards (PCBs). The first demonstration of such an artificial dielectric was at 7T (Vorobyev et al., 2020), with rapid extension to 3T (Vorobyev et al., 2021) using an artificial dielectric produced on a single double-sided PCB, with capacitors formed by the overlap of conductive patches on either side of the flexible PCB. Results, shown in Fig. 2.7, indicated very similar improvement in image quality as for a dielectric pad.

2.5 **Parallel transmit technology**

Parallel transmit technology, using a multielement transmit array, is present in almost all modern-day 7T scanners. Although some neuroimaging studies are still performed in fixed B_1-shim mode using either a circularly or elliptically polarized field from a two-element transmit coil, the majority of neuroimaging systems have an eight-element transmit head coil. Body imaging universally uses between eight and thirty-two transmit elements, with dipole-based elements being the most commonly used element. Multielement transmit array systems were effectively developed with very similar chronology at 7 and 3T. The first transmit arrays designed for 7T neuroimaging were described by the Minnesota group in 2005 (Adriany et al., 2005), and the first experimental eight-channel transmit array for body imaging in 2007 (Vernickel et al., 2007). Shortly afterward, results from the first commercial dual-transmit 3T systems were reported in 2010 (Willinek et al., 2010).

Extended (>2 independent channels) parallel transmit systems for B_1 homogenization at 3T have not been commercially produced due to the limited improvement compared with increased complexity. However, several research groups have started to show how a four- or eight-channel system can be used to improve safety when scanning metallic implants, and in particular long guidewires used for interventional MRI or discarded pacemaker leads and deep brain stimulation implants. In such cases, the electric field produced by the transmit coil drives currents on the guidewire, which produce heat at locations along the guidewire at which charge can be displaced in the surrounding dielectric medium, with the most extreme case being at a noninsulated tip. The general principle to mitigate these effects is that certain combinations of inputs to the individual channels of the array result in usable B_1^+ distributions, but minimize the total electric field at the location of maximum heating (Etezadi-Amoli et al., 2015; McElcheran et al., 2017; Godinez et al., 2020, 2021).

As one example, Godinez et al. (2021) designed an eight-element parallel transmit coil at 1.5T and performed cardiac imaging experiments on sheep with implanted guidewires. Two operating modes were used, corresponding to different settings for the elements of the transmit array, with the settings calculated using the approach of Etezadi-Amoli et al. (2015). First, images were acquired using very low transmit power, operating in "maximum currents mode," also known as "coupling mode." In this mode, the electric field produced by the transmit array couples strongly to the guidewire, producing currents in the wire which then create a secondary magnetic field, which enables visualization of the wire. This mode uses very low transmit power since its safety cannot be guaranteed in terms of SAR. The second set of images is acquired in "null-currents mode," which produces usable images but has an extremely low SAR due to the cancellation of electric fields.

2.6 **Clinical applications**

In some applications, the translation from UHF to lower fields lies not so much in the transfer of specific technology, but more so in that the increased spatial resolution achievable with optimized hardware and imaging protocols at UHF provides clinically useful information. This encourages a greater degree of optimization at lower fields to replicate as much as possible the improved image quality, and therefore clinical relevance, with the obvious advantage that the applications can be much more widespread. One example comes from the field of ophthalmological MRI, and in particular the diagnosis and treatment of uveal melanoma (UM) which is the most common primary intraocular malignant tumor in adults, with an incidence rate of 6 per million per year. The main treatment options for UM consist of either eye-preserving therapies, such as proton beam therapy and episcleral brachytherapy, or enucleation, i.e., surgical removal of the eye. Diagnosis, treatment planning, and follow-up are conventionally performed using a combination of optical imaging techniques and ultrasound. Funduscopic evaluation is generally the primary means of detecting UM and the optical characteristics of the lesion provide an important first indication of the type of lesion. Additionally, ultrasound imaging is used to assess the lesion's internal reflectivity, an important aid in the differential diagnosis, and to measure its dimensions, which determine to a great extent the optimal treatment modality.

In the last decade, MRI has become a valuable imaging tool for UM. In the past, its diagnostic value was limited due to relatively low spatial resolution and image artifacts due to eye motion. Advances in ocular MRI, such as dedicated eye-coils and eye-specific acquisition strategies, have resolved many of these limitations, improving the care for UM patients. Using specialized RF coils and cued-blinking acquisition protocols, very high-resolution images were first acquired at 7T (Beenakker et al., 2013). It was shown that three-dimensional visualization of the tumor extent had a direct implication on the chosen therapy in a group of UM patients where there were doubts on the conventional ultrasound measurements, enabling eye-preserving therapy in two of the ten patients (Beenakker et al., 2016). In more recent years, these techniques have been translated to 3T with a recent comparison of optimized protocols concluding that the diagnostic performance of the evaluated 3T protocol proved to be as good as 7T, with the addition of 3T being superior in assessing tumor growth into nearby anatomical structures compared with 7T (Tang et al., 2021). Fig. 2.8 shows data acquired during this study comparing the quality of 7 and 3T images acquired from a patient with UM.

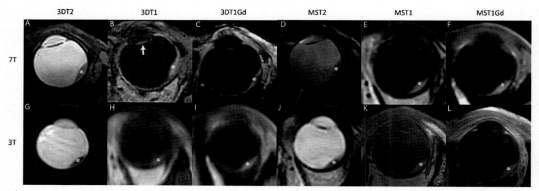

FIG. 2.8

A side-by-side comparison of the scans of one patient with uveal melanoma (UM) (asterisk) on 7T (A–F) and 3T (G–L). (A,G) $3DT_2$ SPIR. (B,H) $3DT_1$. Note the intraocular lens after cataract surgery (arrow). (C,I) Contrast enhanced $3DT_1$ SPIR (D) MST_2 SPIR (J) MST_2 without fat suppression. (E,K) MST_1 SPIR. (F) Contrast enhanced MST_1 without fat suppression. (L) Contrast enhanced MST_1 SPIR. *Figures adapted from Tang et al. (2021).*

2.7 Discussion

Just as the unicorn "killer UHF application" so desperately desired by commercial MR marketeers proved to be (predictably) elusive, in the same way, there has been no one "killer UHF technology," which has transformed systems at lower field strength. Instead, in common with many other high-tech industries, there has been a gradual and systematic exchange of information and ideas between the UHF and more clinically driven MRI communities, many of whom have a foot in both camps and therefore have much to benefit from a healthy exchange of ideas. In addition to the specific, mainly hardware-based examples outlined in this chapter, there is also an active interplay in sequence design and optimization, as well as image reconstruction methods. For example, although qualitative susceptibility weighted imaging (SWI) and quantitative susceptibility mapping (QSM) techniques were not specifically developed for high field MRI, with the original papers having being published before the commercialization of 7T scanners, the much greater sensitivity of the measurements at higher fields has led to an increase in the number of techniques used to process the data. A similar situation exists for techniques based on chemical exchange saturation transfer (CEST). CEST contrast increases significantly at high field, and many examples of this have been shown clinically. For example, glucoCEST was first demonstrated in vivo at 7T (Xu et al., 2015). Its translation to lower field is challenging, but results have been shown in patients with head and neck cancer (Wang et al., 2016). Related techniques such as chemical exchange spin locking (CESL) have also been developed at high field and translated to 3T (Paech et al., 2017).

References

Adriany, G., Van de Moortele, P.F., Wiesinger, F., et al., 2005. Transmit and receive transmission line arrays for 7 tesla parallel imaging. Magn. Reson. Med. 53 (2), 434–445.

Barmet, C., De Zanche, N., Pruessmann, K.P., 2008. Spatiotemporal magnetic field monitoring for MR. Magn. Reson. Med. 60 (1), 187–197.

Beenakker, J.W.M., van Rijn, G.A., Luyten, G.P.M., Webb, A.G., 2013. High-resolution MRI of uveal melanoma using a microcoil phased array at 7T. NMR Biomed. 26 (12), 1864–1869.

Beenakker, J.W.M., Ferreira, T.A., Soemarwoto, K.P., et al., 2016. Clinical evaluation of ultra-high-field MRI for three-dimensional visualisation of tumour size in uveal melanoma patients, with direct relevance to treatment planning. Magn. Reson. Mater. Phys., Biol. Med. 29 (3), 571–577.

Brink, W.M., Webb, A.G., 2014. High permittivity pads reduce specific absorption rate, improve B-1 homogeneity, and increase contrast-to-noise ratio for functional cardiac MRI at 3T. Magn. Reson. Med. 71 (4), 1632–1640.

Darnell, D., Truong, T.K., Song, A.W., 2017. Integrated parallel reception, excitation, and shimming (iPRES) with multiple shim loops per radio-frequency coil element for improved B-0 shimming. Magn. Reson. Med. 77 (5), 2077–2086.

de Heer, P., Brink, W.M., Kooij, B.J., Webb, A.G., 2012. Increasing signal homogeneity and image quality in abdominal imaging at 3T with very high permittivity materials. Magn. Reson. Med. 68 (4), 1317–1324.

Engel, M., Kasper, L., Barmet, C., Schmid, T., Vionnet, L., Wilm, B., Pruessmann, K.P., 2018. Singleshot spiral imaging at 7T. Magn. Reson. Med. 80 (5), 1836–1846.

Etezadi-Amoli, M., Stang, P., Kerr, A., Pauly, J., Scott, G., 2015. Controlling radiofrequency-induced currents in guidewires using parallel transmit. Magn. Reson. Med. 74 (6), 1790–1802.

Godinez, F., Scott, G., Padormo, F., Hajnal, J.V., Malik, S.J., 2020. Safe guidewire visualization using the modes of a PTx transmit array MR system. Magn. Reson. Med. 83 (6), 2343–2355.

Godinez, F., Tomi-Tricot, R., Delcey, M., et al., 2021. Interventional cardiac MRI using an add-on parallel transmit MR system: in vivo experience in sheep. Magn. Reson. Med. 86, 3360–3372.

Haines, K., Smith, N.B., Webb, A.G., 2010. New high dielectric constant materials for tailoring the B1+ distribution at high magnetic fields. J. Magn. Reson. 203 (2), 323–327.

Juchem, C., Nixon, T.W., McIntyre, S., Boer, V.O., Rothman, D.L., de Graaf, R.A., 2011. Dynamic multi-coil shimming of the human brain at 7T. J. Magn. Reson. 212 (2), 280–288.

Juchem, C., Theilenberg, S., Kumaragamage, C., et al., 2020. Dynamic multicoil technique (DYNAMITE) MRI on human brain. Magn. Reson. Med. 84 (6), 2953–2963.

Lemke, C., Hess, A., Clare, S., et al., 2015. Two-voxel spectroscopy with dynamic B_0 shimming and flip angle adjustment at 7T in the human motor cortex. NMR Biomed. 28 (7), 852–860.

Lindley, M.D., Kim, D., Morrell, G., et al., 2015. High-permittivity thin dielectric padding improves fresh blood imaging of femoral arteries at 3T. Invest. Radiol. 50 (2), 101–107.

Maclaren, J., Armstrong, B.S.R., Barrows, R.T., et al., 2012. Measurement and correction of microscopic head motion during magnetic resonance imaging of the brain. PloS One 7 (11), e48088.

Manoliu, A., Spinner, G., Wyss, M., et al., 2015. Magnetic resonance imaging of the temporomandibular joint at 7.0T using high-permittivity dielectric pads: a feasibility study. Invest. Radiol. 50 (12), 843–849.

McElcheran, C.E., Yang, B.S., Anderson, K.J., Golestanirad, L., Graham, S.J., 2017. Parallel radiofrequency transmission at 3 tesla to improve safety in bilateral implanted wires in a heterogeneous model. Magn. Reson. Med. 78 (6), 2406–2415.

Paech, D., Schuenke, P., Koehler, C., et al., 2017. T_1 rho-weighted dynamic glucose-enhanced MR imaging in the human brain. Radiology 285 (3), 914–922.

Rupprecht, S., Sica, C.T., Chen, W., Lanagan, M.T., Yang, Q.X., 2018. Improvements of transmit efficiency and receive sensitivity with ultrahigh dielectric constant (uHDC) ceramics at 1.5T and 3T. Magn. Reson. Med. 79 (5), 2842–2851.

Sica, C.T., Rupprecht, S., Hou, R.J., et al., 2020. Toward whole-cortex enhancement with a ultrahigh dielectric constant helmet at 3T. Magn. Reson. Med. 83 (3), 1123–1134.

Stockmann, J.P., Witzel, T., Keil, B., et al., 2016. A 32-channel combined RF and B-0 shim array for 3T brain imaging. Magn. Reson. Med. 75 (1), 441–451.

Stucht, D., Danishad, K.A., Schulze, P., Godenschweger, F., Zaitsev, M., Speck, O., 2015. Highest resolution in vivo human brain MRI using prospective motion correction. PloS One 10 (7), e0133921.

Tang, M.C.Y., Ferreira, T.A., Jaarsma-Coes, M.G., Marinkovic, M., Luyten, G.P.M., Beenakker, J.W.M., 2021. A comparison between 7T and 3T MR-imaging for Uveal Melanoma. Acta Ophthalmol. 99, 26–27.

van der Jagt, M.A., Brink, W.M., Versluis, M.J., et al., 2015. Visualization of human inner ear anatomy with high-resolution MR imaging at 7T: initial clinical assessment. Am. J. Neuroradiol. 36 (2), 378–383.

Vernickel, P., Roschmann, P., Findeklee, C., et al., 2007. Eight-channel transmit/receive body MRI coil at 3T. Magn. Reson. Med. 58 (2), 381–389.

Versluis, M.J., Peeters, J.M., van Rooden, S., et al., 2010. Origin and reduction of motion and f0 artifacts in high resolution T-2*-weighted magnetic resonance imaging: application in Alzheimer's disease patients. Neuroimage 51 (3), 1082–1088.

Versluis, M.J., Sutton, B.P., de Bruin, P.W., Bornert, P., Webb, A.G., van Osch, M.J., 2012. Retrospective image correction in the presence of nonlinear temporal magnetic field changes using multichannel navigator echoes. Magn. Reson. Med. 68 (6), 1836–1845.

Vorobyev, V., Shchelokova, A., Zivkovic, I., et al., 2020. An artificial dielectric slab for ultra high-field MRI: proof of concept. J. Magn. Reson. 320, 106835.

Vorobyev, V., Shchelokova, A., Efimtcev, A., et al., 2021. Improving B_1^+ homogeneity in abdominal imaging at 3T with light, flexible, and compact metasurface. Magn. Reson. Med. 87, 496–508.

Wang, J.H., Weygand, J., Hwang, K.P., et al., 2016. Magnetic resonance imaging of glucose uptake and metabolism in patients with head and neck cancer. Sci. Rep. 6, 1–7.

Willinek, W.A., Gieseke, J., Kukuk, G.M., et al., 2010. Dual-source parallel radiofrequency excitation body MR imaging compared with standard MR imaging at 3.0T: initial clinical experience. Radiology 256 (3), 966–975.

Wilm, B.J., Barmet, C., Gross, S., Kasper, L., Vannesjo, S.J., Haeberlin, M., Dietrich, B.E., Brunner, D.O., Schmid, T., Pruessmann, K.P., 2017. Single-shot spiral imaging enabled by an expanded encoding model: demonstration in diffusion MRI. Magn. Reson. Med. 77 (1), 83–91.

Xu, X., Yadav, N.N., Knutsson, L., et al., 2015. Dynamic glucose-enhanced (DGE) MRI: translation to human scanning and first results in glioma patients. Tomography 1 (2), 105–114.

Yang, Q.X., Mao, W., Wang, J., et al., 2006. Manipulation of image intensity distribution at 7.0T: passive RF shimming and focusing with dielectric materials. J. Magn. Reson. Imaging 24 (1), 197–202.

Zivkovic, I., Teeuwisse, W., Slobozhanyuk, A., Nenasheva, E., Webb, A., 2019. High permittivity ceramics improve the transmit field and receive efficiency of a commercial extremity coil at 1.5 Tesla. J. Magn. Reson. 299, 59–65.

Acquisition at ultra-high field: Practical considerations

Practical solutions to practical constraints: Making things work at ultra-high field

3

Christopher Wiggins[a], Richard Bowtell[b], and Michela Tosetti[c]

[a]*Institute of Neuroscience and Medicine Imaging Core Facility, INM-ICF, Forschungszentrum Jülich, Jülich, Germany*
[b]*Sir Peter Mansfield Imaging Centre, School of Physics and Astronomy, University of Nottingham, Nottingham, United Kingdom* [c]*Laboratory of Medical Physics and Magnetic Resonance, IRCCS Stella Maris, Pisa, Italy*

Highlights
- Translation of protocols is more complicated than simply copying from lower field.
- Development has reduced SAR limitations for virtually all sequences.
- Higher spatial resolution comes at the cost of limited anatomical coverage or longer scan time.

3.1 Introduction

Much to your amazement, it seems your friends have put their money together to buy you a shiny new 7T system for your birthday. It took a while to work out the installation instructions, but now it is up and running and the keys have been handed over by the vendor. You and your team have put a grocery store worth of vegetables and fruits through the system, and all is looking fine. Eventually, though, it is time to get the researchers and clinicians running studies on this expensive system. How does one get started with this?

It is crucial to understand that an ultra-high field MRI scanner is not just "a better camera," no matter how shiny. To get good results, one must understand the advantages and limitations of 7T MRI, some of which are not obvious at first and some of which can also be counterintuitive. Only then can one judge which research questions will truly benefit from the investment in running a 7T project.

3.2 Translation of workflows to 7T

A frequent situation is that the operator of a 7T is requested to reproduce an established workflow from lower field strength. Such an approach is likely to be difficult and ignores some of the differences, limitations, and indeed advantages of higher fields.

3.2.1 Contrast changes at higher field

As a general rule, T_1 tends to increase while T_2 and T_2^* tend to decrease as the field is increased (Rooney et al., 2007; Bartha et al., 2002; Peters et al., 2007), with the reduction in T_2^* being the most significant effect. These changes can present advantages and disadvantages, depending on the technique being applied. The longer T_1 of blood, for instance, is beneficial for time-of-flight angiography as well as for bolus tagging for, e.g., arterial spin labeling methods, because it means that the labeling of blood persists longer. However, longer T_1 also leads to a requirement for increased inversion times in MPRAGE image acquisitions (Mugler and Brookeman, 1990). The shorter T_2^* can present challenges for, e.g., accessing the optimal echo time for EPI, but also allows gradient echo-based scanning with shorter TEs and TRs while still showing significant contrast. The larger local field variations that arise at high field due to differences in magnetic susceptibility equate to a faster phase accumulation, which is a significant benefit for quantitative susceptibility mapping (QSM) (Wang and Liu, 2015). The combination of faster phase evolution and T_2^* relaxation makes the implementation of susceptibility-weighted imaging a very clear win at high field (Deistung et al., 2008).

3.2.2 SAR limitations

One of the more restrictive aspects of moving to a higher field for MRI is the unfortunate relation of magnetic field strength (B_0) to RF heating of the tissue, as the heating is proportional to the square of the magnetic field. RF heating is normally controlled by limiting the specific absorption rate (SAR). SAR can be reduced by increasing the repetition time TR, so that fewer RF pulses are applied in a given time, or by reducing the amplitude of the RF pulses, so that less energy is deposited by each pulse. If the RF pulse amplitude is reduced, the pulse duration must be increased to achieve the same flip angle, and this often leads to an increase in the minimum TE that can be achieved.

Techniques and protocols that are already operating close to the SAR limits at 3T are restricted to a much greater degree at 7T. Lowering the SAR to allowed values usually results in reduced coverage or increased scan times. In particular, techniques that rely on saturating the MR signal (e.g., to establish T_1 contrast) can often be so restricted that they become unusable.

While SAR limitations can render some protocols from lower field strength unusable, there are usually approaches that can achieve the desired contrast at 7T. The researcher or clinician must therefore be prepared for a change of sequence and protocol.

For T_1-weighted imaging, where sometimes a short TR/higher flip angle gradient echo or even spin echo sequence is used at lower field strength, the common approach at 7T is to use MPRAGE or a variant of this. In recent years, MP2RAGE (Marques et al., 2010) has become popular, as it allows for correction of the effect of B_1 inhomogeneities, as well as calculation of semiquantitative T_1 values.

For T_2-weighted imaging, a standard multiple spin echo sequence with fixed flip angle refocusing pulses is almost always so SAR limited, also at 3T, that any protocol built from it becomes either too long or too limited in anatomical coverage to be valuable at 7T. Thankfully, the developments in spin manipulation over the past years have resulted in 3D fast spin echo sequences such as SPACE/CUBE/VISTA (Mugler, 2014) that can achieve good T_2-weighting while being very efficient in terms of SAR. These developments include the use of variable flip angle pulse trains that minimize SAR while maintaining favorable signal characteristics and the use of RF pulses that have been optimized to limit power deposition.

In both of these cases, the suggested alternate sequence is generally run as a 3D scan. While this allows for nice features such as isotropic voxels, it is also the case that some of the people who read images are used to a particular 2D slice orientation. Depending on the software they use to visualize the data, this may not be available to them when examining the resulting data set. In this case, reformatting the data—which is a feature usually available on the MR console—to the appropriate orientation may be needed.

Inversion recovery techniques can also quickly hit SAR limits, or limited inversion efficacy, or both. Reducing the peak power and, therefore, the SAR by lengthening the inversion pulse reduces the effective bandwidth of the inversion. The greater susceptibility-induced frequency offsets in areas such as the inferior frontal lobes (which are close to the sinuses) can cause the inversion to fail and contrast to be lost in these regions. Here again, developments in SAR-efficient pulses have been of great benefit, e.g., MP2RAGE acquisitions with uniform inversion contrast (Marques et al., 2010).

3.2.3 Image quality

Just as abdominal imaging at 3T can be affected by image quality issues due to the inhomogeneous B_1^+ fields, imaging of the brain at 7T can suffer from contrast changes and signal dropouts. The shape of the B_1^+ inhomogeneities at 7T localizes these effects particularly in the inferior parts of the frontal lobes and the cerebellum. This can be addressed to some extent by the use of dielectric pads (Yang et al., 2006), although the results can show improvement they are rarely perfect. Additionally, care must be taken with the positioning of the pads, as in some geometries there is the potential to generate SAR hotspots (Fiedler et al., 2015), and careful steps must be taken to ensure that pads are consistently positioned in longitudinal studies. Parallel transmission (pTx) in which different RF waveforms can be applied to the individual elements of an array of RF transmit coils offers a powerful approach to reducing effects of B_1^+ inhomogeneity (Padormo et al., 2016). In its simplest form, this involves adjusting the phase and amplitude of the RF waveforms applied to each element, so as to maximize the homogeneity of the combined B_1^+ in a region of interest. This process, known as B_1-shimming, requires knowledge of the complex B_1^+ fields generated by each transmit element. Further improvements in image quality can be achieved by playing out different waveforms on the individual transmit elements and even changing these waveforms for acquisition of different regions of k-space.

The effects of B_0 inhomogeneity also increase at higher field. These effects are especially significant for sequences using an EPI readout, where susceptibility variations will result in increased distortions. For this reason, most 7T systems are equipped with gradients that are higher in performance than standard clinical systems, and often with higher order shim coils. Higher performance gradient systems produce larger field gradients that reduce the size of image distortions due to susceptibility-induced field variation, while the availability of second-order shim coils helps to reduce the magnitude of the unwanted field variation. There are also now several different approaches that can be used to remove distortion in postprocessing (Schallmo et al., 2021), although these require acquisition of additional data—e.g., field maps or images with reversed gradient polarity.

Dephasing effects, such as the signal dropout particularly seen over the sinuses in transverse 2D T_2^*-weighted images of the brain, will also worsen. Thankfully, these effects are dependent on slice thickness, so if the protocol is optimized for the higher resolution that should be possible on higher field systems, the effect will be reduced due to the use of thinner slices.

3.2.4 Inversion recovery-based techniques

While the relatively high B_1^+ inhomogeneity of 7T compared with lower field strengths is, in general, a problem that can be dealt with by the methods described above, getting a homogeneous inversion across an entire organ such as the brain can be extremely difficult. This is in part due to the fact that B_0 inhomogeneity—and so spatial variation of MR frequency—is also increased at 7T. In principle, the broader range of MR frequencies could be countered by using an inversion pulse with wider bandwidth. However, this usually implies a shorter RF pulse with higher peak power, and so such an approach quickly hits SAR limitations. The use of special RF techniques, such as the use of FOCI (Ordidge et al., 1996) for MP2RAGE acquisitions, has allowed for e.g., T_1 anatomical images of high quality. However, very sensitive techniques, such as FLAIR, are challenging to perform with the same quality and image appearance as at lower field strengths (Zwanenburg et al., 2010).

3.2.5 fMRI

The use of 7T systems for fMRI is extremely popular, due to the enhanced sensitivity and better spatial localization (e.g., Barth and Poser, 2011). The concept of first repeating a lower field fMRI experiment at 7T, with the same parameters, would normally be seen as a very appropriate, incremental approach. However, an important factor is the influence of physiological noise. As the resolution is decreased (i.e., voxel sizes increase), a plateau in the signal-to-noise ratio (SNR) is reached when physiological noise (whose magnitude scales with signal strength) dominates (Triantafyllou et al., 2005). This effect differs by field strength, so that resolutions that are reasonable at lower field strength may be dominated by physiological noise at higher field strength. In practice, this means that a 7T experiment replicating the resolution at lower field strength may not show any benefit from the higher field. Therefore, this conservative approach to initial fMRI experiments at 7T is likely to give disappointing results, and instead higher resolutions that lie in the optimal noise regime for 7T should be used.

This phenomenon becomes clearer when viewing a plot of the time series signal-to-noise (tSNR) versus the image signal-to-noise (SNR_0) as shown in Fig. 3.1 (which is reproduced from Triantafyllou et al., 2005). If we take note of the datapoints at 3×3 mm^2 resolution, we can see that the 7T data (black) show a significant increase in SNR_0 compared with 3T (red), from approximately 100 to approximately 200. However, the tSNR shows only a minor increase from around 68 to around 76 (i.e., an increase of around 12%). Since the tSNR is the key for distinguishing between neuronal activity and rest, this implies that an fMRI experiment using 3×3 mm^2 resolution at 3T will not produce improved statistics if repeated at 7T. If instead we look at the data from 1.5×1.5 mm^2 resolution, the tSNR will increase from approximately 38 to over 50 (roughly 30%), which would then translate into improved fMRI statistics at 7T.

In addition to the intrinsic gain in SNR that can be realized by moving from lower field to 7T, the blood oxygenation level dependent (BOLD) signal changes upon which fMRI relies are also significantly enhanced at 7T (Gati et al., 1997; van der Zwaag et al., 2009). This additional increase in BOLD contrast-to-noise ratio (CNR) can be exploited in pushing to finer spatial resolution. At higher field, the BOLD signal changes due to the small venules and capillaries are also relatively enhanced compared to the effects of large veins (Boxerman et al., 1995). Since small-vessel effects are more closely tied to the site of neuronal activity, spatial specificity of fMRI measurements is improved at 7T. This further encourages the use of 7T fMRI in the study of the fine detail of brain organization in individual subjects (Viessmann and Polimeni, 2021).

Nevertheless, the higher spatial resolution generally has to be paid for in terms of reduced coverage of the acquired brain volume. In the end, the physics of MRI remains the same: if the spatial resolution is increased, it is necessary to reduce the spatial extent of the imaging volume or increase the acquisition time for each volume and so worsen temporal resolution.

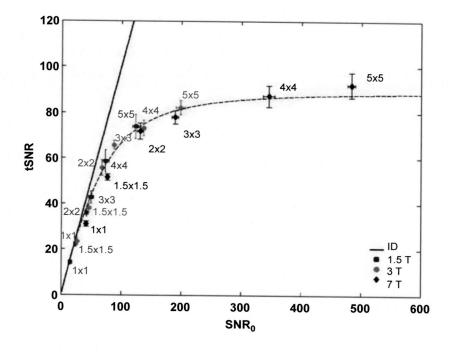

FIG. 3.1

Measured SNR in fMRI time series (tSNR) as a function of image SNR (SNR$_0$) for different spatial resolutions. The labels indicate the in-plane resolution in mm^2 at 3 mm slice thickness, with the different colors indicating field strength. The measurements are derived from areas of cortical gray matter and averaged over five subjects at each field strength. The solid line represents the line of identity (tSNR $=$ SNR$_0$), and the dashed line shows a model fit to all the data points. *Reprinted from Triantafyllou et al. (2005). Copyright (2005), with permission from Elsevier.*

When translating lower field protocols to 7T, it should also be noted that echo times will need to be adapted to obtain the optimal fMRI contrast-to-noise. In some cases, the added SNR at 7T will mean that the signal amplitude can rise above the noise baseline at the edges of *k*-space. This in turn can lead to truncation artifacts when the images are reconstructed, giving the false impression that 7T images are disturbed by a higher level of artifacts.

3.2.6 Time limitations

Especially in clinical settings, where there are issues with both the compliance of patients and institutional demand for high throughput, there is a desire to keep scan times short (or at least comparable to those of lower field strengths). This can lead to problems at 7T for a variety of reasons. Firstly, the more restricted scanning due to SAR limitations can be addressed by, e.g., longer TRs, but these in turn increase the scan times. Secondly, scanning at higher resolution generally involves increasing the matrix size for a given field of view, which also inherently increases the scan times. Acceleration techniques, and in particular the use of compressed sensing (Lustig et al., 2007), can help mitigate these effects. Thirdly, the necessity for more careful (and sometimes anatomically specific) calibration of both B_0 homogeneity and B_1 strength can increase the amount of setup time. The latter is unfortunately a form of "dead time," as no clinical information is being acquired.

The situation generally worsens when parallel transmission (pTx) is used. While the initial pTx experiments took a very long amount of time to acquire the necessary B_1^+ maps and calculate pulses, the field has come a long way in reducing the acquisition and calculation times needed for this down to a few minutes. Some researchers have pushed things even further by developing "Universal pulses" (Gras et al., 2017) that are calculated in advance using B_1^+ maps acquired from a cohort. The precalculated pulses can then be applied to other subjects to produce high-quality images. Here, though, there are some limits based on software (only those sequences for which pulses have already been prepared are available for use) and hardware (the pulses are based on the B_1^+ maps for a particular multielement RF transmit coil and so are not suitable for use with a different design of coil).

3.2.7 Safety of implants at 7T

While this will be discussed in more detail in Chapter 4, a limitation of 7T for clinical use is the fact that very few implants, if any at all, have MR labeling that includes 7T. This is not surprising, as FDA- and CE-certified 7T systems are a relatively recent development, and before this, there was little clinical reason to test these devices at higher field. As a consequence, scanning of most implants at 7T will be "off label," and so will require consideration about the safety of scanning with the implant and weighing of the clinical benefit vs. risk. This consideration is often restrictive, especially in the case of healthy research subjects who gain no benefit from the examination. However, other aspects of 7T scanning can help reduce the risk to the subject. In particular, none of the presently clinically certified 7T systems use body transmit coils, and all the coils used are local transmit coils. For implants that are in a remote part of the body (e.g., knee implants when scanning the brain), this often results in considerably less concern regarding elevated SAR near the implant. Due to the common need for subject-specific decisions to be made about whether or not to scan in the presence of implants, many 7T sites have specific review processes for the subjects who will be scanned at 7T. Safety procedures at 7T have been the subject of a small number of publications, particularly that by Fagan et al. (2021), and of the guidelines suggested by the German Ultrahigh Field Imaging network (https://mr-gufi.de/im ages/documents/Approval_of_subjects_for_measurements_at_UHF.pdf).

3.2.8 Vendor nomenclature

The number of vendors offering clinically certified 7T systems is presently quite low, and considerably less than the number of vendors at lower fields. This can often mean that the vendor at 7T is not the same as that of the other MR scanners used at a given site. When combined with clinical protocol descriptions that are effectively a form of shorthand, e.g., "2D T_1 COR," this can result in some difficulty in understanding what exactly the original sequence was and then from there working out what is an optimal sequence and protocol at 7T that could be used in its place.

3.3 **Researcher acceptance of higher field**

While much is written about subject perception of higher fields, the acceptance by researchers and clinicians is less widely discussed. The objections can be divided into several different areas.

3.3.1 **Certification of the system**

While at the time of writing, two vendors are offering FDA/CE-certified 7T scanners, a substantial portion of the installed 7T scanner base consists of systems not certified for medical use. Additionally, even the presently certified systems are only certified for specific body regions and methods. This "lack of certification" is often put forward as an objection to scanning subjects, with an implication that the lack of certification implies that the systems are somehow lacking in safety. This is a misunderstanding of the role of such certification for these devices. In general, the vendors will have manufactured the devices utilizing the exact same safety standards (e.g., ISO 60601) as are used for the clinically certified devices, often with additional safety margins. Clinical certification is something different than a safety assessment and is meant to ensure that the devices will deliver results that are of clinical value.

3.3.2 **"Unknown" risk of exposure to high fields**

Since to many outside the MR research community, higher field strengths are considered new, there is a worry about what appears to be the unknown effects of these higher fields on the subjects. However, neither the considerable experience with human 7T scanning over the past 20 years nor preclinical studies at considerably higher fields have provided any evidence of chronic effects.

3.3.3 **Vestibular effects**

It is known that the strong magnetic fields can produce vestibular effects and phosphenes in the subjects. While such effects certainly exist, their prevalence can be overstated, and reports show that the acceptance of 7T by subjects is generally very good with very low dropout rates (e.g., Cosottini et al., 2014; Heilmaier et al., 2011; Versluis et al., 2013). Care must be taken with, e.g., the speed of the patient bed, and vendors have addressed this issue in their control of the systems. For further discussion of these issues, see Chapter 5.

3.4 **Peripheral equipment**
3.4.1 **General considerations for peripheral equipment**

In a similar fashion to the labeling of medical implants, not all peripheral equipment has been tested at fields above 3T. Even though these devices often have a static field limit, this can be accommodated by siting the device slightly farther from the magnet. Of greater concern is RF interference of the device with the MR acquisition. While this is certainly a possibility, in practice the RF shielding and filtering that will have been integrated for operation at lower field strengths often works well also at the 7T RF frequency. However, it is advisable to test any device in the 7T MR environment to evaluate RF interference.

Higher field magnets have longer bores, and longer distances to the 5 Gauss lines or to other limits for operation of devices (often 20–40 mT). For physiological monitoring, this can result in the need for longer cabling. It can also cause difficulties with, e.g., expiratory CO_2 measurements if longer tubing with larger dead volume is needed.

For fMRI, it can be challenging to provide suitable stimuli equipment. For projectors, the increased distance of projection that is needed may require the use of custom lenses. Often there is little room within the RF coil, limiting the visual angle of the subject and also making the use of, e.g., headphones for auditory stimulation problematic.

3.4.2 Electrocardiogram (ECG)

ECG electrodes and the connected cabling are considered a potential burning hazard at 3T and lower field strengths. At 7T, the lack of body RF transmission can be considered an advantage as the cabling and electronics needed for ECG are remote from the RF coils (e.g., brain or knee). (An exception is of course the case of torso RF coils.) This considerably reduces the risks of RF focusing and SAR hotspots due to the ECG equipment.

Unfortunately, other effects come into play, particularly the cardioballistic effect. In this, the pulsatile movement of an ionic fluid—the blood—in the strong magnetic field causes its own electric potential. This signal is effectively overlaid onto the ECG signal, resulting in an ECG with a very unexpected shape. Standard ECG-triggering methods consequently often don't give reliable results. Various approaches have been put forward to address this, including acoustic cardiac triggering via the use of a microphone and appropriate filtering (Frauenrath et al., 2009) and the vectorcardiogram approach (Fischer et al., 1999).

3.4.3 Electroencephalography (EEG)

Simultaneous MRI and EEG setups are relatively routinely available at field strengths up to 3T. Some EEG system vendors also have devices that have been approved for use at 7T. However, the use of these is still very much a research prospect. This is in part due to problems in acquiring EEG data of good quality due to, e.g., cardioballistic induced movement of the subject's head in the field (Mullinger et al., 2008). Some researchers find it beneficial to turn off the cryopumps while performing simultaneous MR and EEG to limit artifacts due to vibration. Until recently, the magnets used by most vendors were provided by third parties and so are not always fully integrated into the system software. Shutting down the cryopumps may then require a manual shutdown and start-up of the system.

While the shielding effects of the EEG cables and electrodes could create situations that increase SAR, this can be approached by appropriate modeling and limit setting. However, such shielding effects, even if safety is properly considered, may reduce the SNR of the MR experiment.

3.5 Tailoring the study to the individual

While developments are leading to better and better images of large target volumes, the difficulties with B_0 and B_1 inhomogeneities and SAR limitations, as well as the inherent trade-off between resolution and acquisition duration, still weigh down on the desire to routinely acquire images that exceed those of lower field, especially in a clinical setting.

Another approach exists. If the clinical or research questions allow, benefit can often be gained from limiting the desired anatomical coverage to a smaller region. Both B_0 and B_1^+ variations generally still have fairly low spatial frequency and are often significantly reduced with a more limited field of view. At the same time, the problem of higher resolution protocols resulting in longer scan times can be countered by the time savings due to the reduced anatomical coverage.

3.6 Conclusions

There are many issues to consider when setting out on the mission "to make things work" on a new 7T system, and here, we have collated some practical solutions to practical constraints that will help in this task. Many of these constraints and solutions are described in more detail in other chapters of this book. By building an understanding of the advantages and limitations of ultra-high field MRI, we hope to help users identify the research and clinical studies that will most quickly benefit from the power of 7T. We hope your 7T birthday present brings you and your user base much joy, results, and publications!

References

Barth, M., Poser, B.A., 2011. Advances in high-field BOLD fMRI. Materials 4 (11), 1941–1955.

Bartha, R., Michaeli, S., Merkle, H., et al., 2002. In vivo (H_2O)-H-1 T-2(dagger) measurement in the human occipital lobe at 4T and 7T by Carr-Purcell MRI: detection of microscopic susceptibility contrast. Magn. Reson. Med. 47 (4), 742–750.

Boxerman, J.L., Hamberg, L.M., Rosen, B.R., Weisskoff, R.M., 1995. MR contrast due to intravascular magnetic-susceptibility perturbations. Magn. Reson. Med. 34 (4), 555–566.

Cosottini, M., Frosini, D., Biagi, L., et al., 2014. Short-term side-effects of brain MR examination at 7T: a single-centre experience. Eur. Radiol. 24 (8), 1923–1928.

Deistung, A., Rauscher, A., Sedlacik, J., Stadler, J., Witoszynskyj, S., Reichenbach, J.R., 2008. Susceptibility weighted imaging at ultra high magnetic field strengths: theoretical considerations and experimental results. Magn. Reson. Med. 60 (5), 1155–1168.

Fagan, A.J., Bitz, A.K., Björkman-Burtscher, I.M., et al., 2021. 7T MR safety. J. Magn. Reson. Imaging 53 (2), 333–346.

Fiedler, T.M., Ladd, M.E., Bitz, A.K., 2015. Local SAR elevations in the human head induced by high-permittivity pads at 7 Tesla. Proc. Int. Soc. Magn. Reson. Med. 23, 3213.

Fischer, S.E., Wickline, S.A., Lorenz, C.H., 1999. Novel real-time R-wave detection algorithm based on the vectorcardiogram for accurate gated magnetic resonance acquisitions. Magn. Reson. Med. 42 (2), 361–370.

Frauenrath, T., Hezel, F., Heinrichs, U., et al., 2009. Feasibility of cardiac gating free of interference with electromagnetic fields at 1.5 Tesla, 3.0 Tesla and 7.0 Tesla using an MR-stethoscope. Invest. Radiol. 44 (9), 539–547.

Gati, J.S., Menon, R.S., Ugurbil, K., Rutt, B.K., 1997. Experimental determination of the BOLD field strength dependence in vessels and tissue. Magn. Reson. Med. 38 (2), 296–302.

Gras, V., Vignaud, A., Amadon, A., Le Bihan, D., Boulant, N., 2017. Universal pulses: a new concept for calibration-free parallel transmission. Magn. Reson. Med. 77 (2), 635–643.

Heilmaier, C., Theysohn, J.M., Maderwald, S., Kraff, O., Ladd, M.E., Ladd, S.C., 2011. A large-scale study on subjective perception of discomfort during 7 and 1.5 T MRI examinations. Bioelectromagnetics 32 (8), 610–619.

Lustig, M., Donoho, D., Pauly, J.M., 2007. Sparse MRI: the application of compressed sensing for rapid MR imaging. Magn. Reson. Med. 58 (6), 1182–1195.

Marques, J.P., Kober, T., Krueger, G., van der Zwaag, W., Van de Moortele, P.F., Gruetter, R., 2010. MP2RAGE, a self bias-field corrected sequence for improved segmentation and T1-mapping at high field. Neuroimage 49 (2), 1271–1281.

Mugler III, J.P., 2014. Optimized three-dimensional fast-spin-echo MRI. J. Magn. Reson. Imaging 39 (4), 745–767.

Mugler III, J.P., Brookeman, J.R., 1990. Three-dimensional magnetization-prepared rapid gradient-echo imaging (3D MP RAGE). Magn. Reson. Med. 15 (1), 152–157.

Mullinger, K., Brookes, M., Stevenson, C., Morgan, P., Bowtell, R., 2008. Exploring the feasibility of simultaneous electroencephalography/functional magnetic resonance imaging at 7 T. Magn. Reson. Imaging 26 (7), 969–977.

Ordidge, R.J., Wylezinska, M., Hugg, J.W., Butterworth, E., Franconi, F., 1996. Frequency offset corrected inversion (FOCI) pulses for use in localized spectroscopy. Magn. Reson. Med. 36 (4), 562–566.

Padormo, F., Beqiri, A., Hajnal, J.V., Malik, S.J., 2016. Parallel transmission for ultrahigh-field imaging. NMR Biomed. 29 (9), 1145–1161.

Peters, A.M., Brookes, M.J., Hoogenraad, F.G., et al., 2007. T_2^* measurements in human brain at 1.5, 3 and 7 T. Magn. Reson. Imaging 25 (6), 748–753.

Rooney, W.D., Johnson, G., Li, X., et al., 2007. Magnetic field and tissue dependencies of human brain longitudinal (H_2O)-H-1 relaxation in vivo. Magn. Reson. Med. 57 (2), 308–318.

Schallmo, M.P., Weldon, K.B., Burton, P.C., Sponheim, S.R., Olman, C.A., 2021. Assessing methods for geometric distortion compensation in 7 T gradient echo functional MRI data. Hum. Brain Mapp. 42 (13), 4205–4223.

Triantafyllou, C., Hoge, R.D., Krueger, G., et al., 2005. Comparison of physiological noise at 1.5 T, 3 T and 7T and optimization of fMRI acquisition parameters. Neuroimage 26 (1), 243–250.

van der Zwaag, W., Francis, S., Head, K., et al., 2009. fMRI at 1.5, 3 and 7 T: characterising BOLD signal changes. Neuroimage 47 (4), 1425–1434.

Versluis, M.J., Teeuwisse, W.M., Kan, H.E., van Buchem, M.A., Webb, A.G., van Osch, M.J., 2013. Subject tolerance of 7T MRI examinations. J. Magn. Reson. Imaging 38 (3), 722–725.

Viessmann, O., Polimeni, J.R., 2021. High-resolution fMRI at 7 Tesla: challenges, promises and recent developments for individual-focused fMRI studies. Curr. Opin. Behav. Sci. 40, 96–104.

Wang, Y., Liu, T., 2015. Quantitative susceptibility mapping (QSM): decoding MRI data for a tissue magnetic biomarker. Magn. Reson. Med. 73 (1), 82–101.

Yang, Q.X., Mao, W., Wang, J., et al., 2006. Manipulation of image intensity distribution at 7.0 T: passive RF shimming and focusing with dielectric materials. J. Magn. Reson. Imaging 24 (1), 197–202.

Zwanenburg, J.J.M., Hendrikse, J., Visser, F., Takahara, T., Luijten, P.R., 2010. Fluid attenuated inversion recovery (FLAIR) MRI at 7.0 Tesla: comparison with 1.5 and 3.0 Tesla. Eur. Radiol. 20 (4), 915–922.

Practical considerations on ultra-high field safety

4

Oliver Kraff[a] and Stephan Orzada[b]

[a]*University Duisburg-Essen, Erwin L. Hahn Institute for MRI, Essen, Germany* [b]*German Cancer Research Center (DKFZ), Medical Physics in Radiology (E020), Heidelberg, Germany*

Highlights

- The same rigorous precautions apply at ultra-high fields as established at lower field strengths.
- 3T MR conditional implants can experience critical deflection at 7T, but this is unlikely for implants made of titanium.
- Gradient-induced heating and peripheral nerve stimulation are comparable on 3T and 7T.
- Shorter RF wavelength at 7T commits a greater risk of RF-induced heating. The critical implant length for resonance effects is about 5 cm at 7T.
- 7T MRI systems are not standardized. Safety tests on implants must always be critically questioned, and their applicability to the respective specific case must be discussed.
- Scanning of implants may be approved if the distance between the implant and the local RF transmission coil is sufficiently large and after limiting the SAR load of the MRI protocol.

4.1 Introduction

Safety considerations are always present in our daily work with a magnetic resonance imaging (MRI) system. MRI operators are trained to rigorously check their pockets for metallic objects before entering the scanner room. Installation of peripheral technical equipment is not straightforward but requires safety evaluations beforehand. The most obvious safety question affecting our daily work with the MRI system, however, typically arises during interviews for in vivo scans when the subject reports the presence of implanted medical devices (IMD). A decision on whether to scan the subject and under which limitations must then be taken, in the case of both a clinically indicated examination and a scientific study. At ultra-high magnetic field strengths (UHF), the decision-making is additionally complicated for three reasons. First, most scans are still performed in scientific studies with no direct benefit for the subject. Second, almost no medical implant has yet been labeled MR conditional for 7T, which places the responsibility of the risk-benefit analysis for a clinically indicated scan with the individual institution. And third, there is still no integrated standardized radiofrequency (RF) body coil available at UHF, but a variety of different local RF transmit coils and transmit strategies, rendering transferability of available safety assessments to the actual exposure scenario difficult.

This chapter starts with a general introduction of technical differences between 3T and 7T systems by recapitulating potential safety hazards from the different components of an MRI system. The focus on safety assessments regarding interactions between implant and RF transmit fields, aspects of RF coil safety, and different RF transmission strategies will finally lead the reader to practical considerations on how to ensure access at 7T. For patient screening, bioeffects, and worker safety regarding UHF exposure, the reader is referred to Chapter 5.

4.2 System overview

Every MRI system utilizes static and time-varying electromagnetic (EM) fields to generate images. The most defining component of an MRI system is the superconducting magnet that generates a homogeneous static magnetic field (B_0) for spin polarization. During imaging, radio waves (50–500 MHz) are switched to manipulate the tissue magnetization. These B_1 pulses are played out via an RF transmit (Tx) coil. For spatial encoding, a set of gradient coils generates magnetic gradient fields, which are switched in the kHz range. Finally, receiver (Rx) RF coils detect the MRI signal, which is then processed for image reconstruction. Fig. 4.1 shows a schematic overview of the hardware components along with a comparison of the relative magnitudes of magnetic fields used in MRI.

4.2.1 Standards and guidelines

Various safety standards and guidelines for MRI are available, with the most relevant being the International Electrotechnical Commission (IEC) standard 60601-2-33 "Medical electrical equipment - Part 2-33: Particular requirements for the basic safety and essential performance of magnetic resonance equipment for medical diagnosis" (IEC, 2022). This technical document addresses all aspects of the MRI system and equipment related to both patient and worker safety. Besides general safety instructions, organizational aspects of safety, and standardized methodologies for measuring system-related field parameters, it includes different modes of operation and exposure limits for patients and workers. Regarding scanning modes, the IEC standard distinguishes between three settings. In the normal mode

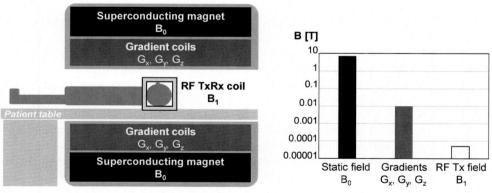

FIG. 4.1

Schematic overview of the main components of an MR system. At UHF, there is no integrated whole-body RF coil for spin excitation. Instead, local RF coils are used for both RF transmission and reception. The bar chart on the right shows the relative magnitudes of magnetic fields used for MRI.

operation, none of the EM fields may cause physiologic stress to the patient. If one or more of the MRI system components reach an output level that may cause physiologic stress to the patient, the MRI operator must acknowledge that this scan shall be performed within the first level controlled mode of MRI operation, necessitating medical supervision of the patient. Explicit ethical approval is required for scans within the second level controlled mode, in which output levels may be of significant risk to the patient. Regarding the static magnetic field, UHF MRI systems are either in first level mode (7T) or in second level mode (>8T). In addition, national guidelines have been developed in different countries to establish the safety of MRI in everyday clinical practice, such as the American College of Radiology (ACR) white papers (United States; ACR, 2020) and the Medicines and Healthcare Products Regulatory Agency (MHRA) guidelines (United Kingdom; MHRA, 2021). Interactions of items with the EM fields of the MR environment have been physically described and translated into standardized labeling (ASTM, 2013) and testing procedures. Items may be labeled either MR safe (no risk at all static magnetic field strengths; basically, plastic material only), MR conditional (no risk under specific conditions, which may range from simple to highly complex conditions), or MR unsafe (poses a significant risk to the patient and/or staff; also includes nonlabeled items).

4.2.2 Static magnetic field

Like any 1.5T or 3T system, UHF MRI systems use superconducting magnets, whose windings are made of a material which loses its electrical resistance below a certain critical temperature. If the windings of the magnet are kept below this critical temperature in a bath of liquid helium (boiling temperature of 4.3 K), a once-induced electric current and hence the accompanied magnetic field persist. Since the first installation of a 7T magnet at the Center for Magnetic Resonance Research at the University of Minnesota in 1999, there have been different 7T magnet designs for human MRI applications. The first magnet generation consists of whole-body systems with passive shielding of the magnetic field realized by installing about 400 tons of steel in the cabin. In the second generation, after the year 2010, actively shielded magnets were introduced, both as whole-body and as head-only systems. These magnet types are no longer manufactured and will be replaced by the latest and third generation of actively shielded 7T whole-body magnets that have been cleared for (partially) diagnostic imaging by the U.S. Food and Drug Administration (FDA). As a visual difference compared to 3T, a modern 7T magnet with a typical length of 2.7 m is at least 1 m longer than magnets of lower field strengths. In addition, to prevent physiologic side effects, the patient table speed is much slower with approximately 3.5 cm/s at 7T compared to 20 cm/s at 3T (values taken from MRI systems of one vendor). In emergency situations, this might render evacuations from the magnet bore difficult and should be discussed during MR safety training.

From a safety point of view, the attractive force on magnetizable objects is the number one risk factor in the MRI environment. Practically, all materials, including the components of the human body, are magnetically active. When brought into an external magnetic field, they themselves generate an additional magnetic field. The magnetic susceptibility χ is the material or tissue property that describes how strong this additional field inside the material is compared to the applied field strength B_0. A negative susceptibility means that the additional magnetic field inside is directed opposite to the external magnetic field B_0. This behavior is known as diamagnetism and occurs, for example, in pure water and in the human body. Paramagnetic substances (e.g., magnesium, aluminum, titanium), on the other hand, have a small positive susceptibility and strengthen the external magnetic field.

A third group of substances (iron, cobalt, and nickel as well as many iron-containing alloys) are called ferromagnetic. Here, electron spins can align themselves permanently in extensive regions and thus generate an even stronger additional magnetic field. Ferromagnetic substances retain their additional magnetic field, even if they are removed from the magnetic field of the MRI system. In the case of ferromagnetic materials, the term susceptibility therefore makes no sense since the additional field is not proportional to the applied field B_0. Instead, two other parameters need to be considered: the demagnetization factors, which strongly depend upon the object's shape, and its saturation, which is the degree of additional field that can be sustained by a material (e.g., around 2T for pure iron).

In a very homogeneous field, i.e., within the center of the magnet, no translatory forces act, not even on ferromagnetic objects. In contrast, strong translational forces can be observed in the inhomogeneous fringe field region around the bore. The force on a paramagnetic or (nonsaturated) ferromagnetic device is proportional to the product of magnetic field (B_0) and spatial magnetic field gradient (dB/dx).

The type of shielding has an influence on the spatial magnetic field gradient, which is significantly steeper with active shielding than with passive shielding. A more compact design of the magnet also influences the course of the magnetic field. Various types of magnets are shown schematically in Fig. 4.2. The course of the spatial magnetic field gradient of an actively shielded 3T magnet is very similar to that of the passively shielded 7T magnet (first generation of 7T magnets). With the new actively shielded 7T magnet, the spatial magnetic field gradients are slightly higher at 5–10 T/m than with the passively shielded 7T or actively shielded 3T magnets (3–7 T/m). In conclusion, the projectile effect on the 7T MRI can be up to 2.3 times stronger than on the 3T MRI. However, for saturated ferromagnetic metals, on the other hand, B_0 becomes irrelevant once saturation occurs, leaving the spatial magnetic gradient, specified in T/m, the only variable. Likewise, already at 3T, ferromagnetic objects reach projectile velocities of tens of meters per second, i.e., traversing the distance toward the magnet in under half a second. Hence, the same rigorous precautions apply at UHF as already established at lower field strengths.

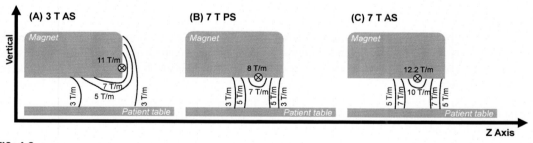

FIG. 4.2

Side view comparison of various magnet types and their respective, exemplary distribution of the spatial, static magnetic field gradient at the MR system's front quadrant, patient end. (A) shows a MAGNETOM Skyra 3T actively shielded (AS) magnet compared to a passively shielded (PS) 7T (first generation) magnet in (B), and an actively shielded 7T magnet of type MAGNETOM Terra (latest generation) in (C). The values given were taken from the respective compatibility data sheets with the kind permission of Siemens Healthineers GmbH, Germany. The plots were schematically drawn and do not reflect the exact course. The points where the force on a magnetically saturated ferromagnetic object is greatest are marked.

Besides the translational force, a twisting force acts on a magnetically active material. The torque τ aligns a nonspherical object with magnetic moment m and an axis at an angle φ to the magnetic field B_0 according to $\tau = m \cdot B_0 \cdot sin(2\varphi)$. Maximum torque occurs when an object is at 45 degrees with respect to B_0 and at the center of the magnet. However, twisting forces are also present in the inhomogeneous fringe field around the scanner and, in many cases, will be greater than translational forces. Hence, scissors or hemostatic clips made of ferromagnetic material, for example, will be twisted first to align with the magnetic field direction, which is then the optimal orientation for translational projectile effects.

4.2.3 Gradient fields

Magnetic field gradients are used during acquisition, for example, to spatially encode the MR signal. A set of three gradient coils G_x, G_y, and G_z are driven by hundreds of amperes of electricity pulses to form strong gradient fields across the imaging field-of-view (FOV). This results in two potential hazards: (1) acoustic noise because of the Lorentz force exerted on the current-carrying wires of the gradient coils within the static magnetic field, and (2) peripheral nerve stimulation as a consequence of Faraday's law describing that a time-varying magnetic field induces an electric field and, hence, an accompanied current density in tissue.

Temporary excessive noise exposure above 100 dB(A) sound pressure level (SPL) can lead to short-term hearing losses. If these exposures are repetitive or continuous, or in case of a single large noise exposure above 120 dB(A), the result may even be a permanent hearing defect. MRI systems can produce SPL of up to 140 dB(A), which is far above the pain and damage thresholds. Hence, proper hearing protection for both subjects to be scanned, and staff remaining in the examination room are an indispensable necessity. Keep in mind that there are different classes of protection. Ear plugs (if properly inserted!) typically provide better attenuation (10–30 dB) compared to the MRI system's headphones (10–15 dB), which are only suited for communication purposes according to the MRI system operator manual. In addition, decibels are multiplicative but not additive, meaning that the use of double ear protection, i.e., ear plugs and ear defenders, may only provide 5–10 dB additional protection over that of the most attenuating device. However, double-hearing protection may be recommended for long and loud acquisitions, e.g., diffusion imaging or functional MRI, and it may even be required for certain landmarks within the scanner bore according to the MRI system operator manual. Additional care must be taken in the sedated or anesthetized patient, in children, and in subjects who already suffer from hearing deficits like tinnitus.

Since the Lorentz force scales with the magnitude of the static magnetic field, one would expect higher SPL for higher magnetic fields. However, stronger vibrations of the gradient coil can also lead to greater mechanical damping, so that there is not a linear scaling of vibrations and acoustics with B_0. This nonlinear dependency is called Lorentz-damping (Winkler et al., 2018). In addition, with improved insulation against sound and vibration, and magnets of larger inert mass, SPL are in practice only slightly higher at 7T compared to 3T. On the other hand, the gain in intrinsic signal-to-noise ratio (SNR) by increasing the static magnetic field, which is usually invested in images of high spatial resolution, also necessitates higher gradient amplitudes and, thus, results in more acoustic noise. Table 4.1 provides a practical overview of pulse sequence parameters that influence acoustic noise. In addition, the MR vendors provide software and hardware packages with reduced noise.

Although peripheral nerve stimulation (PNS) during MRI is not harmful and usually well tolerated, its avoidance is highly desirable for maximum patient comfort and acceptance as well as to minimize

Table 4.1 **While there are various levels of acoustic noise for different pulse sequences, the MR operator can influence the acoustic noise by varying scanning parameters for each sequence.**

MR imaging parameter	Effect on acoustic noise
Field-of-view FOV	Increasing FOV will reduce gradient amplitude and noise.
In-plane resolution	Smaller pixel sizes will result in higher gradient amplitude and noise.
Slice thickness	Increasing the slice thickness in 2D sequences will reduce the acoustic noise as it is inversely proportional to the slice selection gradient.
Low SAR RF pulses	Low SAR pulses are longer and have a narrower bandwidth compared to standard RF pulses, so that a lower slice selection gradient will be needed.
Echo Time (TE)	Increasing TE may reduce the reception bandwidth, resulting in lower noise.
Echo spacing (ES)	Increasing ES or reducing the turbo factor (echo train length) reduces the noise.
Repetition time (TR)	Increasing TR reduces the overall noise.
Number of slices/echoes	Reducing the number of slices or echoes will reduce the overall noise.

movement artifacts. The change of the magnetic field (dB/dt) induces an electric field and thus an accompanying current density producing nerve or muscle depolarization (Schaefer et al., 2000). As dB/dt is maximized during the ramp up and ramp down portions of the gradient waveform, PNS therefore typically occurs in pulse sequences that are built upon rapid gradient switching, such as echo-planar imaging, or balanced steady-state free precession. Since only the most linear central segments of the magnetic gradient fields are used for imaging, the largest gradient fields may occur outside the FOV. Hence, the strongest induced E fields are typically located in the more superficial portions of the patient where many peripheral nerves run. The MRI system's software can predict the likely onset of stimulation if the MRI operator filled in correct data for the patient registration (i.e., age, sex, and body part to be imaged).

The gradient coils used in UHF systems are not different from those of current 1.5T or 3T MRI devices. Across field strengths, standard gradient strengths are around 40–80 mT/m with slew rates of 100–200 mT/m/s. Slew rate is defined as the maximum amplitude divided by the rise time to achieve that amplitude. There is a long history of safe use with the clinically established gradient coils. However, some research systems are outfitted with stronger gradients of up to 300 mT/m (McNab et al., 2013), while even 500 mT/m gradients with a tripled slew rate of 600T/m/s are currently discussed (Huang et al., 2021). Here, cardiac stimulation remains theoretically possible, and hence could have serious consequences, so that special care must be exercised in such environments. Similarly, in case of large and distal implants (approx. 30–50 cm away from isocenter), potential risks of gradient-induced heating (Bruhl et al., 2017) should also be considered.

4.2.4 RF field

The most frequent MRI-related incidents are thermal events (excessive heating, burns), followed by mechanical (cuts, fractures, lifting injuries), projectiles, and hearing losses (Delfino et al., 2019). A dramatic example of excessive RF-induced heating is the case of a fourth degree burn in an extremity of an anesthetized child due to an ignored MR unsafe pulse oximeter wrapped around the child's forearm (Haik et al., 2009). Hence, in addition to the rightly thoroughly presented projectile effect in MRI safety training sessions, the interaction between the emitted RF transmit fields and the human body poses another great safety risk during an MRI scan that requires the same level of attentiveness.

During the electromagnetic exposure, energy is absorbed in human body tissue causing a heat deposition in the tissue. The degree of power deposition is described by the associated specific absorption rate (SAR) in units of W/kg. SAR depends quadratically upon the electric field induced in tissue and is also related to the tissue's electrical conductivity and density. Tissues with higher conductivity or lower density will experience higher SAR. Furthermore, conductivity increases with frequency, and thus with static magnetic field strength, contributing not only to higher SAR for UHF MR systems but also to much more complex and nonuniform patterns throughout the subject. At 7T, the current density distributions are significantly more complex compared to lower field strength. Besides polarization effects, local SAR elevations now appear much deeper in the tissue, as shown in Fig. 4.3. However, in contradiction to the traditionally cited quadratic dependency of SAR with B_0, studies at UHF, and in combination with parallel transmission strategies (see below), have shown a flattening of the SAR distribution above 3T, which adheres closely to a linear increase with magnetic field strengths (Deniz et al., 2016).

RF heating becomes more severe when going to higher field strengths since localized effects can be more pronounced due to a transition from the quasistationary to the electromagnetic field regime (Fiedler et al., 2018). The latter allows waves to separate from the source and travel through space. At 7T, the wavelength of the transmitted RF is small enough compared to the bore diameter of the MR scanner, so that the lower limit frequency of the lowest waveguide mode is just exceeded and the so-called traveling waves can propagate in the MR scanner. Consequently, this results in B and

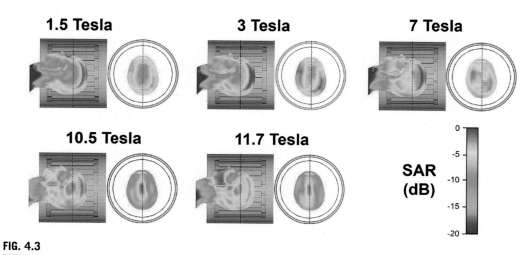

FIG. 4.3

10 g-averaged SAR distribution in a sagittal and transversal slice for a male body model inside a head coil tuned to frequencies from 64 MHz for 1.5T to 500 MHz for 11.7T MRI. Plots are normalized to the individual maximum, i.e., at 0 dB. At 1.5T, the SAR distribution is correlated with typical eddy current patterns known from quasistatic approximations and the maximum SAR is located in superficial tissues. With increasing frequency, local SAR elevations occur deeper in the head. *Reprinted with permission from Fiedler et al. (2018). Elsevier.*

E fields extending well beyond the RF coil's housing. RF energy may be absorbed by the body further away from the RF transmit source or interact with distant metallic objects, which has implications for subjects with IMD.

To avoid thermal injuries from RF-induced heating in MRI, the IEC standard provides limits for core temperature in humans (IEC, 2022). For the first level controlled mode, the rise in core temperature may be nearly doubled compared to the normal operating mode. However, keep in mind that limits for temperature rise are only given for core temperature. Hence, stronger rises of temperature may occur locally, and physiologic stress for the subject being imaged should be expected. MRI operators must review each case before switching the RF system into this mode as presence of IMD, light fever of the subject ($\leq$39.5°C), or a primary disease affecting the subject's thermoregulation (e.g., diabetes) may be a contraindication.

As in vivo temperature cannot be monitored during the MRI examination, limits are given in terms of SAR. The IEC standard requires an averaging time of 6 min for different types of exposed mass (Table 4.2). At UHF, and in general for local transmit RF coils, the local SAR calculated over any 10 g of tissue is the most critical aspect. For short averaging durations of up to 10 s, the SAR limit may be doubled. Table 4.3 provides an overview of parameters for the MRI operator to control SAR in practice.

Table 4.2 Classification of SAR averaging types according to the IEC safety guideline.

RF coil	SAR averaging	Definition
Volume RF Tx coil	Whole Body	SAR averaged over the total mass of the body.
	Partial Body	SAR averaged over the body mass within the effective volume of the RF Tx coil, in which no more than 95% of the total RF power is absorbed
	Head SAR	SAR averaged over mass of the head approximated by a suitable model
Local RF Tx coil	Local Head SAR	SAR averaged over any 10 g of tissue of the head determined by a suitable model
	Local Trunk SAR	SAR averaged over any 10 g of tissue of the trunk determined by a suitable model
	Local Limbs SAR	SAR averaged over any 10 g of tissue of the limbs determined by a suitable model
Volume and local RF Tx coil	Short-term SAR	SAR is averaged over any 10-s period and shall not exceed two times the stated values
	MR Examination Specific Absorption	RF energy absorbed per unit of mass (kJ/kg, or W·min/kg), calculated from Whole Body SAR. It is also known as SED (specific energy dose) or SAE (specific absorbed energy)

Note that the averaging time is any 6-min period for all SAR types. The transition from normal operating mode to first level controlled operating mode allows a factor of two to comply with the IEC SAR limits, with exclusion of Head SAR which remains fixed at 3.2 W/kg in both operating modes. At UHF, usually the 10-g-averaged local SAR is the most critical aspect due to absence of an integrated volume body coil.

Table 4.3 Practical methods for reducing SAR.

MR imaging parameter	Effect on SAR
Pulse sequence protocol	It is recommended to set up an imaging protocol with alternately applying pulse sequences of high SAR load (spin echo) with cooling times of low SAR load (gradient echo). Some sequences may also introduce scan delays to comply with the 6-min SAR averaging limit
Flip angle (FA)	As a rule of thumb, a reduction of 10 degrees of FA reduces the SAR by 10%–15%. Image contrast and SNR may be affected
Pulse duration	Prolonging the pulse duration is usually more effective for large FA (greater than 60 degrees) than reducing the amplitude. It will affect the minimum allowable echo time (TE) and potentially number of slices
Low SAR RF pulses	Low SAR RF pulses are scaled down and prolonged and are therefore an easy and effective way to reduce SAR
Repetition time (TR)	A 50% increase in TR will reduce the SAR by one third. Increasing TR will affect the image contrast, and it is not recommended for T_1-weighted sequences
Number of slices/echoes	Reducing the spatial coverage or number of echoes in an echo train is an effective way to reduce the number of RF pulses per TR, but it will increase the scan time
Hyperechoes/Variable-Rate Selective Excitation (VERSE)	When hyperechoes are enabled, an RF pulse train with small FA pulses is used but flanked with full amplitude RF refocusing pulses to restore SNR and contrast. VERSE pulses modify the envelope of the RF pulse with a corresponding dip in gradient amplitude at times where the RF pulse is highest
Parallel imaging	Acceleration techniques like parallel imaging reduce the overall number of RF pulses in a sequence and hence, indirectly reduce the SAR
Parallel transmission	Besides mitigating B_1 inhomogeneities, parallel transmission techniques can also be designed to find an excitation of reduced SAR. However, this requires extensive knowledge of RF fields and (time-consuming) calculation of RF pulses and/or shims for the individual exposure scenario
Ventilation/Room temperature	SAR hotspots typically occur deep within the human tissue, so maximum ventilation or a reduced room temperature will have no effect on SAR. On the other hand, for temperatures above 25°C within the MR bore the MR scanners safety supervision will limit the RF exposure and may even prevent further scans

4.3 RF coil safety

Many different RF coil designs can be used to perform UHF neuroimaging. A detailed overview on different designs will be provided in Chapter 8. Here, we will give a brief overview on how the necessities of UHF imaging influence coil design and impact RF coil safety.

In contrast to clinical MRI systems at 1.5 and 3T, there are no vendor-provided Tx body coils installed in UHF MRI systems. A birdcage body coil as used at lower field strengths would not be able to produce a sufficiently homogenous transmit field due to the pronounced inhomogeneities associated with the short RF wavelength at UHF. Therefore, coils for imaging at UHF need to contain a transmit part. Furthermore, to cope with the difficulties introduced by the short wavelength, the transmit part of the coils often is an array of multiple Tx elements. The relation of amplitudes and phases between the channels can either be fixed by design or varied using a multichannel transmit system. It is obvious that this increase in complexity also makes coil safety more complex.

All RF coils used on human subjects have to conform to the relevant norms, most notably, the IEC (IEC, 2022). A well-written guideline on how to ensure that self-developed coils fulfill the requirements of the IEC guideline can be found in the literature (Hoffmann et al., 2016). In addition, a working group of members of the Safety and Engineering Study Groups of the International Society for Magnetic Resonance in Medicine published a very detailed consensus recommendation on best practices for safety testing of experimental RF hardware (ISMRM, 2022). In short, patients must always be protected from hazards. These hazards include electrical shock, contact to nonbiocompatible materials and tissue damage through heating, either by RF heating or direct contact to hot parts of the housing.

To ensure protection from electrical shock, coils must be enclosed by a biocompatible, nonconducting housing with a high melting point and low flammability. On the user side, regular visual inspection is recommended to ensure that no damage of the housing reduces its capability of protecting the patient. Visual inspection should also include the cables and connectors of the coil. The cable coating should be intact, and no conducting material should be visible, connectors should be undamaged, and should connect securely. It is the responsibility of the MRI operator to visually inspect the RF coil for defects.

During RF coil development and safety testing, extensive EM simulations and validation measurements are necessary to ensure safe operation of the coil array. These simulations include highly detailed models of the coil as well as detailed human body models. It must be emphasized that the results from these simulations are only valid for the intended use of the coil as it was modeled, which includes the coil setup and its alignment with respect to the patient. Using a coil differently to its intended use might harm the patient because the same RF exposition can lead to completely different SAR levels in different tissues. Kopanoglu et al. investigated implications of mispositioning on SAR in a head coil at 7T (Kopanoglu et al., 2020). In their setup, they found increases in peak local SAR of more than a factor of two when the patient's head was misaligned. Therefore, due to the coils at UHF being actively transmitting parts, training the users on their correct use is even more important than at lower field strengths.

4.4 Dielectric pads

The B_1 fields of single-channel Tx coils are often a compromise between FOV, efficiency, and homogeneity. A simple and cheap way of improving the Tx field homogeneity or increasing the Tx field in certain areas is the use of dielectric pads. Dielectric pads are bags filled with materials of very high permittivity like barium titanate ($BaTiO_3$) or calcium titanate ($CaTiO_3$), and other non-MRI-visible high permittivity materials like heavy water (D_2O), for example.

Since dielectric pads change the field distribution of the Tx field, it is obvious that they can have an impact on SAR. This impact depends on the Tx coil used, the position and size of the dielectric pads, and their permittivity. Studies give different reports on the impact of the dielectric pads on SAR. While Teeuwisse et al. report almost no effect of the pads on SAR (Teeuwisse et al., 2012), Brink et al. show a reduction of SAR for optimal configurations but also report an increase in SAR by up to 20% at 3T (Brink et al., 2015), while Bitz et al. even show an increase of up to 64% for certain configurations in a 7T head coil (Bitz et al., 2014). Care should be taken to ensure that the SAR limits are not exceeded when using dielectric pads. For commercial pads, the respective datasheet should be consulted for the correct positioning and eventual SAR increase provided by the vendor. While EM simulations are a suitable tool to evaluate the impact of dielectric pads on SAR, a pragmatic solution would be to restrict the MRI protocol to be applicable within limits of the normal operation mode only.

In addition, pads should be checked for leakages before use as some of the materials can be a potential health risk or damage the RF coil.

4.5 Parallel transmission

With the use of multichannel Tx arrays, it is possible to use more sophisticated methods of increasing homogeneity and reducing SAR at UHF. Since parallel transmission (pTx) techniques will be presented in detail in Chapter 7, this chapter provides a few practical considerations only. The simplest form of parallel transmission is RF shimming. In RF shimming, the same RF pulse is transmitted from each Tx element of an array, albeit with a different amplitude and phase for each Tx element.

For each choice of amplitudes and phases, not only the B_1 is different but also the E-fields. This in turn means that each so called B_1-shim produces a different SAR distribution.

The SAR for a certain RF shim can be precalculated by appropriate EM-simulations. If the shim, the coil, and the subject remain the same throughout the measurement, the SAR scales linearly with the input power, making supervision simple. Yet, care must be taken that those above assumptions hold. Hofmann et al. show an example where the phase of one out of eight elements of a head coil is changed by 180 degrees, leading to more than a two-fold increase in peak local SAR (Hoffmann et al., 2016). In the same paper, the authors also show that switching off a single element can increase the peak local SAR per unit power. Therefore, even for RF shimming using a full amplitude and phase supervision of all channels including a coil check is advisable.

In contrast to static RF shimming, where a single shim is used throughout a sequence or even throughout the whole measurement, dynamic RF shimming changes the shim much faster. Examples for such dynamic RF shimming techniques are TIAMO, where the shim is changed with every k-space line (Orzada et al., 2010), k_T-points where a train of pulses with different shims is played out each line (Cloos et al., 2012) and Transmit SENSE, where each pulse can be interpreted as consisting of a fast succession of shims (Katscher et al., 2003). Although the speed in which the relation of amplitudes and phases changes is different in the respective techniques, they share a common need for a supervision that rapidly samples the RF in amplitude and phase in all channels to calculate the SAR at any sampled point in time. Due to the complexity of the supervision, today's pTx systems still have conservative safety margins and are less suited for routine use. In this context, "plug and play" techniques such as the concept of Universal Pulses (Gras et al., 2017) or TIAMO based on precalculated optimal RF shims could leverage pTx for a broad and routine use in the near future.

4.6 Implant safety

To examine subjects with IMD safely, it is necessary to clarify the MRI safety status of the various implants in advance of the examination. The clarification process should start as early as possible (e.g., when making an appointment) as detailed information about the implant itself, its MRI safety labeling, and instructions for use, about the landmark of the FOV, and the required MRI examination parameters (field strength, RF coils used, sequences, SAR load, etc.) must be obtained. This is generally not an easy task, and at UHF, it even poses an almost insurmountable obstacle as (i) most scans are performed with a scientific purpose, and not because of a clinical indication, and (ii) so far, only a few implants are labeled MR conditional at 7T by the implant manufacturers. These are mostly rather small, nonferromagnetic implants with lengths up to 20 mm as used in otorhinolaryngology for ventilation, tympanic, or stapes prosthesis (Kraff and Quick, 2017). Passive IMD are tested for magnetically induced force and torque, as well as for RF-induced tissue heating according to methods described by the American Society for Testing and Materials (ASTM) International (ASTM, 2011). For more complex and electrically long IMD (especially active implants, such as defibrillators and pacemakers), the international standards organization technical specification (ISO, 2012) recommends additional safety testing regarding RF- and gradient-induced heating, as well gradient-induced vibration, and malfunction. Extensive numerical simulation is the method of choice here.

Implants made of paramagnetic material are unlikely to experience magnetically induced attraction forces stronger than the gravitational force. Slightly paramagnetic objects made of titanium or aluminum will therefore not show significant translational deflections even at 7T. However, the true problem lies in the description of the IMD information in accordance with the applicable ASTM standard F2503-13 (ASTM, 2013). As the implant information does not specify the measured deflection angle, scaling to the actual exposure scenario remains difficult. Regarding RF-induced heating, the critical implant length for resonance effects and the presence of standing waves typically occurs at half of the wavelength (or integer multiples thereof) of the excitation frequency. However, this serves only as a rough guide, since studies have shown that resonance effects can occur even at a quarter of the wavelength. While the critical lengths at 1.5T correspond to approximately 26 cm and approximately 13 cm at 3T, several studies have shown temperature increases at an implant length of approximately 5 cm at 7T (Noureddine et al., 2018).

Most implants will certainly not receive a dedicated safety evaluation for 7T from the implant manufacturers. Likewise, many of these implants will not be in the direct exposure volume of the local RF coil. Since the power density outside of local Tx RF coils decreases very quickly, access to 7T MRI may be granted under certain conditions. For subjects with passive implants that are labeled MR conditional for 3T, that do not contain magnetizable components, and that are located at a certain distance from the RF coil, the German Ultra-high Field (GUFI) network published a consensus recommendation that an overly conservative exclusion would no longer be warranted, as previously required by many ethics' committees (GUFI, 2015). A flowchart of the decision tree as suggested by the GUFI network is given in Fig. 4.4. Certainly, traveling wave effects need to be considered as well, and implants with dimensions close to or larger than a critical wavelength in the human body need to be treated with additional precautions, especially for partially implanted metallic objects. Another possibility for ensuring access is minimizing the SAR load in a protocol. Noureddine et al. performed numerous thermal simulations for RF-induced tissue heating in case of aneurysm clips of different length, orientation, and location (Noureddine et al., 2019). In practice, the exact orientation of the clip to the electrical field component during a MRI examination remains unknown, as well as maybe even the clip length. This motivated the authors to calculate a conservative power which amounts to 4.6 W for the investigated head coil. Although this is a reduction of the maximum allowable input power by almost a factor of 8 for this case, it would still allow application of clinically relevant pulse sequences such as T_1-weighted 3D gradient echo and susceptibility-weighted imaging at 7T.

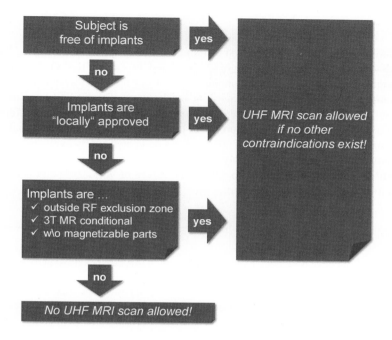

FIG. 4.4

Decision tree for inclusion of subjects for measurements at UHF MRI in suspected case of implants as recommended by the German Ultrahigh Field Imaging (GUFI) network. Please note that the minimum distance between the implant and the local RF coil depends on both components and must always be discussed individually.

4.7 Implants and parallel transmission

Changing the amplitudes and phases of the signals in a multichannel Tx system not only changes the B_1 distribution but also the E-fields. As this can be used to reduce, for example, peak local SAR in the absence of metallic implants, this can also be used to reduce SAR in the presence of such implants. Perhaps, the simplest Tx array is a birdcage when the two quadrature inputs are used as the inputs of a two-channel array. In this case, it can be seen as the superposition of two linear polarized birdcages. A linear polarized birdcage has a large area of very low E-fields. If this area is aligned appropriately with the wire lead of for example a brain stimulation device, the SAR at the tip of the device can dramatically be reduced as was demonstrated by Eryaman et al. in simulations and experiments (Eryaman et al., 2013). Since increasing the number of Tx channels increases the degrees of freedom for RF field manipulation, it is obvious that a multichannel Tx array can potentially be used to dramatically reduce the interaction between the RF transmission and a metallic implant. This was demonstrated in a large simulation study by Guerin et al. for a multitude of coils and body models with realistic deep brain stimulation devices (Guerin et al., 2020). The study found that pTx reduced the absorbed power around stimulation devices by more than an order of magnitude at no cost of flip angle uniformity or global SAR. Exploiting pTx can enable safe imaging of patients with conductive implants when using appropriate techniques that implement constraints for SAR around the implants into the optimization algorithms for pTx pulse calculation.

4.8 Conclusion

Ultra-high field MRI has evolved from the first installation of a 7T system at the turn of the millennium into a medical device for diagnostic imaging of the head and the extremities. On the other hand, it remains an investigational device for other imaging applications and MRI systems at 7T are still less standardized compared to 3T. Especially regarding the RF transmit coil and transmission methods used, there are substantial differences. Hence, it is important to critically question safety assessments of implants and to have a thorough discussion about how this relates to the individual exposure scenario. Although most implants will certainly not receive a dedicated safety evaluation for 7T from the implant manufacturers, access to 7T MRI may be granted under certain conditions. It is the responsibility of the institution and MRI operator to ensure the safety of volunteers and patients during the entire exposure to the UHF MRI environment.

References

ACR, 2020. American College of Radiology guidance document on MR safe practices: updates and critical information 2019. J. Magn. Reson. Imaging 51, 331–338.

ASTM, 2011. American Society for Testing and Materials (ASTM) International: Standard test method for measurement of radio frequency induced heating on or near passive implants during magnetic resonance imaging. F2182-19e2.

ASTM, 2013. American Society for Testing and Materials (ASTM) International: Standard Practice for Marking Medical Devices and Other Items for Safety in the Magnetic Resonance Environment. F2503-13.

Bitz, A.K., Kraff, O., Orzada, S., et al., 2014. RF safety evaluation of different configurations of high-permittivity pads used to improve imaging of the cerebellum at 7 Tesla. Proc. Int. Soc. Magn. Reson. Med. 22, 4892.

Brink, W.M., Van Den Brink, J.S., Webb, A.G., 2015. The effect of high-permittivity pads on specific absorption rate in radiofrequency-shimmed dual-transmit cardiovascular magnetic resonance at 3T. J. Cardiovasc. Magn. Reson. 17, 82.

Bruhl, R., Ihlenfeld, A., Ittermann, B., 2017. Gradient heating of bulk metallic implants can be a safety concern in MRI. Magn. Reson. Med. 77, 1739–1740.

Cloos, M.A., Boulant, N., Luong, M., et al., 2012. kT-points: short three-dimensional tailored RF pulses for flip-angle homogenization over an extended volume. Magn. Reson. Med. 67, 72–80.

Delfino, J.G., Krainak, D.M., Flesher, S.A., Miller, D.L., 2019. MRI-related FDA adverse event reports: a 10-yr review. Med. Phys. 46, 5562–5571.

Deniz, C.M., Vaidya, M.V., Sodickson, D.K., Lattanzi, R., 2016. Radiofrequency energy deposition and radiofrequency power requirements in parallel transmission with increasing distance from the coil to the sample. Magn. Reson. Med. 75, 423–432.

Eryaman, Y., Turk, E.A., Oto, C., Algin, O., Atalar, E., 2013. Reduction of the radiofrequency heating of metallic devices using a dual-drive birdcage coil. Magn. Reson. Med. 69, 845–852.

Fiedler, T.M., Ladd, M.E., Bitz, A.K., 2018. SAR simulations & safety. Neuroimage 168, 33–58.

Gras, V., Vignaud, A., Amadon, A., Le Bihan, D., Boulant, N., 2017. Universal pulses: a new concept for calibration-free parallel transmission. Magn. Reson. Med. 77, 635–643.

Guerin, B., Angelone, L.M., Dougherty, D., Wald, L.L., 2020. Parallel transmission to reduce absorbed power around deep brain stimulation devices in MRI: impact of number and arrangement of transmit channels. Magn. Reson. Med. 83, 299–311.

GUFI, 2015. German Ultra-High Field Imaging Network: Recommendations Regarding Access Procedures and User Access Rules at German Ultra-High-Field Sites. https://mr-gufi.de/index.php/en/documents.

Haik, J., Daniel, S., Tessone, A., Orenstein, A., Winkler, E., 2009. MRI induced fourth-degree burn in an extremity, leading to amputation. Burns 35, 294–296.

Hoffmann, J., Henning, A., Giapitzakis, I.A., et al., 2016. Safety testing and operational procedures for self-developed radiofrequency coils. NMR Biomed. 29, 1131–1144.

Huang, S.Y., Witzel, T., Keil, B., et al., 2021. Connectome 2.0: developing the next-generation ultra-high gradient strength human MRI scanner for bridging studies of the micro-, meso- and macro-connectome. Neuroimage 243, 118530.

IEC, 2022. 60601-2-33: Particular requirements for the safety of magnetic resonance diagnostic devices. IEC 60601-2-33. 4.0 ed. International Electrotechnical Commission.

ISMRM Working Groups, 2022. ISMRM Best Practices for Safety Testing of Experimental RF Hardware. https://www.ismrm.org/safety/RF_Hardware_Safety_Testing_2022-03.pdf.

ISO, 2012. International Standards Organization Technical Specification 10974: Requirements for the safety of magnetic resonance imaging for patients with an active implantable medical device.

Katscher, U., Bornert, P., Leussler, C., Van Den Brink, J.S., 2003. Transmit SENSE. Magn. Reson. Med. 49, 144–150.

Kopanoglu, E., Deniz, C.M., Erturk, M.A., Wise, R.G., 2020. Specific absorption rate implications of within-scan patient head motion for ultra-high field MRI. Magn. Reson. Med. 84, 2724–2738.

Kraff, O., Quick, H.H., 2017. 7T: physics, safety, and potential clinical applications. J. Magn. Reson. Imaging 46, 1573–1589.

Mcnab, J.A., Edlow, B.L., Witzel, T., et al., 2013. The human connectome project and beyond: initial applications of 300 mT/m gradients. Neuroimage 80, 234–245.

MHRA, 2021. Medicines and Healthcare Products Regulatory Agency Safety Guidelines for Magnetic Resonance Imaging Equipment in Clinical Use.

Noureddine, Y., Kraff, O., Ladd, M.E., et al., 2018. In vitro and in silico assessment of RF-induced heating around intracranial aneurysm clips at 7 Tesla. Magn. Reson. Med. 79, 568–581.

Noureddine, Y., Kraff, O., Ladd, M.E., et al., 2019. Radiofrequency induced heating around aneurysm clips using a generic birdcage head coil at 7 Tesla under consideration of the minimum distance to decouple multiple aneurysm clips. Magn. Reson. Med. 82, 1859–1875.

Orzada, S., Maderwald, S., Poser, B.A., Bitz, A.K., Quick, H.H., Ladd, M.E., 2010. RF excitation using time interleaved acquisition of modes (TIAMO) to address B1 inhomogeneity in high-field MRI. Magn. Reson. Med. 64, 327–333.

Schaefer, D.J., Bourland, J.D., Nyenhuis, J.A., 2000. Review of patient safety in time-varying gradient fields. J. Magn. Reson. Imaging 12, 20–29.

Teeuwisse, W.M., Brink, W.M., Webb, A.G., 2012. Quantitative assessment of the effects of high-permittivity pads in 7 Tesla MRI of the brain. Magn. Reson. Med. 67, 1285–1293.

Winkler, S.A., Schmitt, F., Landes, H., et al., 2018. Gradient and shim technologies for ultra high field MRI. Neuroimage 168, 59–70.

Biological effects, patient experience, and occupational safety

5

Boel Hansson[a] and Isabella M. Björkman-Burtscher[b,c]

[a]*Department of Medical Imaging and Physiology, Skane University Hospital, Lund, Sweden* [b]*Department of Radiology, Institute of Clinical Sciences, Sahlgrenska Academy, University of Gothenburg, Gothenburg, Sweden* [c]*Department of Radiology, Sahlgrenska University Hospital, Gothenburg, Sweden*

Highlights

- Exposure to the three electromagnetic fields—the static magnetic field, the time-varying gradient magnetic field, and the radiofrequency field—is the main cause for bioeffects experienced by patients, research subjects, and personnel.
- Individual predisposition, psychological aspects, and patient care will affect the experience not only regarding frequency of occurrence but also regarding experienced strength of the bioeffect and discomfort.
- Information and communication as well as de-dramatization are key factors in increasing patient comfort and compliance.
- MR safety at UHF MR must focus equally on patients, research subjects, personnel, and visitors.
- If MR safety routines are in place, injuries related to projectiles, implants, and burns can be prevented completely.

5.1 Biological effects

Biological effects—also including physiological effects and health implications—experienced in MR are mainly attributed to the three electromagnetic fields used in MR—the static magnetic field, the time-varying gradient magnetic field, and the radiofrequency field—which are described in detail in other chapters. These electromagnetic fields affect the human body differently during different phases of an MR examination and thus may cause effects experienced with varying frequency and strength. The biological effects referred to are, for example, dizziness, inconsistent movement, peripheral nerve stimulation (PNS), headache, nausea, metallic taste, and light flashes. These effects depend for example on the location of the body part in the field, potential motion of the body part in the field, and strength and variation of the applied field. Individual predisposition of subjects will influence the occurrence of biological effects as well as how they are perceived. The individual's experience can be further influenced by psychological aspects triggered by for example expectations or fears associated with the examination (Lo Re et al., 2016) or the exam situation and thus also by patient care.

5.2 **Static magnetic field**

Acute biological effects arising from movement through the high static magnetic field include dizziness or vertigo, unrealistic motion, and nausea. The Lorentz force acts on electric charges that move in a magnetic field. In the case of a head moving in a magnetic field, this affects the vestibular system and causes dizziness and a sense of unrealistic motion (McRobbie, 2020; Glover, 2015). During normal head movement, vestibular hair cells show an electrophysiological response to mechanical displacement. The displacement of hairs causes a change in firing rate which the brain interprets as movement (Glover et al., 2007). Nausea might be the effect of a conflict in the position information supplied by the visual and perceptive systems and vestibular position-sensing system affected by the translation of the body through the static magnetic field (Shellock and Crues, 2014). In the 2015 amendment of the International Electrotechnical Commission (IEC) 60601-2-33 standard, the first level controlled operating mode for the static magnetic field was increased to 8T. At the first level controlled operating mode, caution must be taken for subjects under physiological stress and medical supervision in addition to routine monitoring may be necessary (Fagan et al., 2021).

5.2.1 **Dizziness**

A range of scientific publications document dizziness, a subjective experience reported by patients, research subjects, and personnel alike (Heilmaier et al., 2011; Rauschenberg et al., 2014; Theysohn et al., 2008; Versluis et al., 2013). Head movement at the center of a 7T magnet resulted in mild or severe dizziness in nine out of ten subjects (Glover et al., 2007). Considering normal circumstances with movement through the static field while lying still on the table and going into a passively shielded 7T scanner, approximately 20% to 50% of study subjects experienced dizziness (Theysohn et al., 2008; Rauschenberg et al., 2014). This wide range is due to varying scoring approaches, installation types, and variation in table speed. More recent 7T data from actively shielded magnets (Hansson et al., 2019, 2020a) report occurrence of dizziness in more than 80% of subjects. Actively shielded (AS) magnets have a higher magnetic field gradient at the bore opening but a lower magnetic field strength in the close vicinity of the magnet than passively shielded magnets. The higher field gradient at the bore opening is partly counteracted by lower table speed when bringing the table into the bore in 7T AS compared to passively shielded 7T scanners, but further patient care adaptations for AS 7T scanners might be needed. In addition, the lower magnetic field outside the magnet bore of the actively shielded magnet gives the subject less time to adapt to the strong magnetic field while being prepared for the examination.

5.2.2 **Nausea**

Although uncommon, MR examinations may be terminated due to nausea as an acute reaction to biological effects caused by the high static magnetic field, if experienced strongly. Nausea, thought to be related to dizziness, is more severe if subjects perform head movement at the center of the magnet but occurs much less frequent than dizziness, reported by less than 35% of subjects (Rauschenberg et al., 2014; Hansson et al., 2020a). It needs to be noted that both nausea and dizziness might affect subjects' ability to perform daily life tasks and the affected subjects should be informed to abstain from risk tasks such as driving or work in risk environments until the effect has worn off completely.

5.2.3 **Nystagmus**

Dizziness is associated with nystagmus, a condition characterized by involuntary eye movements. Head rotational movement is linked to eye viewing direction. When the head moves in one direction, the eyes automatically move in the opposite direction to enable a consistent visual field (McRobbie, 2020). Nystagmus is induced by high magnetic fields as the interaction between ionic currents in the vestibular system and the high static magnetic field evokes a vestibular-ocular reflex (Glover et al., 2014).

5.2.4 **Unrealistic motion**

It can be difficult to distinguish unrealistic motion from dizziness if the two sensations are closely related. The term "unrealistic motion" summarizes complex sensations such as experiencing body movement in a direction other than the actual straight direction through the bore, perception of rotation such as traveling along a curvilinear path through the scanner (Mian et al., 2013), feeling of unreality (Theysohn et al., 2008), or feeling of insubstantiality (Rauschenberg et al., 2014). Subjects who can identify a particular direction of apparent motion when going into the bore experience a reversed apparent motion when going into the opposite end of the magnet (Glover, 2015). With up to 70% of subjects at UHF reporting the effect, unrealistic motion is a common effect, however, only experienced while moving through the static magnetic field and often rapidly decreasing when reaching exam position (Glover, 2015; Hansson et al., 2019).

5.2.5 **Heart rate and blood pressure**

Motion of conductive tissue within a magnetic field produces a force perpendicular to the direction of the motion. The electromotive force induced by blood flow in the heart may produce large distortions of the ECG signal, especially during the T-wave phase of the cardiac cycle. This effect contributes to difficulties in obtaining acceptable electrocardiograms (ECG) during MR examinations at higher field strengths (Shellock and Crues, 2014). In two publications regarding subjects inside 8T scanners, the only physiologic and statistically significant parameter shown to correlate with increased field strength was a small but measurable increase in systolic blood pressure. Observed characteristic changes of the ECG during the MR examination were not apparent to the subject, had no clinical significance, and were presumed to represent an artifact due to magnetic interference (Chakeres and de Vocht, 2005; Chakeres et al., 2003). At 10.5T, only a mix of small changes to heart rate and blood pressure were noted, suggesting no major or unexpected field effects at 10.5T. The blood pressure change was statistically significant but smaller than the change observed when moving from supine to lateral or supine to standing position or even a change in arm position (Grant et al., 2020).

5.2.6 **Metallic taste**

As a result of the strong field gradient at the magnet bore, shaking the head vigorously can evoke a metallic taste. Metallic taste might be described as "tasting blood." The effect is thought to arise from either direct stimulation of taste buds or from electrolysis of saliva (McRobbie, 2020) but not likely from electrolysis of metallic chemicals in teeth fillings (Cavin et al., 2007). Metallic taste is experienced by less than 10% of individuals in study populations and with low intensity (Hansson et al., 2020a).

5.2.7 Cognition

Evidence of a biological effect on cognition caused by the exposure to the electromagnetic fields is currently scarce, and effects described are very subtle, transient, not harmful (McRobbie, 2020), and not statistically significant (Fagan et al., 2021), independently of field strength. However, a potential effect on performing complex everyday tasks such as driving a car, not the least considering reaction time, cannot be excluded for subjects experiencing, for example, dizziness or nausea (Heinrich et al., 2013). Thus, transient altered cognitive performance secondary to dizziness and nausea should be considered as stated earlier.

5.2.8 Projectile risk

High static magnetic fields pose known risks related to the forces exerted on magnetic materials and objects. The forces may affect material both inside and outside of the human body. The magnetic field causes translational (attractive) forces on magnetic objects, pulling them into the magnet, as well as torque when objects pass through the field. Material damage, malfunction of devices, or human injury will occur if appropriate safety precautions are not in place or are ignored by personnel, patients, or research subjects (McRobbie, 2020; Hansson et al., 2020b) (see further Chapter 4).

5.3 The time-varying gradient magnetic field

The gradient dB/dt is the rate of change of the magnetic field induced using gradient coils during the MR examination. Short-term effects caused by the gradient field are muscle twitches (peripheral nerve stimulation (PNS)), light flashes (magnetophosphenes), and metallic taste. In addition, the gradients cause acoustic noise. The gradient field is a low-frequency pulsed magnetic field, which is used for localization of the signal in the imaging process and for various signal encodings such as flow and diffusion (Shellock and Crues, 2014). The gradient systems in 7T MR scanners do not necessarily have higher amplitudes or slew rates than 3T MR scanners, but the gradient system is pushed further because of the increasing focus on, for example, high-resolution and fMRI studies.

5.3.1 Peripheral nerve stimulation

The most common biological effect of time-varying gradient magnetic fields is peripheral nerve stimulation. The mechanism is described as a change in the induced electric field along axons of peripheral nerves (McRobbie et al., 2017). PNS is more likely to occur when using rapid sequences such as echo planar imaging, diffusion imaging, and fast multiecho gradient sequences (such as QSM), where fast gradients and strong gradient amplitudes are used. Relevant for UHF, high-resolution imaging is also likely to cause PNS, especially with oblique slices as they demand high gradient amplitudes (McRobbie, 2020). Subjects describe PNS as anything between a sensation of mild tingling and pain. To be able to minimize PNS, MR scanners predict a PNS value for each sequence. The estimate is given as a percentage, where 100% is defined as the level of gradient output at which 50% of humans are expected to experience PNS (Glover, 2009). Safety limits are in place to avoid excess PNS and cardiac stimulation. Occurrence of PNS varies greatly between different studies, and although occurrence of PNS has been reported for more than 40% of subjects in some study populations (Theysohn et al., 2008; Hansson et al., 2020a), most of these subjects reported the sensation as not uncomfortable at all or very little uncomfortable (Hansson et al., 2020a). In a comparison study of 1.5T and 7T, there was no significant difference in reported PNS (Heilmaier et al., 2011). However, in clinical and research practice and reported in 7T studies with more than 40% of the subjects reporting PNS (Theysohn et al., 2008; Hansson et al., 2020a), PNS can be expected to occur more frequently during 7T examinations than at lower field strength.

5.3.2 Magnetophosphenes

Magnetophosphenes are perceived as light flashes, which are caused by direct stimulation of retinal receptors. Magnetophosphenes can be experienced if the gradient switching frequency is in the range of around 20 Hz (Glover, 2009), but most MR sequences do not operate in this range. Therefore, magnetophosphenes are likely not related to the gradient switching but might occur when moving inside or close to the magnet (McRobbie, 2020). In two UHF studies, magnetophosphenes have been reported by 7% and 8% of the subjects, respectively (Theysohn et al., 2008; Hansson et al., 2020a). There was no significant difference in reporting magnetophosphenes for subjects in a 1.5T versus a 7T (Heilmaier et al., 2011). A limitation and source of error in reporting magnetophosphenes is the difficulty to distinguish true magnetophopenes from phosphenes experienced when closing the eyes in a lit-up environment when the retina continues to produce electrical charges.

5.3.3 Acoustic noise

As a result of varying Lorentz force distribution on the gradient coil, acoustic noise is generated due to gradient coil displacement. Further, the gradient coil's mechanical vibrations contribute to the knocking sound (Shellock and Crues, 2014). Acoustic noise levels at 7T systems are similar to those at 3T systems, and maximum noise levels are regulated and limited by standards. However, 7T head coils tend to have a tight design, making it more difficult to use headphones compared to standard clinical head coils (Fagan et al., 2021). In "MRI bioeffects, safety, and patient management," the authors give examples of MR systems with reported acoustic noise levels up to approximately 130 dB (Shellock and Crues, 2014). For comparison, sound pressure levels of 120 dB are also reached with a chainsaw. Ear protection is necessary and mandatory for all MR scans irrespective of field strength (Shellock and Crues, 2004). Harm to the auditory system caused by excessive noise exposure or a single large noise exposure can vary between a short-term hearing deficit or loss and a permanent hearing loss (McRobbie, 2020). As acoustic noise exposure in everyday lives is common, exposure during an MR examination needs to be treated as part of the subject's cumulative noise exposure and not as a standalone exposure. Therefore, acoustic noise protection is of utmost importance.

Despite protection, the maximum noise level at some point of an MR examination independent of field strength may be experienced as uncomfortable or not acceptable by many subjects as shown in a large 7T study (Hansson et al., 2020a), and acoustic noise was one of the top four causes of discomfort experienced during an MR examination, together with examination duration, room temperature, and general discomfort (Theysohn et al., 2008).

5.4 Radio-frequency (RF) fields

The radio-frequency (RF) energy deposition in the tissue is expressed as the power absorbed per unit mass measured in watts per kilogram (W/kg) in the Specific Absorption Rate (SAR). All MR systems have built-in safety mechanisms to avoid excess of SAR limits. However, it is important to ensure that patients with health conditions potentially causing impaired thermoregulation such as fever, spinal cord or brain injury, or obesity are not subjected to the risk of increasing the body temperature (Safety ACR, 2020). It is also important to notice that patient care and individual preferences will impact the subjects' experience of the temperature in the scanner room and during the examination. The goal of patient care is to provide a comfortable experience avoiding not only a potential body temperature increase but also to avoid that a subject feels cold (Hansson et al., 2019). At 7T, coils are in general locally transmitting and SAR calculations are specific for the body part to be examined. To avoid excess of SAR limits, unintentional use of coils for body parts not covered by the intended use of the coil must be eschewed.

Burns are among the most common human injuries related to MR and are caused by RF exposure. Skin burns can for example arise from the use of electrodes or monitoring leads that are not MR safe, incorrectly positioned cables, receive coil faults, skin contact with the surface of the bore (McRobbie, 2020), or skin-to-skin contact leading to electrical circuits in the body. Further, RF interference with implants and medical devices may cause human injury and device malfunction, and need to be prevented by MR safety routines concerning subject screening and use of medical devices within electrical fields associated with the use of MR.

5.5 Patient care at UHF

Patient care in MR is based on medical, technical, and interpersonal and communication skills adjusted for the imaging modality in question. To ensure safe and effective patient care in UHF MR, key concepts on handling MR safety, biological effects, and psychological aspects need to be established and applied at UHF MR facilities and any MR facility alike.

5.5.1 Patient safety

MR safety procedures including, e.g., site planning, education of personnel, screening of subjects for hazards, and implant and device handling, must be in place and known by everybody working with or in the proximity of MR. Personnel needs to be MR safety conscious and always look out for objects and actions that might pose a danger to patients, research subjects, or personnel. International recommendations should be adapted at any MR facility (Safety ACR, 2020; MHRA, 2021), and the compliance with the established regulatory framework by the personnel needs to be followed up upon.

The most important safety risks in MR considering human injury and material damage are the projectile risk related to the static magnetic field and the risk of burns related to the RF field. This applies to all field strengths, and incidents and near miss incidents do occur. In a national study, a risk assessment of the potential worst-case scenario of all reported MR incidents and close calls classified 16% of these with the highest potential severity score defined as potentially leading to a catastrophic outcome (death, persistent major sensory, motor, physiological, intellectual, or mental disability) (Hansson et al., 2020b). UHF MR safety concepts are discussed in detail in Chapter 4.

5.5.2 Psychological aspects and physical comfort

Every subject has different physical and psychological prerequisites for coping with exposure to the MR environment, and it is important to consider individual variations. General aspects influencing the experience of comfort and compliance in healthcare are physical pain, biological effects, fear or anxiety, motivation, and the ability to communicate.

To avoid or minimize biological and psychological effects that do not pose a physical danger but still might be experienced as uncomfortable by individual subjects, a welcoming atmosphere, the opportunity to maintain confidentiality, and distinct patient care efforts are as important at UHF MR facilities as at any MR facility. Professionalism from the personnel provides a sense of security for the subject and facilitates communication.

Although fear or anxiety upfront or during an examination may be expected to be more pronounced in patients affected by a disease or dreading an unfavorable examination result, these psychological effects should not be underestimated in healthy research subjects exposed to an unfamiliar environment. Despite disease-related physical pain or anxiety concerning exam results, a well-informed patient who is motivated to undergo an examination might experience a higher level of comfort and comply better during the MR examination than a healthy subject in a research study who is ill-informed about the aim and proceedings related to the examination. The support and information given to subjects need to be individualized, and some subjects will need more support to be able to relax and others need help to experience control over the situation (Tornqvist et al., 2006). As examinations in UHF MR tend to be long, a need of reassurance during the examination might occur, necessitating continuous communication. Further, as prevalence of biological effects is higher at UHF, subjects need to be provided with adequate information and coping strategies to ensure compliance.

Physical comfort is facilitated by adapting the subject's position, adjusted padding, adequate noise protection, adjustment of the environment regarding temperature and lighting, and mediated by professionalism, empathy, and communication.

5.6 Occupational safety

MR safety concerns not only patients and research subjects but also all human and material resources within an MR environment. Occupational safety for personnel meets the same challenges as general occupational safety in addition to MR-specific areas. To mitigate adverse health effects from static magnetic field exposure, occupational exposure limits are set by the International Commission on Non-Ionizing Radiation Protection (ICNIRP, 2009). Personnel needs to be subjected to the same MR-screening procedures as care recipients or research subjects. Personnel can experience the same biological effects as patients depending on the proximity to the scanner—exposure to the stray field—when performing work tasks, depending on motion within the stray field, motion-induced time-varying magnetic fields, and whether presence within the scanners proximity during scanning is necessary (Schaap et al., 2014). Evidence is lacking whether exposure to MR-related electromagnetic fields in clinical routine affects work performance and health in MR workers. However, a study of simultaneous exposure to static magnetic field at the bore of a passively shielded 7T scanner, and low-frequency head movement-induced time-varying magnetic fields showed affected neurocognitive performance in two of five tasks compared with a mock scanner situation. In this study, it is pointed out that this might possibly hamper performance, especially when careful professional action is important (van Nierop et al., 2015).

MR personnel has an active role in preventing and handling patient and occupational safety hazards and incidents. Implementation of safety routines and follow-up of compliance with routines are essential for prevention of adverse events (Hansson et al., 2022). In case of incidents, routines and training need to be adapted to meet the causes of the incidents. Considering the potential risk of human injury, personnel should not operate alone with patients or study subjects in any MR suite, regardless of field strength (Blankholm and Hansson, 2019; Kihlberg et al., 2022).

5.7 Practical guide to avoid or minimize biological effects, to facilitate patient comfort, and increase MR safety at UHF MR

Patient care and MR safety procedures in UHF MR are in general subject to the same considerations as at lower magnetic field strengths. The following guide is thus designed to complement standard procedures to maintain safety and improve patient care and comfort with items more specific for UHF MR and relevant for the technique's translation from research to clinical practice.

5.7.1 The MR environment

The design and site planning of UHF facilities need to project medical professionalism and offer patient care and MR safety standards comparable to clinical routine independent of their use as research and/or clinical facilities.

5.7.2 Patient and occupational safety

MR safety routines must cover patients, research subjects, visitors, and any personnel entering the facility. All personnel must undergo adequate documented clinical and technical education ensuring the safety of themselves and others.

UHF MR facilities often operate in research-oriented environments with personnel from diverse work cultures. It is important to highlight the importance of MR safety, to involve all team members and multidisciplinary personnel, to facilitate handling of safety procedures with structure and documentation, to schedule safety activities in patient workflow, to ensure sufficient staffing, and to introduce joint responsibility for safety routines among members of the personnel (signature and countersigning of safety documentation).

Safety procedures for emergencies at UHF MR including magnet quench and subject evacuation may differ compared to lower field strengths. For example, 7T magnets may contain more helium which prolongs the time needed to reach zero field in a quench (Fagan et al., 2021), patient tables may not be detachable and much higher than in clinical MR systems, and response times of medical emergency teams may be longer in case of siting outside hospital environments. Thus, at least two persons trained to handle safety procedures for emergencies at the site in question should always be present when the scanner is in operation or during site visits (Safety ACR, 2020).

To avoid injuries and hazards related to the static magnetic field, the following precautions need to be followed:

- MR-safety screening procedures need to be in place. The procedures should have several checkpoints to ensure that if one fails another one can step in.
- To allow evaluation of compliance with routines, MR safety screening and made decisions require accessible documentation.
- International recommendations on UHF MR Safety including the establishment of local 7T MR safety committees (Fagan et al., 2021) should be accommodated in local routines.
- Educate and train emergency procedures including subject evacuation periodically (Fagan et al., 2021).
- MR safety also includes knowledge and approval of any additional equipment brought into the scanner room or used for examinations. Instructions for use for coils (also off label use), power

injectors, patient monitoring equipment, dielectric pads, and other experimental equipment should be well known by the personnel using the equipment to avoid incidents and provide a safe environment.
- At UHF MR scanners, the transmit-receive RF coils tend to be heavier than coils on lower field MR systems. To optimize ergonomic working conditions and minimize material damage, a coil cart for the magnet room is recommended (Fagan et al., 2021).
- To be able to adjust routines and avoid future incidents, all incidents and near miss incidents need to be documented, reported, and followed up upon.

5.7.3 Biological effects and patient comfort

Very few subjects experience the biological effects that are common at UHF MR as very uncomfortable or to be a reason for scan abortion. However, biological effects might be experienced as uncomfortable and, if not anticipated, may induce anxiety. Personnel should therefore be trained to recognize and handle biological effects that may be attributed to the MR environment. Routines on how to inform subjects regarding the potential occurrence, cause, duration, and individual variability of perception of biological effects need to be established, and the communication of the information should be practiced. Giving the subjects relevant information about potential biological effects in a calm manner will likely increase the compliance of the subjects. It further allows subjects to develop coping strategies and supports risk-benefit assessment and decision-making considering informed consent.

To avoid or minimize biological effects, the following precautions are suggested.
Information and communication
- Educate and train personnel.
- Inform subjects regarding the most common potential biological effects, variability of perception of the effects, and coping strategies at hand prior to entering the stray field.
- Ensure continuous communication throughout the complete stay of the subject at the facility and initiate communication prior to, under, and after the examination.
- Repetition of information and active invitation to ask questions and to express uncomfortable perception of adverse experiences should be encouraged.
- Make sure that the subject fully understands the information (Hansson et al., 2019).
- Besides giving the opportunity for slight movement to relax tension, it is important to inform subjects during an examination on the approximate duration of the next scan and remaining exam time, and to notify subjects before a high PNS risk sequence or a sequence with a high acoustic noise level is scanned (Hansson et al., 2020a).

The static magnetic field
- Any movement including head movement within the stray field or the scanner, especially in the proximity of the bore opening, should be avoided or be performed slowly.
  - This includes that instructions and actions ensuring safe positioning and patient comfort need to be given and performed outside the bore.
- Consider the necessity to adapt to the strong magnetic field and the higher field gradient in actively shielded 7T magnets compared to the setting in a passively shielded 7T magnet.
  - Assure that the table speed is lower for UHF scanners compared to $\leq$3T scanners.
  - Inform on common biological effects related to movement in the static field and their short-term character.

  ○ Instruct subjects to keep the head still even if other body parts are examined to minimize biological effects.

The radiofrequency and gradient field
- Noise exposure related to MR should be considered as part of the complete noise exposure for individuals and be kept as low as possible at any instance.
- Head coils at UHF may pose a challenge concerning application of hearing protection, making it an even higher priority to adhere strictly to routines and adjust suboptimal hearing protection. Optimal earplugs should be used, applied with care, and checked prior to examinations. If included in local routines, double-component clay for extra sound attenuation and to keep earplugs in place can be used in addition to headsets and padding (Fig. 5.1).
- PNS cannot be completely avoided at UHF MR. As it is potentially experienced as uncomfortable and causing anxiety, adequate information is crucial for coping.
- To avoid burns, it is important to use sufficient padding and ensure that no loops of cables are formed and no skin to skin or direct skin to equipment contact is present. Checklists like the FDA and SMRTs "MRI burn prevention tips to keep patients safe" are instructive and easy to use (Fig. 5.2) (ISMRM org, 2022).

Comfort and compliance
- Provide information, establish, and maintain communication; check functionality of the alarm bulb by asking the subject to squeeze it.
- Provide coping strategies for biological effects.
- Provide padding for comfort and to avoid burns and readjust if necessary.

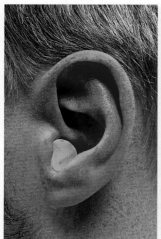 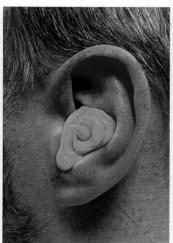 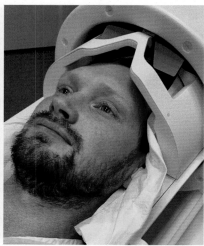

FIG. 5.1

Application of the earplug and a double-component clay for extra sound attenuation. The shown clay has the intended use of casting a mold for the manufacturing of hearing protections. When the subject is placed inside the coil, there is just about room for the dielectric pads.

MRI BURN PREVENTION
Tips for Keeping Patients Safe

Screen patients for implants, devices, and other metallic objects. Assume anything unknown is MR Unsafe.

 Screen objects to ensure that anything entering the scan room is MR Conditional or MR Safe. Match conditions on MR Conditional devices with your scanner. All metals, even non-ferromagnetic ones, have the potential to heat up and cause burns.

Have patients change out of street clothes whenever possible.

 Position patients to avoid skin-to-skin contact (e.g. no hands on hips, no crossed arms, no crossed legs, etc.).

Always use the manufacturer-provided padding to insulate the patient. Sheets and blankets may be added for patient comfort but are not a substitute for manufacturer-provided padding.

 Route cables out of the scanner in a straight line. Don't coil cables or allow them to touch the patient.

Use only Normal Operating Mode and the lowest SAR, whenever possible.

Lowest SAR Possible

 Keep your eyes and ears on the patient at all times. Stay in communication with patients to identify warming. Monitor sedated patients using MR Conditional monitoring equipment.

FIG. 5.2

FDA and ISMRTs "MRI burn prevention tips to keep patients safe." *Reprint with permission of ISMRM Executive Director (n.d.).*

- Dielectric pads are often used at 7T scanners to improve image uniformity. Assure comfort in tight head coils in addition to training on how to use these pads and follow the intended use (Fagan et al., 2021).
- Ensure sufficient staffing to be able to accommodate focus on challenging examination procedures and the subject at the same time. Participation of two trained members of the personnel in the examination ensures correct handling of the system without losing focus on the subject in the scanner and facilitates handling of potential emergency situations.
- Routines need to be established to facilitate adequate communication and potentially treatment if dizziness, nausea, or any other biological effect causes discomfort to the subject. Further, communication with subjects needs to include the information that these biological effects potentially might affect cognitive and daily function irrespective of the cause and that the subject needs to adapt activities after leaving the facility (driving, high risk occupations, etc.) until the effect has worn off completely (Fagan et al., 2021). This is true also for personnel performing activities requiring repair or cleaning inside the bore. A space for the subject to sit down after the 7T examination should be provided (Fig. 5.3).

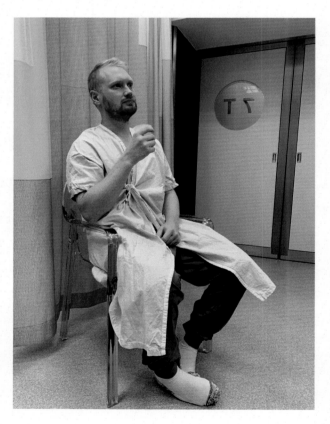

FIG. 5.3

Example of a dedicated space in the proximity of the scanner room to prepare subjects for examinations and handle biological effects after the examination. It is encouraged that subjects have the possibility to sit down, relax, and have some water after the 7T examination.

References

Blankholm, A., Hansson, B., 2019. Incident reporting and level of MR safety education: a Danish national study. Radiography 26, 147–153. https://doi.org/10.1016/j.radi.2019.10.007.

Cavin, I.D., Glover, P.M., Bowtell, R.W., Gowland, P.A., 2007. Thresholds for perceiving metallic taste at high magnetic field. J. Magn. Reson. Imaging 26 (5), 1357–1361.

Chakeres, D.W., de Vocht, F., 2005. Static magnetic field effects on human subjects related to magnetic resonance imaging systems. Prog. Biophys. Mol. Biol. 87 (2–3), 255–265.

Chakeres, D.W., Kangarlu, A., Boudoulas, H., Young, D.C., 2003. Effect of static magnetic field exposure of up to 8 tesla on sequential human vital sign measurements. J. Magn. Reson. Imaging 18 (3), 346–352.

Fagan, A.J., Bitz, A.K., Bjorkman-Burtscher, I.M., et al., 2021. 7T MR safety. J. Magn. Reson. Imaging 53 (2), 333–346.

Glover, P.M., 2009. Interaction of MRI field gradients with the human body. Phys. Med. Biol. 54 (21), R99–r115.

Glover, P.M., 2015. Magnetic field-induced vertigo in the MRI environment. Curr. Radiol. Rep. 3 (8).

Glover, P.M., Cavin, I., Qian, W., Bowtell, R., Gowland, P.A., 2007. Magnetic-field-induced vertigo: a theoretical and experimental investigation. Bioelectromagnetics 28 (5), 349–361.

Glover, P.M., Li, Y., Antunes, A., Mian, O.S., Day, B.L., 2014. A dynamic model of the eye nystagmus response to high magnetic fields. Phys. Med. Biol. 59 (3), 631–645.

Grant, A., Metzger, G., Van de Moortele, P.-F., et al., 2020. 10.5 T MRI field effects on human cognitive, vestibular, and physiological function. Magn. Reson. Imaging 73, 163–176.

Hansson, B., Hoglund, P., Markenroth Bloch, K., et al., 2019. Short-term effects experienced during examinations in an actively shielded 7 T MR. Bioelectromagnetics.

Hansson, B., Markenroth Bloch, K., Owman, T., Nilsson, M., Latt, J., Olsrud, J., et al., 2020a. Subjectively reported effects experienced in an actively shielded 7T MRI: a large-scale study. J. Magn. Reson. Imaging.

Hansson, B., Olsrud, J., Wilen, J., Owman, T., Hoglund, P., Bjorkman-Burtscher, I.M., 2020b. Swedish national survey on MR safety compared with CT: a false sense of security? Eur. Radiol. 30 (4), 1918–1926.

Hansson, B., Simic, M., Olsrud, J., et al., 2022. MR- safety: evaluation of compliance with screening routines using a structured screening interview. J. Patient Saf. Risk Manag. 27 (2), 76–82.

Heilmaier, C., Theysohn, J.M., Maderwald, S., Kraff, O., Ladd, M.E., Ladd, S.C., 2011. A large-scale study on subjective perception of discomfort during 7 and 1.5 T MRI examinations. Bioelectromagnetics 32 (8), 610–619.

Heinrich, A., Szostek, A., Meyer, P., et al., 2013. Cognition and sensation in very high static magnetic fields: a randomized case-crossover study with different field strengths. Radiology 266 (1), 236–245.

ICNIRP, 2009. Guidelines on limits of exposure to static magnetic fields. Health Phys. 96, 504–514. Available from: http://www.icnirp.org/cms/upload/publications/ICNIRPstatgdl.pdf.

ISMRM Executive Director, n.d. https://www.ismrm.org/smrt/safety_page/burn_prevention_poster/MRI_Burn_Prevention_8.5x11.pdf.

ISMRM org, 2022. Available from: https://www.ismrm.org/mr-safety-links/.

Kihlberg, J., Hansson, B., Hall, A., Tisell, A., Lundberg, P., 2022. Why are MRI incidents severely underreported? A multicenter interviews survey. Eur. Radiol. 32 (1), 477–488.

Lo Re, G., De Luca, R., Muscarneri, F., et al., 2016. Relationship between anxiety level and radiological investigation. Comparison among different diagnostic imaging exams in a prospective single-center study. Radiol. Med. 121 (10), 763–768.

McRobbie, D.W., 2020. Essentials of MRI safety. Wiley-Blackwell.

McRobbie, D.W., Moore, E.A., Graves, M.J., 2017. MRI from Picture to Proton. Cambridge University Press, Cambridge.

MHRA Medicines and Healthcare Products Regulatory Agency, 2021. Safety Guidelines for Magnetic Resonance Imaging Equipment in Clinical Use 2021. Available from: https://assets.publishing.service.gov.uk/government/uploads/system/uploads/attachment_data/file/958486/MRI_guidance_2021-4-03c.pdf.

Mian, O.S., Li, Y., Antunes, A., Glover, P.M., Day, B.L., 2013. On the vertigo due to static magnetic fields. PLoS One 8 (10), e78748.

Rauschenberg, J., Nagel, A.M., Ladd, S.C., et al., 2014. Multicenter study of subjective acceptance during magnetic resonance imaging at 7 and 9.4 T. Investig. Radiol. 49 (5), 249–259.

Safety ACR Committee on MR Safety, 2020. ACR Manual on MR Safety 20201-56. Available from: https://www.acr.org/-/media/ACR/Files/Radiology-Safety/MR-Safety/MR-Safety-Screening-Form.pdf?la=en.

Schaap, K., Christopher-de Vries, Y., Mason, C.K., de Vocht, F., Portengen, L., Kromhout, H., 2014. Occupational exposure of healthcare and research staff to static magnetic stray fields from 1.5-7 Tesla MRI scanners is associated with reporting of transient symptoms. Occup. Environ. Med. 71 (6), 423–429.

Shellock, F.G., Crues, J.V., 2004. MR procedures: biologic effects, safety, and patient care. Radiology 232 (3), 635–652.

Shellock, F.G., Crues, J.V., 2014. MRI Bioeffects, Safety, and Patient Management. Biomedical Research Publishing Group, Los Angeles.

Theysohn, J.M., Maderwald, S., Kraff, O., Moenninghoff, C., Ladd, M.E., Ladd, S.C., 2008. Subjective acceptance of 7 Tesla MRI for human imaging. MAGMA 21 (1–2), 63–72.

Tornqvist, E., Mansson, A., Larsson, E.M., Hallstrom, I., 2006. It's like being in another world–patients' lived experience of magnetic resonance imaging. J. Clin. Nurs. 15 (8), 954–961.

van Nierop, L.E., Slottje, P., van Zandvoort, M., Kromhout, H., 2015. Simultaneous exposure to MRI-related static and low-frequency movement-induced time-varying magnetic fields affects neurocognitive performance: a double-blind randomized crossover study. Magn. Reson. Med. 74 (3), 840–849.

Versluis, M.J., Teeuwisse, W.M., Kan, H.E., van Buchem, M.A., Webb, A.G., van Osch, M.J., 2013. Subject tolerance of 7 T MRI examinations. J. Magn. Reson. Imaging 38 (3), 722–725.

Ultra-high field challenges and technical solutions

B_0 inhomogeneity: Causes and coping strategies

Nicolas S. Arango[a], Bruno Pinho-Meneses[b], and Jason P. Stockmann[c,d]

[a]*Department of Electrical Engineering, Massachusetts Institute of Technology, Cambridge, MA, United States* [b]*Siemens Healthineers, MR Magnet Technology, Eynsham, Oxon, United Kingdom* [c]*A. A. Martinos Center for Biomedical Imaging, Massachusetts General Hospital, Charlestown, MA, United States* [d]*Harvard Medical School, Boston, MA, United States*

Highlights

- B_0 inhomogeneity grows linearly with B_0 field strength, leading to serious artifacts at UHF which cannot be completely mitigated using postprocessing approaches.
- Prospective correction by a variety of active and passive shim hardware systems has been shown to improve brain B_0 homogeneity at UHF and reduce artifacts.
- Shim coil wire patterns can be designed to optimize shim efficacy for a "typical" human brain.
- There are fundamental limits for shim performance using sources outside the head, which we characterize in this chapter.
- The spherical harmonic rating provides a way to compare B_0 shimming setups at different sites.

6.1 Scope of this chapter

Several review articles have discussed B_0 shimming technology in the context of ultra-high field (UHF) brain imaging (de Graaf and Juchem, 2016; Stockmann and Wald, 2018) as well as spectroscopy (Juchem et al., 2021; Juchem and de Graaf, 2017). In this chapter, we reiterate the importance of addressing B_0 inhomogeneity at UHF and highlight common B_0 artifacts that arise in UHF applications. Methods for coping with these artifacts either in postprocessing or by optimizing the MR acquisition are then considered, with an emphasis on echo-planar imaging sequences that are widely used for functional and diffusion MRI. We briefly review B_0 field mapping methodology and discuss sources of noise and bias. We also describe ways to track B_0 field fluctuations during scans including navigators and NMR field probes. B_0 shimming hardware including spherical harmonic coils, multicoil shim arrays, and optimized shim arrays is then considered in the context of the "ultimate achievable B_0 shim." Lastly, we briefly highlight new ways that shim array coils are being used to provide flexible field control for a variety of spatial encoding applications.

Advances in Magnetic Resonance Technology and Applications. Volume 10. ISSN 2666-9099. https://doi.org/10.1016/B978-0-323-99898-7.00010-9

6.2 Origins of ΔB_0 inhomogeneity and implications for UHF MR

Modern MRI magnets for human imaging typically achieve a main field ("B_0") homogeneity of approximately 1 ppm or less over the field-of-view (FOV). However, when the body is inserted in this field, tissues become slightly magnetized, and small differences in tissue magnetic susceptibility generate local perturbations of the B_0 field. At UHF, tissue magnetization increases, which can be beneficial at the *microscopic* scale when it provides enhanced intrinsic T_2^* contrast as compared to 3T, for example, in susceptibility weighted imaging, quantitative susceptibility mapping, blood oxygen level-dependent functional MRI, and T_2^* mapping (see Chapter 13). However, at UHF, the unwanted *macroscopic* susceptibility effects also become larger. Specifically, paramagnetic oxygen in the air of the sinuses, oral cavity, ear canals, and temporal bone causes susceptibility discontinuities with the adjacent diamagnetic tissues, leading to local field perturbations that reach 1–2 ppm in the worst-impacted brain areas. Since most MRI pulse sequences rely on a high degree of field uniformity, these B_0 perturbations cause artifacts in a wide variety of acquisitions. Because BOLD fMRI contrast-to-noise-ratio (CNR) is typically maximized highest when TE$=T_2^*$, the wide variability in T_2^* over the brain at UHF makes it difficult to get optimal BOLD weighting in every brain region with a single choice of TE.

Similarly, while UHF MR spectroscopic imaging holds great potential for improved metabolic mapping of the brain compared to 3T—due to the boosted SNR and increased spectral separation of metabolites—B_0 inhomogeneity at UHF poses a serious obstacle in the form of spectral line broadening and chemical shift. Similar challenges arise in chemical exchange saturation transfer (CEST) imaging, which benefits from the increased T_1, SNR, and spectral separation of UHF but unfortunately also suffers from ΔB_0 since CEST relies on spectrally selective RF pulses at precise off-resonance frequencies for each chemical species of interest.

Fig. 6.1a shows a typical distribution of magnetic field sources in the cavities of the head along with the maps of ΔB_0 at 7T. The ΔB_0 fields are especially pronounced in the ventral and orbitofrontal cortex, medial temporal lobes, anterior temporal horns, and deep brain areas (e.g., brainstem and cervical spine). The sharply varying ΔB_0 field in the temporal lobes and brainstem can be appreciated by looking at the T_2^*-weighted phase image in Fig. 6.1b.

In most MRI and MR spectroscopic imaging (MRSI) acquisitions, a high degree of background field homogeneity is typically required for performing accurate RF excitation and spatial encoding. Nuisance ΔB_0 fields disrupt these processes, leading to a wide variety of artifacts for diverse MR pulse sequences (see Fig. 6.1), and this problem grows much more severe at UHF compared to 3T. One artifact that grows dramatically more severe at UHF is banding in balanced steady-state-free precession (Fig. 6.1c), posing an obstacle to the use of this technique for fMRI (Aghaeifar et al., 2020). Another major obstacle for fMRI and other T_2^*-sensitive acquisitions are signal voids in gradient echo images caused by through-slice B_0 field gradients which lead to intravoxel dephasing (Fig. 6.1D). For diffusion and functional imaging acquisitions that rely on echo-planar imaging (EPI) sequences, both geometric distortion and blurring along the in-plane phase-encoding direction increase linearly with the B_0 field strength. This makes multichannel receive arrays (Chapter 8) and parallel imaging acquisition and reconstruction (Chapter 9) key technologies for fMRI at UHF. In off-resonance voxels, unwanted phase accumulates during the EPI echo train, leading to voxel shifts in the image domain. Registering these distorted EPI slices to anatomic images can be difficult. The distortion, D, depends on ΔB_0 (in Hz), the echo spacing (ESP), and the parallel imaging acceleration factor (R):

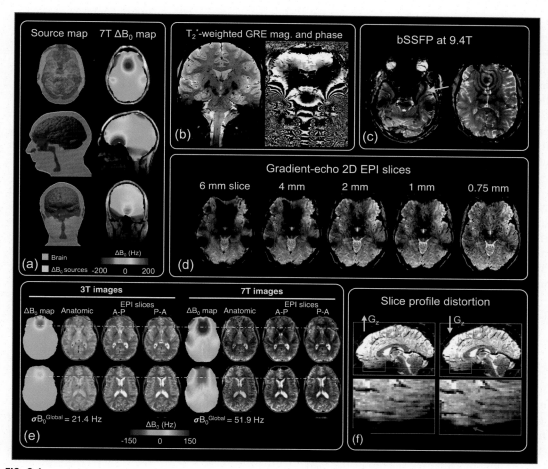

FIG. 6.1

(A) Example in vivo B_O field map acquired at 7T after second-order SH shimming. Note the areas of focal B_O inhomogeneity near the frontal and temporal lobes adjacent to the sinus and oral cavities, the ear canals, and temporal bone. (B) T_2^*-weighted gradient echo magnitude and phase brain image (300 μm in-plane) with densely packed phase wraps in areas of focal B_O inhomogeneity in the temporal lobes, brainstem, and cervical spine. (C) Banding artifacts in balanced SSFP imaging. (D) Through-plane field gradients cause spin dephasing which results in signal voids in gradient echo images. The effect grows more severe at UHF but can be mitigated by using thinner slices. (E) Echo-planar images with matched echo spacing and acceleration factor ($R = 2$) acquired at 3 and 7T, showing linearly increased geometric distortion at UHF. (F) Strong focal B_O hotspots bend slices in 2D images if the off-resonance is comparable to the slice-select pulse bandwidth. In these gradient echo images acquired axially and presented sagittally, voxel shifts are seen in the S-I direction when the direction of the slice-select gradient is reversed. Materials are courtesy of (B), (D) Jon Polimeni, MGH; (C) Klaus Scheffler, MPI Tuebingen; (F) Anna Blazejewska, MGH.

$$D = \Delta B_0 \frac{\text{ESP FOV}}{R} = \Delta B_0 ESP_{eff} \text{FOV}.$$

Finally, ΔB_0 offsets and spatial gradients present challenges for RF pulse design. Field inhomogeneity distorts slice-select profiles, as shown in Fig. 6.1f, when ΔB_0 is comparable to the slice-select pulse bandwidth. Further, ΔB_0 widens water and lipid peaks and reduces their spectral separation, limiting the efficacy of frequency-selective water excitation or lipid suppression pulses. Off-resonance also complicates parallel transmit (pTx) methods for improving flip angle homogeneity at UHF (Guérin et al., 2016). Robustness to ΔB_0 can be included in the pTx pulse design process but often comes at the expense of added SAR. This highlights the interdependence of B_0 and B_1^+ mitigation strategies at UHF and the importance of addressing ΔB_0 as part of an overall strategy to improve image quality. A detailed discussion of parallel transmission is found in Chapter 7.

In addition to static ΔB_0 fields, *time-varying* field fluctuations caused by subject motion and physiological processes also grow more severe at UHF. Head motion alters the shape of susceptibility-induced fields inside the brain, leading to time-varying spatial distortions in EPI time series (Dymerska et al., 2018). Similarly, motion of the chest wall and the changing volume of oxygen in the lungs create gradients in ΔB_0, leading to deleterious effects especially in cervical spine and brainstem imaging. These spatiotemporal field variations introduce k-space phase instability which leads to ghosting in T_2^*-weighted gradient echo scans and multishot EPI.

Further details on how B_0 inhomogeneity generates image artifacts are available in Koch et al. (2009).

6.3 Measuring ΔB_0

In order to perform both prospective and retrospective corrections of off-resonance artifacts, it is important to first acquire ΔB_0 field maps that are accurate (unbiased) and precise (high contrast-to-noise ratio). For a detailed and fully illustrated discussion of ΔB_0 mapping, see de Graaf and Juchem (2016) or Hetherington et al. (2006). In this chapter, we briefly review the mechanics of ΔB_0 mapping, with an emphasis on (i) how to deal with challenges that arise in UHF ΔB_0 mapping and (ii) how to assess the quality of the maps.

ΔB_0 is most commonly mapped with a gradient echo sequence using multiple echo-times, exploiting the fact that spin phase evolution depends on the background field offset: $\phi(\text{TE}) = 2\pi f t = \gamma/2\pi \Delta B_0 \text{TE}$. $\gamma/2\pi \Delta B_0$ in Hz can thus be estimated by linear fitting to the phase across TE. Fig. 6.2A outlines the process of computing the maps beginning with combining multichannel RF receive data into a single-phase image for each TE. At UHF, care must be taken to avoid "singularities" in areas where uncombined single-channel images have low SNR and poorly behaved phase wraps. Techniques for removing coil background phase include ESPIRIT (Uecker et al., 2014) and ASPIRE (Eckstein et al., 2018). Once coil-combined phase images are obtained, the remaining phase wraps must be unwrapped either using spatial-domain (e.g., FSL PRELUDE (Jenkinson et al., 2012)) or time-domain techniques (Hetherington et al., 2006). Typically, a mask derived from the gradient echo magnitude image is used to remove the background prior to unwrapping. The phase in each voxel across TEs is then fit to a line to generate the final ΔB_0 map. The standard deviation of ΔB_0 over the whole brain ($\sigma_{B_0}^{WB}$), or over a specific brain Region of Interest (ROI), is the most commonly used benchmark for the severity of the field inhomogeneity.

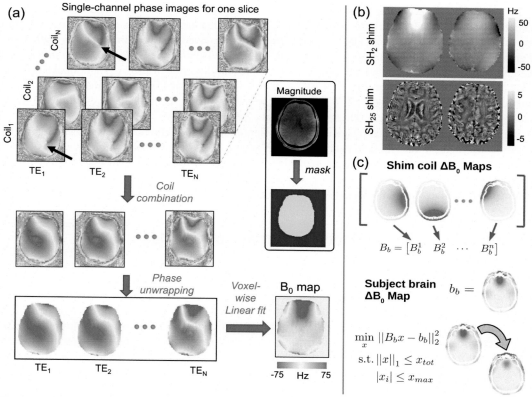

FIG. 6.2

B_O field mapping typically uses gradient echo images acquired at multiple echo-times (TEs). (A) This figure outlines B_O map image formation for a single slice. The magnitude image is used to create a brain mask. Uncombined images from different receive channels are combined to create a single phase image for each TE. At UHF, care must be taken to remove the background receive coil phase in order to avoid phase singularities (see black arrows) from propagating through to the combined phase images. Phase unwrapping is then performed either in the spatial domain, time domain, or a hybrid of the two. Finally, in each voxel, the phase evolution vs TE is fit to a line to compute the B_O field map. (B) It is important to consider the accuracy (bias) and precision (CNR) of a given field mapping protocol. One way to assess the precision of field maps is to apply simulated B_O shimming on each slice up to a high spatial order (25th-order spherical harmonic shimming shown here). If the B_O maps have high CNR, the residual B_O map should show intrinsic T_2^* contrast between gray and white matter. (C) To perform B_O shimming, a basis set of shim coil B_O maps is first acquired. During in vivo scans, a B_O map of the subject's head is acquired. The shim basis maps are interpolated into the coordinate system of the in vivo maps and a brain mask is typically applied. A quadratic program is then used to solve for optimal shim currents on each channel. The optimizer minimizes the least squares residual ΔB_O over the masked region of interest, with practical constraints on the total shim current and current in each channel.

In practice, it is important to assess the impact of noise and bias in field maps. Care should be taken in choosing the field map voxel size, since severe dephasing in areas like the frontal lobes can result in very noisy maps even when short TEs are used. Noise can be reduced and CNR improved by using three or more TEs to reduce uncertainty in the linear fit. To better visualize the CNR, the smoothly varying overlaying ΔB_0 field can be removed using either a Laplacian filter or by fitting out spherical harmonic fields up to a high spatial order. Fig. 6.2B shows that for high-CNR maps at UHF, the residual ΔB_0 in superior slices is dominated by the 4–5 Hz difference in intrinsic T_2^*-contrast between gray and white matter (similar to QSM images) (Hetherington et al., 2021).

Imperfections in spatial encoding arising from gradient-induced eddy currents can bias B_0 maps by adding erroneous spatially varying field patterns. Another source of bias is chemical shift in the lipids, which will alter the ΔB_0 estimate in voxels containing significant lipid fractions. This issue can be addressed by setting ΔTE so that water and the primary lipid peak remain in-phase (1.02 ms at 7T) or by using DIXON-style methods (Glover and Schneider, 1991) to simultaneously obtain water, lipid, and B_0 maps.

6.4 Reducing image artifacts without adjusting fields

6.4.1 Postacquisition correction for echo-planar imaging

A variety of methods exist for mitigating ΔB_0-induced image artifacts in postprocessing. We will focus our discussion here on artifacts arising in EPI acquisitions most commonly used for fMRI and dMRI. Many fMRI processing pipelines include an unwarping step to remove geometric distortion in EPI slices. Unwarping tools such as FSL FUGUE use conventional ΔB_0 maps while methods like FSL TOPUP create a voxel-displacement map by combining two spin echo EPI acquisitions with opposite phase-encode polarities (which also captures some eddy current effects) (Andersson et al., 2003). However, these methods have limited ability to undo distortion when severe voxel pile-up occurs, since this causes the unwarping problem to become poorly conditioned.

A further challenge faced in fMRI distortion correction is head motion which changes the ΔB_0 field in the brain and thus the pattern of geometric distortion. One way to track these ΔB_0 fluctuations is to use the EPI phase images themselves as a guide (Dymerska et al., 2018). The ΔB_0 map derived from each time-series volume can then be used to perform more accurate distortion correction. An alternative method is to interleave volumetric 3D EPI-based navigators ("vNAVs") into the time series (Bogner et al., 2014). vNAVs rapidly acquire low-resolution B_0 maps with minimal impact on the spin history. An approach known as "FIDnavs" uses free induction decay signals acquired with multichannel receive arrays to estimate the B_0 field distribution in the body (Wallace et al., 2020). While FIDnavs do not alter the spin history, they generally provide field estimates only for low spatial orders (up to second-order or possibly third-order spherical harmonics). Finally, NMR field probes can be used to monitor ΔB_0 in real time by acquiring FID readouts from small water droplets placed inside probes arranged around the head (Vannesjo et al., 2015). While field probes enable concurrent monitoring of B_0 fields, they are also limited in their ability to track high-spatial frequency field components (i.e., second-order field tracking for an array of 16 field probes).

6.4.2 Desensitizing echo-planar acquisitions against ΔB_0 at scan time

The limitations of postprocessing corrections highlight the need to limit artifacts during the acquisition itself using pulse sequence parameter optimization and/or specialized hardware.

One way to reduce EPI distortion is to leverage massively parallel RF receive arrays to accelerate the acquisition by undersampling k-space along the phase-encode direction, and then restore a full-FOV image using methods such as SENSE or GRAPPA (Larkman and Nunes, 2007). By skipping k-space lines, the effective echo spacing (ESP_{eff}) and the distortion are both reduced proportional to the acceleration factor (R). While these techniques are now widely used successfully, in practice there is a limit to the achievable acceleration factor, beyond which residual artifacts and/or noise amplification become too severe. In a similar vein, multishot EPI can be used to further reduce distortion but often at the expense of increased ghosting due to shot-to-shot phase variations introduced by motion or physiological B_0 fluctuations.

A second way to limit distortion is to reduce ESP_{eff} by employing gradient coils with increased slew rate and maximum amplitudes. Prototypes with slew rates of 500 T/m/s or higher have been demonstrated (Foo et al., 2020), as compared with 200 T/m/s for conventional gradients. However, increasing gradient performance without exceeding peripheral nerve stimulation safety thresholds is challenging, and high-performance gradient coils are only available at a handful of research sites around the world.

The aforementioned techniques help with geometric distortion, but they do not recover signal caused by intravoxel dephasing in areas with short T_2^*. The z-directed gradient of the B_0 field in the brain is roughly proportional to the magnitude of ΔB_0 offset (Guérin et al., 2016). B_0 z-gradients can be counteracted by applying an extra pulse to the z-gradient coil before signal readout to rephase the spins, but this comes at the expense of dephasing the rest of the slice. In this "z-shimming" approach, baseline and z-shimmed images are separately acquired and then combined to fill in the dephased "holes."

6.5 Shim devices for controlling magnetic field in vivo

A fundamental approach is to eliminate the off-resonance artifacts *at their source* by generating a compensating "B_0 shim" field that offsets the nuisance ΔB_0 fields in the body. By improving homogeneity, B_0 shimming works synergistically with all of the above B_0-mitigation methods. Shimming reduces the burden on unwarping methods and can potentially provide *multiplicative reductions in distortion in EPI* when combined with parallel imaging or high-performance gradient coils.

This section will review passive and active B_0 shimming approaches for nulling ΔB_0 fields on a subject-specific basis. In both approaches, the shim hardware aims to generate a field that is equal in amplitude but opposite in polarity to the unwanted ΔB_0 fields in the body, approximating their spatial profile as closely as possible using the available degrees of freedom. While in general, both passive and active shims generate ΔB_0 vector field perturbations along all three axes, only the z-component is relevant for restoring the homogeneity of the main magnetic field, since the x- and y-terms are too small to have a measurable effect.

6.5.1 Passive shimming of subject-induced inhomogeneity

In passive shimming approaches, pieces of magnetic material are placed close to the body at strategic locations in order to perturb the local B_0 field in an effort to null unwanted nuisance ΔB_0 fields. Commonly ferromagnetic (e.g., iron) and paramagnetic (e.g., zirconium) materials are used, but diamagnetic materials (pyrolytic graphite or bismuth) can also be useful for generating field offsets in the opposite direction. Fig. 6.3 shows graphite intraoral graphite shim inserts targeting the frontal lobes (Wilson et al., 2002)

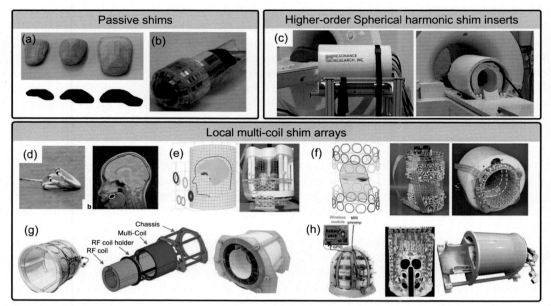

FIG. 6.3

Examples of hardware used for passive and active shimming. (A) Pyrolytic graphite intraoral shims based on a mouth mold for targeting prefrontal cortex. (B) Subject-specific, optimized array of diamagnetic and paramagnetic material (bismuth and zirconium) for shimming rat brain. (C) Spherical harmonic shim insert coil with 18 higher-order channels, shown here with RF transmit-receive coils nested inside. (D) Intraoral active multiturn shim loops targeting frontal lobes. (E) Array of six local multiturn shim loops placed over the face to shim the frontal lobes. (F) Generic "multicoil" shim array of 48 multiturn loops patterned over a cylinder that is nested inside a 7T RF Tx/Rx array. There is a gap in the coil layout (white dotted lines) to expose the RF coil elements. (G) 16-ch array of multiturn shim loops placed outside the shield of a transmit coil to avoid interactions between shim and RF elements. (H) Integrated RF/B_0 shim arrays in which RF receive loops are modified to add B_0 shim current-carrying capability (both 3 and 7T examples shown). Images are provided courtesy of (A) Peter Jezzard, Oxford Univ.; (B) Kevin Koch, Medical College of Wisconsin; (C) Piotr Starewicz, Resonance Research Inc.; (D) Gary Glover, Stanford Univ.; (E,F) Christoph Juchem, Columbia Univ.; (G) Klaus Scheffler, MPI Tuebingen; (H) Dean Darnell, Duke Univ. (3T example).

as well as a scaffold that holds pieces of diamagnetic and paramagnetic material for shimming rat brain (Koch et al., 2006). Since efficacy is improved by tailoring the spatial distribution of material on a subject-specific basis, passive shimming may not be practical in a routine imaging setting.

6.5.2 Active shimming

The most common B_0 shimming approach is to drive independent electric currents in a set of wire windings placed around the body. The resulting local magnetic fields can be tuned electronically by changing the current amplitude in the coils to optimize the B_0 shim field for different subjects or target ROIs. The resulting fields can be simulated accurately in the body using Biot-Savart's law since they interact only weakly with tissue.

6.5.2.1 Spherical harmonic shims

The most widely used active shim coils are those which generate fields approximating terms of the spherical harmonic (SH) basis (Roméo and Hoult, 1984). SH functions are an orthogonal basis that forms the solution to Laplace's equation in a source-free spherical ROI. For the set of SH terms up to order n (SH_n), each order contributes $2n+1$ terms, for a total of $(n+1)^2$ overall. As the order increases, so too does the spatial frequency content of the magnetic fields.

Most clinical MRI scanners are equipped with first-to-second-order (SH_2) shim coils, providing eight terms in total. The zeroth-order uniform field offset is usually realized by adjusting the RF carrier frequency. The first-order fields are generated by applying DC offsets to the scanner's linear gradient coils. The second-order fields are generated by five dedicated shim coils (Roméo and Hoult, 1984) that are typically embedded within the gradient coil housing. While the first-order shims can be adjusted dynamically during scans, the second-order shim coils are usually considered "static" since they are not configured for rapid switching.

The SH_2 basis set provides large improvements in homogeneity over the whole brain when compared to the unshimmed case. They can also be highly effective for shimming small brain ROIs, for example, in single-voxel MR spectroscopy. However, SH_2 shims have limited efficacy in areas of focal ΔB_0 due to their low spatial order. This has motivated the introduction of higher-order SH insert coils (Fig. 6.3C) for research applications (Hetherington et al., 2021).

Fig. 6.4 shows simulated whole-brain ("global") shimming up to SH_{100} on a 100-field map database at 7T. Average inhomogeneity across the database is shown as a function of the SH order, using the

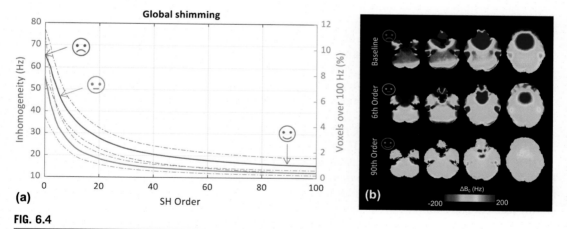

(a)   **(b)**

FIG. 6.4

(A) Spherical harmonic shimming simulation on a large field map database of 100 subjects acquired at 1.70 mm isotropic resolution. The average standard deviation of ΔB_0 over the whole brain ($\sigma_{B_0}^{WB}$) across the database and percentage of voxels with absolute field excursion above 100 Hz is used as performance evaluation metrics (dotted line shows +/1 standard deviation from the mean for the 100 maps). The 100 Hz frequency was chosen as it generates 10 mm shift in a voxel when using typical EPI acquisition parameters of 200 mm phase FOV and 0.5 ms interecho spacing (before adjusting for parallel imaging acceleration factor). (B) ΔB_0 field map across a few selected slices on a single subject after SH shimming simulations at different orders. High-intensity field excursions are observed at baseline. SH_6 shimming provides considerable improvement, but large inhomogeneity hotspots remain. With SH_{90} shimming, the slices show good homogeneity overall, but significant field excursions located next to magnetic field sources remain, demonstrating the fundamental limitations on global shim performance even when many shim orders are used.

standard deviation of residual ΔB_0 as well as outlier voxels ($|\Delta B_0| > 100$ Hz) as metrics. A steep drop is observed up until $\sim SH_{10}$, when inhomogeneity has improved by 43%. Further improving the homogeneity to match 3T would require a SH_{20} basis with up to 400 additional coils, which would be impractical from a space and power consumption perspective.

In the context of an empty magnetic bore, the SH basis set is a natural choice for shimming, since any level of homogeneity can be achieved if enough SH terms are added. However, when a human is introduced into the bore, the conditions of Laplace's equation are violated by the susceptibility interfaces inside the body. As a consequence, it is no longer intuitively obvious that the SH basis is the natural and most effective way to perform high spatial order shimming in the body.

6.5.2.2 Local multicoil shim arrays

An alternative and/or complementary approach to the orthogonal SH shim basis is to place arrays of local shim coil elements around the head close to the regions of interest. The loops may then be independently driven with shim currents of a few amperes or less. Examples of these "multicoil" shim arrays (MCA) are shown in Fig. 3D–H. The fields generated by these loops are no longer orthogonal. But by bringing many degrees of freedom to bear, high-spatial frequency B_0 fields can still be synthesized.

MC arrays typically have both low self-inductance and low mutual-inductance with the scanner's built-in gradient system. Thus, the driver voltages required to rapidly switch shim currents and reject gradient disturbances are low when compared to larger shim coils such as those built into gradient coils or used in SH insert coils. Additionally, the low inductance of MCA shim elements and the relatively large distance from cold structures in the bore tend to limit MCA-induced eddy currents (Aghaeifar et al., 2018).

Fig. 3D,E shows early realizations of low channel-count local MCAs designed to specifically target focal ΔB_0 in the frontal lobes with multiturn shim loops placed in the mouth (Hsu and Glover, 2005) and in front of the face (Juchem et al., 2010), respectively. The approach was then extended to generic arrays of loops driven with modest current amplitudes (1 ampere or less) patterned around the head on a cylindrical former to provide whole-brain coverage (Juchem et al., 2011). Fig. 6.3G–F shows example MC arrays for 9.4T (Aghaeifar et al., 2018) and 7T (Juchem et al., 2011) applications, respectively.

As an alternative to stand-alone MCAs, B_0 shimming capability can be added into the loop coils that are used in RF receive array coils. In this approach, known as "iPRES" (Truong et al., 2014) or "AC/DC" (Stockmann et al., 2016), the same single-turn wire windings are used simultaneously for RF signal reception and for carrying B_0 shim currents. Fig. 6.3H shows two examples of integrated RF/B_0-shim coils that have been demonstrated at 3T (Truong et al., 2014; Stockmann et al., 2016) and 7T (Stockmann et al., 2022). In studies to date, the added DC hardware has introduced either very modest (Stockmann et al., 2016) or undetectable (Stockmann et al., 2022; Truong et al., 2014) changes in RF receive sensitivity. This approach leverages the following synergies between parallel imaging and B_0 shimming: (i) both methods benefit from using large arrays of coils with independent field profiles, and (ii) close proximity to the body benefits B_0 shim efficient (more ΔB_0 field per amp of current) while also boosting RF receive SNR.

6.5.3 Active shimming as an optimization problem

As illustrated in Fig. 6.2C, active shimming is conveniently stated as an optimization problem. Given a set of coils, a collection of spatially varying field profiles generated per unit current for each coil needs to be measured, providing a so-called shim basis. The basis is assembled as a matrix $B_b = [B_b^1 \, B_b^2 \ldots B_b^n]$

from vectorized individual shim-coil field profiles B_b^i, with each row a voxel in the target volume. Field maps of the head are acquired to measure the subject-induced magnetic field perturbations to be corrected and put into vector form b_b. Shim currents are then calculated to minimize the ΔB_0 field variation, often in an l_2-sense under hardware-based current constraints. This means minimizing $\|B_b x - b_b\|_2^2$ with respect to x, the currents for each channel.

Typical hardware constraints on maximum current per channel and maximum total current supplied to the shim system may be written as two linear constraints: $|x_i| \leq$ max channel current and $\|x\|_1 \leq$ max total current, respectively. This optimization problem with a quadratic objective and linear inequality constraints may be solved efficiently using quadratic program solvers.

The l_2-norm is not the only possible choice for the optimization objective. Recent studies aiming to improve both signal dropout and image distortion in gradient echo EPI minimize a dual objective function, jointly minimizing both R_2^* (through ∇B_0 minimization) and ΔB_0 in each voxel (Willey et al., 2021).

The framework above leaves a choice of which voxels to include in the optimization problem. Typically, vendor shimming includes the entirety of the adjust-volume in a user-prescribed slab. However, performance may be improved by shimming voxels within only the target brain anatomy, typically excluding the scalp, peripheral fat, eyes, etc. Because of the geometry of the human brain, sinuses, and ear canals, partitioning the brain into smaller shim volumes yields significant performance gains (Poole and Bowtell, 2008).

Multislice 2D imaging provides a natural partitioning that can be exploited in dynamic shim updating (DSU) B_0 shimming (Blamire et al., 1996). By rapidly updating shim currents on a slice-by-slice basis, the encoded tissue within the slice is optimally shimmed and the inhomogeneity outside the target volume does not impact the slice acquisition. Effective DSU requires rapidly switchable shim coils and has been demonstrated with SH insert coils (Schwerter et al., 2019) as well as local MCAs (Aghaeifar et al., 2018; Juchem et al., 2011; Stockmann et al., 2022). Regularization of the shim optimization problem has been shown to reduce slice-to-slice variation in shim current amplitudes and limit unwanted eddy current effects from SH insert coils (Schwerter et al., 2019). Recently, slice-by-slice shimming has been extended to simultaneous multislice acquisitions (Hetherington et al., 2021; Stockmann and Wald, 2018). While helpful for MB-2 and MB-3, as the multiband factor increases further, simultaneously acquired slices become less separated from each other in space, causing shim performance to fall off, eventually converging to global shimming.

6.6 Simulated and experimental B_0 shimming results for different hardware setups

Examples of improved shim performance achieved using advanced shimming hardware are shown in Figs. 6.5 and 6.6. Fig. 6.5 shows how higher-order shimming can benefit MR spectroscopy, balanced SSP, and EPI acquisitions. Both global and dynamic shimming provide powerful options for artifact mitigation, with DSU providing better results, at the cost of increased current-driving complexity. Fig. 6.6 shows how dynamic shimming can be applied to simultaneous multislice scans by computing optimal shims over all N slices that are acquired at the same time, for multiband factor N. As expected, with increasing N, the dynamic shim performance converges toward the global static shim.

Table 6.1 summarizes whole-brain B_0 standard deviation ($\sigma_{B_0}^{WB}$) for a range of simulations and experiments reported in the literature. We note significant variation in the reported values, even for the

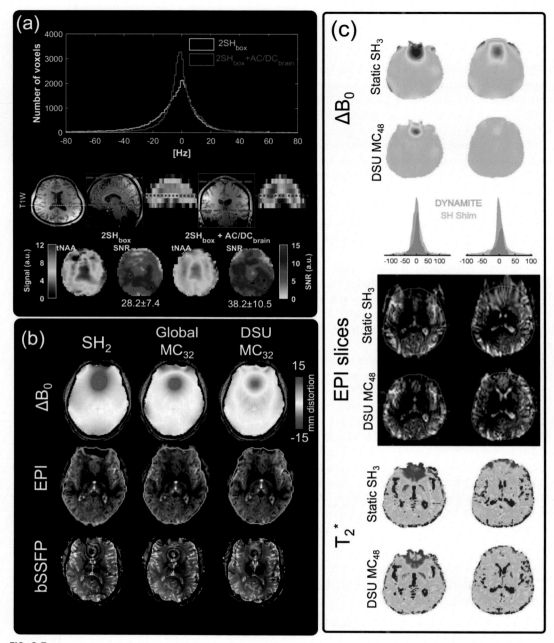

FIG. 6.5

Examples of improved data quality achieved with higher-order B_0 shimming. (A) MC_{31} shimming in MRSI reduces linewidths and improves metabolite maps. Note that the MC shims are switched off during lipid suppression pulses to avoid disrupting the pulse performance with off-resonance effects. (B) Global and DSU shimming at 9.4T with an optimized MC_{32} array reduces geometric distortion in GRE-EPI and banding artifacts in bSSFP images. (C) DSU shimming at 7T with a generic MC_{48} array improves GRE-EPI distortion and increases T_2^* in problem areas. Materials are courtesy of (A) Ovidiu Andronesi, MGH; (B) Klaus Scheffler, MPI Tübingen; (C) Christoph Juchem, Columbia Univ.

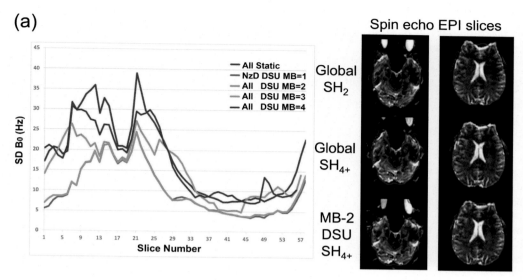

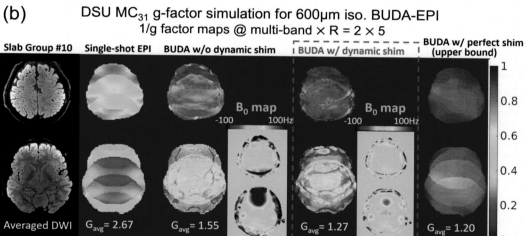

FIG. 6.6

For simultaneous multislice acquisitions, the shim fields can be optimized for each slice-pack to enable dynamic shim updating. (A) Degeneracy in spherical harmonic shim terms can be exploited to improve multiband imaging of axial slices. With a SH_{4+} shim insert coil, MB-2 DSU shim performance is equivalent to the MB-1 DSU case, improving distortion in SE-EPI slices as well as the standard deviation of ΔB_0 within each slice. (B) DSU shimming at 3T with a MC_{31} "AC/DC" array is used to reduce ΔB_0 and improve the g-factor in "BUDA" distortion-free high-resolution SE-EPI diffusion-weighted imaging. Materials are courtesy of (A) Hoby Hetherington, Resonance Research Inc.; (B) Congyu Liao, Stanford Univ.

Table 6.1 Summary of B_0 shim performance ($\sigma_{B_0}^{WB}$: standard deviation over the whole brain) described in the literature.

Study	Field strength	Scanner baseline	Static[a]	MB-1	MB-2	MB-3	MB-4
(Hetherington et al., 2021) 4th + SH	7T	32.4 ± 2.6	24 ± 2.5	14.3 ± 1.5	14.4 ± 2.0	18.6 ± 3.2^{a}	21 ± 3.4^{a}
(Stockmann and Wald, 2018) 4th order SH	7T	48.7 ± 6.2^{a}	38.7 ± 6.3^{a}	23.9 ± 5.2^{a}	25.8 ± 5.1^{a}	31.5 ± 5.8^{a}	–
(Stockmann and Wald, 2018) 32MC	7T	48.7 ± 6.2^{a}	41.2 ± 6.2^{a}	23.7 ± 5.0^{a}	27.6 ± 5.6^{a}	33.3 ± 5.7^{a}	–
(Juchem et al., 2011) 3rd-order SH	7T	–	43 ± 10^{a}	30 ± 7^{a}	–	–	–
(Juchem et al., 2011) 48MC	7T	–	–	25 ± 6	–	–	–
(Juchem et al., 2015) 4th-order SH	7T	40.6 ± 3.6^{a}	30.8 ± 4.0^{a}	17.2 ± 0.9^{a}	–	–	–
(Juchem et al., 2015) 48MC	7T	–	–	13.5 ± 0.5^{a}	–	–	–
(Aghaeifar et al., 2020) 32 MC	9.4T	71.9	48.4	31.9	–	–	–
(Chang et al., 2018) 3rd-order SH	9.4T	55.1 ± 6.4	48.7 ± 6.39	–	–	–	–
(Chang et al., 2018) 4th-order SH	9.4T	55.1 ± 6.4	44.7 ± 6.39	–	–	–	–

Significant discrepancies are reported in different studies even when relatively similar shim hardware is used. This could reflect differences in methodological details such as shim volume, the B_0 field mapping protocol, masking, and phase unwrapping.
[a]Statistics algorithm of simulated B_0 shimming.

SH_2 baseline static shim at 7T. Factors that may contribute to these discrepancies are discussed later in this chapter. Regardless of the hardware used, all studies show significant improvements compared to baseline SH_2 shimming.

6.7 Optimizing shim coil wire patterns to target brain anatomy

Successful B_0 shimming systems tend to share common features for combatting the large ΔB_0 inhomogeneity. For example, regularly arranged MCAs tend to demand higher currents in loops over the face (Stockmann et al., 2022). Such commonality comes from brain ΔB_0 patterns presenting similarities across different subjects. This naturally motivates the exploration of shim coil designs tailored to the brain anatomy.

Early explorations analyzed the principal components of the in vivo ΔB_0 field so that coils matching the dominant terms could be designed (Adalsteinsson et al., n.d.; Poole, 2007). More recently, principal component decompositions were applied to surface currents (expressed by stream functions) instead of the in vivo magnetic fields themselves (Jia et al., 2020; Pinho Meneses and Amadon, 2021). In this approach, optimal current patterns to minimize a target field excursion are calculated on a predefined surface. This is repeated for a collection of brain field maps, and the set of subject-optimal surface currents is decomposed into principal components. The most significant components are selected and transformed into independently driven coils, where currents are adjusted for shimming each subject. Finally, degrees of freedom can be added to the surface current decomposition design if the winding patterns of principal coils are used as template to optimize channel shape and position of a MCA (Pinho Meneses et al., 2022).

Fig. 6.7A illustrates the surface current decomposition and shows an early experimental realization. The bilateral symmetry and the high coil density near the nose and eyes of this computationally designed coil match common intuition regarding local ΔB_0 shim coil design.

Simulation results for different shim systems are shown in Fig. 6.8A for illustration. A large field map database at 7T was used. The simulations compare shim systems designed with different methodologies on a 280 mm diameter and 300 mm height coil former, using 1 mm diameter copper wire. Unconstrained ideal SH shimming performance is also shown.

It is assumed that ultimate performance when shimming a brain under constrained power dissipation is achieved using a bespoke coil. Therefore, a SF-based coil is designed for each subject in the database under increasing power dissipation bounds. Realistic matrix and optimized MCA designs serving the entire subject population are then simulated for comparison.

SF-based subject-optimized designs can provide homogeneity levels better than SH_7 system while consuming only 10 W (ignoring cabling, etc.). At 20 W, performance rivals a SH_8 system, but as power dissipation continues to increase, homogeneity improvement is only marginal. Increasing power dissipation by 60 W is still insufficient to move from SH_8 to SH_9. Also, from SH_8 to SH_9, inhomogeneity drops by less than 2 Hz, a small change with high engineering effort (19 additional SH coils).

A 48-ch matrix array can almost reach SH_6 with low average power dissipation, with the advantage for MCAs of being potentially easier to build than an equivalent-performance SH system. The complete SH_6 system requires 40 coils on top of the usual second-order SH shims, and each may require a cylindrical coil former of its own. Doubling the number of channels of the matrix MCA brings shimming performance slightly better than a SH_7 system. This is accompanied however by a significant increase in power dissipation.

By optimizing the MCA channels' geometry and positions for brain shimming, an optimized 48-ch MCA shows virtually the same performance as the generic 96-ch matrix MCA. Thus, the number of channels is not a fundamental limitation on performance.

What does it all mean for shim system design? If targeting the brain, a tight-fitting MCA appears to be a promising alternative to SH coils as MCAs tend to be more compact, versatile, and potentially better-suited to nulling local field excursions. As channel count increases, performance does improve, but electronics become more complex and power dissipation increases exponentially. When more performance is required, optimized MCAs are a powerful tool, as they can significantly increase performance at a fixed number of channels. Since power dissipation will still increase, a cooling system may become necessary. A potential way to circumvent the power dissipation barrier would be to increase the number of turns per channel. But if using the same wire gauge, the coils become bulkier

FIG. 6.7

(A) Illustration of ultimate shim performance calculation and few-channel optimized shim coil wire patterns. A surface current basis is used to shim a library of ΔB_0 maps. The library of currents is decomposed into dominant components and approximated with discrete wires. (B) Optimized surface current shim performance over database as compared to second-order SH shim performance. The target volume library includes a combination of global, slice-by-slice, and multiband shim regions. (C) Comparison between optimized few-channel shim coil performance and uniform circular coil performance over the off-resonance library as a fraction of ultimate shim performance. In simulation, 18 SVD-decomposed channels are needed for comparable performance to 50-channel generic MCA. (D) Optimized MCA design obtained when some of the highest energy SVD modes are decomposed into multiple independently driven channels. The choice of windings that should be segmented into individual channels can be done based on wire density. Notice how the channels are naturally positioned in front of the head and around the ears, regions where magnetic field inhomogeneity is known to be high due to air cavities near the brain.

(a)

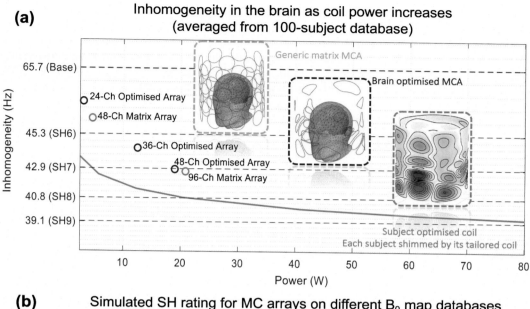

Inhomogeneity in the brain as coil power increases
(averaged from 100-subject database)

(b)

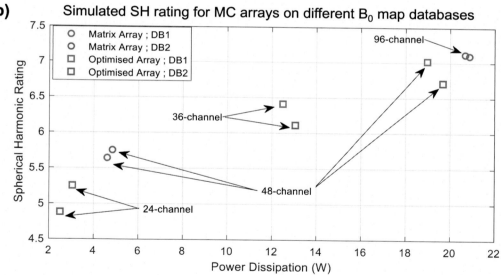

Simulated SH rating for MC arrays on different B_0 map databases

FIG. 6.8

(A) Average residual 7T B_0 inhomogeneity across the 100-subject field map database after shimming simulations with ideal and realistic shimming systems is shown as a function of the system's power dissipation. Resulting inhomogeneity from subject optimized shim coils, brain optimized MCAs, and generic matrix MCAs are shown for comparison. All shim system designs were assumed to be on a cylindrical former of 280 mm diameter and 300 mm length with windings made of copper wire of 1 mm diameter and inter-wire spacing of 1 mm used for discretization into windings of the subject-optimized coil system. MCA channels have 20 turns and each

(Continued)

and the winding will deviate more and more from the ideal wire path, which could be detrimental to performance. If the coil volume is to remain the same, the wire section has to decrease linearly as the number of turns increases, and power will remain the same. As an alternative to changing the wire pattern, another way to boost performance is to increase the max current. Increasing performance means the shim system starts to focus on more localized inhomogeneity hotspots, but it becomes more sensitive to small head movements, which are unavoidable and could put all the homogeneity improvement to waste.

It is clear that increasing performance always comes at a cost, and in practice, it may be prudent to find the "sweet spot" between performance and hardware complexity, beyond which performance gains become marginal.

6.8 Shim system performance evaluation

The common metric to assess shim performance is to compare standard deviation within the target ROI before and after shimming. In isolation, however, it does not provide information about the field distribution before and after shimming (or whether it was locally degraded despite global improvement). A fuller picture of the impact of ΔB_0 on imaging may therefore require standard deviations, percentiles, field maps, and even estimated artifact intensity maps.

Adding to the ambiguity, high variability in population $\sigma_{B_0}^{WB}$ values is seen across the literature (cf. Table 6.1). This is observed in both SH_2 baselines and higher-order shimming, making it difficult to assess robustness of a shimming system across different sites. Voxel size and exact brain mask boundaries are known to have a considerable effect on $\sigma_{B_0}^{WB}$. The averaging effect and T_2^*-signal losses associated with large field map voxels also artificially reduce apparent inhomogeneity. Such factors accumulate and can contribute to $\sigma_{B_0}^{WB}$ estimation errors of several Hz.

FIG. 6.8—Cont'd

channel is limited to 3 A current. The subject-optimized coil is assumed to be an ideal shim system where each subject would have a bespoke coil designed using surface current-based inverse methods with a power constraint. The green solid line shows how the inhomogeneity behaves as the power constraint is relaxed. It also appears to be a lower bound to the achievable inhomogeneity of "less optimized" alternative systems at any level of power dissipation. (B) Simulated shimming performance at 7T (averaged across database field maps), evaluated using the Spherical Harmonic Rating, as a function of power dissipation for different MCA designs when shimming different databases, denoted as DB1 and DB2. Optimized and generic matrix MCA designs were considered. MCAs are assumed to be built from 1 mm diameter round copper wire with 20 turns per channel and with currents limited to 3 A on each channel. DB1 contains 100 field maps and DB2 contains 127 field maps. These were acquired at different sites, with different scanners, sequence parameters, resolutions, and masking. Despite methodological differences in database acquisition, the SHR shows very similar performance for a same shimming system when employed on the different databases, contrasting to the large variations shown in Table 1 when using the standard deviation metric. Unconstrained ideal SH shimming simulations are marked on the y-axis. In this case, no coil design was performed and the simulations use ideal SH fields. A 100-subject brain field map database at 1.70 mm isotropic resolution at 7T is employed in the simulations. All other systems are designed considering a 280 mm diameter and 300 mm height coil former.

For illustration, simulations of a generic 48-ch matrix MCA (described in Section 6.5) on two different field map databases, DB1 (100 field maps, 1.7 mm isotropic) and DB2 (127 field maps, 4 mm isotropic), show that DB1 average inhomogeneity drops from 65.7 to 46.4 Hz, while DB2 average inhomogeneity is reduced from 67.2 to 39.3 Hz. Despite similar baselines, final inhomogeneity on each DB is quite different, with apparently superior 42% reduction on DB2 and only 29% on DB1. Even doubling the number of channels used on DB1 leads to 42.7 Hz average $\sigma_{B_0}^{WB}$, which still does not match the 48-ch DB2 performance, despite the use of a generic MCA design, which should have performed equally well on both databases.

A metric that can address cross-site shim array comparisons is the spherical harmonic rating (SHR) (Pinho Meneses et al., 2022). It compares the particular shimming system to an ideal SH shim system. For a given field map, if the resulting inhomogeneity σ_{shim} after shimming by some arbitrary system is between that obtained by unconstrained SH shimming of orders n and $n+1$ ($\sigma_{SH_n} \geq \sigma_{shim} > \sigma_{SH_n}+1$), then the SHR of the system on the field map is defined as

$$SHR = n + \frac{\sigma_{SH_n} - \sigma_{shim}}{\sigma_{SH_n} - \sigma_{SH_{n+1}}}.$$

Application of the metric to different shim systems simulated on DB1 and DB2 is shown in Fig. 6.8B. SHR and power dissipation now converge for matrix arrays, showing equivalent performance on both databases, whereas the standard deviation by itself was insufficient, or even misleading.

Simulations with an optimized MCA have a standard deviation indicating better performance on DB2, despite DB1 being employed as the design database. In contrast, assessment based on the SHR shows that performance over DB2 is only marginally worse than on DB1, indicating a more consistent performance of the coil system across data sets.

Overall, despite not giving a direct measure of image quality, the SHR seems useful in comparing systems across different databases, tackling intersite variability, which is not properly addressed by other metrics. The SHR therefore facilitates shim system performance comparison and can be used in conjunction with conventional metrics to provide a richer set of information.

6.9 Emerging applications

Finding new uses of ΔB_0 field control is an active area of research. One evolving research area is real-time correction of time-varying patient-specific ΔB_0 both due to patient respiration (Vannesjo et al., 2015) and patient motion (Deelchand et al., 2019), often using navigators or field probes to guide the real-time shim updates.

While switchable, high-spatial-order active B_0 shim devices were initially designed for applications in magnetic field homogenization, access to time-varying control of high spatial order ΔB_0 fields has enabled a number of new applications. Just as shims can be switched between slices in 2D acquisitions, they can also be switched within a single TR to apply different shims for each sequence module. Fig. 6.9A,B illustrates methods that take advantage of this insight in different ways. Fig. 6.9A shows zoomed 3D EPI enabled by a frequency-selective RF pulse combined with ΔB_0 field control for target volume selection. The shim field is rapidly switched between a "spatial selection shim" and "homogeneity shim" in between the RF excitation and readout.

Similarly, Fig. 6.9B shows a variety of lipid suppression approaches that are improved by applying switchable, nonlinear ΔB_0 fields. The first two methods enhance frequency-selective lipid suppression by using field control to increase the spectral separation between brain metabolites and lipids. The third

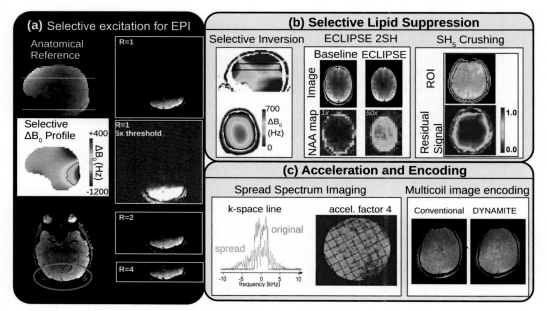

FIG. 6.9

(A) Emerging applications of ΔB_0 field control beyond conventional homogeneity shimming. High-order, switchable shim systems in a variety of applications: (A) Zoomed 3D functional imaging using frequency selective pulses and ΔB_0 field control for volume selection. (B) Spatially tailored, pulsed higher-order ΔB_0 fields used for improving lipid suppression: AC/DC coils used to improve the efficacy of lipid-selective inversion; ECLIPSE SH_2 fields for inner volume selection; and SH_5 field gradients at the periphery for spatially selective lipid crushing. (C) Image acceleration and spatial encoding using MCAs in addition to and in place of conventional scanner gradient systems. Materials are courtesy of (B) Robin de Graaf, Yale Univ (ECLIPSE) and Hoby Hetherington, Resonance Research Inc. (crushing); (C) Klaus Scheffler, MPI Tübingen (sinusoidal waveform encoding) and Christoph Juchem, Columbia Univ. (DYNAMITE).

method uses field control to apply large ΔB_0 gradients with spatial selectivity for localized crushing. We note that switching B_0 shims to a different setting (e.g., zeroing the shims) during lipid suppression is also useful for avoiding artifacts when DSU is applied during 2D multislice acquisitions including EPI (Stockmann et al., 2022).

Recent advances in active shim control electronics have enabled the use of arbitrary current waveforms for continuously varying ΔB_0 field control. For example, MCAs driven in a linear gradient mode using sinusoidal temporal waveforms can provide supplementary spatial encoding to boost parallel imaging performance. Fig. 6.9C shows spread spectrum imaging in which multicoil array encoding enables a fourfold accelerated acquisition using only a single RF receive channel In "DYNAMITE" multicoil imaging, the MCA completely replaces the scanner gradients for slice selection and/or spatial encoding.

Advances in B_0 shimming hardware have helped spawn a new research field around flexible spatial encoding that we hope will mature and bear fruit in the years ahead, benefiting the versatility and robustness of MRI.

Acknowledgments

The authors wish to thank Bastien Guerin for helpful discussions of off-resonance effects in RF pulse design and Hoby Hetherington for insights on B_0 field mapping protocols and ways to assess field map data quality.

References

Adalsteinsson, Conolly, Xu, n.d. Design of dedicated shim fields. Proc. Int. Soc. Magn. Reson. Med. Sci. Meet. Exhib.

Aghaeifar, A., Mirkes, C., Bause, J., et al., 2018. Dynamic B0shimming of the human brain at 9.4 T with a 16-channel multi-coil shim setup. Magn. Reson. Med. 80, 1714–1725.

Aghaeifar, A., Zhou, J., Heule, R., et al., 2020. A 32-channel multi-coil setup optimized for human brain shimming at 9.4T. Magn. Reson. Med. 83, 749–764.

Andersson, J.L.R., Skare, S., Ashburner, J., 2003. How to correct susceptibility distortions in spin-echo echo-planar images: application to diffusion tensor imaging. Neuroimage 20, 870–888.

Blamire, A.M., Rothman, D.L., Nixon, T., 1996. Dynamic shim updating: a new approach towards optimized whole brain shimming. Magn. Reson. Med. 36, 159–165.

Bogner, W., Hess, A.T., Gagoski, B., et al., 2014. Real-time motion- and B0-correction for LASER-localized spiral-accelerated 3D-MRSI of the brain at 3T. Neuroimage 88, 22–31.

Chang, P., Nassirpour, S., Henning, A., 2018. Modeling real shim fields for very high degree (and order) B0 shimming of the human brain at 9.4 T. Magn. Reson. Med. 79(1), 529–540. https://doi.org/10.1002/mrm.26658. Epub 2017 Mar 20. PMID: 28321902.

Deelchand, D.K., Joers, J.M., Auerbach, E.J., Henry, P.-G., 2019. Prospective motion and B0 shim correction for MR spectroscopy in human brain at 7T. Magn. Reson. Med. 82, 1984–1992.

Dymerska, B., Poser, B.A., Barth, M., Trattnig, S., Robinson, S.D., 2018. A method for the dynamic correction of B0-related distortions in single-echo EPI at 7T. Neuroimage 168, 321–331.

Eckstein, K., Dymerska, B., Bachrata, B., et al., 2018. Computationally efficient combination of multi-channel phase data from multi-echo acquisitions (ASPIRE). Magn. Reson. Med. 79, 2996–3006.

Foo, T.K.F., Tan, E.T., Vermilyea, M.E., et al., 2020. Highly efficient head-only magnetic field insert gradient coil for achieving simultaneous high gradient amplitude and slew rate at 3.0T (MAGNUS) for brain microstructure imaging. Magn. Reson. Med. 83, 2356–2369.

Glover, G.H., Schneider, E., 1991. Three-point Dixon technique for true water/fat decomposition with B0 inhomogeneity correction. Magn. Reson. Med. 18, 371–383.

de Graaf, R., Juchem, C., 2016. B0 shimming technology. In: Magnetic Resonance Technology: Hardware and System Component Design. Royal Society of Chemistry, pp. 166–207.

Guérin, B., Stockmann, J.P., Baboli, M., Torrado-Carvajal, A., Stenger, A.V., Wald, L.L., 2016. Robust time-shifted spoke pulse design in the presence of large B0 variations with simultaneous reduction of through-plane dephasing, B1+ effects, and the specific absorption rate using parallel transmission. Magn. Reson. Med. 76, 540–554.

Hetherington, H.P., Chu, W.-J., Gonen, O., Pan, J.W., 2006. Robust fully automated shimming of the human brain for high-field 1H spectroscopic imaging. Magn. Reson. Med. 56, 26–33.

Hetherington, H.P., Moon, C.H., Schwerter, M., Shah, N.J., Pan, J.W., 2021. Dynamic B0 shimming for multiband imaging using high order spherical harmonic shims. Magn. Reson. Med. 85, 531–543.

Hsu, J.-J., Glover, G.H., 2005. Mitigation of susceptibility-induced signal loss in neuroimaging using localized shim coils. Magn. Reson. Med. 53, 243–248.

Jenkinson, M., Beckmann, C.F., Behrens, T.E.J., Woolrich, M.W., Smith, S.M., 2012. FSL. Neuroimage 62, 782–790.

Jia, F., Elshatlawy, H., Aghaeifar, A., et al., 2020. Design of a shim coil array matched to the human brain anatomy. Magn. Reson. Med. 83, 1442–1457.

Juchem, C., Cudalbu, C., Graaf, R.A., et al., 2021. B_0 shimming for in vivo magnetic resonance spectroscopy: Experts' consensus recommendations. NMR Biomed.

Juchem, C., de Graaf, R.A., 2017. B0 magnetic field homogeneity and shimming for in vivo magnetic resonance spectroscopy. Anal. Biochem. 529, 17–29.

Juchem, C., Nixon, T.W., McIntyre, S., Boer, V.O., Rothman, D.L., de Graaf, R.A., 2011. Dynamic multi-coil shimming of the human brain at 7 T. J. Magn. Reson. 212, 280–288.

Juchem, C., Nixon, T.W., McIntyre, S., Rothman, D.L., de Graaf, R.A., 2010. Magnetic field homogenization of the human prefrontal cortex with a set of localized electrical coils. Magn. Reson. Med. 63, 171–180.

Juchem, C., Umesh Rudrapatna, S., Nixon, T.W., de Graaf, RA., 2015. Dynamic multi-coil technique (DYNAMITE) shimming for echo-planar imaging of the human brain at 7 Tesla. Neuroimage 105, 462–472. https://doi.org/10.1016/j.neuroimage.2014.11.011. Epub 2014 Nov 8. PMID: 25462795; PMCID: PMC4262558.

Koch, K.M., Brown, P.B., Rothman, D.L., de Graaf, R.A., 2006. Sample-specific diamagnetic and paramagnetic passive shimming. J. Magn. Reson. 182, 66–74.

Koch, K.M., Rothman, D.L., de Graaf, R.A., 2009. Optimization of static magnetic field homogeneity in the human and animal brain in vivo. Prog. Nucl. Magn. Reson. Spectrosc. 54, 69–96.

Larkman, D.J., Nunes, R.G., 2007. Parallel magnetic resonance imaging. Phys. Med. Biol. 52, R15–R55.

Pinho Meneses, B., Amadon, A., 2021. A fieldmap-driven few-channel shim coil design for MRI of the human brain. Phys. Med. Biol. 66, 015001.

Pinho Meneses, B., Stockmann, J.P., Arango, N., et al., 2022. Shim coils tailored for correcting B0 inhomogeneity in the human brain (SCOTCH): design methodology and 48-channel prototype assessment in 7-Tesla MRI. Neuroimage 261, 119498.

Poole, M.S., 2007. Improved Equipment and Techniques for Dynamic Shimming in High Field MRI. University of Nottingham. Ph.D. thesis.

Poole, M., Bowtell, R., 2008. Volume parcellation for improved dynamic shimming. MAGMA 21, 31–40.

Roméo, F., Hoult, D.I., 1984. Magnet field profiling: analysis and correcting coil design. Magn. Reson. Med. 1, 44–65.

Schwerter, M., Hetherington, H., Moon, C.H., et al., 2019. Interslice current change constrained B0 shim optimization for accurate high-order dynamic shim updating with strongly reduced eddy currents. Magn. Reson. Med.

Stockmann, J.P., Arango, N.S., Witzel, T., et al., 2022. A 31-channel integrated "AC/DC" B_0 shim and radiofrequency receive array coil for improved 7T MRI. Magn. Reson. Med.

Stockmann, J.P., Wald, L.L., 2018. In vivo B0 field shimming methods for MRI at 7T. Neuroimage 168, 71–87.

Stockmann, J.P., Witzel, T., Keil, B., et al., 2016. A 32-channel combined RF and B_0 shim array for 3T brain imaging. Magn. Reson. Med.

Truong, T.-K., Darnell, D., Song, A.W., 2014. Integrated RF/shim coil array for parallel reception and localized B0 shimming in the human brain. Neuroimage 103, 235–240.

Uecker, M., Lai, P., Murphy, M.J., et al., 2014. ESPIRiT—an eigenvalue approach to autocalibrating parallel MRI: where SENSE meets GRAPPA. Magn. Reson. Med. 71, 990–1001.

Vannesjo, S.J., Wilm, B.J., Duerst, Y., et al., 2015. Retrospective correction of physiological field fluctuations in high-field brain MRI using concurrent field monitoring. Magn. Reson. Med. 73, 1833–1843.

Wallace, T.E., Afacan, O., Kober, T., Warfield, S.K., 2020. Rapid measurement and correction of spatiotemporal B0 field changes using FID navigators and a multi-channel reference image. Magn. Reson. Med. 83, 575–589.

Willey, D., Darnell, D., Song, A.W., Truong, T., 2021. Application of an integrated radio-frequency/shim coil technology for signal recovery in fMRI. Magn. Reson. Med.

Wilson, J.L., Jenkinson, M., Jezzard, P., 2002. Optimization of static field homogeneity in human brain using diamagnetic passive shims. Magn. Reson. Med. 48, 906–914.

Parallel transmission: Physics background, pulse design, and applications in neuro MRI at ultra-high field

Vincent Gras[a], Xiaoping Wu[b], and Nicolas Boulant[a]

[a]*University of Paris-Saclay, CEA, CNRS, BAOBAB, NeuroSpin, Gif sur Yvette, France* [b]*Center for Magnetic Resonance Research, Radiology, Medical School, University of Minnesota, Minneapolis, MN, United States*

Highlights

- RF field inhomogeneity inside the body is a major hindrance for the adoption of UHF MRI for imaging the human body, despite the SNR gain offered by high magnetic fields.
- Parallel transmission (pTx) offers a powerful means to tackle this problem.
- Optimal exploitation of pTx-equipped MRI systems requires the development of dedicated RF pulse design techniques.
- A seamless pTx workflow and a reliable estimation of the local RF energy deposition inside the body remain key to bringing UHF MRI to its full potential and to strengthening its use in clinical routine and brain research.

7.1 Introduction

In magnetic resonance imaging, the well-known increase in signal-to-noise (SNR) and the expected gains in contrast-to-noise ratios (CNR) in vivo have fueled a race for working at higher magnetic fields (B_0). Unfortunately, imaging at ultra-high magnetic field (UHF) and thus at high frequency (298 MHz at 7 Tesla against 64 MHz at 1.5 Tesla) brings new difficulties, and among those is the necessity to cope with an inhomogeneous radiofrequency (RF) field. In the human brain at 7 Tesla, the RF field distribution using volume coil excitation is such that important zones of signal and contrast loss can arise, leading to suboptimal image quality and unusable images in the worst case. Furthermore, a loss of contrast is generally not recoverable by postprocessing because the MR contrast is multiparametric and may exhibit a nonlinear dependence with the underlying parameters, in particular the flip angle and the MR relaxation times. Aside from higher costs, RF field inhomogeneity has been one of the greatest obstacles that has prevented UHF MRI from being fully embraced by the community. An illustration of the problem is provided in Fig. 7.1.

Being a long-standing problem in magnetic resonance, RF field inhomogeneity arose in the early days of liquid- and solid-state nuclear magnetic resonance (NMR). Today's UHF community stands on NMR giants' shoulders, and this review would be incomplete if the historical developments for tackling RF field inhomogeneity were not presented at least briefly. Although some of these techniques have limited usage in MRI at UHF because of long pulse durations and high power demand, they have

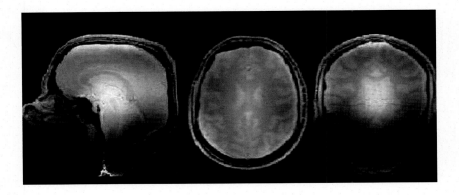

FIG. 7.1

Gradient echo in vivo acquisition at 7T with a conventional birdcage coil. RF field inhomogeneity yields the center brightening and an important loss of signal/contrast in some zones. The cerebellum, temporal, and occipital lobes are the most severely affected regions.

provided considerable insights into more sophisticated methods. After introducing the physics of RF field inhomogeneity and the historical mitigation techniques, this chapter focuses on parallel transmission (pTx) and some of its milestone developments and applications in neuro MRI. In particular, this chapter will cover the key pulse parametrizations and algorithms for 2D selective and 3D nonselective pTx RF designs targeting small and large flip angles and will provide concrete in vivo demonstrations with cornerstone MR sequences. This chapter finishes by outlining unmet needs and challenges that the authors foresee. Since its inception, nearly 20 years ago, pTx has been an active field of research, leading to a large body of publications. As a result, we ask for the readers' forgiveness if their favorite work is not included. We hope that this chapter will constitute a good basis for the student or researcher interested in pursuing this exciting research.

7.2 B_1^+ inhomogeneity
7.2.1 Physics background

Hoult and Phil (Hoult and Phil, 2000) gave considerable insight into RF field inhomogeneity by studying the transmit B_1 (B_1^+) field and power deposition in a homogeneous spherical phantom. The phantom was enclosed in a spherical probe to create a simplified scenario in which analytical expressions could be obtained. No matter how sophisticated the RF coil is, a perfectly homogeneous field is not a solution of Maxwell's equations, making RF field inhomogeneity an unavoidable phenomenon. Its severity depends on the details of the setup, such as the type of RF coil, sample size, and frequency. Field focusing is the effect of boosting the B_1^+ field at the center, whereas dielectric resonances arise from reflections at the boundaries of the sample (from strong discontinuities of the electric properties) likewise leading to an amplification of the B_1^+ field at some locations when the wavelength matches certain conditions with respect to sample size. Dielectric resonances therefore only occur at specific frequencies while field focusing can occur for every frequency. Both effects result in nonuniform B_1^+ field distribution inside

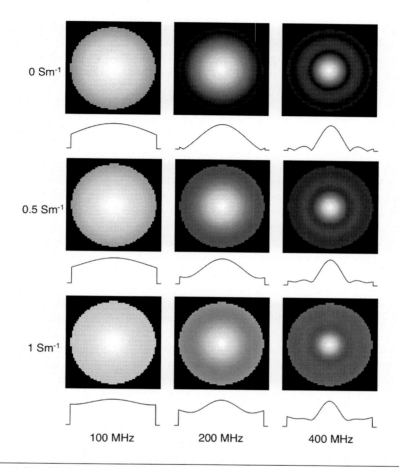

FIG. 7.2

Field focusing and dielectric resonances. Simulated B_1^+ field distribution in the quadrature mode (axial view) and in a saline spherical phantom versus frequency and conductivity (courtesy of David Hoult). The line profile through the center is also provided for each case.

the object. Interestingly, although a nonzero conductivity of the sample would normally suggest a loss of B_1^+ and thus a decrease in RF homogeneity, it can in fact dampen these effects and help control the B_1^+ field inhomogeneity inside the body, unless it becomes too high leading to the skin effect (Yang et al., 2002).

The phenomena are illustrated in Fig. 7.2 showing the B_1^+ field distribution in a representative axial slice of a sphere as a function of frequency and conductivity. For the same conductivity, increasing the frequency (or B_0 field strength) yields a field distribution with a more peaked profile. For the same frequency, increasing the conductivity on the other hand decreases the maximum over minimum ratio.

By the same token, the authors showed that the total RF power absorbed by the sample (proportional to the Specific Absorption Rate or SAR) for the same target B_1^+ field at the center follows a quadratic law with respect to the B_0 field strength at low frequencies. However, the corrections arising from the inhomogeneous RF field in Maxwell-Faraday's equation reveal a much less severe trend (e.g., a five-fold smaller power than that of the quadratic law at 400 MHz and for a sphere of 10 cm in radius). Nevertheless, the trend remains that power deposition increases with field strength.

7.2.2 Composite and adiabatic pulses

A composite pulse consists of a train of subpulses each parametrized by a flip angle and phase. Conventionally, the flip angle is the nominal one, i.e., achieved on resonance for a given nutation (Rabi) frequency and pulse duration. The general goal is to achieve increased robustness against variations of any parameter involved in the equation governing the dynamics. These variations involve the control parameters such as B_1^+ field magnitude and phase in the spin ensemble, coupling strengths between nuclei, but they can also reflect experimental limitations or uncertainties. In the early days of NMR, many of these techniques were designed to compensate for some drawbacks such as lack of accuracy in RF pulse shapes and lack of RF power. As spectrometers became more and more sophisticated, research on composite pulses started to focus almost exclusively on compensating for RF field inhomogeneity and off-resonance frequencies to achieve a desired rotation or magnetization state. The former was caused by the spatial extent of the sample while the latter was mostly a natural consequence of studying multinuclei molecules with a broad range of chemical shifts. As a result, a great application of composite pulses is broadband decoupling of heteronuclear species in liquid-state NMR.

Although numerical techniques can be used to determine optimal parametrizations of composite pulses, symmetries are at the heart of many achievements. So unsurprisingly, the same tools and ideas have inspired the resolution of some pTx pulse design problems that will be presented later on. The use of spinor SU(2) formalisms and occasionally average Hamiltonian theory can be less familiar to the MRI community. In the simplest cases, pictorial and geometrical representations of the spin dynamics can provide a valuable insight. The reader is encouraged to consult Levitt (2008) for an excellent presentation of the basic concepts. The problem with composite pulses is that the larger the degree of desired compensation, the more the RF pulses and the higher the RF integrated power. For instance, the simple $(90)_0 - (180)_{90} - (90)_0$ inversion scheme, an equivalent to a 2π integrated pulse, represents a good example of obtaining first-order compensation for B_1^+ field inhomogeneity. Although this can be tolerated in NMR with larger nutation frequencies and longer T_2 relaxation times, the approach is no longer possible in in vivo MRI because RF power and T_2 values in biological tissues combined are more than two orders of magnitude smaller than those in NMR. The maximum SAR allowed for in vivo NMR experiments would also make it problematic to implement composite pulses in many in vivo applications.

An attractive alternative to composite pulses is adiabatic pulses (De Graaf and Nicolay, 1997). The design of adiabatic pulses follows the elegant idea that if the effective field (composed of the transverse RF and offset longitudinal fields in the rotating frame) aligns with the magnetization and varies slowly in its direction, it can "lock" and force the magnetization to stay aligned with itself. To give the reader some intuition about the phenomenon, imagine walking while holding by its tip a pendulum that is initially aligned with the gravitational field: walking too fast will lead to chaotic oscillations, whereas walking slowly enough will maintain the pendulum straight, i.e., keep it aligned with the gravitational field. With the appropriate modulation of the amplitude and phase of the B_1^+ field, a magnetization can be flipped into the transverse plane or be inverted. Examples of adiabatic pulses include the B_I^+ -insensitive rotation (BIR-4) pulses with adapted phase shifts that can generate arbitrary flip angles, or when applied in pairs, can yield plane rotations for refocusing. Like composite pulses, adiabatic pulses find limited application for excitation and refocusing in UHF neuro MRI due to their long durations and high RF power. Yet, they can be accommodated if used scarcely with a long repetition time (TR), for instance as inversion preparation. In this context, the hyperbolic-secant (Silver et al., 1984) pulse is a popular choice for the preparation module in some anatomical sequences.

7.3 Parallel transmission

In 2001, Ibrahim and colleagues proposed to transform a single-port high-pass birdcage RF coil into a four-port drive system to gain control over the B_1^+ spatial distribution and thereby mitigate the field focusing effect obvious at 3T onward (Ibrahim et al., 2000). A few years later, the use of multiport systems allowing for an independent control of the RF signal at each port was proposed and studied from a theoretical point of view (Katscher et al., 2003). Owing to the so-called Transmit SENSE principle, such a system was shown to offer great benefits for implementing multidimensional spatially selective excitations (Pauly et al., 1991). The actual realization of multitransmit RF array yet represents a challenge as the techniques commonly used to decouple two receive elements (preamplifier decoupling) are not particularly effective for decoupling two such resonators in transmission. An early realization of such multiport systems exploiting transmission lines was reported in Adriany et al. (2005). The insertion of a power divider and phase shifter enabled tuning the RF phase of each transmitter to optimize the B_1^+ profile homogeneity across the brain, a method that is usually referred to as (static) RF phase shimming. Using independent RF sources (full pTx) comes at the expense of additional hardware and complexity but offers a much greater control of spin excitation through space. Static RF shimming, where the RF phases *and* amplitudes of a given RF waveform (typically a hard pulse or sinc shape) are adjusted across channels, can be considered in this context. This provides more degrees of freedom than RF phase shimming to shape the B_1^+ spatial distribution. Finally, yet importantly, dynamic RF shimming, wherein fully independent temporal waveforms can be played out on each channel, can be designed as well. In what follows, dynamic RF shimming is shown capable of providing much higher excitation homogeneity, especially when static RF (phase) shimming is often deemed insufficient for achieving uniform excitation over an extended volume. For UHF neuro MRI, the number of independent transmitters N_c is usually 8 and can reach 16 in research setups (Shajan et al., 2014). For a detailed discussion on RF coils, see Chapter 8.

7.3.1 RF shimming

RF shimming consists of applying optimized complex-valued RF voltages $v_1, \cdots, v_{N_c}$ on each transmitter in order to achieve the best possible total RF field distribution across the ROI, typically the volume of the brain. Let $B_{1,j}^+(\boldsymbol{r})$ denote the RF field at position $\boldsymbol{r}$ generated by channel j when driven by a unit voltage. The total RF field B_1^+ is the sum of the RF fields generated by individual channels (weighted by their respective voltages v_j) of the transmit RF array:

$$B_1^+(\boldsymbol{r}) = \sum_{j=1}^{N_c} B_{1,j}^+(\boldsymbol{r})v_j. \qquad (7.1)$$

We note here that for a vast majority of the MRI applications, one is concerned with the spatial distribution of the flip angle. The latter being proportional to the magnitude of the total B_1^+ for an on-resonance pulse, RF shimming may simply target a uniform $|B_1^+|$, especially when the B_1^+ phase is irrelevant (which is the case in many neuro MRI applications where the information is only carried in the image magnitude).

By discretizing the ROI into a set of N_p positions $r_1, \cdots, r_{N_p}$, one can represent the transmit sensitivity profiles in a $N_p \times N_c$ complex matrix:

$$\mathbf{A} = \left(B_{1,j}^+(r_m)\right)_{m,j}. \tag{7.2}$$

RF shimming then boils down to solving one of the following two optimization problems:

$$\boldsymbol{\xi} = \arg\min_x \|\mathbf{A}x - b\|_2^2, \tag{7.3A}$$

$$\boldsymbol{\xi} = \arg\min_x \||\mathbf{A}x| - b\|_2^2, \tag{7.3B}$$

where b is a vector of dimension N_p representing the target complex field or magnitude, and $x = (v_1, \cdots, v_{N_c})^T$ is the vector composed of the N_c RF drive voltages to be optimized. Solving the magnitude least squares (MLS) optimization problem (Setsompop et al., 2008) in Eq. 7.3B (applicable when the B_1^+ phase is irrelevant) generally yields better performance than tackling the least-squares (LS) counterpart in Eq. 7.3A (needed when the B_1^+ phase is relevant). The MLS problem however is nonconvex (Hoyos-Idrobo et al., 2014) and, therefore, subject to local minima. Without constraints, one effective way to solve the problem is the use of an iterative method called the variable-exchange (Setsompop et al., 2008), or Glechberg-Saxton (Hoyos-Idrobo et al., 2014) algorithm. In each iteration of this algorithm, an LS problem is first solved, yielding

$$\boldsymbol{\xi} = \mathbf{A} \backslash b = \left(\mathbf{A}^\dagger \mathbf{A}\right)^{-2} \mathbf{A}^\dagger b, \tag{7.4}$$

where $\mathbf{A}^\dagger$ denotes the conjugate transpose of $\mathbf{A}$. The product $\mathbf{A}\boldsymbol{\xi}$ is then used to give a phase distribution to be reinjected into b at the next iteration. The process is repeated until convergence. RF shimming is capable of achieving relatively good RF homogeneity (reducing the normalized root mean square error (NRMSE) down to ~10%) (Wu et al., 2019) when targeting 2D slices in the brain at 7T using an eight-loop coil design similar to that proposed by Adriany et al., 2005. However, when targeting the whole brain in a 3D acquisition, RF shimming is shown to only lead to marginal improvements in RF homogeneity when compared to the circularly polarized (CP) mode (the mode mimicking a single-channel transmit (sTx) setup wherein all transmit channels are approximately in phase at the center of the coil array) with NRMSE of ~21%. In other words, RF shimming per se does not entirely solve the transmit field inhomogeneity problem for 3D neuro MRI at UHF. This is where two additional "ingredients" play a critical role, namely, the use of linear B_0 gradients for phase modulation and time to take advantage of the spins' dynamics and their phase evolution.

7.3.2 Transmit-SENSE

In an early work, Katscher et al. (2003) demonstrated the added value of pTx to implement short multidimensional pulses. The methodology was inspired by the ingenious principle of parallel imaging where multireceive coil elements are used to enable image reconstruction from accelerated (i.e., not fully encoded spatially) data acquisition. Starting with an initial magnetization at thermal equilibrium thus aligned with the z axis, the small tip angle (STA) approximation (Pauly et al., 1989) for the complex magnetization's tip angle θ in response to the time-varying RF voltages $v_1(t), \cdots, v_{N_c}(t)$ and time-varying magnetic field gradients (MFG) $g(t) = (G_x(t), G_y(t), G_z(t))$ of duration T (is)

$$\theta(r) \simeq -i\gamma \int_0^T B_1^+(r,t)e^{ik(t)\cdot r}e^{-i\gamma \Delta B_0(r)(T-t)}dt, \tag{7.5}$$

where i denotes the imaginary number $\sqrt{-1}$, γ is the gyromagnetic ratio (in rad/s/T), $B_1^+(r,t)$ is the time- and space-dependent total resonant RF field (see Eq. 7.1, wherein the RF voltage signals are now varying in time), $k(t) = -\int_t^T \gamma g(t')dt'$ is the so-called excitation k-space trajectory, $k(t)$. r denotes the scalar product of $k(t)$ and r, and ΔB_0 is the susceptibility-induced off-resonance field (in Tesla). Discretizing Eq. 7.5 in time yields

$$\theta(r) \approx -i\gamma \Delta t \sum_{n=1}^{N_t} \sum_{j=1}^{N_c} B_{1,j}(r)v_j(n\Delta t)e^{ik(n\Delta t)\cdot r}e^{-i\gamma \Delta B_0(r)(T-n\Delta t)}, \tag{7.6}$$

where Δt is the dwell time and $N_t = T/\Delta t$ is the total number of time steps. Then, by discretizing in space and by matrix concatenation, the same design problem as in Eq. 7.3 can be proposed for pulse calculation, where b now represents the target flip angle while the matrix $\mathbf{A}$ is a $N_p \times (N_c N_t)$ complex matrix whose m-th line ($1 \leq m \leq N_p$) is constructed as follows:

$$\mathbf{A}_m = (a_{m,1,1} \ a_{m,1,2} \cdots a_{m,1,N_t} \ a_{m,2,1} \cdots a_{m,N_c,N_t}), \tag{7.7}$$

where $a_{m,j,n}$—the complex coefficient associated with the mth position r_m, channel j, and time step n—is given by

$$a_{m,j,n} = -i\gamma \Delta t B_{1,j}(r_i)e^{ik(n\Delta t)\cdot r_m}e^{-i\gamma \Delta B_0(r_m)(T-n\Delta t)}, m = 1, 2, \ldots, N_p. \tag{7.8}$$

The vector x is now the stack of the discretized RF waveforms of individual channels

$$x = (v_1(\Delta t), \ldots, v_1(N_t\Delta t), v_2(\Delta t), \ldots, v_{N_c}(N_t\Delta t))^T \in \mathbb{C}^{(N_c N_t)\times 1}. \tag{7.9}$$

A pulse design formulation in which fields and targets are all expressed in space is called the spatial domain method (Grissom et al., 2006). This has become the most commonly used formulation because of its advantages over the frequency domain method (Katscher et al., 2003), such as easy incorporation of masks or spatial weights to exclude regions from the optimization, and spatially dependent static field offsets into the design problem formulation. Depending on the complexity of the target flip angle pattern, a relatively long pulse duration with a long k-space trajectory may be necessary for achieving a good performance. Mathematically speaking, this can be intuited with the rank of the matrix $\mathbf{A}$ growing with the number of time steps, provided the k-space trajectory is appropriately modulated in time. Once the matrix is full rank, i.e., equal to the number of spatial locations (rows), any arbitrary excitation pattern (e.g., a university logo) can in principle be achieved (Stenger et al., 2002). From a physics perspective, ideally all spatial frequencies of the discretized domain should be covered to faithfully reproduce a pattern. When k-space points are skipped to return a shorter k-space trajectory and RF pulse, solving the Transmit-SENSE pulse design problem consists of "filling the gaps" by using the spatial encoding capabilities of the individual channels' transmit sensitivity profiles.

Besides boosting the quality of multidimensional (2D or 3D selective) excitations (Katscher et al., 2003), the basic principle of shortening excitation k-space trajectories while targeting simple, homogeneous, target magnetization patterns ($b_m = \theta_T \forall m$) is still at the heart of mitigating B_1^+ inhomogeneity with 3D nonselective and 2D selective pulses, whereby pulse durations ideally should remain short compared to relaxation times. For this application of Transmit-SENSE, we may speak about *dynamic* RF shimming, as the use of the temporal dimension is essential to exploiting the dynamics of the spins. Before going into the details of some pTx pulse design approaches, we want to stress that the model presented so far idealizes the experimental conditions. As already noted, relaxation mechanisms are usually ignored for simplicity. Likewise, k-space trajectories are assumed ideal but can be affected by eddy currents. Unless characterized and properly accounted for, the k-space errors can result in great deterioration of pulse performance (Jankiewicz et al., 2010). Finally, it should be kept in mind that static or dynamic RF shimming, and more generally any Transmit-SENSE method, relies on some measurement of the transmit sensitivity profiles. The limited precision of these measurements and, in the context of in vivo imaging, their stability across time can lead to discrepancies between the desired and the actual pulse performances.

7.3.3 Pulse design

As shown above, pTx offers the ability to control the RF field itself, and thus the spatial distribution of the magnetization output state, by modulating multichannel transmit amplitudes and phases through time. The design formulation given by Eq. 7.3 can be used when solving multiple practical problems in the linear STA regime (from nonselective to 3D selective excitations). For any given k-space trajectory, the solution obtained using the Glechberg-Saxton algorithm to induce a uniform target flip angle θ_T is given by

$$\xi = \mathrm{GS}(\mathbf{A}, \theta_T),\tag{7.10}$$

where $\mathrm{GS}(\cdot)$ denotes the application of the Glechberg-Saxton algorithm, the dependence of matrix $\mathbf{A}$ on the k-space trajectory parameterization $k(t)$ being that provided in Eq. 7.8. Naturally, the choice for the k-space trajectory (and the associated gradient waveforms) greatly influences the performance of the resulting RF pulse. In this problem formulation, the entire difficulty lies in the adequate choice of the k-space trajectory $\mathbf{K} = \{k(t), 0 \leq t \leq T\}$. For instance, the spiral nonselective (SPINS) RF pulse (Malik et al., 2012) is suitable for short uniform nonselective excitations and exploits a 3D spiral trajectory with the following parameterization:

$$k(t) = \frac{k_{max}}{1 + e^{1+\alpha\left(\frac{t}{T}-\beta\right)}} \begin{pmatrix} \sin(ut)\cos(u't) \\ \sin(ut)\sin(u't) \\ \cos(ut) \end{pmatrix},\tag{7.11}$$

where k_{max}, α, β, u, and u' are parameters that can be adjusted to obtain the adequate density (u, u') and extent (k_{max}, α, β) of sampling in the k-space and a preferred trade-off between pulse duration and excitation uniformity.

7.3.3.1 Composite pulses revisited

The framework for design of composite pulses is also very helpful to the pulse design for uniform nonselective excitation. Having in hand two transverse rotations $\alpha_\perp^{(1)}$ and $\alpha_\perp^{(2)}$ (with the two corresponding rotation-inducing excitation vectors $x^{(1)}$, $x^{(2)} \in \mathbb{C}^{N_c \times 1}$), we can think of a generalized construction of composite pulses

$$\alpha_{\perp}^{(1)} - \alpha_z - \alpha_{\perp}^{(2)}, \tag{7.12}$$

where α_z denotes a z-rotation which can be easily obtained by the insertion of MFG blips in the 3 directions of space between the $\alpha_{\perp}^{(1)}$ and $\alpha_{\perp}^{(2)}$ transverse rotations. Let Δk denote the first moment of the blip multiplied by $-\gamma$. The rotation angle of α_z amounts to $\Delta k \cdot r$. Given that $x^{(1)}$, $x^{(2)}$, and Δk are the free variables, there are a total of $4N_c + 3$ real parameters (2 per channel per excitation vector and 3 for the MFG blip) that can be optimized to minimize the RMS deviation from the target excitation b. Naturally, this strategy can be easily generalized to N square pulses ($x^{(1)}, \cdots, x^{(N)}$) and $N-1$ MFG blips ($\Delta k^{(1)}, \cdots, \Delta k^{(N-1)}$), leading to the construction of the so-called k_T-points pulses (Cloos et al., 2012a). Drawing here the link with Transmit-SENSE by applying Eq. 7.5 to this particular pulse type, we observe that the k-space trajectory for k_T-points is now a broken line made of $N-1$ segments. The n-th segment is defined by $\Delta k^{(n)}$ and the n-th RF shim $x^{(n)}$ is applied at a fixed location in k-space (leading to energy deposition in a stationary manner). For this type of pulse, the integral in Eq. 7.5 can be decomposed into $2N+1$ segment integrals, with each having a simple analytical expression. It follows that the encoding matrix $\mathbf{A}$ is of size $N_p \times (NN_c)$ and Eq. 7.8 can be rewritten as

$$a_{m,j,n} = -i\gamma\tau B_{1,j}^{+}(r_m)e^{ik^{(n)}\cdot r_m}e^{-i\gamma\Delta B_0(r_m)\left(T-n(\tau+\tau_b)+\frac{\tau}{2}\right)}\mathrm{sinc}\left(\gamma\Delta B_0(r)\frac{\tau}{2}\right), \tag{7.13}$$

where τ (respectively τ_b) denotes the RF square pulse (respectively MFG blip) duration, and $k^{(n)}$ is given by

$$k^{(n)} = \Delta k^{(n+1)} + \ldots + \Delta k^{(N)}. \tag{7.14}$$

Slice-selective rotations $\alpha_{\perp}^{(n)}$ (usually achieved by applying a sinc-shaped RF pulse in the presence of a linear slice-selective gradient) can be viewed as a 2D-analog of k_T-points. When targeting a thin slice, the z component of the k-space displacement (usually in the slice direction) can be ignored, leaving only the two transverse components $\Delta k^{(i)} \cdot \hat{x}$ and $\Delta k^{(i)} \cdot \hat{y}$ ($\hat{x}$, $\hat{y}$, and $\hat{z}$ representing the unit vectors aligned with the x, y, and z directions, respectively) to be optimized. The resulting composite pulses are called fast-k_z or spoke pulses (Saekho et al., 2006) and in fact preceded k_T-point pulses. An illustration of various types of RF pulses, along with corresponding gradient waveforms and excitation k-space trajectories, is provided in Fig. 7.3.

In essence, although sharing some similarities, pTx k_T-point/spoke pulses differ from traditional composite pulses in the sense that MFGs (yielding z-rotations with no SAR penalty) are exploited and that pTx allows the total B_1^+ spatial profile to be modulated through time. By contrast, in sTx, this profile is entirely fixed and determined by the spatial sensitivity of the transmit RF coil. RF field inhomogeneity mitigation using k_T-point/spoke pulses is naturally possible in sTx but generally requires more subpulses to reach the same performance. This is often problematic as RF pulse durations ideally must be short (for improved sequence timing, reduced relaxation effects, and increased robustness to off-resonance).

7.3.3.2 K-space trajectory optimization
As already noted in Section 7.3.2, the Transmit-SENSE concept can be applied for the computation of short RF pulses that can be used to create a 2D (e.g., a circle cross-section) or a 3D (e.g., a cube) selective excitation. For 2D selective excitations, EPI or spiral trajectories are most commonly chosen because of their ability to rapidly traverse the 2D k-space. For 3D selective excitations, various excitation k-space trajectories have been proposed to cover the 3D k-space, including stack of spirals and shell trajectories (Stenger et al., 2002; Davids et al., 2016; Geldschläger et al., 2021). In practice, pulse

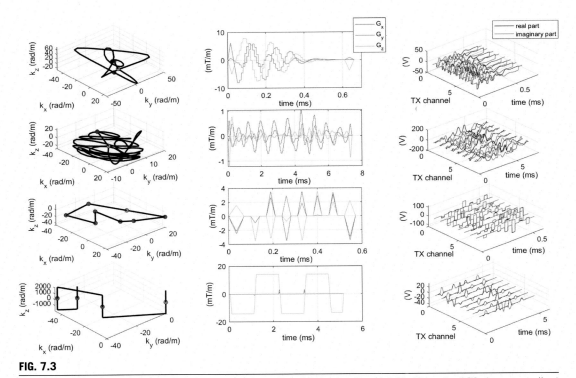

FIG. 7.3

Graphical representation of a 10 degree k_T-point (A–C), a 10-degree k_T-point (D–F), and a 180-degree gradient ascent pulse engineered (GRAPE) pTx pulse (G–I). Further description for the construction of the 180-degree GRAPE pulse is provided in the subsection "Large tip angle and refocusing." The respective k-space trajectories are represented in subfigures (A), (D), and (G). The underlying magnetic field gradient waveforms are represented in subfigures (B), (E), and (H). The RF waveforms (1 per TX channel, here eight) are displayed in subfigures (C), (F), and (H). In subfigures (A), (D), and (G), the green dot indicates the center of k-space. The red portions of the k-space trajectories indicate where RF energy is deposited. For the case of k_T points (A), this portion reduces to a discrete number of points scattered across the 3D k-space. For the case of spokes (D), these portions of the k-space trajectory are vertical segments. For the GRAPE pulse (G), it consists of a continuous differentiable curve which starts and ends at two locations of k-space which are distinct from the origin.

design is more difficult for 3D than for 2D selective excitation as the considerably increased length of the 3D k-space trajectory poses the problem of long excitations (arising from relaxation and off-resonance effects). Fig.7.4 demonstrates the potential of pTx to enable inner volume excitation in less than 5 ms. Here, resorting to a MFG waveform optimization (e.g., using a multishell model of the excitation k-space trajectory) appears effective in boosting the excitation performance. Without MFG optimization, the pulse duration necessary for reaching the same performance would be prohibitively long. Optimization of the k-space trajectory itself hence plays a major role in pTx pulse design. For the design of k_T-point or spokes pulses, k-space trajectory optimization can also be used to improve pulse performance with regard to pulse duration, uniformity of the excitation profile, and immunity to off-resonance effects. Unfortunately, the relationship between k-space trajectory and θ (see Eq. 7.5)

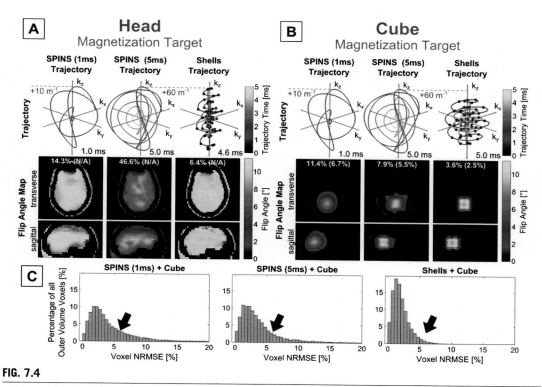

FIG. 7.4

Joint MFG and RF waveform optimizations to selectively excite the magnetization in the volume of the brain only (A) and a $4 \times 4 \times 4$ cm^3 cube inside the brain. In each case, a 1-ms SPINS pulse, a 5-ms SPINS pulse, and ~5-ms long solution implementing the so-called shells trajectory where optimized and tested. Excitation performance is visible through retrospective flip angle simulations. In (C), the flip angle histograms over the complementary of the target region show that optimized shells trajectory yields better outer volume suppression than SPINS trajectories. *Courtesy of Mathias Davids, MGH.*

is non-linear and, in general, not "linearizable" since $k(t) \cdot r$ can reach a large value ($\gg 2\pi$). In the absence of static field offsets ($\Delta B_0 = 0$) and in the STA regime, it is noted from Eq. 7.3 that $|\theta|$ is independent of the order in which the k-space displacements occur. Consequently, if a pulse with N k_T-points emerges as a solution to the MLS problem, a total of $N!$ *equivalent* solutions can be obtained simply by shuffling the order in which every k-space location is traversed (see Fig. 7.3A). Those solutions, however, lose their equivalence when $\Delta B_0 \neq 0$. In this case, many local minima exist when searching for the solution. The concurrent optimization of the k-space trajectory and the RF pulses thus is considerably more complex than the optimization of the RF pulses alone.

For the design of spokes or k_T-point pulses, the difficulty arises from the potentially large number of k-space trajectory parameters. To date, several algorithms have been proposed that can be used to return an optimized k-space trajectory. One effective algorithm is the iterative greedy method. The idea is to initialize the k-space trajectory with the origin of the k-space ($\mathbf{K}^{(0)} = \{0\}$) and to iteratively aggregate new k-space locations. At each iteration, the $N_c \times N$ RF coefficients along with the $2 \times (N-1)$ and $3 \times (N-1)$ k-space displacements for spokes and k_T-points, respectively, are optimized (Grissom et al., 2012) (N being the number of subpulses). The aggregation procedure stops when the number of added k-space locations exceeds a prescribed limit or when the performance of the solutions (fidelity to the target excitation pattern) reaches a predefined threshold. Alternative approaches have also been proposed that consist in setting in advance the number of subpulses, choosing a random set of initial trajectories, and running a second-order optimization algorithm with respect to control parameters which in this case are the k-space trajectory and the RF coefficients (Gras et al., 2015)

$$(\boldsymbol{\xi}, \boldsymbol{\psi}) = \arg\min_{\boldsymbol{x}, \boldsymbol{g}} J(\boldsymbol{x}, \boldsymbol{g}) \text{ where } J(\boldsymbol{x}, \boldsymbol{g}) = \||\mathbf{A}(\boldsymbol{g})\boldsymbol{x}| - \boldsymbol{b}\|_2^2. \tag{7.15}$$

When using such optimization methods to solve nonconvex optimization problems, the result will often depend on the initialization of the algorithm and on the constraints. Fortunately, to validate an RF pulse, one does not need to fulfill the extremely difficult (if not impossible) task of verifying that the solution obtained is the global optimum. Instead, it suffices to verify that the value of the objective function is acceptably low. For joint optimization of the RF pulses and the k-space trajectory, to reduce the risk of convergence toward an overly suboptimal local minimum, multiple initializations may be tested. Furthermore, the first- and second-order derivatives of $J(\boldsymbol{x}, \boldsymbol{g})$ in Eq. 7.15 with respect to the control parameters can be obtained analytically using the chain rule and can be used to improve the accuracy and speed of the algorithm.

7.3.3.3 Hardware and safety constraints

For the RF and MFG waveforms to be implementable in practice, various constraints need to be satisfied due to hardware limitations and safety issues. Peak amplitude of the RF and the MFG waveforms, which are often imposed on all RF channels and all gradient channels at all time points, are given by

$$|x(j, t_n)| \leq x_{max}; j = 1, 2, \ldots, N_c; n = 1, 2, \ldots N_t, |g(j', t_n)| \leq g_{max}, j' = x, y, z, \tag{7.16}$$

where x_{max} and g_{max} are hardware-dependent maximum allowed RF amplitude and gradient strength, respectively. Due to the large inductance of the B_0 gradient coils, limitations also need to be taken into account regarding the time derivative (dg/dt) of the waveform. This type of constraints takes the following form:

$$\left|\frac{dg}{dt}(j', t_n)\right| \leq S_{max}; j' = x, y, z; n = 1, 2, \ldots, N_t, \tag{7.17}$$

where S_{max} denotes the maximum slew rate (T/m/s). Another set of constraints concerns the total average power applied to each RF channel. For patient safety and coil protection (heating, detuning), the total RF power needs to be restricted over a time-sliding window. The average RF power constraints are given by

$$\Delta t \sum_{n=1}^{N_t} |x(j, t_n)|^2 \leq Z E_{max}; j = 1, 2, \ldots, N_c; n = 1, 2, \ldots N_t, \tag{7.18}$$

where E_{max} denotes the maximum allowed total RF energy (in J) per channel and Z is the nominal impedance of the transmit array (usually $50\,\Omega$). Another set of constraints concerns the local and global SAR. For local SAR constraint, the so-called virtual observation point (VOP) approach (Eichfelder and Gebhardt, 2011) was proposed as an efficient and effective means of handling the 10 g-SAR during the acquisition. Mathematically, a VOP is a $N_c \times N_c$ complex Hermitian matrix $\mathbf{Q}$ which allows evaluating a representative local SAR value. The set of VOPs is constructed in such a way that the maximum local

SAR over all voxels (usually on the order of millions) is always no greater than the maximum local SAR value estimated using the VOPs. Likewise, a $N_c \times N_c$ complex Hermitian matrix $\boldsymbol{Q}_{glob}$ can also be constructed to estimate the global SAR. The SAR constraints can be written as

$$\forall \mathbf{Q}, \mathrm{SED}(\mathbf{Q}, \boldsymbol{x}) = \Delta t \sum_{n=1}^{N_t} \boldsymbol{x}^{\dagger}(., t_n) \mathbf{Q} \boldsymbol{x}(., t_n) \leq \mathrm{SED}_{max}, \tag{7.19A}$$

$$\mathrm{SED}\left(\mathbf{Q}_{glob}, \boldsymbol{x}\right) = \Delta t \sum_{n=1}^{N_t} \boldsymbol{x}^{\dagger}(., t_n) \mathbf{Q}_{glob} \boldsymbol{x}(., t_n) \leq \mathrm{gSED}_{max}, \tag{7.19B}$$

where SED($\cdot$) represents the specific energy dose (J/kg), i.e., the energy deposition in tissues, and SED_{max} and gSED_{max} are, respectively, the maximum allowed SED values prescribed to comply with the local and global SAR limits per RF safety guidelines.

To satisfy the RF power constraints, a simple approach can be used that consists in augmenting the objective function $J(\boldsymbol{x}, \mathbf{g})$ by adding a regularization term $E(\boldsymbol{x}) = \|\boldsymbol{x}\|_2^2$ to penalize the total RF power. The new objective then is given by

$$J_c(\boldsymbol{x}, \mathbf{g}) = J(\boldsymbol{x}, \mathbf{g}) + \beta E(\boldsymbol{x}), \tag{7.20}$$

where β is a parameter that can be adjusted to balance between excitation fidelity and total RF power. Increasing β will lead to a decrease in $E(\boldsymbol{x})$, thus the total RF power but at the cost of an increase in excitation error. For large β, it is possible to ensure that all RF-related constraints (including those constraining RF peak amplitude and SAR) are satisfied. When this approach is used to solve the LS problem, the solution is given by (Grissom et al., 2012)

$$\boldsymbol{\xi}_{\beta} = \left(\mathbf{A}^{\dagger}\mathbf{A} + \beta\mathbf{I}\right)^{-1}\mathbf{A}^{\dagger}\boldsymbol{b}. \tag{7.21}$$

To take into account explicitly the various hardware and safety constraints, a more effective and versatile way to solve the problem is by formulating a *constrained* optimization problem. Such a problem can be effectively solved using the state-of-the-art solvers (Hoyos-Idrobo et al., 2014; Vinding et al., 2017) tailored for nonlinear problems. Since most constraints described above are either linear or quadratic in the control parameters, their derivatives with respect to the control parameters can easily be calculated analytically and used to facilitate the computation of the solution.

7.3.3.4 Large tip angle and refocusing pulses

When designing large-tip-angle (LTA) pulses (i.e., targeting a flip angle no smaller than 90 degree), using the STA linear approximation (i.e., Eq. 7.5) usually does not lead to satisfying results because the nonlinearity of the Bloch equations (governing how the magnetization evolves in response to the application of RF and MFG waveforms) cannot be ignored in this regime. Therefore, a more exact expression of the magnetization state as a function of the RF and MFG waveforms is needed. An effective way to design LTA pTx pulses is by using optimal control. For improved computation efficiency, the evolution of the magnetization can be treated in SU(2) (Pauly et al., 1991) or equivalently using quaternions (Majewski and Ritter, 2015). Further, when dealing with time-dependent RF and MFG waveforms, the hard-pulse approximation can be used, in which both RF and MFG waveforms are decomposed into a train of hard pulses by discretizing in time the respective waveforms with a dwell time Δt and by modeling each time interval as a square pulse. Within the nth time interval, the combined effect of the RF and MFG hard pulses is a 3D rotation $\mathbf{R}(\widehat{\boldsymbol{u}}_n, a_n \Delta t)$ characterized by its rotation axis $\widehat{\boldsymbol{u}}_n$ and a rotation frequency a_n (rad/s) that satisfy the following relationship:

$$a_{r,n}\widehat{\boldsymbol{u}}_{r,n} = \Re(\omega_{1,r,n})\widehat{\boldsymbol{x}} + \Im(\omega_{1,r,n})\widehat{\boldsymbol{y}} - \gamma(\Delta B_0 + \mathbf{G}(t_n).\boldsymbol{r})\widehat{\boldsymbol{z}}, \tag{7.22}$$

where $\Re(\cdot)$ and $\Im(\cdot)$ denote, respectively, the real part and the imaginary part of a complex number, and $\omega_{1,r,n}$ is the nutation frequency due to the RF pulse

$$\omega_{1,r,n} = -\gamma \sum_{j=1}^{N_c} B_{1,j}^+(r)x(j,t_n) . \tag{7.23}$$

The overall transformation of the magnetization resulting from application of the entire RF and MFG waveforms thus can be approximated by

$$M^+(r) = R(\widehat{u}_{r,N_t}, a_{r,N_t}\Delta t)R(\widehat{u}_{r,N_t-1}, a_{r,N_t-1}\Delta t)\cdots R(\widehat{u}_{r,1}, a_{r,1}\Delta t)M^-(r), \tag{7.24}$$

where a "+" superscript is used to refer to the resulting magnetization, whereas a "−" superscript to the initial magnetization.

In contrast to the STA approximation, we have now modeled the overall effect of RF and MFG waveforms by the *product* of a time series of 3D rotations (as opposed to a time integration). A nonlinear operator can be defined to act on the initial magnetization (at $t=0$) to produce the resulting magnetization by taking the RF and MFG waveforms as control parameters

$$\overline{R}(x,g,r) \mapsto R(\widehat{u}_{r,N_t}, a_{r,N_t}\Delta t)R(\widehat{u}_{r,N_t-1}, a_{r,N_t-1}\Delta t)\cdots R(\widehat{u}_{r,1}, a_{r,1}\Delta t). \tag{7.25}$$

For example, in the case of k_T-point pulses, the operator $\widehat{R}$ is the multiplication of $2N-1$ rotations, each corresponding to a transverse (induced by the RF sub-pulse) or a z (induced by the gradient blip) rotation.

Assuming that the magnetization has unit length, the flip angle can then be obtained by

$$|\theta(r)| = \mathrm{acos}\big(\widehat{z} \cdot \overline{R}(x,g,r)M^-(r)\big). \tag{7.26}$$

In this framework, seeking optimum RF and MFG waveforms to achieve a target flip angle requires the computations of $\overline{R}$ and its partial derivatives with respect to the control parameters (which in this case are the discretized RF and gradient values within individual time intervals). Being an important topic in the fields of NMR and quantum control, this has been extensively studied (Khaneja et al., 2005) and later on introduced to the field of MRI (Maximov et al., 2010, Vinding et al., 2017; Van Damme et al., 2021). Because the optimization process involved is computationally intensive, parallel computing (e.g., with GPUs) is often desired to ensure that the pulse computation can be done within a reasonable timeframe.

The generalization to the LTA regime also opens to other types of pulse design not evoked so far when the initial magnetization (M^- in Eq. 7.21) is not longitudinal. This is the case for instance for the design of 180-degree *refocusing* pulses which act on a magnetization that can be anywhere on the Bloch sphere and where ideally the rotation induced by the RF pulses is purely transverse. This pulse design problem thus potentially involves *all* coefficients of the rotation operator $\overline{R}(x,g)$. Using the Cayley-Klein parameters (Pauly et al., 1991), the operator $\overline{R}(x,g,r)$ of rotation axis $\widehat{u}$ and rotation angle ϕ is represented by a unitary matrix $\overline{U}$ of the form

$$\overline{U} = \begin{pmatrix} \overline{\alpha} & -\overline{\beta}^* \\ \overline{\beta} & \overline{\alpha}^* \end{pmatrix}, \tag{7.27}$$

where a "*" superscript indicates the complex conjugate and where

$$\overline{\alpha} = \cos\left(\frac{\phi}{2}\right) - i(\widehat{u} \cdot \widehat{z})\sin\left(\frac{\phi}{2}\right), \tag{7.28A}$$

$$\overline{\beta} = -i(\widehat{\boldsymbol{u}} \cdot \widehat{\boldsymbol{x}} + i\widehat{\boldsymbol{u}} \cdot \widehat{\boldsymbol{y}}) \sin\left(\frac{\phi}{2}\right), \tag{7.28B}$$

$$|\overline{\alpha}|^2 + |\overline{\beta}|^2 = 1. \tag{7.28C}$$

Noting (see Eqs. 7.28A and 7.28B) that a perfect plane rotation of angle ϕ imposes $\overline{\alpha} = \cos\left(\frac{\phi}{2}\right)$, the design of a ϕ refocusing pulse with phase-free rotation axis thus may simply be written as

$$(\boldsymbol{\xi}, \boldsymbol{\psi}) = \arg\min_{x,g} \sum_{m=1}^{N_p} \left| \overline{\alpha}(x, g, \boldsymbol{r_m}) - \cos\left(\frac{\phi}{2}\right) \right|^2. \tag{7.29}$$

This example shows that, for the design of refocusing pulses, the Cayley-Klein parameters can concisely describe the desired properties for $\overline{\mathbf{R}}(g, x, r)$ (rotation angle ϕ and properties of the rotation axis $\widehat{\boldsymbol{u}}$).

7.3.3.5 Direct signal control

So far, the pTx pulse design has been formulated to achieve a target flip angle or rotation operator with minimum residual error. However, in reality, it is the resulting MR signal that is of the most relevance. For some MR sequences (especially multipulse sequences), optimizing the pulses independently may not necessarily result in the optimal MR signal due to the complex interplay of individual pulses. To obtain the optimal MR signal, the direct signal control (DSC) framework has been proposed, in which the pulse design is formulated to directly target a desired MR signal. A DSC approach assumes an analytical signal model (f) to express the MR signal (s) as a function of the rotations induced by each pulse of the sequence ($\mathbf{R}_1$, $\mathbf{R}_2$, ...) and noncontrol parameters ($\boldsymbol{p}$) relevant to the formation of MR signal (including relaxation times and imaging parameters)

$$s = f(\boldsymbol{p}, \mathbf{R}_1, \mathbf{R}_2, \ldots). \tag{7.30}$$

For example, the pulse design for a 2-pulse sequence can be formulated using an objective function of the form

$$J_{DSC}\left(\boldsymbol{x}^{(1)}, \boldsymbol{g}^{(1)}, \boldsymbol{x}^{(2)}, \boldsymbol{g}^{(2)}\right) = \sum_{m=1}^{N_p} \left\| f\left(\boldsymbol{p}(\boldsymbol{r_m}), \overline{\mathbf{R}}\left(\boldsymbol{x}^{(1)}, \boldsymbol{g}^{(1)}, \boldsymbol{r_m}\right), \overline{\mathbf{R}}\left(\boldsymbol{x}^{(2)}, \boldsymbol{g}^{(2)}, \boldsymbol{r_m}\right)\right) - \boldsymbol{s}_T(\boldsymbol{r_m}) \right\|^2, \tag{7.31}$$

where $s_T(\boldsymbol{r_m})$ is the target signal at the position $\boldsymbol{r_m}$, $\boldsymbol{x}^{(1)}$, $\boldsymbol{g}^{(1)}$, $\boldsymbol{x}^{(2)}$, $\boldsymbol{g}^{(2)}$ are the control parameters for the first and second pulse of the sequence, and $\|\cdot\|$ denotes a desired norm that measures the distance between actual and target signals. The effectiveness of DSC for addressing the problem of RF nonuniformity at UHF has been demonstrated in 7T T_2-weighted (T_2w) FLAIR neuroimaging (Beqiri et al., 2018), in which DSC is applied to obtain the desired MR signal for a 3D TSE readout. The concept of DSC has also been applied to the joint design of a STA excitation pulse and a LTA inversion pulse for a Magnetization-Prepared Rapid Acquisition Gradient Echo (MPRAGE) sequence when used to acquire 7T T_1w neuroimaging (Gras et al., 2016).

7.4 Neuroimaging applications of pTx

To date, the pTx method has been demonstrated within the context of a large array of potential neuro MRI applications covering various image contrasts. In particular, RF shimming has been explored to a large extent as it can easily be integrated into an MRI protocol. Dynamic RF shimming on the other hand has shown its usefulness, especially for whole brain 3D image acquisition.

7.4.1 Anatomical T_1-, T_2^*-, and T_2-weighted imaging

The utility of pTx has been demonstrated for acquiring high-quality T_1w MPRAGE brain images at 7T. MPRAGE is the most commonly used 3D sequence for T_1w imaging that employs a nonselective inversion RF pulse for magnetization preparation followed by a 3D FLASH readout. In a pioneering study (Cloos et al., 2012b), the authors showed that the use of pTx pulses could substantially improve the image quality for MPRAGE in comparison to the CP mode. Both excitation and inversion pTx pulses were designed with the k_T-point parameterization. The designed pTx excitation and inversion pulses were utilized in an MPRAGE sequence to acquire human brain images at 0.8-mm isotropic resolutions. The images obtained with pTx presented largely enhanced tissue contrasts between gray and white matter, especially in lower brain regions such as cerebellum and occipital lobe, allowing intricate structures to be resolved with greater detail across the entire brain. The performance boost was found to allow automated tissue segmentation to be conducted across the entire brain. Obtained morphometric results (such as cortical thickness) were brought closer to what was achievable with a clinical setup at 3T serving as a reference (see Fig. 7.5), indicating an effective mitigation of the RF field inhomogeneity problem.

Parallel transmission has also enabled high-quality T_2w 3D SPACE brain imaging at 7T. The 3D SPACE (known as the sampling perfection with application optimized contrasts using different flip angle evolutions (Mugler, 2014)), also called variable flip angle Turbo Spin Echo (TSE), is a widely used sequence for acquiring T_2w images, exploiting a nonselective 90-degree excitation followed by a train of nonselective refocusing pulses with variable flip angles. In their work, Eggenschwiler et al. (2014) illustrated how the use of pTx pulses can help improve the image quality for 3D T_2w brain imaging relative to the CP mode. For this application, the pulse optimization problem in principle should inspect the Cayley-Klein parameters of the output rotation matrix $\overline{\mathbf{R}}$ (see Eq. 7.25) or its equivalent representation in SU(2), $\overline{\mathbf{U}}$, to ensure correct rotation angles and rotation axes. However, symmetries may be enforced in the construction of RF and MFG waveforms such that the STA formalism (i.e., Eq. 7.3) can still be used in this particular case. Indeed, by application of Average Hamiltonian Theory, neglecting here the static field offset ΔB_0, the temporal symmetry is shown to cancel every odd term in the Magnus expansion of the generator (For any rotation matrix $\mathbf{U}$ in SU(2), there exists a matrix $\mathbf{A} \in \mathbb{C}^{2\times2}$, called the generator of $\mathbf{U}$, that satisfies $\mathbf{U} = e^{i\mathbf{A}}$) of $\overline{\mathbf{U}}$, making the STA approximation a reasonable model for the generator of the refocusing pulse (Gras et al., 2018).

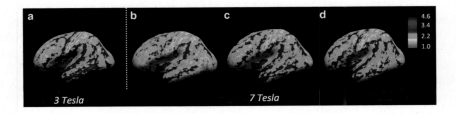

FIG. 7.5

Cortical thickness (in mm) of the inflated brain from automated analysis. From left to right: CP mode result at 3T (A), CP mode (B), tailored RF shimming (C), and dynamic RF shimming method at 7T (D). *Courtesy of Martijn Cloos.*

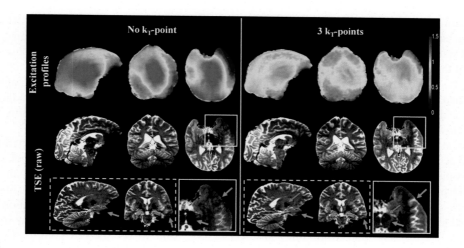

FIG. 7.6

Turbo spin echo results. Top row is the excitation profile normalized to the nominal flip angle. Bottom rows are raw TSE data with arrows pointing toward noticeable improvements. *Courtesy of José Marques.*

Hence, in this case, a single time-symmetric k_T-point pulse was designed in the STA (Eq. 7.15) and embedded into the 3D TSE sequence. To implement the prescribed flip angle pattern of the TSE readout (Mugler, 2014), the amplitude of the RF waveforms was scaled according to the prescribed flip angle (Eggenschwiler et al., 2014). The in-vivo results were compared to those obtained with CP mode square pulses. The images obtained with pTx exhibited largely improved contrast between gray and white matter across the entire brain. The signal void observed with the CP mode was effectively recovered especially in the temporal lobes and in the deep nuclei (see Fig. 7.6).

Finally, the utility of pTx was also demonstrated for multislice anatomical T_2^*-weighted imaging when designing 2D spoke pulses in both small- and large-flip angle regimes (Gras et al., 2017). Simultaneous optimization of RF and gradient waveforms was implemented for best RF performance. Moreover, despite an increase in computation time, the joint design of all pulses for the 25 image slices prescribed to cover the whole brain was chosen (rather than separate and independent designs for individual slices) to reduce SAR, thanks to SAR-hopping effects (Guérin et al., 2015). When compared to the CP mode, the image obtained with pTx exhibited a 40% signal increase on 70% of the voxels.

7.4.2 Functional MRI

UHF functional MRI (fMRI) with the BOLD contrast can also benefit from the use of pTx. In an exploratory human study (De Martino et al., 2012), the authors demonstrated the feasibility of RF shimming to facilitate T_2w fMRI studies of bilateral auditory cortices at 7T when using a spin echo EPI (SE-EPI) sequence for data acquisition. The calculated RF coefficients were applied to both the excitation and refocusing pulses of a standard 2D SE-EPI sequence. Multislice T_2w fMRI images were collected at 1.5-mm isotropic resolutions to measure functional responses to simple tones and to complex sounds (e.g., voices and tools). The results showed that the use of RF shimming substantially improved the homogeneity and efficiency of the B_1^+ fields over the bilateral auditory cortices. Correspondingly, the required RF power was found far less than when using a CP-like mode, enabling 27 (as opposed to only 9) image slices to be acquired with a 3-s repetition time without exceeding SAR limits. The improvement in B_1^+ was shown to translate into a large enhancement in image quality, which in turn allowed more reliable tonotopy mapping.

Wu et al. (2019) also investigated the utility of pTx for whole-brain resting-state fMRI (rfMRI) at 7T when acquiring T_2^*w images with a slice-accelerated 2D GRE-EPI sequence. Single-spoke multiband pTx pulses were designed following a generalized slab-wise design framework (Wu et al., 2016), in which band-specific RF shim values were calculated to produce uniform B_1^+ fields inside 30 contiguous slabs or bands prescribed to jointly cover the entire brain. The multiband pTx excitation pulses were enabled to acquire Human Connectome Project (HCP)-style rfMRI data (1.6-mm isotropic resolution, fivefold slice, and twofold in-plane acceleration), and the results were compared to those of the original 7T HCP protocol using an sTx setup combined with dielectric padding. The use of pTx significantly improved B_1^+ uniformity across the brain, with the coefficient of variation (std/mean) of whole-brain B_1^+ field distribution reduced on average by ~39%. This improvement in B_1^+ field uniformity in turn yielded ~17% increase in group temporal SNR (tSNR) as averaged across the entire brain and ~10% increase in group functional contrast-to-noise ratio (fCNR). This translated into improved estimation of functional connectivity, leading to stronger correlation of the seeds with the rest of the gray ordinate space (Fig. 7.7).

7.4.3 Diffusion-weighted MRI

Diffusion-weighted MRI (dMRI) is often fulfilled using a 2D SE-EPI with strong field gradients added right before and after the refocusing RF pulse to sensitize the MR signal to water diffusion. This type of acquisition typically involves nonadiabatic slice-selective refocusing pulses, which are particularly sensitive to RF heterogeneities. Wu et al. (2018) demonstrated how pTx can be used to promote the rapid acquisition of high-quality high-resolution whole-brain dMRI at 7T. Again, single-spoke multiband pTx excitation and refocusing pulses were designed following the generalized slab-wise design framework and were used to acquire HCP-style dMRI data (1.05-mm resolution, twofold slice and threefold in-plane accelerations, 71-ms echo time, and double-shell q-space sampling with b-values = 1000/2000 s/mm^2). When compared to those acquired using a sTx setup with dielectric padding, the results showed that pTx on average led to 50% improvement in B_1^+ uniformity and 19% increase in tSNR. This in turn resulted in significantly enhanced performance for estimation of multiple fiber orientations, giving rise to clearer depiction of principal fiber orientations in the temporal lobe and better measurement of second fiber orientations in both the temporal lobe and the cerebellum (Fig. 7.8). Further, because of its ability to reduce SAR, the use of the pTx pulses was shown to permit faster image acquisition with higher slice accelerations, thereby enabling the collection of either the same data in shorter scan time or more data in the same scan time.

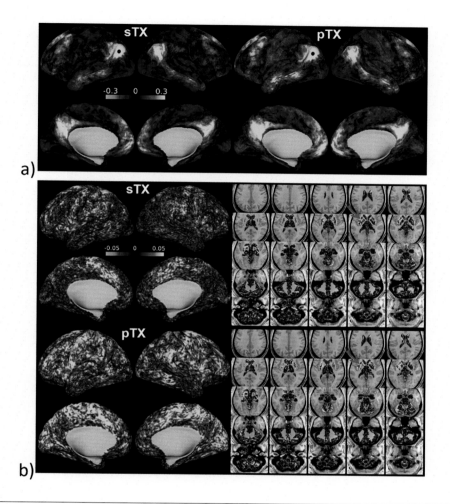

FIG. 7.7

Performance of single transmit plus dielectric padding (sTx) vs. parallel transmit (pTx) when both are used to acquire Human Connectome Project-style resting state fMRI at 7T for the estimation of seed-based dense connectome. Shown are example connectivity maps for (A) a seed (as indicated by a *black* dot) placed in the posterior parietal cortex (part of the default mode networks), and (B) a seed (as highlighted by a *red* arrow) placed in the subcortical gray matter putamen. In both cases, the connectivity shown was averaged across the same five subjects (a total of 20, 16-min resting state fMRI runs). The 20 runs of fMRI data were preprocessed, demeaned, and variance normalized before being concatenated in the time dimension to calculate the correlation of the seed with the rest of the brain. Note that the pTx acquisition yielded stronger correlations as measures of functional connectivity between the seed and the rest of the brain.

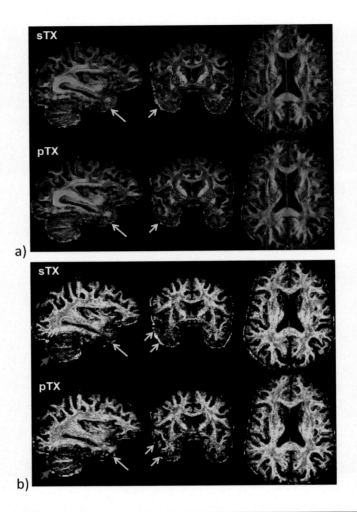

FIG. 7.8

Performances of single transmit plus dielectric padding (sTx) vs. parallel transmit (pTx) when both used to acquire Human Connectome Project-style diffusion MRI at 7 Tesla for estimation of multiple fiber orientations. Data are shown for a representative subject. Shown are (A) color fractional anisotropy (FA) maps and (B) volume fraction maps for second fiber orientations. The color FA is FA (in the range of [0 1]) with the color representing the orientation of the principal fiber (*red*: left-right; *green*: A-P; *blue*: inferior-superior). The volume fraction map is shown in a color scale of [0.05 0.2] (with *yellow* being high and *red* being low in volume fraction), overlaid on the respective FA map (in a grayscale of [0 1]). Total scan time was kept constant for both data sets (i.e., 40 min divided into four segments of 10 min each). Note that the use of pTx largely improved the fiber orientation estimation performances not only in lower temporal lobe (as indicated by *yellow* arrows) but also in cerebellum (as highlighted by *red* arrows).

7.4.4 **Time-of-flight and perfusion imaging**

Owing to the well-known increase in longitudinal relaxation time with field strength, it is of increasing interest to perform blood vessel and perfusion imaging at UHF. Time-of-flight (TOF) MR angiography is usually obtained with a multislab GRE sequence in which a slab-selective excitation pulse targeting a relatively large flip angle (for saturating the "static spins," leaving only the signal from the inflowing blood) is utilized in combination with a relatively short TR to create the artery-to-background contrast (or TOF contrast). Further, a slab-selective saturation RF pulse positioned above the imaging slab is often applied to produce venous saturation. In an exploratory study (Schmitter et al., 2014), the authors investigated the impact of RF shimming on the performance of the excitation and saturation pulses in high-resolution TOF acquisitions at 7T. Images were collected at $0.49\times0.49\times0.50$ mm^3 resolutions from three imaging slabs, in which a traveling saturation slab was placed cranially. TOF images were acquired by optimizing a set of RF shim values for all slab-selective excitation pulses and were compared with those obtained using a CP-like mode for excitation. The use of pTx improved the B_1^+ homogeneities by 55% which resulted in substantial gains in TOF contrast (up to 63% for small arteries in brain periphery) and better visualization of blood vessels (Fig. 7.9). RF shimming was also found very beneficial for saturation performance as it largely improved B_1^+ efficiency within the saturation ROIs, not only enabling stronger venous suppression in the saturation slab but also yielding better subcutaneous fat signal reduction in the imaging slab.

Owing to its relatively high SNR and clinical applicability, pseudo-continuous arterial spin labeling (pCASL) is a prevalent method for perfusion imaging. Prior to the readout, spins in the feeding arteries upstream of the imaging slab are labeled (through inversion or saturation) using a train of slice-selective tagging RF pulses. In a recent study (Tong et al., 2020), the authors investigated the advantages of pTx over the CP-mode for pCASL at 7T. A custom 2D EPI-based pCASL sequence was developed to exploit RF shimming and VERSE for optimizing the labeling pulse (600-μs-long Gaussian shape, 20 degree flip angle, 1-s labeling duration). The results showed that RF shimming substantially improved the labeling efficiency for pCASL. Correspondingly, the quality of the perfusion-weighted images was significantly improved as compared to that obtained using the CP-mode, leading to a tSNR level comparable to what was achievable at 3T using matched imaging parameters. These results are encouraging since performing in-vivo pCASL imaging at UHF is usually challenging due to the high RF power demand of the labeling pulse and the conservative RF power limit that was imposed. Further improvement in sensitivity at 7T is expected for pTx if a less conservative RF power limit can be used to increase the labeling efficiency.

7.4.5 **MR spectroscopy and chemical exchange saturation transfer**

Thanks to the increased spectral resolution, single-voxel proton MR spectroscopy (MRS) at UHF can be used to reliably and precisely quantify region-specific neurochemical profiles in the human brain. In an early work, Emir et al. (2012) demonstrated the feasibility of acquiring and quantifying short-echo, single-voxel proton MR spectra from multiple brain regions at 7T using the STEAM sequence and 16-channel pTx. For each volume of interest, a single RF phase shimming solution was calculated to maximize the transmit efficiency over the ROI. The set of optimized phases was then applied for all RF pulses, namely, the 90 degree STEAM pulses as well as the 3D outer volume suppression and VAPOR (variable-power RF pulses with optimized relaxation delays) water suppression pulses. Comparison against the CP mode in terms of transmit efficiency revealed largely enhanced transmit

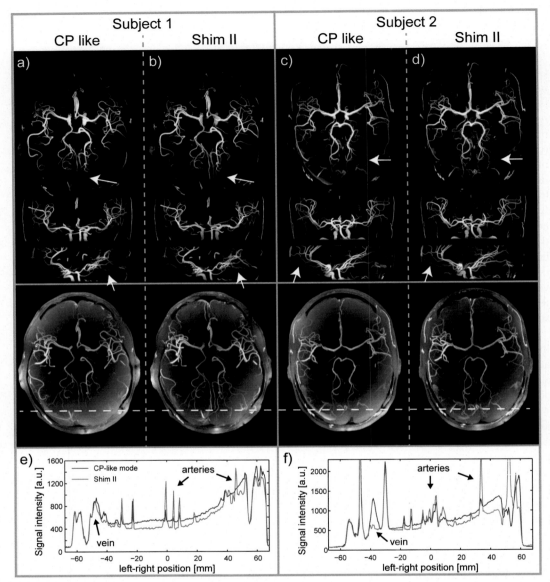

FIG. 7.9

Performance of CP-like mode (mimicking a single transmit setup) vs. pTx RF shimming when both are used for excitation in acquisition of submillimeter cerebral time of flight (TOF) images at 7T with a 16-channel RF transceiver head array. Shown are (A) 50 mm thick axial (*top row*), coronal (*middle row*), and sagittal (*bottom row*) maximum intensity projection (MIP) views obtained from receive profile corrected native TOF images, (B) thinner (30 mm) axial MIP images of the same data set but without correction of the receive profile, and (C) line plots through the MIP images at the location indicated by the white horizontal dashed line, all in two representative subjects. In all cases, the saturation RF pulses (aimed at venous suppression) were applied in the CP-like mode. Note how the use of pTx RF shimming improved the TOF contrast, giving rise to better depiction of small arteries in the periphery of the brain (as indicated by arrows). *Courtesy of Sebastian Schmitter.*

efficiency for pTx, especially when targeting an ROI in the brain periphery, with the fraction of available transmit B_1 found to increase on average by a factor ranging from 1.2 (in the substantia nigra) to 3.3 (in the cerebellar vermis). Such enhancements improved significantly the quality of the spectra and consequently the precision of the metabolite concentrations.

More recently, the usefulness of pTx has also been demonstrated for imaging the chemical exchange saturation transfer (CEST) across the whole brain. In addition to the higher sensitivity and the greater spectral resolution, UHF indeed is beneficial for CEST imaging due to the increased T_1 of the free water pool as well as the shift toward a slower exchange regime between molecular protons (metabolites, mobile macromolecules). By optimizing short pTx SPINS pulses combined with a narrow-band Gaussian modulation for spectral selectivity, Tse and colleagues were able to improve visualization of APT-weighted and nuclear Overhauser effect (NOE)-weighted images as compared to standard CP-mode pulses (Tse et al., 2017). In a subsequent work (Liebert et al., 2021), the authors proposed to use a pTx-specific CEST saturation pulse called MIMOSA (multiple interleaved mode saturation) and demonstrated its ability to improve the homogeneity of CEST saturation and the SAR budget relative to the standard CP-mode saturation pulse. Here, the effectiveness of the MIMOSA approach lies in the fact that the molecular protons being saturated have a fast exchange rate or a short T_2 relaxation or both and are only sensitive (to first-order approximation) to the RMS B_1^+ field (i.e., the time average of the saturation pulse).

7.5 Perspectives and conclusion

The field of RF parallel transmission has bloomed over the last two decades. Developments include faster B_1^+ mapping sequences, more powerful pulse design algorithms, more advanced coil designs, and better SAR management strategies. The technology and methods today are mature enough to solve the problem, provided the right human resources and equipment are available. However, for long, pTx has not been adopted in routine due largely to its cumbersome workflow. With the traditional workflow, calibration scans (including B_1^+, B_0 field mapping) and pTx pulse calculations (including ROI definition, RF and MFG pulse optimizations, pulse performance, and validity checks) necessary before conducting anything clinically useful could cumulate tens of minutes in the early days and require expertise. Despite that great progress has been made in accelerating calibration scans and pulse calculations, the complexity of pTx still remains to this day an obstacle to the user. In this context, Universal Pulses (UPs) have been proposed to present pTx to the end-user as a "plug-and-play" method. As opposed to subject-specific pTx pulses, UPs are designed offline on a database of field maps acquired with the same RF coil. The optimization criterion for UPs is to minimize the flip angle error *simultaneously* across all subjects of the database. In practice, the UPs approach yields remarkable robustness against intersubject variability. That way, RF and gradient solutions can be thoroughly preoptimized and injected in the sequences without the extra burden originally imposed by pTx. The ability of this technique to counteract RF field inhomogeneity has been demonstrated experimentally for various applications (including anatomical imaging (Fig. 7.10) (Gras et al., 2018, 2019b), fMRI (Gras et al., 2019a), spectroscopy (Berrington et al., 2021), 3D-selective excitations (Geldschläger et al., 2021)) and across many laboratories sharing the same setup. Hundreds of healthy volunteers and tens of patients with occasionally large brain abnormalities (Herrler et al., 2021) have been tested. Naturally, the price to pay is a loss of performance compared to the subject-specific approach, and it relies on coil stability. Nevertheless, across all tests performed so far, the NRMSE in the brain at 7T has never exceeded

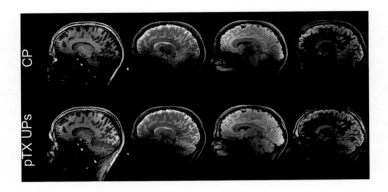

FIG. 7.10

Universal pulse anatomical results. The gain provided by parallel transmission universal pulses and for different contrasts and sequences is shown (from left to right: sagittal views for MPRAGE, vFA-TSE, FLAIR with T_1-preparation and DIR).

the inhomogeneity obtained in CP mode at 3T. As recently demonstrated UPs can also be used to accelerate and consolidate the pTx workflow by serving as initialization for subject-specific online pulse optimizations (Herrler et al., 2021). However, even with that framework, computation-expensive techniques such as optimal control approaches (Vinding et al., 2017; Van Damme et al., 2021) may still remain incompatible with clinical routine due to their current time-demands in computations. A drastically different approach that will most likely gain in importance in the future is the use of machine learning for pulse design where key factors based on easily accessible information and quick measurements guide algorithms toward more optimal solutions (Ianni et al., 2018; Tomi-Tricot et al., 2019; Vinding et al., 2021).

SAR management is another reason that has slowed down the applicability of pTx in routine. SAR results from the interference of the electric fields generated by the different coil elements and therefore the details of the time-dependent amplitudes and phases. It is no longer a function of the incident power only and thus has increased the demand in accuracy of the electromagnetic simulations used to predict SAR in human head models. To be safe, first in-vivo experiments with pTx were thus conducted with very conservative safety margins, inapplicable in routine. Procedures have been iterated and refined over the years to validate the electromagnetic simulations of the RF coils, and tremendous effort has been made by the scanner manufacturers to realize real-time SAR supervision (Homann et al., 2011). Today, safety factors related to different uncertainties (real-time supervision, modeling, and intersubject variability) commonly verge on a total safety margin of ~2. Individualized SAR models (Milshteyn et al., 2020) or switching to temperature limits are interesting perspectives to monitor RF safety. In the future, these techniques could also provide leeway to gain pTx performance without compromising patient safety.

In conclusion, pTx is an ingenious and promising technique that can solve the challenges posed by RF field inhomogeneity at UHF. Yet more work is needed to fully deploy pTx to cover all neuro MRI applications. We hope that the reader will become interested in this exciting research topic after reading this chapter. Integration of a seamless workflow on a global scale and with reasonable safety margins yet remains to the authors a prerequisite to fully leverage this powerful technology. We would adopt the optimistic view that while nearly two decades of research in this field have been devoted to methods and tools development, the next decade will be marked by the exploitation of the pTx technology in routine for UHF MRI on a broad scale.

References

Adriany, G., Van de Moortele, P.-F., Wiesinger, F., et al., 2005. Transmit and receive transmission line arrays for 7 Tesla parallel imaging. Magn. Reson. Med. 53, 434–445. https://doi.org/10.1002/mrm.20321.

Beqiri, A., Hoogduin, H., Sbrizzi, A., Hajnal, J.V., Malik, S.J., 2018. Whole-brain 3D FLAIR at 7T using direct signal control. Magn. Reson. Med. 80, 1533–1545. https://doi.org/10.1002/mrm.27149.

Berrington, A., Považan, M., Mirfin, C., et al., 2021. Calibration-free regional RF shims for MRS. Magn. Reson. Med. 86, 611–624. https://doi.org/10.1002/mrm.28749.

Cloos, M.A., Boulant, N., Luong, M., et al., 2012a. Parallel-transmission-enabled magnetization-prepared rapid gradient-echo T1-weighted imaging of the human brain at 7T. Neuroimage 62, 2140–2150. https://doi.org/10.1016/j.neuroimage.2012.05.068.

Cloos, M.A., Boulant, N., Luong, M., et al., 2012b. kT-points: short three-dimensional tailored RF pulses for flip-angle homogenization over an extended volume. Magn. Reson. Med. 67, 72–80. https://doi.org/10.1002/mrm.22978.

Davids, M., Schad, L.R., Wald, L.L., Guérin, B., 2016. Fast three-dimensional inner volume excitations using parallel transmission and optimized k-space trajectories. Magn. Reson. Med. 76, 1170–1182. https://doi.org/10.1002/mrm.26021.

De Graaf, R.A., Nicolay, K., 1997. Adiabatic rf pulses: applications to in vivo NMR. Concepts Magn. Reson. 9, 247–268. https://doi.org/10.1002/(SICI)1099-0534(1997)9:4<247::AID-CMR4>3.0.CO;2-Z.

De Martino, F., Schmitter, S., Moerel, M., et al., 2012. Spin echo functional MRI in bilateral auditory cortices at 7T: an application of B1 shimming. Neuroimage 63, 1313–1320. https://doi.org/10.1016/j.neuroimage.2012.08.029.

Eggenschwiler, F., O'Brien, K.R., Gruetter, R., Marques, J.P., 2014. Improving T2-weighted imaging at high field through the use of kT-points. Magn. Reson. Med. 71, 1478–1488. https://doi.org/10.1002/mrm.24805.

Eichfelder, G., Gebhardt, M., 2011. Local specific absorption rate control for parallel transmission by virtual observation points. Magn. Reson. Med. 66, 1468–1476. https://doi.org/10.1002/mrm.22927.

Emir, U.E., Auerbach, E.J., Moortele, P.-F.V.D., et al., 2012. Regional neurochemical profiles in the human brain measured by ^{1}H MRS at 7 T using local B_1 shimming: SINGLE-VOXEL MRS AT 7 T WITH TRANSCEIVER ARRAY COIL. NMR Biomed. 25, 152–160. https://doi.org/10.1002/nbm.1727.

Geldschläger, O., Bosch, D., Glaser, S., Henning, A., 2021. Local excitation universal parallel transmit pulses at 9.4T. Magn. Reson. Med. 86, 2589–2603. https://doi.org/10.1002/mrm.28905.

Gras, V., Luong, M., Amadon, A., Boulant, N., 2015. Joint design of kT-points trajectories and {RF} pulses under explicit {SAR} and power constraints in the large flip angle regime. J. Magn. Reson. 261, 181–189. https://doi.org/10.1016/j.jmr.2015.10.017.

Gras, V., Vignaud, A., Mauconduit, F., et al., 2016. Signal-domain optimization metrics for MPRAGE RF pulse design in parallel transmission at 7 tesla: signal-domain optimization metrics for MPRAGE RF pulse design. Magn. Reson. Med. 76, 1431–1442. https://doi.org/10.1002/mrm.26043.

Gras, V., Vignaud, A., Amadon, A., Mauconduit, F., Bihan, D.L., Boulant, N., 2017. In vivo demonstration of whole-brain multislice multispoke parallel transmit radiofrequency pulse design in the small and large flip angle regimes at 7 tesla. Magn. Reson. Med. 78, 1009–1019. https://doi.org/10.1002/mrm.26491.

Gras, V., Mauconduit, F., Vignaud, A., et al., 2018. Design of universal parallel-transmit refocusing kT-point pulses and application to 3D T2-weighted imaging at 7T: universal pulse design of 3D refocusing pulses. Magn. Reson. Med. 80, 53–65. https://doi.org/10.1002/mrm.27001.

Gras, V., Poser, B.A., Wu, X., Tomi-Tricot, R., Boulant, N., 2019a. Optimizing BOLD sensitivity in the 7T Human Connectome Project resting-state fMRI protocol using plug-and-play parallel transmission. Neuroimage, 195, 1–10. Epub 2019/03/30. https://doi.org/10.1016/j.neuroimage.2019.03.040. PMID: 30923027.

Gras, V., Pracht, E.D., Mauconduit, F., Le Bihan, D., Stöcker, T., Boulant, N., 2019b. Robust nonadiabatic T2 preparation using universal parallel-transmit kT-point pulses for 3D FLAIR imaging. Magn. Reson. Med. 81, 3202–3208. https://doi.org/10.1002/mrm.27645.

Grissom, W., Yip, C., Zhang, Z., Stenger, V.A., Fessler, J.A., Noll, D.C., 2006. Spatial domain method for the design of RF pulses in multicoil parallel excitation. Magn. Reson. Med. 56, 620–629. https://doi.org/10.1002/mrm.20978.

Grissom, W.A., Khalighi, M.-M., Sacolick, L.I., Rutt, B.K., Vogel, M.W., 2012. Small-tip-angle spokes pulse design using interleaved greedy and local optimization methods. Magn. Reson. Med. 68, 1553–1562. https://doi.org/10.1002/mrm.24165.

Guérin, B., Setsompop, K., Ye, H., Poser, B.A., Stenger, A.V., Wald, L.L., 2015. Design of parallel transmission pulses for simultaneous multislice with explicit control for peak power and local specific absorption rate. Magn. Reson. Med. 73, 1946–1953. https://doi.org/10.1002/mrm.25325.

Herrler, J., Liebig, P., Gumbrecht, R., et al., 2021. Fast online-customized (FOCUS) parallel transmission pulses: a combination of universal pulses and individual optimization. Magn. Reson. Med. 85, 3140–3153. https://doi.org/10.1002/mrm.28643.

Homann, H., Börnert, P., Eggers, H., Nehrke, K., Dössel, O., Graesslin, I., 2011. Toward individualized SAR models and in vivo validation. Magn. Reson. Med. 66, 1767–1776. https://doi.org/10.1002/mrm.22948.

Hoult, D.I., Phil, D., 2000. Sensitivity and power deposition in a high-field imaging experiment. J. Magn. Reson. Imaging, 12(1), 1.

Hoyos-Idrobo, A., Weiss, P., Massire, A., Amadon, A., Boulant, N., 2014. On variant strategies to solve the magnitude least squares optimization problem in parallel transmission pulse design and under strict SAR and power constraints. IEEE Trans. Med. Imaging 33, 739–748. https://doi.org/10.1109/TMI.2013.2295465.

Ianni, J.D., Cao, Z., Grissom, W.A., 2018. Machine learning RF shimming: prediction by iteratively projected ridge regression. Magn. Reson. Med. 80, 1871–1881. https://doi.org/10.1002/mrm.27192.

Ibrahim, T.S., Lee, R., Baertlein, B.A., Kangarlu, A., Robitaille, P.-M.L., 2000. Application of finite difference time domain method for the design of birdcage RF head coils using multi-port excitations. Magn. Reson. Imaging 18, 733–742. https://doi.org/10.1016/S0730-725X(00)00143-0.

Jankiewicz, M., Zeng, H., Moore, J.E., et al., 2010. Practical considerations for the design of sparse-spokes pulses. J. Magn. Reson. 203, 294–304. https://doi.org/10.1016/j.jmr.2010.01.012.

Katscher, U., Börnert, P., Leussler, C., van den Brink, J.S., 2003. Transmit SENSE. Magn. Reson. Med. 49, 144–150. https://doi.org/10.1002/mrm.10353.

Khaneja, N., Reiss, T., Kehlet, C., Schulte-Herbrüggen, T., Glaser, S.J., 2005. Optimal control of coupled spin dynamics: design of {NMR} pulse sequences by gradient ascent algorithms. J. Magn. Reson. 172, 296–305. https://doi.org/10.1016/j.jmr.2004.11.004.

Levitt, M.H., 2008. Symmetry in the design of NMR multiple-pulse sequences. J. Chem. Phys. 128, 052205. https://doi.org/10.1063/1.2831927.

Liebert, A., Tkotz, K., Herrler, J., et al., 2021. Whole-brain quantitative CEST MRI at 7T using parallel transmission methods and correction. Magn. Reson. Med. 86, 346–362. https://doi.org/10.1002/mrm.28745.

Majewski, K., Ritter, D., 2015. First and second order derivatives for optimizing parallel {RF} excitation waveforms. J. Magn. Reson. 258, 65–80. https://doi.org/10.1016/j.jmr.2015.06.010.

Malik, S.J., Keihaninejad, S., Hammers, A., Hajnal, J.V., 2012. Tailored excitation in 3D with spiral nonselective (SPINS) RF pulses. Magn. Reson. Med. 67, 1303–1315. https://doi.org/10.1002/mrm.23118.

Maximov, I.I., Salomon, J., Turinici, G., Nielsen, N.C., 2010. A smoothing monotonic convergent optimal control algorithm for nuclear magnetic resonance pulse sequence design. J. Chem. Phys. 132, 084107. https://doi.org/10.1063/1.3328783.

Milshteyn, E., Guryev, G., Torrado-Carvajal, A., et al., 2020. Individualized SAR calculations using computer vision-based MR segmentation and a fast electromagnetic solver. Magn. Reson. Med. 85, 429–443. https://doi.org/10.1002/mrm.28398.

Mugler, J.P., 2014. Optimized three-dimensional fast-spin-echo MRI. J. Magn. Reson. Imaging 39, 745–767. https://doi.org/10.1002/jmri.24542.

Pauly, J., Nishimura, D., Macovski, A., 1989. A k-space analysis of small-tip-angle excitation. J. Magn. Reson. 81, 43–56. https://doi.org/10.1016/0022-2364(89)90265-5.

Pauly, J., Le Roux, P., Nishimura, D., Macovski, A., 1991. Parameter relations for the Shinnar-Le Roux selective excitation pulse design algorithm [NMR imaging]. IEEE Trans. Med. Imaging 10, 53–65. https://doi.org/10.1109/42.75611.

Saekho, S., Yip, C., Noll, D.C., Boada, F.E., Stenger, V.A., 2006. Fast-kz three-dimensional tailored radiofrequency pulse for reduced B1 inhomogeneity. Magn. Reson. Med. 55, 719–724. https://doi.org/10.1002/mrm.20840.

Schmitter, S., Wu, X., Adriany, G., Auerbach, E.J., Uğurbil, K., Van de Moortele, P.-F., 2014. Cerebral TOF angiography at 7T: Impact of B_1^+ shimming with a 16-channel transceiver array: cerebral TOF angiography at 7T: Impact of B_1^+ shimming. Magn. Reson. Med. 71, 966–977. https://doi.org/10.1002/mrm.24749.

Setsompop, K., Wald, L.L., Alagappan, V., Gagoski, B.A., Adalsteinsson, E., 2008. Magnitude least squares optimization for parallel radio frequency excitation design demonstrated at 7 tesla with eight channels. Magn. Reson. Med. 59, 908–915. https://doi.org/10.1002/mrm.21513.

Shajan, G., Kozlov, M., Hoffmann, J., Turner, R., Scheffler, K., Pohmann, R., 2014. A 16-channel dual-row transmit array in combination with a 31-element receive array for human brain imaging at 9.4 T: a transmit and receive array combination for human brain MRI at 9.4 T. Magn. Reson. Med. 71, 870–879. https://doi.org/10.1002/mrm.24726.

Silver, M.S., Joseph, R.I., Chen, C.-N., Sank, V.J., Hoult, D.I., 1984. Selective population inversion in NMR. Nature 310, 681–683. https://doi.org/10.1038/310681a0.

Stenger, V.A., Boada, F.E., Noll, D.C., 2002. Multi-shot 3D slice-select tailored RF pulses for MRI. Magn. Reson. Med. 48, 157–165. https://doi.org/10.1002/mrm.10194.

Tomi-Tricot, R., Gras, V., Thirion, B., et al., 2019. Smart pulse, a machine learning approach for calibration-free dynamic RF shimming: preliminary study in a clinical environment. Magn. Reson. Med. https://doi.org/10.1002/mrm.27870.

Tong, Y., Jezzard, P., Okell, T.W., Clarke, W.T., 2020. Improving PCASL at ultra-high field using a VERSE-guided parallel transmission strategy. Magn. Reson. Med. 84, 777–786. https://doi.org/10.1002/mrm.28173.

Tse, D.H.Y., da Silva, N.A., Poser, B.A., Shah, N.J., 2017. B1+ inhomogeneity mitigation in CEST using parallel transmission: B1+ inhomogeneity mitigation in CEST using pTx. Magn. Reson. Med. 78, 2216–2225. https://doi.org/10.1002/mrm.26624.

Van Damme, L., Mauconduit, F., Chambrion, T., Boulant, N., Gras, V., 2021. Universal nonselective excitation and refocusing pulses with improved robustness to off-resonance for Magnetic Resonance Imaging at 7 Tesla with parallel transmission. Magn. Reson. Med. 85(2), 678–693. https://doi.org/10.1002/mrm.28441.

Vinding, M.S., Guérin, B., Vosegaard, T., Nielsen, N.C., 2017. Local SAR, global SAR, and power-constrained large-flip-angle pulses with optimal control and virtual observation points. Magn. Reson. Med. 77, 374–384. https://doi.org/10.1002/mrm.26086.

Vinding, M.S., Aigner, C.S., Schmitter, S., Lund, T.E., 2021. DeepControl: 2DRF pulses facilitating inhomogeneity and B0 off-resonance compensation in vivo at 7 T. Magn. Reson. Med. 85, 3308–3317. https://doi.org/10.1002/mrm.28667.

Wu, X., Schmitter, S., Auerbach, E.J., Uğurbil, K., Van de Moortele, P.-F., 2016. A generalized slab-wise framework for parallel transmit multiband RF pulse design: slab-wise pTx multiband pulse design. Magn. Reson. Med. 75, 1444–1456. https://doi.org/10.1002/mrm.25689.

Wu, X., Auerbach, E.J., Vu, A.T., et al., 2018. High-resolution whole-brain diffusion MRI at 7T using radiofrequency parallel transmission. Magn. Reson. Med. 0. https://doi.org/10.1002/mrm.27189.

Wu, X., Auerbach, E.J., Vu, A.T., et al., 2019. Human connectome project-style resting-state functional MRI at 7 tesla using radiofrequency parallel transmission. Neuroimage 184, 396–408. https://doi.org/10.1016/j.neuroimage.2018.09.038.

Yang, Q.X., Wang, J., Zhang, X., et al., 2002. Analysis of wave behavior in lossy dielectric samples at high field. Magn. Reson. Med. 47, 982–989. https://doi.org/10.1002/mrm.10137.

RF coils for ultra-high field neuroimaging

Özlem Ipek[a] and Jérémie D. Clément[b]

[a]*School of Biomedical Engineering and Imaging Sciences, King's College London, London, United Kingdom* [b]*System Technologies, Siemens Healthcare GmbH, Erlangen, Germany*

Highlights

- Imaging deep regions at UHF neuroimaging is challenging due to RF inhomogeneity imposed by decreased electromagnetic wavelength in the body tissues.
- MRI signal homogeneity is increased with using parallel-transmit RF coil arrays by modulating the complex excitation of the individual channels.
- The number of receivers has usually to be a trade-off between the size of the region to cover, the size of receive coils, and the MR scanner hardware.
- The combination of proton and X-nuclei coil designs in one structure is challenging in terms of maintaining the transmit and receive efficiencies similar to a single-nuclei coil.
- The validation of the electromagnetic simulation RF coil model includes the use of cosimulation to tune to the Larmor frequency and match to 50 Ohm load of the simulated setup similarly to the measured configuration, and the comparison of simulated and measured, individual and shimmed, B_1^+ field maps.

8.1 Introduction

UHF systems (7T and above) offer the potential to provide truly comprehensive structural, functional, and metabolic imaging. RF coils are the physically closest MRI component to the subject as they are placed surrounding or next to the region of imaging for transmitting and receiving the MRI signal. So far, the RF coils have been developed by the research groups for UHF MRI scanners dedicated to human imaging, and their commercialization has been taken by third-party companies rather than the main MRI vendors. In this chapter, we describe the design considerations and challenges of RF coils for UHF human neuroimaging. We discuss B_1^+ (transmit) and B_1^- (receive) behavior, coil types and designs dedicated to whole head, and local applications with covering X-nuclei coil types. The validation methods of electromagnetic field simulations for safe human imaging with in-house-built RF coils are also briefly addressed.

8.2 Behavior of transmit/receive at ultra-high field

Magnetic resonance at ultra-high field ($\geq$7T, UHF) benefits from higher signal-to-noise ratio (Vaughan et al., 2001) and better spectral (Gruetter et al., 1998) and spatial resolution (Webb and Collins, 2010), compared to lower field MR scanners.

Advances in Magnetic Resonance Technology and Applications. Volume 10. ISSN 2666-9099. https://doi.org/10.1016/B978-0-323-99898-7.00039-0

8.2.1 Transmit field at ultra-high field

While at 1.5T or 3T, the RF field is relatively homogeneous over the human body, pronounced inhomogeneity emerges when increasing the B_0 field to 7T and above. The electromagnetic wavelength inside the body tissue is decreased and is comparable to the brain size at 7T ($\sim$13 cm). Consequently, destructive interference of the magnetic field causes degradation in image quality and the so-called central brightening effect (Collins et al., 2005). This effect is particularly pronounced for the birdcage coil design, typically used at lower field strengths (Ipek, 2017).

The following approaches have been proposed to address the inhomogeneities at UHF. One of the earliest methods aimed to passively shim the transmit field using high dielectric material padding (Yang et al., 2006). By placing the pad near low transmit-field areas, the transmit field is locally enhanced and the overall transmit field is more homogeneous (Webb, 2011). Another passive approach to address the RF inhomogeneity is the use of metamaterials as they describe a material engineered to have specific properties that cannot be achieved naturally. They are usually arranged in repeating patterns and can be used to influence the propagation of electromagnetic waves. The transmit or receive field can be locally enhanced, as for dielectric pads, but with the advantage of being smaller structures with more controlled properties (Alipour et al., 2021).

Parallel transmit systems, where an array of multiple independent RF coils is used, are an alternative to the previous methods to mitigate RF inhomogeneity. By modulating the complex excitations of the individual channels, constructive transmit field interferences can be generated over the region-of-interest and thus improve signal homogeneity (Metzger et al., 2008). An extensive number of coil arrays have been developed through years for body or head imaging at 7T and above. In Section 8.2, we give a short introduction to existing designs. Strategies for the mitigation of B_1^+ field inhomogeneities by RF pulse design and parallel transmission are also discussed in depth in Chapter 7.

8.2.2 Receive at ultra-high field

At lower field strength, the transmit signal is usually ensured by large volume coils built in the MR scanner to provide an efficient full-body coverage. However, such coils lack receive sensitivity as they encompass a large volume. Parallel imaging was originally proposed as a method to combine the high signal-to-noise ratio (SNR) achieved by small coils with the large field-of-view obtained on transmit side (Roemer et al., 1990). In addition, the simultaneous acquisition of spatial harmonics (SMASH) (Sodickson and Manning, 1997) method made use of the subsequent multiple-receiver signals to enable accelerated image encoding without compromising the SNR. It was followed by the sensitivity encoding (SENSE) (Pruessmann et al., 1999) and later the generalized auto-calibrating partially parallel acquisitions (GRAPPA) (Griswold et al., 2002) methods, making parallel imaging an important tool for MR applications. At ultra-high field, although the transmit coils are built in proximity with the region to cover, the number of elements is usually by the RF transmit path of the MR scanner to 8 or 16 independent elements. Therefore, to improve the acceleration capabilities and the SNR levels, independent receive arrays are often included in addition to the transmit coil array, closer to the region being imaged.

The number of receivers has usually to be a trade-off between the size of the region to cover, the size of receive coils, and the MR scanner hardware, although it is generally acknowledged that increasing the number of receivers for a given volume is beneficial in terms of SNR and acceleration capabilities (Kim et al., 2019). With more receive channels, the g-factor, which quantifies the loss in SNR in undersampled acquisitions, is improved. Receive coil arrays with 32 (Clement et al., 2019a,b; Gunamony et al., 2014), 64 (May et al., 2022; Uğurbil et al., 2019), or even 128 (Gruber et al., 2021) channels were investigated at different ultra-high field strengths. However, it is important to note that increasing the number of receivers is mainly beneficial for peripheral SNR rather than central when imaging the brain region. To address this, and while the receive arrays are usually built with identical RF coil designs (mainly loop coils), an original design was recently proposed where 24-channel receive loops are combined with 8-channel dipoles, also used for the RF transmit signal (Avdievich et al., 2022). With this hybrid approach, a significant increase in SNR was achieved at the periphery and in central brain locations compared to a commercial 32-channel receive array.

8.3 Nonstandard head coils and applications

At ultra-high field, the observed RF inhomogeneity makes whole-head or body MR applications more challenging compared to lower B_0 field strengths. Therefore, while at lower field, the birdcage coils are extensively used due to high intrinsic B_1^+ field homogeneity, the RF coil arrays are preferred at ultra-high field together with the parallel transmission methods that were introduced in Chapter 7.

8.3.1 RF coil arrays for whole-head applications

When it comes to designing a RF coil for whole head applications, several designs approaches have been reported with the aim to address one of or the multiple challenges described previously. In the following paragraphs, a few examples of RF coil arrays developed for ultra-high fields with their distinct advantages for whole-head applications are presented.

Loop coil arrays have been largely used and are still very popular for head coils at 7T or 9.4T. Whether they are placed in a tight configuration (Gilbert et al., 2012; Avdievich et al., 2022) or an larger cylindrical housing (Williams et al., 2021), they provide good transmit field efficiency (B_1^+ field generated per unit power) and cover the brain regions.

On a different note, the Tic-Tac-Toe RF coil is a good example of variability in design approaches possible at 7T and above. Built with square-shaped transmission lines that are electrically connected to each other, it demonstrated robustness of input impedance against load variations and better B_1^+ field to specific-absorption-rate ratio value compared to more conventional approaches as the TEM coil array arrangement (Krishnamurthy et al., 2019).

Dipole antennas, introduced in 2011 (Ipek et al., 2012; Raaijmakers et al., 2011), are an alternative design approach for the individual transmit elements of RF coil arrays. They were shown to have a good RF signal penetration depth and field symmetry at 7T (Ipek et al., 2013). Therefore, dipoles are also investigated for 10.5T systems where a head-conformal dipole array was shown to excite the tissue more uniformly, compared, for example, to transverse electromagnetic (TEM) coil. Dipole arrays were also used to acquire in vivo MR brain images for the first time at 10.5T (Sadeghi-Tarakameh et al., 2020).

The 8Tx/32Rx dipole coil array is an example of RF coil array designed to address the challenge of longitudinal coverage along head foot direction (z-direction) (Clement et al., 2019a,b, 2022) (Fig. 8.1C and D). Taking advantage of the large longitudinal coverage inherent to the dipole antenna structure (elongated in z-direction), full coverage of the adult brain could be achieved. Combined with a nested 32-channel receive loop coil array, the SNR was, for example, increased by 83% over the cerebellum compared to a standard birdcage coil with 32-channel receivers (Clement et al., 2019a,b).

The significant increase in SNR was, for example, used for a functional MRI study on the auditory pathway (Costa et al., 2021). The auditory pathway is composed of different elements that extend from the auditory cortices (in the temporal lobes) to subcortical regions as the inferior-colliculi or superior olivary complex and cochlear nuclei. The latter being located deep inside the brain and around the cerebellum area. Taking advantage on the improved performances of the 8Tx/32Rx dipole coil array for the whole-brain coverage, a qualitative evaluation of the simultaneous left and right auditory response was shown along the entire auditory pathway. In addition, the increased SNR allowed for inner-ear MR imaging at high resolution.

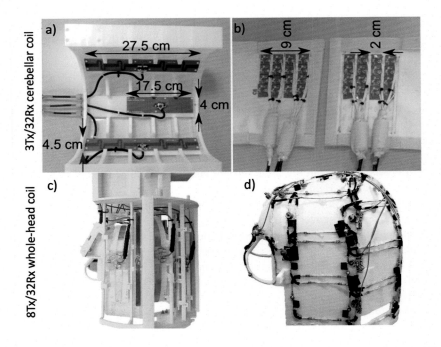

FIG. 8.1

(A) 3-Channel dipole transmit and (B) 32-ch flexible receive loop coil array for 7T cerebellar imaging, and (C) 8-channel dipole/loop transmit array and (D) 32-channel conformal loop receive array for whole-head imaging. *(A) Image from Priovoulos et al. (2020); (C) Image from Clement et al. (2019a,b).*

8.3.2 Dedicated RF coils for local applications

Although covering the whole head is necessary for general research purpose on the adult brain, the target region is sometimes smaller and therefore it can be beneficial to optimize the RF coil design accordingly. In the next paragraphs, a few dedicated RF coils are presented with their corresponding applications and benefits.

The RF inhomogeneity observed in the brain at UHF when using standard birdcage coils is particularly problematic in temporal lobes regions (see also Chapter 7). The significant drop in B_1^+ field efficiency amends the feasibility of performing, for example, proton (^{1}H) spectroscopy. Indeed, the power requirements to achieve the needed B_1^+ field are often constrained by the safe RF power limits determined for the coil.

A possible solution consists in designing local RF coils that are placed directly over the region-of-interest. As an example, we present here the ear-to-ear loop coils (ETE-loops) (Clement et al., 2016) that were designed to be placed on each side of the adult head with an appropriate coil former (Fig. 8.2A–C). Compared to the birdcage coil, the loop coil presents the distinct advantage to produce high B_1^+ field efficiency over a localized region. In addition, having a focused signal contributes to limit the risk of lipid contamination from regions outside the region-of-interest when performing MR spectroscopy. With the ETE loops, the B_1^+ field efficiency was, for example, increased by 109% from 9.03 μT/√kW for the birdcage coil to 18.9 μT/√kW over the voxel-of-interest for ^{1}H spectroscopy in temporal lobes (Fig. 8.2D). Using the semiadiabatic spin-echo full intensity-acquired localized (SPECIAL) sequence (VOI $= 20 \times 20 \times 20$ mm^3, TR/TE $= 6500/16$ ms, NA $= 64$), the increased B_1^+ field efficiency obtained with the ETE loops allowed to acquire a ^{1}H spectrum while it was not possible with the birdcage coil due to the RF power limits.

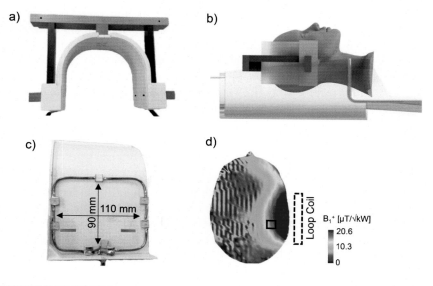

FIG. 8.2

(A–B) CAD view of the ear-to-ear (ETE) loop coils. (C) Picture of one side of the ETE loops. (D) B_1^+ field map shown for one-side loop coil. The voxel-of-interest for MR spectroscopy is indicated (continuous line *black* box).

Another example is the cerebellar region that is located at the bottom of the head and is usually poorly covered with whole-head RF coils. In addition, only a limited number of receivers can be dedicated to this region. This hinders the performance for fMRI studies due to the lack of sensitivity and acceleration capabilities.

A solution proposed by Priovoulos et al. (2020) was to build dedicated transmit elements together with a 32-channel dense receive array specifically targeting the cerebellum area (Fig. 8.1A and B). Using three dipole antennas to transmit the RF signal and 32 small loops as receivers, a median increase of 27.51% in SNR was achieved over the whole cerebellum compared to a whole-head RF coil (8Tx32Rx, Nova Medical, USA). In terms of temporal SNR (tSNR), crucial for fMRI applications, a gain was also shown using the dedicated RF coil.

8.4 Multituned and non-H-coils

The increased SNR at higher field strengths brings advantages for X-nuclei MRI/MRS, which compared to proton MRI/MRS is challenging due to the low tissue concentrations and hence inherently low SNR. At 7T, the Larmor frequencies of X-nuclei are much lower than that of the ^{1}H proton, 297.2 MHz: Sodium, ^{23}Na: 78.6 MHz, Phosphorous, ^{31}P: 120.3 MHz, Deuterium, ^{2}H: 45.6 MHz, Potassium, ^{39}K: 13.9 MHz. At these frequencies the B_1^+ inhomogeneities are relatively unproblematic compared to proton MRI/MRS. It is therefore preferable to transmit with a birdcage volume coil and to receive with a conformal multichannel local loop coil array to maximize receive sensitivity. This arrangement is generally combined with a volume transmit/receive proton coil to be used for acquiring a localizer image of the object and B_0 shimming. The combination of proton and X-nuclei coil designs in one structure is challenging in terms of maintaining the transmit and receive efficiencies similar to a single-nuclei coil. In practice, one often sacrifices some proton signal efficiency in favor of keeping the X-nuclei at a good level (Choi et al., 2020). One combined structure example for a three-layered ^{23}Na/^{1}H coil array from Shajan et al. (2016) includes a 4-channel ^{23}Na transceiver loops, 27-channel ^{23}Na receive array, and 4-channel ^{1}H transceiver dipoles. Another example of two layers with dual-tuned coil design would be a dual-tuned ^{1}H/^{31}P birdcage volume transmit and 30-channel ^{1}H/^{31}P loop receive array (Rowland et al., 2020). Moreover, a dual-tuned coil arrays provide an opportunity to acquire simultaneous proton and X-nuclei quantitative brain mapping (Wang et al., 2021).

8.5 Coil safety considerations

Coil safety evaluation must be a focus of concern when designing a RF coil for in-vivo MR applications. Besides material protection, it is crucial to ensure that none of the potential hazards can constitute a threat for living subjects. While some practical aspects were already introduced in Chapter 5, in this section, we will consider the safety aspects from the coil validation perspective using electromagnetic field simulations. In Section 8.5.1, we define the local and global SAR that are the main quantities used to assess the RF coil safety with respect to the electromagnetic fields for human applications. However, before running simulations on human models and determining the appropriate RF power limits, the first validation step consists of assessing the accuracy of the simulation model. This is usually done using a phantom, and in Section 8.5.2, we provide a detailed description of this step.

8.5.1 Local and global SAR

Eq. 8.1 defines the SAR quantity, where V is the volume of the sample, σ is the electrical conductivity, E is the RMS electric field, and ρ is the density

$$\text{SAR} = \frac{1}{V} \int_{sample} \frac{\sigma(r)|E(r)|^2}{\rho(r)} \, dr. \tag{8.1}$$

Electric fields are obtained from electromagnetic field simulations using an exact model of the RF coil under investigation. In Section 8.5.2, details are given on RF modeling for simulations and validation of the results.

8.5.1.1 Global SAR

$$P_{absorbed}^{ROI} = \frac{1}{2} * \left| \sum_{m=1}^{M} E_m * \overline{J_m} * V_m \right| \tag{8.2}$$

The SAR value calculated, using Eq. 8.1, for each voxel of the simulated model is usually averaged over a given mass region and is referred as the *global SAR*. This quantity is directly related to the total power sent to the RF coil and deposited in human tissue. A straightforward method to compute the global SAR is to calculate first the total absorbed power in the tissue using Eq. 8.2, where M is the total number of voxels in the region-of-interest (ROI), E_m and J_m are the per-voxel electric and current field values, respectively (with the bar denoting the complex conjugate), and V_m is the voxel's volume.

Once the total absorbed power is obtained, the total mass of the ROI can be calculated using the per-voxel mass density. The global SAR is then calculated as the ratio between the total absorbed power in tissue and the total mass of the ROI (Eq. 8.3)

$$\text{SAR}_{global}^{ROI} = \frac{P_{absorbed}^{ROI}}{\text{Mass}_{ROI}}. \tag{8.3}$$

8.5.1.2 Local SAR

Local regions with high SAR levels at UHF are more likely to appear due to the inherent inhomogeneity of the RF field. Therefore, using exclusively the global mass averaged SAR value may not accurately cover all potential RF safety hazards. These risks are increased as local RF coils, placed near the body regions, are used at ultra-high field to transmit the RF signal. A second quantity was defined and is referred as the *local SAR*. One way to evaluate it would be to use the per-voxel SAR values calculated using Eq. 8.1 and to find its maximum.

Nevertheless, in adult subjects with a healthy vascular system, the local heating caused by high SAR levels is temporally dissipated. The phenomenon, also known as *perfusion*, can be for example analytically studied using the Pennes' bioheat equation (Wang et al., 2007). In this scenario, using the per-voxel SAR value to assess the local SAR maxima is very conservative and does not appropriately represent tissue heating. To better represent the effect of local heating, the local SAR is usually averaged over 10-g-tissue regions. For each tissue-containing voxel, the SAR is averaged over surrounding voxels until the 10 g mass of tissue is reached. The 10-g value was chosen as it has shown good correlation between temperature elevation in the brain and the local mass-averaged SAR. Different algorithms were introduced to create the 10-g-tissue regions (Ipek et al., 2014; de Greef et al., 2013), and the simulation software packages usually also include a method to compute the local SAR.

8.5.1.3 Regulatory limits
Global and local SAR limits are defined by the International Electrotechnical Commission (IEC 60601–2-33:2010) for safe MRI procedures. In Table 8.1, the main limits are indicated as reference for normal operating mode. The whole-body SAR and head SAR correspond to global SAR (Eq. 8.3).

The values given in Table 8.1 are time-averaged over 6 min. Eq. 8.4 is used to correlate these numbers with the quantities calculated in simulation and with the sequence parameters

$$SAR_{6\,min} = \frac{SAR_{1W} * P_{pulse} * \#pulses_{6\,min} * T_{pulse}}{T_{6\,min}}. \tag{8.4}$$

In Eq. 8.4, the numerator gives either the total or the maximum energy deposited for a given sequence over 6 min when the global or local SAR are considered, respectively. The quantity SAR_{1W} corresponds to the global or maximum local SAR as calculated in simulations and normalized to 1 W total input power. The P_{pulse} corresponds to the power of the RF pulse, $\#pulses_{6min}$ to the number of RF pulses during a time window of 6 min, and T_{pulse} is the duration of a single RF pulse. The denominator in Eq. 8.4 corresponds to the time-averaging window of 6 min. For any sequence, none of the SAR limits defined in Table 8.1 should be exceeded when calculating the SAR_{6min}. However, under certain circumstances, the sequences can be run in first level controlled mode where all limits in Table 8.1 are doubled, except for global head SAR.

8.5.2 RF simulations and validation
Prior to evaluate the maximum SAR levels achieved in the human for a given RF coil design, the RF coil model used for simulations must be itself validated. Phantom experiments are done and compared to the simulated results for the RF coil. To illustrate this essential step, we take as example an 8-channel dipole array designed and built for MR imaging of very young infants at 7T (Clement et al., 2022), but comparable processes are available and were used by different groups (Sadeghi-Tarakameh et al., 2020; Williams et al., 2021).

8.5.2.1 Electromagnetic field simulations
To perform the simulations, different software suits are commercially available to solve the Maxwell's equations and obtain the RF field distributions such as CST Studio Suite (CST, Darmstadt, Germany), XFDTD (Remcom, State College, PA, USA), or HFSS (ANSYS, Canonsbury, PA, USA). Here, the simulations were performed using the finite-difference time-domain (FDTD) simulation software Sim4life (ZMT, Switzerland).

Table 8.1 SAR limits as defined by the IEC guidelines.

Body region	Whole-body SAR	Head SAR	Local SAR (10 g)		
	Whole body	Head	Head	Trunk	Extremities
SAR limit	2 W/kg	3.2 W/kg	10 W/kg	10 W/kg	20 W/kg

8.5.2.2 Model representation and simulation setup

The phantom CAD model should be easily available to be used within the chosen simulation software package. In addition, its dielectric properties must be known so that it is accurately simulated. For the 8-channel dipole array, a realistic infant-size phantom was designed in-house, and its dielectric properties were measured ($\epsilon_r = 79$, $\sigma = 0.95$ S/m) using a dielectric assessment kit (DAK 12, SPEAG, Switzerland).

The RF coil should be represented as precisely as possible, including notably the printed-circuit board, if any, as well as all the components used. Fig. 8.3A and B shows the CAD model of the 8-channel dipole array as it was represented in Sim4Life. The copper traces were included as in the built circuit. The magnet RF shield is also included (diameter = 600 mm, length = 1150 mm). To accurately place the RF coil with respect to the load, the CAD model of the housing should be included. However, it does not necessarily need to be simulated if the material was already tested and shown to be MR transparent. To tune and match the RF coil and validate simulation results, the measured S-matrix can be used as the reference to achieve. One way is to adjust manually the lumped element values until the right values are found. However, this operation can be time-consuming since the simulations need to be done every time the component values are modified. Alternatively, a cosimulation approach can be used. To allow this, all RF ports (8 sources/ports and 40 lumped elements) are driven individually by

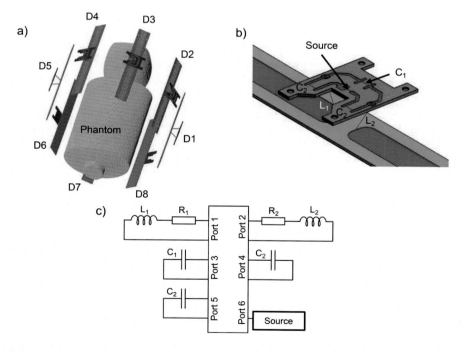

FIG. 8.3

(A) Simulated voxel model including the infant phantom and dipole coil elements. The magnet bore was simulated but is not shown for better visualization of the coil array. (B) Detailed view of the tuning/matching circuit. Each lumped elements were represented at its exact position. (C) Corresponding diagram as implemented in the cosimulation software.

a Gaussian excitation centered at 297.2 MHz with a 200 MHz bandwidth for 300 periods with auto-termination when the convergence reaches to −50 dB. The impedance data for each port can then be sent to a cosimulation software to be processed. Software packages such as ADS (Keysight Technologies, USA) or Optenni (Optenni Ltd., Finland) are available. Each port can then be defined either as an inductor, capacitor, or source/port (Fig. 8.3C).

8.5.2.3 Cosimulation configuration

To accurately represent the physical array, RF losses must be considered that arise from coaxial cables or from the lumped elements. Since the capacitors have low losses, a general Q-factor of 1500 at 300 MHz was applied. The two series capacitors (Fig. 8.3B, C_2) were defined using a subcircuit, which forces the optimizer to assign them identical values, as it is for the built coil array. To mimic the RF losses along the line from RF power amplifiers to the coil input, a series resistor was added to both inductors, as it is expected to appropriately represent the power attenuation from the nonsimulated coaxial cables. Fig. 8.3C shows the typical port configuration for a given dipole. The optimizer was, in addition, constrained to assign lumped elements values within a given realistic range with respect to the built coil array. The measured reflection coefficients and 1st and 2nd neighbor coupling values were used as targets for the optimizer. Furthest coupling values are low and are not expected to have a significant influence on the simulation results.

8.5.2.4 Validation of the model simulations

Using the cosimulation approach, high correlation can be achieved between simulated and measured reflection coefficients (~1% relative difference) but also for the coupling terms with an averaged relative difference of ~4.2% for the 1st coupling terms (S_{12}), and ~9.4% for the 2nd coupling terms (S_{13}) (Fig. 8.4).

Once this is achieved, the next step is to assess the correlation between simulated and measured individual B_1^+ field maps and RF shimmed cases. Individual scaling of the individual B_1^+ field maps can be applied so that the averaged simulated B_1^+ field value matches with the measured one (Fig. 8.5A). The correlation can be quantified using the normalized root-mean square error

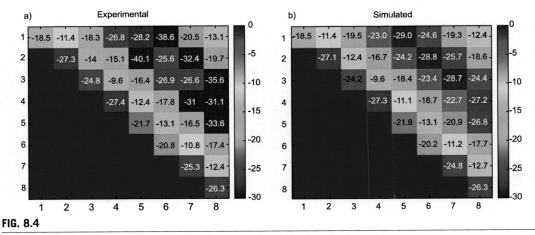

FIG. 8.4

(A) Experimental and (B) simulated S-matrices shown for the 8Tx dipole coil array.

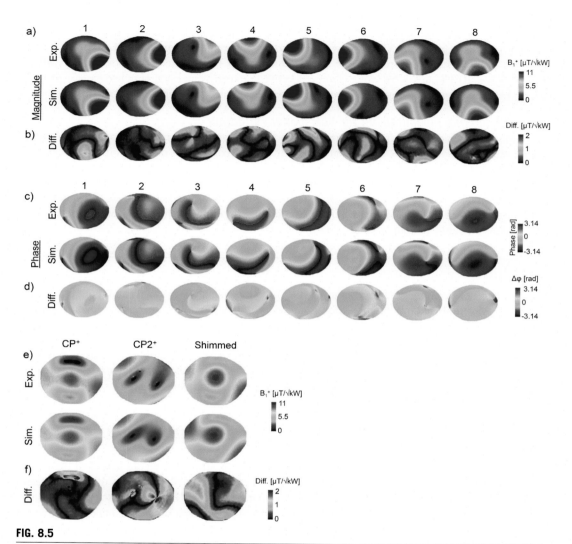

FIG. 8.5

Experimentally measured and simulated B_1^+ field maps, normalized to 1 kW total input power, shown in (A) for individual transmit elements and (E) for CP$^+$ mode, CP2$^+$ mode, and one RF shim configuration ([155 200 328 0 0 7 83 132] degrees). (C) Experimentally measured and simulated individual phase maps corresponding to the transmit elements shown in (A). The phase maps were computed relative to the CP mode. The slice position for all the results shown is indicated in (A), (B), (D), and (F) Difference maps calculated for the combined maps (E) and individual B_1^+ field maps (A and C).

(NRMSE) between simulated and measured data. In the case of the 8-channel dipole array, the NRMSE values for individual B_1^+ field maps ranged from 2% for channel 2% to 4.8% for channel 3 (Fig. 8.5A and B). For the individual phase maps, an averaged difference of 15 degrees in simulation and measurements was found across all channels (Fig. 8.5C and D).

The combined field is evaluated using three different sets of transmit RF phases (Fig. 8.5E). These are usually the circularly polarized (CP) mode ($\Delta\varphi = 45$ degree increments from dipole 1 to 8), C2P mode ($\Delta\varphi = -45$ degree increments from dipole 1 to 8), and one set of shimmed RF phases. The NMRSE values of 6.2%, 10.3%, and 7.5% were observed between experimental and simulated maps in CP$^+$, CP2$^+$, and shimmed modes, respectively, for the 8-channel dipole array (Fig. 8.5E and F).

8.5.2.5 RF heating measurement for SAR model validation

The approach presented in the previous paragraphs can be completed with fiber-optic temperature probe measurements during MR experiments, to validate the spatial SAR distribution and values predicted by the accurately simulated model. After inserting the fiber-optic temperature probes inside a phantom at distinct locations, various excitations patterns could be tested, and the local SAR is estimated based on the temperature increase at the probe tips. Good correspondence was shown between the measured-derived local SAR value and the simulation providing a further validation of the simulation model (Sadeghi-Tarakameh et al., 2020).

8.6 Outlook

The use of parallel transmit systems with at least eight independent RF channels and integration with sensors for SAR, field, and motion monitoring sensors is a requirement for the further development of UHF neuroimaging. Enabling the full platform capability of parallel transmit system would be achieved with real-time update of subject-specific SAR values during the MR acquisition. In addition, with an integration of B_0 shim AC-DC coils and field/motion sensors, RF coil arrays will gain further capability of controlled MR signal acquisition (Chapter 6). Further development on massively parallel transmit and receive RF coil arrays integrated with metamaterials/composite designs would be the next step for high-resolution whole-head MRI.

8.7 Summary

This chapter has provided an overview of transmit and receive arrays for whole-head and dedicated brain region neuroimaging applications. The current state-of-art by the example of an integrated X-nuclei coil with a proton coil for unified structural and metabolic MRI has been discussed. We have illustrated the procedure of coil validation by simulation and in phantom for an 8-channel dipole array designed for young infant MR imaging at 7T and introduced further methods that are used to validate a simulation model. The different steps were described to provide a clear understanding of the key aspects when preparing the simulation model.

References

Alipour, A., Seifert, A.C., Bradley, N.D., et al., 2021. Improvement of magnetic resonance imaging using a wireless radiofrequency resonator array. Sci. Rep. 11, 23034. https://doi.org/10.1038/s41598-021-02533-3.

Avdievich, N.I., Nikulin, A.V., Ruhm, L., et al., 2022. A 32-element loop/dipole hybrid array for human head imaging at 7 T. Magn. Reson. Med. 88, 1912–1926. https://doi.org/10.1002/mrm.29347.

Choi, C.-H., Hong, S.-M., Felder, J., Shah, N.J., 2020. The state-of-the-art and emerging design approaches of double-tuned RF coils for X-nuclei, brain MR imaging and spectroscopy: a review. Magn. Reson. Imaging 72, 103–116. https://doi.org/10.1016/j.mri.2020.07.003.

Clement, J.D., Gruetter, R., Ipek, Ö., 2019a. A human cerebral and cerebellar 8-channel transceive RF dipole coil array at 7T. Magn. Reson. Med. 81, 1447–1458. https://doi.org/10.1002/mrm.27476.

Clement, J., Gruetter, R., Ipek, Ö., 2019b. A combined 32-channel receive-loops/8-channel transmit-dipoles coil array for whole-brain MR imaging at 7T. Magn. Reson. Med. 82, 1229–1241. https://doi.org/10.1002/mrm.27808.

Clement, J., Tomi-Tricot, R., Malik, S.J., Webb, A., Hajnal, J.V., Ipek, Ö., 2022. Towards an integrated neonatal brain and cardiac examination capability at 7T: electromagnetic field simulations and early phantom experiments using an 8-channel dipole array. MAGMA, 1–14. https://doi.org/10.1007/s10334-021-00988-z.

Clement, J., Xin, L., Gruetter, R., Ipek, Ö., 2016. Dedicated surface coils for MR studies in the temporal and the frontal lobes of the human brain at 7T. In: Presented at the 24th Annual Meeting of ISMRM, #3513, Singapore.

Collins, C.M., Liu, W., Schreiber, W., Yang, Q.X., Smith, M.B., 2005. Central brightening due to constructive interference with, without, and despite dielectric resonance. J. Magn. Reson. Imaging 21, 192–196. https://doi.org/10.1002/jmri.20245.

Costa, S.D., Clément, J., Gruetter, R., Ipek, Ö., 2021. Evaluation of the whole auditory pathway using high-resolution and functional MRI at 7T parallel-transmit. PLoS One 16, e0254378. https://doi.org/10.1371/journal.pone.0254378.

Gilbert, K.M., Belliveau, J.-G., Curtis, A.T., Gati, J.S., Klassen, L.M., Menon, R.S., 2012. A conformal transceive array for 7 T neuroimaging. Magn. Reson. Med. 67, 1487–1496. https://doi.org/10.1002/mrm.23124.

de Greef, M., Ipek, Ö., Raijmakers, A.J.E., Creeze, J., van den Berg, C., 2013. Specific absorption rate intersibject variability in 7T parallel transmit MRI of the head. Magn. Reson. Med. 69, 1476–1485. https://doi.org/10.1002/mrm.24378.

Griswold, M.A., Jakob, P.M., Heidemann, R.M., et al., 2002. Generalized autocalibrating partially parallel acquisitions (GRAPPA). Magn. Reson. Med. 47, 1202–1210. https://doi.org/10.1002/mrm.10171.

Gruber, B., Stockmann, J.P., Keil, B., Ghotra, A., Feinberg, D.A., Wald, L.L., 2021. A 128-channel head coil array for cortical imaging at 7 tesla. In: 2021 International Conference on Electromagnetics in Advanced Applications (ICEAA). Presented at the 2021 International Conference on Electromagnetics in Advanced Applications (ICEAA), p. 367, https://doi.org/10.1109/ICEAA52647.2021.9539808.

Gruetter, R., Weisdorf, S.A., Rajanayagan, V., et al., 1998. Resolution improvements inin Vivo1H NMR spectra with increased magnetic field strength. J. Magn. Reson. 135, 260–264. https://doi.org/10.1006/jmre.1998.1542.

Gunamony, S., Kozlov, M., Hoffmann, J., Turner, R., Scheffler, K., Pohmann, R., 2014. A 16-channel dual-row transmit array in combination with a 31-element receive array for human brain imaging at 9.4 T. Magn. Reson. Med. 71, 870–879. https://doi.org/10.1002/mrm.24726.

Ipek, Ö., 2017. Radiofrequency coils for ultra-high field magnetic resonance. Anal. Biochem. 529, 10–16. https://doi.org/10.1016/j.ab.2017.03.022.

Ipek, Ö., Raaijmakers, A., Klomp, D., Lagendijk, J., Luijten, P., Van den Berg, C., 2012. Characterization of transceive surface elements designs for 7 tesla magnetic resonance imaging of the prostate: radiative antenna and microstrip. Phys. Med. Biol. 57, 343–355. https://doi.org/10.1088/0031-9155/57/2/343.

Ipek, Ö., Raaijmakers, A., Lagendijk, J., Luijten, P., van den Berg, C., 2013. Optimization of the radiative antenna for 7T magnetic resonance imaging. Concepts Magn. Reson. Part B: Magn. Reson. Eng. 43, 1–10. https://doi.org/10.1002/cmr.b.21224.

Ipek, Ö., Raaijmakers, A.J., Lagendijk, J.J., Luijten, P.R., van den Berg, C.A.T., 2014. Intersubject local SAR variation for 7T prostate MR imaging with an eight-channel single-side adapted dipole antenna array. Magn. Reson. Med. 71, 1559–1567. https://doi.org/10.1002/mrm.24794.

Kim, K.-N., Hernandez, D., Seo, J.-H., et al., 2019. Quantitative assessment of phased array coils with different numbers of receiving channels in terms of signal-to-noise ratio and spatial noise variation in magnetic resonance imaging. PLoS One 14, e0219407. https://doi.org/10.1371/journal.pone.0219407.

Krishnamurthy, N., Santini, T., Wood, S., et al., 2019. Computational and experimental evaluation of the tic-tac-toe RF coil for 7 tesla MRI. PLoS One 14, e0209663. https://doi.org/10.1371/journal.pone.0209663.

May, M.W., Hansen, S.-L.J.D., Mahmutovic, M., et al., 2022. A patient-friendly 16-channel transmit/64-channel receive coil array for combined head-neck MRI at 7 tesla. Magn. Reson. Med. 88, 1419–1433. https://doi.org/10.1002/mrm.29288.

Metzger, G.J., Snyder, C., Akgun, C., Vaughan, T., Ugurbil, K., Van de Moortele, P.-F., 2008. Local B1+ shimming for prostate imaging with transceiver arrays at 7T based on subject-dependent transmit phase measurements. Magn. Reson. Med. 59, 396–409. https://doi.org/10.1002/mrm.21476.

Priovoulos, N., Roos, T., Ipek, Ö., et al., 2020. A local multi-transmit coil combined with a high-density receive array for cerebellar fMRI at 7 T. NMR Biomed. 34, e4586. https://doi.org/10.1002/nbm.4586.

Pruessmann, K.P., Weiger, M., Scheidegger, M.B., Boesiger, P., 1999. SENSE: sensitivity encoding for fast MRI. Magn. Reson. Med. 42, 952–962. https://doi.org/10.1002/(SICI)1522-2594(199911)42:5<952::AID-MRM16->3.0.CO;2-S.

Raaijmakers, A.J.E., Ipek, O., Klomp, D.W.J., et al., 2011. Design of a radiative surface coil array element at 7 T: the single-side adapted dipole antenna. Magn. Reson. Med. 66, 1488–1497. https://doi.org/10.1002/mrm.22886.

Roemer, P.B., Edelstein, W.A., Hayes, C.E., Souza, S.P., Mueller, O.M., 1990. The NMR phased array. Magn. Reson. Med. 16, 192–225. https://doi.org/10.1002/mrm.1910160203.

Rowland, B.C., Driver, I.D., Tachrount, M., et al., 2020. Whole brain ^{31}P MRSI at 7T with a dual-tuned receive array. Magn. Reson. Med. 83, 765–775. https://doi.org/10.1002/mrm.27953.

Sadeghi-Tarakameh, A., DelaBarre, L., Lagore, R.L., et al., 2020. In vivo human head MRI at 10.5T: a radiofrequency safety study and preliminary imaging results. Magn. Reson. Med. 84, 484–496. https://doi.org/10.1002/mrm.28093.

Shajan, G., Mirkes, C., Buckenmaier, K., Hoffman, J., Pohmann, R., Scheffler, K., 2016. Three-layered radio frequency coil arrangement for sodium MRI of the human brain at 9.4 tesla. Magn. Reson. Med. 75, 906–916. https://doi.org/10.1002/mrm.25666.

Sodickson, D.K., Manning, W.J., 1997. Simultaneous acquisition of spatial harmonics (SMASH): fast imaging with radiofrequency coil arrays. Magn. Reson. Med. 38, 591–603. https://doi.org/10.1002/mrm.1910380414.

Uğurbil, K., Auerbach, E., Moeller, S., et al., 2019. Brain imaging with improved acceleration and signal-to-noise ratio at 7 tesla obtained with 64 channel receive array. Magn. Reson. Med. 82, 495–509. https://doi.org/10.1002/mrm.27695.

Vaughan, J.T., Garwood, M., Collins, C.M., et al., 2001. 7T vs. 4T: RF power, homogeneity, and signal-to-noise comparison in head images. Magn. Reson. Med. 46, 24–30. https://doi.org/10.1002/mrm.1156.

Wang, Z., Lin, J.C., Mao, W., Liu, W., Smith, M.B., Collins, C.M., 2007. SAR and temperature: simulations and comparison to regulatory limits for MRI. J. Magn. Reson. Imaging 26, 437–441. https://doi.org/10.1002/jmri.20977.

Wang, B., Zhang, B., Yu, Z., et al., 2021. A radially interleaved sodium and proton coil array for brain at 7 T. NMR Biomed. 34, e4608. https://doi.org/10.1002/nbm.4608.

Webb, A.G., 2011. Dielectric materials in magnetic resonance. Concept. Magn. Reson. A 38A, 148–184. https://doi.org/10.1002/cmr.a.20219.

Webb, A.G., Collins, C.M., 2010. Parallel transmit and receive technology in high-field magnetic resonance neuroimaging. Int. J. Imaging Syst. Technol. 20, 2–13. https://doi.org/10.1002/ima.20219.

Williams, S.N., Allwood-Spiers, S., McElhinney, P., et al., 2021. A nested eight-channel transmit array with open-face concept for human brain imaging at 7 tesla. Front. Phys. 9. https://doi.org/10.3389/fphy.2021.701330.

Yang, Q.X., Mao, W., Wang, J., et al., 2006. Manipulation of image intensity distribution at 7.0 T: passive RF shimming and focusing with dielectric materials. J. Magn. Reson. Imaging 24, 197–202. https://doi.org/10.1002/jmri.20603.

Parallel imaging and reconstruction techniques

Berkin Bilgic[a,b] and Tolga Cukur[c,d]

[a]*Athinoula A. Martinos Center for Biomedical Imaging, Charlestown, MA, United States* [b]*Department of Radiology, Harvard Medical School, Boston, MA, United States* [c]*Department of Electrical and Electronics Engineering, Bilkent University, Ankara, Turkey* [d]*National Magnetic Resonance Research Center (UMRAM), Bilkent University, Ankara, Turkey*

Highlights

- The encoding power of receive arrays has significantly improved over the last two decades, and acceleration factors of an order of magnitude became attainable through parallel imaging. This implies that receive arrays now perform most of the image encoding, whereas gradient coils are contributing a much smaller portion.
- Spatial variation in coil sensitivities increases at ultra-high fields, which permit yet higher acceleration factors. Combined with the SNR advantage of higher fields, this renders submillimeter-resolution imaging feasible.
- While controlled aliasing strategies have enabled optimal utilization of the degrees of freedom in modern dense receive arrays, compressed sensing, low-rank constraints, and deep learning priors have provided a yet better trade-off between image SNR and contrast versus scan time.

9.1 Introduction

Image encoding in MRI has been mainly performed using gradient coils, which create spatially varying magnetic fields that encode spins' position into their resonant frequencies. The spatial encoding power of radiofrequency receive arrays has significantly improved over the last two decades, and acceleration factors of an order of magnitude and higher have become attainable through parallel imaging reconstruction. This implies that receive arrays are now performing most of the image encoding, whereas gradient coils are contributing a much smaller portion at high accelerations. As such, parallel imaging and advanced reconstruction algorithms have emerged as important tools in our MR physics arsenal, especially at ultra-high fields (UHF) where high acceleration rates permit acquisitions that probe brain structure and function at mesoscale resolutions.

Spatial variations in coil sensitivity profiles increase at higher fields, and these increased degrees of freedom allow higher acceleration rates to be achieved compared to lower field strength. Unfortunately, undersampling in k-space leads to an intrinsic $\sqrt{R}$ SNR penalty (where R is the acceleration factor) since less data points are acquired, and thus, there is less "noise averaging" being performed. Indeed, at high acceleration factors, this intrinsic SNR penalty can prohibit high-resolution imaging at 3T or lower field strengths as the resulting images may become too noisy for practical use. The SNR boost provided by going to UHF directly counteracts this penalty and thus renders high acceleration

Advances in Magnetic Resonance Technology and Applications. Volume 10. ISSN 2666-9099. https://doi.org/10.1016/B978-0-323-99898-7.00019-5

factors feasible. Coupled with the increased degrees of freedom in coil sensitivity profiles, high acceleration factors are well suited for UHF imaging, which enables unprecedented spatial and temporal resolutions to be achieved.

This chapter will start by focusing on the basics of parallel imaging and controlled aliasing that aim to fully utilize the degrees of freedom in dense receive arrays for highly undersampled acquisitions, calibration scans, and coil sensitivity estimation approaches that permit robust utilization of such techniques, and advanced model-based reconstructions and deep learning approaches that can utilize a priori or learned regularizers to further push the acceleration. The chapter will conclude by looking at the effect of going to higher field strengths on parallel imaging capability and examples that illustrate the power and potential of image encoding at UHF.

9.2 Undersampled acquisitions and fundamental parallel imaging approaches

Parallel imaging (PI) methods use the extra degrees of freedom in multichannel receive arrays to reconstruct images from undersampled acquisitions, thereby reducing the scan time. The reduction factor (R) denotes the amount of subsampling performed during the acquisition and is also called the acceleration factor. PI relies on the fundamental relation between the imaging field of view (FOV) and the spacing between the successive k-space lines, Δk, where $\text{FOV} = 1/\Delta k$. This implies that a large FOV requires dense sampling of k-space, and if the prescribed FOV is smaller than the object that is being imaged, aliasing occurs. PI reduces the FOV deliberately by skipping lines in k-space and then tries to resolve the aliasing in image space or estimate the missing lines by interpolating the acquired data in k-space. In Fig. 9.1A, $R = 2$-fold acceleration is obtained by skipping every other k-space line, thereby

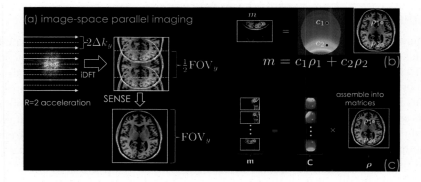

FIG. 9.1

(A) SENSE is a fundamental parallel imaging approach that operates in image space, where aliased signal replicas are unfolded using the coil sensitivity profiles explicitly. This is demonstrated in (B), where each coil contributes a linear equation that relates the aliasing voxels to the acquired coil signal. In (C), equations coming from all coils are assembled into a matrix, which leads to an overdetermined linear system that can be inverted to unalias the signal.

increasing the spacing between successive lines to $2\Delta k$. This, in turn, reduces the imaging FOV by half and causes the voxels that are FOV/2 apart to alias on top of each other.

Sensitivity encoding (SENSE) (Pruessmann et al., 1999) is a fundamental image-space approach where coil sensitivity profiles are used explicitly to unalias voxels by solving a set of linear equations. Generalized auto-calibrating partially parallel acquisition (GRAPPA) (Griswold et al., 2002) uses the spatial variations in coil sensitivities implicitly to synthesize missing k-space lines using a linear combination of the acquired data. Both image- and k-space approaches rely on auto-calibration signal (ACS) data to estimate either coil sensitivity maps or the linear combination weights required for k-space data interpolation.

The simultaneous acquisition of spatial harmonics (SMASH) technique (Sodickson and Manning, 1997) precedes both SENSE and GRAPPA and contains underlying principles of both of these influential approaches. SMASH seeks a linear combination of coil sensitivities that can explicitly form Fourier harmonics (resembling SENSE) and then uses these linear weights to synthesize missing k-space data (akin to GRAPPA). In the following, we will examine these image- and k-space PI algorithms in detail.

9.2.1 PI in image space

As shown in Fig. 9.1B, two voxels that are FOV/2 apart, ρ_1 and ρ_2, will alias on top of each other in an acquisition at $R = 2$-fold acceleration. Focusing on a particular coil with sensitivities denoted by c_1 and c_2 in these voxel positions, SENSE models the relation between the acquired aliased signal, m, and the unknown voxel intensities ρ_1 and ρ_2 as

$$m = c_1\rho_1 + c_2\rho_2 \tag{9.1}$$

indicating that the unknown magnetization is weighted by the coil sensitivity, then aliased in image space. Given that we have multiple coils, each providing one additional observation, we can assemble these linear equations into matrix format (Fig. 9.1C)

$$\mathbf{m} = C\rho. \tag{9.2}$$

Here $\mathbf{m}$ is an $N_c \times 1$ vector of aliased signals in each coil, ρ are the unknown $R \times 1$ voxel intensities ($R = 2$ in this example), C is the $N_c \times R$ coil sensitivity matrix, and N_c denotes the number of coils.

The linear system in Eq. 9.2 can be solved in the least squares sense by minimizing

$$\rho^* = \text{argmin}_\rho \|C\rho - \mathbf{m}\|_2^2,$$
$$= (C^H C)^{-1} C^H \mathbf{m}. \tag{9.3}$$

If present, an $N_c \times N_c$ channel noise covariance matrix, $\boldsymbol{\Psi}$, which describes the levels and correlation of noise in receiver coils, can be incorporated to obtain an SNR-optimal solution (Pruessmann et al., 1999)

$$\rho^*_{optSNR} = (C^H \boldsymbol{\Psi}^{-1} C)^{-1} C^H \boldsymbol{\Psi}^{-1} \mathbf{m}. \tag{9.4}$$

9.2.2 Geometry factor (g-factor)

The matrix inversion in Eq. 9.4 becomes more ill-conditioned at high acceleration rates, which leads to mathematical noise amplification during image reconstruction. This noise amplification is captured by the geometry factor (or g-factor) map and is given by (Pruessmann et al., 1999)

$$g_\rho = \left(\left[\left(C^H \mathbf{\Psi}^{-1} C \right)^{-1} \right]_{\rho,\rho} \left[C^H \mathbf{\Psi}^{-1} C \right]_{\rho,\rho} \right)^{1/2} \geq 1, \tag{9.5}$$

where the indices $[]_{\rho,\rho}$ denote the diagonal elements corresponding to voxel ρ. Since the g-factor is greater than or equal to 1, it is common to report the inverse of the g-factor to ensure that it remains in the interval [0,1]. 1/g-factor reports the retained SNR after parallel imaging reconstruction as shown in Fig. 9.2. Since coil sensitivity profiles are less spatially varying in the middle of the FOV, g-factor is often worse in these regions. This can be better visualized in the $R = 4$ case in Fig. 9.2, where the zoomed-in region of interest (ROI) exhibits higher noise in the middle (white and deep gray matter) and less noise in the periphery (cortex).

   Although an $N_c = 8$ channel array was used in this simulation experiment, acceleration factors beyond $R = 4$ lead to prohibitive noise amplification. We still have more observations than unknowns in Eq. 9.2 since $N_c > R$, but not all these observations are linearly independent because coils that are in close proximity around the head contribute similar encoding information. Further, the acceleration in this experiment is performed only along the phase encoding direction (vertical axis), whereas the eight coils are distributed around the head in 2 dimensions. As such, variations in these eight coils are shared among the vertical and horizontal axes, which makes $R > 4$-fold acceleration in only one direction difficult.

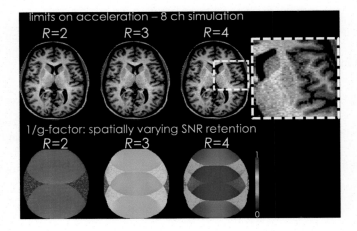

FIG. 9.2

An 8ch SENSE reconstruction simulation is conducted to show the limits of acceleration. While $R=2$- and 3-fold accelerations lead to successful reconstructions, noise amplification is visible especially in the $R=4$ case. The noise amplification is spatially varying and more severe in the middle of the FOV. This can also be seen in the 1/g-factor maps in the bottom row, where up to ~80% of SNR is lost during parallel imaging reconstruction in the middle of the FOV. The shape of the 1/g-factor maps also reflects the acceleration factor, e.g., 4 bands of aliased replicas are visible at $R=4$.

9.2.3 Generalized SENSE reconstruction

The encoding matrix in Eq. 9.4, $(C^H \Psi^{-1} C)^{-1} C^H \Psi^{-1}$, is very small (of size $R \times N_c$) and the equation can be computed rapidly, yet this needs to be performed for each of the collapsed voxels in the image, which may be computationally intensive. Apart from computing these small problems in parallel, another way to facilitate rapid computation is to represent the entire unknown 2D image as a vector $\boldsymbol{\rho}$, which is now of size $(N_x N_y) \times 1$ where N_x and N_y are the number of voxels in readout and phase-encoding axes. This leads to the more flexible relation

$$\boldsymbol{\rho}^* = \mathrm{argmin}_{\boldsymbol{\rho}} \sum_i \|DFC_i \cdot \boldsymbol{\rho} - y_i\|_2^2 \text{ with } i = 1, \dots, N_c, \tag{9.6}$$

where C_i now denotes a matrix whose diagonal entries are the sensitivities of the ith coil for the entire slice, F is a 2D discrete Fourier transform (DFT) operator, D is a k-space undersampling mask, and y_i denotes the acquired k-space data for the ith coil. Though represented as matrix-vector operations, this formulation permits rapid computations through element-wise multiplications that implement $(C_i \cdot \boldsymbol{\rho})$, whereas F is conveniently evaluated using the 2D fast Fourier transform (FFT). While it would still be possible to operate in image space by replacing the DFT operator with a "point spread function" matrix that explains image aliasing, the transition to k-space allows us to use nonuniform sampling patterns where the spacing between successive lines is not held constant. Such sampling strategies can be easily represented by the diagonal sampling mask D that has binary elements. Eq. 9.6 can be solved using least squares solvers such as conjugate gradients (CG) and provides the additional flexibility of incorporating regularization, which will be detailed in Section 9.4.

9.2.4 PI in *k*-space using GRAPPA

Unlike SENSE where coil sensitivity profiles are explicitly used in the reconstruction, GRAPPA uses them implicitly to estimate missing k-space data. This estimation is performed across coils and within a small neighborhood in k-space as described in the following:

$$s_j(k_x, k_y) = \sum_i \sum_{\mu \in U} \sum_{v \in V} w_j(i, \mu, v) \, s_i(k_x + \mu \Delta k_x, k_y + v \Delta k_y) \text{ with } i = 1, \dots, N_c. \tag{9.7}$$

Here, $s_j(k_x, k_y)$ is the target missing k-space sample in the jth coil (black point in Fig. 9.3A), and w_j is the k-space "kernel" used for interpolating the data for the jth coil. This kernel computes a linear combination of the acquired points $s_i(k_x + \mu \Delta k_x, k_y + v \Delta k_y)$ not only inside small neighborhoods in k-space (denoted with U and V for the k_x and k_y axes) but also across all the coils. The underlying assumption in GRAPPA is that there are linear dependencies across coils that permit such estimation, which is akin to SMASH.

As demonstrated in Fig. 9.3B, GRAPPA suffers from similar limitations as SENSE when the acceleration factor is pushed beyond $R > 4$ along a single dimension. At $R = 5$, this reconstruction using a 32ch head array begins to suffer from aliasing artifacts, which become severe at $R = 6$. At this latter acceleration factor, noise amplification especially in the middle of the FOV becomes apparent.

An advantage of GRAPPA over SENSE is in its kernel calibration. Until recently, estimation of coil sensitivities for SENSE has suffered from robustness issues, as they need to be smoothed and carefully masked to exclude nontissue signals (Section 9.5 will detail new techniques that boosted the robustness of sensitivity estimation). GRAPPA, on the other hand, does not need coil sensitivities to be explicitly known, but only requires the estimation of the kernels w_j. To make this possible, fully sampled ACS

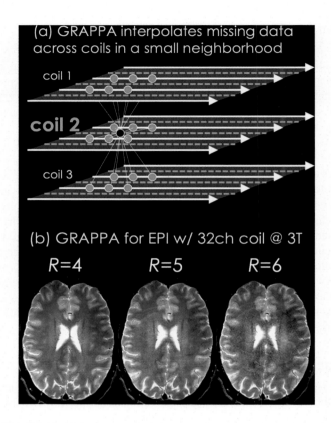

FIG. 9.3

(A) GRAPPA uses a linear combination of acquired k-space data in a small neighborhood across all coils to estimate a missing point. (B) Similar to SENSE, GRAPPA suffers from residual aliasing and noise amplification especially at higher acceleration factors of $R=5$ and 6. Data were acquired using a single-shot echo planar imaging (EPI) readout with 32ch reception at 3T.

data are used. Here, both the target $s_j(k_x,k_y)$ and the neighboring k-space data $s_i(k_x + \mu\Delta k_x, k_y + \nu\Delta k_y)$ in Eq. 9.7 are known. As such, a large "calibration matrix" can be built by creating one row for each (k_x,k_y) point inside the ACS region. This then permits the estimation of the kernels in the least squares sense due to $W_j = S^\dagger S_j$, where W_j is the vectorized version of the k-space kernel w_j, $S^\dagger = (S^H S)^{-1} S^H$ is the pseudo-inverse of the calibration matrix, and S_j is the vector made from all the target points inside the ACS. The kernel calibration step also admits Tikhonov regularization, where the kernel estimate becomes $W_j = (S^H S + \lambda I)^{-1} S^H S_j$, with λ being the regularization parameter.

Another parameter that needs to be selected in GRAPPA reconstruction is the kernel size. Popular choices include 3×3 and 5×5 in $k_x \times k_y$ axes, but larger kernel sizes can be used as well. The trade-off is that smaller kernel sizes provide better g-factor performance, and larger kernels better mitigate potential reconstruction artifacts. This can be understood by thinking of GRAPPA kernels as k-space filters, where a smaller kernel will have more of a "low-pass" effect on the data, thus denoising it more effectively. On the other hand, larger kernels can help synthesize higher order Fourier harmonics and thus reduce potential aliasing artifacts especially at higher accelerations. Finally, it is important to note that the ACS data that allow for kernel estimation do not have to have the same contrast as the actual undersampled imaging data. This point is valid for both sensitivity estimation for SENSE and kernel estimation for GRAPPA. As such, low-resolution, short echo time (TE) and short repetition time (TR) gradient echo, ACS data can be used for calibration, which usually require a couple of seconds to acquire. By this way, it becomes unnecessary to incorporate a fully sampled ACS region inside the actual imaging scan, which often has longer TE/TR combinations to provide the desired contrast. Significant time savings can be achieved with such "external" calibration scans.

Similar to SENSE, an analytical expression for g-factor for the jth coil in GRAPPA reconstructions can be defined using the matrix W made from *image-space* kernels (Breuer et al., 2009)

$$g_j = \left([W^H \mathbf{\Psi} W]_{j,j} / [\mathbf{\Psi}]_{j,j} \right)^{1/2} \geq 1. \tag{9.8}$$

Alternatively, Monte Carlo simulations can be performed by injecting noise to k-space and running GRAPPA reconstruction several times, then taking ratio between the standard deviation across these reconstructions and the standard deviation of the added noise to obtain an empirical g-factor estimate (Robson et al., 2008). This approach is powerful since it provides a general way to estimate g-factor maps for arbitrary trajectories and advanced reconstructions. A caveat is that, with CS regularization (e.g., L1 or low-rank), using different levels of standard deviation for the added noise may lead to different g-factor maps, since these regularizers may threshold the noise entirely depending on its level. In such cases, it might be helpful to acquire a noise-only reference scan to be able to synthesize noise with appropriate power.

9.2.5 PI in *k*-space using SPIRiT

Inspired by GRAPPA, SPIRiT takes a different approach to provide a more general solution that uses data more efficiently and also formulates the reconstruction as an optimization problem that can admit additional, e.g., compressed sensing (CS) regularizers (Lustig and Pauly, 2010). The main difference is that GRAPPA enforces consistency between the synthesized points and the neighboring acquired data, whereas SPIRiT enforces consistency between every point and its neighborhood across all coils. In other words, the acquired data should be able to generate the missing points, but also the missing points need to be able to synthesize the acquired points as well as other missing data. This also leads to a different definition of the reconstruction kernel. In GRAPPA, a kernel spans a large extent in k-space since only the acquired data are counted in the kernel size. For example, at $R_y = 3$-fold acceleration, a 3×3 kernel would have a k-space extent of 3×7 in (k_x, k_y) axes. In SPIRiT, a 3×3 kernel implies a literal 3×3 neighborhood, where all 9 points contribute to each other. This is expressed via

$$s_j = \sum_i g_{ij} \otimes s_i \text{ with } i = 1, \ldots, N_c$$
$$\text{or} \tag{9.9}$$
$$s = Gs,$$

where g_{ij}s denote the SPIRiT kernels, which are convolved with the entire k-space data s_i in the ith coil, then summed over all coils to yield the jth coil's reconstructed k-space, s_j. This is written more succinctly as $s = Gs$, where s now denotes entire k-space concatenated across all coils, and G is a matrix containing g_{ij}s in appropriate positions. Finally, SPIRiT enforces data consistency via

$$y = D \cdot s, \tag{9.10}$$

where D is a linear operator that selects only the acquired k-space locations out of the entire k-space grid, and y is a vector of the acquired k-space data concatenated together. The self- and data-consistency constraints in Eqs. 9.9 and 9.10 can be combined to yield the SPIRiT loss function

$$s^* = \text{argmin}_s \, \|Ds - y\|_2^2 + \lambda \, \|(G - I) \, s\|_2^2, \tag{9.11}$$

where λ is a regularization parameter. We can eliminate the need for selecting this parameter by solving only for the missing k-space data, $\hat{s}$, through the formulation $s = D^T y + D_c^T \hat{s}$, where D^T and D_c^T select the acquired and nonacquired data and put them back in the full k-space grid (Lustig and Pauly, 2010). This leads to

$$\text{argmin}_s \, \left\| D \left(D^T y + D_c^T \hat{s} \right) - y \right\|_2^2 + \lambda \left\| (G - I) \left(D^T y + D_c^T \hat{s} \right) \right\|_2^2$$
$$= \|y + 0 - y\|_2^2 + \lambda \left\| (G - I) \left(D^T y + D_c^T \hat{s} \right) \right\|_2^2, \tag{9.12}$$
$$= \text{argmin}_{\hat{s}} \, \left\| (G - I) D^T y + (G - I) D_c^T \hat{s} \right\|_2^2,$$

which can be solved using a standard CG solver.

SPIRiT is also auto-calibrating, where the kernel estimation is performed similar to GRAPPA and can admit Tikhonov regularization. Unlike GRAPPA which functions as a k-space filter, the iterative nature of Eq. 9.11 allows SPIRiT to use more involved regularizers during the reconstruction stage as well (Lustig and Pauly, 2010; Murphy et al., 2012), which will be detailed in Section 9.4.

9.3 Controlled aliasing in parallel imaging (CAIPI) and non-Cartesian trajectories

Modern head coils have large channel counts (32ch or higher) which are often distributed uniformly around the head. This makes it possible to accelerate in more than one phase encoding axis. 2D acceleration is a powerful concept and easily permits $R = 4$-fold acceleration to be distributed as $R = 2 \times 2$ between two-phase encoding axes in 3D-encoded acquisitions (Weiger et al., 2002; Blaimer et al., 2006). Importantly, the concept of 2D acceleration can be generalized to multislice imaging through simultaneous multislice (SMS) encoding (Feinberg et al., 2011; Setsompop et al., 2012; Moeller et al., 2010; Nunes et al., 2006; Larkman et al., 2001). In SMS, multiple slices are excited simultaneously, which causes the acquired signal to be the superposition of all of these excited slices. Either image- or k-space based PI reconstruction is then used to unalias the collapsed slices (Zahneisen et al., 2015). SMS encoding admits undersampling in the phase encoding axis within each slice as well, which is denoted as "$R_{inplane}$" acceleration. Simultaneous excitation of multiple slices is performed using tailored MultiBand (MB) RF pulses, thus leading to the nomenclature $R_{total} = R_{inplane} \times MB$, where R_{total} is the combined acceleration factor and MB is the number of simultaneously excited slices.

Acceleration in 2D allows the utilization of Controlled Aliasing in Parallel Imaging (CAIPI), where aliasing voxels can be pushed further apart in image space to improve g-factor performance. CAIPI is

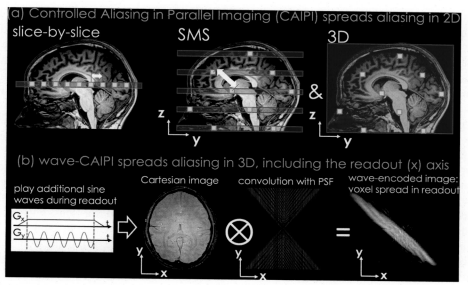

FIG. 9.4

(A) Standard 2D (slice-by-slice) imaging does not lend itself well to high acceleration, as aliasing voxels are very close to each other. When Simultaneous MultiSlice (SMS) or 3D encoding are used, two axes, phase encoding (y) and slice/partition (z) directions, become available to spread aliasing. Controlled aliasing in parallel imaging (CAIPI) improves on this by introducing slice-shifting in SMS and staggered sampling in 3D encoding to further push the distance between aliasing voxels. (B) In wave-CAIPI, the conventionally "fully-sampled" readout (x) direction can be used to spread aliasing in addition to the y- and z-axes, thus better harness the degrees of freedom in receive arrays in all three dimensions.

applicable to both 3D (Breuer et al., 2006) and SMS encoding (Breuer et al., 2005). In 3D imaging, this is achieved by altering the sampling pattern in the 2D phase encoding plane, which changes the aliasing pattern of the collapsing voxels in image space (Fig. 9.4A, right). This is particularly helpful for uniformly distributing the total acceleration factor across the 2D phase encoding axes. For instance, at $R_{total} = 8$, standard 2D sampling would be constrained to distribute aliasing either as $R_y \times R_z = 4 \times 2$ or 2×4. The high R = 4-fold acceleration in one of the axes would lead to a high g-factor penalty. Instead, with CAIPI, this can be distributed more evenly (i.e., $\sim\sqrt{8}$) by staggering the sampling pattern using Δk_y or Δk_z gradient blips.

Application of the CAIPI concept to SMS encoding is slightly more involved. In spin-warp imaging where k-space is acquired line-by-line, controlled aliasing can be achieved by modulating the phase of the MB RF pulse (Breuer et al., 2005). This permits shifting the aliasing slices with respect to each other in the phase encoding direction, thus increasing the distance between aliasing voxels (Fig. 9.4A, middle). In an $MB = 2$ experiment, the phase of the RF pulse exciting one of the slices can be alternated between 0 and π radians across successive phase encoding lines. This creates a phase ramp in k-space and causes an FOV/2 shift in image space in the y-direction. Such phase modulation ideas can be generalized to higher MB cases. For EPI readouts, it is not possible to alternate the phase of the RF pulse between k-space lines since there is only a single RF per entire k-space. In these cases, blipped-CAIPI (Setsompop et al., 2012) can be utilized. Instead of RF phase modulation, FOV shifting is made possible by playing G_z gradient blips across k-space lines. G_z blips create a linearly varying phase deposition in the slice axis, whose amplitude can be adjusted to provide the desired FOV shift in the target slice positions. Application of SMS in EPI has been impactful, as it has allowed rapid diffusion and functional imaging acquisitions and has been popularized by the Human Connectome Project (Setsompop et al., 2013; Sotiropoulos et al., 2013).

It is possible to push the CAIPI idea further by also utilizing the conventionally fully sampled readout axis to spread aliasing. Zigzag GRAPPA achieves this by playing rapidly oscillating gradients on the G_y gradient during the readout (Breuer et al., 2008). As the name implies, this leads to a zigzag trajectory in k-space, which spreads the aliasing in x- as well as y-axes and improves acceleration capability. The reconstruction is performed using multiple GRAPPA kernels that conform to the shape of the non-Cartesian trajectory. In Bunched Phase Encoding (BPE), signal processing concepts were introduced to reconstruct such zigzag sampled data without the need for sensitivity encoding (Moriguchi and Duerk, 2006). Wave-CAIPI is a generalization of zigzag GRAPPA and BPE, where oscillating gradients are played on both G_y and G_z gradients (Bilgic et al., 2015). Using a sine on, e.g., G_y and cosine waveform on G_z gradients creates a "corkscrew" trajectory in k-space. Different from the preceding methods, wave-CAIPI represents this non-Cartesian trajectory as a convolution with a point spread function (PSF) so that a fully Cartesian reconstruction becomes possible (Fig. 9.4B). This PSF formalism also helps explain the g-factor benefit of playing sinusoidal waveforms: taking an inverse DFT of the non-Cartesian data leads to image-space picture (Fig. 9.4B, right) where voxels are spread out in the readout direction. The amount of this spreading is a function of the y-position, e.g., there is little spreading in the middle of the FOV, but this increases toward the edge of the object. This way, aliasing voxels are pushed further apart from each other in the x-direction, in addition to the y- and z-axes that are exploited through standard controlled aliasing.

Controlled aliasing can be applied in other non-Cartesian trajectories as well. In radial-CAIPI, RF phase modulation is performed across radial k-space lines. In an $MB = 2$ experiment, alternating the phase between 0 and π radians in one of the slices largely cancels out the aliasing signal contributions from this slice (Yutzy et al., 2011). This permits separating out the two slices even without the aid of sensitivity encoding and renders total acceleration rates of $R_{total} = 10$ or higher feasible using a 12ch array. Blipped-spiral trajectory is another powerful way to spread aliasing across three spatial axes (Zahneisen et al., 2014). Generalizing blipped-CAIPI to spiral imaging permits distributing MB acceleration across slice, as well as between k_x and k_y axes. Further, it is possible to rotate the interleaves in the k_x-k_y plane across different k_z partitions during 3D stack-of-spirals acquisitions, thus exploiting another degree of freedom to introduce complementary sampling for rapid imaging (Deng et al., 2016).

9.4 Model-based reconstruction for parallel imaging

Image reconstruction in PI involves inverting the forward system model expressed in Eq. 9.2. For relatively limited R, traditional PI methods such as SENSE or GRAPPA can offer satisfactory reconstruction performance. However, the inverse problem becomes heavily ill-conditioned due to the reduced number of measurements at higher R (Pruessmann et al., 1999). This results in heavy residual artifacts and/or noise amplification in reconstructed images. To improve conditioning, prior knowledge on the distribution of MRI data can be incorporated to constrain the solution set of the reconstruction problem. This is commonly achieved by augmenting the inverse problem based on the system model with a regularization term. For image-domain reconstructions such as SENSE, the modified optimization problem can be expressed as

$$\boldsymbol{\rho}^* = \text{argmin}_{\boldsymbol{\rho}} \sum_i \|A_i\boldsymbol{\rho} - y_i\|_2^2 + \lambda_r R(\boldsymbol{\rho}), \tag{9.13}$$

where $\boldsymbol{\rho}$ is the MR image, y_i are k-space data for the ith coil, $A_i = \text{DFC}_i$ is the system matrix component for the ith coil, $R(.)$ is the regularization function, and λ_r is the regularization weight. For k-space reconstructions such as SPIRiT, the regularized reconstruction is instead expressed as follows:

$$s^* = \text{argmin}_s \sum_i \|Ds_i - y_i\|_2^2 + \lambda_1 \|(G - I)s\|_2^2 + \lambda_r R(s), \tag{9.14}$$

where y_i are acquired k-space data for the ith coil and s is the aggregated k-space data across all coils. Differing in terms of their assumptions regarding the data distribution, main-stream regularization functions used in parallel MRI reconstruction include smoothness (Lustig and Pauly, 2010), sparsity (Murphy et al., 2012), low-rank (Haldar and Zhuo, 2016), and recently deep priors (Hammernik et al., 2017). These fundamental approaches to regularized reconstruction are detailed below.

9.4.1 Smoothness priors

The spectrum of MR images rapidly decay from low- toward high-spatial frequencies in k-space. A corollary is that tissue signals show relatively gradual spatial variation in MR images. Furthermore, bodily organs typically contain tissue blocks with relatively uniform signal levels. As such, a traditional approach to separate tissue signals from white noise in MRI has been incorporation of smoothness priors either in image domain or k-space (Lustig et al., 2007). Common regularization functions include total-variation (TV) norm (i.e., l1-norm of the gradient) and l2-norm:

$$R(\rho) = \|\nabla\rho\|_1 \text{ or } R(s) = \|s\|_2^2. \tag{9.15}$$

Smoothness priors allow separation of additive white noise from gradually varying tissue signals in MR images. However, excessive regularization leads to spatial blurring or block artifacts in reconstructions.

9.4.2 Sparsity priors

MR images are considered to have sparse representations in known linear transform domains such as wavelet transform, where they can be represented with much fewer coefficients than would be required in image domain (Murphy et al., 2012). In turn, compressed sensing theory dictates that it should be possible to recover MR images from randomly undersampled acquisitions by enforcing a sparsity prior (Lustig et al., 2007). Although theoretically motivated, random undersampling in k-space yields low SNR efficiency due to the inhomogeneous distribution of energy across the spectrum of MR images. In practice, random undersampling with a variable density across k-space to mimic the image spectrum enhances measurement efficiency while still generating spatially incoherent artifacts in the image domain. Afterward, the sparsity prior can be incorporated to the reconstructions via an l1-norm term:

$$R(\rho) = \|\Phi\{\rho\}\|_1 \text{ or } R(s) = \|\Phi\{F^{-1}s\}\|_1, \tag{9.16}$$

where Φ stands for the transform domain where the images have sparse representations, e.g., wavelet transform. Sparsity priors coupled with random sampling can allow separation of incoherent aliasing artifacts from tissue signals. However, excessive regularization typically leads to loss of detailed, small image features in reconstructions.

9.4.3 Low-rank priors

Multicoil MR images reflect multiplicative modulation of the underlying MR image with sensitivities of individual coils. Multiplication via broad coil sensitivities in the image domain corresponds to convolution with relatively compact kernels in k-space. As such, k-space samples from multiple coils can be cast in the form of a matrix with block Hankel structure, inherently possessing low rank (Haldar and Zhuo, 2016; Shin et al., 2014). Recovery of missing k-space samples in undersampled acquisitions is then equivalent to recovering missing entries in the matrix via structured low-rank matrix completion. This completion can be achieved by enforcing the matrix to have low rank. Thus, low-rank priors can be incorporated via a regularization term

$$R(s) = \sum_i \sigma_i^2(H(s)) \text{ such that rank } (H) \leq r, \tag{9.17}$$

where H is the structured low-rank matrix, σ_i is the ith singular value of H, and r denotes the upper bound for matrix rank. Structured low-rank matrix completion has dualities to smoothness or sparsity priors, so prescribing excessively low r values during recovery can cause loss of image features during reconstruction.

9.4.4 Deep priors

Smoothness, sparsity, or low-rank priors commonly involve hand-constructed regularization terms that rely on certain assumptions regarding the MR image distribution. When these assumptions diverge from the properties of the actual data distribution, they can introduce undesirable reconstruction biases and suboptimal performance. To surmount this difficult challenge, recent studies have adopted deep learning models for constructing priors for MRI reconstruction. Given a training set of undersampled and corresponding fully sampled acquisitions, a neural network can learn an indirect prior to suppress aliasing artifacts encountered in examples of training data (Dar et al., 2020). To do this, the network can be trained via solving a regularized optimization problem

$$w^* = \text{argmin}_w \sum_i \|A_i N_w\{\rho_u\} - y_i\|_2^2 + \lambda_r \|N_w\{\rho_u\} - \rho_o\|_1, \tag{9.18}$$

where N_w is the network mapping with parameters w, ρ_u are MR images obtained via Fourier reconstruction of undersampled acquisitions, and ρ_o are ground-truth MR images based on fully sampled acquisitions. The data-consistency term based on the forward system model can also be incorporated into the network architecture via unrolling based on estimated coil sensitivities (Hammernik et al., 2017), or end-to-end estimation of coil sensitivity and the MR image can be performed (Shin et al., 2014). Afterward, the trained network can unalias Fourier reconstructions of undersampled acquisitions (Fig. 9.5).

Alternatively, a network can learn a direct prior that captures the distribution of MR data to constrain the set of reconstructions to high-quality images. The high-quality MRI prior can be trained using either fully sampled auto-calibration data in undersampled acquisitions, or else trained using MR images derived from fully sampled acquisitions (Korkmaz et al., 2022). Reconstructions based on direct

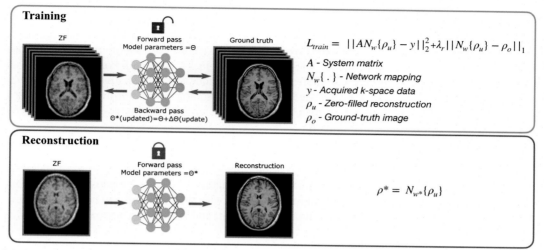

FIG. 9.5

Given a training set of undersampled and corresponding fully sampled acquisitions, a neural network can learn an indirect prior to suppress aliasing artifacts encountered in examples of training data. To do this, the network can be trained via solving a regularized optimization problem that weights a data-consistency loss based on the forward system model against a pixel-wise loss between the network output and the ground truth image. Afterward, the trained network can de-alias Fourier reconstructions of undersampled acquisitions.

MRI priors involve an iterative inference procedure to minimize the data-consistency loss on acquired k-space samples:

$$w^*, \rho^* = \mathrm{argmin}_w \sum_i \|A_i N_w \{\rho_u\} - y_i\|_2^2, \text{where } \rho^* = N_{w*}\{\rho_u\}. \tag{9.19}$$

Building a network model requires prolonged training procedures on a large array of training data. Yet, reconstructions based on deep priors typically offer higher performance than those based on hand-constructed priors as they can learn from and adapt to data flexibly, and they often offer faster inference.

9.5 Estimation of coil sensitivities

Coil sensitivity profiles determine the spatial encoding capabilities introduced by coil arrays over gradient-based encoding. Accordingly, coil sensitivities must be known to set up the forward system model in image-domain methods such as SENSE. While coil sensitivities are not explicitly derived in k-space methods, they are still implicitly embedded in k-space interpolation kernels due to the duality between image and Fourier domains. Therefore, regardless of the reconstruction domain, PI reconstructions must be informed regarding coil sensitivities to leverage coil-driven spatial encoding. In this section, we overview common approaches for the estimation of coil sensitivities including external calibration methods, auto-calibration methods, joint sensitivity estimation and reconstruction methods, and calibrationless methods.

9.5.1 **External calibration**

A straightforward approach for coil sensitivity estimation is to perform external calibration measurements (Pruessmann et al., 1999). This method requires access to a body coil that offers a homogeneous sensitivity profile over the imaged volume. UHF systems often lack a body coil. For such magnets, an alternative is to operate the coil array of interest in birdcage mode to attain relatively uniform sensitivity across the field-of-view. Images collected with spatially homogeneous sensitivity are taken as a reference, and coil sensitivity profiles can then be estimated by normalizing images collected with the coil array by the reference image (Fig. 9.6A)

$$C_i = \rho_i / \rho_{ref}, \tag{9.20}$$

where ρ_{ref} denotes the reference image and ρ_i is the image for the ith element in the coil array. External calibration is a powerful approach that allows estimation of absolute sensitivity information. However, inadvertent movement in between measurements with the body coil and coil array, or any drifts in coil sensitivities between the calibration measurements and the actual scans, can cause errors in sensitivity estimates.

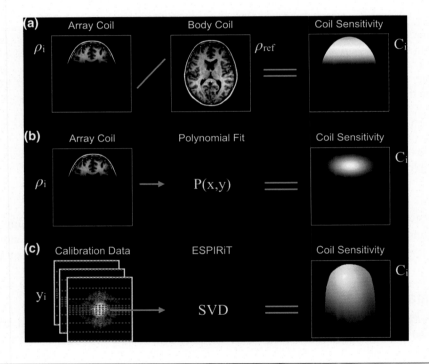

FIG. 9.6

Common methods for coil sensitivity estimation. (A) External calibration method. Images acquired with the coil array of interest are normalized by a reference image acquired separately via a body coil with homogeneous sensitivity. (B) Assuming that coil sensitivity should show gradual spatial variation, a low-order polynomial is fit to individual coil images. (C) Calibration data aggregated across coils are subjected to a singular value decomposition to estimate coil sensitivity profiles.

Indeed, the acquisition of high-quality external calibration data plays an important role for robust echo planar imaging (EPI) reconstruction. For high-resolution whole-brain EPI data often acquired at UHF, reference scans can be lengthy (10 s or longer), which increases the vulnerability to subject motion as well as B_0 changes due to respiration. Since B_0 fluctuations scale with the field strength, it is crucial to perform calibration scans robust to physiologic variations. Standard calibration scans rely on multishot EPI readouts, which obtain "fully-sampled" reference data when their k-space is averaged across multiple shots. These standard reference scans run through all the slices to cover the imaging FOV for the first shot, then proceed to acquire all the slices for the second shot. As such, when the multishot data are combined, each slice receives contributions from several seconds of scan time. An alternative, motion-robust calibration approach is the fast low-angle excitation echo-planar technique (FLEET) method (Polimeni et al., 2016). In FLEET, all shots belonging to slice 1 are acquired first, then all shots for the next slice position are sampled. By this way, each slice's k-space data are subject to a much shorter acquisition time frame of 100–200 ms, thereby significantly boosting the robustness of such external calibration scans.

9.5.2 Auto-calibration

To mitigate the need to perform separate calibration measurements, coil sensitivities can instead be estimated based on the very data subject to PI reconstruction. For image-domain methods that require explicit sensitivity estimates, polynomial fitting can be used. Coil sensitivity profiles reflect the receive B_1 field expected to vary gradually across space, so they predominantly contain low-spatial-frequency components. In turn, a limited degree polynomial can be fit to individual coil images to capture gradual intensity modulations due to coil sensitivities (Fig. 9.6B)

$$P(x,y) = \sum_{k=0}^{n} \alpha_k \cdot x^q \cdot y^r, \text{ such that } (q + r) \leq k, \tag{9.21}$$

where P denotes a polynomial over two spatial dimensions (x,y) of degree n and α_k denotes the scaling factor of the kth term in the polynomial fit. Since polynomial fitting can be cast as a linearized regression problem, the solution can be obtained via least-squares minimization (Pruessmann et al., 1999)

$$C_i = \text{argmin}_\alpha \| P(x,y) - \rho_i(x,y) \|_2^2. \tag{9.22}$$

An alternative approach is the ESPIRiT method that estimates coil sensitivity via an eigenvalue problem expressed using fully sampled calibration data at the center of k-space (Uecker et al., 2014). Aggregating auto-calibration data across coils into a calibration matrix, ESPIRiT observes that this matrix has a nonempty null space and calibration data that lie entirely in the row space of the calibration matrix. Since these fundamental observations should also hold for other k-space regions outside the auto-calibration region, aggregated k-space data in remaining regions should be consistent with calibration data. Assuming that linear relationships between k-space patches across coils are characterized with a reconstruction operator W, consistency to calibration data can be expressed as

$$Ws = s, \tag{9.23}$$

where s denotes k-space data. Substituting the forward system model in Eq. 9.23, we get

$$WFC\rho = FC\rho, \tag{9.24A}$$

$$(F^{-1}WF)C\rho = C\rho. \tag{9.24B}$$

It follows from Eq. 9.24B that coil sensitivities are an eigenvector of $(F^{-1}WF)$ and thereby W with an eigenvalue of 1. Thus, coil sensitivities that form a basis for the row space can be derived based on eigendecomposition of W (Fig. 9.6C).

9.5.3 Joint sensitivity estimation and reconstruction

Both external and auto-calibration methods perform a priori estimation of coil sensitivities, and the derived estimates are then used as fixed variables in the forward system model during PI reconstruction. Therefore, any estimation errors for coil sensitivities will translate into reconstruction errors due to inaccuracies in the forward system model. To help mitigate errors in sensitivity estimation, a joint optimization problem can be solved instead that simultaneously estimates coil sensitivities along with the reconstructed image. For image-domain methods, this can be achieved by modifying the problem formulation in Eq. 9.13 as

$$\rho^*, C^* = \text{argmin}_{\rho,C} \sum_i \|\text{DFC}_i\rho - y_i\|_2^2 + \lambda_r R(\rho). \tag{9.25}$$

Meanwhile, for k-space methods, the modified problem formulation is

$$s^*, G^* = \text{argmin}_{s,G} \sum_i \|Ds_i - y_i\|_2^2 + \lambda_1 \|(G - I)s\|_2^2 + \lambda_r R(s), \tag{9.26}$$

where G is the k-space interpolation operator that is to be estimated. Optimization over two distinct sets of variables can be performed via alternating minimization approaches.

9.5.4 Calibrationless reconstruction

Acquiring fully sampled k-space lines is common in PI applications as it enables either explicit estimation of coil sensitivities or implicit sensitivity estimation in the form of interpolation kernels in k-space. However, in certain cases, it may be impractical to perform Nyquist sampling within a dedicated k-space region such as time-interleaved k-space sampling, or imaging at very high acceleration rates. In such cases, performing PI reconstruction in the absence of calibration data can be attempted via calibrationless approaches such as P-LORAKS or SAKE (Haldar and Zhuo, 2016; Shin et al., 2014). Observing that k-space samples from multiple coils should form a system matrix with block Hankel structure, reconstruction is formulated as a structured low-rank matrix completion problem. In this framework, enforcing low rank in the Hankel matrix implicitly enables estimation of missing k-space entries in the matrix, without the need for explicit estimates of coil sensitivities or interpolation kernels. For instance, a k-space reconstruction can be implemented as

$$s^* = \text{argmin}_s \sum_i \|Ds_i - y_i\|_2^2 + \lambda_r \sum_n \sigma_n^{\ 2}(H(s)) \text{ such that rank } (H) \leq r, \tag{9.27}$$

where H is the structured low-rank matrix, σ_n is the nth singular value of H, and r denotes the upper bound for matrix rank.

9.6 Coil sensitivity profiles vary more rapidly across space at UHF, thereby improving g-factor performance

As coil sensitivity profiles become more localized and spatially varying at higher field strengths, it is expected that similar coil geometries will have better g-factor performance at UHF. This expectation

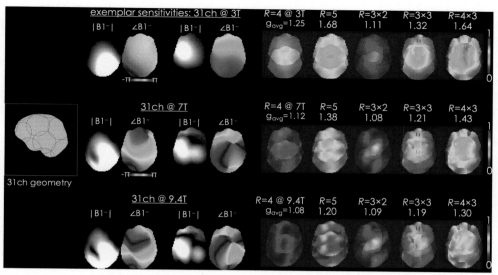

FIG 9.7

(Top) Exemplar magnitude and phase coil sensitivities for two channels out of a 31ch numerical simulation are depicted. 1/g-factor maps report results from 1-dimensional undersampling (at $R = 4$ and 5) as well as 2-dimensional CAIPI reconstructions (at $R = 3 \times 2$, 3×3 and 4×3). *(Middle)* Going to 7T, coil sensitivity profiles become more spatially varying, and "singularities/fringe lines" become visible in the phase of the sensitivity maps. G-factor performance improves over 3T. *(Bottom)* At 9.4T, coil profiles are yet more rapidly varying and this leads to further gains in g-factor. For instance, $R = 4 \times 3$ acceleration at 9.4T has slightly better performance as the $R = 3 \times 3$ case at 3T. This is also true for $R = 5$ at 9.4T, compared to the reconstruction at $R = 4$-fold acceleration at 3T.

has been demonstrated through numerical simulations (Wiesinger et al., 2004a) and experimental data (Wiesinger et al., 2004b). We have used the MARIE electromagnetic simulation toolbox (Villena et al., 2016) to explore the field strength dependence of g-factor performance across 3T, 7T, and 9.4T using the same 31ch coil geometry in Fig. 9.7. Noise covariance was taken to be identity ($\mathbf{\Psi} = I$). As demonstrated in the exemplar profiles, both phase and magnitude of coil sensitivities become more spatially varying toward higher fields. This is reflected in the g-factor performance, where SENSE at UHF clearly outperformed 3T reconstructions. For example, the average g-factor at 9.4T using $R = 4 \times 3$ acceleration was better than that of the 3T g-factor at the lower $R = 3 \times 3$-fold rate. The ability to support higher undersampling factors is complemented by the SNR increase at higher field strengths, which should more than compensate for the increased $\sqrt{R}$ intrinsic SNR penalty and render such acceleration factors feasible at submillimeter resolutions. An active research field is the development of very dense coil arrays at UHF. The construction of 64ch (Uğurbil et al., 2019) and 128ch head arrays (Gruber et al., 2021) increased the PI capability well beyond the commercially available 32ch UHF coils, whereas simulations of 256ch designs helped underline the potential of massively parallel arrays in pushing the acceleration factors even further (Hendriks et al., 2019).

9.7 Exemplar applications enabled by the increased encoding power of UHF systems

Going to higher fields provides two complementary benefits for efficient image encoding. As detailed in the previous section, coil sensitivity profiles are more localized at UHF, thus permitting higher acceleration factors to be achieved. Additionally, the SNR boost provided by higher field strengths renders such high acceleration factors practical. For instance, wave-CAIPI readily permits $R = 3 \times 3$-fold acceleration with negligible g-factor penalties (Polak et al., 2018), yet the impact of the intrinsic $\sqrt{R}$ penalty on SNR causes the images to be relatively noisy for routine practical use at 3T. As such, with the advent of advanced parallel imaging strategies, we have become SNR limited, rather than encoding limited, especially for high-resolution ($\sim$1 mm isotropic) data at 3T or lower field strengths. While regularization techniques can help boost the SNR, going to UHF directly makes such acceleration factors practical and impactful. An example to this is the wave-encoded MPRAGE acquisition at 1 mm isotropic resolution in Fig. 9.8A, which was completed in under a minute with near-perfect g-factor

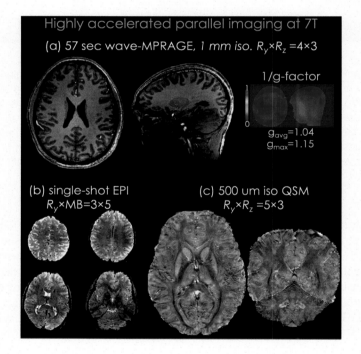

FIG. 9.8

(A) A 57-s, 1-mm isotropic MPRAGE acquisition with adequate SNR became possible at $R = 4 \times 3$-fold acceleration using wave encoding by capitalizing on the SNR gain of 7T imaging. (B) Single-shot EPI with SMS encoding at $R_y \times MB = 3 \times 5$-fold acceleration yielded high-quality gradient echo data for functional imaging studies. (C) The superlinear boost of UHF gradient echo imaging permits trading off SNR for resolution, in this case permitting a 500 μm isotropic QSM acquisition at $R = 5 \times 3$-fold acceleration using wave encoding. All acquisitions were made using a 31ch head receiver array.

performance. Such a rapid acquisition at $R = 4 \times 3$-fold acceleration would have been too noisy at 3T when using a standard wave-CAIPI reconstruction.

There is a superlinear relation between the SNR and the field strength for gradient echo (GRE) imaging, e.g., going from 3T to 7T provides a $\sim$3.1-fold SNR boost instead of the expected $\sim$2.3-fold (Pohmann et al., 2016). This makes highly accelerated, high-resolution GRE acquisitions extremely favorable at UHF. Fig 9.8 provides two important example applications. In Fig. 9.8B, whole-brain single-shot EPI with high-quality reconstructions became possible at $R_y \times MB = 3 \times 5$ acceleration, thus providing high temporal resolution and high geometric fidelity simultaneously for functional imaging applications. In Fig. 9.8C, the superlinear SNR gain is traded off for spatial resolution in an $R_y \times R_z = 5 \times 3$-fold accelerated wave-GRE acquisition at 500 μm isotropic resolution. This permitted quantitative susceptibility mapping (QSM) reconstruction from a $\sim$20 min scan where three acquisitions were made with different head orientations relative to the main magnetic field. Combination of the mesoscale resolution and susceptibility contrast mechanism revealed exquisite contrast in the cortex and deep gray matter (axial) as well as in the cerebellum (coronal view).

Acknowledgments

We would like to thank Drs Jason Stockmann and Jonathan Polimeni for their insight and help with figures and coil sensitivity simulations across field strengths.

References

Bilgic, B., Gagoski, B.A., Cauley, S.F., et al., 2015. Wave-CAIPI for highly accelerated 3D imaging. Magn. Reson. Med. 73, 2152–2162.

Blaimer, M., Breuer, F.A., Mueller, M., et al., 2006. 2D-GRAPPA-operator for faster 3D parallel MRI. Magn. Reson. Med. 56, 1359–1364. https://doi.org/10.1002/mrm.21071.

Breuer, F.A., Blaimer, M., Heidemann, R.M., Mueller, M.F., Griswold, M.A., Jakob, P.M., 2005. Controlled aliasing in parallel imaging results in higher acceleration (CAIPIRINHA) for multi-slice imaging. Magn. Reson. Med. 53, 684–691.

Breuer, F.A., Blaimer, M., Mueller, M.F., et al., 2006. Controlled aliasing in volumetric parallel imaging (2D CAIPIRINHA). Magn. Reson. Med. 55, 549–556.

Breuer, F.A., Kannengiesser, S.A.R., Blaimer, M., Seiberlich, N., Jakob, P.M., Griswold, M.A., 2009. General formulation for quantitative G-factor calculation in GRAPPA reconstructions. Magn. Reson. Med. 62, 739–746. https://doi.org/10.1002/mrm.22066.

Breuer, F.A., Moriguchi, H., Seiberlich, N., et al., 2008. Zigzag sampling for improved parallel imaging. Magn. Reson. Med. 60, 474–478.

Dar, S.U.H., Özbey, M., Çatlı, A.B., Çukur, T., 2020. A transfer-learning approach for accelerated MRI using deep neural networks. Magn. Reson. Med. 84, 663–685

Deng, W., Zahneisen, B., Andrew, S.V., 2016. Rotated stack-of-spirals partial acquisition for rapid volumetric parallel MRI. Magn. Reson. Med. 76, 127–135. https://doi.org/10.1002/mrm.25863.

Feinberg, D.A., Moeller, S., Smith, S.M., et al., 2011. Correction: multiplexed echo planar imaging for sub-second whole brain FMRI and fast diffusion imaging. PLoS One 6. https://doi.org/10.1371/annotation/d9496d01-8c5d-4d24-8287-94449ada5064.

Griswold, M.A., Jakob, P.M., Heidemann, R.M., et al., 2002. Generalized autocalibrating partially parallel acquisitions (GRAPPA). Magn. Reson. Med. 47, 1202–1210.

Gruber, B., Stockmann, J., Mareyam, A., et al., 2021. A 128-channel head coil array for cortical imaging at 7 tesla. In: Proceedings of the 2021 ISMRM & SMRT Virtual Conference & Exhibition, p. 176.

Haldar, J.P., Zhuo, J., 2016. P-LORAKS: low-rank modeling of local k-space neighborhoods with parallel imaging data. Magn. Reson. Med. 2016 (75), 1499.

Hammernik, K., Klatzer, T., Kobler, E., et al., 2017. Learning a Variational network for reconstruction of accelerated MRI data. Magn. Reson. Med. 79, 3055–3071.

Hendriks, A.D., Luijten, P.R., Klomp, D.W.J., Petridou, N., 2019. Potential acceleration performance of a 256-channel whole-brain receive array at 7 T. Magn. Reson. Med. 81, 1659–1670.

Korkmaz, Y., Dar, S.U.H., Yurt, M., Özbey, M., Çukur, T., 2022. Unsupervised MRI reconstruction via zero-shot learned adversarial transformers. IEEE Trans. Med. Imaging 41, 1747–1763.

Larkman, D.J., Hajnal, J.V., Herlihy, A.H., Coutts, G.A., Young, I.R., Ehnholm, G., 2001. Use of multicoil arrays for separation of signal from multiple slices simultaneously excited. J. Magn. Reson. Imaging 13, 313–317.

Lustig, M., Donoho, D., Pauly, J.M., 2007. Sparse MRI: the application of compressed sensing for rapid MR imaging. Magn. Reson. Med. 58, 1182–1195.

Lustig, M., Pauly, J.M., 2010. SPIRiT: iterative self-consistent parallel imaging reconstruction from arbitrary k-space. Magn. Reson. Med. 64, 457–471.

Moeller, S., Yacoub, E., Olman, C.A., et al., 2010. Multiband multislice GE-EPI at 7 tesla, with 16-fold acceleration using partial parallel imaging with application to high spatial and temporal whole-brain fMRI. Magn. Reson. Med. 63, 1144–1153. https://doi.org/10.1002/mrm.22361.

Moriguchi, H., Duerk, J.L., 2006. Bunched phase encoding (BPE): a new fast data acquisition method in MRI. Magn. Reson. Med. 55, 633–648.

Murphy, M., Alley, M., Demmel, J., Keutzer, K., Vasanawala, S., Lustig, M., 2012. Fast l1-SPIRiT compressed sensing parallel imaging MRI: scalable parallel implementation and clinically feasible runtime. IEEE Trans. Med. Imaging 31, 1250–1262.

Nunes, R.G., Hajnal, J.V., Golay, X., Larkman, D.J., 2006. Simultaneous slice excitation and reconstruction for single shot EPI. Proc. Int. Soc. Magn. Reson. Med. 14, 293.

Pohmann, R., Speck, O., Scheffler, K., 2016. Signal-to-noise ratio and MR tissue parameters in human brain imaging at 3, 7, and 9.4 tesla using current receive coil arrays. Magn. Reson. Med. 75, 801–809.

Polak, D., Setsompop, K., Cauley, S.F., et al., 2018. Wave-CAIPI for highly accelerated MP-RAGE imaging. Magn. Reson. Med. 79, 401–406.

Polimeni, J.R., Bhat, H., Witzel, T., et al., 2016. Reducing sensitivity losses due to respiration and motion in accelerated echo planar imaging by reordering the autocalibration data acquisition. Magn. Reson. Med. 75 (2), 665–679.

Pruessmann, K.P., Weiger, M., Scheidegger, M.B., Boesiger, P., 1999. SENSE: sensitivity encoding for fast MRI. Magn. Reson. Med. 42, 952–962.

Robson, P.M., Grant, A.K., Madhuranthakam, A.J., Lattanzi, R., Sodickson, D.K., McKenzie, C.A., 2008. Comprehensive quantification of signal-to-noise ratio and g-factor for image-based and k-space-based parallel imaging reconstructions. Magn. Reson. Med. 60, 895–907.

Setsompop, K., Gagoski, B.A., Polimeni, J.R., Witzel, T., Wedeen, V.J., Wald, L.L., 2012. Blipped-controlled aliasing in parallel imaging for simultaneous multislice echo planar imaging with reduced g-factor penalty. Magn. Reson. Med. 67, 1210–1224.

Setsompop, K., Kimmlingen, R., Eberlein, E., et al., 2013. Pushing the limits of in vivo diffusion MRI for the human connectome project. NeuroImage 80, 220–233.

Shin, P.J., Larson, P.E.Z., Ohliger, M.A., et al., 2014. Calibrationless parallel imaging reconstruction based on structured low-rank matrix completion. Magn. Reson. Med. 72, 959–970.

Sodickson, D.K., Manning, W.J., 1997. Simultaneous acquisition of spatial harmonics (SMASH): fast imaging with radiofrequency coil arrays. Magn. Reson. Med. 38, 591–603. https://doi.org/10.1002/mrm.1910380414.

Sotiropoulos, S.N., Jbabdi, S., Xu, J., et al., 2013. Advances in diffusion MRI acquisition and processing in the human connectome project. NeuroImage 80, 125–143.

Uecker, M., Lai, P., Murphy, M.J., et al., 2014. ESPIRiT-an eigenvalue approach to autocalibrating parallel MRI: where SENSE meets GRAPPA. Magn. Reson. Med. 71, 990–1001.

Uğurbil, K., Auerbach, E., Moeller, S., et al., 2019. Brain imaging with improved acceleration and SNR at 7 tesla obtained with 64-channel receive array. Magn. Reson. Med. 82, 495–509.

Villena, J.F., Polimeridis, A.G., Eryaman, Y., et al., 2016. Fast electromagnetic analysis of MRI transmit RF coils based on accelerated integral equation methods. IEEE Trans. Biomed. Eng. 63, 2250–2261.

Weiger, M., Pruessmann, K.P., Boesiger, P., 2002. 2D SENSE for faster 3D MRI. MAGMA 14, 10–19.

Wiesinger, F., Boesiger, P., Pruessmann, K.P., 2004a. Electrodynamics and ultimate SNR in parallel MR imaging. Magn. Reson. Med. 52, 376–390.

Wiesinger, F., Van de Moortele, P.-F., Adriany, G., De Zanche, N., Ugurbil, K., Pruessmann, K.P., 2004b. Parallel imaging performance as a function of field strength—an experimental investigation using electrodynamic scaling. Magn. Reson. Med. 52, 953–964.

Yutzy, S.R., Seiberlich, N., Duerk, J.L., Griswold, M.A., 2011. Improvements in multislice parallel imaging using radial CAIPIRINHA. Magn. Reson. Med. 65, 1630–1637.

Zahneisen, B., Ernst, T., Poser, B.A., 2015. SENSE and simultaneous multislice imaging. Magn. Reson. Med. 74, 1356–1362.

Zahneisen, B., Poser, B.A., Ernst, T., Stenger, A.V., 2014. Simultaneous Multi-Slice fMRI using spiral trajectories. NeuroImage 92, 8–18.

Motion correction

Vincent Oltman Boer

*Center for Functional and Diagnostic Imaging and Research, Danish Research Centre for Magnetic Resonance,
Copenhagen University Hospital—Hvidovre and Amager, Hvidovre, Denmark*

Highlights

- Motion correction is an important aspect in MR, especially in high-resolution imaging using long scans, as typically used at ultra-high field.
- Motion correction can be performed during scanning or in reconstruction.
- Many solutions are available for motion tracking, either using external devices (such as cameras), MR-based navigators, or purely data-driven corrections.

10.1 Introduction

Subject motion can be a severe issue for ultra-high field MR and was for example identified as a confounder for use of 7T MR in epilepsy (Opheim et al., 2021). As MR data are collected sequentially to build up a 2D/3D k-space, there is a need for data consistency between k-space lines sampled over the complete scanning time. Motion occurring during data collection causes inconsistencies in the acquired data. After Fourier reconstruction, this can lead to various image artifacts, such as blurring or ghosting, depending on the type of scan and the amount of motion. In clinical practice, subject motion leads to frequent repeat examinations and potential for missed pathologies (Andre et al., 2015).

At ultra-high field, more issues arise. First, there is a desire to use the increased signal-to-noise ratio at ultra-high field for higher-resolution imaging. The higher resolution requires longer scanning times, and consequently, the chance of significant movement occurring during a scan increases. Second, higher-resolution scans are intrinsically sensitive to smaller motion. This puts more stringent requirements on the used motion correction technique and requires more attention for correction of also small motion. Third, the motion correction techniques developed for lower field scanners are typically not directly applicable to ultra-high field. For example, standard ultra-high field RF coil technology obscures the view for some existing optical tracking systems. Also, susceptibility effects are increased at higher field, compromising the use of EPI image navigators for motion correction.

In this chapter, motion correction approaches will be discussed with a specific focus on challenges arising in ultra-high field neuro-applications.

Advances in Magnetic Resonance Technology and Applications. Volume 10. ISSN 2666-9099. https://doi.org/10.1016/B978-0-323-99898-7.00022-5

10.2 Prospective or retrospective motion correction?

The many approaches for MR motion correction can in general be split up in two branches. There are techniques that during data acquisition can correct prospectively for motion. Then there are techniques that after data acquisition attempt to retrospectively correct for motion artifacts in image reconstruction. Prospective approaches have the advantage that the motion artifacts are reduced directly in the acquired data, and after a scan, one can directly judge if the data quality is sufficient or if rescanning is needed. With retrospective techniques, offline processing is typically needed, which, depending on the technique and level of automation, can take a significant amount of time. On the other hand, for prospective correction, the data acquisition needs to be adapted during scanning. This implies that real-time changes to the scan encoding need to be performed based on motion estimates. This requires some changes to the sequence programming, making it more complex to implement widely. Also, prospective techniques can employ data reacquisition, an approach where a real-time decision is made to repeat some part of the data acquisition in case large motion was detected. Retrospective techniques on the other hand can only use data rejection for highly corrupted parts of the data. This leads to gaps in the acquired data which need to be corrected for in the reconstruction pipeline (Federau and Gallichan, 2016).

Both strategies require some methods to estimate the motion trace, so that either the scanner acquisition can be updated or the k-space data can be corrected for the occurred motion. Various techniques exist for motion estimation, but here again two main lines of approach exist. First, various motion-tracking systems that use external hardware to capture the motion of a subject have been used (see Section 10.3). This could be, for example, an optical camera, a miniature motion-tracking device, or other hardware that can be added to the MR system to capture subject motion. These systems typically produce a continuous stream of motion estimates with a high frame rate, which is independent of the MR system and scanning technique. These methods depend on a "calibration" step to convert the collected motion trace to the MR frame of reference. In the second branch of techniques, the MR system itself is used to capture motion by collecting a series of low-resolution navigator scans (see Section 10.4). This can be interleaved with the acquisition of a longer high-resolution scan to provide an interleaved motion trace. This inherently leads to a gapped acquisition with a lower temporal resolution, but the acquired motion trace is already in the correct frame of reference. The interleaving of navigator acquisitions is dependent on available dead-time in a sequence and needs to be optimized for each sequence. Both approaches are described in further detail below.

Spin history effects have to be considered in both prospective and retrospective motion correction. For 3D sequences, this is not so much of an issue as long as all RF pulses are nonselective and affect all magnetization globally. However, for example, in multislice sequences, or any other sequences with spatially selective RF pulses, motion will cause the imaging slice to move into tissue that has a different steady-state magnetization. This effect can lead to undesired signal fluctuations (Muraskin et al., 2013). In prospective correction approaches, this issue can be tackled by reacquisition, where the parts of k-space where large motion occurred can be sampled again after the movement has stopped (White et al., 2010). This leads to an increase in scan time, which varies depending on the amount of motion during the scan. In retrospective correction, this cannot be done, and it is more common to remove, or put a low weighting factor, on the parts of the data set that are most corrupted by motion. Similarly, gaps in k-space can occur after correcting for rotations, where k-space lines are spaced more than the Nyquist sampling criteria. Both effects lead to an uneven sampling in k-space which reduces the quality of the final image. However, ways can be found to minimize their impact, for example, by using parallel imaging techniques to recover missing parts of k-space.

An additional complication is a more indirect effect of motion on the susceptibility distribution in the magnet. Motion of the head (Liu et al., 2018) or arms or even respiration leads to a redistribution of the susceptibility in the magnet, which changes the induced magnetic field. This causes changes in the B_0 field in the head, which can lead to artifacts in B_0-sensitive sequences, such as high-resolution T_2^*-weighted imaging at ultra-high field (Versluis et al., 2010). This can be corrected for prospectively by actively updating the shim fields (Van Gelderen et al., 2007) or retrospectively by correcting the k-space data for B_0 fluctuations (Versluis et al., 2010).

10.3 Motion-tracking systems

The most obvious way to detect motion of the subject is perhaps the placement of an optical camera close to the subject and record the movement for either prospective or retrospective MR data correction.

Apart from that, several other approaches have been proposed for motion tracking with external systems at 7T, including both optical and MR active markers. With these techniques, high temporal frame rates can be reached, but they require installation of additional hardware in the scanner room. Furthermore, most approaches require some kind of marker to be placed on the subject which, depending on the type of marker, can hinder a clinical workflow.

The data collected with motion tracking can be used to correct data retrospectively or prospectively. For a prospective correction, an interface is needed between the external system and the MR system to allow for position updates of the field-of-view during scanning. Typically, the motion updates are then performed once per repetition time or similar.

10.3.1 Optical motion tracking

Many systems for optical motion tracking have been proposed for use with MR. At ultra-high field, this started with stereotactic tracking systems (Fig. 10.1A) using multiple reflecting markers and infra-red LEDs and cameras (Qin et al., 2009), which were later improved to include image processing directly in the bore (Schulz et al., 2012). A potential drawback is the requirement of open RF coils with a free line-of-sight from the camera(s) to the subject markers. Also, care was taken to minimize RF interference between the camera equipment and the MRI. Later, the development of markers including 3D patterns allowed for the use of single markers and cameras (Stucht et al., 2015). Unfortunately, the standard coil for ultra-high field (NOVA Medical Inc., Wilmington, MA, USA) only has a narrow viewing angle on the subject. To this end, a marker on a lever from a bite-bar was proposed in order to have a marker moving with the subject head outside of the RF coil (Fig. 10.1B). Later, development of slimmer cameras and a new marker allowed the placement of the camera inside the RF coil with a marker attached to the subject forehead to track motion (Digiacomo et al., 2020).

A factor in marker-based motion correction is the correlation between motion of the marker and motion of the brain. The approach using a bite bar gives a very rigid link between the skull and the marker but can be uncomfortable and less practical in routine use. On the other hand, an adhesive maker to the forehead improves patient compliance but is less tightly coupled to the motion of the head.

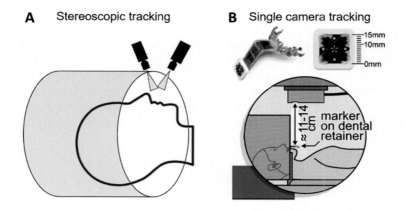

FIG. 10.1

Two examples of optical tracking approaches proposed in the literature for use at ultra-high field. Stereotactic tracking systems (A) can be used with relatively open coils where several cameras have different view angles on the subject and/or markers. Further development led to a single marker and single camera system (B) that can still track 3D motion, but the line-of-sight for the camera system can be obscured by a standard head coil. Here, a dental retainer was used to put the tracker on a lever outside of the coil (Stucht et al., 2015).

A second factor of consideration is the calibration stage, where the coordinate system of the motion-tracking system and marker have to be translated to the magnet and gradient coordinate system (Maclaren et al., 2018). This is typically only needed after installation of the tracking device. Lastly, due to significant image processing times, note should be taken of the delay between the measurement of motion and the time point where the motion update can be performed.

Nevertheless, these tracking approaches have shown very high accuracy motion estimates at a high frame rate and have enabled very high-resolution imaging (Stucht et al., 2015, Mattern et al., 2018).

10.3.2 Motion tracking using NMR markers

To overcome the limitations of optical systems, which require a line-of-sight between the camera and the marker placed on the subject, NMR markers have been investigated for motion tracking. A small NMR-visible sample can be combined with a micro-RF coil to give a very localized signal in the MR system, and this can be used as a motion-tracking marker when attached to the subject. Prospective correction with NMR makers was shown with three gadolinium-doped water markers on a head band (Ooi et al., 2009). To localize the samples in the magnet, the gradient system is used to read the x-, y-, and z position of the sample and hence tracks motion of the maker. Notably, gradient nonlinearity correction might be required for accurate position estimates (Eschelbach et al., 2019).

To minimize interference between the ^{1}H MR imaging and the NMR maker, NMR probes based on ^{19}F were proposed (De Zanche et al., 2008) which were also shown for motion tracking (Haeberlin et al., 2015). The motion tracking of the NMR probes required some modification of the sequence to insert fast readouts to localize the probes; however, later work also showed that the original sequence can even be used to encode the probe position (Aranovitch et al., 2018).

A comparison between optical tracking and tracking using NMR field probes showed that optical systems outperformed the NMR probes on tracking accuracy, but prospective image correction can give similar image quality with both methods (Eschelbach et al., 2019). Notably, the attachment of the field probes to the subject was possible despite the limited space in the receiver array, by taping the probes to the nose bridge and temples of a subject.

An additional advantage of NMR makers is that they can both be used to encode the position of the probe and track the B_0 field offset in the probe. The latter can be used to track, e.g., scanner drift, subject-induced B_0 field changes, or concurrent measurement of the k-space trajectory (Haeberlin et al., 2015). This information can be used for image correction.

10.4 Motion tracking: MR-based tracking

Instead of using external systems for motion tracking, the MR acquisition itself can be used to track motion of the subject. This has the main advantage that no additional hardware or markers are needed, improving patient compliance and ease of use. Also, the acquired motion information is directly in the scanner coordinate system and can be used directly for tracking motion.

10.4.1 Navigator-based motion tracking

The most straightforward way for MR-based tracking is to acquire a series of short low-resolution 3D images interleaved with the acquisition of higher-resolution data, or "host" scan (Tisdall et al., 2012). Most sequences already have significant dead time, for example, in the T_1 recovery period of an MPRAGE scan, so a navigator acquisition can be inserted in the host scan without lengthening the scan (Fig. 10.2). This results in acquisition of one navigator scan after every shot, which has an interval of around 2 s. Therefore, the temporal resolution of this approach is much lower than the external motion-tracking systems. Note that not all sequences have inherent dead time, but typically a host sequence can be adapted to allow for insertion of navigator scans, albeit sometimes at the cost of an increased scan time.

A rigid body registration of the low-resolution navigator scans is performed, resulting in six motion parameters (translation and rotation in x, y, and z) for each time point where a navigator is acquired. The motion parameters can be applied prospectively during scanning or extracted afterward for retrospective data correction. Prospective correction requires a fast, but accurate, online registration, while time constraints in the registration are not relevant for retrospective correction, and more time is available for the registration algorithm. Especially in cases with very large motion, this could be needed, as iterative algorithms take longer to solve for larger motion. On the other hand, recent developments in computer hardware and artificial intelligence might alleviate these computational limits in the very near future.

Also, for prospective correction, the required dead time in the sequence is longer, as not only the data acquisition but also image reconstruction, image registration, and geometry updates need to happen before continuing with the high-resolution scan. Depending on the implementation, this could require a significant amount of time in the sequence (typically a few hundred milliseconds).

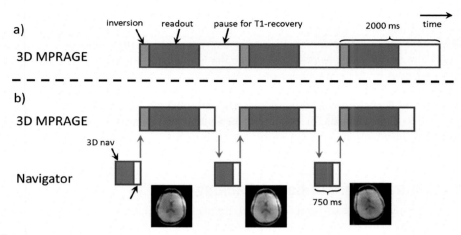

FIG. 10.2

Prospective motion correction using navigators. An MPRAGE sequence (A) typically has a long pause for T_1 recovery of the magnetization (M_z). In (B), it is shown how a 3D navigator scan can be interleaved in this gap of the "host" scan for motion correction, without increasing the total scan time. The inserted block for the navigator consists of data acquisition, image reconstruction, realignment, and a geometry update of the field-of-view of the MPRAGE, and in this example takes 750 ms. A navigator scan is acquired every 2000 ms for updating the geometry of the MPRAGE prospectively.

10.4.2 Reacquisition

Navigator-based motion correction inherently has a low temporal resolution, as the navigators are typically only acquired once every few seconds. This makes the approach "blind" to the motion occurring between subsequent navigators. With small motion, or slow drifting motion, this is not a problem. However, for large motion or fast or erratic motion, the data acquired from the host scan in between the two navigators can be severely corrupted and cannot be corrected with the navigator information. To this end, reacquisition can be employed, where a threshold is put on the allowed motion between two navigators. If the motion exceeds this threshold, the data acquired for the host scan, between the navigators, is recollected. As reacquisition increases the scan time, the threshold is chosen as a balance between reducing image artifacts and increase in scan time when motion occurs. Additionally, one can decide on a maximum allowed amount of reacquisition, or prioritize the center of k-space for reacquisition, as to not prolong the scan excessively when the subject moves a lot.

10.4.3 Navigator sequences

The navigator sequence can be set up in many different ways. 3D volumes, perpendicular 2D scans, or even k-space based navigators have been proposed. The main requirement for a navigator scan is that it is a fast acquisition, as to fit into the available dead time of the host sequence. At the same time, it should deliver an accurate motion estimate, something that can be a complex optimization as most acceleration techniques have a penalty in either image quality (parallel imaging) or introduce image distortions (EPI). On top of this, for prospective correction, data reconstruction should be fast, which complicates the use of time-demanding reconstruction techniques (e.g., compressed sensing) for navigators.

Another consideration when designing navigators concerns the interaction of the navigator with the magnetization pattern for the host scan. Due to added excitation pulses, insertion of a navigator scan interferes with the steady-state magnetization, which can lead to changes in image contrast in the high-resolution scan. To reduce this effect, navigator scans are set up as low flip angle gradient echo scans. Also, EPI is a good approach to reduce the number of excitations and accelerate data acquisition, although geometric distortions at 7T can be high. Care should be taken that, especially with large motion, EPI-induced image distortions do not negatively impact the navigator accuracy. Effect of motion and EPI on the registration quality can be simulated to estimate the impact in motion accuracy (Andersen et al., 2022). Furthermore, parallel imaging can be used to accelerate and reduce the number of excitations, although too high-acceleration factors can introduce image artifacts, and for large motion, the coil sensitivity maps might need updating.

3D fat navigators seem to provide very good overall performance at ultra-high field (Gallichan et al., 2016). Here, the excitation pulse is spectrally selective for fat tissue and only the skull and skin are visible in the images, which also allows for increased parallel imaging factors (Gallichan, 2017). This also fully avoids excitation of brain tissue, and effects on the magnetization of the host scan are minimal. An example of motion correction using fat navigators in an MPRAGE is shown in Fig. 10.3. The combination of fat navigators with single-shot EPI is not recommended due to the short T_2 and large susceptibility effects in the fat tissue around the brain (Andersen et al., 2022).

Notably, the contrast in the navigator scan is also affected by the host scan. For example, in sequence with background signal suppression, like a time-of-flight scan, there is not much signal available from brain tissue for a navigator scan. Also, single-voxel spectroscopy or multislice host scans can leave unexpected patterns in the magnetization that can be visible in a navigator scan and affect the registration. Again, fat-selective navigators can be a solution, as the fat has a short T_1, and the magnetization is restored much faster than the brain tissue.

10.5 Self-navigating sequences

Instead of using external motion-tracking systems, or interleaving low-resolution navigators, some scans allow for self-navigation. One of the best examples of this is the propellor technique (Pipe, 1999). With this approach, the k-space is not sampled in a Cartesian way but rather using rotating blades. In each blade, a number of parallel lines in k-pace are sampled. In this way, each blade contains the central part of k-space, which can be used to reconstruct a low-resolution image. These low-resolution images can be used as navigators and can be aligned. Afterward, the blades can be aligned, and the full image can be reconstructed (Fig. 10.4).

A disadvantage of the propellor technique is that the technique is mainly used to correct in-plane motion, as there is no motion information in the slice direction. Also, the k-space sampling is not Cartesian and requires a more complex reconstruction, although large improvements in that have been shown in the last years.

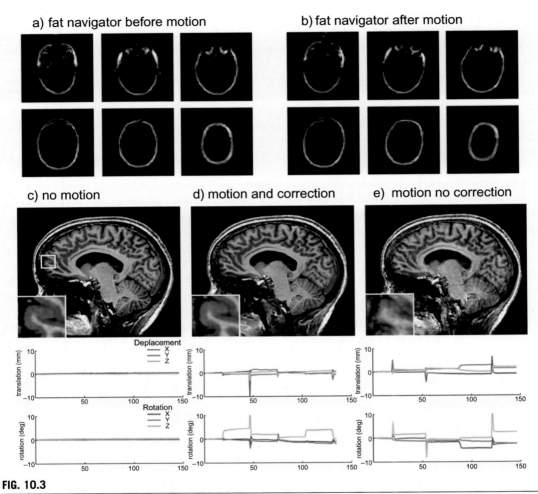

FIG. 10.3

Six axial slices of a 3D fat navigator used at 7T before (A) and after (B) motion. Registration of the navigators provides the rigid body motion estimate. This can be used in, for example, T_1-weighted MPRAGE scans, where image quality is good when no motion occurs (C). Using fat selective navigators, the instructed motion can be tracked and corrected for in the T_1 scan (D). Disabling motion correction during instructed motion (E) still shows the measured motion trace but without correction leads to severe image blurring and artifacts.

10.6 Motion tracking: Data-driven approaches

A final alternative that is discussed here is fully data-driven motion-correction approaches. With these techniques, there is no need for acquisition of additional data. Instead, one can manipulate the k-space data to iteratively find a better outcome, by some image measure. Image entropy is one measure that was proposed in the auto-focusing approach (Atkinson et al., 1997). Here, the k-space lines are

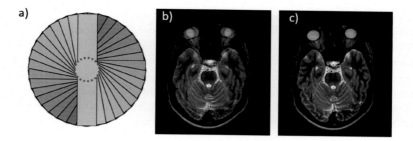

FIG. 10.4

Propellor imaging can be used to reduce motion artifacts. In propellor, the k-space is sampled by rotating blades (A), where every blade collects the center of k-space (in red circle). This can be reconstructed to a low-resolution image for each blade acquisition. These can be aligned to get motion parameters for each blade, which can be corrected for afterward. In the presence of subject motion, the T_2 propellor acquisition is corrupted (B), but after performing motion correction on the blades, data quality can be restored (C).

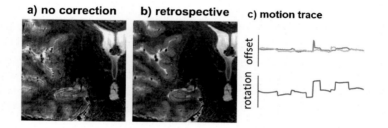

FIG. 10.5

Example of retrospective motion tracking using sensitivity encoding for aligned reconstruction. The image before (A) and after (B) retrospective motion correction shows great improvement. The reconstruction is able to estimate the motion trace (C) from the imaging data directly in a joint optimization. For this 2D scan, the motion estimation was limited to in-plane transformations only.

corrected for translation and rotation parameters. During an iterative optimization process, an algorithm evaluates the image entropy until the best set of translation and rotation parameters are found. As each line in k-space now has six degrees of freedom (translation in $x/y/z$ and rotation in $x/y/z$), this quickly becomes a very large optimization process. For a 128×128 2D image, there are already 768 motion parameters to estimate. And especially at ultra-high field, larger image matrices are used, increasing complexity more. Fortunately, most image quality improvement is made in the center of k-space. Optimization in the outsize of k-space is less critical. Furthermore, grouping k-space segments that have been acquired closely together in time can be used to reduce the number of parameters or constrain them.

Various versions of such data-driven corrections have been proposed, but one promising technique extended this strategy to include parallel imaging, as the coil sensitivity patterns can provide additional redundancy in the k-space data that can be exploited (Cordero-Grande et al., 2016). In this approach, a combined optimization of the image and motion parameters is performed to maximize the consistency between the acquired data and an estimate of the acquired data from the reconstructed image, taking the motion parameters, k-space sampling, and coil sensitivities into account (Fig. 10.5).

The iterative optimization process here consists of a joint optimization, where alternatingly the reconstructed image and the motion parameters are optimized. This is done to reduce the very large number of parameters and provide a more stable optimization.

Lastly, artificial intelligence approaches have started to enter the scene, where it shows to be beneficial to use deep learning in motion correction. For example, in image registration, this can be used to either get a quick initial estimate for the motion parameters or to help speed and convergence and improve the motion estimation and image reconstruction process. Second, artificial intelligence might be able to recognize and correct motion-induced artifacts in the image reconstruction process.

10.7 Conclusion

In conclusion, motion correction at ultra-high field is an important aspect in maximizing data quality. The drive to higher-resolution imaging set more stringent limits on the acceptable maximum movement during a scan, and especially in clinical studies, motion correction can be essential to optimally benefit from the increase in field strength.

In this chapter, several approaches for motion correction have been described. Unfortunately, at this moment, there is currently not one single technique that is universally applicable. It seems navigator sequences are easiest to implement in daily routine, as they do not require additional hardware. However, this approach is not yet widely implemented in MRI systems and navigator scans still require some user input as the optimal timing and scan settings are different for each MR sequence. On the other hand, (optical) tracking systems have shown amazing results in research settings, so as long as additional hardware can be installed and subject markers can be used. Data-driven approaches seem very promising as they are fully user-independent and do not require additional hardware. As computing power is increasing and artificial intelligence is maturing, approaches that can cover a large range of sequences at ultra-high field MR imaging might be on the horizon. Before that, combinations of prospective and data-driven approaches could be a good way to tackle motion in a large range of sequences.

References

Andersen, M., Laustsen, M., Boer, V., 2022. Accuracy investigations for volumetric head-motion navigators with and without EPI at 7 T. Magn. Reson. Med. 88(3), 1198–1211. https://doi.org/10.1002/mrm.29296.

Andre, J.B., Bresnahan, B.W., Mossa-Basha, M., et al., 2015. Towards quantifying the prevalence, severity, and cost associated with patient motion during clinical MR examinations. J. Am. Coll. Radiol. 12, 689–695.

Aranovitch, A., Haeberlin, M., Gross, S., et al., 2018. Prospective motion correction with NMR markers using only native sequence elements. Magn. Reson. Med. 79, 2046–2056.

Atkinson, D., Hill, D.L., Stoyle, P.N., Summers, P.E., Keevil, S.F., 1997. Automatic correction of motion artifacts in magnetic resonance images using an entropy focus criterion. IEEE Trans. Med. Imaging 16, 903–910.

Cordero-Grande, L., Teixeira, R.P., Hughes, E., Hutter, J., Price, A., Hajnal, J., 2016. Sensitivity encoding for aligned multishot magnetic resonance reconstruction. IEEE Trans. Comput. Imaging 2, 1.

De Zanche, N., Barmet, C., Nordmeyer-Massner, J.A., Pruessmann, K.P., 2008. NMR probes for measuring magnetic fields and field dynamics in MR systems. Magn. Reson. Med. 60, 176–186.

Digiacomo, P., Maclaren, J., Aksoy, M., et al., 2020. A within-coil optical prospective motion-correction system for brain imaging at 7T. Magn. Reson. Med. 84, 1661–1671.

Eschelbach, M., Aghaeifar, A., Bause, J., et al., 2019. Comparison of prospective head motion correction with NMR field probes and an optical tracking system. Magn. Reson. Med. 81, 719–729.

Federau, C., Gallichan, D., 2016. Motion-correction enabled ultra-high resolution in-vivo 7T-MRI of the brain. PLoS One 11, e0154974.

Gallichan, D., 2017. Optimizing the acceleration and resolution of three-dimensional fat image navigators for high-resolution motion correction at 7T. Magn. Reson. Med. 77, 547–558.

Gallichan, D., Marques, J.P., Gruetter, R., 2016. Retrospective correction of involuntary microscopic head movement using highly accelerated fat image navigators (3D FatNavs) at 7T. Magn. Reson. Med. 75, 1030–1039.

Haeberlin, M., Kasper, L., Barmet, C., et al., 2015. Real-time motion correction using gradient tones and head-mounted NMR field probes. Magn. Reson. Med. 74, 647–660.

Liu, J., De Zwart, J.A., Van Gelderen, P., Murphy-Boesch, J., Duyn, J.H., 2018. Effect of head motion on MRI B0 field distribution. Magn. Reson. Med. 80, 2538–2548.

Maclaren, J., Aksoy, M., Ooi, M.B., Zahneisen, B., Bammer, R., 2018. Prospective motion correction using coil-mounted cameras: cross-calibration considerations. Magn. Reson. Med. 79, 1911–1921.

Mattern, H., Sciarra, A., Godenschweger, F., et al., 2018. Prospective motion correction enables highest resolution time-of-flight angiography at 7T. Magn. Reson. Med. 80, 248–258.

Muraskin, J., Ooi, M.B., Goldman, R.I., et al., 2013. Prospective active marker motion correction improves statistical power in BOLD fMRI. NeuroImage 68, 154–161.

Ooi, M.B., Krueger, S., Thomas, W.J., Swaminathan, S.V., Brown, T.R., 2009. Prospective real-time correction for arbitrary head motion using active markers. Magn. Reson. Med. 62, 943–954.

Opheim, G., Van Der Kolk, A., Markenroth Bloch, K., et al., 2021. 7T epilepsy task force consensus recommendations on the use of 7T MRI in clinical practice. Neurology 96, 327–341.

Pipe, J.G., 1999. Motion correction with PROPELLER MRI: application to head motion and free-breathing cardiac imaging. Magn. Reson. Med. 42, 963–969.

Qin, L., Van Gelderen, P., Derbyshire, J.A., et al., 2009. Prospective head-movement correction for high-resolution MRI using an in-bore optical tracking system. Magn. Reson. Med. 62, 924–934.

Schulz, J., Siegert, T., Reimer, E., et al., 2012. An embedded optical tracking system for motion-corrected magnetic resonance imaging at 7T. MAGMA 25, 443–453.

Stucht, D., Danishad, K.A., Schulze, P., Godenschweger, F., Zaitsev, M., Speck, O., 2015. Highest resolution in vivo human brain MRI using prospective motion correction. PLoS One 10, e0133921.

Tisdall, M.D., Hess, A.T., Reuter, M., Meintjes, E.M., Fischl, B., Van Der Kouwe, A.J., 2012. Volumetric navigators for prospective motion correction and selective reacquisition in neuroanatomical MRI. Magn. Reson. Med. 68, 389–399.

Van Gelderen, P., De Zwart, J.A., Starewicz, P., Hinks, R.S., Duyn, J.H., 2007. Real-time shimming to compensate for respiration-induced B0 fluctuations. Magn. Reson. Med. 57, 362–368.

Versluis, M.J., Peeters, J.M., Van Rooden, S., et al., 2010. Origin and reduction of motion and f0 artifacts in high resolution T2*-weighted magnetic resonance imaging: application in Alzheimer's disease patients. NeuroImage 51, 1082–1088.

White, N., Roddey, C., Shankaranarayanan, A., et al., 2010. PROMO: real-time prospective motion correction in MRI using image-based tracking. Magn. Reson. Med. 63, 91–105.

Ultra-high field structural imaging: Techniques for neuroanatomy

PART

4

Ultra-high field
structural imaging:
Techniques for
neuroanatomy

High-resolution T_1-, T_2-, and T_2^*-weighted anatomical imaging

11

Shaihan J. Malik[a], Tom Hilbert[b,c,d], and José P. Marques[e]

[a]*School of Biomedical Engineering and Imaging Sciences, King's College London, London, United Kingdom* [b]*Advanced Clinical Imaging Technology, Siemens Healthcare AG, Lausanne, Switzerland* [c]*Department of Radiology, Lausanne University Hospital and University of Lausanne, Lausanne, Switzerland* [d]*LTS5, EPFL, The Swiss Federal Institute of Technology in Lausanne, Lausanne, Switzerland* [e]*Radboud University, Donders Institute for Brain, Cognition and Behaviour, Centre for Cognitive Neuroimaging, Nijmegen, The Netherlands*

Highlights

- Ultra-high field scanners facilitate high-spatial-resolution imaging, thanks to both the increased SNR and the possibility to use increased sampling acceleration.
- B_1^+ field inhomogeneity is one of the main caveats of ultra-high field often resulting in spatially varying contrast.
- Despite T_1 relaxation times becoming longer and relatively closer together at ultra-high field, high-quality contrast-weighted imaging can be achieved using inversion recovery methods.
- T_2^* contrast is significantly enhanced at ultra-high field due to the increased interaction between magnetic susceptibility and static.

11.1 Introduction

The advent of ultra-high field (UHF) came with the promise that some major imaging and contrast improvements would be found in functional imaging and spectroscopy. Functional imaging benefits strongly from the improved magnetic susceptibility contrast origin associated with deoxygenated blood, while the increased spectral width improves the sensitivity in spectroscopy. Yet, one of the unexpected big beneficiaries was structural imaging, particularly T_1- and T_2^*-weighted imaging. Key to this improvement has been increasing the spatial resolution that is achievable within a given amount of time, due to the intrinsically higher signal-to-noise ratio (SNR) at UHF. SNR has been shown to increase supra-linearly with the magnetic field (B_0) as SNR $\propto B_0^{1.65}$ (Pohmann et al., 2016).

In practice for most imaging contrasts, the impact of increased SNR is offset by changes in relaxation times at UHF. In general, longitudinal relaxation times (T_1) are longer, and transverse relaxation times (T_2, T_2^*) are shorter than at lower field, as discussed in the next section. Longer T_1 leads to a need for longer recovery times that reduce the efficiency of data acquisition, such that the effective SNR and contrast-to-noise ratio (CNR) improvement is approximately linear with B_0 (Marques et al., 2019). This results in the observation that when going from a low ($B_{0,L}$) to a higher field ($B_{0,H}$), at the same SNR level and in the same amount of time, an increase in the isotropic spatial resolution of voxels (res_H) can be obtained:

$$\frac{res_H}{res_L} = \left(B_{0,L} / B_{0,H} \right)^{\frac{1}{3}}. \tag{11.1}$$

An increased spatial resolution in MRI requires an increased number of encoding steps, which suggests that acquisitions would necessarily become longer. Various advances in efficient image encoding and image reconstruction techniques (discussed in detail in Chapter 9) and the generalizability of the large number receive arrays (discussed in Chapter 8) have allowed to further benefit from an intrinsic advantage of UHF. The reduced radio frequency wavelength and its increased interaction with the tissue dielectric properties (see Chapters 1, 4, and 7) further result in lower g-factor penalty for similar hardware and encoding strategies, thanks to the better spatial encoding power of local receive arrays (Wiesinger et al., 2004) at UHF.

When acquisition speed is not the priority, but rather spatial resolution, motion correction techniques can make extremely long acquisitions feasible, thus achieving even higher spatial resolution at a sufficient CNR than suggested by Eq. 11.1. As motion sensitivity increases with spatial resolution and acquisition time, motion-tracking and correction techniques have their own chapter in this book (Chapter 10). Fig. 11.1 shows examples of the exquisite detail that can be obtained at UHF using motion correction to acquire whole brain 3D volumes at $\sim$0.35 mm isotropic resolution with a variety of sequence types (Federau and Gallichan, 2016). While the highly detailed anatomical information obtained at UHF is clear, unfortunately so is the signal and contrast inhomogeneity due to the increased B_0 and B_1^+ inhomogeneities.

The next section discusses the observed relationships between relaxation times and B_0 and briefly explores the underlying physical mechanisms. Knowledge of field dependence of relaxation properties is important for optimizing contrast at a particular field strength and for interpreting information conveyed in contrast-weighted images when comparing across field strengths. The remainder of this chapter will briefly discuss the main sequence types used for structural imaging at UHF, before focusing on details specific to obtaining T_1-weighted, T_2-weighted, and T_2^*-weighted contrasts. It should be noted that we will focus only on approaches that are currently available as part of MRI products and that are routinely used to obtain submillimeter resolution. The focus will be on the timing of sequences rather than particular readouts and image acceleration that can be used to further improve acquisition efficiency.

11.2 Field dependence of relaxation times

NMR relaxation characterizes return to thermal equilibrium, largely driven by the randomly fluctuating "local" magnetic fields experienced by spins, caused by their molecular environment. The nature of these fluctuating fields (i.e., their frequency and strength) is a fundamental property of the material, and this leads to the differences in relaxation times that are observed for different tissues. Transverse (spin-spin) relaxation is caused by randomly varying magnetic fields oriented in the same direction as the applied field; these lead to randomly varying local precession frequencies and hence a loss of coherence of transverse magnetization driving the system to the state of maximum entropy. T_2 is expected to be largely independent of the B_0 magnetic field since the "local" fluctuating fields are not B_0 dependent. On the other hand, longitudinal (spin-lattice) relaxation is driven by local fluctuating fields stimulating state transitions that drive the spin system back to its minimum energy state. This is more efficient if local field fluctuations occur close to the Larmor frequency, and so field dependence of T_1 is expected (Bloembergen et al., 1948).

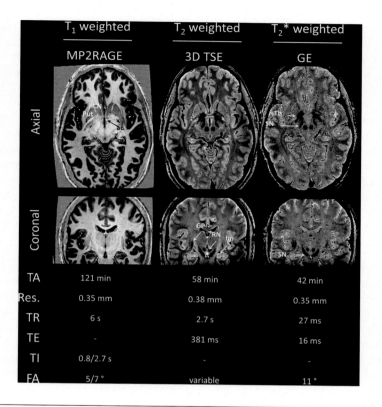

	T$_1$ weighted	T$_2$ weighted	T$_2$* weighted
	MP2RAGE	3D TSE	GE
Axial			
Coronal			
TA	121 min	58 min	42 min
Res.	0.35 mm	0.38 mm	0.35 mm
TR	6 s	2.7 s	27 ms
TE	-	381 ms	16 ms
TI	0.8/2.7 s	-	-
FA	5/7 °	variable	11 °

FIG. 11.1

Examples of axial (top) and coronal slices (bottom) of T_1-weighted (left), T_2-weighted (center), and T_2^*-weighted (right) whole-brain acquisitions on the same subject. The figure is created from the ultra-high-spatial-resolution dataset released by Federau and Gallichan (2016) using fatnav motion compensation. *White arrows* point various brain substructures: *SN*—substantia nigra; *RN*—red nucleus; *hp*—hippocampus; *hCN*—head of the caudate nucleus; *Put*—putamen; *GP*—globus pallidus; *sTh*—subthalamic nucleus; *ac*anterior commissure. It is possible to observe the large effect of B_1^+ inhomogeneity in the temporal lobe of the TSE sequence (see the *red arrow*). *TA*—acquisition time; *Res.*—resolution (isotropic in each case); *TR*—repetition time; *TE*—echo time; *TI*—inversion time; *FA*—flip-angle.

In a wide-ranging survey of animal and human tissues, Bottomley et al. (1984) found that the key determinants of T_1 are the tissue type and the resonance frequency (i.e., B_0). B_0 dependence for all data could be fitted using a relationship of the form $T_1(\text{ms}) = a(\gamma B_0)^b$, where γ is the gyromagnetic ratio (Hz/T) and a and b are constants. Rooney et al. (2007) confirmed this with an observational study using 0.2T, 1T, 1.5T, 4T, and 7T MRI of three healthy human subjects and estimated parameters a and b as 0.71/1.16/3.35 and 0.382/0.376/0.340 for white matter, gray matter, and blood, respectively. CSF on the other hand was found to have no discernible field dependence. Rooney et al. also highlighted that a key determinant of the relaxation time of a given tissue is strongly influenced by the presence of macromolecules, though the exact mechanism for this influence was not made explicit.

A more recent study by Wang et al. (2020) looked explicitly at the influence of macromolecules, acknowledging that these contain protons which cross-relax with liquid water. Wang et al. postulated a model for white matter tissue that consists of MRI visible liquid water whose T_1 is not field dependent, exchanging with MRI invisible macromolecules with $T_1 = aB_0$. This model was found to fit well to data obtained in healthy human subjects at 0.55T, 1.5T, 3T, and 7T with $a \approx 0.082\ s\ T^{-1}$. The implication is that the field dependence of longitudinal relaxation in human tissue (or at least white matter) is primarily in the macromolecules—indeed, this is consistent with the lack of field dependence observed in CSF by Rooney et al. A key difference is that Wang's model explicitly includes a two-compartment system, which can then exhibit more complex behavior such as biexponential relaxation.

Although the intrinsic transverse decay time T_2 should be independent of B_0, in practice, there are many contributions to transverse relaxation in a complex material like biological tissue, such that the observed T_2 tends actually to change in the opposite direction to that of T_1. It is well known that transverse decay times can be written as follows:

$$\frac{1}{T_2^*} = \frac{1}{T_2} + \frac{1}{T_2'}, \tag{11.2}$$

where T_2 is the intrinsic transverse decay time, T_2' is a contribution of local (static) B_0 field dispersion due to microstructure, and T_2^* is then the overall observed decay time. In terms of measurement, T_2 is distinguished from T_2^* by use of spin echo measurements that refocus on contributions from static B_0 field dispersion (T_2'). Since T_2' is due to local B_0 dispersion, it is strongly dependent on the applied B_0 field; for example, Peters et al. (2007), observed T_2^* in both cortical gray and white matter reduces by a factor of 2.5 when moving from 1.5T to 7T. Indeed, this is responsible for the increased T_2^* contrast available at UHF, often exploited for susceptibility-weighted imaging or BOLD contrast for example. Perhaps somewhat less expectedly, Michaeli et al. (2002) also demonstrated that T_2 observed with spin echo measurement also falls with increasing B_0. This is attributed to diffusion of spins through the locally variable B_0 fields that lead to T_2'. Since diffusion in these spatially varying fields results in random and temporally variable phase dispersion, this will not be refocused in a spin echo sequence and hence appears as a reduction in the apparent T_2 decay time. Unlike the "intrinsic" transverse relaxation effect, the diffusion-related term depends on the water diffusion properties of the tissue and the sequence parameters used (e.g., echo spacing and strengths of applied gradients) and is B_0 dependent.

11.3 Commonly used sequence types for UHF structural imaging

High-resolution imaging requires the acquisition of large k-space matrices (i.e., large amounts of data) favoring sequences with high data acquisition rates, preferably avoiding blurring or distortion that can be inherent to some rapid imaging methods (e.g., echo-planar imaging, EPI). The two most used sequence types for UHF structural imaging are spoiled gradient recalled echo (GE) and turbo spin echo (TSE), both of which come in many variants that can be used to generate different required contrasts. The main challenges in adapting sequences used at lower field to UHF arise mainly from: (i) elevated specific absorption rate (SAR) for equivalent transmit field, B_1^+; (ii) more spatially inhomogeneous B_1^+; and (iii) altered relaxation properties. Elevated SAR means that we reach regulatory limits more quickly when replicating protocols that would otherwise work well at lower field, and this may, for example, limit the flip angle or number of slices that can be interleaved. Different relaxation properties mean that sequences must be optimized to give good contrast: Some protocols that yield good results at low field may not work acceptably at UHF, while others will produce even better results than at lower field.

Inhomogeneity of B_1^+ leads to spatial variation of contrast weighting. This is because the flip angle(s) specified in the imaging sequence are themselves spatially variable; usually, they change in proportion to B_1^+ such that $\frac{\theta}{\theta_{nom}} = \frac{B_1^+}{B_{1,nom}} = B_{1,rel}^+$. Here, the suffix "nom" refers to the "nominal" value as defined in the protocol. A detailed discussion on B_1^+ inhomogeneity and parallel RF transmission technique for its mitigation can be found in Chapter 7. Typically, within the brain, the spread of transmit sensitivity on a single-channel transmit system is characterized by a standard deviation of ~25%–30% with a peak near the center of the brain that can be 40% higher than the brain average while more inferior regions such as temporal lobe and cerebellum can see much lower values (50% or greater reduction compared to the brain average). The consequences of this variability are sequence-specific and will be discussed in subsequent sections. It should be noted that the receiver sensitivity (typically denoted as B_1^-) is also more spatially variable at UHF. This does not affect image *contrast* since the effect is always only multiplicative on the signal; however, it can lead to uneven image shading. At lower field, this nonuniform sensitivity can be removed by using the scanner's built-in body coil (which has an approximately homogenous reception profile) as a reference. This is not possible at UHF since at these frequencies, a volume transmit coil has highly variable sensitivity—indeed, current UHF scanners generally do not have a built-in body coil. Instead, small flip angle GE images, whose signal is approximately given by $M_0 B_1^- B_1^+$, can be acquired to estimate B_1^- and hence to remove its effect (Van de Moortele et al., 2009).

GE is perhaps the simplest type of imaging sequence, consisting of repeated excitation and readouts as depicted in Fig. 11.2A, and can be applied in either 2D (often with interleaved slices) or 3D. The latter benefits from higher intrinsic SNR—all other factors being equal, 3D sequences have an SNR increase of the square root of the number of slices when compared to 2D—they can also be very efficient in terms of spatial encoding if short TRs are used. Sensitivity to B_1 inhomogeneity depends on the flip angles used; typically, the smaller flip angles used for 3D imaging lead to a larger spread in signal for the same spread in B_1 (and hence higher contrast variability) than 2D imaging which typically employs higher flip angles. Fig. 11.3A shows that the GE level of transmit B_1 sensitivity is also dependent on the regime used for imaging.

Turbo spin echo (TSE) sequences employ long trains of refocusing pulses to collect multiple echoes per TR (Fig. 11.2B). This approach, first named RARE (Hennig et al., 1986), but also known as fast spin echo (FSE), is one of the most commonly used clinical sequences at lower field strengths. TSE can also be applied in either 2D or 3D variants, and encodes signal as magnetization changes transiently over the echo train. As a result, time for magnetization recovery must be built in periodically. This makes the 3D variant less time efficient since the whole field of view must be left to recover during this time, while with a 2D TSE sequence, data can be acquired from one slice while magnetization recovers in another (once the number of slices requires a $TR \gg T_1$, the 2D TSE becomes increasingly inefficient). Furthermore, at UHF, SAR limits may be easily reached due to the use of multiple refocusing pulses applied in close succession. To address this problem, refocusing flip angles can be reduced or even varied throughout the echo train. While reducing SAR, this also allows for

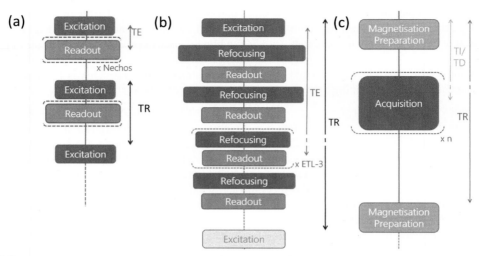

FIG. 11.2

Simplified standard acquisition strategies used for T_1-weighted and T_2-weighted protocols. (A) Example of a 3D GE readout as it is used in the MP(2)RAGE, T_2 prep, and T_2^*-weighted imaging sequence. (B) TSE acquisition strategy where various refocusing pulses are used with constant or varying amplitudes throughout the echo train length. Note that the readout can be Cartesian, wave, or EPI-like. In this acquisition strategy, TE is the time between excitation and encoding of center of k-space. TSE readout train, where TE refers to the time between excitation and the encoding of the center of k-space. Note that in the case of variable flip angle, the effective echo time is lower than TE and represents the average time spins have spent in the transverse plane between during the TE period. (C) A magnetization preparation block might be used in some of the T_1-weighted or T_2-weighted flavors consisting of one or more inversion pulses (one 180 for inversion recovery, two 180s for double inversion recovery) or a T_2 preparation (sequence of 90–180–180-90 RF pulses that stores along the z direction the MRI signal depending on the level of T_2 decay). *TR*—repetition time (time between successive magnetization preparation pulses applied to a given spin population). *TD*—delay time (referred to as TI/ inversion time if magnetization preparation is an inversion pulse) (time between magnetization preparation block and excitation of spins that will be encoded in the center of k-space).

manipulation of contrast since the partial refocusing mixes T_1 and T_2 relaxation into the resulting signal, and enables lengthening of the echo train to potentially hundreds of echoes before the signal has fully decayed (Mugler, 2014). 3D TSE with nonselective excitation and refocusing pulses with variable angles is also referred to as SPACE, CUBE, VISTA, or 3D FSE (Busse et al., 2008).

In addition to the intrinsic contrast of these sequences, "magnetization preparation" modules can be added before the readout acquisition (Fig. 11.2C) to change or enhance contrast. Typical preparation modules are adiabatic inversion pulses for T_1 weighting or a T_2 preparation module. The latter typically consists of a 90° tip-down, pair of 180° refocusing adiabatic pulses (needed to ensure full rephasing of the signal), and finally, the magnetization is stored in the longitudinal axis using either 90° tip-up or a 90° tip-down pulse. The use of adiabatic (Hurley, 2011) or dynamic parallel transmit pulses (Gras et al., 2018) for preparation modules allows contrast weighting to be achieved relatively uniformly over a range of B_1^+ and B_0 inhomogeneities. It should be noted that the adiabaticity requirements become more

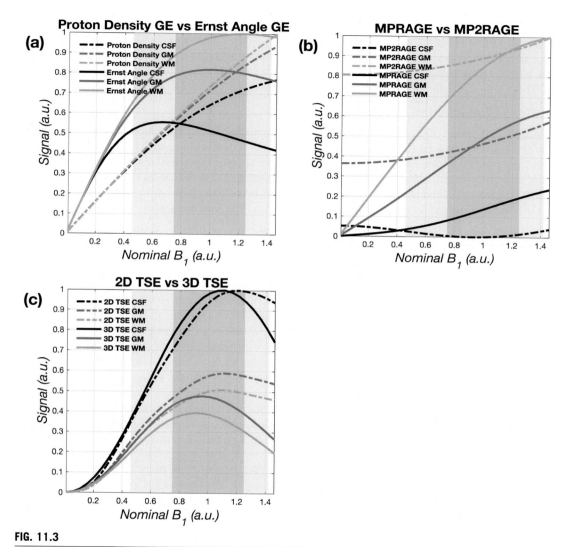

FIG. 11.3

Plots of the signal intensity as a function of relative transmit B_1 for CSF (black, $T_1/T_2 = 4/0.02$ s), GM (*dark gray*, $T_1/T_2 = 1.8/0.06$ s), and WM (*light gray*, $T_1/T_2 = 1.2/0.05$). Signal intensities of each sequence were rescaled to ensure that maximum and minimum signals in the given range of relative B_1 for any of the tissues of interest were 1 and 0, respectively. *Light-blue*-shaded areas represent the typical 9–95 percentile range found within the brain using a single-channel transmit volume head coil, while the *dark-blue*-shaded areas represent the standard deviation of the distribution of relative B_1 found within the brain. (A) shows the signal intensity transmit B_1 dependence for a GE sequence with TR 7 ms in the proton density-weighted regime (*dashed line*, flip angle 1.7°) and in the Ernst angle regime (i.e., flip angle yielding maximum signal) for GM (*full line*, flip angle 5°). (B) shows the MP2RAGE (*dashed line*) and MPRAGE (*full line*) signal dependence on the transmit field when using the sequence parameters reported in Fig. 11.4. (C) shows the 2D TSE (*dashed line*) and 3D TSE (*full line*) signal dependence on the transmit field.

stringent with increasing B_0 strength, requiring, for example, larger frequency sweeps and thus longer RF pulses. While these RF pulses typically require larger RF power levels, the relatively long dead times needed to allow magnetization recovery between preparations can help to keep sequence SAR levels within allowed limits.

11.3.1 Sequences for T_1-weighted imaging

T_1-weighted sequences are very popular, particularly in neuroscience applications, as they deliver the strongest contrast between CSF ($T_1 \sim 4$ s), gray ($T_1 \sim 1.8$ s), and white matter ($T_1 \sim 1.2$ s), and relatively little contrast within each of these tissue compartments. These properties are valuable in the context of brain segmentation (see Chapter 12) but also to visualize demyelination lesions in white matter or in the cortical gray matter (see Chapters 32), and visualize cortical malformations (Chapter 31).

There are two main strategies for incorporating T_1 contrast into an image:

- Using the inherent saturation of the acquisition strategy as a mean to create T_1 contrast (Fig. 11.2A–B).
- Using an inversion pulse to prepare the T_1 contrast prior to the image readout (Fig. 11.2C).

Common examples of inherent saturation-based T_1 weighting are as follows: (i) GE using a short TE (compared to T_2^* of tissues) and appropriately chosen flip angle to maximize the contrast between gray and white matter, Fig. 11.5; and (ii) TSE, Fig. 11.2B, with a TR of approximately the average T_1 of gray and white matter and a center-out k-space encoding to reduce the T_2 weighting of the readout. An advantage of using a TSE acquisition, particularly one with many refocusing pulses, is that the T_1 saturation obtained is relatively insensitive to B_1^+ inhomogeneities. This is because the repeated refocusing pulses lead to effective saturation of longitudinal magnetization for a range of T_1 and B_1^+ values, so that saturation recovery occurs relatively uniformly over the field of view from the end of the echo train until the next excitation. Conversely, one of the main limitations of GE approaches is that the amount of saturation (i.e., T_1 weighting) is strongly B_1^+ dependent, as can be clearly seen in the variable level of contrast between tissues as a function of relative B_1^+ for a GE sequence in the Ernst angle regime as shown in Fig. 11.3A.

The choice of 2D vs 3D readout variants for these two saturation methods is often related to the volume coverage and the number of slices required. 2D can be a valid choice in the cases when a small number of slices are desired. In this regime (and SAR allowing), 2D TSE readouts can be more efficient than their 3D variants since the latter require a longer dead time for magnetization recovery. In the case of GEs, a 2D strategy with interleaved slice acquisition requires lengthening the effective TR, which in turn requires higher flip angles to maintain T_1 contrast; this can quickly come up against SAR limits.

Magnetization preparation is the most common way to obtain T_1 contrast at UHF. The longer T_1 times typically necessitate the use of longer inversion delay times than at lower field strengths to ensure good T_1 contrast. The most popular examples arising from lower field are the MPRAGE and the IR-TSE which use GE and TSE readouts, respectively. TI is traditionally chosen to ensure CSF signal nulling, although other options might be used to increase the sensitivity to gray matter signal but require a phase-sensitive reconstruction (Mougin et al., 2016). Because the T_1 contrast is mostly achieved using an inversion pulse, anything affecting the efficiency of the inversion will result in spatially varying T_1 contrast. The two main factors affecting inversion efficiency are low local B_1^+ (in the temporal lobes or cerebellum) and the large B_0 frequency shifts (in regions close to air-tissue interfaces), resulting in very localized intensity and contrast variations.

The increased tissue T_1 at UHF means that the inversion delay and repetition times for MPRAGE must be increased to maintain contrast, while longer readout trains can be used without increasing the point spread function associated with acquiring the different phase-encoding steps at various inversion times. The B_1^+ sensitivity of the MPRAGE sequence closely follows the proton density like B_1^+ dependency (see Fig. 11.3B), justifying the approach of using a PD image to partially remove these effects. The increased amount of dead time makes this less efficient. The MP2RAGE (Marques et al., 2010) follows up on this principle by adding a second train of imaging readouts, while even further extending the repetition time. By having two images acquired at different inversion times, it is straightforward to combine them to correctly estimate the polarity of the signal at each pixel in the first inversion time. This offers the possibility to use shorter inversion times than the CSF nulling point, maximizing the contrast between tissues with different $T_1's$. By combining the images using the ratio of product to sum of squared intensities, B_1^- and T_2^* weighting is divided out, and the result is only weakly sensitive to B_1^+ (as can be seen in Fig. 11.3B). The MP2RAGE sequence has been used in three different contexts:

- Generation of a uniform image with excellent T_1 contrast.
- Selective nulling of particular tissue signals by tuning inversion times as with fluid and white matter suppression (FLAWS) (Tanner et al., 2012). An UHF example is shown in Fig. 11.5.
- Obtaining quantitative T_1 maps (with lower flip angles to reduce B_1 sensitivity).

Various developments have also been performed to accelerate the image encoding to accommodate 2D parallel imaging acceleration without affecting the observed T_1 contrast. It should be noted that the simple use of a ratio of two images does not completely cancel B_1^+ inhomogeneity effects, both because of the B_1^+ dependence associated with the excitation pulse and the accumulated spin history. The inherent and complex sensitivity to B_1^+ inhomogeneity of standard-weighted images motivates the development of faster quantitative methods that would be independent of such effects. Advancements have since been made to the MP2RAGE sequence with respect to quantitative T_1 estimation (Marques and Gruetter, 2013) or increasing the number of inversion times to ensure it is less biased by the biexponential behavior of magnetization recovery in white matter. A fuller treatment of quantitative techniques is given in Chapter 14.

Double-inversion recovery involves application of two inversion pulses in order to suppress the signal from two tissues. Use of adiabatic inversion pulses with TSE readout (Madelin et al., 2010) yields acceptable contrast homogeneity; however, the lengthening of tissue T_1s toward the T_1 of CSF reduces the SNR available once CSF is nulled compared to lower field.

Fig. 11.4 shows example images obtained with the GE, MPRAGE, and MP2RAGE sequences. All images show excellent T_1 contrast while the MP2RAGE sequence shows the least spatial bias, which led to its popularity at UHF.

11.3.2 Sequences for T_2- and T_2^*-weighted imaging

The most basic experiment to generate a T_2-weighted image is a spin echo (SE) sequence. Spin echo formation refocuses static field related contributions to transverse relaxation (T_2') as discussed above, and so this sequence is vital for generating T_2, opposed to T_2^* weighting. The echo time (TE) should be chosen to approximately match the T_2 of the tissues of interest to maximize T_2 contrast. This basic sequence has good T_2 specificity but is still biased by proton density, diffusion effects, magnetization

FIG. 11.4

Example T_1-weighted images acquired with a GE sequence (left), MPRAGE (middle), and MP2RAGE (right). Respective acquisition parameters are listed below. *TA*—acquisition time; *Res.*—resolution (isotropic in each case); *TR*—repetition time; *TI*—inversion time; *Acc.*—acceleration, *CS*—compressed sensing.

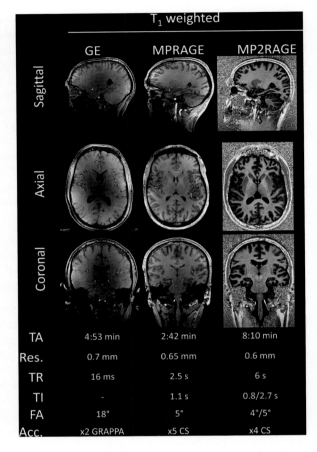

	GE	MPRAGE	MP2RAGE
TA	4:53 min	2:42 min	8:10 min
Res.	0.7 mm	0.65 mm	0.6 mm
TR	16 ms	2.5 s	6 s
TI	-	1.1 s	0.8/2.7 s
FA	18°	5°	4°/5°
Acc.	x2 GRAPPA	x5 CS	x4 CS

transfer, and deviations from the nominal flip angle $\sin^3\left(\frac{\pi}{2}B^+_{1,rel}\right)$. The major drawback of the basic SE sequence is the acquisition time, since only one k-space line is acquired per TR, and longitudinal magnetization should recover (fully if pure T_2-w is desired) before the next excitation to achieve a high SNR.

The TSE sequence therefore is a more common and faster alternative that still can generate T_2 weighting. It should be noted, however, that the use of reduced or variable refocusing flip angles as described above reduces the T_2 weighting, by also introducing a greater dependence on T_1. Fortunately, the longer T_1s at UHF reduce this effect since the echo train duration is usually short compared to T_1. TSE sequences can experience blurring related to T_2 since k-space lines are acquired while the signal is decaying, and this decay is faster at UHF. The high RF duty cycle of 2D TSE and the need to minimize the duration of each RF pulse to acquire sufficient phase-encoding lines make SAR particularly high. SAR in 2D TSE sequences can be reduced by using variable-rate selective excitation (VERSE) (Hargreaves et al., 2004) pulses which are nonuniformly stretched to minimize peak RF amplitudes,

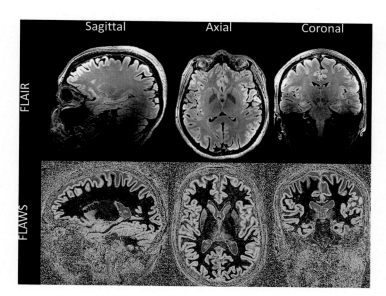

FIG. 11.5

Example images at UHF for FLAIR (top) and FLAWS (bottom) which both null the signal of tissues in order to better depict pathology. These images were acquired on healthy subjects and, therefore, do not show any hyperintensities caused by pathology.

resulting in slightly longer RF pulses with poorer slice profile. Despite these shortcomings, whole-brain 2D T_2-weighted images with high in-plane image resolution can be acquired in short acquisition times (see Fig. 11.6). The use of long echo train durations can make acquisition of multiple slices inefficient, as the TR becomes unnecessarily long ($>1.1\ T_1$). This has led researchers to use simultaneous multi-slice, but such implementations further increase SAR and have not found wide use at UHF. Current research shows promising results that B_1^+ effects may be mitigated in the TSE sequence with pTx (Sbrizzi et al., 2017). The B_1^+ sensitivity of 2D TSE is rather complex as can be appreciated in Fig. 11.3C. The asymmetric behavior around relative $B_1^+ = 1$ is due to the "slice profile" effect: Since a range of flip angles exist throughout the slice profile, in regions of high B_1^+, the flip angle at the center of the slice exceeds the optimal value leading to lower signal, but this is compensated by an increase in signal from the slice edges where the flip angle is closer to optimal.

    Many of the above limitations can be addressed by using a 3D TSE approach with very long echo trains of varying flip angle amplitude. 3D acquisitions are inherently more efficient in terms of SNR, and they also allow use of parallel imaging acceleration in two spatial dimensions, which is particularly effective at UHF. As a result, the 3D TSE sequence is often used to generate images with high isotropic resolution. Care must be taken when designing the refocusing flip angle train since blurring can occur. As mentioned in the previous paragraph, contrast may be biased by T_1 due to the long echo train but also the shorter TRs used to further increase efficiency. As opposed to spin echo sequences, interpretation of the level of T_2 weighting cannot be fully understood from the reported echo time, as the effective echo time also depends on the k-space ordering in the echo train.

    3D TSE is sensitive to B_1^+ inhomogeneity, though the degree of sensitivity depends on the refocusing flip angles used. The effect can lead to signal modulation and a loss of contrast, for example, in the temporal lobes in Fig. 11.1. This effect is particularly visible between gray and white matter in regions of low transmit B_1 (see Fig. 11.3C). Ongoing research addresses these problems with pTx either by dynamically modulating along the echo train (Sbrizzi et al., 2017) or by use of dynamic pTx pulses (Gras et al., 2018) or by using k_T-points for both excitation and refocusing (Eggenschwiler et al., 2013).

A related and common clinically used variant of T_2-weighted 3D TSE is the fluid-attenuated inversion recovery (FLAIR) sequence, which uses an inversion pulse to null CSF signal followed by a T_2w readout to provide tissue contrast (see Fig. 11.5 for an example). One issue at UHF, where tissue T_1 times are longer, is that the tissue signal is still strongly attenuated at the inversion delay times needed to null fluids. A way to mitigate this is to use a tip-down T_2 preparation module prior to the inversion pulse, essentially to encode T_2 weighting into the longitudinal magnetization. Since tissue T_2 is very different to that of CSF, a long T_2 preparation time (longer than the T_2 of tissues, but shorter than the T_2 of CSF) results in CSF magnetization being inverted while tissue magnetization is saturated. Hence, at the inversion delay time required to null the CSF signal, tissue signal has more substantially recovered, resulting in a stronger signal (Visser et al., 2011) and a more SNR efficient FLAIR contrast (see Fig. 11.5). Research into use of pTx for reducing B_1^+ sensitivity to this variant of 3D TSE is ongoing (Beqiri et al., 2018; Gras et al., 2019).

As an alternative to T_2-weighted 3D TSE, T_2 preparation can also be performed in the tip-up variant preceding a GE readout. To maximize the T_2-weighting, the T_2 preparation time should be chosen as in a classical spin echo sequence. Center-out readouts should be used to ensure the image retains the T_2-prepared contrast, since this will reduce over the GE readout as the magnetization state is also affected by successive excitation pulses and T_1 recovery. The center-out readout with a changing signal will lead to some image blurring; nevertheless, high-resolution T_2-weighted brain images with good T_2 contrast can be achieved at UHF and may provide a good alternative to the 3D TSE sequence (see Fig. 11.6).

Figs. 11.1 and 11.6 show that T_2 contrast at 7T has a large contrast between white matter and the iron-rich deep gray matter nuclei, even though the natural form to observe contrasts of susceptibility origin is via T_2^*-weighted imaging. This is due to fast dephasing around ferritin iron cores. T_2^* contrast is more commonly obtained using GE with echo times close to the T_2^* of the tissues of interest. This is particularly attractive at UHF since T_2^* decreases linearly with B_0, allowing short TE and hence also short TRs to be used, leading to faster imaging.

In order to enhance T_2^* contrast, particularly for imaging veins and other small features at 1.5 and 3T, susceptibility-weighted imaging (SWI) was proposed as a technique that combines the magnitude of T_2^*-weighted images with high-pass-filtered phase images (Haacke et al., 2004). This method can also be employed very successfully at UHF, though the shorter T_2^* of venous blood and intra voxel signal dephasing in the surrounding of veins already delivers strong contrast in magnitude images without further enhancement from phase information. One very interesting observation in the early days of ultra-high field systems (Duyn et al., 2007) was that susceptibility effects can also be seen in the phase of gradient echo images (as opposed to the conventional magnitude image). Moreover, they were not limited to venous contrast but could also be used to generate subtle contrast within both gray and white matter (see Fig. 11.7A). As a result, SWI has been used as a means to increase tissue contrast and conspicuity into magnitude images to better visualize, for example, thalamic nuclei in presurgical planning (Abosch et al., 2010) (see Fig. 11.7B). Chapter 13 will further discuss on how phase images can be used to obtain quantitative susceptibility maps.

A challenge for T_2^*-weighted GE is that the sequence is very sensitive to B_0 field inhomogeneity, both in terms of static effects due to anatomy (e.g., above the nasal cavity or ear canals) and dynamic

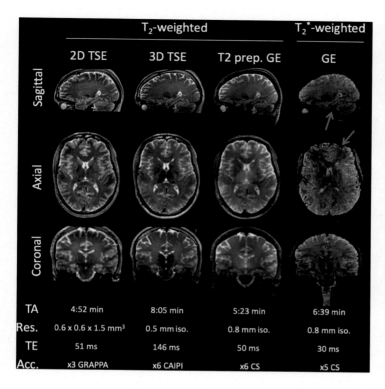

FIG. 11.6

Example T_2 and T_2^* images acquired from one subject using different techniques (2D and 3D turbo spin echo, TSE; T_2-prepared gradient recalled echo GE, and T_2^*-weighted GE). *Blue arrows* indicate signal dropouts in the GE acquisition, and the red arrow indicates large veins that are only visible in the T_2^*-weighted contrast. *TA*—acquisition time, *Res.*—resolution, *TE*—echo time, *Acc.*—acceleration, *GRAPPA*—generalized autocalibrating partial parallel acquisition, *CAIPI*—controlled aliasing in parallel imaging results in higher acceleration, *CS*—compressed sensing.

	T₂-weighted			T₂*-weighted
	2D TSE	3D TSE	T2 prep. GE	GE
TA	4:52 min	8:05 min	5:23 min	6:39 min
Res.	0.6 x 0.6 x 1.5 mm³	0.5 mm iso.	0.8 mm iso.	0.8 mm iso.
TE	51 ms	146 ms	50 ms	30 ms
Acc.	x3 GRAPPA	x6 CAIPI	x6 CS	x5 CS

effects due to B_0 fluctuation driven by subject motion or respiration. Strong local B_0 distortion leads to signal dropout while fluctuations cause phase inconsistencies across k-space. Both effects are most pronounced at the longer TEs used to obtain T_2^* weighting, and lead to blurring or ghosting artifacts. A further practical issue with GE is motion sensitivity: While prospective motion correction has been used to generate high-quality high-resolution data for the T_1- or T_2-weighted sequences described above (both 2D and 3D), the required motion estimation modules cannot trivially be inserted into a GE sequence without breaking its structure. A thorough discussion of motion correction can be found in Chapter 10. For T_2^*-weighted GE, motion leads to subtle changes in B_0 and therefore signal phase in the acquired k-space data, resulting in spatially variable phase inconsistencies and hence image blurring. These B_0 fluctuations can be measured using an MRI-based field navigator (Versluis et al., 2012) or measurement of the effective k-space trajectory with external field cameras (Duerst et al., 2015). This information can be used either to drive a prospective real-time B_0 dynamic shimming or retrospectively accounting for such phase variations (local k-space trajectories) in the image reconstruction.

Fig. 11.6 shows example images for 2D TSE, 3D TSE, T_2-prepared GE, and T_2^*-weighted GE sequences from one subject. These are just examples, and further protocol optimizations may lead to better image quality for one or the other technique. From the images shown here, the TSE sequence appears to show the best WM and GM contrast while 3D TSE has the highest isotropic resolution

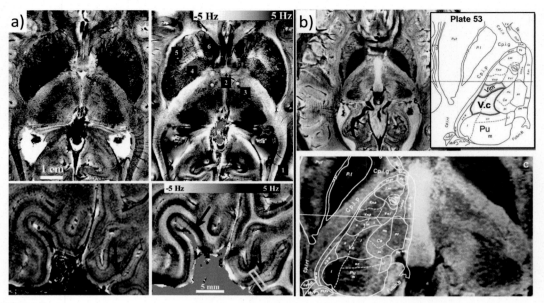

FIG. 11.7

(A) Magnitude (left) and phase(right) images from a 2D GE acquired at 0.24 mm in plane resolution and 1-mm slice thickness, TR/TE = ~750/29 ms. Top part shows how various details are particularly highlighted in the phase data: veins crossing the optic radiations (box 1), columna fornix (box 2), cross-section of the mammillothalamic tract (box 3), globus pallidus (box 4), putamen (box 5), and head of the caudate nucleus (box 6). The bottom part shows cortical layers such as the stria of Gennari (*black arrow*). (B) 2D SWI image shown next to a thalamic segmentation, highlighting its potential use for targeting deep brain stimulation. *Figures adapted with permission from Panel (A) Duyn et al. (2007) and (B) Abosch et al. (2010).*

(0.5 mm). Some of the thalamic contrast observed in 3D TSE though is associated with the large B_1^+ at the centre of the brain that changes the degree of T_2 and T_1 weighting in this region. The T_2-prepared sequence shows similar contrast to the TSE sequences although it suffers from blurring. The T_2^*-weighted GE sequence shows different contrast in comparison to the T_2-weighted images. While tissue susceptibility (e.g., in the substantia nigra) also results a reduced signal intensity, veins are particularly visible, thanks to blooming artifacts and signal cancelation in their surroundings, that in the case of T_2-weighted imaging are fully refocused.

11.4 Conclusion

Although the main motivation for UHF developments originally was functional and susceptibility-weighted imaging, the increased SNR with increased field strength has proven to drastically improve image resolution for structural imaging and tissue contrast. The lengthening of the T_1 of brain tissues opened new opportunities to encode T_1-weighting contrast in a more specific way and T_2 weighting in more efficient manner. The improved resolution in combination with contrast changes with field strength has shown to be advantageous for various clinical applications, allowing not only imaging small focal pathologies but also improving our understanding of their pathophysiology. While this chapter has focused only on contrast-*weighted* imaging, significant effort has also been made in quantitative measurement of relaxation parameters, as discussed in Chapter 14. Physical challenges such as SAR limitations and field inhomogeneity have prompted various developments in the UHF community that have had an impact on both brain and body imaging at lower fields and an increase of attention given to quantitative imaging. With further clinical studies, UHF structural imaging may improve patient diagnosis, surgical planning, and follow-up in the future of clinical routine.

Acknowledgments

The authors would like to thank Dr. Gabriele Bonanno, Dr. Arun Joseph, and Dr. Gian Franco Piredda for the acquisition of example dataset at the Translational Imaging Center in Bern, Switzerland; and Dr. Thomas Wilkinson, Dr. David Carmichael, and Ms. Philippa Bridgen for acquisition of data at the LoCUS 7T facility, King's College London.

Disclosure

Dr. Tom Hilbert is employed by Siemens Healthcare AG, Switzerland.

References

Abosch, A., Yacoub, E., Ugurbil, K., Harel, N., 2010. An assessment of current brain targets for deep brain stimulation surgery with susceptibility-weighted imaging at 7 tesla. Neurosurgery 67, 1745–1756.

Beqiri, A., Hoogduin, H., Sbrizzi, A., Hajnal, J.V., Malik, S.J., 2018. Whole-brain 3D FLAIR at 7T using direct signal control. Magn. Reson. Med. 80, 1533–1545.

Bloembergen, N., Purcell, E., Pound, R., 1948. Relaxation effects in nuclear magnetic resonance absorption. Phys. Rev. 73, 679–715.

Bottomley, P.A., Foster, T.H., Argersinger, R.E., Pfeifer, L.M., 1984. A review of normal tissue hydrogen NMR relaxation times and relaxation mechanisms from 1–100 MHz: dependence on tissue type, NMR frequency, temperature, species, excision, and age. Med. Phys. 11, 425–448.

Busse, R.F., Brau, A.C.S., Vu, A., et al., 2008. Effects of refocusing flip angle modulation and view ordering in 3D fast spin echo. Magn. Reson. Med. 60, 640–649.

Duerst, Y., Wilm, B.J., Dietrich, B.E., et al., 2015. Real-time feedback for spatiotemporal field stabilization in MR systems. Magn. Reson. Med. 73, 884–893.

Duyn, J.H., Van Gelderen, P., Li, T.Q., De Zwart, J.A., Koretsky, A.P., Fukunaga, M., 2007. High-field MRI of brain cortical substructure based on signal phase. Proc. Natl. Acad. Sci. U. S. A. 104, 11796–11801.

Eggenschwiler, F., O'Brien, K.R., Gruetter, R., Marques, J.P., 2013. Improving T 2 -weighted imaging at high field through the use of k T -points. Magn. Reson. Med. 71 (4), 1478–1488.

Federau, C., Gallichan, D., 2016. Motion-correction enabled ultra-high resolution in-vivo 7T-MRI of the brain. PLoS One 11, 1–12.

Gras, V., Mauconduit, F., Vignaud, A., et al., 2018. Design of universal parallel-transmit refocusing kT-point pulses and application to 3D T2-weighted imaging at 7T. Magn. Reson. Med. 80, 53–65.

Gras, V., Pracht, E.D., Mauconduit, F., Le Bihan, D., Stöcker, T., Boulant, N., 2019. Robust nonadiabatic T 2 preparation using universal parallel-transmit k T -point pulses for 3D FLAIR imaging at 7 T. Magn. Reson. Med. 81 (5), 3202–3208

Haacke, E.M., Xu, Y., Cheng, Y.-C.N., Reichenbach, J.R., 2004. Susceptibility weighted imaging (SWI). Magn. Reson. Med. 52, 612–618.

Hargreaves, B.A., Cunningham, C.H., Nishimura, D.G., Conolly, S.M., 2004. Variable-rate selective excitation for rapid MRI sequences. Magn. Reson. Med. 52, 590–597.

Hennig, J., Nauerth, A., Friedburg, H., 1986. RARE imaging: a fast imaging method for clinical MR. Magn. Reson. Med. 3, 823–833.

Hurley, A.C., 2011. Tailored RF Pulse Design for 7T MRI.

Madelin, G., Oesingmann, N., Inglese, M., 2010. Double inversion recovery MRI with fat suppression at 7 tesla: Initial experience. J. Neuroimaging 20, 87–92.

Marques, J.P., Gruetter, R., 2013. New developments and applications of the MP2RAGE sequence - focusing the contrast and high spatial resolution R1 mapping. PLoS One 8. https://doi.org/10.1371/journal.pone.0069294.

Marques, J.P., Kober, T., Krueger, G., van der Zwaag, W., Van de Moortele, P.-F., Gruetter, R., 2010. MP2RAGE, a self bias-field corrected sequence for improved segmentation and T1-mapping at high field. NeuroImage 49, 1271–1281.

Marques, J.P., Simonis, F.F.J., Webb, A.G., 2019. Low-field MRI: an MR physics perspective. J. Magn. Reson. Imaging 49, 1528–1542.

Michaeli, S., Garwood, M., Zhu, X.H., et al., 2002. Proton T2 relaxation study of water, N-acetylaspartate, and creatine in human brain using Hahn and Carr-Purcell spin echoes at 4T and 7T. Magn. Reson. Med. 47, 629–633.

Mougin, O., Abdel-Fahim, R., Dineen, R., Pitiot, A., Evangelou, N., Gowland, P., 2016. Imaging gray matter with concomitant null point imaging from the phase sensitive inversion recovery sequence. Magn. Reson. Med. 76, 1512–1516.

Mugler, J.P., 2014. Optimized three-dimensional fast-spin-echo MRI. J. Magn. Reson. Imaging 39, 745–767.

Peters, A.M., Brookes, M.J., Hoogenraad, F.G., et al., 2007. T2* measurements in human brain at 1.5, 3 and 7 T. Magn. Reson. Imaging 25, 748–753.

Pohmann, R., Speck, O., Scheffler, K., 2016. Signal-to-noise ratio and MR tissue parameters in human brain imaging at 3, 7, and 9.4 tesla using current receive coil arrays. Magn. Reson. Med. 75, 801–809.

Rooney, W.D., Johnson, G., Li, X., et al., 2007. Magnetic field and tissue dependencies of human brain longitudinal 1H2O relaxation in vivo. Magn. Reson. Med. 57, 308–318.

Sbrizzi, A., Hoogduin, H., Hajnal, J.V., et al., 2017. Optimal control design of turbo spin-echo sequences with applications to parallel-transmit systems. Magn. Reson. Med. 373, 361–373.

Tanner, M., Gambarota, G., Kober, T., et al., 2012. Fluid and white matter suppression with the MP2RAGE sequence. J. Magn. Reson. Imaging 35, 1063–1070.

Van de Moortele, P.F., Auerbach, E.J., Olman, C., Yacoub, E., Uğurbil, K., Moeller, S., 2009. T1 weighted brain images at 7 tesla unbiased for proton density, T2* contrast and RF coil receive B1 sensitivity with simultaneous vessel visualization. NeuroImage 46, 432–446.

Versluis, M.J., Sutton, B.P., De Bruin, P.W., Börnert, P., Webb, A.G., Van Osch, M.J., 2012. Retrospective image correction in the presence of nonlinear temporal magnetic field changes using multichannel navigator echoes. Magn. Reson. Med. 68, 1836–1845.

Visser, F., Zwanenburg, J.J.M., Luijten, P.R., 2011. Whole brain high resolution T2w 3D TSE at 7Tesla with a tissue specific non linear refocus pulse angle sweep; initial results. In: Proc ISMRM. 57, p. 4242.

Wang, Y., van Gelderen, P., de Zwart, J.A., Duyn, J.H., 2020. B0-field dependence of MRI T1 relaxation in human brain. NeuroImage 213, 116700.

Wiesinger, F., Van de Moortele, P.-F., Adriany, G., De Zanche, N., Ugurbil, K., Pruessmann, K.P., 2004. Parallel imaging performance as a function of field strength—an experimental investigation using electrodynamic scaling. Magn. Reson. Med. 52 (5), 953–964. https://doi.org/10.1002/mrm.20281.

Brain segmentation at ultra-high field: Challenges, opportunities, and unmet needs

12

Jonathan R. Polimeni[a,b,c], Saskia Bollmann[d], and Martin Reuter[a,b,e]

[a]*Athinoula A. Martinos Center for Biomedical Imaging, Massachusetts General Hospital, Charlestown, MA, United States* [b]*Department of Radiology, Harvard Medical School, Boston, MA, United States* [c]*Division of Health Sciences and Technology, Massachusetts Institute of Technology, Cambridge, MA, United States* [d]*School of Information Technology and Electrical Engineering, Faculty of Engineering, Architecture and Information Technology, The University of Queensland, Brisbane, QLD, Australia* [e]*German Center for Neurodegenerative Diseases (DZNE), Bonn, Germany*

Highlights

- Increased image contrast at UHF can improve brain segmentation accuracy.
- While tissue boundaries can be better delineated, several sources of bias confound segmentation.
- Segmentation and bias correction approaches adapted to UHF MRI data are needed.
- Sensitivity, specificity, and resolution-SNR trade-offs must be considered and balanced.
- Region-specific, EPI-based, multimodal, and ML-based segmentation methods hold promise.

12.1 Introduction

Brain image segmentation is key to the interpretation of neuroimaging data. It is performed to *delineate* tissue borders, nuclei, or distinct brain areas and to *identify* anatomical and functional regions. For studies of brain anatomy, segmentation is needed to estimate the geometry of structures, such as the thickness of the cerebral cortex or the volume of the hippocampus—to quantify morphometric changes cross-sectionally across groups or longitudinally across time. In studies of brain function, segmentation determines which regions are engaged/activated to interpret functional responses and compare them across subjects.

This chapter focuses on segmentation of human brain data acquired at ultra-high field (UHF) MRI (field strengths 7 Tesla and higher). Segmentation of UHF MRI data poses several distinct challenges and opportunities. As explained below, many features of brain architecture can be detected using UHF MRI that cannot be seen with conventional imaging. This opens exciting possibilities to quantify brain anatomy in vivo through segmentation and to attempt to relate structure to function.

All segmentation methods leverage prior information, and today most brain segmentation methods developed for MRI data tacitly expect conventional field strengths and standard imaging resolutions. This means that many implicit and explicit assumptions are violated when applying standard methods to UHF MRI data, and existing segmentation methods may not fully benefit from the unique capabilities afforded by UHF MRI.

When moving to higher magnetic fields, imaging sensitivity and thus signal-to-noise ratio (SNR) increase. Also, many forms of image contrast are promoted, increasing the contrast-to-noise ratio (CNR) dramatically. This boost in CNR acts as a currency to be "spent" in various ways: either reducing scan times or improving resolution to increase the detectability of smaller anatomical structures and sharpen tissue borders. This increased flexibility adds complexity to the task of image segmentation, making it challenging to develop generalizable segmentation methods that perform well on data acquired with a wide range of possible imaging parameters. Nevertheless, the unique capabilities of UHF MRI have enabled successful segmentation of subtle anatomical features that cannot be detected at conventional field strengths, or segmentation of common structures with greater clarity and confidence than what could be achieved previously (see Fig. 12.1).

Here we survey key topics of brain segmentation at UHF. One central theme is the classic, ubiquitous trade-off between bias and variance (i.e., accuracy and precision) in the estimated segmentation, and the appropriate balance will depend on the priorities of the given study.

12.2 Differentiating tissues at UHF

Many image contrasts change with increasing field strength; Chapters 11 and 14 provide detailed discussions on contrasts at UHF. Image contrasts based on magnetic susceptibility effects (such as T_2^*) are promoted, some imaging methods benefit from longer T_1 values while others suffer, and techniques such as diffusion imaging face multiple challenges. There are several considerations related to trade-offs between sensitivity and specificity.

12.2.1 MPRAGE

The workhorse of brain segmentation at any field strength is T_1-weighted MPRAGE. This sequence can provide strong contrast between gray matter, white matter, and cerebrospinal fluid (CSF) to delineate cortical and subcortical gray matter and is used mainly for whole-brain segmentation. T_1 values of gray and white matter increase with field strength, such that the intrinsic gray-white contrast is reduced at UHF. Protocol adaptations can partly compensate for this.

MPRAGE is vulnerable to various bias fields, and their removal during preprocessing can be challenging. Instead, it is common to attempt to remove bias by acquiring multiple image volumes that all contain the same bias field and then remove the bias through normalization. One approach computes the ratio of nominally resolution- and distortion-matched MPRAGE and T_2-weighted data (Glasser and Van Essen, 2011). Because both contrasts are sensitive to myelin (often through magnetization transfer or MT effects in the T_2-weighted data), these ratio images are called "myelin maps." However, each image of the pair has a different weighting to myelin across the brain; thus, this method produces a complicated tissue contrast. Nevertheless, it appears to provide good specificity to myelin, especially in cerebral gray matter.

Another similar approach is MP2RAGE, proposed to correct for intensity and contrast biases in brain anatomical data acquired at 7T (see Chapter 11). This method produces impressively high image quality and contrast, although the ratio of these two images introduces complications for segmentation if standard methods developed for MPRAGE are unmodified. The ratio causes nonlinear partial volume effects (Duché et al., 2017)—such that the intensity of any voxel containing two or more tissue types

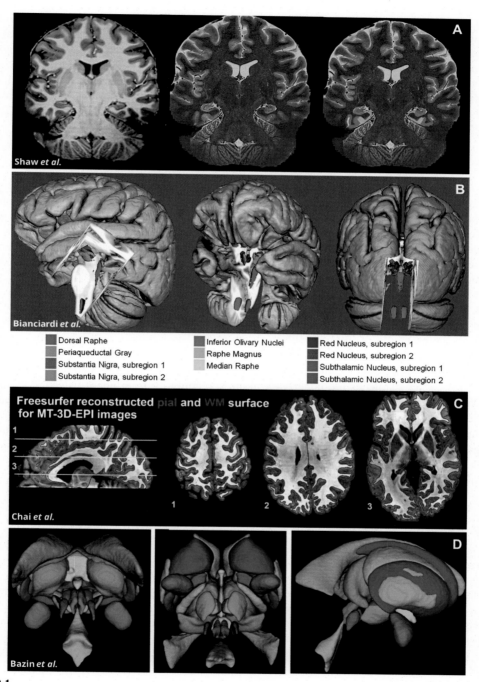

Dorsal Raphe
Periaqueductal Gray
Substantia Nigra, subregion 1
Substantia Nigra, subregion 2
Inferior Olivary Nuclei
Raphe Magnus
Median Raphe
Red Nucleus, subregion 1
Red Nucleus, subregion 2
Subthalamic Nucleus, subregion 1
Subthalamic Nucleus, subregion 2

FIG. 12.1

See legend on next page

will not be a simple linear combination of the intensities of those tissues, e.g., a voxel at the gray-white border that contains equal amounts of gray and white matter will have an intensity that is not halfway between those of gray and white matter—which will violate the signal model used in many segmentation methods. The ratio operation also affects the noise distribution (Bazin et al., 2014), which can violate the noise model assumed in many methods. Thus, segmentations computed from MP2RAGE may differ systematically from those from MPRAGE (Fujimoto et al., 2014); however, segmentation methods that update these models accordingly can remove these unwanted discrepancies (Duché et al., 2017).

12.2.2 T_2^* and susceptibility contrasts

The most striking change in contrast observed when moving to UHF is in susceptibility-weighted methods such as T_2^*-weighted imaging. T_2^* contrast is enhanced with increasing field strength and reflects tissue iron and myelin content, as well as deoxyhemoglobin-rich venous blood. Fig. 12.2 shows examples in which various anatomical features are observable. Because of the well-known extravascular blooming effect, signal dephasing occurs around venous structures, enabling veins smaller than the voxel size to be detected; however, venous segmentation must be corrected for blooming to avoid overestimating vessel diameters.

The boost in CNR seen in T_2^*-weighted imaging is counterbalanced by its poor specificity since myelin, nonheme iron, and deoxygenated blood all contribute. Furthermore, T_2^* depends on the local orientation of the anatomical structure. This poses challenges to accurate segmentation in most structures, with the exception of iron-rich substructures of the basal ganglia that exhibit prominent T_2^* contrast.

This limited specificity is addressed with quantitative susceptibility mapping (QSM) (see Chapter 13), which estimates the underlying tissue susceptibility from phase-valued T_2^*-weighted data. QSM can remove orientation and blooming effects, improving geometric accuracy, but susceptibility estimation requires dedicated processing steps to avoid artifacts at brain boundaries. QSM has been successfully applied to segmenting subcortical structures at 7T, including deep-gray nuclei and basal ganglia, and penetrating veins. Still, because of the generally reduced contrast between gray and white matter in QSM compared to T_1-weighted data, QSM is not widely used for brain segmentation.

FIG. 12.1—Cont'd

Examples of brain segmentation based on 7 Tesla MRI taken from the literature, showcasing the diversity of brain structures targeted and demonstrating how different contrasts may be suitable to different segmentation tasks. (A) Segmentation of the hippocampus using multi-contrast data based on a T_2-weighted turbo-spin-echo acquisition and a T_1-weighted MP2RAGE acquisition. (B) Segmentation of brainstem and sub-cortical nuclei using a diffusion-weighted EPI acquisition. (C) Segmentation of cerebral cortical gray matter using magnetization transfer contrast using a 3D EPI acquisition. (D) Segmentation of 17 subcortical structures (including striatum, ventricles, thalamus, basal ganglia, and white matter structures) based on estimates of R_1 and R_2^* relaxation rates and QSM. *Panel (A) Adapted from Shaw et al. (2020), with permission. Panel (B) Adapted from Bianciardi et al. (2015), with permission. Panel (C) Adapted from Chai et al. (2021), with permission. Panel (D) Adapted from Bazin et al. (2020), with permission.*

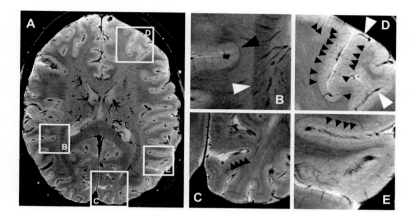

FIG. 12.2

Complexities of segmenting T_2^*-weighted data at 7T. (A) An axial slice of a typical high-resolution 2D (0.23 × 0.23 × 1.0 mm^3) gradient-echo acquisition used for T_2^*-weighted imaging at 7T. (B–E) Zoomed-in views of regions of the brain showcasing prominent features that complicate tissue segmentation. (B) Heterogeneity of the white matter intensity due to regional variations in myelin content and orientation, as well as iron, including dark bands in superficial white matter subjacent to the cortical gray matter (indicated by *black arrowhead*) as well as the optic radiation connecting the visual thalamus and primary visual cortex (indicated by *white arrowhead*). (C) Heterogeneity of the gray matter intensity again due to variations in myelin and iron content, here seen in the presumptive stria of Gennari in Layer IVb of primary visual cortex (indicated by *black arrowheads*). (D) Examples of vascular features, such as mesoscale venules within the cortex (indicated by *black arrowheads*) and large macroscale pial veins on the pial surface (indicated by *white arrowheads*). (E) Another example of heterogeneous gray matter, in this case different intensities seen in deep cortical layers, known to have higher myelin content, and superficial layers (the interface between which is indicated by *black arrowheads*).

Multimodal imaging and segmentation approaches extend the concept of intensity normalization to remove biases and delineate tissues that cannot be easily discriminated using a single contrast (Viviani et al., 2017). For example, cortical gray matter and surrounding tissues with similar T_1 values, such as dura mater and walls of the cerebral sinuses, may not be separable with T_1-weighted data alone, but combining T_1-weighted and T_2^*-weighted data can help discriminate these structures; recent attempts have shown that T_2^*-weighted FLAIR data help suppress dura (Viviani et al., 2017). Multimodal segmentation jointly estimates gray matter borders from multiple contrasts rather than forming ratio images or masking one image with the other.

12.2.3 Magnetization transfer contrast

A promising contrast for improved specificity is based on MT (see Chapter 14). While MT contrast is often used at conventional field strengths, it is not common at UHF due to the high RF power required and increased SAR at higher fields. However, one workaround is to reduce the number of MT pulses, which reduces contrast but small brainstem nuclei can still be delineated (Priovoulos et al., 2018).

A new MT contrast, "inhomogeneous MT," provides even greater specificity to myelin. This has been incorporated into "MT-RAGE" acquisition schemes with limited numbers of pulses that achieve high anatomical quality and promising cortical segmentation at 3T.

12.2.4 Blood vessel contrast

A useful contrast promoted at UHF but often overlooked is time-of-flight (TOF) contrast used for MR angiography (MRA). Because of prolonged T_1 values of blood and tissue at higher fields, blood signal persists longer while tissue signal is more effectively suppressed, enhancing blood-tissue contrast. Superior venous saturation and MT-based tissue suppression are not used at UHF due to SAR constraints; however, the intrinsic blood-tissue contrast boost enables higher resolutions and improved vessel segmentation. To image small vessels with slower flow, multiple thin slabs are employed, and both arteries and veins appear in these data. However, they can be distinguished either using vessel tracking from known major vessels (such as the sagittal sinus) or using auxiliary T_2^*-weighted data. Because smaller voxels reduce partial-volume effects, increased TOF contrast can be achieved, which enables the detection of smaller vessels, as demonstrated in Fig. 12.3; vessels one voxel in diameter can be detected down to isotropic voxel sizes of 140–160 μm (Bollmann et al., 2022). Segmentation of vessels typically exploits their elongation in one direction through vessel enhancement operations such as the well-known Frangi filter. However, at high resolutions, a wide range of vessel diameters are present in the data, necessitating multiscale enhancement (Bernier et al., 2020). Because of the lack of

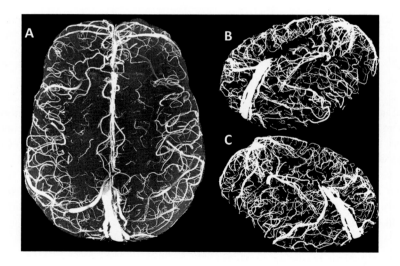

FIG. 12.3

Segmentation of high-resolution time-of-flight MR angiography acquired at 7T. (A) Maximum intensity projection of multi-slab 3D TOF-MRA data acquired at 160-μm isotropic resolution and 50-mm coverage in the head-foot direction. (B–C) Oblique views of 3D segmentation of the vasculature using a multiscale 3D CNN with data augmentation. *Figure courtesy of Siyu Liu, University of Queensland.*

quantitative ground-truth brain vasculature data, validating these segmentations is challenging; fortunately, priors can be exploited to evaluate performance, such as all noncapillary vessels branch off larger vessels, and vessels tend to branch at nearly-right angles.

12.2.5 Diffusion contrast

Diffusion MRI is increasingly important for investigating tissue microstructure beyond its standard application to white-matter fiber architecture. Diffusion MRI is not common at UHF due to shorter tissue T_2 values and B_1^+ nonuniformity; it is viewed as a method in which one "fights against" the increased magnetic field. However, in acquisitions with moderate diffusion weighing—which help reduce TE values and associated T_2 signal decay—diffusion MRI can achieve high SNR and image quality. This so-called high-k/low-b diffusion acquisition (Bianciardi et al., 2015) has been applied to segmenting subcortical gray matter and brainstem nuclei by filtering out surrounding anisotropic tissue structures. Similar diffusion MRI approaches have delineated depth-dependent features in the cerebral cortex imparted by its laminar architecture (Assaf, 2019).

12.3 Intensity, contrast, and geometric biases in UHF MRI

While higher field strengths can increase CNR (thus reducing imaging *variance*), they also increase vulnerability to several forms of image artifacts (thus increasing imaging *bias*). These biases include intensity, contrast, and geometric bias. These are well-known and routinely addressed—either by estimating bias fields before segmentation or jointly alongside the tissue segmentation itself. While they are to some extent present at conventional field strengths, the nature and the severity of many forms of bias change with field strength; thus, standard bias estimation and removal methods fail on UHF data.

12.3.1 Intensity bias from receive coil inhomogeneity

Perhaps, the most apparent bias at UHF is receiver coil bias caused by spatially varying receive or B_1^- fields. This becomes more severe at UHF, as discussed in Chapter 9. At conventional field strengths, receiver bias can be readily estimated using a second reference receive coil with spatially uniform sensitivity, such as a built-in body coil typically used for transmission. Body coils, however, are currently unavailable for UHF MRI due to engineering challenges. A common correction is to jointly estimate receive sensitivity and tissue segmentation, known as "unified segmentation," which leverages prior information regarding brain anatomy and tissue contrast. It includes a prior on the smoothness of the bias field that must be adapted to UHF data (Zaretskaya et al., 2018). However, because it is not straightforward to separate intensity variations due to changes in rapidly changing receive sensitivity from those due to the underlying anatomy, these methods can mistake meaningful variations in intensity driven by, e.g., regional variations in gray matter T_1 values across cortical areas with varying levels of myelination for bias. As a result, overcorrection occurs, stripping away tissue contrast, and impacting downstream segmentation accuracy. Perhaps, the most common approach is to acquire a pair of anatomical images, one ideally with tissue contrast and one without, such that each image contains the same multiplicative bias fields, and divides these images. This is the basis of the MP2RAGE method, described above.

12.3.2 Contrast bias from transmit field nonuniformity

Another prominent bias at UHF is the B_1^+ transmit field nonuniformity over the head, described in Chapter 7. Since image contrast is determined partly by flip angle, this leads to a form of contrast bias that cannot be simply removed in postprocessing. This bias is best addressed during acquisition, either by judicious calibration of the RF transmission to achieve an accurate flip angle in the region of interest, by using adiabatic RF pulses, when possible, or by using parallel transmission. Given the practical challenges with pTx, incorporating an acquired B_1^+ map into the image reconstruction is a pragmatic way to improve segmentation at 7T (Haast et al., 2018).

12.3.3 Geometric bias from distortion

Geometric distortion is mainly caused by B_0 field inhomogeneities induced by tissue susceptibility gradients, most prominently near air-tissue interfaces. This effect scales linearly with field strength. B_0 inhomogeneity interferes with image encoding, causing local geometric distortions and spatially varying voxel sizes and image intensities; thus, there are secondary intensity and contrast biases associated with geometric distortion. Distortions occur along any image encoding direction in which encoding bandwidth is low relative to the B_0 offset—an effect most clearly observed in echo-planar imaging (EPI), which typically uses low bandwidths in the phase-encoding direction. Still, they can also occur in conventional non-EPI acquisitions in the frequency-encoding (readout) direction and the slice-encoding (slice-select) direction that use relatively low bandwidths for high-resolution imaging. Therefore, distortions are present in non-EPI anatomical imaging, but are rarely acknowledged. Increasing encoding bandwidth reduces vulnerability to distortion at the cost of reducing SNR. Advanced methods such as field sensing and control (see Chapter 6) may soon become more widely available to help reduce distortion. Fully removing B_0 inhomogeneity during postprocessing is challenging, and for studies that use anatomical reference data to interpret fMRI data, geometric distortion is a major obstacle. For this reason, newer strategies seek to segment distorted fMRI data directly (see Section 12.6).

12.4 Higher imaging resolutions

The increased CNR at UHF is often exploited to achieve higher imaging resolution. Several brain regions require high resolutions to delineate their borders—for example, hippocampus requires isotropic voxel sizes below 1 mm (Wisse et al., 2021), whereas the cerebellar cortex may require 0.2 mm to segment the folia (Sereno et al., 2020), and the smallest pial blood vessels, the anastomoses, may require 0.1 mm. While smaller voxel sizes help sharpen tissue borders and adequately sample small structures, many sources of intrinsic blurring occur during image acquisition due to the long readouts required for small voxels, especially when using echo-train methods like EPI, 3D-GRASE, TSE, SPACE, or MPRAGE. These effects can be mitigated somewhat during acquisition. Nevertheless, because true voxel sizes may be larger than nominal voxel sizes, care must be taken when evaluating the data to account for these losses of resolution, especially when quantifying geometric properties of the anatomy.

Typically, segmentation methods developed for conventional resolutions must be adapted for higher resolutions because assumptions based on low-resolution data no longer hold, such as smoothness priors (Bazin et al., 2014; Lüsebrink et al., 2013; Zaretskaya et al., 2018). Practical considerations related to computing time, memory, and storage must be addressed as the number of voxels grows with increased resolution. This is especially challenging for algorithms whose complexities scale supralinearly with voxel count.

With higher resolution, several new anatomical features emerge that were unseen at conventional resolutions, which pose both opportunities and challenges. For example, when segmenting the cerebral cortex, higher resolutions enable more straightforward detection of surrounding anatomical structures that can be easily mistaken for gray matter, including the claustrum, a gray-matter region interior to the insular cortex separated by the white matter of the extreme capsule. Resolving the claustrum and distinguishing it from the insula can help improve the delineation of the insular cortex. Similarly, resolving the space between gray matter and adjacent dura mater, the walls of the cerebral sinuses, and subarachnoid vasculature helps improve segmentation accuracy. In many regions, the space between dura and gray matter is vanishingly small and challenging to resolve; thus, combining high resolutions with the multimodal approaches described above may be needed to prevent tissue misidentification.

When segmenting cortical gray matter using submillimeter data, several groups have reported apparent changes in cortical thickness compared with segmentations based on standard 1-mm data, with some cortical areas appearing thinner and others appearing thicker (Glasser and Van Essen, 2011; Lüsebrink et al., 2013; Zaretskaya et al., 2018). In particular, the thickness of thin and heavily myelinated areas such as primary sensory and visual cortex tends to be underestimated in low-resolution data. This is due to partial volume effects: the intensity of gray matter in these heavily myelinated areas tends to be more similar to that of white matter, causing the estimated location of the gray-white interface to be placed within gray matter (Zaretskaya et al., 2018). This may also cause the estimated location of the gray matter-CSF interface to be placed within gray matter (Glasser and Van Essen, 2011), leading to inaccurate segmentation. Analogously, dura mistaken for gray matter can cause the estimated location of gray matter-CSF interfaces to be placed within CSF. Thus, improved segmentation accuracy of cortical gray matter with higher resolution may cause several counter-acting changes in cortical thickness as estimates of both boundaries improve.

Accurate estimation of tissue borders requires subvoxel accuracy, which can be achieved either using volume-based segmentation that explicitly accounts for partial-volume effects by estimating the mixture of tissues within each voxel, or using surface-based segmentation that implicitly accounts for partial-volume effects by placing the tissue boundary within voxels based on nearby image intensities. Both approaches improve with higher resolution. This inference of tissue classes within voxels based on partial-volume models is well known in PET literature and is increasingly applied in MRI (Polimeni et al., 2018). In one notable study, partial-volume estimation was applied to inferring infragranular and supragranular layers of cortical gray matter based on the knowledge that infragranular layers tend to be more myelinated (Shafee et al., 2015). While generally these two compartments cannot be resolved in T_1-weighted data (likely due to insufficient contrast), the thickness of the infragranular and supragranular layers could be reasonably estimated from standard 1-mm MPRAGE data (Lambert et al., 2014; Shafee et al., 2015).

12.4.1 Balancing resolution and SNR

As new acquisition technologies enable higher resolutions, it is tempting to shrink voxel sizes to resolve smaller structures and improve segmentation quality. However, one must maintain sufficient SNR to ensure segmentation accuracy. It is often difficult to judge "by eye" when image SNR is insufficient for

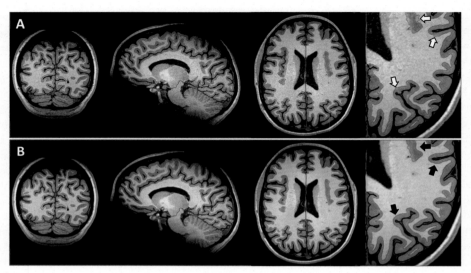

FIG. 12.4

High imaging resolution can improve segmentation accuracy, but adequate imaging SNR is also necessary. (A) Single average of an 0.6-mm isotropic 3D MPRAGE volume acquired at 3T using a slab-selective pulse and an oblique-axial orientation, shown in coronal, sagittal, axial, and axial zoom-in views. Cross-section of cortical surface reconstruction derived from segmentation is shown as *black contours*. While surface placement is largely accurate, in several locations, clear errors can be seen (indicated by *arrows*). (B) The same data averaged over six repeated acquisitions to increase SNR. The accuracy of the surface placement is improved (indicated by *arrows*). *Figure courtesy of Natalia Zaretskaya, Massachusetts General Hospital & University of Graz.*

segmentation, so with high-resolution data, segmentation performance can suffer even though tissue boundaries appear more salient (see Fig. 12.4). One strategy is to obtain multiple averages of high-resolution data to increase SNR; however, this can make acquisition times impractical, and blurring will occur when participants inevitably move within or between scans.

Recently, there has been a resurgence of image denoising applied to high-resolution MRI. Techniques ranging from traditional edge-preserving smoothing and classical machine learning, to patched-based learning (BM4D) and other "benchmark" denoising approaches, to low-rank approaches based on random matrix theory (Moeller et al., 2021; Veraart et al., 2016), and to deep learning (Tian et al., 2021) have been proposed. These all seek to remove unstructured noise while preserving signal—in this case, boundaries of anatomical structures—and can perform well when algorithm assumptions are met. Care must be taken when applying these approaches, which may decrease variance yet increase bias, leading to false-positive or false-negative detections of subtle anatomical features.

12.5　Region-specific segmentation

As discussed in Chapters 15–18, limiting the imaging field of view to the anatomical region of interest is often advantageous in high-resolution imaging. Approaches developed for whole-brain segmentation and labeling cannot always be readily applied to partial-brain data; thus, new tools are required.

Whole-brain segmentation (e.g., provided by FreeSurfer, FSL, and SPM) typically exploits priors regarding neighborhood relationships between individual regions, which provide context for segmentation. This information is missing in partial-brain data. Still, region-specific segmentation can exploit local priors to label structures of interest—key examples are atlas-based segmentation of hippocampal subfields, labeling of brainstem subnuclei, and identification of layers within individual cerebral cortical areas.

Today, whole-brain segmentation is synonymous with separating gray matter from white matter, and often uses T_1 contrast. Region-specific segmentation of UHF MRI data, however, is applied to separate substructures, often deep-gray nuclei, and is tailored to "dedicated" imaging protocols (often using higher resolutions). Many cutting-edge segmentation methods are being developed and applied in this domain.

Region-specific segmentation can be fully automatic, guided by whole-brain data used to home in on the region of interest using template matching or atlases (e.g., Fig. 12.1B); however, it is often performed using semiautomatic methods with manual guidance. These range from fully manual hand-labeling to adaptive methods based on active contours that build smoothness or other geometric constraints into the tracing combined with local edge detection. While these methods are powerful, they are time-consuming, and results can be biased by subjective definitions of tissue borders, which cause variance when multiple operators segment larger datasets. Seed-based or other methods that allow for coarse identification of regions of interest are less biased and time-consuming; newer learning-based adaptive user-guided methods also show promise. Operator intervention can be helpful for posthoc correction of segmentation results, and is most successful when the user interface is simple and intuitive. Combinations of manual and semiautomatic segmentation have been applied to 7T brain data (Gulban et al., 2018) that outperform fully automatic methods. Specialized training in the specific features and biases of UHF MRI data, and straightforward operating procedures/guidelines, help ensure consistency.

Regional segmentation approaches are increasingly used to delineate the cortical surface for high-resolution fMRI studies. In this application, tailored segmentation approaches aimed at the accurate definition of gray-white borders in the anatomical reference data are desired; however, registration of the segmented border to the fMRI data is often the factor that limits accuracy, and for this reason, segmentation approaches are being developed for the fMRI data themselves.

12.6 Direct segmentation of EPI data

EPI is the main acquisition method for functional, perfusion, and diffusion imaging. EPI is well known to be vulnerable to geometric distortion along the phase-encoding direction. Severe differential distortion can be found between EPI data and anatomical reference data at UHF. As the quality and resolution of EPI data have improved, EPI has become suitable for anatomical segmentation—much to the surprise of long-time UHF MRI practitioners! At UHF, EPI resolution can exceed that of conventional anatomical imaging, as submillimeter-scale voxels are readily achievable. This opens new possibilities to directly segment anatomical EPI data that are distortion-matched to the target functional, diffusion, or perfusion data, which overcomes a major limitation to segmentation accuracy for many studies.

This approach has become popular in high-resolution fMRI, especially in the emerging field of laminar fMRI (see Chapters 22–25), where accurate alignment of functional and anatomical data is critical for the interpretation of the data. While standard BOLD fMRI uses T_2^* weighting for functional contrast, direct segmentation of T_2^*-weighted images is challenging and not recommended. Instead, a contrast preparation such as an inversion recovery can impose T_1 weighting in the EPI data to facilitate segmentation while using a readout that is distortion-matched to the fMRI data. Because EPI is fast, it is possible to efficiently generate a quantitative T_1 map by collecting several EPI volumes at various inversion times (see Renvall et al., 2016 and references therein). This has the added benefit of separating T_1 effects from unwanted T_2^* weighting and B_1-related biases that impact segmentation accuracy. This approach provides accurate, automatic full-brain segmentations based on 1-mm isotropic 7T data acquired in under 3 min (Renvall et al., 2016). The accuracy of these segmentations of the cerebral cortex is high enough to be recommended for surface-based analysis of fMRI data.

This concept of anatomical segmentation using distortion-matched EPI data has been extended to 3D EPI, which is increasingly utilized for high-resolution fMRI, including a T_1-weighted 3D EPI approach that mimics MP2RAGE (van der Zwaag et al., 2018). Other contrast preparations are possible, such as MT (Chai et al., 2021).

In some cases, it is possible to segment the target fMRI data directly. For non-BOLD fMRI, the fMRI data themselves can possess sufficient anatomical contrast to be accurately segmented. This strategy has been extended to EPI-based diffusion MRI which exhibits sufficient gray-white contrast (Little and Beaulieu, 2021).

The major drawback of segmenting brain structures using EPI is the increased vulnerability to geometric distortion compared to conventional anatomical data. While the distortion in anatomical EPI data allows for the resulting segmentation to be distortion-matched to the functional EPI data, it will cause inaccuracy and imprecision in any morphological estimates such as cortical thickness, which will depend on B_0 inhomogeneity. Naturally, any uncorrected distortions will leave geometric biases in the fMRI data, so care must be taken with this approach.

12.7 Machine learning-based segmentation

As with many aspects of neuroimaging, machine learning (ML) is increasingly playing a major role in brain segmentation, mainly deep learning (DL) based on convolutional neural networks (CNNs). This trend has been fueled by the following: (i) the power of these methods, (ii) the availability of software packages (such as PyTorch and TensorFlow) that facilitate the implementation of sophisticated networks and training algorithms, (iii) access to large, freely available datasets, and (iv) massively parallel computational resources such as graphics processing units (GPUs). An advantage of DL-based segmentation is that, once a network is trained, computing a segmentation can be remarkably fast, making previously intractable tasks feasible and allowing new applications enabled by near-real-time solutions. While ML-based segmentation has not yet been widely applied to UHF data, it is expected to provide benefits—especially for high-resolution images, where traditional methods become excruciatingly slow.

ML-based methods have been used to preprocess the data to be more amenable to segmentation. Most commonly, however, ML-based methods are applied directly to image segmentation, frequently employing supervised learning approaches that require high-quality ground-truth data for training. There are many ML-based approaches for segmenting specific brain regions and pathologies, and several DL approaches have been successfully applied to whole-brain segmentation (e.g., Wachinger et al.,

2018). These methods have been validated against manual segmentations and conventional methods, such as the segmentations provided by FreeSurfer or FSL, with comparable or even improved performance achieved in a small fraction of the computational time. The *FastSurfer* method (Henschel et al., 2022), in particular, utilizes DL-based segmentation of volumetric data followed by sped-up cortical surface reconstruction to provide all relevant FreeSurfer-conforming outputs.

Like atlas-based approaches, DL-based methods demonstrate excellent performance on cases from the training domain, trained mostly using 3T data, but do not necessarily generalize to "out-of-distribution" contrasts or resolutions, and are likely to fail on UHF data. DL-based methods, however, can cover a wide range of anatomies during training—often hundreds or thousands of cases, if they are available—compared to only relatively few cases that are employed to construct probabilistic atlases. Furthermore, DL approaches can be adapted more easily to other domains than atlas-based approaches. The *PSACNN* method, for example, provides fast, whole-brain segmentations that perform well on data acquired with a variety of contrasts and bias fields to be agnostic to the details of the pulse sequence (Jog et al., 2019). This is a promising avenue for exploring whether networks trained on 3T data perform well on 7T data.

Other advances permit spanning different resolutions. Training separate individual models for each resolution (Fig. 12.5A) would not be feasible due to limited available ground-truth and potential biases, such as the lack of diseased or very old cases at particularly high resolutions (or at UHF in general). ML-based segmentation approaches can be made to handle input data from a range of resolutions

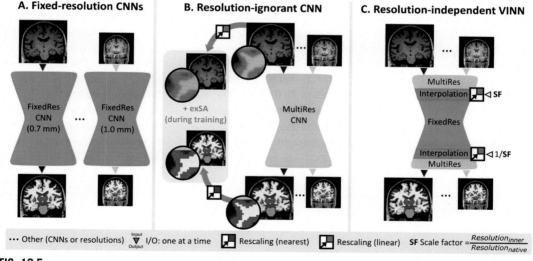

FIG. 12.5

Resolution independence in deep learning networks. (A) Multiple dedicated fixed-resolution CNNs are limited by the availability and quality of training datasets. (B) One single resolution-ignorant CNN can be trained on a diverse dataset where external scale augmentation (+exSA; B, left) simulates resolutions with few or no training cases, while losing structural details due to interpolation artifacts. (C) *FastSurferVINN* avoids interpolation of the images and discrete labels by integrating the interpolation step into the network architecture, and can, thus, focus on learning anatomical features at a fixed internal resolution rather than scale differences. *Adapted from Henschel et al. (2022), with permission.*

through extensive augmentation (Fig. 12.5B) during training as in *SynthSeg* (Billot et al., 2020), where ground-truth segmentations must be available at the highest resolution (which in this study was 1 mm). *SynthSeg* uses augmentation based on synthetically generated data to segment real images acquired across multiple lower resolutions and contrasts. It, furthermore, provides segmentations that are aware of partial-volume effects and can thus provide subvoxel accuracy up to the training resolution.

FastSurferVINN is a novel approach to directly segment images at their native resolution, ranging from 1.0-mm down to 0.7-mm isotropic and beyond (Henschel et al., 2022), which holds promise for high-resolution UHF MRI (see Fig. 12.5C). *FastSurferVINN* introduces a voxel-size-independent neural network (VINN) that avoids the lossy label interpolation of external scale augmentation approaches (Fig. 12.5B). It further allows the network to learn from different age groups or diseases, available at different resolutions, transferring this information across resolutions and thus reducing potential biases of individual fixed-resolution models (Fig. 12.5A).

Thus far, there has been limited application of these techniques to UHF data. Recently, a global 3D CNN-based whole-brain segmentation method, *CEREBRUM-7T*, was developed for 7T MRI that can segment six tissue classes from high-resolution (0.65-mm iso.) MP2RAGE data (Svanera et al., 2021). It operates directly on the acquired high-resolution 7T MP2RAGE data without requiring preprocessing and shows promise for augmentation and fine-tuning using data from different imaging protocols across multiple sites (Svanera et al., 2021).

For most ML-based segmentation methods, performance and generalizability critically depend on the quality of training data. Some evidence suggests that, with sufficient data augmentation, ML-based methods can, remarkably, outperform the segmentation used to generate the training data (Henschel et al., 2022; Svanera et al., 2021), including improved test–retest reliability, improved sensitivity to disease effects, and better generalizability. These observations suggest that ML-based methods may reduce segmentation noise. Still, the network likely inherits systematic errors in the training data.

The key challenge for ML-based segmentation is generalizability, especially given the broad diversity of data that can be acquired with modern UHF MRI. This can be addressed by expanding the diversity of training data, either through incorporating more datasets, through augmentation, or by applying domain transfer methods. One promising direction is "physics-informed" ML approaches that aim to generate augmentation data that adhere to the physics of the data acquisition, potentially enabling ML-based segmentation that can perform well on data acquired across field strengths.

12.8 Conclusions and outlook

There is clear potential to improve segmentation performance; in particular, more effort will be required to remove biases that confound segmentation. Either prior knowledge of bias fields must be updated, or physics-based priors that account for field strength may improve generalizability. Also, methods that can generalize across the wide variety of imaging protocols and resolutions in use, as well as the variety of *instrumentation* used across sites, will be needed; many UHF MRI scanners are not standardized product scanners, and there is substantial heterogeneity across sites and vendors. Efforts into cross-site harmonization and protocol standardization can facilitate the development of segmentation methods that perform well across laboratories.

Segmentation can be improved by using better data—the best cortical segmentation method cannot be expected to perform well when gray and white matter are isointense due to B_1^+ errors, or when gray matter and dura are isointense due to their similar T_1 values, or when voxel size is insufficient to resolve the folia of the cerebellar cortex. Thus, collaboration is needed between researchers developing data acquisition methods and those developing segmentation algorithms. Often the factors limiting data quality stem from "biological" limits imposed by the human body—such as safety limits, e.g., PNS or SAR, and motion, both rigid head movement and nonrigid tissue deformation—rather than limitations of the MRI hardware. Today, many important brain regions cannot be reliably resolved, such as many brainstem nuclei and layers of cortical gray matter, and efforts to improve resolution while addressing motion will be required.

Consensus is growing that no one contrast may suffice for accurate segmentation, even for classic problems such as segmenting the cerebral cortex. Acquiring multiple images with different contrast weightings, in combination with auxiliary data for estimating bias fields, is promising. "Multimodal" imaging (Lambert et al., 2014) can help remove biases, better distinguish tissue classes, and improve data interpretability in terms of the underlying microanatomical features of interest. This, combined with quantitative imaging, can enhance anatomical specificity and enable segmentation based on relevant anatomical features such as myelin content or neuronal density rather than on T_1 or fractional anisotropy. As in vivo data continue to improve, they will increasingly be capable of relating to microanatomical architectonic features, achieving the goals of "in vivo histology" (Weiskopf et al., 2021).

Finally, while most segmentation methods leverage prior knowledge to improve performance, standard assumptions may not always hold. As UHF MRI methods continue to evolve, and resolutions and contrasts continue to increase, even the most accurate segmentation methods developed for conventional 3T data are likely to fail when applied to UHF data without adaptation. Approaches based on registration to atlases may also fail to capture fine-scale details of brain anatomy known to vary across individuals, such as distal branches of the vasculature, borders of higher-order cortical areas, and varying patterns of myelination across cortical columnar systems. Future work toward improving the accuracy of brain segmentation of individual subjects enabled by UHF MRI will aid the investigation of subtle brain anatomy changes with development, plasticity, aging, and disease progression, and help understand how brain structure shapes and reflects brain function, cognition, and behavior.

Acknowledgments

We thank Drs. Daniel Gomez, Leonie Henschel, Qiyuan Tian, Divya Varadarajan, and Natalia Zaretskaya for helpful comments. Special thanks to Ms. Siyu Liu for providing the images in Fig. 12.3, Dr. Zaretskaya for providing the images in Fig. 12.4, and Mr. Thomas Shaw, Dr. Marta Bianciardi, Dr. Yuhui Chai, and Dr. Pilou Bazin for agreeing to include figures from their work in Fig. 12.1.

References

Assaf, Y., 2019. Imaging laminar structures in the gray matter with diffusion MRI. Neuroimage 197, 677–688. https://doi.org/10.1016/j.neuroimage.2017.12.096.

Bazin, P.-L., Weiss, M., Dinse, J., Schäfer, A., Trampel, R., Turner, R., 2014. A computational framework for ultra-high resolution cortical segmentation at 7Tesla. Neuroimage 93 (Pt 2), 201–209. https://doi.org/10.1016/j.neuroimage.2013.03.077.

Bazin, P.L., Alkemade, A., Mulder, M.J., Henry, A.G., Forstmann, B.U., 2020. Multi-contrast anatomical subcortical structures parcellation. eLife 9, e59430.

Bernier, M., Bilgic, B., Bollmann, S., Fultz, N.E., Polimeni, J.R., 2020. Multimodal quantitative arterial-venous segmentation of the human brain at 7T: structure, susceptibility and flow. Proc. Int. Soc. Magn. Reson. Med. 28, 0158.

Bianciardi, M., Toschi, N., Edlow, B.L., et al., 2015. Toward an in vivo neuroimaging template of human brainstem nuclei of the ascending arousal, autonomic, and motor systems. Brain Connect. 5, 597–607. https://doi.org/10.1089/brain.2015.0347.

Billot, B., Robinson, E., Dalca, A.V., Iglesias, J.E., 2020. Partial volume segmentation of brain MRI scans of any resolution and contrast. In: Lect. Notes Comput. Sci. (including Subser. Lect. Notes Artif. Intell. Lect. Notes Bioinformatics) 12267 LNCS, pp. 177–187, https://doi.org/10.1007/978-3-030-59728-3_18.

Bollmann, S., Mattern, H., Bernier, M., et al., 2022. Imaging of the pial arterial vasculature of the human brain in vivo using high-resolution 7T time-of-flight angiography. Elife 11. https://doi.org/10.7554/ELIFE.71186.

Chai, Y., Li, L., Wang, Y., et al., 2021. Magnetization transfer weighted EPI facilitates cortical depth determination in native fMRI space. Neuroimage 242. https://doi.org/10.1016/J.NEUROIMAGE.2021.118455.

Duché, Q., Saint-Jalmes, H., Acosta, O., et al., 2017. Partial volume model for brain MRI scan using MP2RAGE. Hum. Brain Mapp. 38, 5115–5127. https://doi.org/10.1002/hbm.23719.

Fujimoto, K., Polimeni, J.R., van der Kouwe, A.J.W., et al., 2014. Quantitative comparison of cortical surface reconstructions from MP2RAGE and multi-echo MPRAGE data at 3 and 7 T. Neuroimage 90, 60–73. https://doi.org/10.1016/j.neuroimage.2013.12.012.

Glasser, M.F., Van Essen, D.C., 2011. Mapping human cortical areas in vivo based on myelin content as revealed by T1- and T2-weighted MRI. J. Neurosci. 31, 11597–11616. https://doi.org/10.1523/JNEUROSCI.2180-11.2011.

Gulban, O.F., Schneider, M., Marquardt, I., Haast, R.A.M., De Martino, F., 2018. A scalable method to improve gray matter segmentation at ultra high field MRI. PloS One 13. https://doi.org/10.1371/journal.pone.0198335.

Haast, R.A.M., Ivanov, D., Uludağ, K., 2018. The impact of B1+ correction on MP2RAGE cortical T1 and apparent cortical thickness at 7T. Hum. Brain Mapp. 39, 2412–2425. https://doi.org/10.1002/hbm.24011.

Henschel, L., Kügler, D., Reuter, M., 2022. FastSurferVINN: building resolution-independence into deep learning segmentation methods—a solution for HighRes brain MRI. Neuroimage 251, 118933. https://doi.org/10.1016/j.neuroimage.2022.118933.

Jog, A., Hoopes, A., Greve, D.N., Van Leemput, K., Fischl, B., 2019. PSACNN: pulse sequence adaptive fast whole brain segmentation. Neuroimage 199, 553–569. https://doi.org/10.1016/J.NEUROIMAGE.2019.05.033.

Lambert, C., Lutti, A., Frackowiak, R., Ashburner, J., 2014. Fine grain cortical segmentation using multiparametric maps at 3T. In: 20th Annu. Meet. Organ. Hum. Brain Mapp. 3887.

Little, G., Beaulieu, C., 2021. Automated cerebral cortex segmentation based solely on diffusion tensor imaging for investigating cortical anisotropy. Neuroimage 237. https://doi.org/10.1016/J.NEUROIMAGE.2021.118105.

Lüsebrink, F., Wollrab, A., Speck, O., 2013. Cortical thickness determination of the human brain using high resolution 3T and 7T MRI data. Neuroimage 70, 122–131. https://doi.org/10.1016/j.neuroimage.2012.12.016.

Moeller, S., Pisharady, P.K., Ramanna, S., et al., 2021. NOise reduction with distribution corrected (NORDIC) PCA in dMRI with complex-valued parameter-free locally low-rank processing. Neuroimage 226. https://doi.org/10.1016/J.NEUROIMAGE.2020.117539.

Polimeni, J.R., Renvall, V., Zaretskaya, N., Fischl, B., 2018. Analysis strategies for high-resolution UHF-fMRI data. Neuroimage 168, 296–320. https://doi.org/10.1016/j.neuroimage.2017.04.053.

Priovoulos, N., Jacobs, H.I.L., Ivanov, D., Uludağ, K., Verhey, F.R.J., Poser, B.A., 2018. High-resolution in vivo imaging of human locus coeruleus by magnetization transfer MRI at 3T and 7T. Neuroimage 168, 427–436. https://doi.org/10.1016/j.neuroimage.2017.07.045.

Renvall, V., Witzel, T., Wald, L.L., Polimeni, J.R., 2016. Automatic cortical surface reconstruction of high-resolution T1 echo planar imaging data. Neuroimage 134, 338–354. https://doi.org/10.1016/j.neuroimage.2016.04.004.

Sereno, M.I., Diedrichsen, J., Tachrount, M., Testa-Silva, G., d'Arceuil, H., De Zeeuw, C., 2020. The human cerebellum has almost 80% of the surface area of the neocortex. Proc. Natl. Acad. Sci. U. S. A. 117, 19538–19543. https://doi.org/10.1073/PNAS.2002896117.

Shafee, R., Buckner, R.L., Fischl, B., 2015. Gray matter myelination of 1555 human brains using partial volume corrected MRI images. Neuroimage 105, 473–485. https://doi.org/10.1016/j.neuroimage.2014.10.054.

Shaw, T., York, A., Ziaei, M., Barth, M., Bollmann, S., Alzheimer's Disease Neuroimaging Initiative, 2020. Longitudinal Automatic Segmentation of Hippocampal Subfields (LASHiS) using multi-contrast MRI. Neuroimage 218, 116798.

Svanera, M., Benini, S., Bontempi, D., Muckli, L., 2021. CEREBRUM-7T: fast and fully volumetric brain segmentation of 7 Tesla MR volumes. Hum. Brain Mapp. 42, 5563–5580. https://doi.org/10.1002/HBM.25636.

Tian, Q., Zaretskaya, N., Fan, Q., et al., 2021. Improved cortical surface reconstruction using sub-millimeter resolution MPRAGE by image denoising. Neuroimage 233. https://doi.org/10.1016/j.neuroimage.2021.117946.

van der Zwaag, W., Buur, P.F., Fracasso, A., et al., 2018. Distortion-matched T1 maps and unbiased T1-weighted images as anatomical reference for high-resolution fMRI. Neuroimage 176, 41–55. https://doi.org/10.1016/j.neuroimage.2018.04.026.

Veraart, J., Novikov, D.S., Christiaens, D., Ades-aron, B., Sijbers, J., Fieremans, E., 2016. Denoising of diffusion MRI using random matrix theory. Neuroimage 142, 394. https://doi.org/10.1016/J.NEUROIMAGE.2016.08.016.

Viviani, R., Pracht, E.D., Brenner, D., Beschoner, P., Stingl, J.C., Stöcker, T., 2017. Multimodal MEMPRAGE, FLAIR, and R2* segmentation to resolve dura and vessels from cortical gray matter. Front. Neurosci. 11, 258. https://doi.org/10.3389/fnins.2017.00258.

Wachinger, C., Reuter, M., Klein, T., 2018. DeepNAT: deep convolutional neural network for segmenting neuroanatomy. Neuroimage 170, 434–445. https://doi.org/10.1016/J.NEUROIMAGE.2017.02.035.

Weiskopf, N., Edwards, L.J., Helms, G., Mohammadi, S., Kirilina, E., 2021. Quantitative magnetic resonance imaging of brain anatomy and in vivo histology. Nat. Rev. Phys. 3, 570–588. https://doi.org/10.1038/s42254-021-00326-1.

Wisse, L.E.M., Chételat, G., Daugherty, A.M., et al., 2021. Hippocampal subfield volumetry from structural isotropic 1 mm3 MRI scans: a note of caution. Hum. Brain Mapp. 42, 539–550. https://doi.org/10.1002/hbm.25234.

Zaretskaya, N., Fischl, B., Reuter, M., Renvall, V., Polimeni, J.R., 2018. Advantages of cortical surface reconstruction using submillimeter 7 T MEMPRAGE. Neuroimage 165, 11–26. https://doi.org/10.1016/j.neuroimage.2017.09.060.

Phase imaging: Susceptibility-Weighted Imaging and Quantitative Susceptibility Mapping

13

Simon Daniel Robinson[a,b,c] and Ferdinand Schweser[d,e]

[a]*High Field MR Centre, Department of Biomedical Imaging and Image-Guided Therapy, Medical University of Vienna, Vienna, Austria* [b]*Department of Neurology, Medical University of Graz, Graz, Austria* [c]*Centre of Advanced Imaging, University of Queensland, Brisbane, QLD, Australia* [d]*Buffalo Neuroimaging Analysis Center, Department of Neurology, Jacobs School of Medicine and Biomedical Sciences, University at Buffalo, The State University of New York, New York, NY, United States* [e]*Center for Biomedical Imaging, Clinical and Translational Science Institute, University at Buffalo, The State University of New York, New York, NY, United States*

Highlights

- Gradient echo MRI signal phase provides a rich source of information about tissue composition and integrity.
- Susceptibility-Weighted Imaging (SWI) and Quantitative Susceptibility Mapping (QSM) are the most widely used phase imaging methods.
- Phase imaging at ultra-high field enables unique clinical and research applications.

13.1 Introduction

Most MRI techniques rely exclusively on the magnitude, or absolute value, of the complex-valued MR signal, but the phase provides a rich source of complementary information about tissue composition and integrity. This chapter focuses on gradient echo (GE)-based applications in which the phase signal reflects local shifts in the Larmor frequency due, primarily, to the presence of tissues with differing magnetic susceptibilities. The principal sources of susceptibility variation between tissues are iron, calcium, and myelin, leading to clinical applications in imaging stroke, venous anomalies, tumors, and neurodegenerative disorders associated with demyelination and iron accumulation, such as multiple sclerosis.

This chapter concentrates on two techniques. The first, Susceptibility-Weighted Imaging (SWI), uses a high-pass filtered phase to increase magnitude image contrast between paramagnetic inclusions and surrounding tissues, yielding exquisite representations of veins and iron-laden deep gray matter. The second, Quantitative Susceptibility Mapping (QSM), reconstructs the underlying tissue susceptibility distribution, offering the potential to provide reproducible measurements of disease status and progression. This chapter introduces the sources of frequency shifts, practical considerations in processing phase images, and the steps involved in generating SWI and QSM from phase images. In QSM, the wide range of approaches under development reflect the complexity of the problem and the relative youth of the field; we have supplied the reader with links to benchmarking comparisons and toolboxes to serve as possible starting points. For practical recommendations on using QSM in clinical research, we refer the reader to a recent consensus paper (The ISMRM Study Group for EMTP, n.d.), which, although it focuses on QSM at 3T, provides recommendations which also apply to QSM at ultra-high field. We conclude this chapter with example applications that showcase the enormous clinical potential of SWI and QSM at ultra-high field.

13.2 The physics of magnetic susceptibility and phase

All matter magnetizes when it is exposed to a magnetic field, such as the MRI scanner's main magnetic field. The magnetization stems from an interaction of the field with the spin magnetic moments of the elementary particles in the material, primarily with those of the electrons. *Magnetic susceptibility* (χ) is the physical quantity that describes how *susceptible* a material is to magnetization: $\overrightarrow{M} = \chi \cdot \overrightarrow{H}_0$, where $\overrightarrow{M}$ describes the magnetization and $\overrightarrow{H}_0 = \mu_0^{-1} \overrightarrow{B}_0$ the external magnetic field.

Susceptibility is dimensionless (no unit) and can be negative ($-1 \leq \chi < 0$; diamagnetism) or positive (paramagnetic), depending on the substance's electron configuration (chemical composition, structure, and bonds) and temperature. The voxel-average susceptibility value of most tissues is close to that of water, the most abundant molecule: $\chi_{water} = -9.04 \times 10^{-6}$, or -9.04 parts per million (ppm). Other tissue constituents like iron (which is paramagnetic), lipids, or calcium (both of which are diamagnetic) shift susceptibility values by only a few tens or hundreds of parts per billion (ppb; $\pm 0.01 \ldots \pm 0.1$ ppm).

The magnetized tissue adds its own magnetic field, the *demagnetization field* $\overrightarrow{B}_{demag}$, to the externally applied field (Fig. 13.1, top right). The total field, as sensed by the imaging protons, is then $\overrightarrow{B} = (1 - \sigma) \cdot \left(\overrightarrow{B}_0 + \overrightarrow{B}_{demag} \right)$, where the *chemical shift* σ represents the shielding of the proton by its surrounding electron cloud. The subtle field perturbation $\overrightarrow{B} - \overrightarrow{B}_0$ causes a Larmor frequency shift Δf.

Larmor frequency shifts due to demagnetization fields cause phase shifts in gradient echo MRI (Fig. 13.1, middle). Other factors that can shift the voxel-average Larmor frequency are tissue microstructure and chemical exchange effects. If the frequency shift varies substantially at a length scale below that of the voxel size, it will also give rise to signal dephasing, resulting in a magnitude signal decay (T_2^*).

Neglecting the multicompartment nature of biological tissues, in a multiecho acquisition with j echoes acquired at echo times TE_j, the true (i.e. wrap-free) jth phase, φ_j^c, from the cth coil is:

$$\varphi_j^c = \varphi_0^c + TE_j \cdot \Delta f, \tag{13.1}$$

where φ_0^c are the phase offsets (the phase at time zero). Eq. 13.1 allows Δf to be determined from the phase images of a multiecho GE scan.

The exact mathematical relationship between χ and the observed, voxel-average Δf is still an area of active research and debate, primarily as it relates to microscopic tissue heterogeneity. However, an elegant convolution equation can be obtained when chemical shift as well as structural and molecule anisotropy is ignored, which is the current practice in the QSM field:

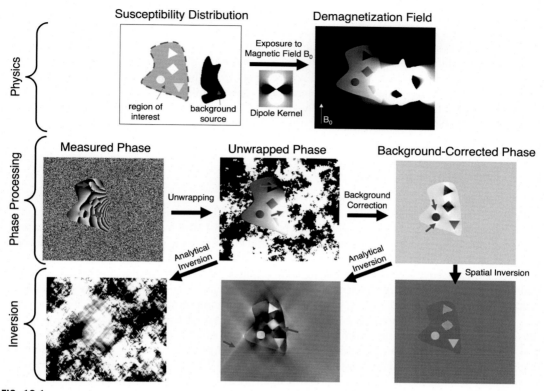

FIG. 13.1

Illustration of the relationship between magnetic susceptibility and image phase. Spatially varying magnetic susceptibility within a homogeneous magnetic field causes field inhomogeneities (demagnetization fields). The relationship between susceptibility and field perturbation is described by physics (Eq. 13.2; top row). Gradient echo MRI produces wrapped phase images (Eq. 13.4), which are unwrapped and corrected for background contributions (middle row; *arrows* highlight phase wraps, background fields, and internal fields, from left to right). Finally, susceptibility maps are computed from the processed phase images (bottom row). Naïve inversion without background correction (bottom left) results in severely degraded image quality. Simple analytical inverse filtering of the background-corrected phase images suffers from characteristic-streaking artifacts (bottom middle), whereas inversion with spatial priors results in a susceptibility map close to the ground truth (bottom right).

$$\Delta f / f_0 = \chi * D, \qquad (13.2)$$

where Δf and $f_0 = \gamma \cdot B_0$ is the center frequency, $*$ denotes 3D convolution, and D is a unit dipole corrected for near fields (Lorentz sphere). This equation allows the estimation of an apparent scalar χ with basic deconvolution methods ($*^{-1}$): $\chi = (\Delta f / f_0) *^{-1} D$. These "inversion" methods are discussed later.

The use of ultra-high field is enormously advantageous in susceptibility imaging. In addition to the approximately linear increase in the image signal-to-noise ratio (SNR) with the field strength which is associated with the increase in the number of protons aligned with the static magnetic field

(Pohmann et al., 2016), a linear increase in tissue magnetization also increases the susceptibility contrast, which accrues rapidly due to the decrease in T_2^* with the field (Yao et al., 2009), while the shorter RF wavelength in the tissue reduces g-factors in accelerated imaging. These conditions allow an increase in the resolution which reduces the partial volume of the dipole field around the small veins, bringing an additional contrast benefit to SWI (see Fig. 13.4). In contrast to relaxation rates (e.g., T_2^*) and the Larmor frequency itself, the magnetic susceptibility of biological tissues is field-independent at the field strengths currently used for MRI, facilitating the translation of quantitative findings to lower field strengths, which are still more widely available in the clinical setting.

13.3 Acquisition methods

The sensitivity of the GE signal to field inhomogeneity makes high-resolution, 3D, spoiled GE the sequence of choice for susceptibility imaging in most contexts. Acquisition of more than one echo makes it possible to separate Δf from phase offsets φ_0^c in Eq. 13.1 (Robinson et al., 2011) and to capture the signal from tissues with fast T_2^* relaxation. Phase and magnitude images can be combined with echoes to reduce signal dropouts and maximize CNR as well as sample the magnitude signal decay for T_2^* mapping. Bipolar sequences in which the signal is acquired under both positive and negative readout gradient lobes allow more efficient sampling, thereby higher CNR than monopolar sequences with fly-back gradients (Eckstein et al., 2021), particularly for high-resolution acquisitions and short echo spacings. However, corrections may be needed for chemical shift displacement and susceptibility distortions, which occur in opposite directions along the readout axis for odd and even echoes (Eckstein et al., 2018). First-order flow compensation can be applied to correct the phase accumulation due to spins in vessels moving with constant velocity (Xu et al., 2014), but the additional time required for the gradient moment nulling and relatively a small correction effect on QSM values has precluded its widespread use in multiecho acquisitions.

The need for faster acquisition for multiorientation QSM (Liu et al., 2009), functional QSM (Balla et al., 2014), and patients with low tolerance to long exams has led to increased adoption of ultra-fast sequences including 2D EPI, 3D EPI (Langkammer et al., 2015), PROPELLER (Stäb et al., 2017), and WAIVE-CAIPI (Bilgic et al., 2016). In the processing of data acquired with these methods for QSM, it should be noted that these fast methods are generally acquired as single-echo scans and that some are affected by distortion, T_2^* blurring, and lower SNR. In the spinal cord and neck, where the structures of interest are close to fatty tissues, the susceptibility-related field perturbations can be isolated from chemical shift effects using in-phase imaging (Karsa et al., 2020), joint estimation (Dimov et al., 2015), preconditioned water-fat total field inversion (Boehm et al., 2022), or simultaneous multiple resonance frequency imaging (SMURF) (Bachrata et al., 2021), which allows correction of a chemical shift and relaxation time bias on QSM (Bachrata et al., 2022).

SWI and QSM both rely on T_2^*-weighted GE data and benefit from high spatial resolution, but there are some discrepancies in the optimum acquisition parameters for the two methods which result from the fact that the focus in SWI is primarily on maximizing CNR between small veins and surrounding tissues. The contributions from the positive and negative lobes of the dipole distribution around the small veins tend to cancel in isotropic voxels, resulting in reduced phase contrast. However, the contrast can be increased in SWI for these small structures using an axial slice orientation and a slice thickness that is at least twice that of the in-plane resolution (Deistung et al., 2008). A general guideline is that optimum CNR is achieved in phase images when the echo time is equal to the T_2^* of the tissue of interest. Since the focus of SWI is generally on the veins, which have short T_2^*, the optimum echo train length is often slightly shorter for SWI than for QSM. For whole-brain QSM at 7T, a useful starting point for imaging parameters would be axial acquisition, matrix size (AP LR HF) 296×234×190, 0.75 mm isotropic voxels, $TE = \{4.5,9,13.5,18,22.5\}$ ms, $TR = 25$ ms, FA $= 10°$, elliptical sampling, parallel imaging acceleration factor 2, and TA circa 8 min.

13.4 **Phase processing**
13.4.1 **Coil combination**

Phased array RF coils are used to increase SNR and allow partial parallel imaging. The goal of coil combination is to calculate the true, Larmor frequency-related phase, $TE_j \cdot \Delta f$ in Eq. 13.1, from the individual complex-valued images φ_j^c of the individual coils (Fig. 13.2).

The phase offsets for the array, φ_0^c in Eq. 13.1, comprise contributions which are common to all coils (coil-*independent*), such as the phase of the transmit RF field, the effects of tissue conductivity, gradient mistiming and eddy current effects, and contributions which are unique to each coil, such as the coil sensitivity. Coil-*dependent* contributions must be identified and removed prior to a complex summation of the signals to avoid destructive interference.

Eq. 13.1, relating to the measured phase, φ_j^c, ΔB_0 and phase offsets, φ_0^c, is underdetermined for a single-echo scan and overdetermined for $j > 1$. Accordingly, many solutions to coil combination (which are described in more detail in Robinson et al., 2017) fall into three categories:

1. Those which require only one echo and determine relative phase offsets [e.g., ESPIRiT (Uecker et al., 2014) and virtual reference coil (Parker et al., 2014)].
2. Those which require a separate reference measurement [e.g., Roemer et al. (1990), SENSE (Pruessmann et al., 1999)].
3. Those which require multiple echoes [e.g., phase contrast/Hermitian inner product (Bernstein et al., 1994), and ASPIRE (Eckstein et al., 2018)].

The drawbacks of category 1 methods are that they introduce a spatial-varying background phase and tend to be less robust, while category 2 and 3 methods require reference or multiecho data, which may be impractical in some contexts (such as UHF MR systems without a body coil or other suitable reference coils). With the phase offsets (or relative phase offsets) defined, the combined phase can be calculated as:

$$\theta_{j,combined} = \angle \sum_c \left(m_j^c\right)^2 \cdot \exp\left(i \cdot \left(\theta_j^c - \varphi_{0,s}^c\right)\right), \tag{13.3}$$

where θ_j^c is the measured (i.e., wrapped) phase and m_j^c is the corresponding magnitude, which is squared to introduce sensitivity weighting.

13.4.2 **Phase unwrapping**

The phase of the complex signal, $\theta_{j,combined}$, is wrapped into a range of 2π radians given by $(\varphi_L, \varphi_L + 2\pi]$, where φ_L, the lower limit of the range, is usually chosen to be $-\pi$. The wrapped phase θ is related to the underlying phase φ by

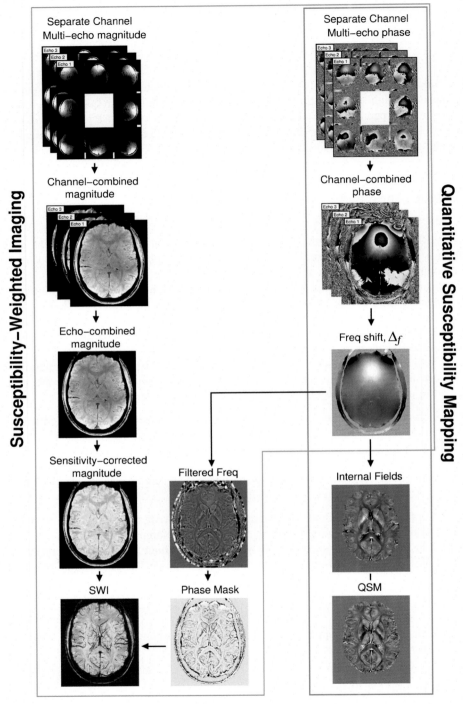

FIG. 13.2

Steps in Susceptibility-Weighted Imaging (SWI) and Quantitative Susceptibility Mapping (QSM), from acquisition to the final image. Both SWI and QSM require data to be combined over coils and echoes. In SWI (left column), the frequency shift map Δf is high-pass filtered and converted, using a positive linear function, to a phase mask, which is multiplied by a homogeneity-corrected magnitude to generate the SWI and minimum intensity project (mIP) SWI (mIP not shown). In QSM (right column), Δf is corrected for the background fields to generate a map of internal fields, the dipole inversion of which yields the QSM. These steps and processes are described more fully in the following sections.

$$\theta = (\varphi - \varphi_L) \bmod 2\pi + \varphi_L. \tag{13.4}$$

The number of wraps is given by

$$n = \left\lfloor \frac{\varphi - \varphi_L}{2\pi} \right\rceil, \tag{13.5}$$

the determination of which allows the underlying phase to be restored;

$$\varphi = \theta + n2\pi. \tag{13.6}$$

Phase wraps can be removed using temporal unwrapping, e.g., by calculating the four-quadrant tangent inverse (or atan2) of the phase difference between echoes, if the interval between echoes is sufficiently short. Path-based or region-growing spatial unwrapping, in contrast, relies on the assumption that the phase gradient is less than π per voxel. Differences of more than π between voxels [BEST-PATH (Abdul-Rahman et al., 2007) and ROMEO (Dymerska et al., 2021)] or regions [PRELUDE (Jenkinson, 2003) and SEGUE (Karsa and Shmueli, 2019)] are taken to be indicative of wraps, and 2π is added to or subtracted from the voxel or region under consideration to minimize the difference. Because path-following and region-growing approaches restore the original phase, we will refer to them as quantitative methods.

Rather than determining n, Laplacian unwrapping attempts to identify the unwrapped phase, the local derivatives of which are almost similar to the derivatives of the wrapped phase (Schofield and Zhu, 2003). This removes wraps but introduces a background phase, so—in contrast to quantitative approaches—the unwrapped phase is not equal to the true or underlying phase (see Fig. 13.3). Laplacian unwrapping is fast and performs well in low SNR conditions, and the background field it introduces can be removed by background field correction (see below), making it applicable for QSM despite its qualitative nature (Fig. 13.3). Temporal, path-following, region-growing, and Laplacian approaches are discussed in more detail in Robinson et al. (2017).

13.4.3 Echo combination

Data from each echo can be processed (unwrapped and background corrected) and inverted into susceptibility maps individually, which allows investigation of the echo-time evolution of susceptibility estimates. More widely used, though, are approaches which combine the information from echoes at different stages of the pipeline to benefit from averaging-related increases in CNR. One such is to calculate a frequency shift map from each individual, unwrapped echo (if phase offsets have been removed), or pairs of echoes (if they have not), and combine these in a weighted average (see Fig. 13.3, panel B, blue area). Optimum CNR can be generated by inverse variance-weighting, in which the frequency estimate from each echo is φ_i/TE_i and the inverse variance weighting $TE_i^2 M_i^2$;

$$\Delta f = \frac{\sum \frac{w_i \varphi_i}{TE_i}}{\sum w_i}, \text{ where } w_i = TE_i^2 M_i^2. \tag{13.7}$$

An alternative approach, which allows the use of Laplacian unwrapping, is to perform nonlinear fitting over echo time (Liu et al., 2013), and Laplacian-unwrap the result (see Fig. 13.3, panel B, gold area). While the frequency shift maps estimated with these two approaches are hugely different (because of the harmonic phase introduced by the Laplacian operation), discrepancies are removed by background field correction, resulting in susceptibility maps that agree well, barring differences in noise and errors arising from unwrapping (in the weighted frequency shift map method) and fitting (in the nonlinear fit approach).

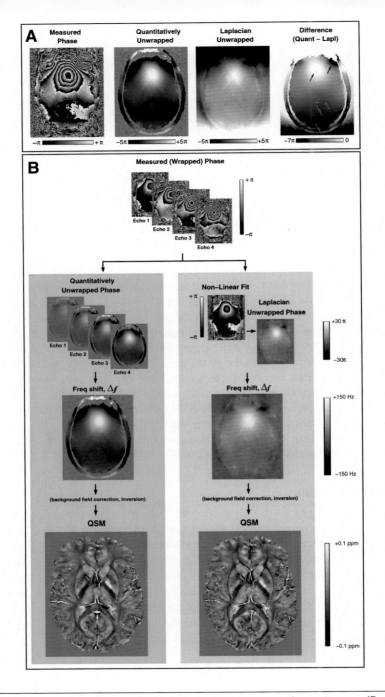

FIG. 13.3

Comparison of path-based (quantitative) and Laplacian phase unwrapping outcomes (Panel A), and two approaches to combining information over echoes (Panel B). Panel A: The true/underlying phase is restored by the quantitative (path-based) method, albeit with some errors in vessels (*red arrows* in difference image). The Laplacian method removes wraps throughout the image but introduces a background phase (*blue arrows* in the difference image). Panel B: The echo combination steps in the blue area show the unwrapping of each echo (using a quantitative method), before weighted combination to a frequency shift map. Alternatively, in the steps in the gold area, a nonlinear fit to the phase evolution approach is performed prior to Laplacian unwrapping and conversion to frequency shift. Note the differences in the frequency shift between the two approaches and that these are largely removed by background field correction (step not shown), leading to similar QSMs.

13.5 **Susceptibility-Weighted Imaging**

Susceptibility-Weighted Imaging (SWI; Haacke et al., 2004) uses the sensitivity of the phase of the MR signal in gradient echo acquisitions to the demagnetization field to generate contrast between tissues with different susceptibilities; primarily calcium, deoxygenated blood, blood products, and iron. The original SWI implementation, which was for data acquired with a single, circularly polarized head coil at 1.5T, involved high-pass filtering of the complex-valued images (homodyne filtering), which resulted in a partially unwrapped, high-pass filtered phase image. The filtered phase was converted into a mask by setting positive filtered phase values to 1 and scaling negative values from 1 to 0. Multiplication of this mask with the magnitude image led to an enhancement of hypointensities already present in the magnitude images due to T_2^* effects, particularly due to paramagnetic deoxyhemoglobin, leading to this originally being termed MR venography.

The use of phased array coils and the inhomogeneous B_0 and B_1 fields at UHF have forced developments in the processing of SWI. Foremost among these is the replacement of homodyne filtering, which not only high-pass filters the phase but (at low and intermediate field strength) removes the slow-phase variation in coil sensitivities. This allows coil signals to be combined while eliminating most phase wraps. For coil-combined images to retain relevant low-frequency information and to be usable for QSM, however, phase images need to be combined with one of the solutions outlined in Section 13.4.1. The larger B_0 variations at UHF also require unwrapping using a quantitative or Laplacian approach (see Section 13.4.2), which additionally allows the phase data to be combined over echoes (see Section 13.4.3). In converting high-pass filtered to a phase mask, the use of a smoother sigmoid function provides a less noisy and more natural phase contrast than multiple applications of a linear function, and magnitude images can be combined over echoes to minimize the signal dropout and corrected for B_1 inhomogeneity. In their totality, these steps (illustrated in Fig. 13.2) yield susceptibility-weighted images that are free of the phase artifacts associated with homodyne filtering and provide homogeneous contrast throughout the brain (see Fig. 13.4, reference 4 and references therein).

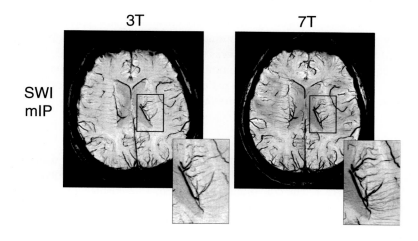

FIG. 13.4

Comparison of SWI at 3T and 7T in the same subject. Whole-brain, multiecho imaging protocols were matched for acquisition time (5′30″) and estimated SNR (with 0.4*0.4*1.6 mm³ voxels and *TE/TR* = {8,16,24,32,40}/47 ms at 3T, 0.3*0.3*1.2 mm³ voxels and *TE/TR* = {4.5,9,13.5,18,22}/28 ms at 7T, in both cases GRAPPA factor 2 and same FOV). Many more vessels are visible with improved contrast in the higher-resolution 7T mIP SWI.

13.6 Quantitative Susceptibility Mapping
13.6.1 Background fields

All tissues in the MRI bore generate demagnetization fields, not only those within the imaging region of interest. In the case of a brain scan, strong background demagnetization fields also originate from the skull, neck, and torso and superimpose the brain's demagnetization fields. The strongest contributions originate from the air-filled lungs and sinus cavities where susceptibility changes abruptly from $\chi \approx, -9$ ppm within the tissue to $\chi \approx 0$ in the air. The resulting fields often overpower, by orders of magnitude those caused by susceptibility variations within the region of interest (Fig. 13.1, top row).

Background fields pose challenges for the calculation of susceptibility when the source tissue of the background fields is outside the imaging region (e.g., lungs in a brain exam) or the field cannot accurately be estimated within the magnetized tissue causing the background fields (skull and air). Most inversion algorithms cannot properly interpret background fields and create susceptibility maps with strong inhomogeneities in their presence (Fig. 13.1, bottom row, left).

To facilitate the inversion, background field correction algorithms correct field maps (or, equivalently, frequency maps) for background fields and determine the *internal fields* of the region of interest (Fig. 13.1, middle row, right). These algorithms employ analytical strategies that capitalize on differences in the mathematical properties of background and nonbackground (internal) fields.

Benchmarking studies suggest only marginal differences in the performance of different approaches when applied in a laboratory setting (Schweser et al., 2017), with the accuracy increasing toward the center of the ROI. However, in the clinical setting, background correction is prone to (i) inaccuracies in the segmentation of the "region of interest" for the susceptibility calculation (ROI; e.g., brain tissue) and (ii) frequency map errors at the boundary of the ROI, e.g., from incomplete unwrapping. In general, segmentation (masking) must be more conservative compared to other applications if the tissue region is surrounded by signal voids (as is the case in the brain) because the background field correction is mathematically defined by the field at the region boundary and, hence, the inclusion of pure phase noise in signal void regions causes strong artifacts. Neuroimaging tools for brain masking like FSL BET, followed by slight binary erosion, usually produce satisfactory results at all field strengths when the brain anatomy is normal. To exclude all regions with strong phase noise, it can be necessary to include in the masking process information on the magnitude image intensity, the reliability of the frequency map, such as the temporal phase fitting residuals, or the quality map used in phase unwrapping. Automated segmentation in patients with brain abnormalities close to the brain's surface can be more challenging and may require tailored algorithms.

13.6.2 Inversion

The goal of the inversion step (Fig. 13.1, bottom) is to calculate a susceptibility distribution, χ, that is consistent with the observed frequency map, Δf. Most efforts have focused on solutions to the simplified physical model in Eq. 13.2. The convolution type of Eq. 13.2 enables a highly efficient computation of the forward problem, i.e., the simulation of the frequency map from a given susceptibility distribution, which is achieved by the voxel-wise multiplication of the Fourier-transformed quantities:

$$F\{\Delta f/f_0\} = F\{\chi\} \cdot F\{D\}, \tag{13.8}$$

where F denotes Fourier transformation. Analysis of $F\{D\}$ shows that the dipole attenuates certain spatial frequency components of χ. With the measurement noise added, information on related components of χ is practically irrecoverable from Δf, rendering the inverse problem numerically unstable (or "ill-conditioned"). The issue can be overcome by rotating the object (i.e., χ) relative to the main magnetic field and acquiring Δf at least three times, a method widely considered to be the gold standard of QSM and known as COSMOS (Liu et al., 2009). Due to the infeasibility of head rotations in the clinical setting, research has focused on addressing the ill-conditioning of the single-orientation problem through the use of numerical regularization. For example, regularization may impose reasonable assumptions on χ, such as spatial smoothness in relatively homogeneous tissue regions.

Eq. 13.8 suggests a straightforward analytical calculation of χ through voxel-wise division in the Fourier domain: $F^{-1}[F\{\Delta f/f_0\} \cdot F\{D'\}^{-1}] = \chi$. The use of a modified dipole kernel, D', addresses the ill-conditioning in this formalism. This computationally highly efficient "k-space approach" was used widely in the early days of QSM (Shmueli et al., 2009) but suffers from cone-shaped streaking artifacts along the main field direction (Fig. 13.1, bottom row, middle). More sophisticated approaches have demonstrated a superior reconstruction quality by solving Eq. 13.2 in the spatial domain (Fig. 13.1, bottom row, right). They iteratively improve estimations of χ and use Eq. 13.8 only to ensure the consistency of χ with the measured Δf. While computationally costly, spatial domain approaches benefit from the ability to incorporate explicit spatial assumptions on χ, such as edge priors or local homogeneity.

Deep neural networks represent a promising tool to overcome the high computational complexity of spatial domain algorithms and further increase the quality through more flexible regularization. Networks have been trained with sample pairs of $\Delta f/f_0$ and χ, either simulated (e.g., through Eq. 13.8) or acquired with the COSMOS method. Trained networks can then either infer χ directly from $\Delta f/f_0$ or be incorporated as regularization terms in spatial domain algorithms. Since neural networks do not require linearization of the mathematical problem, they may enable the solution of more realistic biophysical tissue models than Eq. 13.2 in the future. In benchmarking studies, however, the performance of neural network-based algorithms is not yet at the level of the best conventional algorithms (QSM Challenge 2.0 Organization Committee et al., 2021). These investigations have also illustrated that inversion results can differ greatly between algorithms and often depend on algorithmic parameter values (QSM Challenge 2.0 Organization Committee et al., 2021; Langkammer et al., 2018). The clinical relevance of these differences and the impact on study outcomes has yet to be determined but may be negligible when the same algorithm is applied at the same site. Field strength dependence has not yet been investigated systematically for different algorithms, but it may be assumed that differences in field map CNR and resolution theoretically affect the requirement for regularization as well as convergence rates. A comprehensive list of inversion algorithms with download hyperlinks was provided in Ref. (QSM Challenge 2.0 Organization Committee et al., 2021, including Supporting Information Table S1; see also https://www.emtphub.org/).

13.7 Clinical applications and outlook

SWI has become well established in imaging stroke, traumatic brain injury (TBI), tumors, and multiple sclerosis (Liu et al., 2017), whereas, despite its potential, a number of factors have limited the clinical adoption of QSM. Generating susceptibility maps is involved and currently needs to be performed offline, and the results are highly sensitive to the algorithms and parameters used, reflecting the complexity of the relationship between susceptibility and phase epitomized by the ill-posed nature of the inverse problem. With QSM being newer than SWI by some 10 years, it has also had less time to gain traction with radiologists, but it too is attracting clinical interest in the diagnosis, therapeutic response assessment, and monitoring of vascular, oncological, and neurodegenerative disorders. Applied clinically, SWI and QSM have been shown to benefit enormously from the use of the ultra-high field (Trattnig et al., 2016, 2018).

In stroke imaging, SWI can be used to define the ischemic penumbra circumscribing tissue which may be saved from progressing to infarction by reperfusion (Liu et al., 2017), while QSM may both remove the orientation dependence of the appearance of vessels in asymmetrically prominent cortical veins (APCVs) and allow quantification of venous oxygenation saturation in APCVs. Brain tumors may be distinguished on the basis of the intratumoral microvasculature, allowing lymphomas and gliomas to be differentiated in SWI, for instance (Trattnig et al., 2018). Tumor vascularization also provides a means to monitor the response to antiangiogenic therapy. Multiple sclerosis has benefitted particularly from susceptibility imaging, with SWI showing peripheral enhancement of some ("iron rim") lesions and the central vein sign which are distinguishing hallmarks of the disease. The appearance of such lesions on SWI and QSM is shown in Fig. 13.5. Susceptibility values of lesions increase as they change from enhancing to nonenhancing, offering the possibility that QSM may replace contrast-agent-enhanced T_1 in the identification of active lesions (Vinayagamani et al., 2021).

Other neurodegenerative diseases are associated with more or less specific patterns of iron accumulation which may be visualized with SWI and quantified with QSM. Increases in susceptibility have

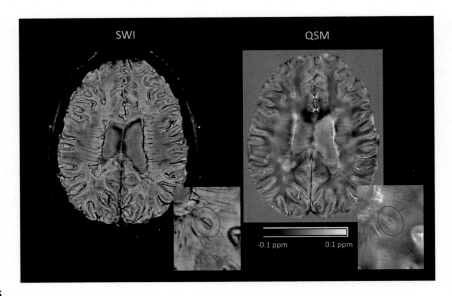

FIG. 13.5

Susceptibility-weighted image (left) and quantitative susceptibility map (right) of a patient with multiple sclerosis. Iron rims and central/penetrating veins are clearly resolved even in lesions as small as that figured in the inset, which is just 4 mm in extent *(red circle)*.

been observed in the putamen in Alzheimer's disease (AD) and in the brainstem and basal ganglia in Wilson's disease. The central globus pallidus appears to be a site of particular iron accumulation in neurodegeneration with brain iron accumulation (NBIA) while the motor cortex has been reported to be affected in motor neuron disease (MND). Parkinson's disease has been associated with increases in susceptibility in the putamen and substantia nigra while the dentate and red nuclei have been reported to be affected in Friedreich's ataxia (Vinayagamani et al., 2021). Much work still needs to be done to establish how distinct and predictive these patterns of susceptibility changes are. Combined analyses of QSM with other quantitative MRI metrics such as R_2^* (Elkady et al., 2019), myelin water fraction mapping (Yao et al., 2018), or diffusion MRI (Yu et al., 2019) can provide additional insights into the biophysical underpinnings of susceptibility alterations and lead to derived imaging metrics that are more specific to the underlying pathobiology than QSM alone.

In the technical sections of this chapter, we have reviewed the steps involved in QSM. Some of these are currently somewhat fragile and subject to an uncomfortable number of assumptions. Nonetheless, the quantitative nature (or perhaps better, potential) of QSM makes it a method of huge interest to the diagnostic imaging community, with the prospect of it taking a place next to, or possibly supplanting, SWI in routine clinical use over the coming decades. The increasingly comprehensive tools we have introduced constitute a promising environment for characterizing neuropathologies using susceptibility. Simultaneously, community challenges are driving improvement, consensus, and insight into how to accurately—or at least reproducibly—calculate susceptibility from phase (QSM Challenge 2.0 Organization Committee et al., 2021; Langkammer et al., 2018; The ISMRM Study Group for EMTP, n.d.). Parallel clinical work will establish whether susceptibility changes observed in pathologies occur early enough and are sufficiently specific to serve as imaging biomarkers.

References

Abdul-Rahman, H.S., Gdeisat, M.A., Burton, D.R., Lalor, M.J., Lilley, F., Moore, C.J., 2007. Fast and robust three-dimensional best path phase unwrapping algorithm. Appl. Opt. 46, 6623. https://doi.org/10.1364/AO.46.006623.

Bachrata, B., Strasser, B., Bogner, W., et al., 2021. Simultaneous multiple resonance frequency imaging (SMURF): fat-water imaging using multi-band principles. Magn. Reson. Med. 85, 1379–1396. https://doi.org/10.1002/mrm.28519.

Bachrata, B., Trattnig, S., Robinson, S.D., 2022. Quantitative susceptibility mapping of the head-and-neck using SMURF fat-water imaging with chemical shift and relaxation rate corrections. Magn. Reson. Med. 87(3), 1461–1479. https://doi.org/10.1002/mrm.29069. Epub 2021 Nov 30. PMID: 34850446; PMCID: PMC7612304.

Balla, D.Z., Sanchez-Panchuelo, R.M., Wharton, S.J., et al., 2014. Functional quantitative susceptibility mapping (fQSM). NeuroImage 100, 112–124. https://doi.org/10.1016/j.neuroimage.2014.06.011.

Bernstein, M.A., Grgic, M., Brosnan, T.J., Pelc, N.J., 1994. Reconstructions of phase contrast, phased array multi-coil data. Magn. Reson. Med. 32, 330–334.

Bilgic, B., Xie, L., Dibb, R., et al., 2016. Rapid multi-orientation quantitative susceptibility mapping. NeuroImage 125, 1131–1141. https://doi.org/10.1016/j.neuroimage.2015.08.015.

Boehm, C., Sollmann, N., Meineke, J., et al., 2022. Preconditioned water-fat total field inversion: application to spine quantitative susceptibility mapping. Magn. Reson. Med. 87, 417–430. https://doi.org/10.1002/mrm.28903.

Deistung, A., Rauscher, A., Sedlacik, J., Stadler, J., Witoszynskyj, S., Reichenbach, J.R., 2008. Susceptibility weighted imaging at ultra high magnetic field strengths: theoretical considerations and experimental results. Magn. Reson. Med. 60, 1155–1168. https://doi.org/10.1002/mrm.21754.

Dimov, A.V., Liu, T., Spincemaille, P., et al., 2015. Joint estimation of chemical shift and quantitative suscepti- bility mapping (chemical QSM). Magn. Reson. Med. 73, 2100–2110. https://doi.org/10.1002/mrm.25328.

Dymerska, B., Eckstein, K., Bachrata, B., et al., 2021. Phase unwrapping with a rapid opensource minimum span- ning tree algorithm (ROMEO). Magn. Reson. Med. 85, 2294–2308. https://doi.org/10.1002/mrm.28563.

Eckstein, K., Dymerska, B., Bachrata, B., et al., 2018. Computationally efficient combination of multi-channel phase data from multi-echo acquisitions (ASPIRE). Magn. Reson. Med. 79, 2996–3006. https://doi.org/ 10.1002/mrm.26963.

Eckstein, K., Bachrata, B., Hangel, G., et al., 2021. Improved susceptibility weighted imaging at ultra-high field using bipolar multi-echo acquisition and optimized image processing: CLEAR-SWI. NeuroImage 237, 118175. https://doi.org/10.1016/j.neuroimage.2021.118175.

Elkady, A.M., Cobzas, D., Sun, H., Seres, P., Blevins, G., Wilman, A.H., 2019. Five year iron changes in relapsing- remitting multiple sclerosis deep gray matter compared to healthy controls. Mult. Scler. Relat. Disord. 33, 107–115. https://doi.org/10.1016/j.msard.2019.05.028.

Haacke, E.M., Xu, Y., Cheng, Y.C., Reichenbach, J.R., 2004. Susceptibility weighted imaging (SWI). Magn. Reson. Med. 52, 612–618.

Jenkinson, M., 2003. Fast, automated, N-dimensional phase-unwrapping algorithm. Magn. Reson. Med. 49, 193–197.

Karsa, A., Shmueli, K., 2019. SEGUE: a speedy region-growing algorithm for unwrapping estimated phase. IEEE Trans. Med. Imaging 38, 1347–1357. https://doi.org/10.1109/TMI.2018.2884093.

Karsa, A., Punwani, S., Shmueli, K., 2020. An optimized and highly repeatable MRI acquisition and processing pipeline for quantitative susceptibility mapping in the head-and-neck region. Magn. Reson. Med. 84, 3206–3222. https://doi.org/10.1002/mrm.28377.

Langkammer, C., Bredies, K., Poser, B.A., et al., 2015. Fast quantitative susceptibility mapping using 3D EPI and total generalized variation. NeuroImage 111, 622–630. https://doi.org/10.1016/j.neuroimage.2015.02.041.

Langkammer, C., Schweser, F., Shmueli, K., et al., 2018. Quantitative susceptibility mapping: report from the 2016 reconstruction challenge. Magn. Reson. Med. 79, 1661–1673. https://doi.org/10.1002/mrm.26830.

Liu, T., Spincemaille, P., de Rochefort, L., Kressler, B., Wang, Y., 2009. Calculation of susceptibility through multiple orientation sampling (COSMOS): a method for conditioning the inverse problem from measured magnetic field map to susceptibility source image in MRI. Magn. Reson. Med. 61, 196–204. https://doi. org/10.1002/mrm.21828.

Liu, T., Wisnieff, C., Lou, M., Chen, W., Spincemaille, P., Wang, Y., 2013. Nonlinear formulation of the magnetic field to source relationship for robust quantitative susceptibility mapping. Magn. Reson. Med. 69, 467–476. https://doi.org/10.1002/mrm.24272.

Liu, S., Buch, S., Chen, Y., et al., 2017. Susceptibility-weighted imaging: current status and future directions: SWI review. NMR Biomed. 30, e3552. https://doi.org/10.1002/nbm.3552.

Parker, D.L., Payne, A., Todd, N., Hadley, J.R., 2014. Phase reconstruction from multiple coil data using a virtual reference coil. Magn. Reson. Med. 72, 563–569. https://doi.org/10.1002/mrm.24932.

Pohmann, R., Speck, O., Scheffler, K., 2016. Signal-to-noise ratio and MR tissue parameters in human brain im- aging at 3, 7, and 9.4 tesla using current receive coil arrays. Magn. Reson. Med. 75, 801–809. https://doi.org/ 10.1002/mrm.25677.

Pruessmann, K., Weiger, M., Scheidegger, M., Boesiger, P., 1999. SENSE: sensitivity encoding for fast MRI. Magn. Reson. Med. 42, 952–962.

QSM Challenge 2.0 Organization Committee, Bilgic, B., Langkammer, C., et al., 2021. QSM reconstruction chal- lenge 2.0: design and report of results. Magn. Reson. Med. 86, 1241–1255. https://doi.org/10.1002/ mrm.28754.

Robinson, S., Grabner, G., Witoszynskyj, S., Trattnig, S., 2011. Combining phase images from multi-channel RF coils using 3D phase offset maps derived from a dual-echo scan. Magn. Reson. Med. 65, 1638–1648.

Robinson, S.D., Bredies, K., Khabipova, D., Dymerska, B., Marques, J.P., Schweser, F., 2017. An illustrated comparison of processing methods for MR phase imaging and QSM: combining array coil signals and phase unwrapping. NMR Biomed. 30, e3601. https://doi.org/10.1002/nbm.3601.

Roemer, P.B., Edelstein, W.A., Hayes, C.E., Souza, S.P., Mueller, O.M., 1990. The NMR phased array. Magn. Reson. Med. 16, 192–225.

Schofield, M.A., Zhu, Y., 2003. Fast phase unwrapping algorithm for interferometric applications. Opt. Lett. 28, 1194–1196.

Schweser, F., Robinson, S.D., de Rochefort, L., Li, W., Bredies, K., 2017. An illustrated comparison of processing methods for phase MRI and QSM: removal of background field contributions from sources outside the region of interest. NMR Biomed. 30, e3604. https://doi.org/10.1002/nbm.3604.

Shmueli, K., de Zwart, J.A., van Gelderen, P., Li, T.Q., Dodd, S.J., Duyn, J.H., 2009. Magnetic susceptibility mapping of brain tissue in vivo using MRI phase data. Magn. Reson. Med. 62, 1510–1522.

Stäb, D., Bollmann, S., Langkammer, C., Bredies, K., Barth, M., 2017. Accelerated mapping of magnetic susceptibility using 3D planes-on-a-paddlewheel (POP) EPI at ultra-high field strength. NMR Biomed. 30. https://doi.org/10.1002/nbm.3620.

The ISMRM Study Group for EMTP, n.d. Recommended Implementation of Quantitative Susceptibility Mapping for Clinical Research in the Brain: Consensus of the QSM Community (in preparation).

Trattnig, S., Bogner, W., Gruber, S., et al., 2016. Clinical applications at ultrahigh field (7 T). Where does it make the difference? NMR Biomed. 29, 1316–1334. https://doi.org/10.1002/nbm.3272.

Trattnig, S., Springer, E., Bogner, W., et al., 2018. Key clinical benefits of neuroimaging at 7T. NeuroImage 168, 477–489. https://doi.org/10.1016/j.neuroimage.2016.11.031.

Uecker, M., Lai, P., Murphy, M.J., et al., 2014. ESPIRiT—an eigenvalue approach to autocalibrating parallel MRI: where SENSE meets GRAPPA. Magn. Reson. Med. 71, 990–1001. https://doi.org/10.1002/mrm.24751.

Vinayagamani, S., Sheelakumari, R., Sabarish, S., et al., 2021. Quantitative susceptibility mapping: technical considerations and clinical applications in neuroimaging. J. Magn. Reson. Imaging 53, 23–37. https://doi.org/10.1002/jmri.27058.

Xu, B., Liu, T., Spincemaille, P., Prince, M., Wang, Y., 2014. Flow compensated quantitative susceptibility mapping for venous oxygenation imaging. Magn. Reson. Med. 72, 438–445. https://doi.org/10.1002/mrm.24937.

Yao, B., Li, T.-Q., van Gelderen, P., Shmueli, K., de Zwart, J.A., Duyn, J.H., 2009. Susceptibility contrast in high field MRI of human brain as a function of tissue iron content. NeuroImage 44, 1259–1266. https://doi.org/10.1016/j.neuroimage.2008.10.029.

Yao, Y., Nguyen, T.D., Pandya, S., et al., 2018. Combining quantitative susceptibility mapping with automatic zero reference (QSM0) and myelin water fraction imaging to quantify iron-related myelin damage in chronic active MS lesions. AJNR Am. J. Neuroradiol. 39, 303–310. https://doi.org/10.3174/ajnr.A5482.

Yu, F.F., Chiang, F.L., Stephens, N., et al., 2019. Characterization of normal-appearing white matter in multiple sclerosis using quantitative susceptibility mapping in conjunction with diffusion tensor imaging. Neuroradiology 61, 71–79. https://doi.org/10.1007/s00234-018-2137-7.

Quantitative MRI and multiparameter mapping

Kerrin Pine and Evgeniya Kirilina

Department of Neurophysics, Max Planck Institute for Human Cognitive and Brain Sciences, Leipzig, Germany

Highlights

- Quantitative magnetic resonance imaging aims at mapping water proton spin characteristics in the tissue.
- qMRI maps are free of biases induced by inhomogeneities of static magnetic field and transmit- and receive radiofrequency fields.
- qMRI maps can be linked to the brain's microstructural characteristics such as tissue myelination and iron content.

14.1 Quantitative MRI at UHF

Quantitative magnetic resonance imaging (qMRI) is a family of methods aimed at mapping quantitative parameters of water proton spins or physiological processes in biological tissues. Instead of optimizing the image contrast for the best visibility of anatomical structures (i.e., in weighted images), qMRI provides maps of tissue spin characteristics (i.e., maps of longitudinal and transverse relaxation times T_1 or T_2) or physiological processes (tissue oxygenation and blood flow) in calibrated physical units.

This goal is usually achieved by a combination of serial measurements with varying acquisition parameters [i.e., flip angles, echo times (TE), repetition times (TR), and inversion times (TI)] and calibration scans for instrumental biases (such as magnetic field B_0 or transmit/receive radiofrequency fields B_1^+ and B_1^-) and involves inverse physical modeling inferring quantitative parameters from the spin system response.

The main objective of qMRI is to lift the three following limitations of conventional anatomical imaging. First, the mapping of quantitative parameters minimizes instrumental biases, making maps acquired at different time points, at different imaging sites, or with different instruments directly comparable. This property is particularly important to facilitate longitudinal investigations of anatomy, multicenter, and across-vendor studies. Second, the acquisition of multiple quantitative parameters allows the creation of synthetic MRI images with variable or even adjustable contrasts, again free of instrumental biases. Such synthetic images with multitudes of anatomical contrast could be utilized for the visualization or automated segmentation of multiple anatomical structures. Third, quantitative parameters of water proton spins in biological tissues carry information about interactions of water with their microscopic environment and are therefore sensitive probes of tissue microscopic properties. Thus, most quantitative parameters (T_1, T_2, T_2^*, and magnetization transfer rate) are influenced by

Advances in Magnetic Resonance Technology and Applications. Volume 10. ISSN 2666-9099. https://doi.org/10.1016/B978-0-323-99898-7.00011-0

the degree of tissue myelination and tissue iron content. Therefore, quantitative MRI parameters could be used to infer valuable biological information about tissue composition and microstructures in vivo, which previously was only accessible using *postmortem* histology.

All three above-described objectives are particularly relevant in the context of ultra-high field (UHF) MRI of brain neuroanatomy but are not without challenges. The inhomogeneity in B_0 within the brain increases linearly with the field strength. The shorter wavelength of the radiofrequency (RF) fields and their increased absorption in the body at UHF result in stronger inhomogeneity of transmit and receive B_1^+ and B_1^- fields, increasing respective image biases. If these biases can be properly corrected, UHF qMRI promises to push the limits of sensitivity, specificity, and spatial resolution. Ultra-high resolution (well below 1 mm isotropic) in combination with multiple contrasts provided by multimodal qMRI yields rich neuroanatomical information allowing visualization of submillimeter neuroanatomical structures including cortical layers and a multitude of subcortical nuclei. Finally, quantitative MRI parameters are sensitive biomarkers of biologically relevant brain tissue properties including axonal myelination, vessel calcification, and brain iron, providing unique quantitative insights into brain development, plasticity, and neurodegeneration. Therefore, quantitative multiparameter mapping of brain anatomy at UHF is a rapidly developing area of research with a constantly increasing number of neuroscientific applications.

In this chapter, we focus on qMRI of the brain at UHF. We describe the potentials of ultra-high field strength for qMRI and the challenges specific to it. We will focus on quantitative relaxometry including proton density and relaxation times T_1, T_2, and T_2^*. Quantitative susceptibility imaging and quantitative metrics related to diffusion, spectroscopy, magnetization, and chemical exchange are described in more depth in other chapters of this book. We provide an overview of frequently used sequences and data analysis strategies and describe applications to mapping biophysical quantities in the brain using qMRI and how it might transform research and utility in clinical practice. For interested readers, we recommend classical (Cercignani et al., 2018) and recent comprehensive literature on qMRI in general (Weiskopf et al., 2021 and references there) and its applications.

14.2 Quantitative MRI parameters of the brain at UHF

The minimal set of quantitative MR parameters, which are necessary (and often sufficient) to describe the dynamics of water proton spins in most MRI acquisitions, are (i) the total spin magnetic moment within the voxel (proportional to the voxel water proton density), (ii) longitudinal (T_1), (iii) transverse (T_2), and (iv) effective transverse (T_2^*) spin relaxation times, and (v) the rate of magnetization transfer between water protons and protons within tissue macromolecules. In qMRI, the relaxation rates ($R_1 = 1/T_1, R_2 = 1/T_2, R_2^* = 1/T_2^*$) are frequently used instead of relaxation times. Since times and rates are inversely related, they can be used interchangeably. One convenient property of relaxation rates, which does not hold for relaxation times, is that the contributions from different independent processes and different tissue components to the relaxation rate are often simply additive and can be easily disentangled.

All quantitative MR parameters are dependent on the static magnetic field B_0 as described in the following sections. Note that assigning a single value of a qMRI parameter to the entire spin ensemble within a tissue voxel with its complex molecular composition and heterogeneous cellular organization on meso- and microscales is an oversimplification. This simplification works well for many neuroscience applications but sometimes needs to be finessed using more complex tissue models that take into account several compartments for a more precise description of MRI parameters (Labadie et al., 2014).

14.2.1 Proton density

Proton density (PD) is a parameter describing the concentration of MR-visible protons within a voxel. It is typically given in percentage units referenced to an external water standard, or to a voxel with known water content, such as cerebral fluid. Proton density is related to tissue water content, but not identical to it since biological tissues also contain MR-invisible water.

Importantly, PD is high in tissues with high water content and decreases as the density of MR-invisible macromolecules (e.g., lipids and proteins) in a voxel increases. Therefore, PD can be used to estimate the macromolecular tissue content. In the brain, PD is a sensitive marker of brain myelination (Mezer et al., 2013). PD can be used to map differences in myelination between white matter tracts, cortical layers, and cortical areas. In pathology, increased PD is an indicator of demyelination or edema.

The proton density can be inferred from the amplitude of the MRI signal when the amplitude weighting due to other parameters (R_1, R_2, and R_2^*) is minimized or regressed out, and the maps are calibrated for instrumental biases induced by the inhomogeneity of transmission and reception RF fields B_1^+ and B_1^-. The calibration of the bias induced by B_1^- is particularly challenging at UHF.

The signal-to-noise (SNR) of PD measurement is proportional to the spin magnetization at thermal equilibrium, which increases linearly with magnetic field B_0 according to Curie's law. In addition, SNR of PD measurements is proportional to the sensitivity of the radiofrequency receive coil and inversely proportional to the amplitude of the measurement noise, which in the case of ultra-high resolution ultra-high field acquisition is often dominated by the noise induced in the receive coils by thermal electrical fluctuations within the imaged object. The dependences of RF coil sensitivity and the thermal noise amplitude on B_0 are more complex (Guérin et al., 2017; Pohmann et al., 2016), resulting in a supralinear increase in SNR for PD measurements and the inhomogeneous SNR across the brain with SNR decrease from the brain surface to deep brain regions (see Fig. 14.1; Guérin et al., 2017; Pohmann et al., 2016). Thus, while the SNR for PD measurements is increasing at UHF, the bias induced by B_1^- field inhomogeneity becomes more severe.

14.2.2 Longitudinal relaxation rate R_1

Longitudinal relaxation rate R_1 is the rate constant for the return of the disturbed longitudinal magnetization to its equilibrium value, with the magnetization parallel to B_0.

In the brain, the main sources of longitudinal relaxation are the molecular interactions of water with macromolecules of myelin and spin interactions of water proton spins with macromolecular spins and paramagnetic iron atoms. Therefore, R_1 maps provide excellent contrast between the gray and white matters (Fig. 14.1) as well as intracortical contrast. For example, the highly myelinated cortical layer IV is hyperintense in R_1 maps (and therefore hypointense in T_1 maps). R_1 maps acquired with ultra-high resolution and sampled at mid-cortical depth reflect the differences in myelination between the areas with different cyto- and myeloarchitecture (Figs. 14.3 and 14.4; Dinse et al., 2015).

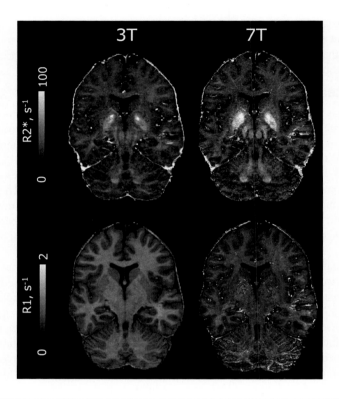

FIG. 14.1

Whole-brain maps of MR spin parameters R_2^* (upper row) and R_1 (bottom row) of the human brain acquired at (left column) clinical (3T) and (right column) ultra-high (7T) magnetic field strength. R_2^* contrast increases at the ultra-high field and iron-rich subcortical structures show better contrast with increasing field strength. Contrarily, R_1 decreases with an increase in the magnetic field, and the gray white matter contrast in R_1 becomes lower at 7T as compared to 3T. In addition, biases induced by the inhomogeneity of transmission field B_1^+ become more prominent at the ultra-high field.

Longitudinal relaxation rates in the brain are of the order of one inverse second, are higher in the white matter as compared to the gray matter, and decrease with the increase in the magnetic field B_0 (Figs. 14.1 and 14.2). Longitudinal relaxation is a dissipative process, which requires the exchange of Zeeman energy between proton spins and their surroundings. This energy exchange is facilitated by stochastic fluctuations of intra- and intermolecular spin interactions in the tissues and is particularly efficient for fluctuations with frequencies close to the Larmor frequency. Since with the increasing magnetic field the fraction of efficiently interacting protons is decreasing, the longitudinal relaxation rate generally decreases with increasing B_0. The decrease in R_1 with B_0 results in two challenges for R_1 mapping, generally for qMRI at UHF. Firstly, lower R_1 results in a stronger spin system saturation, therefore a decrease in MR signal intensity and inefficient spoiling for acquisitions where TR $< T_1$. Secondly, the differences in R_1 between the anatomical structures are smaller at UHF resulting in lower

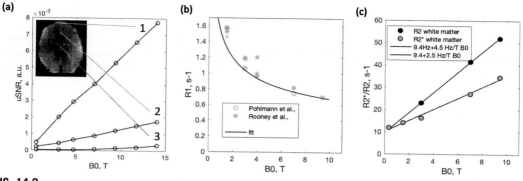

FIG. 14.2

Field dependence of quantitative MR parameters and their SNR on B_0. (A) Theoretical estimation for the highest achievable SNR for purely PD-weighted acquisition of the human brain as a function of B_0. Higher SNR, which is linearly dependent on B_0, is achieved on the brain periphery in regions close to receiving array elements, while deep brain structures show lower SNR and supralinear dependence on B_0. (B) Field dependence of longitudinal relaxation rate R_1 in the human brain. R_1 decreases with higher B_0 following a power law. (C) Field dependence of transverse and effective transverse relaxation rate R_2^*. R_2^* is higher for the white matter and shows a linear dependence on B_0. *Plots (B) and (C) are generated using data from Pohmann et al. (2016) and Rooney et al. (2007).*

contrast in R_1 maps. Due to the decrease in contrast, a general increase in SNR at UHF does not generally translate into the increased contrast-to-noise ratio in R_1 maps.

14.2.3 Transverse and effective transverse relaxation rates R_2 and R_2^*

Transverse and effective transverse relaxation rates R_2 and R_2^* are the rate constants for the irreversible and reversible dephasing of magnetization components transverse with respect to B_0.

In the biological tissues, R_2^* results from the dephasing induced by spatial variation of the local magnetic field on a microscopic scale due to microscopic tissue heterogeneity (Kiselev and Novikov, 2018). In the brain, the main sources of R_2^* are the local magnetic field perturbations in the microscopic vicinity of diamagnetic myelinated fibers and paramagnetic iron-rich cells (Fukunaga et al., 2010; Kirilina et al., 2020; Stüber et al., 2014). Different from the quantitative magnetic susceptibility (QSM) contrast, where the negative contribution to the susceptibility of diamagnetic myelin can be disentangled from the positive contribution of paramagnetic iron, these tissue components contribute to R_2^* and cannot be easily separated. Such separation is further complicated by the fact that iron and myelin are partly co-localized (Fukunaga et al., 2010), with highly myelinated parts of the cortex having higher iron content. Due to the anisotropy of myelin magnetic susceptibility and the ordered structure of myelinated fibers in white and gray matter, R_2^* depends on the orientation of the brain with respect to B_0 (Wharton and Bowtell, 2012). The mechanisms of transverse relaxation R_2 are far less understood and more complex. Two important sources for R_2 are the dynamic averaging of the above-described microscopic magnetic field perturbation by water diffusion and interactions of water with lipid membranes of myelin (Laule et al., 2006).

R_2^* contrast is a clear winner at UHF. Magnetic field inhomogeneities increase linearly with B_0 resulting in signal de-phasing and therefore R_2^* increasing approximately linearly with B_0, similar to the QSM contrast described in detail in Chapter 13. Interestingly, R_2 is much less field dependent compared to R_2^*, most probably due to the contribution of dipole-dipole interactions, which are magnetic field independent.

14.3 Methods for mapping quantitative spin parameters at UHF

14.3.1 Proton density

Measurement of PD requires the acquisition of images with minimal T_1, T_2, and T_2^* weightings and compensation for inhomogeneity of transmit and receive RF fields. By minimizing these weightings by an appropriate choice of sequence parameters (i.e., minimal TE and low flip angles) and/or compensating them using quantitative maps of R_1 and R_2/R_2^*, the fully relaxed PD-weighted signal (extrapolated to TR $= +\infty$ to minimize R_1 weighting and to TE $= 0$ to minimize R_2/R_2^* weightings) can be inferred and converted from arbitrary units to percentage units with reference to a known standard, usually water (or CSF). Inhomogeneity of receive RF field B_1^- must be removed, making it more difficult on ultra-high field systems, where the presence of a more uniform body coil is uncommon and the reciprocity theorem cannot easily be applied. Taking advantage of the known low spatial frequency of B_1^-, analytic approaches for the compensation of B_1^- inhomogeneity biases provide promising alternative correction strategies (Tustison et al., 2010). Because of the need to remove so many factors, PD is usually measured simultaneously with other parameters including R_1 and R_2^*/R_2 (see multimodal mapping methods below).

14.3.2 Longitudinal relaxation rate R_1

Quantitative R_1 mapping builds upon the techniques for T_1-weighted imaging described in detail in Chapter 11. The gold standard for measuring R_1 is the inversion recovery experiment, in which several images are acquired with a varying delay TI between spin inversion and signal readout. R_1 is then obtained by fitting the exponential recovery curve pixel-wise. For an accurate measurement, a delay of four to five times the sample T_1 should be left between inversions. This leads to a lengthy measurement even when the signal readout is performed by echo-planar imaging (EPI) (Preibisch and Deichmann, 2009). For this reason, several accelerated methods for measuring R_1 have been proposed; among them are Look-Locker and variable flip angle (Stikov et al., 2015).

The most popular method at UHF is the magnetization-prepared[2] rapid gradient echo (MP2RAGE) sequence which combines two 3D gradient echo volumes acquired at different TI after an inversion pulse (Marques et al., 2010). Inhomogeneity is improved by the use of a TR-FOCI inversion pulse (Hurley et al., 2010). Correction of residual B_1^+ effects has proven to be useful for reproducibility and more accurate cortical thickness estimation (Haast et al., 2021). Other sequences with even higher temporal efficiency were proposed; among them is multislice multishot inversion recovery EPI (Sanchez Panchuelo et al., 2021).

14.3.3 **Transverse relaxation rate R_2**

In an R_2 measurement, the classical Hahn spin echo sequence is repeated with varying TE delays to give a signal weighted by R_2 only. The measurement can be made more time-efficient by using multiple $180°$ RF pulses (the so-called multiecho T_2 method) and refocusing efficiency enhanced by modulating the RF phase to create the Carr-Purcell-Meiboom-Gill sequence. Remnant imperfect refocusing leads to image artifacts, e.g., stimulated echoes. Strategies such as crusher gradients or post hoc correction by extended phase graph or Bloch simulations can be used to recover accuracy. At higher fields, the CPMG sequence is less suitable due to SAR restrictions and B_1^+ inhomogeneity. Therefore, lower refocusing flip angles are used. A dictionary method can be used to recover R_2 from a decay curve which depends not only on R_2 but also on an imperfect slice profile and secondary/stimulated echoes (Emmerich et al., 2019). Different approaches to CPMG-derived methods include gradient spin echo (GraSE) and T_2 preparation, in which a T_2 contrast module is inserted before a fast imaging sequence. Similar to T_2-weighted imaging described in detail in Chapter 11, quantitative R_2 mapping is most often very SAR-intensive.

14.3.4 **Effective transverse relaxation rate R_2^***

The multiecho gradient-echo sequence is the most frequently applied method for mapping R_2^*, but other sequences can be extended into multiecho readouts. Log-linear weighted least square fitting provides good results in reasonable computation time. The multicompartmental nature of the brain tissue leads to some residual dependence on the chosen measurement flip angle and echo times. Background field gradients can lead to an overestimation of R_2^*, which can be compensated for (Cohen-Adad et al., 2012).

14.3.5 **Simultaneous multimodal mapping and fingerprinting**

Until this point, sequences which were described measure a single quantitative parameter. Increasingly, protocols are being developed to map two or more parameters simultaneously, providing a great many advantages. Firstly, clinical applications are better served by estimating a range of parameters in the least possible acquisition time. It also enables the derivation of multimodal biophysical models. The combination of different parameters can potentially provide access to tissue microstructure information not available with any individual measurement. Simultaneous measurement means that spatial distortions or effects due to the head motion manifest in the same way, avoiding misalignments that could otherwise result from different readout schemes.

Quantitative multiparameter mapping (MPM) is one such approach, providing maps of R_1, R_2^*, PD, and magnetization transfer saturation intrinsically in the same space. It is based on a FLASH readout and extended for use at 7T at resolutions of up to 0.4 mm (Trampel et al., 2019). Interleaved multishot EPI with controlled aliasing was proposed to improve scan time feasibility (Wang et al., 2022). Variable flip angle echo planar time-resolved imaging (vFA-EPTI) was recently proposed for the simultaneous acquisition of myelin water fraction, PD, and multicompartmental R_1 and R_2^* maps (Dong et al., 2021).

MP2RAGE can be extended to acquire multiple gradient echoes at each phase-encoding step, permitting the calculation of R_1, R_2^*, and QSM (Metere et al., 2017) at isotropic resolutions of up to 0.6 mm. MP2RAGEME is an alternative with gradient echoes acquired after the second inversion only (Caan et al., 2019).

The balanced steady-state free precession (bSSFP) signal following an inversion pulse can be used to deduce R_1, R_2, and PD at lower field strengths but is so far unstable at UHF. The unbalanced variant is used with the configuration state formalism to simultaneously map PD, flip angle, R_1, and R_2 at 7T but at the lower resolution of $1 \times 1 \times 3$ mm^3 (Leroi et al., 2020).

MR fingerprinting also maps multiple parameters within a session but approaches the problem from a different angle. By undersampling balanced SSFP acquisitions and pseudorandomly varying the imaging parameters TR and flip angle, the unique signal evolution can be matched to a calculated dictionary (Ma et al., 2013). It is implemented together with a spiral readout to measure R_1, R_2, and B_1^+ at 7T at a relatively low resolution (Buonincontri et al., 2017, p. 2).

Another suite of sequences addresses the challenge of efficiently acquiring diffusion and relaxometry data, for example, the MESMERIZED sequence for mapping R_1, R_2, and DWI by echo shifting (Fritz et al., 2021).

14.4 Measurement of quantitative MRI parameters

The requirements for acquiring and analyzing quantitative measurements are necessarily more stringent, taking greater physics input and development time, than conventional weighted imaging.

The use of isotropic voxels is common, to ensure that quantification is independent of sampling direction (for example, in layers or fiber bundles).

Processes must be established to minimize variability introduced by the operator (e.g., through consistent subject positioning on the scanner couch, fixing the choice of sequence parameters) and the measurement device (e.g., by discovering scanner instability, confirming performance continuity after equipment upgrades, or characterizing coil imperfections). To ensure consistent measurements over time, a good quality assurance practice is beneficial and could be extended to include quantitative measurements of a suitable phantom.

14.4.1 Assessing accuracy and precision

Traditionally in the physical sciences, measurement techniques are characterized by their accuracy and precision. Accuracy is the extent to which the measured values are consistently different from their true values. Since the brain tissue itself is not readily accessible, the ground truth is usually unknown, but comparisons can be made to gold-standard measurement techniques or measurements on phantoms of known properties. Precision, how close the agreement is between repeated measurements under the same condition, is evaluated by intraclass correlation, coefficient of variation, or sometimes other image similarity metrics.

The most demanding test of measurement performance is the multicenter study, where the same measurement technique is implemented at several sites and occasionally with scanners of different hardware/software versions or even vendors. One approach is the traveling head study, where the same subject or group of subjects is scanned repeatedly across sites (Voelker et al., 2021).

14.4.2 Sources of error and limiting factors

14.4.2.1 B_0 inhomogeneity

Differences in the magnetic susceptibility of tissues lead to inhomogeneity in the static field B_0 and worsen with field strength. It causes a range of problems depending on the measurement technique: spatial distortion especially in EPI, signal dropout due to intravoxel dephasing, changes to the excitation profile, and systematic errors where the absolute signal level is a term in the map calculation (e.g., PD measurements).

Adjustment procedures provided by the vendor may be by themselves insufficient. When the measurement is particularly sensitive to B_0, the homogeneity can be improved by performing several iterations or customizing the optimization volume. However, nonuniformity is likely to remain, especially around tissue-air interfaces such as those close to the temporal lobes. The dynamic variation of B_0 due to respiration and other forms of subject motion can be addressed by navigators, field probes, or fitting during reconstruction.

For a more in-depth treatment of B_0 inhomogeneity and compensation strategies, the reader is referred to Chapter 6.

14.4.2.2 B_1^+ inhomogeneity

Nonuniformity in radiofrequency fields represents the most significant measurement imperfection and the largest source of errors in quantitative MRI. Transmit field distribution in the head is increasingly nonuniform as the field strength increases and at 7T may lead to as much as a 60% reduction in B_1^+ at the edges of the brain. Low B_1^+ levels in the temporal lobes and cerebellum are especially a problem, not only affecting the measurement accuracy but also the precision and reliability of measurements. The transmitter gain calibration strategy may shift toward achieving a certain minimum B_1^+ in these regions.

Measuring the distribution of B_1^+ allows for the estimation of errors in parameter maps and is essential for an accurate mapping of some parameters. The process of B_1^+ mapping can be broken down into two stages, namely a magnetization preparation stage in which the signal depends on a flip angle and a readout stage. In practice, the magnetization preparation rarely depends only on the flip angle and can be subject to errors from T_1 relaxation and magnetization transfer effects among other sources. The readout can be a further source of errors when the flip angle itself is unknown. Nonetheless, several methods are in wide use at UHF (Pohmann and Scheffler, 2013), including spin/stimulated-echo 3D EPI (Lutti et al., 2012), Bloch-Siegert shift (Sacolick et al., 2010), and DREAM (Nehrke et al., 2014).

A comprehensive overview of the topic of B_1^+ inhomogeneity, B_1^+ mapping, and ways to correct it can be found in Chapter 7.

14.4.2.3 Other sources of error

Other potential sources of error include nonlinearity in the RF transmit chain (leading to divergence of the nominal and actual flip angles), slice profile variations (made it more complex by the distribution of flip angle), insufficient spoiling of transverse magnetization (Corbin and Callaghan, 2021), image noise from random thermal processes, patient positioning, and movement.

14.5 Translating qMRI maps to maps of tissue composition

Multiparametric qMRI at UHF delivers unique quantitative information on brain tissue composition. qMRI provides in vivo, quantitative, 3D-, and whole-brain measures of tissue myelin and iron content and may even outperform classical histology, which usually gives only qualitative 2D information on small *postmortem* brain sections. To link UHF qMRI measures to histological observables and quantitative iron and myelin measures, a "triple jump" approach is commonly used. It compares in vivo to *postmortem* qMRI measures as the first step and *postmortem* qMRI to histology or advanced physical measures of tissue composition as the second step.

Using this approach, the spatial distribution of R_1 and R_2^* maps in the gray matter was explained by Fukunaga et al. (2010) and quantitatively linked to the spatial distribution of myelin and iron as main qMRI contrast sources in the brain (Stüber et al., 2014; Fig. 14.3). While R_1, R_2, and R_2^* of white matter

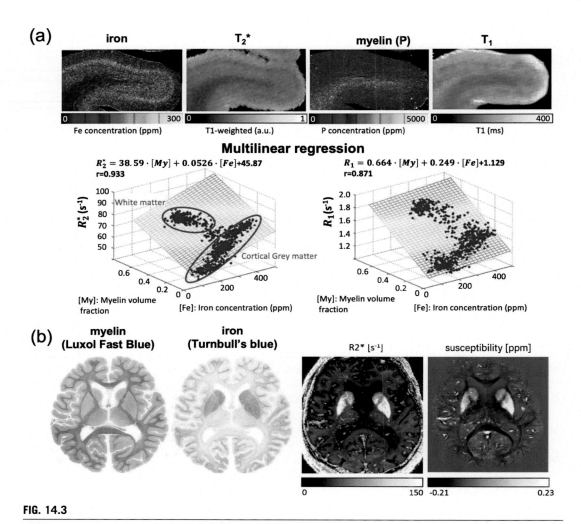

FIG. 14.3

qMRI parameters can be quantitatively related to metrics of tissue composition using the "triple jump" approach. (A) Combining quantitative MRI and 7T and quantitative maps of tissue elemental composition obtained by proton-induced X-ray emission on *postmortem* brain tissue sample, Stüber et al. (2014) demonstrated that R_1 and R_2^* in the brain are well described by the weighted linear combination of tissue iron concentration and myelin content. (B) This approach was extended by Hametner et al. (2018) to whole *postmortem* brains. *Reproduced with permission from (A) Stüber et al. (2014); (B) Hametner et al. (2018).*

at UHF mostly reflect tissue myelin content (Laule et al., 2006; Wharton and Bowtell, 2012), iron strongly contributes to R_2^* and magnetic susceptibility in the iron-rich subcortex (Deistung et al., 2013; Hametner et al., 2018; Langkammer et al., 2012), cortex (Fukunaga et al., 2010; Stüber et al., 2014), and superficial white matter (Kirilina et al., 2020). The contrast mechanisms across the entire brain and particularly in the subcortex remain largely unexplored and most likely differ between the brain regions and between subcortical nuclei with their complex anatomy and different degree of myelination (Fig. 14.3). Recently published datasets combining ultra-high resolution, ultra-high field multicontrast qMRI with 3D multimodal (Alkemade et al., 2022) or quantitative histology (Hametner et al., 2018) across several *postmortem* brains promise to foster progress in this area (Fig. 14.3).

To go beyond the above-described correlative analysis, biophysical models predicting qMRI parameters from brain tissue composition and microscopic organization using first principles were developed. While recently a lot of progress has been achieved to describe myelin-driven (Wharton and Bowtell, 2012) and iron-driven R_2^* contrasts (Kirilina et al., 2020), the models of R_1 and R_2 relaxation in the brain linking these parameters to myelin composition and microstructures at the time of writing remain scarce (Diakova et al., 2012; Labadie et al., 2014; Laule et al., 2006).

14.6 Neuroscience application of qMRI at UHF

QMRI of the brain anatomy at ultra-high field has an ever-increasing number of neuroscience applications, fostered by recent clinical approval and the growing availability of 7T systems in clinical and research settings. Here, we describe only two exciting examples to illustrate the potential of qMRI at UHF: in vivo Brodmann mapping of the human neocortex and cartography of subcortical nuclei (Fig. 14.4).

14.6.1 In vivo Brodmann mapping

The human neocortex is organized into multiple areas with different functional roles facilitated by their differing cyto- and myeloarchitecture. Area- and layer-dependent density of myelinated fibers and co-laterals in the cortex as well as area- and layer-dependent cortical iron content are reflected by all quantitative MRI parameters. Thus, quantitative MRI parameters sampled at mid-cortical depth demonstrate boundaries between the cortical areas opening the possibility to segment cortical areas in a single subject. Moreover, the submillimeter resolution achievable with ultra-high field makes the distinction between cortical layers feasible and potentially allows the distribution of lateral cortical structures, such as cortical columns or septa in motor and somatosensory cortices (Fig. 14.4).

14.6.2 Subcortical cartography

Ultra-high field ultra-high resolution multimodal quantitative MRI holds unique potential for neuro-anatomical studies of the human subcortex, with its largely unexplored anatomy. The subcortical nuclei are very small; thus, high resolution is particularly important for their imaging. The contrasts in the R_2^* and QSM maps of the subcortex are strongly enhanced at UHF due to the high iron content in these structures. Moreover, multimodal quantitative MRI maps are particularly powerful to discriminate subcortical structures, where iron-rich gray matter structures are interleaved with densely myelinated fiber tracts (Fig. 14.4). Quantitative MRI parameters with their high comparability between individuals are particularly suitable to detect subtle changes in the subcortex, e.g., due to neurodegeneration.

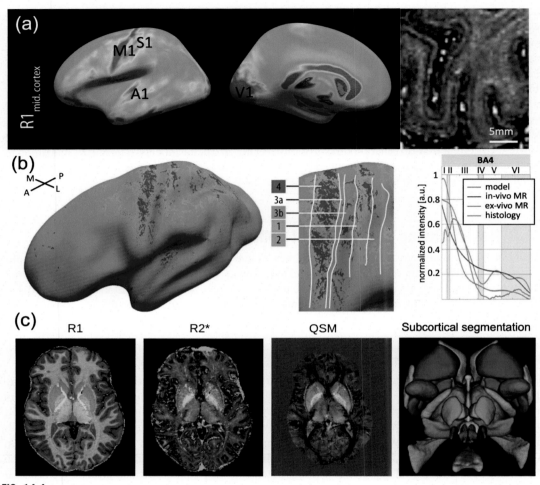

FIG. 14.4

Two example applications of ultra-high resolution ultra-high field quantitative MRI for studies of brain anatomy: in vivo Brodmann mapping (A, B) and subcortex cartography (C). (A) Whole-brain cortical map of R_1 (left and middle panels) sampled at mid-cortical depth and presented as the inflated cortical surface of the left hemisphere (0.4 mm resolution, prospective motion correction, average across four healthy participants) highlights the primary cortical areas including motor (M1), somatosensory (S1), visual (V1), and auditory (A1) cortexes as areas with high intracortical R_1 reflecting high cortical myelin and iron contents. Different myelination of cortical layers is visible in the quantitative maps when a submillimeter resolution is used (right panel). (B) The cortical profiles of qMRI parameters can be quantitatively related to cortical myeloarchitectonic profiles (right panel) as known from *postmortem* MRI and classical histology and used for a fine-grained parcellation of cortical areas (left and middle panels). (C) Subcortical structures in the subcortex can be parcellated (right panels) using multicontrast ultra-high resolution quantitative MRI (three left panels) due to their different iron, myelin, and calcium contents and small sizes. *Reproduced with permission from (B) Dinse et al. (2015); (C) Bazin et al. (2020).*

14.7 Outlook and conclusions

Ultra-high field quantitative MRI is a unique tool to study the brain anatomy in health and pathology. It minimizes instrumental biases and provides quantitative anatomical metrics which are directly comparable across time points, individuals, and imaging sites. Quantitative MRI parameters are markers of brain tissue microstructure reflecting tissue vascularization, myelination, macromolecular, and iron content. qMRI, therefore, provides information about the living brain, which previously was only accessible with histology after autopsy. To obtain these metrics, qMRI relies on biophysical modeling of the MRI acquisition process and MR contrast mechanisms in biological tissues. qMRI is an active area of research, strongly profiting from recent advances in MRI hardware, motion correction techniques, and improvements in MRI image acquisition acceleration and image reconstruction. Moreover, anatomical insights obtained from ultra-high field and ultra-high resolution qMRI are of unique importance for explaining contrast mechanisms and informing qMRI imaging at lower, clinically available fields.

References

Alkemade, A., Bazin, P.-L., Balesar, R., et al., 2022. A unified 3D map of microscopic architecture and MRI of the human brain. Sci. Adv. 8, eabj7892. https://doi.org/10.1126/sciadv.abj7892.

Bazin, P.-L., Alkemade, A., Mulder, M.J., Henry, A.G., Forstmann, B.U., 2020. Multi-contrast anatomical subcortical structures parcellation. eLife 9, e59430. https://doi.org/10.7554/eLife.59430.

Buonincontri, G., Schulte, R.F., Cosottini, M., Tosetti, M., 2017. Spiral MR fingerprinting at 7T with simultaneous B1 estimation. Magn. Reson. Imaging 41, 1–6. https://doi.org/10.1016/j.mri.2017.04.003.

Caan, M.W.A., Bazin, P.-L., Marques, J.P., de Hollander, G., Dumoulin, S.O., van der Zwaag, W., 2019. MP2RA-GEME: T1, T2*, and QSM mapping in one sequence at 7 tesla. Hum. Brain Mapp. 40, 1786–1798. https://doi.org/10.1002/hbm.24490.

Cercignani, M., Dowell, N.G., Tofts, P.S., 2018. Quantitative MRI of the Brain: Principles of Physical Measurement, second ed. CRC Press.

Cohen-Adad, J., Polimeni, J.R., Helmer, K.G., et al., 2012. T2* mapping and B0 orientation-dependence at 7 T reveal cyto- and myeloarchitecture organization of the human cortex. NeuroImage 60, 1006–1014. https://doi.org/10.1016/j.neuroimage.2012.01.053.

Corbin, N., Callaghan, M.F., 2021. Imperfect spoiling in variable flip angle T1 mapping at 7T: quantifying and minimizing impact. Magn. Reson. Med. 86, 693–708. https://doi.org/10.1002/mrm.28720.

Deistung, A., Schäfer, A., Schweser, F., Biedermann, U., Turner, R., Reichenbach, J.R., 2013. Toward in vivo histology: a comparison of quantitative susceptibility mapping (QSM) with magnitude-, phase-, and R2*-imaging at ultra-high magnetic field strength. NeuroImage 65, 299–314. https://doi.org/10.1016/j.neuroimage.2012.09.055.

Diakova, G., Korb, J.-P., Bryant, R.G., 2012. The magnetic field dependence of water T1 in tissues. Magn. Reson. Med. 68, 272–277. https://doi.org/10.1002/mrm.23229.

Dinse, J., Härtwich, N., Waehnert, M.D., et al., 2015. A cytoarchitecture-driven myelin model reveals area-specific signatures in human primary and secondary areas using ultra-high resolution in-vivo brain MRI. NeuroImage 114, 71–87. https://doi.org/10.1016/j.neuroimage.2015.04.023.

Dong, Z., Wang, F., Chan, K.-S., et al., 2021. Variable flip angle echo planar time-resolved imaging (vFA-EPTI) for fast high-resolution gradient echo myelin water imaging. NeuroImage 232, 117897. https://doi.org/10.1016/j.neuroimage.2021.117897.

Emmerich, J., Flassbeck, S., Schmidt, S., Bachert, P., Ladd, M.E., Straub, S., 2019. Rapid and accurate dictionary-based T2 mapping from multi-echo turbo spin echo data at 7 Tesla. J. Magn. Reson. Imaging 49, 1253–1262. https://doi.org/10.1002/jmri.26516.

Fritz, F.J., Poser, B.A., Roebroeck, A., 2021. MESMERISED: super-accelerating T1 relaxometry and diffusion MRI with STEAM at 7 T for quantitative multi-contrast and diffusion imaging. NeuroImage 239, 118285. https://doi.org/10.1016/j.neuroimage.2021.118285.

Fukunaga, M., Li, T.-Q., van Gelderen, P., et al., 2010. Layer-specific variation of iron content in cerebral cortex as a source of MRI contrast. Proc. Natl. Acad. Sci. USA 107, 3834–3839. https://doi.org/10.1073/pnas.0911177107.

Guérin, B., Villena, J.F., Polimeridis, A.G., et al., 2017. The ultimate signal-to-noise ratio in realistic body models. Magn. Reson. Med. 78, 1969–1980. https://doi.org/10.1002/mrm.26564.

Haast, R.A.M., Lau, J.C., Ivanov, D., Menon, R.S., Uludağ, K., Khan, A.R., 2021. Effects of MP2RAGE B1+ sensitivity on inter-site T1 reproducibility and hippocampal morphometry at 7T. NeuroImage 224, 117373. https://doi.org/10.1016/j.neuroimage.2020.117373.

Hametner, S., Endmayr, V., Deistung, A., et al., 2018. The influence of brain iron and myelin on magnetic susceptibility and effective transverse relaxation—a biochemical and histological validation study. NeuroImage 179, 117–133. https://doi.org/10.1016/j.neuroimage.2018.06.007.

Hurley, A.C., Al-Radaideh, A., Bai, L., et al., 2010. Tailored RF pulse for magnetization inversion at ultrahigh field. Magn. Reson. Med. 63, 51–58. https://doi.org/10.1002/mrm.22167.

Kirilina, E., Helbling, S., Morawski, M., et al., 2020. Superficial white matter imaging: contrast mechanisms and whole-brain in vivo mapping. Sci. Adv. 6, eaaz9281. https://doi.org/10.1126/sciadv.aaz9281.

Kiselev, V.G., Novikov, D.S., 2018. Transverse NMR relaxation in biological tissues. NeuroImage 182, 149–168. https://doi.org/10.1016/j.neuroimage.2018.06.002.

Labadie, C., Lee, J.-H., Rooney, W.D., et al., 2014. Myelin water mapping by spatially regularized longitudinal relaxographic imaging at high magnetic fields. Magn. Reson. Med. 71, 375–387. https://doi.org/10.1002/mrm.24670.

Langkammer, C., Schweser, F., Krebs, N., et al., 2012. Quantitative susceptibility mapping (QSM) as a means to measure brain iron? A post mortem validation study. NeuroImage 62, 1593–1599. https://doi.org/10.1016/j.neuroimage.2012.05.049.

Laule, C., Leung, E., Lis, D.K.B., et al., 2006. Myelin water imaging in multiple sclerosis: quantitative correlations with histopathology. Mult. Scler. 12, 747–753. https://doi.org/10.1177/1352458506070928.

Leroi, L., Gras, V., Boulant, N., et al., 2020. Simultaneous proton density, T1, T2, and flip-angle mapping of the brain at 7 T using multiparametric 3D SSFP imaging and parallel-transmission universal pulses. Magn. Reson. Med. 84, 3286–3299. https://doi.org/10.1002/mrm.28391.

Lutti, A., Stadler, J., Josephs, O., et al., 2012. Robust and fast whole brain mapping of the RF transmit field B1 at 7T. PLoS One 7, e32379. https://doi.org/10.1371/journal.pone.0032379.

Ma, D., Gulani, V., Seiberlich, N., et al., 2013. Magnetic resonance fingerprinting. Nature 495, 187–192. https://doi.org/10.1038/nature11971.

Marques, J.P., Kober, T., Krueger, G., van der Zwaag, W., Van de Moortele, P.-F., Gruetter, R., 2010. MP2RAGE, a self bias-field corrected sequence for improved segmentation and T1-mapping at high field. NeuroImage 49, 1271–1281. https://doi.org/10.1016/j.neuroimage.2009.10.002.

Metere, R., Kober, T., Möller, H.E., Schäfer, A., 2017. Simultaneous quantitative MRI mapping of T1, T2* and magnetic susceptibility with multi-echo MP2RAGE. PLoS One 12, e0169265. https://doi.org/10.1371/journal.pone.0169265.

Mezer, A., Yeatman, J.D., Stikov, N., et al., 2013. Quantifying the local tissue volume and composition in individual brains with magnetic resonance imaging. Nat. Med. 19, 1667–1672. https://doi.org/10.1038/nm.3390.

Nehrke, K., Versluis, M.J., Webb, A., Börnert, P., 2014. Volumetric B1+ mapping of the brain at 7T using DREAM. Magn. Reson. Med. 71, 246–256. https://doi.org/10.1002/mrm.24667.

Pohmann, R., Scheffler, K., 2013. A theoretical and experimental comparison of different techniques for B_1 mapping at very high fields. NMR Biomed. 26, 265–275. https://doi.org/10.1002/nbm.2844.

Pohmann, R., Speck, O., Scheffler, K., 2016. Signal-to-noise ratio and MR tissue parameters in human brain imaging at 3, 7, and 9.4 tesla using current receive coil arrays. Magn. Reson. Med. 75, 801–809. https://doi.org/10.1002/mrm.25677.

Preibisch, C., Deichmann, R., 2009. T1 mapping using spoiled FLASH-EPI hybrid sequences and varying flip angles. Magn. Reson. Med. 62, 240–246. https://doi.org/10.1002/mrm.21969.

Rooney, W.D., Johnson, G., Li, X., Cohen, E.R., Kim, S.-G., Ugurbil, K., Springer, C.S., 2007. Magnetic field and tissue dependencies of human brain longitudinal 1H2O relaxation in vivo. Magn. Reson. Med. 57, 308–318. https://doi.org/10.1002/mrm.21122.

Sacolick, L.I., Wiesinger, F., Hancu, I., Vogel, M.W., 2010. B1 mapping by Bloch-Siegert shift. Magn. Reson. Med. 63, 1315–1322. https://doi.org/10.1002/mrm.22357.

Sanchez Panchuelo, R.M., Mougin, O., Turner, R., Francis, S.T., 2021. Quantitative T1 mapping using multi-slice multi-shot inversion recovery EPI. NeuroImage 234, 117976. https://doi.org/10.1016/j.neuroimage.2021.117976.

Stikov, N., Boudreau, M., Levesque, I.R., Tardif, C.L., Barral, J.K., Pike, G.B., 2015. On the accuracy of T1 mapping: searching for common ground. Magn. Reson. Med. 73, 514–522. https://doi.org/10.1002/mrm.25135.

Stüber, C., Morawski, M., Schäfer, A., et al., 2014. Myelin and iron concentration in the human brain: a quantitative study of MRI contrast. NeuroImage 93 (Part 1), 95–106. https://doi.org/10.1016/j.neuroimage.2014.02.026.

Trampel, R., Bazin, P.-L., Pine, K., Weiskopf, N., 2019. In-vivo magnetic resonance imaging (MRI) of laminae in the human cortex. NeuroImage 197, 707–715. https://doi.org/10.1016/j.neuroimage.2017.09.037.

Tustison, N.J., Avants, B.B., Cook, P.A., et al., 2010. N4ITK: improved N3 bias correction. IEEE Trans. Med. Imaging 29, 1310–1320. https://doi.org/10.1109/TMI.2010.2046908.

Voelker, M.N., Kraff, O., Goerke, S., et al., 2021. The traveling heads 2.0: multicenter reproducibility of quantitative imaging methods at 7 Tesla. NeuroImage 232, 117910. https://doi.org/10.1016/j.neuroimage.2021.117910.

Wang, D., Ehses, P., Stöcker, T., Stirnberg, R., 2022. Reproducibility of rapid multi-parameter mapping at 3T and 7T with highly segmented and accelerated 3D-EPI. Magn. Reson. Med. 88, 2217–2232. https://doi.org/10.1002/mrm.29383.

Weiskopf, N., Edwards, L., Helms, G., Mohammadi, S., Kirilina, E., 2021. Quantitative magnetic resonance imaging of brain anatomy: towards in-vivo histology. Nat. Rev. Phys. 3, 570–588.

Wharton, S., Bowtell, R., 2012. Fiber orientation-dependent white matter contrast in gradient echo MRI. PNAS 109, 18559–18564. https://doi.org/10.1073/pnas.1211075109.

Ultra-high field structural imaging: Zooming in on the brain

5

Ultra-high-field
structural imaging:
Zooming in on the brain

Cerebellar imaging at ultra-high magnetic fields

Wietske van der Zwaag[a,b], **Dagmar Timmann**[c,d], **Andreas Deistung**[d,e], **and Nikos Priovoulos**[a,f]

[a]*Spinoza Centre for Neuroimaging, Royal Netherlands Academy of Arts and Sciences (KNAW), Amsterdam, Netherlands*
[b]*Computational Cognitive Neuroscience and Neuroimaging, Netherlands Institute for Neuroscience, KNAW, Amsterdam, Netherlands* [c]*Department of Neurology and Center for Translational Neuro- and Behavioral Sciences (C-TNBS), Essen University Hospital, University of Duisburg-Essen, Duisburg, Germany* [d]*Erwin L. Hahn Institute for Magnetic Resonance Imaging, University of Duisburg-Essen, Duisburg, Germany* [e]*University Clinic and Outpatient Clinic for Radiology, University Hospital Halle (Saale), Halle (Saale), Germany* [f]*Department of Biomedical Engineering and Physics, Amsterdam UMC, Amsterdam, Netherlands*

Highlights

- Visualization of the fine anatomical structure of the cerebellum requires high spatial resolution, which can be achieved at ultra-high field.
- Most common sequences can be applied with good use in the cerebellum, although B_0 and B_1 inhomogeneities have to be dealt with.
- There are many possible clinical applications of human cerebellar imaging at UHF. To date, multiple sclerosis (MS) has been studied in the greatest detail at UHF.

In this chapter, we first discuss the functional and structural organization of the cerebellum, followed by the benefits, challenges, and optimizations of ultra-high field (UHF) MRI for cerebellar imaging and the MRI sequences and processing strategies used for cerebellar imaging. Imaging cerebellar morphology at UHF is discussed next, followed by clinical applications of cerebellar imaging at UHF.

15.1 Functional and structural cerebellar organization

Anatomically, the cerebellum resembles a little brain: it has a white matter core, which houses several iron-rich deep nuclei and a thin layer of gray matter covering the surface of the white matter tree. The thin cerebellar cortex allows for very tight folding of the cortical sheet (Fig. 15.1). In contrast to the neocortex, the cerebellar gray matter consists of three separate layers. The most superficial is the molecular layer. The middle layer consists of a single layer of Purkinje cells and is only approximately 12 μm thick. The deepest layer contains very small and densely packed neurons and is aptly named the granular layer. The granular cells are so small that even though the cerebellum as a whole covers approximately 10% of the brain's volume, it contains 80% of the total neuron population (Herculano-Houzel, 2012).

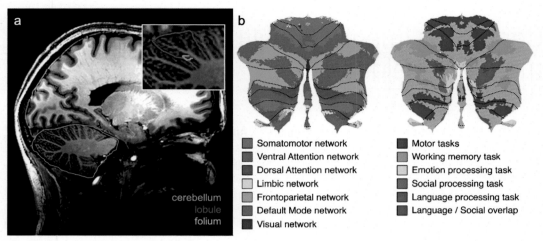

FIG. 15.1

Anatomical and functional outline of the human cerebellum. (A) Sagittal slice through the cerebellum, outlined in *blue*. A single lobule (*red*) and folium (*green*) are outlined in the enlarged area. (B) Cerebellar functional resting state (*right*) and task-based (*left*) networks. *Reproduced from Guell et al. (2018) (Fig. 1); licensed under a Creative Commons Noncommercial 4.0 international license.*

The white matter structure strongly resembles a tree, where the main branches are called lobules and the smallest ones are folia. As can be observed from the image in Fig. 15.1A, lobules, an example of which is outlined in red, are relatively easy to depict, while the much smaller folium, outlined in green, is barely discernable. Lobules I–V form the cerebellar anterior lobe, with lobules VI–IX making up the posterior lobe. Between lobules VI and VIIB, we find crus I and crus II. Lobule X corresponds to the flocculonodular lobe.

Neurons in the cerebellar cortex are connected to the forebrain via the dentate and other deep nuclei and the thalamus and occasionally via the red nucleus as an intermediate station. Ascending information enters the cerebellum from the spine and the inferior olive in the brainstem predominantly through the inferior cerebellar peduncle. Feedback from the neocortical regions is brought to the cerebellum via the pons through the middle cerebellar peduncle (Marzban et al., 2018).

The human cerebellum contains four deep nuclei. The largest, the dentate nucleus, is clearly visible in MRI data (see Figs. 15.3 and 15.5 in this section). The emboliform, globose, and fastigial nuclei are found more medial and anterior to the dentate nucleus. Those three nuclei are much smaller and rarely visible on MR images.

Historically, the cerebellum was thought of as a motor structure while, in fact, the cerebellar cortex is part of all major functional networks (Fig. 15.1B). Separate areas of the cerebellar cortex are connected to distinct cerebral areas and are often activated during similar tasks as their neocortical counterparts. For example, the motor areas in the anterior lobe are connected to the primary motor cortex, while crus I is connected to cerebral default mode network hubs in the posterior cingulate cortex, temporal lobe, and medial frontal cortex (Buckner et al., 2011). The dentate nucleus is similarly divided into motor and cognitive domains, each connected to the relevant areas of the cerebellar cortex.

Cerebellar functional maps (Guell et al., 2018; King et al., 2019) demonstrate the involvement of specific cerebellar regions in motor tasks, as well as mathematics, spatial imagery, movie watching, and working memory tasks, among others. Within the motor areas in the anterior and posterior lobes, two complete homunculi are found, with the feet in both body maps positioned most anterior, or at the top and bottom in the flattened surface presented in Fig. 15.1B. The representation of the head or eyes is found most posterior, near the middle of the flattened surface, overlapping the area where activation related to saccades is found. A third body representation in the posterior lobe has also been suggested. Because of the double crossing of the spinocerebellar tract, information from the right body parts ends up in the right cerebellar hemisphere, unlike the contralateral body representations found in the cerebrum. Likewise, language tasks are found to engage the right cerebellar crus I/crus II areas while mental arithmetic and divided attention are more left-lateralized (King et al., 2019).

15.2 Benefits, challenges, and optimization of cerebellar imaging at UHF

Resolving the highly complex cerebellar anatomy necessitates high spatial resolution and, consequently, high SNR. Since SNR scales supralinearly with the B_0 field, moving to UHF can provide the necessary increased signal for anatomical and functional cerebellar imaging. Along with SNR, the sensitivity to susceptibility increases with B_0, which provides increased contrast for susceptibility-based techniques, such as blood oxygenation level dependency (BOLD) weighted fMRI (Stockmann and Wald, 2018). Finally, the more independent coil-sensitivity profiles at UHF allow higher acceleration factors in parallel imaging and therefore more efficient high-resolution sampling. In short, cerebellar imaging benefits especially from the advantages of UHF.

Human brain imaging at UHF, however, comes with multiple challenges, several of which are exacerbated at the cerebellum. At UHF, the B_1 shows a spatially variant profile: at 7T, the B_1 tends to destructively interfere in the cerebellum with typical RF coils, resulting in large signal voids, which are particularly evident in T_1-weighted images (Fig. 15.2) (Oliveira et al., 2021), though they can also lead to decreased statistical power in BOLD fMRI (Priovoulos et al., 2021). The cerebellum is also relatively close to areas with high susceptibility differences compared to the brain tissue, such as air cavities and the fat around the skull. The induced B_0 variations can result in increased signal loss and distortions, which limit the imaging fidelity, particularly for EPI-based techniques (Stockmann and Wald, 2018). Importantly, susceptibility changes are also dynamically induced due to respiration. This effect is more pronounced in UHF and its magnitude is predominantly dependent on the distance from the thorax. The cerebellum lies at the bottom of the brain and is therefore more sensitive to respiration-related artifacts such as dynamic dephasing, distortions, and blurring. These also result in signal variations in fMRI experiments that can be hard to disentangle from the BOLD signal (Stockmann and Wald, 2018). Finally, the high spatial specificity that is the target of UHF cerebellar imaging is implicitly sensitive to blurring induced by participant motion (Andersen et al., 2019).

The above challenges, while exacerbated in the cerebellum, are ubiquitous in UHF brain imaging and, therefore, multiple solutions already exist. The B_1 profile can be improved with several methods, ranging from the usage of dielectric pads (Vaidya et al., 2018) to dedicated transmit coils to the static or dynamic combination of multi-transmit coils (parallel transmission, see also Chapter 7). Adiabatic RF pulses, that are less sensitive to B_1 inhomogeneity and frequency offsets, are now also commonly used at UHF. B_1-insensitive inversion pulses and the parallel transmit pulses for excitation can improve the SNR and CNR of T_1-weighted images in the cerebellum (see Fig. 15.2 and Oliveira et al., 2021) while

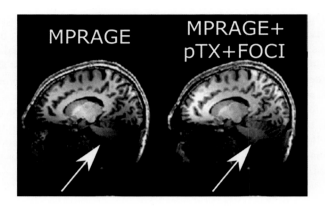

FIG. 15.2

MPRAGE images obtained with and without optimally combined multi-transmit coils (pTx) and an efficient adiabatic inversion at 7T. Note that the cerebellum shows large signal decreases that are reduced when the FOCI pulse and pTx are employed (*white arrows*). *From Oliveira et al. (2021), licensed under a Creative Commons NonCommercial 4.0 international license.*

local transmit elements or the optimized combination of multiple transmit elements can increase the statistical power of cerebellar BOLD fMRI (Priovoulos et al., 2021). The utilization of multichannel receive arrays as an additional spatial encoding mechanism allows increased data undersampling and therefore the usage of higher resolution in anatomical and functional imaging methods, as well as read-outs at shorter echo times to reduce the sensitivity to susceptibility artifacts in EPI approaches. High-density local receive arrays have been shown to facilitate highly undersampled, high-resolution BOLD fMRI in the cerebellum (Priovoulos et al., 2021). Careful selection of the phase-encoding direction and slice thickness as well as the usage of higher-order shim coils can increase B_0 homogeneity (see Chapter 6 and Stockmann and Wald, 2018). Real-time B_0 detection and shim updates can mitigate the effect of dynamic B_0 variations due to respiration or participant movement. Off-resonances can also be corrected in a retrospective manner by reconstructing the data while accounting for the ramp induced in the field map due to respiration. Finally, prospective or retrospective motion correction (e.g., camera or navigator based) can reduce blurring in high-resolution acquisitions and is expected to be particularly useful to image the complex cerebellar anatomy (see Chapter 10 and Andersen et al., 2019). Overall, the large benefits to be reaped from UHF and the exacerbation of several of the brain UHF challenges make the human cerebellum an especially good testing ground for UHF technology.

15.3 MRI sequences for cerebellar imaging

Contrary to the title of this section, there are no specific cerebellar sequences and many neuroimaging approaches may be used successfully in the cerebellum. For all sequences, cerebellar imaging may be carried out using a whole-brain or slab-based approach. The beauty of whole-brain imaging is that in the case of 3D sequences, the signal comes from the whole brain and the blood vessels in the vicinity of the cerebellum are saturated, as they are covered by the field of view. When imaging the cerebellum with an axial slab of about 10 cm, unsaturated blood (e.g., in the transverse sinus) may enter the imaging slab and can introduce severe flow artifacts. One solution may be to apply phase encoding in the anteroposterior direction, or alternatively, use saturation bands below and above the slab to saturate the signal within the blood vessels.

T_1-weighted structural imaging at UHF is very well achieved with magnetization-prepared rapid gradient echo (MPRAGE) sequence variants (see also Chapter 11). The resulting MPRAGE images are still affected by T_2^*, proton density, receiver sensitivity, and transmit B_1 field biases resulting in spatially varying signals and lower contrast between brain tissues. These drawbacks can be mitigated by using an MP2RAGE sequence, a variation of the MPRAGE sequence, that acquires two images generated at different inversion times based on which a synthetic T_1-weighted image is computed (Marques and Gruetter, 2013) (Figs. 15.3A and 15.2B), which provides good image contrast, even

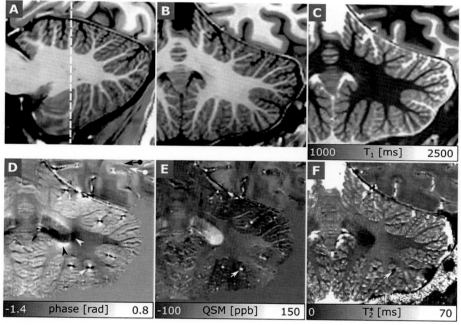

FIG. 15.3

MP2RAGE (*top row*) and multi-echo gradient echo imaging (*bottom row*) of the left hemisphere of the cerebellum of a female healthy subject acquired at 7T in vivo. Synthetic T_1-weighted images in sagittal and coronal views are presented in (A) and (B), respectively. The quantitative T_1 map, background field corrected phase image, quantitative susceptibility map, and the T_2^* map covering the same anatomic regions as in (B) are illustrated in (C) to (F), respectively. The *dashed line* in (A) indicates the location of the coronal slice. The *white and black arrowheads* indicate negative and positive phase contributions originating from the dentate nucleus. The *white arrow* indicates a venous vessel that shows a dipole-shaped pattern in (D) that is overcome in (E). With respect to (E), the same vessel shows an increased diameter due to blooming in (F).

in the low B_1 areas of the cerebellum. Because of the two inversions, the MP2RAGE sequence requires a longer acquisition time than the MPRAGE. In addition, MP2RAGE imaging offers the possibility to quantitatively measure the T_1 relaxation time (Fig. 15.3C). Maps of the transmit B_1 field enable compensation of residual B_1 inhomogeneities in the T_1 maps (Marques and Gruetter, 2013).

Due to the higher sensitivity toward susceptibility effects with increasing magnetic fields, gradient (recalled) echo (GRE) imaging with T_2^*-weighting is achieved already with shorter echo times. The effective transverse relaxation time (T_2^*), a quantitative measure that sensitively indicates the degree of magnetic field inhomogeneity at a microscopic scale, may be determined by analyzing the signal decay of multi-echo GRE magnitude images (Fig. 15.3F) (Deistung et al., 2017). The signal phase of a GRE scan is also driven by the magnetic susceptibility as it reflects the magnetic field distribution originating from the subject and substances within the MRI scanner. Phase unwrapping followed by background field removal of the GRE phase images yields corrected phase images directly reflecting the local magnetic field distribution. Such processed phase images with 120 µm in-plane resolution even enables the depiction of the granular and molecular layers of the cerebellar cortex (Marques et al., 2010). The phase images show a dipole-like pattern in regions surrounding the dentate and venous vessels as well as in the interfaces between the white and gray matters (Fig. 15.3D). Both blooming in GRE magnitude images and the dipole-like pattern in phase images are expected to be overcome by directly mapping the bulk tissue magnetic susceptibility (Fig. 15.3E). Based on GRE phase images processed as described previously, the post-processing technique quantitative susceptibility mapping (QSM) solves the ill-posed inverse problem of determining the magnetic susceptibility from local magnetic field values (Deistung et al., 2017) (see also Chapter 13). Both magnetic susceptibility and T_2^* are highly sensitive to iron, myelin, and calcium, allowing study of tissue composition in controls and patients (Deistung et al., 2017).

In addition to the previously stated challenges for cerebellum imaging at UHF, the RF power deposition, measured as the specific absorption rate (SAR), increases approximately with the square of the magnetic field. Therefore, a tighter limit on the number, duration, and amplitude of applied RF pulses in a given time period exists, limiting the application of some common sequence variants (e.g., turbo spin-echo sequences or inversion-recovery sequences) typically applied at lower magnetic fields. Utilizing RF pulses tailored for low power deposition (e.g., variable flip angle turbo spin echo) is a reasonable solution to control power deposition (Eggenschwiler et al., 2014), bringing TSE imaging of the human cerebellum within reach.

Functional MRI, resting state MRI, and diffusion-weighted imaging typically rely on EPI for fast spatial encoding. These approaches are prone to susceptibility artifacts at tissue interfaces, which abound around the cerebellum, while the readout is also limited in duration due to the fast T_2^* relaxation. These limitations may be alleviated with parallel imaging, multiband imaging, and segmented EPI readout approaches while the well-established sensitivity benefits of UHF in BOLD-based EPI have also been shown for the cerebellum (Gizewski et al., 2007).

15.4 Processing

Cerebellar image processing typically includes segmentation of the cerebellar white and gray matters, including the cerebellar nuclei and potentially the parcellation of the cerebellum into lobules or unfolding of the cortical sheet.

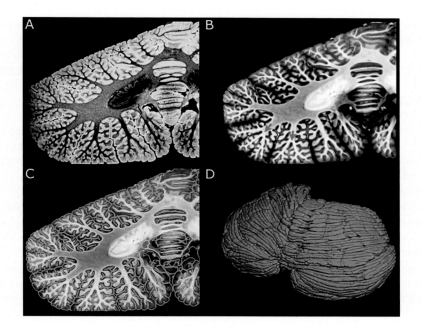

FIG. 15.4

High-resolution (0.2 mm isotropic) ex vivo cerebellum processing with Csurf. (A) T_2^*-weighted gradient echo data. Note that the foliation of the cortex and the dentate nuclei can be clearly discerned. (B) Resultant image after dividing the T_2^*-weighted with the PD-weighted data, brightness inversion, bias field correction, and denoising. (C) Topologically and anatomically consistent white matter (*yellow*) and pial surface (*green*). (D) Surface representation of the pial surface. *Reproduced from Sereno et al. (2020), licensed under a Creative Commons NonCommercial 4.0 international license.*

The main challenge applying these processing techniques in the cerebellum is the complex cerebellar anatomy: the cerebellar cortex is very thin and convoluted to the point that its finest details are not typically resolved in vivo (Fig. 15.4). UHF acquisitions can push the spatial-resolution envelope so that more details can be resolved, but translating this to improved segmentations is not trivial. The cerebellar sulci are so tight that techniques to separate the gray matter banks in the neocortex (e.g., by identifying the likely CSF voxels in between) are challenging to apply due to partial volume effects and the high curvature of the cerebellar cortex (Sereno et al., 2020). Furthermore, the adjacent dura and veins can have a similar signal intensity to the cerebellar gray and white matters, respectively. This complicates tissue identification using intensity-based algorithms. Gradient magnitude approaches to identify ridge-like structures (e.g., veins) can also be challenging to apply since the veins are comparable in size to the convoluted cerebellar anatomy. At UHF, these problems with cerebellar imaging are exacerbated by the frequently lower SNR and CNR in the cerebellum and the increased signal inhomogeneity. The complex and individual-dependent cerebellar foliations hinder spatial homogenization across groups, beyond the larger anatomical structures such as the lobules. The highly complex anatomy also impedes the creation of sphere-equivalent surfaces of the cerebellum and its substructures while inflating or flattening these surfaces typically results in large distortions (Sereno et al., 2020). In practice, several of the standard neuroimaging packages are optimized for lower-resolution datasets. Thus, processing the high-resolution images and meshes that are needed to reap the UHF benefits (that may need to be further upsampled to better capture the cortical curvature) implies an often prohibitive increase in computational requirements (Huntenburg et al., 2018).

Several techniques can help address these issues. Signal intensity bias correction, e.g., using the N4 algorithm, is frequently performed to reduce B_1 signal inhomogeneity. To reduce the noise in very high spatial-resolution images or in later echoes of multi-echo approaches, denoising filters may be applied. Cerebellar tissue classification is commonly performed using a template or a mix of template and intensity-based approaches, which decreases sensitivity to SNR or contrast levels (Diedrichsen et al., 2009). Several approaches to segment the cerebellum and/or its lobules and nuclei in an automated manner exist, ranging from the originally neocortex-focused FreeSurfer to cerebellum-dedicated packages such as SUIT, CERES2, or ACAPULCO (for an overview, see Carass et al., 2018). As a pragmatic choice, such segmentations are frequently performed at a spatial level that smooths over the finer structures of the cerebellum since the current in vivo state-of-the-art MRI scans do not fully resolve the cerebellar anatomy and the computational demands increase quickly with finer sampling grids. For example, typical execution of the FreeSurfer or SUIT pipelines implies resampling to a 1-mm resolution. Subsequent analyses, such as cerebellar cortical surface reconstructions to examine for example fMRI activations in a sulci-accommodating manner, tend therefore to average over anatomical details compared to the neocortex while unfolding and flattening schemes can generate large local distortions. Even so, SUIT and similar packages have been very successful in streamlining cerebellar MRI processing and visualization, which is reflected in their widespread usage in neuroscientific and clinical applications. Tools that accommodate submillimeter resolutions, both in terms of atlases and computational requirements, are starting to become available [e.g., the recently released Nighres package (Huntenburg et al., 2018)]. While in vivo the finest cerebellar anatomical detail is still not depictable, recently, segmentation, reconstruction, and flattening of the complete cerebellar cortical and dentate nuclei surfaces were performed based on data from an ex vivo brain at 9.4T using the processing package Csurf (Sereno et al., 2020). This feat was achieved by obtaining a 0.2 mm isotropic resolution dataset and a subsequent very fine tessellation that proved to be necessary to resolve and unfold the anatomical detail at the level of individual folia (Fig. 15.4D). Further development of dedicated processing methods to leverage the UHF capabilities and reach for that level of detail in vivo is an important target for the cerebellar imaging community.

15.5 Imaging cerebellar morphology

Postmortem ex vivo MRI at UHF is well suited for visualizing the microstructural neuroanatomy of the cerebellum. Microscale information improves the understanding of the MRI signal behavior depending on the underlying tissue composition and, thus, is the foundation to develop and validate biophysical models applicable to understand tissue composition at coarser spatial resolutions achievable in vivo. Ex vivo MRI studies with isotropic spatial resolutions down to 100 μm were recently performed providing an unprecedented view of the three-dimensional neuroanatomy of the human cerebellum (Edlow et al., 2019; Sereno et al., 2020) (Fig. 15.5D and E). Based on PD- and T_2^*-weighted gradient

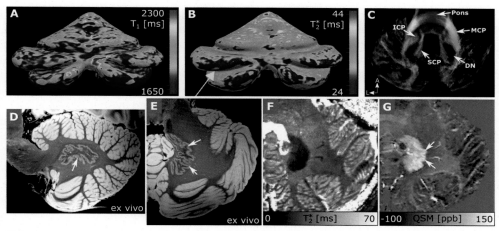

FIG. 15.5

T_1 and T_2^* values mapped on the inflated surface of the CHROMA atlas (middle cortical depth) are shown in (A) and (B), respectively. In (A), the T_1 distribution exhibits a patchy appearance across the hemispheres and shows the highest values in the vermis. The T_2^* distribution presents with lower values on the apex of the folia of the posterior lobe while the fissures exhibit higher values. The *yellow arrow* indicates the "concavity-related" pattern on the folia's apex. (C) Diffusion-based tract-density image (TDI) of the human cerebellum at 0.2 mm isotropic resolution. The major tracts, subcortical structures, and fine details of tract trajectories can be distinguished. *Red, blue, and green* in the tract-density images represent anisotropy along the mediolateral, superoinferior, and anteroposterior directions, respectively. *DN*, dentate nucleus; *SCP, MCP, ICP*, superior, middle, inferior cerebellar peduncles. Sagittal and axial T_1w images obtained with 0.1 mm isotropic resolution ex vivo demonstrating the complex structure of the dentate nuclei (see *white arrows*) and the cerebellar cortex are shown in (D) and (E), respectively. Axial T_2^* (F) and susceptibility (G) maps, obtained in vivo, delineate the dentate nucleus based on its iron distribution. The susceptibility map shows a ribbon with high signal intensity at the lateral border of the dentate (see *arrows*). *Panels A and B were modified from Boillat et al. (2018), with permission; panel C was kindly provided by Dr. Chris Steele; panels D and E were downloaded from Edlow et al. (2019).*

echo MR images with an isotropic spatial resolution of 190 µm, Sereno et al. (2020) were able to reconstruct the human cerebellar surface down to the level of the individual folia (Fig. 15.4) and observed that the cerebellar surface area amounts to 78% of the entire surface area of the human neocortex. This ultra-high resolution surface model can serve as ground truth for evaluating cerebellar surface reconstructions from in vivo data. Relying on MP2RAGE and multi-echo gradient echo imaging with 0.75 mm × 0.75 mm × 0.9 mm voxels, Boillat et al. (2018) studied microstructural properties at three different depths of the cerebellar human cortex in healthy subjects in vivo. Albeit partial volume effects prevented complete recovery of all folia in vivo, the different lobules and the general shape of the arbor vitae were preserved. Mapping quantitative MRI measures (e.g., T_1, T_2^*, and susceptibility) onto the surface allowed the investigation of distinct distribution patterns (Fig. 15.5A and B).

The cerebellar nuclei are characterized by a distinct cytoarchitecture, little myelin content, and high iron content with respect to their surroundings (Koeppen et al., 2012). Because the shape of the nuclei and the internal distribution of iron are likely tightly coupled, iron-sensitive approaches like T_2^*-weighted imaging, susceptibility-weighted imaging, T_2^*-mapping, or quantitative susceptibility mapping provide a unique view into the cerebellar nuclei. As can be seen in Fig. 15.5G, the susceptibility maps nicely show the structure of the dentate nuclei. Higher susceptibility values of the dentate nuclei on MR-susceptibility maps, however, extend beyond these thin walls (see Fig. 15.5D and E as a comparison) and include white matter within the sac formed by the dentate nucleus. The amount of increased iron content in the vicinity of the thin gray matter ribbon is clearly visible by regions of lower signal intensity in T_2^*-weighted images (Figs. 15.4A and 15.5F). Nevertheless, relying on iron content as a contrast mechanism allows for studying the shape and iron accumulation of the dentate nuclei, both of which can be affected by certain diseases. The smaller cerebellar nuclei (emboliform, globose, and fastigial nuclei) have been reported to be visible with susceptibility-weighted images and quantitative-susceptibility maps; however, their depiction is not yet achievable reliably.

The cerebellar cortex projects to the cerebellar nuclei. Recently, ultra-high resolution diffusion-weighted imaging (0.8 mm isotropic) at 7T was able to provide information on the topographical pattern of white matter connectivity between the cerebellar cortex and dentate nucleus supporting the idea of largely segregated corticocerebellar loops (Steele et al., 2017) (Fig. 15.5C). Neuronal fibers exhibited a marked preference for connectivity that was topography consistent with the arrangement of the cerebellar cortex. Classification of the connections between the dentate and cerebellar cortex revealed that over 50% of the classified surface of the dentate nucleus was primarily connected with nonmotor cerebellar cortical regions (Steele et al., 2017). Ultra-high resolution diffusion-weighted imaging offers insights into the organization of fiber architecture to understand and probe the structure and functional significance of corticocerebellar loops in human behavior.

In conclusion, ultra-high field MRI can bridge the gap between histopathology and ex vivo MRI and may develop into in vivo MRI histology.

15.6 Clinical applications

The possible clinical applications of human cerebellar imaging at UHF are manifold. They embrace a wide range of neurological, psychiatric, and developmental disorders, such as the various forms of ataxias, schizophrenia and autism, and prematurity-related disruption in cerebellar development. Clinical applications include early diagnosis, improved differential diagnosis, a deeper understanding of cerebellar pathophysiology, and the use of UHF-MRI parameters as biomarkers to monitor treatment effects. As yet, however, cerebellar imaging at UHF is still in its infancy and not part of the clinical routine.

The clinical application of UHF brain imaging has been studied in the greatest detail in multiple sclerosis (MS) (Filippi et al., 2019; Louapre et al., 2020 for reviews). This is for good reasons because myelin loss results in characteristic changes in T_1 (longer), T_2^* (increased), and magnetic susceptibility (increased), and these changes intensify with increasing field strength (see also Chapter 1). The cerebellum is one of the common lesion sites in MS. Fartaria et al. (2017) showed that the sensitivity to detect cerebellar lesions in the early stages of MS significantly increases in MP2RAGE images acquired with 7T MRI compared with the conventional field strength at 3T (Fig. 15.6). Detection sensitivity increased for cerebellar cortical and white matter lesions. Improved detection of cerebral cortical lesions would have significant clinical implications because it allows differentiation of MS

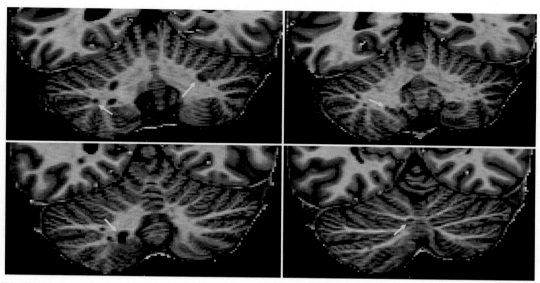

FIG. 15.6

Cerebellar cortical lesions in axial MP2RAGE uniform images acquired at 7T in patients with early-stage MS. *Yellow arrows* indicate individual lesions. *Reproduced from Galbusera et al. (2020) (Fig. 2); licensed under a Creative Commons NonCommercial 4.0 international license.*

from other white matter disorders, and substantial cortical lesions are linked to a poorer outcome. At a resolution of 0.58 mm isotropic voxel size, Fartaria et al. (2017) found that 7T MRI provided a better differentiation between leukocortical lesions, that is lesions affecting both cerebellar cortical gray matter and white matter, and white matter lesions. As yet, it remains to be seen whether UHF MRI allows showing of subpial lesions in the cerebellum, the most frequent cortical lesion localization based on histology (Kutzelnigg et al., 2007), which likely manifest in early MS disease stages (Pardini et al., 2021).

Involvement of the cerebellar cortex in MS, however, is not restricted to focal lesions but likely affects the entire cerebellar cortex (Louapre et al., 2020). Human cerebellar imaging at UHF allows for laminar analysis of the cerebellar cortex based on differences in myelination and iron content, which is higher in the granule cell layer compared to the outer molecular layer (Boillat et al., 2018; Marques et al., 2010). Galbusera et al. (2020) performed quantitative T_1 and T_2^* measurements at 7T using high-resolution MP2RAGE and multi-echo gradient echo imaging in normal-appearing cerebellar cortex in early MS patients. The volume of the cerebellar cortex and cerebellar cortical layers was not reduced in cerebellar patients compared to controls. Early-stage MS patients, however, showed significantly longer T_1 values in all vermis cortical layers and the middle and external (that is subpial) cortical layers of the cerebellar hemispheres likely reflecting diffuse subpial demyelination. It will be of great interest in the future to perform laminar imaging of the cerebellar cortex for disease detection and monitoring in a wide range of disorders. Diseases or disease stages are of particular interest in which the cerebellar cortex appears normal in conventional MRI (for example, essential tremor or pre-clinical spinocerebellar ataxias, SCAs).

UHF brain imaging is not only ideally suited to show the destruction of myelin but also increases in iron concentration. Again, MS is a very good example of a clinical application. The central vein sign, and the paramagnetic rim of slowly evolving lesions in chronic MS, reflecting high iron content in microglia, are highly characteristic of MS lesions (Filippi et al., 2019; Louapre et al., 2020). They are detected with high sensitivity at 7T but not at conventional field strength. This has been demonstrated for cerebral lesions but not yet for the cerebellum.

UHF imaging of the cerebellum is also expected to better demonstrate the pathology of the iron-rich cerebellar nuclei compared to conventional field strength. Marked atrophy of the cerebellar nuclei has been found in patients with spinocerebellar ataxia type 6 (SCA6) and mild atrophy in patients with Friedreich's ataxia and spinocerebellar ataxia type 3 (SCA3) in SWI images acquired at 7T (Stefanescu et al., 2015). Similar results have also been found using QSM at 3T (Deistung et al., 2022). As yet, 7T MRI in vivo does not allow visualization of the cerebellar nuclei with histological detail (Fig. 15.5D–F, Fig. 15.7 bottom row). UHF methods to visualize the cerebellar nuclei need to be improved in the future to allow differentiation of pathology of the neurons and surrounding white matter. Furthermore, as yet, the smaller cerebellar nuclei cannot reliably be visualized at 7T in vivo, neither in healthy people nor in patients with cerebellar disease.

In summary, cerebellar MRI stands to gain immensely from UHF MRI because of the cerebellum's very fine structure, which is difficult to depict accurately at clinical field strengths. Challenges such as B_0 and B_1 inhomogeneities, motion sensitivity, and limited availability of atlases and analytic tools are currently being resolved, which leads us to expect a bright future for clinical and neuroscientific applications of cerebellar imaging at 7T.

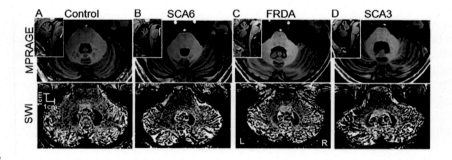

FIG. 15.7

7T MRI imaging of the cerebellar nuclei in three common forms of hereditary ataxias. (A) A control subject (67 years, male); (B) a patient with SCA6 (54 years, male); (C) a patient with Friedreich's ataxia (FRDA; 32 years, female); and (D) a patient with SCA3 (58 years, female). *Top row:* Axial slices of MPRAGE acquisition. *Small inset* shows sagittal images. Marked cerebellar atrophy is visible in the patient with SCA6, a large fourth ventricle in the patient with SCA3, and mild atrophy of the spinal cord in the patient with Friedreich's ataxia. *Bottom row:* Axial slices of SWI acquisition of the same subjects. Dentate nuclei are visible as hypointensities. Drawings of the dentate nuclei used for the quantification of volumes are superimposed on the left (*red*). Dentate nuclei were smaller in the three patients. Dentate atrophy was most marked in the patient with SCA6. *L* = left; *R* = right. *Reproduced from Stefanescu et al. (2015) (Fig. 1) with permission from Oxford University Press.*

References

Andersen, M., Björkman-Burtscher, I.M., Marsman, A., Petersen, E.T., Boer, V.O., 2019. Improvement in diagnostic quality of structural and angiographic MRI of the brain using motion correction with interleaved, volumetric navigators. PLoS One 14, e0217145. https://doi.org/10.1371/journal.pone.0217145.

Boillat, Y., Bazin, P.-L., O'Brien, K., et al., 2018. Surface-based characteristics of the cerebellar cortex visualized with ultra-high field MRI. NeuroImage 172, 1–8. https://doi.org/10.1016/j.neuroimage.2018.01.016.

Buckner, R.L., Krienen, F.M., Castellanos, A., Diaz, J.C., Yeo, B.T.T., 2011. The organization of the human cerebellum estimated by intrinsic functional connectivity. J. Neurophysiol. 106, 2322–2345. https://doi.org/10.1152/jn.00339.2011.

Carass, A., Cuzzocreo, J.L., Han, S., Hernandez-Castillo, C.R., Rasser, P.E., Ganz, M., Beliveau, V., Dolz, J., Ben Ayed, I., Desrosiers, C., Thyreau, B., Romero, J.E., Coupé, P., Manjón, J.V., Fonov, V.S., Collins, D.L., Ying, S.H., Onyike, C.U., Crocetti, D., Landman, B.A., Mostofsky, S.H., Thompson, P.M., Prince, J.L., 2018. Comparing fully automated state-of-the-art cerebellum parcellation from magnetic resonance images. Neuroimage 183, 150–172. https://doi.org/10.1016/j.neuroimage.2018.08.003. Epub 2018 Aug 9. PMID: 30099076; PMCID: PMC6271471.

Deistung, A., Schweser, F., Reichenbach, J.R., 2017. Overview of quantitative susceptibility mapping. NMR Biomed. 30, e3569. https://doi.org/10.1002/nbm.3569.

Deistung, A., Jäschke, D., Draganova, R., et al., 2022. Quantitative susceptibility mapping reveals alterations of dentate nuclei in common types of degenerative cerebellar ataxias. Brain Commun. 4 (1), fcab306. https://doi.org/10.1093/braincomms/fcab306. PMID: 35291442. PMC8914888.

Diedrichsen, J., Balsters, J.H., Flavell, J., Cussans, E., Ramnani, N., 2009. A probabilistic MR atlas of the human cerebellum. Neuroimage 46 (1), 39–46. https://doi.org/10.1016/j.neuroimage.2009.01.045. Epub 2009 Feb 5. PMID: 19457380.

Edlow, B.L., Mareyam, A., Horn, A., et al., 2019. 7 Tesla MRI of the ex vivo human brain at 100 μm resolution. Sci. Data 6, 244. https://doi.org/10.1038/s41597-019-0254-8.

Eggenschwiler, F., O'Brien, K.R., Gruetter, R., Marques, J.P., 2014. Improving T_2-weighted imaging at high field through the use of kT-points. Magn. Reson. Med. 71, 1478–1488. https://doi.org/10.1002/mrm.24805.

Fartaria, M.J., O'Brien, K., Şorega, A., et al., 2017. An ultra-high field study of cerebellar pathology in early relapsing–remitting multiple sclerosis using MP2RAGE. Investig. Radiol. 52, 265–273. https://doi.org/10.1097/RLI.0000000000000338.

Filippi, M., Preziosa, P., Banwell, B.L., et al., 2019. Assessment of lesions on magnetic resonance imaging in multiple sclerosis: practical guidelines. Brain 142, 1858–1875. https://doi.org/10.1093/brain/awz144.

Galbusera, R., Parmar, K., Boillat, Y., et al., 2020. Laminar analysis of the cerebellar cortex shows widespread damage in early MS patients: a pilot study at 7 T MRI. Mult. Scler. J. Exp. Transl. Clin. 6, 2055217320961409. https://doi.org/10.1177/2055217320961409.

Gizewski, E.R., de Greiff, A., Maderwald, S., Timmann, D., Forsting, M., Ladd, M.E., 2007. fMRI at 7 T: whole-brain coverage and signal advantages even infratentorially? NeuroImage 37, 761–768. https://doi.org/10.1016/j.neuroimage.2007.06.005.

Guell, X., Schmahmann, J.D., Gabrieli, J.D., Ghosh, S.S., 2018. Functional gradients of the cerebellum. elife 7. https://doi.org/10.7554/eLife.36652.

Herculano-Houzel, S., 2012. The remarkable, yet not extraordinary, human brain as a scaled-up primate brain and its associated cost. Proc. Natl. Acad. Sci. 109, 10,661–10,668.

Huntenburg, J.M., Steele, C.J., Bazin, P.L., 2018. Nighres: processing tools for high-resolution neuroimaging. Gigascience 7 (7), giy082. https://doi.org/10.1093/gigascience/giy082. PMID: 29982501; PMCID: PMC6065481.

King, M., Hernandez-Castillo, C.R., Poldrack, R.A., Ivry, R.B., Diedrichsen, J., 2019. Functional boundaries in the human cerebellum revealed by a multi-domain task battery. Nat. Neurosci. 22, 1371–1378. https://doi.org/10.1038/s41593-019-0436-x.

Koeppen, A.H., Ramirez, R.L., Yu, D., et al., 2012. Friedreich's ataxia causes redistribution of iron, copper, and zinc in the dentate nucleus. Cerebellum 11, 845–860. https://doi.org/10.1007/s12311-012-0383-5.

Kutzelnigg, A., Faber-Rod, J.C., Bauer, J., et al., 2007. Widespread demyelination in the cerebellar cortex in multiple sclerosis. Brain Pathol. 17, 38–44. https://doi.org/10.1111/j.1750-3639.2006.00041.x.

Louapre, C., Treaba, C.A., Barletta, V., Mainero, C., 2020. Ultra-high field 7 T imaging in multiple sclerosis. Curr. Opin. Neurol. 33, 422–429. https://doi.org/10.1097/WCO.0000000000000839.

Marques, J.P., Gruetter, R., 2013. New developments and applications of the MP2RAGE sequence - focusing the contrast and high spatial resolution R1 mapping. PLoS One 8, e69294. https://doi.org/10.1371/journal.pone.0069294.

Marques, J.P., van der Zwaag, W., Granziera, C., Krueger, G., Gruetter, R., 2010. Cerebellar cortical layers: in vivo visualization with structural high-field-strength MR imaging. Radiology 254, 942–948. https://doi.org/10.1148/radiol.09091136.

Marzban, H., Manto, M., Mariani, J., 2018. Cerebellum: from development to disease-the 8th International Symposium of the Society for Research on the cerebellum and ataxias. Cerebellum 17, 1–3. https://doi.org/10.1007/s12311-018-0919-4.

Oliveira, Í.A.F., Roos, T., Dumoulin, S.O., Siero, J.C.W., van der Zwaag, W., 2021. Can 7 T MPRAGE match MP2RAGE for gray-white matter contrast? NeuroImage 240 (118), 384. https://doi.org/10.1016/j.neuroimage.2021.118384.

Pardini, M., Brown, J.W.L., Magliozzi, R., Reynolds, R., Chard, D.T., 2021. Surface-in pathology in multiple sclerosis: a new view on pathogenesis? Brain J. Neurol. 144, 1646–1654. https://doi.org/10.1093/brain/awaB025.

Priovoulos, N., Roos, T., Ipek, Ö., et al., 2021. A local multi-transmit coil combined with a high-density receive array for cerebellar fMRI at 7 T. NMR Biomed., e4586. https://doi.org/10.1002/nbm.4586.

Sereno, M.I., Diedrichsen, J., Tachrount, M., Testa-Silva, G., d'Arceuil, H., De Zeeuw, C., 2020. The human cerebellum has almost 80% of the surface area of the neocortex. Proc. Natl. Acad. Sci. U. S. A. 117, 19538–19543. https://doi.org/10.1073/pnas.2002896117.

Steele, C.J., Anwander, A., Bazin, P.-L., et al., 2017. Human cerebellar sub-millimeter diffusion imaging reveals the motor and non-motor topography of the dentate nucleus. Cereb. Cortex 1991 (27), 4537–4548. https://doi.org/10.1093/cercor/bhw258.

Stefanescu, M.R., Dohnalek, M., Maderwald, S., et al., 2015. Structural and functional MRI abnormalities of cerebellar cortex and nuclei in SCA3, SCA6 and Friedreich's ataxia. Brain J. Neurol. 138, 1182–1197. https://doi.org/10.1093/brain/awv064.

Stockmann, J.P., Wald, L.L., 2018. In vivo B_0 field shimming methods for MRI at 7 T. NeuroImage 168, 71–87. https://doi.org/10.1016/j.neuroimage.2017.06.013.

Vaidya, M.V., Lazar, M., Deniz, C.M., et al., 2018. Improved detection of fMRI activation in the cerebellum at 7 T with dielectric pads extending the imaging region of a commercial head coil. J. Magn. Reson. Imaging 48, 431–440. https://doi.org/10.1002/jmri.25936.

Ultra-high field imaging of the human medial temporal lobe

16

Xenia Grande[a,b], Laura Wisse[c], and David Berron[b]

[a]*Institute of Cognitive Neurology and Dementia Research, Otto von Guericke University, Magdeburg, Germany* [b]*German Center for Neurodegenerative Diseases, Magdeburg, Germany* [c]*Institute for Clinical Sciences Lund, Lund University, Lund, Sweden*

Highlights

- Ultra-high field structural MRI enables visualization and measurement of subfields of the medial temporal lobe (MTL).
- Ultra-high field structural and functional MRI allows for a more detailed study of the role of MTL subregions in disease mechanisms.
- Ultra-high field functional MRI enables the probing of heterogeneous memory processes and information flow within MTL subregions.
- Ultra-high field structural and functional MRI allows for the translation of spatially specific insights on disease and cognitive processes from the animal to the human brain.

16.1 Introduction

The medial temporal lobe (MTL) is a complex heterogeneous region that is crucially involved in several cognitive, behavioral, and emotional processes (Squire et al., 2004; Fanselow and Dong, 2010; please see the list of recommended readings for this chapter in the electronic Supplementary Material in the online version at https://doi.org/10.1016/B978-0-323-99898-7.00031-6). Changes in the MTL have long been linked to neurological and psychiatric diseases (Small et al., 2011). In this chapter, we will mainly focus on two MTL regions: the hippocampus and parahippocampal gyrus. Both can be further subdivided into cytoarchitectonically, functionally, and connectomically different subregions (see Fig. 16.1) (Ding and Van Hoesen, 2010; Insausti and Amaral, 2012). The hippocampus consists of the subiculum (also including para- and presubiculum), cornu ammonis (CA) 1–3, and dentate gyrus (Insausti and Amaral, 2012). It should be noted that there is some discussion about the actual number and terminology of subregions in the MTL. Some of these subregions can even be further subdivided into distal and proximal zones or deep and superficial layers (Fig. 16.1, lower panel). The parahippocampal gyrus is a macroanatomical annotation of the gyrus inferomedial to the hippocampus which consists of the entorhinal cortex and part of the perirhinal cortex anteriorly and the parahippocampal cortex posteriorly (Insausti et al., 1998). The perirhinal cortex can be further subdivided into Brodmann area (BA) 35 and 36 (Ding and Van Hoesen, 2010). These MTL subregions are of importance because they play different roles in the cognitive processes

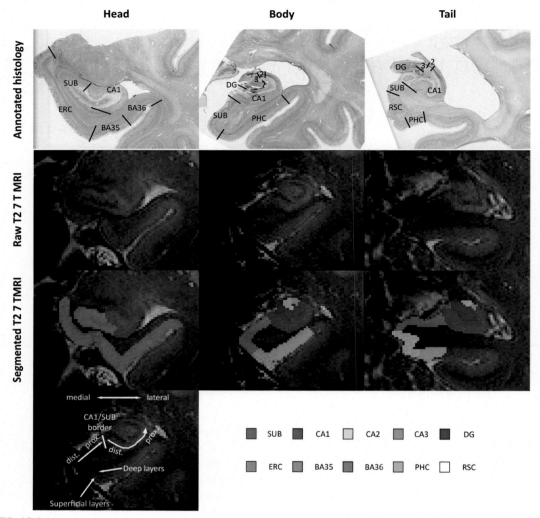

FIG. 16.1

Overview of the anatomy of the medial temporal lobe in the anterior (Head), middle (Body), and posterior (Tail) sections of the hippocampus. The *top row* shows histology sections with annotations of different subregions by the courtesy of Ricardo Insausti and Paul Yushkevich. The *second and third rows* show a 0.4 × 0.4 mm² T_2-weighted 7T MRI with and without segmentations from a different subject with the coronal sections selected at similar locations as the histology sections. The MRI is from a 65-year-old female with mild cognitive impairment by the courtesy of David Wolk. The segmentations are modeled after the histology annotations in the *top row*. At *the bottom row*, the *left figure* indicates additional anatomical information regarding the medial/lateral axes, the superficial and deep layers of the cortex, and the proximal and distal regions of the subiculum and CA1. *SUB*, subiculum; *CA*, cornu ammonis; *DG*, dentate gyrus; *ERC*, entorhinal cortex; *BA*, Brodmann area; *PHC*, parahippocampal cortex; *RSC*, retrosplenial cortex; *dist.*, distal; *prox.*, proximal.

and also show differential vulnerability to disease processes. Studying MTL subregions in vivo, therefore, has the potential to provide new insights into the cognitive processes and disease mechanisms and may even provide new biomarkers for clinical trials and clinical practice.

Ultra-high field magnetic resonance imaging (MRI), which is generally performed at 7T in vivo, has allowed for better interrogation of the structure and functions of these MTL subregions. In this chapter, we will first discuss the advantages of ultra-high field MRI for structural imaging of the MTL and give several examples of the utility of structural imaging in different clinical populations. Then, we will discuss the utility of ultra-high field MRI for functional imaging of the MTL. Finally, we will provide several examples of the knowledge gained on the functional architecture of the MTL using this advancement in functional MRI (fMRI).

16.2 Ultra-high field structural imaging of the MTL

Benefits of ultra-high field imaging: The main advantage of ultra-high field imaging of the MTL structure is the ability to obtain high-resolution images within a reasonable scanning time. The higher resolution is of particular advantage for visualizing the inner structure of the hippocampus which contains crucial information on the border locations of the different hippocampal subfields. The hippocampus consists of folded archicortex (Insausti and Amaral, 2012) which cannot be differentiated on standard-resolution 1 mm^3 images (Wisse et al., 2020). T_2-weighted images have proven to be especially useful for visualizing the inner structure of the hippocampus (Yushkevich et al., 2015a), but other sequences can also be used given that sufficient resolution is obtained. It is most important that the resolution in the coronal plane is sufficient, as this allows for the easiest differentiation of subfields given that anatomical atlases mostly show examples in this plane (e.g., Insausti and Amaral, 2012). The exact resolution required for the visualization of the inner structure of the hippocampus is discussed later in this section.

There are three features that can be visualized within the hippocampus (see Fig. 16.2). The first is the stratum radiatum lacunosum moleculare (SRLM) of the CA subfields and the stratum lacunosum moleculare of the subiculum (Insausti and Amaral, 2012) (for ease both will be referred to as SRLM). SRLM is one of the three layers of the subiculum and CA subfields that is rich in fibers and therefore has a different intensity than the adjacent pyramidal cell layer. SRLM is often referred to as "dark band" as it appears hypointense on T_2-weighted MRI. Given that this layer is present for the full length of the folded CA subfields and subiculum, this hypointense band on T_2-weighted images is helpful for differentiating these subregions from the dentate gyrus. The second feature that can be visualized with high-resolution images is the endfolial pathway (Lim et al., 1997; Berron et al., 2017). This is another hypointense band on T_2-weighted MRI, rich in fibers, that demarcates part of the border between the inward-folded CA3 and dentate gyrus. The third important feature is the alveus which is the outer layer of the CA subregions and subiculum (Insausti and Amaral, 2012), again hypointense on T_2-weighted MRI. This layer clearly outlines the outer surface of the hippocampus, which can be particularly helpful in the complex anterior region of the hippocampus where there is a lot of variation in the depth and number of digitations (de Flores et al., 2019). Better visualization of the outer structure of the hippocampus can also guide the visualization and segmentation of the hippocampus. Of these three features, the alveus can generally be observed on standard-resolution 1 mm^3 images, although not in as much detail. SRLM and the endfolial pathway cannot be visualized on standard-resolution images but can be visualized on specialized high in-plane resolution (often 0.4 × 0.4 mm^2) 3T images

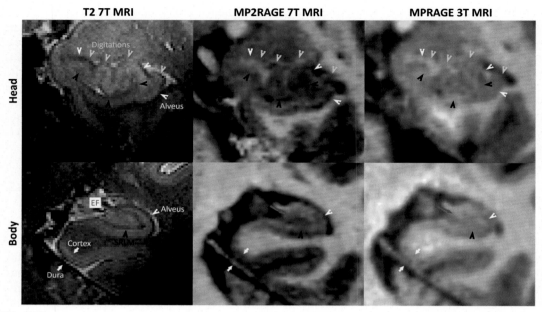

FIG. 16.2

Two examples of improved visualization of the medial temporal lobe at T_2-weighted 7T MRI at the level of the hippocampal head (anterior, *top*) and body (posterior, *bottom*), compared to an MP2RAGE 7T and an MPRAGE 3T MRI. *Top row: In the top row*, two main features of segmentation of the hippocampus are shown; alveus (*white arrowheads*) and SRLM (*black arrowheads*). These features appear as hypointense bands on T_2-weighted MRI, where the alveus helps with the visualization of the outer borders of the hippocampus and the SRLM differentiates the dentate gyrus from the subiculum and cornu ammonis subfields. These features are especially helpful in the anterior portion of the hippocampus where they aid with the visualization of the variable curving (digitations, *blue arrowheads*) of the hippocampus. Note that these features are only to a limited extent visible as hyperintense bands on the MP2RAGE 7T and MPRAGE 3T images, making visualization and segmentation of the hippocampus more difficult. *Bottom row: In the bottom row*, the alveus (*white arrowheads*) and the SRLM (*black arrowheads*) are again easily discernable on the T_2-weighted MRI but more difficult to discern on the MP2RAGE 7T and MPRAGE 3T images. Additionally, the endfolial pathway (*red arrow*), another hypointense band, can be distinguished which is helpful for differentiating the cornu ammonis 3 from the dentate gyrus. This band cannot be observed in other images. Finally, the T_2-weighted MRI and MP2RAGE 7T MRI show clear differentiation between the dura (hypointense) and cortex (*gray; white arrows*). The dura and cortex cannot be separated on the MPRAGE 3T MRI where they have the same intensity. This can lead to oversegmentation of the cortex. *MPRAGE*, magnetization-prepared rapid gradient echo; *MP2RAGE*, magnetization prepared-2 rapid gradient echoes; *SRLM*, stratum radiatum lacunosum moleculare; *EF*, endfolial pathway.

(Yushkevich et al., 2015a). However, this is generally only feasible at the cost of longer scan times or a lower through-plane resolution which ultimately means that the structure of the hippocampus is averaged over a thicker slice leading to less precise measurements. It should be noted that the endfolial pathway cannot be consistently identified in all populations, even with ultra-high field imaging (Berron et al., 2017).

The most important feature to visualize is the SRLM, as this feature is crucial for the segmentation of hippocampal subfields. As the SRLM is generally between 0.52 and 1.04 mm thick (Adler et al., 2018), a resolution of at least 0.5×0.5 mm^2 is recommended to ensure proper visualization. However, lower in-plane resolution, such as 0.7×0.7 mm^2, can also be sufficient to visualize these structures. Interestingly, a recent study indicated that structural postmortem images with a $0.2 \times 0.2 \times 0.2$ mm^3 resolution obtained at 9.4T MRI did not reveal any additional features of the inner structure of the hippocampus that can be useful for the delineation of the different subfields (Wisse et al., 2017). Obtaining an in vivo MRI with an in-plane resolution much higher than 0.5×0.5 mm^2 might, therefore, not be worthwhile. Ultimately, proper visualization of the hippocampus is important for the delineation of hippocampal subfields. This leads to more precise volume and thickness measures which are in turn used to interrogate their involvement in behavior and diseases. Note that while some borders for hippocampal subfields can be visualized with ultra-high field imaging, not all subfield borders are visible on MRI and are therefore approximated based on anatomical atlases.

The advantages of ultra-high field for imaging the structure of the hippocampus are not as evident for the parahippocampal gyrus. However, high-resolution images can help with the differentiation of the dura from the cortex (Fig. 16.2). Dura can be difficult to disentangle from the cortex, especially on standard-resolution T_1-weighted images where they have the same signal intensity (Xie et al., 2019). Clear visualization of this feature will help with the delineation of the parahippocampal gyrus, again in turn leading to better thickness and volume estimates. Note again that high in-plane resolution 3T images can also help with the visualization of the sulci and dura. However, because high in-plane resolution 3T images generally have thicker slices, this may not necessarily improve thickness measurements.

16.2.1 Examples of structural studies

Ultra-high field imaging has improved the visualization of MTL structures. This allows the study of fine-grained subregions, which was not possible at lower field strengths, and has revealed new information on different clinical populations. We provide several compelling examples of the utility of ultra-high field imaging for studying MTL in clinical populations.

Example 1: Neurogenesis as working mechanisms of electroconvulsive therapy in depression. Electroconvulsive therapy (ECT) is an effective treatment for depression, but the working mechanism remains unclear. Animal literature indicates that neurogenesis, which occurs in the granular cell layer of the dentate gyrus, is observed following electroconvulsive seizures (the animal homology of ECT; Nakamura et al., 2013). Nuninga et al. (2020) set up a trial where 23 patients with depression underwent a 7T MRI before and after 10 ECT sessions. They also performed repeated 7T MRI scanning in eight controls at the same time interval. Intriguingly, they observed a volume increase in the dentate gyrus, but not in other subfields, in patients with depression following ECT treatment. No volume changes were observed in the controls. Moreover, the volume increase in the dentate gyrus was related to a decrease in depression scores. These results provide the first clues about the underlying mechanisms of ECT in depression and are supportive of a role in neurogenesis.

Example 2: CA1 apical neuropil atrophy as an early marker of Alzheimer's disease (AD) pathology. The first cortical regions where neurofibrillary tangles, one of the hallmarks of AD, accumulate are in the MTL. One of the regions in the MTL with the earliest accumulation is the apical neuropil layer of

CA1 (Braak and Braak, 1996), also often referred to as the SRLM or "dark band" (see previous section). Kerchner et al. (2010) were the first to show significant thinning of the SRLM in patients with early AD compared to controls using ultra-high field imaging. In their second paper, they also showed that thinning of the SRLM is associated with worse performance of a delayed memory task (Kerchner et al., 2012). Both findings support the utility of the SRLM as an early marker of AD, as measured by ultra-high field imaging.

Example 3: CA3 atrophy in LGI1 voltage-gated potassium channel (VGKC)-complex antibody limbic encephalitis. Autoantibodies in VGKC-complex limbic encephalitis are preferentially expressed in CA1 and CA3 of the hippocampus (Irani et al., 2013) and have been linked to inflammation in rodents (Irani et al., 2013). Miller et al. (2017) used ultra-high field imaging to measure MTL subregions in 18 patients with VGKC-complex limbic encephalitis and 18 controls. Patients with VGKC-complex limbic encephalitis showed significantly smaller CA3 volumes than controls. Interestingly, smaller CA3 volumes were also associated with problems in episodic memory for premorbid autobiographical events, which is one of the main behavioral characteristics of LGI1 VGKC-complex limbic encephalitis. This study showed the utility of ultra-high field imaging in visualizing atrophy in very specific MTL subregions in this clinical population. Moreover, this study provides a link with autoantibody-binding patterns in rodents.

16.3 Ultra-high field functional imaging of the MTL

So far, we focused on the opportunities that ultra-high field imaging holds for measuring and visualizing anatomical structures in the MTL. However, the full potential of ultra-high field imaging is revealed when structural insights are combined with functional meaning. For the scientific endeavor of understanding the functional architecture of the brain, it is not sufficient to grasp the details of its structural design. Cognition emerges when these structures communicate with each other, thereby transferring and shaping information. We will summarize the potential and challenges of ultra-high field functional imaging and provide an overview of the achievements of ultra-high field imaging to understand the mechanisms of MTL function.

Functional and structural organization of the MTL: How the information is processed and flows throughout the MTL and how cognitive functions like memory emerge have been thoroughly conceptualized and elaborated in anatomically inspired theoretical and computational models (McClelland and Goddard, 1996). The medial temporal lobe is seen as a processing hierarchy with the entorhinal-hippocampal circuitry at its core. This circuitry receives and sends information mainly via the parahippocampal gyrus that is the perirhinal cortex with BA35 and BA36 as well as the parahippocampal cortex (Nilssen et al., 2019) (Fig. 16.3).

Within the entorhinal-hippocampal circuitry, the superficial entorhinal layers transfer information into the tri-synaptic loop along which information flows from the dentate gyrus to CA3 and CA1 subfields. From here, the information flows back via the subiculum and deep entorhinal layers toward the adjacent parahippocampal gyrus and cortical areas. Note that the CA3 and CA1 subfields also receive incoming information directly from the entorhinal cortex. Incoming information is separated from similar representations in the dentate gyrus (a process referred to as "pattern separation") whereas attempts to complete the incoming information toward existing representations are made in CA3 (referred to as "pattern completion"; McClelland and Goddard, 1996). When incoming information is successfully

[A]

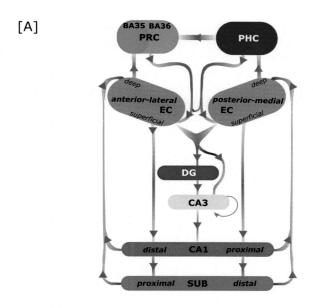

[B]

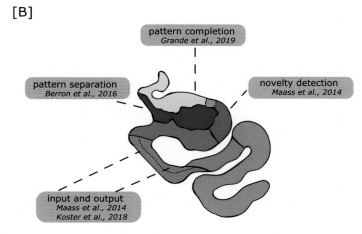

FIG. 16.3

Schematic information flow and empirical evidence obtained with the ultra-high field functional imaging in humans for heterogeneous processing within the parahippocampal-hippocampal system. The hippocampal formation receives information via the superficial entorhinal layers and projects information to the deep entorhinal layers (A). Empirical evidence for these input and output layers, as well as information flow *between* the input and output layers of the entorhinal cortex (recurrence) were obtained by Maass et al. (2014) and Koster et al. (2018) (B). These entorhinal-hippocampal projections follow a highly topographical pattern with the anterolateral EC mainly projecting toward the distal CA1 and receiving information from the proximal subiculum while the posteromedial EC projects to the proximal CA1 and receives information from the distal subiculum. These two pathways are functionally connected to the perirhinal and parahippocampal cortices, respectively, and considered to be part of the two cortical routes, biased to process item- and context-related information. Note, however, that profound crosstalk and projections from the parahippocampal to the

(Continued)

completed, the representation is enriched in CA1 and reinstated in the cortex (McClelland and Goddard, 1996). However, when the information is novel, the dentate gyrus and CA3 regions interact to presumably create storable indices that allow for the retrieval of information later on (Tanaka and McHugh, 2018). In addition to these topographically specific computations, certain types of information seem to flow along specific routes along the medial temporal lobe (Ranganath and Ritchey, 2012). On one hand, the parahippocampal cortices, medial entorhinal cortex, and distal subiculum seem to process contextual information, for instance, the spatial setting in which an event occurs. On the other hand, the perirhinal and lateral entorhinal cortices and subiculum/CA1 border may process item-related information, presumably converged with contextual aspects, such as the location of objects (Nilssen et al., 2019; Grande et al., 2022). Notably, cross-talk exists between these two routes, especially from the parahippocampal cortex toward the perirhinal cortex and lateral entorhinal cortex (Nilssen et al., 2019). Like gears in a clockwork, the structures within the MTL are thus conceptualized as processing different aspects of information, transforming that information at specific locations in the brain, and making the shaped representations disposable for cognitive operations. While these models provide a valuable source for hypotheses, empirical evidence in the human brain require ultra-high spatial resolution due to the highly topographic nature of the information flow and the comparably small size of functionally relevant subregions. This is where ultra-high field imaging comes into play.

Benefits of ultra-high field functional imaging: Firstly and similar to ultra-high field structural imaging, ultra-high field functional imaging allows for significantly higher resolution which has allowed the study of fine-grained subregions of the MTL, their functional connectivity as well as functional involvement. This was not possible at lower field strengths. While conventional functional imaging at 3T usually operates at voxel sizes between $1.5 \times 1.5 \times 1.5$ mm^3 and $3 \times 3 \times 3$ mm^3, 7T reaches a submillimeter resolution of up to $0.7 \times 0.7 \times 0.7$ mm^3. Secondly, functional imaging has increased sensitivity at ultra-high field due to an interplay of contrast changes and physiological factors (see further Chapter 22). Thirdly, combining computational predictions with high anatomical specificity (e.g., layer-specific imaging) may not only allow for the verification of computational models but even allow expanding them further. Finally, the ultra-high resolution technique is an excellent tool to preserve the high anatomical specificity of rodent studies that target highly constrained regions. This opens the door for research that directly verifies and translates insights from the rodent to the human brain.

FIG. 16.3—Cont'd

perirhinal cortex exist ((A); Nilssen et al., 2019). Besides these highly topographical projections from the entorhinal cortex toward the hippocampal CA1, the hippocampal formation receives incoming information directly in the dentate gyrus and CA3 subfield. Information along the dentate gyrus, CA3, and CA1 subfields flows in a rather unidirectional manner (tri-synaptic loop). The entorhinal projections toward the dentate gyrus are sparse, indicative of their ability to separate the similar incoming input. Empirical evidence for such a pattern separation mechanism has been obtained by Berron et al. (2016) (B). Within the subfield CA3, the recurrent collaterals have been proposed to perform a pattern completion computation that allows retrieving more comprehensive information based on the partial input. Empirical evidence for the involvement of subfield CA3 in comprehensive retrieval via pattern completion has been obtained by Grande et al. (2019) (B). Note moreover that the two-folded input that the subfield CA1 receives from CA3 but also directly from the EC puts CA1 in a state to function as a comparator between new incoming information (from EC) and old information (completed in CA3). Empirical evidence with ultra-high field imaging in humans for novelty detection in CA1 has been reported in Maass et al. (2014). *EC*, entorhinal cortex; *CA*, cornu ammonis.

16.3.1 Examples of functional studies

Example 1: Investigating memory processes in the MTL. The very first glimpse of memory function with the 7T imaging was caught by Theysohn and colleagues (Theysohn et al., 2009). Theysohn et al. showed the feasibility of functionally imaging the MTL with 7T in proof-of-concept studies demonstrating a reliable signal from the hippocampus and the benefits of 7T over more common 3T imaging. The functional involvement of hippocampal subfields during the encoding and retrieval of associations was mapped by mainly showing anterior vs posterior differences in a number of subfields (Suthana et al., 2015). Later on, even empirical evidence for different types of information processing in the dentate gyrus vs CA3 subfields was provided in two independent studies (Berron et al., 2016; Grande et al., 2019). These studies were the first to attribute the functions to the respective subfields with a high amount of specificity without merging across the subfields. The study of Berron and colleagues is unique for its high specificity in computational evidence. This study showed strong evidence for pattern separation in the dentate gyrus but not in other subregions. Overall, these studies show a need for high anatomical specificity to understand the clockwork within the MTL, and they underscore the potential of ultra-high field imaging in translating insights from computational models to the human brain when studying functions that are proposed to be highly anatomic specific.

　　Example 2: Investigating information flow within the MTL. Besides the subfield-specific computations, the communication between the subregions can also be tracked by examining the functional connectivity patterns using ultra-high field fMRI. Notably, these functional connectivity patterns correspond to structural routes (Shah et al., 2018). A straightforward approach is to correlate the fluctuation of the BOLD signal over time between the regions of interest, even allowing voxel-wise specificity. Using this method, empirical evidence could be obtained for two functional routes in the human brain that are biased for the processing of item- and context-related information and map onto the perirhinal and parahippocampal cortices, respectively (Ranganath and Ritchey, 2012). These two functional routes have been found to split the entorhinal cortex into an anterolateral and a posteromedial part. This functional connectivity method thus revealed a prerequisite for information-specific processing pathways in the MTL (Maass et al., 2015). These studies show the potential of ultra-high field imaging in translating findings from rodents (i.e., functionally different medial vs lateral entorhinal subregions) to the human brain. In addition, Maass, Berron, and colleagues were able to find further functional segregation in the human brain: the proximal vs distal subiculum which preferentially connects to the anterolateral and posteromedial entorhinal cortices, respectively. A subsequent ultra-high field study indeed confirmed scene-biased processing in the distal subiculum (Hodgetts et al., 2017). Recent studies have started to reveal the routes of information flow within the human hippocampal subfields (Grande et al., 2022).

　　Example 3: Probing memory functions through layer-based functional imaging. Merging the ultra-high resolution functional connectivity technique with computational models shows the extraordinary potential of ultra-high field imaging for testing mechanisms of brain function at the mesoscale level. How can ultra-high field functional imaging reveal the fundamentals of brain function? Let us go back to our brief introduction of the proposed information flow in the entorhinal-hippocampal circuitry. There is a differential topography of the information entering and leaving the circuitry. While the former flows through superficial entorhinal layers, the latter flows through deep entorhinal layers. If we would be able to go to the level of layers to reveal function, we could then infer how information has been shaped in between. Indeed, this is the approach of a pioneering study by Maass et al. (2014).

Ultra-high field imaging allowed them to provide evidence for the superficial vs deep entorhinal layer processing of novel information in vivo in humans. They also showed that subsequent memory performance was related to the functional connectivity between deep entorhinal layers and subfield CA1. Taking all these insights further even allowed for the examination of a fundamental question regarding the information flow in the entorhinal-hippocampal circuitry: does the information flow unidirectionally or is outgoing information entered as new input into the circuitry creating a recurrent loop? In a paired associative inference task, participants learned to associate A-B and B-C. The B stimulus could either be a scene or an object while A and C were always faces. At retrieval, the A-C association had to be inferred, without ever presenting the B stimulus. Remember, B could be either a scene or an object category stimulus. Now, given the unique functionality of the entorhinal layers in holding input (superficial) and output (deep) information from the hippocampus, traces of the not-presented B stimulus category (either scene or object) at retrieval in the superficial entorhinal layers were suggestive of recurrent information flow within the entorhinal-hippocampal circuitry. The authors reasoned that this category of information in the input entorhinal layers is unrelated to sensory input (B is not presented at that moment) but could only have been generated by the hippocampus itself based on the presented A-C stimuli. The B stimulus category would then appear as a hippocampal output in the deep entorhinal layers. The occurrence in superficial entorhinal layers speaks for a feedback mechanism and recurrent information flow. Even more evidence for recurrence could be found, as the retrieval performance was dependent on the interaction between the superficial and deep entorhinal layers. This indicated communication between outgoing and incoming information (Koster et al., 2018). Both studies show how ultra-high resolution functional imaging can move the field of functional imaging away from mere structure-function mapping to the precise investigation of mechanisms. This not only verified but even advanced computational models further. While the examination of the architecture of memory function in the MTL has so far been predominant in research leveraging ultra-high field functional imaging, the benefits and opportunities are not restricted to that. Indeed, representations within the MTL subregions have also been investigated with a focus on navigational mechanisms (Chen et al., 2019) and further aspects may be explored in the future.

Example 4: Feedback to 3T functional imaging at conventional resolution. Functional subregions identified with ultra-high field imaging can be taken to provide meaningful masks for the investigation of these subregions' role within 3T studies (Chen et al., 2019; Berron et al., 2019). Ultra-high field imaging thereby gains broader influence on the whole research area of MTL imaging as insights can directly be transferred to improve studies on lower resolution and, in turn, increase their anatomical specificity.

16.4 Challenges of structural and functional UHF imaging

Despite all these exciting opportunities that ultra-high field imaging can offer, its profound potential can only come into effect with awareness and careful handling of its specific challenges. We, therefore, want to draw the interested readers' attention toward some of these challenges before heading out to acquire and analyze their ultra-high resolution data.

One important challenge is motion. While this is not a specific problem for ultra-high field imaging, the higher resolution images generally required for interrogating MTL structure and function are particularly prone to motion, especially in certain populations such as children or patients with dementia. Imagine a participant in an fMRI study only moving 1–2 mm when the voxel size is 1 mm^3 or smaller, and the aim is to examine the layer-specific activity with one layer not wider than 1–2 voxels. Mislocation of the signal can easily happen, threatening the potential inferences one can draw from the acquired data. Adaptive or real-time motion correction even with the aid of special devices to prevent motion is, therefore, the key. For a discussion on motion correction methods (see Chapter 10).

Another challenge, which is specific for ultra-high field imaging, is the signal dropout in the lateral parahippocampal gyrus. This can be so severe that the gray matter borders of the lateral parahippocampal gyrus subregions (most often BA36) cannot be observed and structural information about these regions can therefore not consistently be obtained in all participants. High-permittivity pads could potentially be used to reduce this issue. Signal dropout is also an issue with functional imaging as the signal is literally lost from these parts. A practical discussion of specific imaging parameters and sequences is beyond the scope of this chapter but we refer the interested reader to an excellent overview by Nau (2019) regarding functional sequences and Chapter 7 for a general discussion on B_1 effects at ultra-high field.

Additionally, there are challenges related to anatomical specificity. A requirement for analyzing MTL subregions is segmentation methods that are reliable and at the same time preserve accurate anatomy as far as possible (see Berron et al., 2017). Even now that time-saving atlas-based segmentation is feasible (Yushkevich et al., 2015b), careful manual inspection still remains mandatory. Likewise, the co-registration between the segmented subregional masks on T_2-weighted images and the functional echo-planar images is a challenge for every new dataset. This usually requires a combination of algorithms from different software packages. We strongly suggest manually checking every step carefully as mislocations occur easily and misplacement of only one row of voxels may have a major effect on results. Please note that this book chapter is not the place to discuss these challenges comprehensively and we only provide a brief insight.

Finally, less a challenge than a point of awareness when conducting and evaluating ultra-high field studies is the reduced brain coverage of functional images (and sometimes structural images), at least when aiming for ultra-high resolution. Focused hypotheses on targeted brain structures are, therefore, the key. It is essential to keep in mind that the number of exploratory findings regarding nontargeted brain structures is therefore limited.

16.5 **An outlook on future developments**

We want to point out that the potential of ultra-high field imaging has not yet come into full effect. For structural imaging, increased resolution in the coronal plane will likely not improve the visualization of MTL structures beyond what is already possible (Wisse et al., 2017). However, obtaining isotropic resolution might help with the visualization of the complicated structures of some parts of the MTL, where visualization in three planes is helpful, such as the hippocampal tail which often shows an upward curve. Isotropic resolution images would allow for resampling of the images along this upward curve and for a better understanding of the anatomy (de Flores et al., 2019). Moreover, better techniques for dealing with motion and signal dropout will certainly increase the usefulness of ultra-high field imaging in clinical and other study populations, especially those prone to motion.

In addition to achieving ultra-high spatial resolution, functional ultra-high field imaging may also achieve ultra-high temporal resolution. This is a potentially interesting feature for revealing the temporal dynamics of cognitive computations, the interaction of brain regions over time, and translating electrophysiological insights into restricted anatomical areas. Yet another exciting field opens up with ultra-high field imaging: the acquisition of individualized functional patterns or "brainprints." The higher SNR of 7T imaging seems to provide an advantage when acquiring reliable patterns of brain functional activity over time (Cai et al., 2021). Certainly, the field of functional imaging has gained profound credibility. It also has gained potential in revealing actual mechanisms of the brain by the powerful features of ultra-high field imaging when applied in strong interaction with computational models, animal insights, and anatomical knowledge.

References

Adler, D.H., Wisse, L.E., Ittyerah, R., et al., 2018. Characterizing the human hippocampus in aging and Alzheimer's disease using a computational atlas derived from ex vivo MRI and histology. Proc. Natl. Acad. Sci. 115, 4252–4257.

Berron, D., Schutze, H., Maass, A., et al., 2016. Strong evidence for pattern separation in human dentate gyrus. J. Neurosci. 36, 7569–7579.

Berron, D., Vieweg, P., Hochkeppler, A., et al., 2017. A protocol for manual segmentation of medial temporal lobe subregions in 7 Tesla MRI. Neuroimage Clin. 15, 466–482.

Berron, D., Cardenas-Blanco, A., Bittner, D., et al., 2019. Higher CSF tau levels are related to hippocampal hyperactivity and object mnemonic discrimination in older adults. J. Neurosci. 39, 8788–8797.

Braak, H., Braak, E., 1996. Development of Alzheimer-related neurofibrillary changes in the neocortex inversely recapitulates cortical myelogenesis. Acta Neuropathol. 92, 197–201.

Cai, Y., Hofstetter, S., van der Zwaag, W., Zuiderbaan, W., Dumoulin, S.O., 2021. Individualized cognitive neuroscience needs 7T: comparing numerosity maps at 3T and 7T MRI. Neuroimage 237, 118184.

Chen, X., Vieweg, P., Wolbers, T., 2019. Computing distance information from landmarks and self-motion cues-differential contributions of anterior-lateral vs. posterior-medial entorhinal cortex in humans. Neuroimage 202, 116074.

de Flores, R., Berron, D., Ding, S., et al., 2019. Characterization of hippocampal subfields using ex vivo MRI and histology data: lessons for in vivo segmentation. Hippocampus 30, 545–564.

Ding, S.L., Van Hoesen, G.W., 2010. Borders, extent, and topography of human perirhinal cortex as revealed using multiple modern neuroanatomical and pathological markers. Hum. Brain Mapp. 31, 1359–1379.

Fanselow, M.S., Dong, H., 2010. Are the dorsal and ventral hippocampus functionally distinct structures? Neuron 65, 7–19.

Grande, X., Berron, D., Horner, A.J., Bisby, J.A., Düzel, E., Burgess, N., 2019. Holistic recollection via pattern completion involves hippocampal subfield CA3. J. Neurosci. 39, 8100–8111.

Grande, X., Sauvage, M.M., Becke, A., Düzel, E., Berron, D., 2022. Transversal functional connectivity and scene-specific processing in the human entorhinal-hippocampal circuitry. eLife 11, e76479. https://doi.org/10.7554/eLife.76479

Hodgetts, C.J., Voets, N.L., Thomas, A.G., Clare, S., Lawrence, A.D., Graham, K.S., 2017. Ultra-high-field fMRI reveals a role for the subiculum in scene perceptual discrimination. J. Neurosci. 37, 3150–3159.

Insausti, R., Amaral, D.G., 2012. Hippocampal formation. In: Mai, J.K., Paxinos, G. (Eds.), The Human Nervous System. Elsevier Academic Press, San Diego.

Insausti, R., Juottonen, K., Soininen, H., et al., 1998. MR volumetric analysis of the human entorhinal, perirhinal, and temporopolar cortices. Am. J. Neuroradiol. 19, 659–671.

Irani, S.R., Stagg, C.J., Schott, J.M., et al., 2013. Faciobrachial dystonic seizures: the influence of immunotherapy on seizure control and prevention of cognitive impairment in a broadening phenotype. Brain 136, 3151–3162.

Kerchner, G.A., Hess, C.P., Hammond-Rosenbluth, K.E., et al., 2010. Hippocampal CA1 apical neuropil atrophy in mild Alzheimer disease visualized with 7-T MRI. Neurology 75, 1381–1387.

Kerchner, G.A., Deutsch, G.K., Zeineh, M., Dougherty, R.F., Saranathan, M., Rutt, B.K., 2012. Hippocampal CA1 apical neuropil atrophy and memory performance in Alzheimer's disease. Neuroimage 63, 194–202.

Koster, R., Chadwick, M.J., Chen, Y., et al., 2018. Big-loop recurrence within the hippocampal system supports integration of information across episodes. Neuron 99, 1342–1354.e6.

Lim, C., Mufson, E.J., Kordower, J.H., Blume, H.W., Madsen, J.R., Saper, C.B., 1997. Connections of the hippocampal formation in humans: II. The endfolial fiber pathway. J. Comp. Neurol. 385, 352–371.

Maass, A., Schütze, H., Speck, O., et al., 2014. Laminar activity in the hippocampus and entorhinal cortex related to novelty and episodic encoding. Nat. Commun. 5, 1–12.

Maass, A., Berron, D., Libby, L.A., Ranganath, C., Düzel, E., 2015. Functional subregions of the human entorhinal cortex. eLife 4, e06426.

McClelland, J.L., Goddard, N.H., 1996. Considerations arising from a complementary learning systems perspective on hippocampus and neocortex. Hippocampus 6, 654–665.

Miller, T.D., Chong, T.T., Aimola Davies, A.M., et al., 2017. Focal CA3 hippocampal subfield atrophy following LGI1 VGKC-complex antibody limbic encephalitis. Brain 140, 1212–1219.

Nakamura, K., Ito, M., Liu, Y., Seki, T., Suzuki, T., Arai, H., 2013. Effects of single and repeated electroconvulsive stimulation on hippocampal cell proliferation and spontaneous behaviors in the rat. Brain Res. 1491, 88–97.

Nau, M., 2019. Functional Imaging of the Human Medial Temporal Lobe. https://www.google.com/url?sa=t&rct=j&q=&esrc=s&source=web&cd=&ved=2ahUKEwiF4v3MjYz5AhXdVPEDHWBLDGgQFnoECAUQAQ&url=https%3A%2F%2Fmatthiasnau.com%2Fepi_guide.pdf&usg=AOvVaw2qkqzobwKWYMxgoc_G-Iwu.

Nilssen, E.S., Doan, T.P., Nigro, M.J., Ohara, S., Witter, M.P., 2019. Neurons and networks in the entorhinal cortex: a reappraisal of the lateral and medial entorhinal subdivisions mediating parallel cortical pathways. Hippocampus 29, 1238–1254.

Nuninga, J.O., Mandl, R.C., Boks, M.P., et al., 2020. Volume increase in the dentate gyrus after electroconvulsive therapy in depressed patients as measured with 7T. Mol. Psychiatry 25, 1559–1568.

Ranganath, C., Ritchey, M., 2012. Two cortical systems for memory-guided behaviour. Nat. Rev. Neurosci. 13, 713–726.

Shah, P., Bassett, D.S., Wisse, L.E., et al., 2018. Mapping the structural and functional network architecture of the medial temporal lobe using 7T MRI. Hum. Brain Mapp. 39, 851–865.

Small, S.A., Schobel, S.A., Buxton, R.B., Witter, M.P., Barnes, C.A., 2011. A pathophysiological framework of hippocampal dysfunction in ageing and disease. Nat. Rev. Neurosci. 12, 585–601.

Squire, L.R., Stark, C.E., Clark, R.E., 2004. The medial temporal lobe. Annu. Rev. Neurosci. 27, 279–306.

Suthana, N.A., Donix, M., Wozny, D.R., et al., 2015. High-resolution 7T fMRI of human hippocampal subfields during associative learning. J. Cogn. Neurosci. 27, 1194–1206.

Tanaka, K.Z., McHugh, T.J., 2018. The hippocampal engram as a memory index. J. Exp. Neurosci. 12, 1179069518815942.

Theysohn, J.M., Kraff, O., Maderwald, S., et al., 2009. The human hippocampus at 7 T—in vivo MRI. Hippocampus 19, 1–7.

Wisse, L., Adler, D.H., Ittyerah, R., et al., 2017. Comparison of in vivo and ex vivo MRI of the human hippocampal formation in the same subjects. Cereb. Cortex 27, 5185–5196.

Wisse, L.E., Chételat, G., Daugherty, A.M., et al., 2020. Hippocampal subfield volumetry from structural isotropic 1 mm3 MRI scans: a note of caution. Hum. Brain Mapp. 42 (2), 539–550.

Xie, L., Wisse, L.E., Pluta, J., et al., 2019. Automated segmentation of medial temporal lobe subregions on in vivo T1-weighted MRI in early stages of Alzheimer's disease. Hum. Brain Mapp. 40, 3431–3451.

Yushkevich, P.A., Amaral, R.S., Augustinack, J.C., et al., 2015a. Quantitative comparison of 21 protocols for labeling hippocampal subfields and parahippocampal subregions in in vivo MRI: towards a harmonized segmentation protocol. Neuroimage 111, 526–541.

Yushkevich, P.A., Pluta, J.B., Wang, H., et al., 2015b. Automated volumetry and regional thickness analysis of hippocampal subfields and medial temporal cortical structures in mild cognitive impairment. Hum. Brain Mapp. 36, 258–287.

Imaging of subcortical deep brain structures with 7T MRI

17

Rémi Patriat, Tara Palnitkar, Henry Braun, Oren Solomona, and Noam Harel
Center for Magnetic Resonance Research/Radiology, University of Minnesota, Minneapolis, MN, United States

Highlights
- 7T MRI enables direct visualization of small deep subcortical gray matter structures.
- 7T MRI enables subject-specific tractography and 3D anatomical reconstructions.
- 7T MRI allows the generation of accurate ground truths for machine learning algorithms.
- 7T MRI has great potential for clinical applications, e.g., deep brain stimulation.

17.1 Introduction

Deep subcortical structures are involved in a myriad of functions and processes. Varying in shapes and sizes, these regions include such structures as the thalamus, the caudate, the putamen, the globus pallidus (GP), the subthalamic nucleus (STN), the substantia nigra (SN), the red nucleus (RN), the zona incerta, the hypothalamus, and the amygdala. Together they are involved in motor, emotional, memory, pleasure, and hormonal processes. Due to their central location within the cranium, deep subcortical structures are further away from the MRI coil elements than the cortex, resulting in typically lower signal sensitivity in these regions, and are, thus, more difficult to visualize. This lower signal sensitivity contributes to lower contrast and lower signal-to-noise ratio (SNR). To mitigate SNR limitations, a common approach is to acquire larger voxels; however, the resulting lower spatial resolution is detrimental to the visualization of many of the aforementioned structures as some are only a few millimeters in size in every direction.

Ultra-high field MRI ($\geq$7 Tesla (T)) can generate images with a higher signal than conventional 1.5T or 3T scanners. This increased sensitivity to signal and improved contrast can be used to acquire high-resolution MR images with adequate SNR (Cho et al., 2010; Ladd et al., 2018). The development of such scanners for research has opened the doors to visualizing and studying deep subcortical structures more clearly. Furthermore, with the recent approval of 7T scanners for clinical use, clinicians can now gather additional information for diagnostic purposes and offer truly patient-specific care for diseases involving deep subcortical structures. In this chapter, we will discuss the advances in subject-specific visualization of deep subcortical structures, reconstruction of their white matter pathways, identification of their functional subterritories, and how these advantages have been applied to deep brain stimulation surgery and research.

Advances in Magnetic Resonance Technology and Applications. Volume 10. ISSN 2666-9099. https://doi.org/10.1016/B978-0-323-99898-7.00018-3

17.2 **Direct visualization of deep subcortical structures**

In structural images of the human brain, 7T (and higher field) imaging provides enhanced resolution and contrast beyond that of conventional MRI scanners (Abosch et al., 2010; Cho et al., 2010; Ladd et al., 2018). This improvement has triggered the development of novel neuroimaging methods that enable direct visualization of the neuroanatomy of deep subcortical structures.

Standard MRI contrasts, such as T_1w and T_2w, benefit from the advent of 7T. Thanks to higher signal sensitivity, these images can now be acquired with submillimeter resolution in vivo and in a timely fashion, allowing visualization of details in the deep gray subcortical regions previously unattainable. For example, in Fig. 17.1, the medullary lamina separating the external and internal parts of the globus pallidus (GPe and GPi, respectively) can now be seen throughout the whole structure on a T_2-weighted image (Patriat et al., 2018).

Another MRI sequence, susceptibility-weighted imaging (SWI), has been shown to especially benefit from the development of ultra-high field MRI. SWI combines the acquired magnitude and phase images to highlight the local magnetic susceptibility variations. These small variations are caused by the close proximity of structures with different magnetic properties, including iron content, deoxyhemoglobin concentration, and densely packed myelinated axons (Abosch et al., 2010), and are easier to measure at a higher field strength. In fact, the increased contrast and submillimeter resolution of 7T SWI have enabled direct visualization of not only the borders of the thalamus but also its nuclei (Abosch et al., 2010; Najdenovska et al., 2019). Furthermore, similar imaging acquisitions have yielded benefits in visualizing and segmenting the main structures of the basal ganglia (Duchin et al., 2018; Keuken et al., 2014; Lenglet et al., 2012; Plantinga et al., 2018) (see Fig. 17.1). T_1, T_2, and SWI images contain information that is often complementary, and together they provide a wealth of qualitative data.

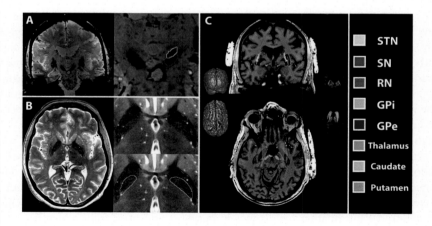

FIG. 17.1

In vivo visualization of deep subcortical brain structures from 7T images. Panel A shows a coronal SWI image as well as the contours of STN and SN. Panel B shows an axial T_2 image as well as the contours of GPi and GPe. Panel C shows subject-specific 3D models of eight subcortical structures with a T_1 image in the background. *STN,* subthalamic nucleus; *SN,* substantia nigra; *RN,* red nucleus; *GPi,* globus pallidus internus; *GPe,* globus pallidus externa.

To go beyond qualitative assessment, researchers have developed a method to compute quantitative metrics based on the T_2^* magnitude and phase images used to generate SWI images. This method is called quantitative susceptibility mapping (QSM). QSM enables iron mapping without blooming artifacts inherent to other sequences, such as SWI, and offers good contrast for deep subcortical structures, such as STN, SN, GPi, and GPe (Eskreis-Winkler et al., 2017).

17.3 Generating subject-specific segmentations of deep subcortical structures

Many deep gray structures are small, and conventional imaging with its relatively low contrast and low resolution (often several millimeters) cannot depict them precisely. Thus, their identification often requires the use of templates for research and, sometimes, clinical applications. Clear direct visualization of deep subcortical structures in submillimeter resolution at ultra-high field opens new avenues for accurate subject-specific three-dimensional representations of an individual's anatomy. Fig. 17.1 shows how T_2 and SWI images can be used to delineate many deep subcortical structures that can be combined for research and clinical applications alike. For instance, Patriat et al. (2020) were able to associate STN volumes with Parkinson's disease diagnosis using manual segmentation of STN, which is a small structure oftentimes only measuring a few millimeters in every direction. For clinical applications, refer to Section 17.6.

Validating the segmentations performed on in vivo imaging is challenging due to the difficulty of obtaining ground truth data. Thankfully, information recorded during deep brain stimulation (DBS) surgery can provide independent data on where the borders of the deep subcortical target structures are located. In fact, prior to implantation of the DBS macroelectrode, a microelectrode is placed down the planned trajectory to identify the cells encountered at different depths based on their firing patterns (Starr et al., 2002). This process is called micro-electrode recording (MER). For example, the firing patterns of STN cells differ greatly from neighboring cells, and neurologists are also able to differentiate the internal and external parts of globus pallidus, enabling accurate identification of their borders. Once the borders have been identified, it is then easy to calculate the length of STN traversed by the electrode. This length can be compared to the length measured directly on the images after fusing a high-resolution postoperative computed tomography (CT) image with the preoperative MRI images and 3D models of a given patient. Duchin et al. (2018) and Patriat et al. (2018) performed this exact test focusing on the subthalamic nucleus and globus pallidus, respectively. The authors reported excellent agreement between MER and the imaging-based measurements (Fig. 17.2).

17.4 Harnessing 7T MRI benefits to develop machine learning algorithms

By facilitating direct visualization of deep subcortical structures, ultra-high field MRI allows for detailed manual segmentation of subcortical anatomical structures. The ability to generate subject-specific segmentations of these structures has several applications including basic scientific studies (Duchin et al., 2018; Patriat et al., 2018, 2020; Plantinga et al., 2018), clinical use (see Section 17.6), and machine learning algorithm development. In fact, these accurate ground truth segmentations, along with the acquired images, can be used to create state-of-the-art machine learning tools that help reduce the

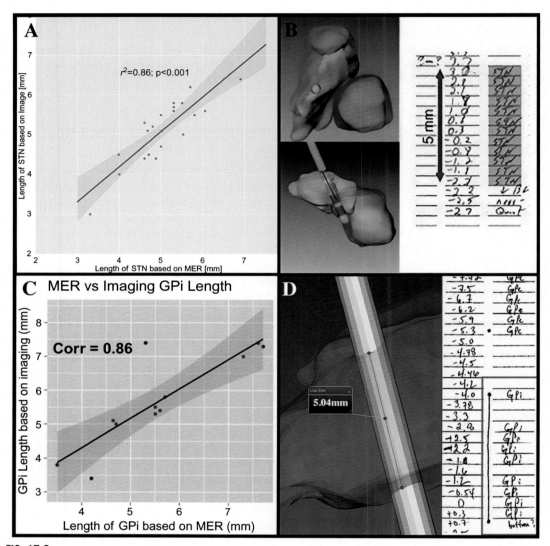

FIG. 17.2

Validation of 7T patient-specific segmentations. Panels A and C show scatter plots, linear fits, and correlation coefficients of the comparison between the length of STN (A) or GPi (C) traversed by the electrode as measured with MER and measured directly on the 3D models. Panels B and D show an example of data measurement for STN (B) and GPi (D). *STN*, subthalamic nucleus; *GPi*, globus pallidus internus; *GPe*, globus pallidus externa; *MER*, microelectrode recording; *Corr*, correlation coefficient. *Figure adapted, in part, with permission under CC BY license from Duchin et al. (2018) and Patriat et al. (2018).*

burden of manual segmentation by providing an accurate and automatic segmentation in a matter of seconds. One such tool, called GP-net, relies on 7T T_2 images from over 100 subjects to train, test, and validate a deep learning-based neural network (Solomon et al., 2021). The authors show improved performance compared to the commonly used template-based approaches. Fig. 17.3 shows examples of machine learning-based outputs of STN and GPi predictions compared to corresponding manually delineated ground truth models.

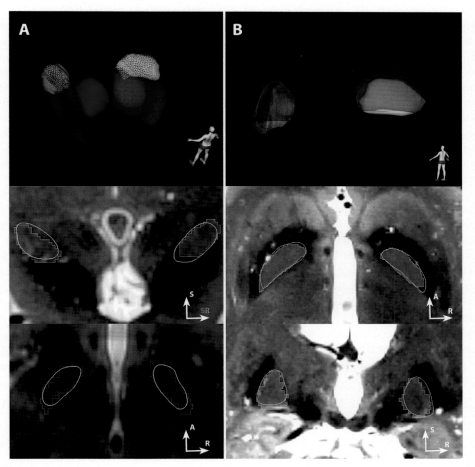

FIG. 17.3

Comparison of machine learning-based segmentation (mesh in 3D, contours in 2D) and manual ground truth segmentation (surface in 3D, filled contours in 2D) for STN (Panel A) and GPi (Panel B). The machine learning algorithm and ground truth were obtained using 7T MRI images. *STN*, subthalamic nucleus; *GPi*, globus pallidus internus; *S*, superior; *R*, right; *A*, anterior.

17.5 Tractography and parcellation

Structural connectivity, or tractography, is computed based on diffusion MRI data that measure the movement of protons in water. A typical diffusion dataset includes a few volumes with no diffusion weighting ($b=0$) and volumes with diffusion weighting ($b>0$), acquired with different gradient directions. From these volumes, a diffusion tensor is computed, and subsequently, white matter pathways can be reconstructed. For more details on diffusion MRI, see Chapter 20.

17.5.1 Subject-specific tractography of deep subcortical structures

The process of reconstructing white matter connections between two or more regions of the brain (i.e., tractography) can be improved greatly by using ultra-high field MRI. In fact, the inherent increase in SNR can be leveraged to achieve higher spatial resolution, faster multishell imaging, and more angular resolution (i.e., acquiring more directions). Thanks to these advances, pathways that had historically only been reported using ex vivo histology data or in vivo group averaged MRI are now visible at the single subject level. This capability is even more relevant for visualizing the connections between the deep subcortical structures as they are typically packed closely together with pathways crossing other important white matter bundles. One caveat of ultra-high field MRI is an increase in B_0 and B_1 inhomogeneities, which can negatively impact images; the former results in image distortions while the latter induces local signal losses. However, these are less likely to be observed at the center of the brain (Duchin et al., 2012).

One example of the utility of 7T imaging is the ability to visualize, in vivo, pathways connecting the basal ganglia structures and thalamic nuclei (Lenglet et al., 2012). Lenglet et al. were able to find consistent tractography results for nigrostriatal, nigropallidal, subthalamopallidal, and pallidothalamic pathways across individuals and brain hemispheres. These subcortical pathways are involved in motor and working memory functions. These visualization capabilities enable a more precise understanding of the physiology and development of brain disorders. For example, the nigropallidal pathway is thought to be upregulated in Parkinson's disease in concordance with the loss of dopaminergic neurons in the substantia nigra (Whone et al., 2003). Lenglet et al. have been able to demonstrate not only that it is possible to reconstruct tracts between deep subcortical structures but also where within those structures the regions involved in those connections were located. For instance, they found that caudolateral STN was most connected to caudoventral GPe. Fig. 17.4 shows examples of tract reconstructions in a Parkinson's disease patient for the nigrostriatal, nigropallidal, subthalamopallidal, and pallidothalamic pathways.

17.5.2 Subject-specific tractography-based parcellation of deep subcortical structures

While tractography can be used to visualize white matter pathways between structures, it can also inform where within a given gray matter structure these connections occur. This process, repeated over multiple targets, helps to create a subdivision of the structure and is commonly referred to as parcellation (Behrens et al., 2003). In essence, tractography-based parcellation enables the identification of subterritories of brain structures most connected to other brain regions.

For example, based on animal and human literature, STN is believed to be organized following a tripartite subdivision including motor, associative, and limbic territories (Lambert et al., 2012; Parent and Hazrati, 1995). Plantinga et al. (2018) used 7T diffusion MRI, in vivo, to parcellate STN and test

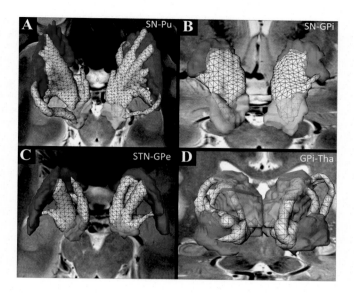

FIG. 17.4

Subject-specific white matter reconstruction of nigrostriatal (A), nigropallidal (B), subthalamopallidal (C), and pallidothalamic (D) pathways using 7T diffusion data. *Figure adapted, with permission under CC BY license, from Lenglet et al. (2012).*

whether this tripartite organization was visible and reproducible in individuals. By fiber tracking from every voxel in STN to motor, associative, limbic, and an "other" region consisting of the rest of the cortex, the authors were able to identify voxels within STN that were most connected to each of these cortical regions. Similar to animal studies, this experiment revealed that the posterior STN was most connected to the motor region of the cortex, followed in the midsection by a region most connected to the associative cortex, while the anterior STN was most connected to the limbic cortical regions. This organizational pattern was consistent across subjects. Note that interindividual variability was also observed in the amount of overlap between these STN parcels. Additional studies on GPi and the thalamus have yielded analogous results and conclusions (Patriat et al., 2018; Plantinga et al., 2018). These patient-specific parcellations can provide scientific and clinical usefulness (see Box 17.1). Fig. 17.5 shows an example of patient-specific parcellations of GPi, STN, and thalamus.

17.6 Clinical application of 7T: Deep brain stimulation

Subcortical structures are involved in many neurological processes and are the focus of much brain disorder research and therapy. Deep brain stimulation (DBS) is a surgical procedure in which an electrical current is delivered to a brain structure or one of its subregions via an implanted electrode. Patients with movement disorders such as essential tremor (ET), Parkinson's disease (PD), and dystonia have now been treated for decades using DBS, and it is becoming even more common.

BOX 17.1 CLINICAL USEFULNESS: A CASE EXAMPLE

The following shows the usefulness of patient-specific models derived from 7T MRI data (see Schrock et al. (2021) for more details).

A 52-year-old patient with a 14-year history of PD underwent bilateral STN DBS for the treatment of motor fluctuations with severe rigidity and bradykinesia during off periods and frequent disabling dyskinesias when on. The patient had a preoperative 7T MRI session for research purposes that was not used for surgical targeting as this patient was part of a clinical trial that included standard imaging in their protocol. The patient had no history of mood disorders. Upon DBS programming, several weeks after the surgery, the patient experienced severe mood side effects when the right DBS electrode was turned ON. These feelings of profound despair dissipated when the electrode was turned OFF unbeknownst to the patient. Given that the patient experienced some motor improvement, the patient was sent home with the right electrode ON at a very low current amplitude. Furthermore, stimulation using the left electrode did not result in any mood side effects and mitigated contralateral motor symptoms effectively.

Months later, the patient was hospitalized due to a suicide attempt from which the patient recovered without medical treatment. The DBS device was turned OFF at that time. The patient returned to clinic for a formal assessment of stimulation effects on mood. Initial assessment with DBS OFF revealed that the patient was without depression, anxiety, or hypomania. For subsequent evaluations, the patient was blinded to the stimulation state. The right DBS lead was first activated to the settings the patient was on at the time of the suicide attempt. The left lead remained OFF. Within 2 min of stimulation onset, the patient reported feeling "a profound sadness, hopelessness, despair, and loss of trust ... I don't think I can make it." At 3 min, the patient started crying and their spouse observed "a noticeable change in [their] eyes, as if [they are] no longer my [spouse]." At 4 min, the negative mood effects seemed to peak, and the patient reported feeling "alone. I feel like I'm pulling away. It's hard to see things will ever get better." DBS was then turned OFF without notifying the patient, and immediately the patient said, "I feel hopeful. The room just became brighter." Within 6 min of turning off the stimulation, the patient's mood had returned to baseline. No mood side effects were observed with the left lead turned ON.

The team generated patient-specific 3D models (see Section 17.3) and parcellations (see Section 17.5) in an attempt to explain what might be happening. It was found that both DBS electrodes were in STN, but the right electrode was in the associative/limbic territories while the left one was in the motor territory of the structure (Fig. 17.7). It was decided to remove the right DBS lead and implant a new lead a few millimeters posterior to the original one. New postoperative models confirmed that the revised electrode was implanted in the motor territory of the right STN. Before lead revision, contralateral motor symptoms were reduced by about 30%; after revision, they were reduced by 92% without any mood side effects.

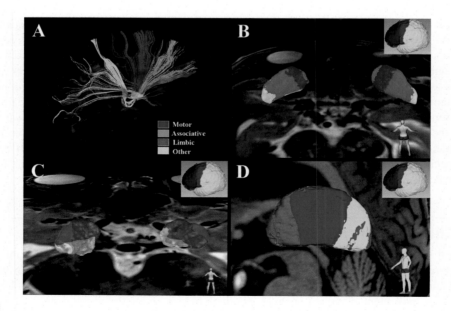

FIG. 17.5

7T MRI parcellation of deep subcortical structures. Panel A shows tracts between a subcortical anatomical seed region and cortical targets. Panels B–D show subject-specific parcellation for GPi (B), STN (C), and thalamus (D) with a T_1 image in the background. *STN*, subthalamic nucleus; *GPi*, globus pallidus internus.

Stimulation sites for these disorders include the ventral intermediate nucleus of the thalamus (VIM), STN, and GPi (Schuurman et al., 2008; Vitek, 2002; Weaver et al., 2012; Welter et al., 2014; Xu et al., 2016). However, there is a large variability in patient outcomes (Vitek et al., 2020) likely due to the electrodes being placed suboptimally, and a relatively high number of patients require additional surgery to place a new electrode in a better location (Rolston et al., 2016).

One of the most impactful factors in placing a DBS electrode optimally is the clinical team's ability to visualize the DBS target when planning the electrode's trajectory. The process of targeting for DBS surgery still relies, in part, on modified atlas-based targeting. Prior to surgery, these atlases are normalized to the patient's images and the target coordinates are obtained based on set distances from the midcommissure point. However, template-based approaches do not account for interindividual variability in the location, shape, and size of the target (Duchin et al., 2018). For small structures, such as STN, these potential inaccuracies can result in missing the target completely, causing no therapeutic effect and sometimes worsening the condition of the patient.

Therefore, there is a need for imaging that enables direct targeting approaches without the use of templates, in a truly patient-specific manner. As described in previous sections, ultra-high field MRI can visualize deep subcortical structures, including DBS targets, making such imaging methods clear candidates to advance the field of personalized DBS targeting. A known drawback of ultra-high field MRI is the increased amount of geometrical distortion of the images. Duchin et al. (2012) characterized the extent of the distortion present at 7T relative to standard clinical imaging. They used seven anatomical landmarks to quantitatively evaluate the registration quality and global distortions. They found that the distortions of 7T MR images are distributed nonuniformly, with more distortion in the regions located further away from the center of the brain—where correcting for the nonlinearity of the gradient field is more challenging—and that minimal distortions compared to 1.5T images are observed in the central and midbrain areas which contain most DBS targets. Other strong distortions include susceptibility artifacts such as air tissue interfaces. Nonetheless, the authors conclude that 7T images can be utilized for clinical applications, such as DBS targeting. Additionally, the authors show that performing co-registration of the patient's MRI and CT images, which is routinely achieved in the clinic, helps correct geometrical distortions at 7T.

Using 7T MRI to create patient-specific segmentations and parcellations of deep subcortical structures also helps DBS therapy postoperatively by providing an accurate visualization of the DBS electrode location with respect to the patient's own anatomy after fusing MRI models with a postoperative CT image (Fig. 17.6). This enhanced visualization not only offers feedback to the surgical team on their electrode placement but also shows actual contact location within the targeted structure that can potentially make DBS programming faster and more optimal.

17.7 Future directions

Future studies using 7T MRI should focus on clinical translation to achieve a fully personalized medical diagnosis, care, and treatment. In the context of DBS, this includes using 7T systems for direct targeting and the creation of postoperative patient-specific models. Likely, improvements in procedure efficiency and therapy outcome should be reported. Furthermore, the improvement of direct targeting using MRI may reduce, or even eliminate, the need for MER which, in turn, would likely result in the widespread adoption of asleep (fully sedated) DBS procedure. Additionally, since awake brain surgery

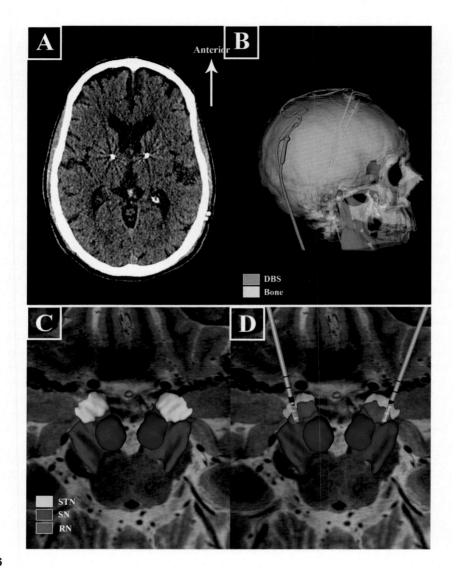

FIG. 17.6

Visualizing lead location with respect to patient-specific 3D models generated from 7T images. Postoperative CT images (Panel A) can be used to create models of DBS electrodes (Panel B) and fused with patient-specific 7T anatomical models (Panel C) to visualize the location of DBS electrodes and their contacts accurately (Panel D). *STN*, subthalamic nucleus; *SN*, substantia nigra; *RN*, red nucleus.

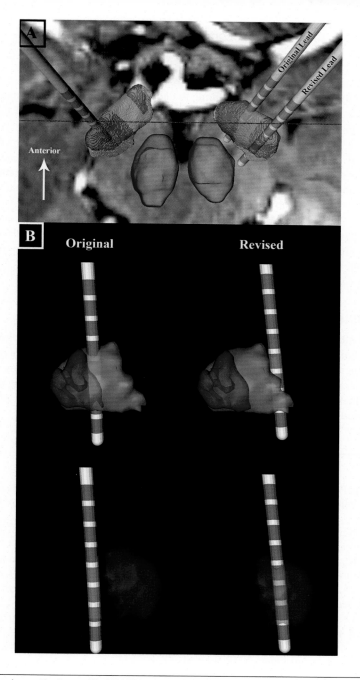

FIG. 17.7

Clinical example of using patient-specific 7T MRI anatomical models and parcellation to help with a unique STN-DBS patient who developed stimulation-induced severe mood side effects requiring revision of the location of the right STN electrode. Panel A shows a top view of lead locations with respect to STN and its motor *(blue)*, associative *(green)*, and limbic *(red)* subterritories. Panel B shows a medial view of the right lead location with respect to STN before and after the revision of the electrode. See Box 17.1 for a full description of the case. *STN*, subthalamic nucleus. Red anatomic structure = red nucleus. *Figure, in part, adapted under CC BY license from Schrock et al. (2021).*

is a likely contributing factor to patients declining to undergo surgery as well as a contributing factor to hospitals and clinics not offering DBS due to the lack of expertise in MER, it will likely increase the access to care for patients who could benefit from DBS.

The ability to use ultra-high field high-resolution and high-quality images to generate patient-specific anatomical models and reconstruct white matter pathways will undoubtedly enable more informative studies of the networks at play in disease development as well as treatment efficacy. In the field of Neuromodulation, this will likely result in better identification of optimal stimulation sites, whether it be in known or unknown gray or white matter anatomical targets.

Finally, future studies should leverage these high-quality datasets to generate state-of-the-art algorithms (e.g., by use of advanced techniques such as deep learning), capable of automatically predicting the optimal stimulation location presurgery as well as the optimal programming settings postsurgery to achieve the best patient care possible.

17.8 Conclusions

While research at ultra-high field strength MRI has been ongoing for many years, clinical applications have only been possible recently. In this chapter, we have described the advantages of this technology and shown its clinical potential. Many brain disorders impact gray matter structures that were heretofore difficult to characterize due to the challenges of visualizing them or quantifying their properties in vivo. While it will take some time for 7T MRI scanners to become the norm worldwide, ultra-high field MRI will undoubtedly markedly improve patient care in the coming years.

References

Abosch, A., Yacoub, E., Ugurbil, K., Harel, N., 2010. An assessment of current brain targets for deep brain stimulation surgery with susceptibility-weighted imaging at 7 tesla. Neurosurgery 67 (6), 1745–1756. Discussion 1756.

Behrens, T.E., Johansen-Berg, H., Woolrich, M.W., et al., 2003. Non-invasive mapping of connections between human thalamus and cortex using diffusion imaging. Nat. Neurosci. 6 (7), 750–757.

Cho, Z.H., Min, H.K., Oh, S.H., et al., 2010. Direct visualization of deep brain stimulation targets in Parkinson disease with the use of 7-tesla magnetic resonance imaging. J. Neurosurg. 113 (3), 639–647.

Duchin, Y., Abosch, A., Yacoub, E., Sapiro, G., Harel, N., 2012. Feasibility of using ultra-high field (7 T) MRI for clinical surgical targeting. PLoS One 7 (5), e37328.

Duchin, Y., Shamir, R.R., Patriat, R., et al., 2018. Patient-specific anatomical model for deep brain stimulation based on 7 Tesla MRI. PLoS One 13 (8), e0201469.

Eskreis-Winkler, S., Zhang, Y., Zhang, J., et al., 2017. The clinical utility of QSM: disease diagnosis, medical management, and surgical planning. NMR Biomed. 30 (4), 1–11.

Keuken, M.C., Bazin, P.L., Crown, L., et al., 2014. Quantifying inter-individual anatomical variability in the subcortex using 7 T structural MRI. NeuroImage 94, 40–46.

Ladd, M.E., Bachert, P., Meyerspeer, M., et al., 2018. Pros and cons of ultra-high-field MRI/MRS for human application. Prog. Nucl. Magn. Reson. Spectrosc. 109, 1–50.

Lambert, C., Zrinzo, L., Nagy, Z., et al., 2012. Confirmation of functional zones within the human subthalamic nucleus: patterns of connectivity and sub-parcellation using diffusion weighted imaging. NeuroImage 60 (1), 83–94.

Lenglet, C., Abosch, A., Yacoub, E., De Martino, F., Sapiro, G., Harel, N., 2012. Comprehensive in vivo mapping of the human basal ganglia and thalamic connectome in individuals using 7T MRI. PLoS One 7 (1), e29153.

Najdenovska, E., Tuleasca, C., Jorge, J., et al., 2019. Comparison of MRI-based automated segmentation methods and functional neurosurgery targeting with direct visualization of the Ventro-intermediate thalamic nucleus at 7T. Sci. Rep. 9 (1), 1119.

Parent, A., Hazrati, L.N., 1995. Functional anatomy of the basal ganglia. I. The cortico-basal ganglia-thalamo-cortical loop. Brain Res. Rev. 20, 91–127.

Patriat, R., Cooper, S.E., Duchin, Y., et al., 2018. Individualized tractography-based parcellation of the globus pallidus pars interna using 7T MRI in movement disorder patients prior to DBS surgery. NeuroImage 178, 198–209.

Patriat, R., Niederer, J., Kaplan, J., et al., 2020. Morphological changes in the subthalamic nucleus of people with mild-to-moderate Parkinson's disease: a 7T MRI study. Sci. Rep. 10 (1), 8785.

Plantinga, B.R., Temel, Y., Duchin, Y., et al., 2018. Individualized parcellation of the subthalamic nucleus in patients with Parkinson's disease with 7T MRI. NeuroImage 168, 403–411.

Rolston, J.D., Englot, D.J., Starr, P.A., Larson, P.S., 2016. An unexpectedly high rate of revisions and removals in deep brain stimulation surgery: analysis of multiple databases. Parkinsonism Relat. Disord. 33, 72–77.

Schrock, L.E., Patriat, R., Goftari, M., et al., 2021. 7T MRI and computational modeling supports a critical role of lead location in determining outcomes for deep brain stimulation: a case report. Front. Hum. Neurosci. 15, 631778.

Schuurman, P.R., Bosch, D.A., Merkus, M.P., Speelman, J.D., 2008. Long-term follow-up of thalamic stimulation versus thalamotomy for tremor suppression. Mov. Disord. 23 (8), 1146–1153.

Solomon, O., Palnitkar, T., Patriat, R., et al., 2021. Deep-learning based fully automatic segmentation of the globus pallidus interna and externa using ultra-high 7 Tesla MRI. Hum. Brain Mapp. 42 (9), 2862–2879.

Starr, P.A., Christine, C.W., Theodosopoulos, P.V., et al., 2002. Implantation of deep brain stimulators into subthalmic nucleus: technical approach and magnetic imaging—verified electrode locations. J. Neurosurg. 97, 370–387.

Vitek, J.L., 2002. Deep brain stimulation for Parkinson's disease. Stereotact. Funct. Neurosurg. 78 (3–4), 119–131.

Vitek, J.L., Jain, R., Chen, L., et al., 2020. Subthalamic nucleus deep brain stimulation with a multiple independent constant current-controlled device in Parkinson's disease (INTREPID): a multicentre, double-blind, randomised, sham-controlled study. Lancet Neurol. 19 (6), 491–501.

Weaver, F.M., Follet, K.A., Stern, M., et al., 2012. Randomized trial of deep brain stimulation for Parkinson disease: thirty-six-month outcomes. Neurology 79 (1), 55–65.

Welter, M.L., Schupbach, M., Czernecki, V., et al., 2014. Optimal target localization for subthalamic stimulation in patients with Parkinson disease. Neurology 82 (15), 1352–1361.

Whone, A.L., Moore, R.Y., Piccini, P.P., Brooks, D.J., 2003. Plasticity of the nigropallidal pathway in Parkinson's disease. Ann. Neurol. 53 (2), 206–213.

Xu, F., Ma, W., Huang, Y., Qiu, Z., Sun, L., 2016. Deep brain stimulation of pallidal versus subthalamic for patients with Parkinson's disease: a meta-analysis of controlled clinical trials. Neuropsychiatr. Dis. Treat. 12, 1435–1444.

Brainstem imaging

18

Olivia K. Harrison[a,b,c], Jonathan C.W. Brooks[d], and Stuart Clare[c,e]

[a]*Department of Psychology, University of Otago, Dunedin, New Zealand* [b]*Translational Neuromodeling Unit, Institute for Biomedical Engineering, University of Zurich and ETH Zurich, Zurich, Switzerland* [c]*Nuffield Department of Clinical Neurosciences, University of Oxford, Oxford, United Kingdom* [d]*Wellcome Wolfson Brain Imaging Centre, University of East Anglia, Norwich, United Kingdom* [e]*Wellcome Centre for Integrative Neuroimaging, University of Oxford, Oxford, United Kingdom*

Highlights

- The increased signal afforded by UHF allows for improvements in brainstem imaging.
- Despite the higher resolution and contrast afforded by UHF, the delineation of individual brainstem nuclei remains difficult.
- Dropout (most notably in the pons), distortion, and physiological noise artifacts can be particularly problematic in the brainstem.
- Approaches that aim to address these problems are available, e.g., field map unwarping, cardiac gating, and physiological noise correction.
- Techniques such as quantitative susceptibility mapping and diffusion tract imaging (or atlases based on these techniques) can be utilized to help delineate brainstem nuclei.

18.1 Introduction

The brainstem is a structure that is vital for sustaining life. Despite this importance, in vivo neuroimaging has remained challenging due to factors such as its small size, its location deep within the brain, and its susceptibility to noise such as that induced from physiological processes. However, the advent of ultra-high field (UHF) magnetic resonance imaging (MRI) at 7T or above has provided a remarkable opportunity to investigate both the structure and function of brainstem nuclei in a way that had not been previously possible. In this chapter, we will provide an overview of the challenges presented when imaging the brainstem, how the physical MR properties are altered at UHF, how this can be optimized for in vivo brainstem imaging, and what potential problems can also be exacerbated at UHF.

The brainstem is made up of three components: the superior midbrain, the pons, and the inferior medulla oblongata (Fig. 18.1). Importantly, the brainstem houses essential life-sustaining nuclei for autonomic functions such as cardiac and respiratory control, and it serves as both a relay station and a white matter "highway" between the brain and body. Ten of the twelve pairs of motor and sensory cranial nerves lie within the brainstem. The brainstem reticular formation and its nuclei are associated with neurotransmitter systems such as the cholinergic, serotonergic, noradrenergic, and dopamine

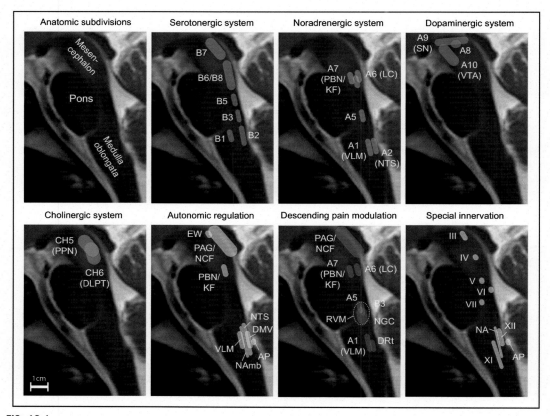

FIG. 18.1

Anatomical subdivisions and important functions of the brainstem. *Colored patches* represent specific brainstem nuclei indicated by abbreviations of their common names; see Sclocco et al. (2018), Fig. 1 for key. *Reprinted from Sclocco et al. (2018). Copyright (2017), with permission from Elsevier.*

systems that are key drivers of arousal, sleep, and attention (Fig. 18.1; see Sclocco et al. (2018) for an overview). While such a pivotal role in our existence should garner extensive interest in brainstem structure and function, the limitations of in vivo imaging at lower field strengths had somewhat tempered and constrained brainstem neuroimaging prior to the introduction of UHF (Sclocco et al., 2018).

The brainstem is located deep and inferior to the majority of the cortical and subcortical structures. Its small size (the human brainstem is approximately the size of a thumb) and distance from the radio-frequency coils mean that it has an inherently low signal-to-noise ratio compared to much of the more readily accessible cortex. Furthermore, many of the nuclei housed within the brainstem are small (1–3 mm in cross-section) and tightly packed and have poor contrast to differentiate them. Therefore, the signal amplification granted at UHF has enormous ramifications for brainstem imaging, making the previously inaccessible potentially accessible when paired with modern neuroimaging techniques. In this chapter, we will outline some of the MR protocols that maximize brainstem imaging qualities, while attempting to minimize issues such as distortion, dropout, and the influence of physiological noise.

18.2 Contrast for brainstem visualization

Identification of anatomical structures in MRI typically depends on sensitizing the image to the differences in the three main MR relaxation parameters: T_1, T_2, and T_2^*. For example, decreased myelination typically manifests as a longer T_1, which will result in a darker contrast in a T_1-weighted image. Similarly, enhanced iron content will shorten T_2^* and appear darker in a T_2^*-weighted scan. Getting good relaxation-based contrast for brainstem imaging at conventional field strengths is challenging. For most nuclei in the brainstem (with some exceptions—notably the red nucleus and substantia nigra), the differences in the relaxation time to the surrounding brainstem is not large. This, coupled with the small size of these nuclei, means that clear delineation of the individual nuclei is only just possible.

Some of the relaxation properties of the sample are strongly field-dependent. T_1 relaxation times lengthen and T_2^* significantly shortens as you move from 3T to 7T. However, the greatest benefit of UHF MRI comes from the increased signal-to-noise ratio (SNR) that scales with field strength. Optimization of MPRAGE images at UHF is mainly achieved by changing the delay between the inversion pulse and the readout (TI). Due to the longer T_1 at 7T, our optimized protocol used a TI = 1050 ms (compared to 880 ms at 3T; see Fig. 18.2). Furthermore, a resolution of 0.7 mm is easily achievable, given the increased SNR. However, despite the higher resolution and contrast, the delineation of individual nuclei is still difficult and needs to be viewed alongside an atlas—and arguably with an "eye of faith."

Those nuclei which exhibit strong T_2^* contrast are significantly easier to visualize, with the higher field strength providing greater contrast. However, T_2^* contrasts demonstrate an orientation dependence, and using the approach of quantitative susceptibility mapping (QSM) gives a more reliable identification of borders. Deistung et al. (2013) demonstrate how the relatively complex acquisition and processing pathway can generate some highly detailed images of the iron-rich nuclei in the brainstem (Fig. 18.3). The quantitative approach can also be used with T_1 or T_2 contrasts. While this does not necessarily make identifying the boundary of the nuclei any easier, it does allow for the identification of nuclei in a multiparametric space (Deistung et al., 2013) and improve the delineation of the structure of the brainstem.

The complex network of nerve fibers that project to and from the brainstem nuclei means that an alternative to classical image contrast is to use diffusion-weighted imaging methods. Since these typically use echo-planar imaging (EPI), they do not have the resolution of other structural approaches and suffer from distortions from the inhomogeneous B_0 field in the region; however, they offer an alternative method for distinguishing brainstem nuclei that lack strong T_2^* contrast.

Researchers wanting to measure the neurochemical state of the brain can use magnetic resonance spectroscopy (MRS) to detect the levels of key brain chemicals. The use of UHF not only gives a boost to the SNR of spectroscopy signals but also has an increased spectral separation allowing brain metabolites that significantly overlap at lower field strengths to be identified (Xin and Tkáč, 2017). Even at UHF, MRS voxels need to be of the order of centimeters in size, meaning that it is not possible to differentiate between individual nuclei. However, brainstem measures of chemicals such as GABA, glutamate, choline, and creatine are all possible (Younis et al., 2020).

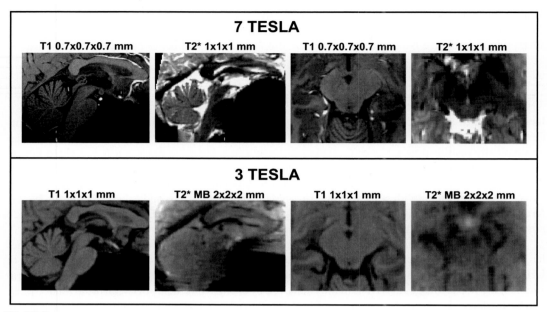

FIG. 18.2

Comparison between T_1 and T_2^* images at 7T and 3T in the same brain. Left two panels are in the sagittal orientation, while the rightmost two panels are in the axial orientation. Images were optimized for each scanning protocol rather than using matching parameters across scanners. Notably, the 3T T_2^* images were conducted with a multiband factor of 4, while no multiband factor was used for the 7T T_2^* images.

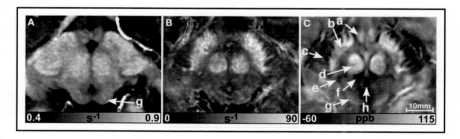

FIG. 18.3

R_1, R_2^*, and susceptibility maps of the same brain region are presented in axial orientation from (A–C), respectively. The *arrows* in the images indicate (a) mammillary body, (b) substantia nigra, (c) crus cerebri, (d) red nucleus, (e) medial lemniscus, (f) central tegmental tract, (g) inferior colliculus, and (h) medial longitudinal fasciculus. *Reproduced under Creative Commons licence from Deistung et al. (2013).*

Functional MRI of the brainstem at UHF also benefits from the increased SNR that the increased field strength brings. In addition, the blood oxygenation level-dependent (BOLD) contrast that most fMRI depends on is also field-dependent, with a potential quadratic dependence of BOLD contrast-to-noise ratio with field strength (Uğurbil, 2012). This means that higher resolution fMRI is possible at 7T, which can be greatly beneficial for brainstem studies. Because the T_2^* of gray matter is shorter at the higher field, the echo time should be reduced, and if coupled with an increase in resolution, this may also mean that the parallel imaging factor needs increasing. Simultaneous multislice, or multiband, acquisitions are increasingly being used for whole brain EPI, but care must be taken when using these, or indeed any parallel imaging techniques for brainstem fMRI, as the brainstem is located where coil sensitivity ("g-factor") losses tend to be greatest.

This leads, then, to the final significant issue when imaging the brainstem at UHF, which is the RF coil. The wavelength of electromagnetic waves in the tissue decreases as the field increases, and at 7T, it becomes of the order of the size of the brain. This leads to significant inhomogeneity in the transmit and receive fields. Inhomogeneity in receive fields is not necessarily a problem for MRI, and in fact can be beneficial, since parallel imaging techniques such as SENSE or GRAPPA rely on such inhomogeneity (Deshmane et al., 2012). However, the inhomogeneity in the transmit field can have a significant impact (see section "Signal dropout and distortion" below). A simple approach to dealing with the bias field generated by the transmit coil in structural scans is to use a scanning method that can compensate, such as MP2RAGE. This approach essentially acquires an additional scan, which can add to the duration of the exam. A more fundamental approach to dealing with this issue is to attempt to make the transmit B_1 field more uniform using a parallel-transmit (pTx) approach. While there has been significant development of these approaches recently, they still require a more complex setup than a conventional scan and again are possibly not necessary for brainstem MRI.

If it is solely the brainstem that is of interest, then dedicated brainstem and cervical spine coils have been developed. These are more closely fitting around the neck than a typical head coil and allow for both better SNR in the brainstem, and also lower g-factors for parallel imaging. Using a dedicated brainstem coil would limit the ability to acquire concurrent cortical images, which, given the brainstem's extensive connectivity, may be a problem.

18.3 Signal dropout and distortion

One of the most significant challenges for functional imaging in the brainstem is overcoming the impact of local field inhomogeneity that causes signal dropout and distortion. While the main magnetic field (B_0) of the scanner is designed to be as uniform as possible, as soon as the head is introduced into the scanner, the susceptibility differences between tissues and sinuses cause a disruption of the field. This is particularly significant in the pons, which sits close to the sigmoid sinus (Fig. 18.4). The field perturbation produced by the sinuses increases with B_0 and causes two main effects.

Firstly, in regions where the B_0 is particularly inhomogeneous, the signal within a voxel can be partially or totally dephased. This dropout effect is more severe in T_2^* sensitive sequences such as EPI and can result in no BOLD signal being detectable. Decreasing the voxel size can help with level of dropout, as can adjusting the echo time; however, reducing the echo time will also reduce the BOLD sensitivity. As well as causing the signal to dephase, B_0 inhomogeneity can also cause a misplacing of the voxel in the

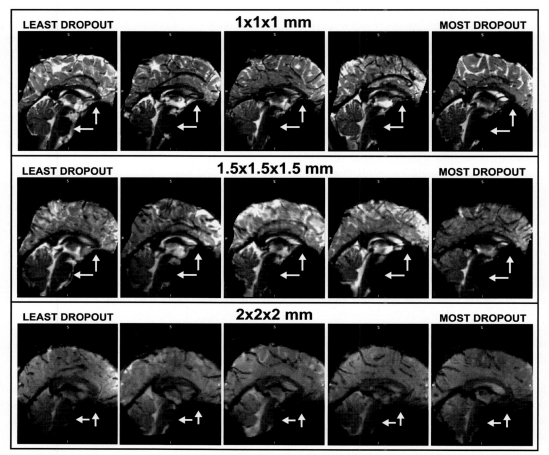

FIG. 18.4

Demonstration of the variable dropout that is most noticeable in the pons and prefrontal areas *(white arrows)* when using T_2^* contrast at 7T, at three different scanning resolutions.

phase encoding direction of the scan, appearing as a distortion in the images. This effect is mitigated by keeping the echo spacing between adjacent phase encoding steps as small as is practical (increasing the bandwidth per pixel in this direction). Consideration of the orientation of the phase encoding direction is also important and is a potential point of optimization for the study protocol.

Ideally, we would try and compensate for B_0 inhomogeneity to improve the quality of the scans. Scanners already use the technique of subject-dependent shimming, which involves measuring the field and applying compensation terms. However, these terms are of very low spatial order and have only small effects. When only interested in the brainstem, it is advisable to optimize the shimming in just that region, by placing the optimization target box appropriately. There have also been some proof-of-principle demonstrations that dynamically updating the shim for every slice that is acquired can also have benefits, but these systems require extra hardware and are not readily available.

18.4 **Physiological factors affecting brainstem imaging**

In addition to its location deep within the brain, which typically hampers signal detection, the brainstem is also particularly susceptible to physiological processes that make it challenging to image. The cardiac cycle produces pulsatile motion of large vessels near the brainstem, but also drives the flow of cerebrospinal fluid (CSF) in the midbrain aqueduct and fourth ventricle, and through the subarachnoid space surrounding it (Greitz et al., 1993). As a consequence, during the cardiac cycle, there are relatively large positional changes in the brainstem of the order of 0.2 mm, compared to the occipital lobe (0.04 mm), cerebellum (0.07 mm), and frontal/parietal lobes (0.09 mm) (Zhong et al., 2009). While the absolute magnitude of movement may seem small, the cross-sectional diameter of some of the structures of interest, e.g., the locus coeruleus, is of the order of 1–2 mm—so increasing the uncertainty in attributing signal to particular nuclei.

When assessing white matter connectivity by using diffusion weighted imaging, bulk motion of the brainstem will reduce the accuracy of apparent diffusion coefficient measurement, estimation of the principal diffusion direction, and therefore fractional anisotropy (Norris, 2001). Furthermore, the brainstem's closer proximity to the lungs means that the contribution of the respiratory cycle to measured signal is increased. This quasiperiodic process has been shown to induce measurable variation in the main magnetic field (due to bulk susceptibility variation as the lung volume changes). The effect of respiration is particularly pronounced on single-shot EPI data due to reduced bandwidth in the phase encoding direction (Raj et al., 2001), giving rise to an image shift. When taken together, these physiological effects may confound the measurement of anatomical connectivity and neuronal activity, and as they scale linearly with magnetic field strength (Triantafyllou et al., 2005), they increase noise in UHF imaging. Indeed, a recent study (Markuerkiaga et al., 2021) showed that physiological noise is the dominant noise source in fMRI studies at 7T when averaging signal over extended regions (>40 mm^3)—as may happen when applying smoothing during preprocessing or averaging within cortical layers to extract signal time courses.

Several approaches exist to mitigate the effect of physiological noise. Cardiac gating can be particularly effective for minimizing noise in diffusion-weighted imaging by acquiring data during the quiescent part of the cardiac cycle (Nunes et al., 2005), though this will inevitably lead to increased scan time. Such approaches have also been proposed for acquisition of fMRI data (e.g., Guimaraes et al., 1998) and used to reveal activity in the inferior colliculi in response to auditory stimulation. The main drawback to cardiac gating data acquisition for fMRI is that it results in a variable repetition time (TR), thus each time point will have a slightly different contribution from T_1-weighting. While schemes have been proposed to adjust the intensity according to the measured TR per sample using an assumed (or measured) T_1 (Guimaraes et al., 1998), such corrections may be problematic if the experiment produces systematic changes in physiological parameters. For example, if the paradigm induces *phasic* changes in heart rate, this correction—e.g., increasing signal to compensate for decreased effective TR (due to increased heart rate)—would increase signal across the whole image and potentially inflate the number of false positives.

Other methods for estimating and removing physiological noise from fMRI data include acquiring data with multiple echo times (Kundu et al., 2017), which can exploit the different T_2^* relaxation properties of non-BOLD like physiological noise and BOLD-like signal change (presumably neuronal in origin) to help distinguish signal from noise. The benefits of such an approach have been nicely demonstrated within the cortex at 7T (Poser and Norris, 2009). While multiecho approaches should (in theory) offer real improvements when studying the brainstem, the impact of magnetic field inhomogeneity and reduced coil sensitivity in this area appears to have limited its application.

An alternative method to addressing the issue of physiological noise was proposed by Glover et al. (2000). Known as RETROICOR (RETROspective Image CORrection), this technique records cardiac and respiratory waveforms from the subject during the experiment, and subsequently attempts to model their contributions to the acquired time series data using a model-based approach (see Brooks et al. (2013) for extended discussion). Typically applied to task-based and resting state fMRI studies, this technique has been shown to be beneficial for imaging at 7T (Hutton et al., 2011). There are relatively few demonstrations of its utility within the brainstem at 7T; however, it has been applied to aid the identification of subdivisions of the periaqueductal gray matter (PAG) responding to respiratory threat (Faull et al., 2015, 2016; Faull and Pattinson, 2017).

While it is relatively straightforward to acquire cardiac and respiratory waveforms using a pulse-oximeter and respiratory belt, not all installations will have this equipment available to them. An alternative, and equally valid, approach is to use the so-called model-free analysis to distinguish between neuronal activity and physiological signals (Beissner et al., 2014; Kundu et al., 2017; Salimi-Khorshidi et al., 2014). These techniques tend to use independent components analysis (ICA) and are typically applied to resting state fMRI to identify structured signal within the data, which can then be "filtered out"—and may be preferable to applying RETROICOR-like models in this situation (Bright et al., 2017). Whatever the chosen method for "denoising" fMRI time series, it is important to gauge how well it has performed. To this end, the temporal signal-to-noise ratio (tSNR) is a relevant measure of intrinsic signal to noise and its fluctuation (Parrish et al., 2000), where high values will generally indicate best conditions for detecting BOLD signal changes associated with neuronal activity (see Fig. 18.5).

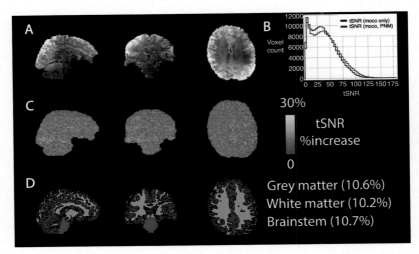

FIG. 18.5

Improvements in temporal signal-to-noise ratio (tSNR) through physiological noise modeling at 7T. (A) Whole-brain (2 mm isotropic) resting state fMRI data acquired at 7T (see Faull and Pattinson (2017) for details) were motion corrected and baseline tSNR calculated. (B) Physiological noise parameters were computed (see Brooks et al. (2008) for details) and regressed from the resting data using FEAT (part of FSL software), the resulting improvement in tSNR can be seen in the histogram of tSNR values (*blue*—baseline, *red*—corrected), which shows a rightward shift (higher values) following correction. (C) The improvement in tSNR was evenly distributed across the brain, with all voxels showing increases (up to 30% in some cases). (D) The average improvement in tSNR (above baseline) for gray matter (*blue mask*), white matter (*green*), and separately, the brainstem (*red*) are shown with their mean percentage increases.

In summary, while UHF imaging offers distinct advantages to resolving signal in small brainstem nuclei, the contribution of physiological noise to measured signal means that it will be necessary to account for these effects through careful selection of voxel size, tailored signal acquisition (e.g., multi-echo approaches), and analysis (e.g., physiological noise modeling, model-free approaches, size of smoothing kernel). While these recommendations are generally applicable to all brainstem imaging studies at 7T, they are particularly relevant for fMRI studies using experimental manipulations that may induce changes in autonomic function (e.g., pain, breathing challenges, learning or reward paradigms, startle, etc.).

18.5 UHF brainstem imaging applications

While early low-field neuroimaging relied on visual comparisons to high-resolution ex vivo atlases (Naidich et al., 2009), the advantages provided by UHF have now allowed for in vivo brainstem imaging at unprecedented detail. Importantly, while some brainstem nuclei (such as the substantia nigra and red nucleus) demonstrate high contrast at UHF across multiple imaging modalities, many nuclei require specific contrast weighting for sufficient delineation from surrounding structures (Deistung et al., 2013). Using high-resolution proton density and T_2-weighted images can aid the depiction of some inner brainstem structures (Gizewski et al., 2014), and multiecho, gradient echo sequences that allow for QSM and effective transverse relaxation rate (R_2^*) maps can more clearly identify a number of brainstem nuclei than T_2-weighted and longitudinal relaxation time maps (Deistung et al., 2013). Additionally, MPRAGE and MP2RAGE can be used for clearly localizing cranial nerves and overall brainstem structure (Gizewski et al., 2014).

Brainstem-specific atlases are a vital tool to assist nuclei localization in UHF neuroimaging. Making use of the power of multiple modalities for brainstem imaging, Bianciardi et al. (2015) utilized both T_2-weighted and fractional anisotropy (FA) images to create an in vivo probabilistic map of arousal, autonomic, and motor brainstem systems, and demonstrated their clinical application in a patient with a traumatic brainstem hemorrhage (Bianciardi et al., 2015). This work has since been extended to localize the lateral parabrachial nucleus, medial parabrachial nucleus, vestibular nuclei complex, and medullary viscero-sensory-motor nuclei complex, providing validated brainstem atlases that can be used for identification of key nuclei in vivo (Singh et al., 2020). Additionally, many nuclei contain subdivisions that appear homogenous within the macroscale resolution of MRI, and thus, further strategies beyond optimizing contrast may be required for their identification. Using this idea, Ezra et al. (2015) utilized the connectivity profile between the midbrain PAG and wider cortex to segment the PAG into its composite subdivisions, resulting in a columnar structure that was highly consistent with those identified in animal models (Fig. 18.6).

Beyond anatomical localization and quantification, UHF has also been used to investigate in vivo functioning of human brainstem nuclei. Researchers have identified dissociable activity within the aforementioned PAG subdivisions related to pain (Satpute et al., 2013) and breathlessness (Faull et al., 2015, 2016; Faull and Pattinson, 2017), and UHF has also been used to identify brainstem functional activity localized to the superior colliculus during emotionally aversive image viewing (Wang et al., 2020), dorsal medulla with a cold pressor test (Hendriks-Balk et al., 2020), trigeminal motor nuclei during jaw clenching (with a particular focus on adequate noise correction to improve both specificity and sensitivity) (Matt et al., 2019), and pain-related nuclei including the rostral ventromedial medulla, ventral nucleus reticularis, nucleus ambiguus, and pontine nuclei (Sclocco et al., 2016).

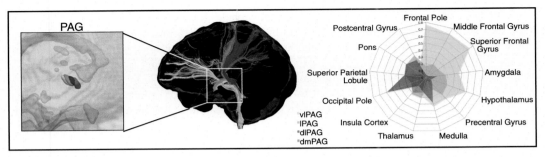

FIG. 18.6

Connections of the PAG columns from human diffusion tractography. Right: Radial diagram of relative connectivity of the clusters to predefined cortical targets. Left: Three-dimensional fiber tracking of cortical and subcortical projections from the four divisions of the human PAG to the cortex, excluding the cerebellum. Tractography demonstrates differential convectively patterns arising from the dorsomedial *(red)*, dorsolateral *(blue)*, lateral *(green)*, and ventrolateral *(yellow)* aspects of the PAG. Image produced using DSI Studio. *Reproduced from Faull et al. (2019), adapted from Ezra et al. (2015) under Creative Commons license.*

Resting state functional MRI has also demonstrated the utility of UHF to understand the integration between brainstem and cortex at high resolution, with the functional connectivity of multiple brainstem nuclei within the ascending arousal, motor and autonomic systems mapped to locations across the cortex (Bianciardi et al., 2015). Lastly, magnetic resonance spectroscopy has also shown efficacy in the brainstem at UHF over slightly larger areas that cover multiple nuclei (Emir et al., 2012a), with elevated GABA levels identified in the pons of patients with Parkinson's disease (Emir et al., 2012b).

18.6 Best practices summary

- T_2^* contrasts demonstrate an orientation dependence and using quantitative susceptibility mapping (QSM) gives a more reliable identification of borders.
- Diffusion tract imaging can be used to distinguish brainstem nuclei that lack strong T_2^* contrast.
- Because the T_2^* of gray matter is shorter at the higher field, the echo time should be reduced, and if coupled with an increase in resolution, this may also require an increase in the parallel imaging factor.
- Simultaneous multislice (or multiband) acquisitions are increasingly being used for whole brain EPI. Care must be taken when using these, or indeed any parallel imaging techniques for brainstem fMRI, as the brainstem is located where coil sensitivity ("g-factor") losses tend to be greatest.
- A simple approach to dealing with the bias field generated by the transmit coil in structural scans is to use a scanning method that can compensate, such as MP2RAGE.
- If it is solely the brainstem that is of interest, then dedicated brainstem and cervical spine coils could be used.

- The levels of brain metabolites such as GABA, glutamate, choline, and creatine can be measured using magnetic resonance spectroscopy, with an elongated voxel to ensure sufficient signal-to-noise ratio while keeping it within the brainstem.
- B_0 inhomogeneity can also cause a misplacing of the voxel in the phase encoding direction of the scan, appearing as a distortion in the images. This effect is mitigated by keeping the echo spacing between adjacent phase encoding steps as small as is practical (increasing the bandwidth per pixel in this direction), tilting the acquisition angle and acquiring field maps to aid distortion-correction.
- Localized shimming within the brainstem can reduce the distortion and dropout observed within this region.
- Acquiring cardiac and respiratory waveforms (alongside scanner triggers) allows model-based physiological noise correction, and it is recommended to test your chosen "denoising" method with resting state data prior to starting your study.
- The benefits of UHF MRI are greatest when small voxels (0.5–2 mm) are used.

Acknowledgments

OKH (née Faull) was supported by a Rutherford Discovery Research Fellowship awarded by the Royal Society of New Zealand, and the Department of Psychology at the University of Otago. SC is part of the Wellcome Centre for Integrative Neuroimaging, which is supported by core funding from the Wellcome Trust (203139/Z/16/Z). JCWB is employed at UWWBIC, which was established with funding from the Wellcome Trust and Wolfson Foundation. Thanks to Jon Campbell and William Clarke for their helpful insights into the content of this chapter.

References

Beissner, F., Schumann, A., Brunn, F., Eisenträger, D., Bär, K.-J., 2014. Advances in functional magnetic resonance imaging of the human brainstem. NeuroImage 86, 91–98. https://doi.org/10.1016/j.neuroimage.2013.07.081.

Bianciardi, M., Toschi, N., Edlow, B.L., et al., 2015. Toward an in vivo neuroimaging template of human brainstem nuclei of the ascending arousal, autonomic, and motor systems. Brain Connect. 5 (10), 597–607. https://doi.org/10.1089/brain.2015.0347.

Bright, M.G., Tench, C.R., Murphy, K., 2017. Potential pitfalls when denoising resting state fMRI data using nuisance regression. NeuroImage 154, 159–168. https://doi.org/10.1016/j.neuroimage.2016.12.027.

Brooks, J.C.W., Beckmann, C.F., Miller, K.L., et al., 2008. Physiological noise modelling for spinal functional magnetic resonance imaging studies. NeuroImage 39 (2), 680–692. https://doi.org/10.1016/j.neuroimage.2007.09.018.

Brooks, J.C.W., Faull, O.K., Pattinson, K.T.S., Jenkinson, M., 2013. Physiological noise in brainstem FMRI. Front. Hum. Neurosci. 7, 623. https://doi.org/10.3389/fnhum.2013.00623.

Deistung, A., Schäfer, A., Schweser, F., et al., 2013. High-resolution MR imaging of the human brainstem in vivo at 7 tesla. Front. Hum. Neurosci. 7, 710. https://doi.org/10.3389/fnhum.2013.00710.

Deshmane, A., Gulani, V., Griswold, M.A., Seiberlich, N., 2012. Parallel MR imaging. J. Magn. Reson. Imaging 36 (1), 55–72. https://doi.org/10.1002/jmri.23639.

Emir, U.E., Auerbach, E.J., Moortele, P.V.D., et al., 2012a. Regional neurochemical profiles in the human brain measured by 1H MRS at 7 T using local B1 shimming. NMR Biomed. 25 (1), 152–160. https://doi.org/10.1002/nbm.1727.

Emir, U.E., Tuite, P.J., Öz, G., 2012b. Elevated pontine and putamenal GABA levels in mild-moderate Parkinson disease detected by 7 tesla proton MRS. PLoS One 7 (1), e30918. https://doi.org/10.1371/journal.pone.0030918.

Ezra, M., Faull, O.K., Jbabdi, S., Pattinson, K.T.S., 2015. Connectivity-based segmentation of the periaqueductal gray matter in human with brainstem optimized diffusion MRI. Hum. Brain Mapp. 36 (9), 3459–3471. https://doi.org/10.1002/hbm.22855.

Faull, O.K., Pattinson, K.T., 2017. The cortical connectivity of the periaqueductal gray and the conditioned response to the threat of breathlessness. Elife 6, e21749–e21767. https://doi.org/10.7554/elife.21749.

Faull, O.K., Jenkinson, M., Clare, S., Pattinson, K.T.S., 2015. Functional subdivision of the human periaqueductal grey in respiratory control using 7 tesla fMRI. NeuroImage 113, 356–364. https://doi.org/10.1016/j.neuroimage.2015.02.026.

Faull, O.K., Jenkinson, M., Ezra, M., Pattinson, K.T.S., 2016. Conditioned respiratory threat in the subdivisions of the human periaqueductal gray. Elife 5, e12047–e12066. https://doi.org/10.7554/elife.12047.

Faull, O.K., Subramanian, H.H., Ezra, M., Pattinson, K.T.S., 2019. The midbrain periaqueductal gray as an integrative and interoceptive neural structure for breathing. Neurosci. Biobehav. Rev. 98, 135–144. https://doi.org/10.1016/j.neubiorev.2018.12.020.

Gizewski, E.R., Maderwald, S., Linn, J., et al., 2014. High-resolution anatomy of the human brain stem using 7-T MRI: improved detection of inner structures and nerves? Neuroradiology 56 (3), 177–186. https://doi.org/10.1007/s00234-013-1312-0.

Glover, G.H., Li, T., Ress, D., 2000. Image-based method for retrospective correction of physiological motion effects in fMRI: RETROICOR. Magn. Reson. Med. 44 (1), 162–167. https://doi.org/10.1002/1522-2594(200007)44:1<162::aid-mrm23>3.0.co;2-e.

Greitz, D., Franck, A., Nordell, B., 1993. On the pulsatile nature of intracranial and spinal CSF-circulation demonstrated by MR imaging. Acta Radiol. 34 (4), 321–328. https://doi.org/10.1177/028418519303400403.

Guimaraes, A.R., Melcher, J.R., Talavage, T.M., et al., 1998. Imaging subcortical auditory activity in humans. Hum. Brain Mapp. 6 (1), 33–41. https://doi.org/10.1002/(sici)1097-0193(1998)6:1<33::aid-hbm3>3.0.co;2-m.

Hendriks-Balk, M.C., Megdiche, F., Pezzi, L., et al., 2020. Brainstem correlates of a cold pressor test measured by ultra-high field fMRI. Front. Neurosci. 14, 39. https://doi.org/10.3389/fnins.2020.00039.

Hutton, C., Josephs, O., Stadler, J., et al., 2011. The impact of physiological noise correction on fMRI at 7 T. NeuroImage 57 (1–4), 101–112. https://doi.org/10.1016/j.neuroimage.2011.04.018.

Kundu, P., Voon, V., Balchandani, P., Lombardo, M.V., Poser, B.A., Bandettini, P.A., 2017. Multi-echo fMRI: a review of applications in fMRI denoising and analysis of BOLD signals. NeuroImage 154, 59–80. https://doi.org/10.1016/j.neuroimage.2017.03.033.

Markuerkiaga, I., Marques, J.P., Bains, L.J., Norris, D.G., 2021. An in-vivo study of BOLD laminar responses as a function of echo time and static magnetic field strength. Sci. Rep. 11 (1), 1862. https://doi.org/10.1038/s41598-021-81249-w.

Matt, E., Fischmeister, F.P.S., Amini, A., et al., 2019. Improving sensitivity, specificity, and reproducibility of individual brainstem activation. Brain Struct. Funct. 224 (8), 2823–2838. https://doi.org/10.1007/s00429-019-01936-3.

Naidich, T.P., Duvernoy, H.M., Delman, B.N., Sorensen, A.G., Kollias, S.S., Haacke, E.M., 2009. Duvernoy's Atlas of the Human Brain Stem and Cerebellum. Springer Science & Business Media, https://doi.org/10.1007/978-3-211-73971-6.

Norris, D.G., 2001. Implications of bulk motion for diffusion-weighted imaging experiments: effects, mechanisms, and solutions. J. Magn. Reson. Imaging 13 (4), 486–495. https://doi.org/10.1002/jmri.1072.

Nunes, R.G., Jezzard, P., Clare, S., 2005. Investigations on the efficiency of cardiac-gated methods for the acquisition of diffusion-weighted images. J. Magn. Reson. 177 (1), 102–110. https://doi.org/10.1016/j.jmr.2005.07.005.

Parrish, T.B., Gitelman, D.R., LaBar, K.S., Mesulam, M.M., 2000. Impact of signal-to-noise on functional MRI. Magn. Reson. Med. 44 (6), 925–932. https://doi.org/10.1002/1522-2594(200012)44:6<925::aid-mrm14>3.0.co;2-m.

Poser, B.A., Norris, D.G., 2009. Investigating the benefits of multi-echo EPI for fMRI at 7 T. NeuroImage 45 (4), 1162–1172. https://doi.org/10.1016/j.neuroimage.2009.01.007.

Raj, D., Anderson, A.W., Gore, J.C., 2001. Respiratory effects in human functional magnetic resonance imaging due to bulk susceptibility changes. Phys. Med. Biol. 46 (12), 3331. http://iopscience.iop.org/0031-9155/46/12/318.

Salimi-Khorshidi, G., Douaud, G., Beckmann, C.F., Glasser, M.F., Griffanti, L., Smith, S.M., 2014. Automatic denoising of functional MRI data: combining independent component analysis and hierarchical fusion of classifiers. NeuroImage 90 (C), 449–468. https://doi.org/10.1016/j.neuroimage.2013.11.046.

Satpute, A.B., Wager, T.D., Cohen-Adad, J., et al., 2013. Identification of discrete functional subregions of the human periaqueductal gray. Proc. Natl. Acad. Sci. 110 (42), 17101–17106. https://doi.org/10.1073/pnas.1306095110/-/dcsupplemental/pnas.201306095si.pdf.

Sclocco, R., Beissner, F., Desbordes, G., et al., 2016. Neuroimaging brainstem circuitry supporting cardiovagal response to pain: a combined heart rate variability/ultrahigh-field (7 T) functional magnetic resonance imaging study. Philos. Trans. R. Soc. A Math. Phys. Eng. Sci. 374 (2067), 20150189. https://doi.org/10.1098/rsta.2015.0189.

Sclocco, R., Beissner, F., Bianciardi, M., Polimeni, J.R., Napadow, V., 2018. Challenges and opportunities for brainstem neuroimaging with ultrahigh field MRI. NeuroImage 168, 412–426. https://doi.org/10.1016/j.neuroimage.2017.02.052.

Singh, K., Indovina, I., Augustinack, J.C., et al., 2020. Probabilistic template of the lateral parabrachial nucleus, medial parabrachial nucleus, vestibular nuclei complex, and medullary viscero-sensory-motor nuclei complex in living humans from 7 tesla MRI. Front. Neurosci. 13, 1425. https://doi.org/10.3389/fnins.2019.01425.

Triantafyllou, C., Hoge, R.D., Krueger, G., et al., 2005. Comparison of physiological noise at 1.5 T, 3 T and 7 T and optimization of fMRI acquisition parameters. NeuroImage 26 (1), 243–250. https://doi.org/10.1016/j.neuroimage.2005.01.007.

Uğurbil, K., 2012. The road to functional imaging and ultrahigh fields. NeuroImage 62 (2), 726–735. https://doi.org/10.1016/j.neuroimage.2012.01.134.

Wang, Y.C., Bianciardi, M., Chanes, L., Satpute, A.B., 2020. Ultra high field fMRI of human superior colliculi activity during affective visual processing. Sci. Rep. 10 (1), 1331. https://doi.org/10.1038/s41598-020-57653-z.

Xin, L., Tkáč, I., 2017. A practical guide to in vivo proton magnetic resonance spectroscopy at high magnetic fields. Anal. Biochem. 529, 30–39. https://doi.org/10.1016/j.ab.2016.10.019.

Younis, S., Hougaard, A., Christensen, C.E., et al., 2020. Feasibility of glutamate and GABA detection in pons and thalamus at 3T and 7T by proton magnetic resonance spectroscopy. Front. Neurosci. 14, 559314. https://doi.org/10.3389/fnins.2020.559314.

Zhong, X., Meyer, C.H., Schlesinger, D.J., et al., 2009. Tracking brain motion during the cardiac cycle using spiral cine-DENSE MRI. Med. Phys. 36 (8), 3413–3419. https://doi.org/10.1118/1.3157109.

Ultra-high field spinal cord MRI

19

Virginie Callot[a,b], Anna J.E. Combes[c,d], Aurélien Destruel[a,b], and Seth A. Smith[c,d]

[a]*Aix-Marseille University, CNRS, CRMBM, Marseille, France* [b]*APHM, Hôpital Universitaire Timone, CEMEREM, Marseille, France* [c]*Vanderbilt University Institute of Imaging Science, Vanderbilt University Medical Center, Nashville, TN, United States* [d]*Department of Radiology and Radiological Sciences, Vanderbilt University Medical Center, Nashville, TN, United States*

Highlights

- Spinal cord imaging at ultra-high field presents particular challenges due to its anatomy and the scarcity of dedicated hardware.
- Visualizing anatomical features such as gray and white matter, CSF, blood vessels, nerve roots, meninges, and pathological features such as multiple sclerosis lesions in greater detail has been demonstrated using structural and quantitative sequences.
- T_1 mapping, diffusion, functional MRI, and some perfusion, spectroscopy, and CEST methods have been successfully translated at 7T, while more work remains for the development of magnetization transfer and sodium imaging techniques.
- While those methods are not currently directly clinically applicable, research studies have shown promise to advance knowledge in neurological conditions such as multiple sclerosis, spinal cord injury, and amyotrophic lateral sclerosis.

19.1 Introduction

The spinal cord (SC) is a long, thin, and highly organized structure (Fig. 19.1) responsible for conducting neural signals between the brain and the peripheral nervous system. Impairment of any SC components, through motor neuron degeneration, white matter (WM) demyelination, or spinal cord injury (SCI), can severely impact its function and lead to symptoms such as loss of sensation, pain, or paralysis.

Currently, conventional anatomical MRI is generally sufficient for diagnosis, and quantitative MRI at 1.5T or 3T is widely used in clinical research to monitor longitudinal studies and provide new knowledge in pathophysiological mechanisms. Yet, 7T systems now also offer new potential to describe tissue changes in small areas contaminated by partial volume effects (PVE) and to go further in characterizing microstructural and functional damages, thanks to increased contrast, sensitivity, and spatial resolution.

However, SC imaging remains challenging. "Usual" intrinsic issues are linked to the thin, tubular, and curved shape of the cord, which requires multiple-slab acquisitions, high resolution, and adequate slice positioning perpendicular to the cord to avoid WM/gray matter (GM) PVE or contamination from cerebrospinal fluid (CSF). In addition, SC MRI at 7T is challenged by various physical/physiological

Advances in Magnetic Resonance Technology and Applications. Volume 10. ISSN 2666-9099. https://doi.org/10.1016/B978-0-323-99898-7.00032-8
301

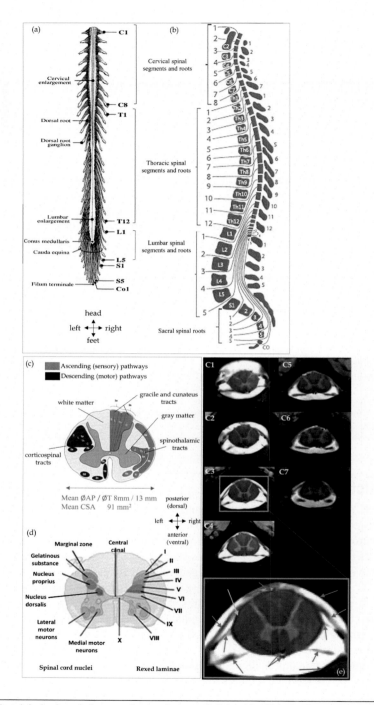

FIG. 19.1

The spinal cord: global description and structures of interest. Schematic coronal (A) and sagittal (B) representations of vertebral and spinal segments. (C, D) Schematic cross-sectional representations of the cord and its WM/GM substructures: the WM consists of myelinated motor and sensory axons grouped into tracts,

(Continued)

constraints, which include (1) deep cord location, which hampers transmission/reception (B_1^+/B_1^-) coil efficiency; (2) inhomogeneous surrounding structures with different tissue magnetic susceptibilities (vertebral bodies, intervertebral disks, etc.), causing increased static (B_0) field inhomogeneities; and (3) physiological noise related to cardiac/CSF pulsatility and dynamic fluctuations, especially respiration, which induces additional B_0 field shift (Vannesjo et al., 2018). Fig. 19.2 illustrates some of these challenges and commonly encountered artifacts.

With this in mind, the objective of this chapter is to provide the readers with a general overview of the various techniques developed up to now at 7T and to illustrate the current state-of-the-art clinical applications of 7T systems. The chapter concludes with some thoughts and identified needs, which are shared here with the hope of driving future developments and motivating further clinical investigations.

19.2 7T spinal cord MRI: What has been achieved so far, challenges, and limitations

Spinal cord MR imaging at 7T emerged a dozen years ago (Kraff et al., 2009), almost a decade after the first 7T brain MRI report. Driven by a smaller community and challenged by numerous limitations (including the lack of adequate RF coils), 7T SC MRI still lags behind brain applications. However, advances over the last 5 years have demonstrated the feasibility and usefulness of both anatomical and quantitative MRI. Table 19.1 proposes an overview of publications available in PubMed on 7T SC MRI (updated version of Barry et al., 2018).

The following sections provide more details about what has been achieved so far in terms of structural, functional, vascular, metabolic, and molecular imaging.

19.2.1 Radiofrequency coils

As large-body radiofrequency (RF) coils have reduced efficiency and uniformity at 7T (cf. Chapter 7), local transmit coils consisting of several elements are typically used to limit this effect. Although some early designs investigated imaging of the whole cord with single coils (Kraff et al., 2009; Vossen et al., 2011), the common trend has been to design RF coils for specific vertebral segments (see Table 19.1).

FIG. 19.1—Cont'd

conventionally divided into dorsal, lateral, and ventral funiculi. The GM, divided into dorsal, intermediate, and ventral horns, is composed of 10 laminae responsible for receiving/transmitting different information (thermal stimuli, proprioception, contraction, etc.). It is made up of dendrites, axons, glial cells, and neuronal cell bodies organized into functional clusters called nuclei. The cord is protected by three membranes called the spinal meninges (pia, arachnoid, and dura matters from inner to outer), not represented here and usually not visible on conventional 3T MR images. (E) T_2^*-weighted MR images (0.18-mm in-plane resolution) acquired at 7T (Massire et al., 2016), at each cervical vertebral level. The GM can be clearly visualized. Additional details can be seen as well, e.g., nerve roots (blue arrows), ligaments (purple), blood vessels (red), dura mater (green), and pia mater (yellow). *(A) Modified from Altman and Bayer (2001). (B) Modified from De Leener et al. (2016). (C) Spinal cord tracts. https://psychology.wikia.org/wiki/Spinothalamic_tracts. Accessed 2021-10-10. (D) Same as (B). (E) Modified from Massire et al. (2016).*

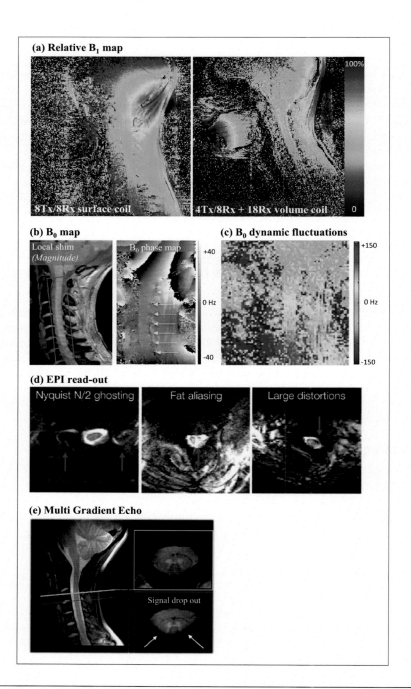

FIG. 19.2

Illustration of some of the challenges encountered at 7T. (A) B_1^+ map obtained with an 8Tx/Rx surface coil (CRMBM-CEMEREM, Marseille, France), and a 4Tx/8Rx+18Rx volume coil (courtesy of Alan Seifert, Biomedical Engineering and Imaging Institute, Mount Sinai Hospital, New York, USA) showing the inhomogeneous RF excitation pattern usually encountered within large FOV and a 25%–40% signal attenuation

(Continued)

Table 19.1 Publications on spinal cord MRI at 7T.

First author, date[a] DOI	Coil design[b]	Main topic	Main sequences	Cohort[c]
Wu et al. (2010) https://doi.org/10.1109/TBME.2009.2030170	4TxRx (TL)	RF design and anatomical MRI	GRE	10 HC
Kraff et al. (2009) https://doi.org/10.1097/RLI.0b013e3181b24ab7	8TxRx (CTL)	RF design and anatomical MRI	3D-FLASH	1 HC, 2 Scoliosis
Vossen et al. (2011) https://doi.org/10.1016/j.jmr.2010.11.004	2Tx/8Rx (CTL)	RF design and anatomical MRI	GRE	10 HC
Grams et al. (2012) https://doi.org/10.1007/s00256-011-1197-0	8TxRx (L)	Evaluation of sequences at 7T	T_2w-TSE, DESS, CISS, VIBE	5 HC, 1 Spina bifida
Sigmund et al. (2012) https://doi.org/10.1002/nbm.1809	4TxRx (Rapid Biomedical) (C)	RF design, comparison between 7T and 3T MRI	T_2w-GRE, T_2w-TSE	10 HC
Dzyubachyk et al. (2013) https://doi.org/10.1002/mrm.24404	10Rx CTL	Automated correction and volume stitching	GRE	23 HC
Andreychenko et al. (2013) https://doi.org/10.1002/mrm.24496	Waveguide antenna (L)	RF design and anatomical MRI	GRE	1 HC
Cohen-Adad et al. (2013) https://doi.org/10.1002/mus.23720	4Tx/19Rx (C)	Evaluation of 7T MRI applied to ALS	T_2^*w-multiecho FLASH	1 HC, 1 ALS
Cohen-Adad et al. (2012) https://doi.org/10.1212/WNL.0b013e31827597ae	4Tx/19Rx (C)	Case report	2-echo T_2^*w-FLASH	1 SCI
Kogan et al. (2013) https://doi.org/10.1016/j.neuroimage.2013.03.072	8TxRx (C)	Feasibility of GluCEST	CEST	7 HC
Zhao et al. (2014) https://doi.org/10.1002/mrm.24911	4Tx/19Rx (C)	4Tx/19Rx (C)	Case report	2 HC
Eryaman et al. (2015) https://doi.org/10.1002/mrm.25246	4Tx (in silico) (C)	Reduction of SAR	N/A	N/A
Barry et al. (2014) https://doi.org/10.7554/eLife.02812	2Tx/16Rx (Nova Medical) (C)	Acquisition and correction of Rs-fMRI	T_2^*w-GRE; 3D multishot GRE	22 HC
Duan et al. (2015) https://doi.org/10.1002/mrm.25817	2Tx/8Rx (T)	RF design and anatomical MRI	GRE	2 HC
Dula et al. (2016a) https://doi.org/10.1177/1352458515591070	2Tx/16Rx (Nova Medical) (C)	Evaluation of 7T MRI applied to MS, compared with 3T MRI	T_1w, T_2^*w, SD FFE	13 HC, 15 MS
Barry et al. (2016) https://doi.org/10.1016/j.neuroimage.2016.02.058	2Tx/16Rx (Nova Medical) (C)	Rs-fMRI reproducibility	T_2^*w-GRE; 3D multishot GRE	23 HC

Continued

FIG. 19.2—Cont'd

in the lower cervical cord. (B) Magnitude and B_0 field map in the cord. A local shim strategy (green box) is usually required to minimize B_0 inhomogeneities along the cord. Small fluctuations at the interface with bones and disks (yellow arrow) subsist. (C) Difference of expired and inspired field maps showing breathing-induced field variations up to 150 Hz at the lower cervical level (courtesy of Johanna Vannesjö, Norwegian University of Science and Technology, Norway). (D) Common artifacts encountered when using EPI readout at 7T. (E) Typical T_2^* signal dropout observed in the vicinity of the spinous process (blue: acquisition performed midvertebra; purple: at the intervertebral disk level).

Table 19.1 Publications on spinal cord MRI at 7T.—cont'd

First author, date[a] DOI	Coil design[b]	Main topic	Main sequences	Cohort[c]
Henning et al. (2016) https://doi.org/10.1002/nbm.3541	2Tx/30Rx (C)	MRS with two-channel RF shimming	semi-LASER	3 HC
Dula et al. (2016b) https://doi.org/10.1002/nbm.3581	2Tx/16Rx (Nova Medical) (C)	Feasibility of CEST	3D-FFE; Fast GRE; Multishot GRE with multishot EPI	10 HC, 10 MS
Massire et al. (2016) https://doi.org/10.1016/j.neuroimage.2016.08.055	8TxRx (Rapid Biomedical) (C)	Multiparametric quantitative MRI (T_1 relaxometry, DTI)	T_2w-TSE; 3D T_1w-MP2RAGE; Multiecho T_2^*w-GRE; SS-SE EPI	10 HC
Zhang et al. (2016) https://doi.org/10.1002/mrm.26538	4Tx/22Rx (C)	RF design and anatomical MRI, BOLD fMRI and DTI	T_1w-GRE; T_2w-TSE; Multiecho FLASH; GRE EPI; SE EPI	2 HC
Barry et al. (2018) https://doi.org/10.1016/j.neuroimage.2017.07.003	Review paper			
Vannesjo et al. (2018) https://doi.org/10.1016/j.neuroimage.2017.11.031	Volume transmit, 16Rx (QED) (C)	Breathing-induced B_0 field fluctuations	Multiecho GRE; FLASH; Multiecho GRE	10 HC
Massire et al. (2018a)[f]	8TxRx (C)	Multiparametric portfolio	SPACE; Multiecho GRE; MP2RAGE; SS-SE EPI	7 HC
Massire et al. (2018b) https://doi.org/10.1002/mrm.27087	8TxRx (C)	Feasibility of DTI	SS-SE-EPI	8 HC
Conrad et al. (2018) https://doi.org/10.1093/brain/awy083	2Tx/16Rx (Nova Medical) (C)	Evaluation of 7T rs-fMRI applied to MS	T_2^*w-GRE; 3D multishot GRE	56 HC, 22 MS
Vannesjo et al. (2019) https://doi.org/10.1002/mrm.27664	Volume transmit, 16Rx (QED) (C)	Correction of breathing artifacts based on respiratory bellows, using T_2^* mapping	Multiecho GRE; multishot EPI	6 HC
Rietsch et al. (2019)[d] https://doi.org/10.1002/mrm.27731	16TxRx or 32TxRx + 16Rx (TL)	RF design and anatomical MRI	3D-GRE; 3D-FLASH	4 HC
Lopez Rios et al. (2019)[g]	3Tx/15Rx (C)	RF design and B_0 shimming	N/A	N/A
Massire et al. (2020) https://doi.org/10.1016/j.neuroimage.2019.116275	8TxRx (Rapid Biomedical) (C)	Investigation of T_1 mapping with MP2RAGE	3D-MP2RAGE; Multiecho T_2^*w-GRE	14 HC
Lévy et al. (2020) https://doi.org/10.1002/mrm.28195	8TxRx (Rapid Biomedical) (C)	In vivo perfusion MRI (intravoxel incoherent motion)	SS-SE EPI; Multiecho GRE	6 HC
Geldschläger et al. (2021) https://doi.org/10.1002/mrm.28455	8TxRx (C)	9.4T SC MRI, anatomical imaging, and T_2^* calculation	T_2^*w-GRE	10 HC
Ouellette et al. (2020)[d] https://doi.org/10.1093/brain/awaa249	4Tx/19Rx (C)	MS patient lesion spatial distribution	Multiecho T_2^*w-FLASH	11 HC, 35 MS
Lévy et al. (2021) https://doi.org/10.1002/mrm.28559	8TxRx (Rapid Biomedical) (C)	In vivo perfusion MRI (DSC)	Multiecho FLASH; SS-SE EPI; FLASH	3 HC, 5 CSM
Galley et al. (2021)[e] https://doi.org/10.1007/s00330-020-07557-3	8TxRx (Rapid Biomedical) (C)	Visualization of nerve rootlets with DESS at 3T and 7T	3D-DESS	21 neck pain
Hernandez et al. (2021) https://doi.org/10.1080/09205071.2021.1871779	4Tx (in silico) (CTL)	RF design (in silico only)	N/A	N/A

Table 19.1 Publications on spinal cord MRI at 7T.—cont'd

First author, date[a] DOI	Coil design[b]	Main topic	Main sequences	Cohort[c]
Callot et al. (2021) https://doi.org/10.1212/WNL.0000000000012072	8TxRx, (Rapid Biomedical) (C)	Case report	Multiecho GRE	2 ALS
Destruel et al. (2021) https://doi.org/10.1109/TMI.2021.3103654	8TxRx (L)	RF design and anatomical MRI	DESS	1 HC
May et al. (2022) https://doi.org/10.1002/mrm.29288	16Tx/64Rx (C)	RF design and anatomical MRI	GRE	5 HC

T_1w, T_1-weighted; T_2w, T_2-weighted; T_2^*w, T_2^*-weighted; SD, spin density; ss-EPI, single-shot spin-echo EPI; QED, quality electrodynamics; HC/P, healthy controls/patients; ALS, amyotrophic lateral sclerosis; CSM, cervical spondylotic myelopathy; DESS, dual-echo steady state; DSC, dynamic susceptibility contrast; FFE, fast field echo; MS, multiple sclerosis.
[a]Publications are sorted in chronological order based on their online availability.
[b]C, cervical; T, Thoracic; L, Lumbar spine.
[c]Volunteers used for optimization of sequences are not included.
[d]Only information about spine imaging is included in this table.
[e]This study includes results acquired at both 3T and 7T. Only information about 7T MRI is included in this table.
[f]MAGNETOM Flash (70) 1/2018.
[g]Conference abstracts were included as latest work on coil design for 7T spine MRI (see "References" section).

Recent designs have particularly focused on the cervical SC, mostly using multiple loops with posterior-only rigid formers (Massire et al., 2016; Sigmund et al., 2012; Zhao et al., 2014), as well as designs with anterior and posterior elements (May et al., 2022; Zhang et al., 2017). Other types of elements such as dipoles and small-volume coils (Barry et al., 2014; Henning et al., 2016; Lopez Rios et al., 2019; Vannesjo et al., 2018) have also been introduced. Some designs focused on increasing the number of receive channels (up to 64) (Henning et al., 2016; May et al., 2022), which improves the parallel imaging capability and the SNR close to the surface, whereas other designs focused on increasing the number of transmit channels (up to 16) to add degrees of freedom to shape the B_1 field distribution (Massire et al., 2016; May et al., 2022). Despite great interest and need, fewer designs have been proposed so far for imaging the thoracolumbar levels where the large size of the torso and abdomen enhances B_1 inhomogeneities. However, a recent work on dipoles (Destruel et al., 2021) has shown potential for such applications.

19.2.2 Structural MRI

19.2.2.1 T_2^*-weighted sequences and T_2^* mapping

With the advent of higher field strengths, T_2^*-weighted MRI (cf. Fig. 19.1) took centerstage, with sharp WM/GM delineation and typically low specific absorption rate (SAR) requirements.

The first publication on SC MRI at 7T in humans (Sigmund et al., 2012) reported on the increased ability of T_2^*-weighted MRI to show GM/WM contrast at high resolution. Similarly Cohen-Adad et al. (2013) showed that T_2^*-weighted scans can specifically detail tissue damage in ALS, Dula et al. (2016a, b) showed that 7T improves on conventional field strengths to highlight lesions in patients with MS, and Callot et al. (2021) showed the power of exceptionally high resolution for demarcating internal SC structure (cf. Fig. 19.5C).

Although the T_2^* of GM at 7T is estimated to be 40% shorter than at 3T, a recent work by Massire et al. (2016) has shown that T_2^* maps can generate excellent GM/WM contrast and highlight specific tracts within the SC. However, the rapid T_2^* decay in the SC at 7T leads to reduced performance of

EPI-based readouts and creates an additional demand for shorter echo spacing when considering multi-echo sequences. Several advancements in shuttered EPI or readout-segmented EPI would offer new opportunities for functional and diffusion MRI. Additionally, the development of gradient and spin echo readout (GraSE) to partially refocus field inhomogeneities may have benefits for targeted SC applications. Finally, susceptibility-weighted imaging (SWI) of the brain at 7T has highlighted intra-cerebral venous networks and aberrations, which, if deployed in the SC, could offer insights into venous abnormalities associated with trauma, MS, and other neurovascular conditions.

19.2.2.2 T_1 mapping

Although T_1 mapping lacks specificity toward a single particular biological feature, it has the potential to discriminate regional tissue organization and characterize tissue microstructural impairments occurring in neurodegenerative pathologies. Among various techniques, the magnetization-prepared two rapid acquisition gradient echoes (MP2RAGE) sequence has emerged as an efficient technique (Marques et al., 2010), thanks to an adiabatic inversion RF pulse, robust gradient echo (GRE) readouts, an intrinsic volume coregistration, and an overall low SAR (depending on the type of inversion pulse used). Optimized for the cord, a 0.7-mm^3-resolution MP2RAGE can be used for diffuse cervical cord investigation with minimal PVE (Massire et al., 2016), while a very high resolution (0.3-mm in plane) can be used to visualize substructures such as anterior fissure, central canal, ventral, and dorsal GM horns, or posterior septum (cf. Fig. 19.3B and C) (Massire et al., 2020). By allowing the investigation of a wider range of functional regions, MP2RAGE opens new perspectives for diagnosis in pathologies, such as motor neuron disease or lesion detection in MS. It is worth noting that a B_1 map is required to correct MP2RAGE T_1 values from B_1^+ inhomogeneity biases (Massire et al., 2016).

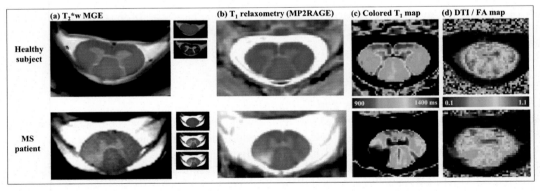

FIG. 19.3

Multiparametric MRI dedicated to morphometric and structural measurements in a healthy subject and a MS patient presenting with a right GM/WM lesion. (A) T_2^*-weighted images (0.18-mm in-plane resolution) along with cord, GM, and lesion segmentations. (B) T_1 relaxometry (0.3-mm in-plane resolution) allowing sharp lesion delineation, (C) color-coded T_1 map. (D) Fractional anisotropy map (0.4-mm in plane resolution). Both T_1 and FA maps demonstrated impaired tissue in the MS patient as compared to the healthy control.

19.2.2.3 Diffusion

Diffusion MRI (dMRI) is frequently used for clinical studies to characterize microstructural impairments in SC diseases. With the expected increased image resolution and SNR, cord dMRI at 7T is particularly attractive to assess tissue changes within specific tracts or GM horns. Yet, translation from clinical field strengths to 7T presents specific technical challenges related to T_2 shortening, B_1 and B_0 inhomogeneities, and SAR increase.

To date, quality improvement of SC dMRI from 3T (especially those equipped with high gradient performance) to 7T has not been realized, but promising results have been demonstrated (Massire et al., 2018b; Massire et al., 2016; Zhang et al., 2017). High in-plane resolution (0.4–0.8 mm) transverse diffusion tensor imaging (DTI) covering the cervical levels from C1 to C7 can be achieved (e.g., Fig. 19.3D), with some improvements needed for lower level imaging. Moderate B_1 drop (up to −30%) along the cord was demonstrated to have limited influence on the accuracy of DTI indices (Massire et al., 2018b); however, a higher drop could lead to insufficient SNR and inefficient fat saturation, which may impact the accuracy of DTI-derived indices.

19.2.3 Functional and vascular MRI

19.2.3.1 fMRI and rs-fMRI

Increased sensitivity to susceptibility effects makes ultra-high field (UHF) advantageous for functional MRI (fMRI). The greater available signal improves temporal SNR (tSNR = mean signal/variance over time), reflecting the ability to detect meaningful blood oxygen level-dependent (BOLD) signal changes. While single-shot EPI sequences are widely used at 3T, 3D multishot GRE (FFE) sequences have been favored for 7T cord imaging, due to higher geometric fidelity with only slightly lower BOLD sensitivity (Seifert et al., 2019). However, physiological noise can negatively impact tSNR in the cord, and motion correction and physiological signal regression are necessary during postprocessing (Barry et al., 2014). Higher resolution can help mitigate the increased contribution of physiological noise relative to thermal noise, as well as the static and time-fluctuating field distortions caused by proximity to the vertebrae, disks, and lungs. So far, resolutions of $0.91 \times 0.91 \times 4$ mm have been achieved (Barry et al., 2014). Smaller voxel sizes are also beneficial for resolving activity in specific neuronal populations (e.g., GM horns underlying motor, sensory, and nociceptive processing).

The first 7T resting state fMRI study revealed the existence of correlations between low-frequency (<0.08 Hz) signal fluctuations forming biologically plausible networks in the cervical cord (Barry et al., 2014) (Fig. 19.4), which subsequently showed moderate within-session reproducibility (Barry et al., 2016). SC fMRI may prove a valuable research tool in the study of human physiology and conditions like MS or fibromyalgia.

19.2.3.2 Perfusion

Vascularization plays a key role in the cascade of events following SCI (from ischemia to neuronal death). Being able to noninvasively map blood perfusion in the cord would thus be beneficial.

Endogenous methods for SC blood perfusion measurements, such as arterial spin labeling, are challenged by the complexity of the vascular network and the currently limited RF coil efficiency that jeopardizes efficient spin-tagging strategies. Alternatively, intravoxel incoherent motion (IVIM) based on a SE-EPI has been proposed to quantify the signal decrease at low b-values (small diffusion

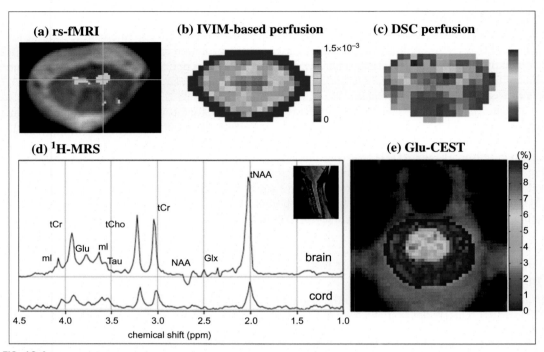

FIG. 19.4

Multiparametric MRI directed toward functional/vascular and metabolic/molecular assessment (healthy subjects). (A) Resting state ventral network observed in a single subject via fMRI, showing correlations ($p < 0.0001$) between a seed voxel (green crosshairs) in the left GM ventral horn and voxels in the contralateral region (from Barry et al., 2016). (B) ($f.D^*$) map (in mm^2/s), with f the vascular fraction and D^* the fast diffusion coefficient, derived from IVIM acquisition (Lévy et al., 2020) and (C) relative blood flow (rBF) map derived from DSC acquisition (Lévy et al., 2021), both showing higher perfusion in the GM structure as compared to WM (CRMBM-CEMEREM, Marseille, France). (D) ^{1}H MR spectra acquired in the brain (voxel size $15 \times 15 \times 15$ mm^3) and the cord (voxel size $6 \times 6 \times 20$ mm^3) (CRMBM-CEMEREM, Marseille, France) using a semi-LASER sequence and a respiratory-gated approach (Roussel et al., 2022). (E) GluCEST$_{asym}$ map corrected for B_0 and B_1 inhomogeneity and MT asymmetry, showing higher values in GM compared to WM (Kogan et al., 2013).

encoding) induced by blood water circulation through capillaries (Lévy et al., 2020). However, the obtained sensitivity at single-slice scale was limited, and averaging across multiple subjects was necessary to map the perfusion difference between GM and WM (see Fig. 19.4B). Using an exogenous contrast, individual submillimetric slice-wise dynamic susceptibility contrast (DSC) maps of relative blood volume and blood flow were demonstrated (Lévy et al., 2021), showing potential for discriminating GM from WM in perfusion maps (see Fig. 19.4C); however, both gradient echo and SE EPI-based DSC perfusion signal stability at 7T were impaired by breathing-induced B_0 fluctuation, hence requiring further developments to be robustly used in a clinical research context.

19.2.4 **Metabolic/molecular MRI**
19.2.4.1 *¹H MR spectroscopy*

Metabolism, assessed through ^{1}H MRS, also plays an important role in various forms of SC dysregulation (hypoxia, neuronal death, cell proliferation, etc.).

Thanks to improved SNR and spectral resolution, 7T MRS should (theoretically) help in measuring and revealing contributions of proton populations hardly visible otherwise. This is especially true in the cord where 4-to-10× smaller voxel sizes compared to the brain are necessary. To fully take advantage of 7T, a good static and RF field homogeneity is mandatory. Additional strategies such as the use of adiabatic pulses, frequency stabilization, and compensation for breathing B_0 field fluctuations (Roussel et al., 2022) and/or new coil design (Henning et al., 2016) may also be adopted to overcome residual B_1^+ heterogeneity, physiological variations, and/or deep location of the cord.

So far, two ^{1}H MRS studies relying on ECG- or respiratory-triggered single-voxel semi-LASER (Localization by Adiabatic SElective Refocusing) acquisitions (Henning et al., 2016; Roussel et al., 2022) have been able to confidently measure the main metabolite ratios (*N*-acetyl aspartate/total creatine (NAA/tCr), total choline containing compounds (Cho/tCr), and myo-inositol (mI/tCr)). However, lower concentration neurotransmitter metabolites such as Glutamine (Glu) or GABA (gamma-amino-butyric acid) remained inaccessible (see Fig. 19.4D).

19.2.4.2 *CEST*

Chemical exchange saturation transfer (CEST) is a spectrally specific saturation of labile protons, such as amide, amine, and hydroxyl protons, followed by a readout of the exchange of that saturation on the water resonance. Amide proton transfer (APT) CEST is sensitive to protons associated with proteins/peptides and is the most widely used. CEST can also provide contrasts from other exchanging moieties and metabolites, neurotransmitters, and pH. CEST benefits from higher field strength through increase in SNR and improved spectral resolution, which in turn allows detection of lower concentration metabolites.

The first report of in vivo CEST in the SC at 7T showed contrast derived from Glutamate (GluCEST) (Kogan et al., 2013) (see Fig. 19.4E), the primary excitatory neurotransmitter in the human CNS. APT CEST was shown in the cervical spine (Dula et al., 2016a,b), focusing on saturation prepulse optimization and transmit B_1^+ field homogeneity. Only APT-CEST and GluCEST have been deployed in the SC due to technical hindrances such as low SNR, temporally fluctuating B_0 inhomogeneities, and spatial B_1 inhomogeneities. By et al. (2018) demonstrated the ability to use the respiratory trace to deconvolve the respiratory impact on B_0 homogeneity at 3T for APT CEST, which could be further exploited at 7T. Improved saturation schemes to minimize B_1 inhomogeneity are considered a valuable next step.

19.3 **Clinical research applications**
19.3.1 **Multiple sclerosis**

Multiple sclerosis (MS) is an autoimmune disease causing inflammation and demyelination in the brain and SC, predominantly in the cervical and thoracic regions (see Chapter 30 on MS). The detection of SC lesions is essential to establish dissemination of the disease in space or following an inconclusive diagnostic brain exam. The ability to detect and quantify tissue damage in and outside of lesions is also important for faster and more efficient clinical trials.

To date, one small study showed a 52% improvement in detection of cervical lesions from 3 to 7T using T_1-weighted and T_2^*-weighted scans compared to a regular 3T protocol (Dula et al., 2016a, b). Lesion conspicuity was also observed superior in the thoracic spine of two MS patients at 7T compared to 3T using sagittal MP-RAGE, multislice T_2^* with navigator correction, and 3D T_2^* radial GRE (Lefeuvre et al., 2016). A preferential spatial distribution of cervical lesions relative to the subpial and central canal CSF in different MS subtypes has additionally recently been shown (Ouellette et al., 2020). A few advanced MRI studies have looked at quantitative and functional parameters in the cervical SC. Feasibility of T_1 mapping and DTI in an MS cohort have been shown in the cervical SC, with T_1 values and axial diffusivity showing sensitivity to lesions, and T_1 mapping revealing morphological features related to tissue atrophy (i.e., enlarged CSF spaces: anterior fissure, central canal, posterior septum) (Massire et al., 2019). Using APT-CEST, Dula et al. (2016a, b) showed differences in Z-spectra between healthy, MS normal-appearing and lesioned tissue, at ranges both up- and downfield of water resonance. Finally, one resting state fMRI study using seed-based connectivity analysis showed both increases and decreases in network connectivity depending on lesion tract and location (Conrad et al., 2018).

19.3.2 Amyotrophic lateral sclerosis

Amyotrophic lateral sclerosis (ALS) is a fatal neuromuscular disease affecting both upper and lower motor neurons, whose diagnosis is predominantly clinical, making conventional anatomical MRI usually only used to rule out alternative pathologies that may mimic ALS. However, resolution achieved at UHF now offers new opportunities to characterize tissue degeneration. This was demonstrated in an early study (Cohen-Adad et al., 2013) showing sharp delineation of T_2^* hyperintensity linked to demyelination in lateral corticospinal tracts, and confirmed recently in a study where the additional involvement of anterior WM tracts was revealed for the first time in vivo (Callot et al., 2021) (see also Fig. 19.5C). Moreover, thanks to improved spatial resolution, earlier changes and refined GM/WM SC atrophy measurements are expected to be seen at UHF. Future multiparametric MRI investigations at 7T are also expected to bring increased sensitivity and spatial accuracy in characterizing anterior horn and motoneuron degeneration/dysfunction.

19.3.3 Spinal cord injury

Physical trauma or compression can result in spinal cord injury (SCI). In the acute setting, the benefits of UHF imaging in its current state have yet to be determined, and its deployment is likely to be hampered by time constraints and safety concerns. There is however a clinical need for assessing chronic tissue microstructure at the injury site, as well as remotely, to help classify and assess lesion severity. The greater anatomical details revealed by UHF have been used to identify a case of Wallerian degeneration following a cervical hemangioma, including features not seen at lower field strength (Cohen-Adad et al., 2012). Characterization using quantitative MRI should now be further encouraged.

19.3.4 Degenerative cervical myelopathy

Degenerative cervical myelopathy (DCM) is a prevalent and disabling condition encompassing cervical spondylotic myelopathy (CSM) and other forms of age-related cord compression. Surgical decompression of the cord is the main treatment available to alleviate symptoms and prevent further deterioration, and

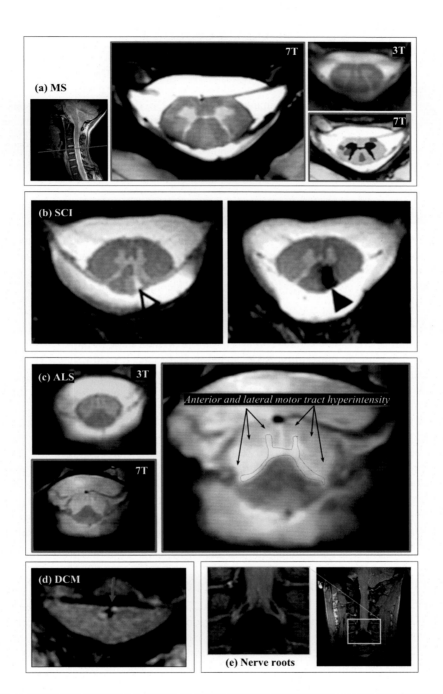

FIG. 19.5

Added value of 7T MRI in the context of spinal cord pathology. (A) 7T T_2^*w MRI in a MS patient showing increased lesion conspicuousness as compared to 3T. In the lower right part, GM (blue) and lesion (red) segmentations are provided (CRMBM-CEMEREM, Marseille, France). (B) T_2^*w hypersignal (empty arrow, left) and hyposignal (filled arrow, right) observed in a patient with spinal cord injury and suggesting dorsal column Wallerian degeneration and hemosiderin deposition, respectively (Cohen-Adad et al., 2012). (C) Upper motor neuron-predominant ALS patient presenting

(Continued)

MRI predictors of postoperative outcomes would have great clinical utility. The visualization of intraspinal anatomy, including denticulate ligaments and nerve roots, is possible at 7T with axial 2D T_2^*-weighted GRE and T_2-weighted TSE sequences (Sigmund et al., 2012). Discrimination of nerve rootlets in great detail using a 3D dual-echo steady-state sequence has been shown (Galley et al., 2021), which may be useful in radiculopathy cases and for presurgical planning. The feasibility of contrast-aided DSC to obtain relative blood volume and flow maps has also been shown in five CSM cases, holding promise to evaluate the impact of compression on perfusion (Lévy et al., 2021).

19.4 What's next? Perspectives, wishes, and dreams

Apart from the usual challenges related to spatial coverage and physiological motion, SC imaging at 7T is currently limited by the lack of fully optimized RF coils, SAR limitations for many pulse sequences (especially true for T_2 TSE, SE-EPI, some adiabatic pulses, etc.), and static/dynamic B_0 inhomogeneities. This last section focuses on promising on-going research and identifies avenues to improve SC MRI at 7T.

19.4.1 pTx and new coil design

Several pTx techniques (Chapter 7) have been successfully applied to brain imaging and showed substantial improvements of B_1 uniformity, SAR decrease, and reduced field-of-view (Padormo et al., 2016). Similar significant gains are expected for SC MRI at 7T but have yet to be implemented. In particular, selected excitation of small tissues using pTx may allow removing signal from artifact-inducing regions (trachea, lungs), and excitation may be optimized to reduce the SAR.

The limited number of commercial RF coils available for 7T SC MRI is an additional challenge, and a greater range of pTx compatible RF coils covering the whole cord, or simultaneously the brain and cervical cord, would be of great benefit, in particular for applications that require whole CNS (e.g., MS, ALS) assessments. Due to the lack of body coils available at 7T, strategies involving scanning and stitching together images from different cord sections are required. Some recent designs using variations of dipole elements for torso and abdomen (Destruel et al., 2021; Raaijmakers et al., 2016) show that the penetration and efficiency of such coils and pTx techniques are expected to enable more comprehensive imaging in the near future. The use of passive elements such as dielectric pads and metamaterials may also provide enhanced field transmission for SC MRI.

19.4.2 Static B_0 inhomogeneities and dynamic B_0 fluctuations

Sequences typically relying on single-shot EPI readout at 3T, such as diffusion or functional MRI, suffer from increased B_0 field inhomogeneities at 7T, resulting in increased susceptibility-induced image distortions despite the use of second-order localized B_0 shim. From the authors' point of view and

FIG. 19.5—Cont'd

with T_2^*w bilateral motor tracts degeneration (CST and others) with sign of impairment of the anterior tracts revealed at 7T but not visible at 3T (modified from Callot, Neurology, 2021). (D) 7T T_2^*w MRI in a patient presenting with degenerative cervical myelopathy and showing loss of contrast between WM and GM presumably linked to vascular involvement (CRMBM-CEMEREM, Marseille, France). (E) Nerve roots visualization using T_2-space imaging (Massire et al., 2018a) (CRMBM-CEMEREM, Marseille, France).

experience, the use of a third-order shimming, if available, has no benefit in the (cervical) cord due to the temporal and spatial periodicity of B_0 inhomogeneities, and could even be detrimental to image quality.

To date, distortion mitigations have been demonstrated using reversed-phase-encoding methods for DTI (Massire et al., 2018b), or segmented readout for fMRI, which is less prone to susceptibility artifacts but at the cost of a substantial acquisition time increase (Seifert and Vannesjo, 2020). Other strategies such as z-shimming (Finsterbusch et al., 2012) or dynamic shimming with integrated coil (Topfer et al., 2016) would help to further improve region-based shimming. More importantly, compensation/correction of breathing-induced B_0 field fluctuation (Vannesjo et al., 2019) have been proposed for gradient echo-based sequences and should now be more widely implemented and made available by MR vendors.

19.4.3 Multiparametric MRI

Some sequences of interest, available at lower field strength, have yet to be deployed at 7T (e.g., multi-echo T_2 mapping for myelin water imaging).

Magnetization transfer (MT) also faces several challenges at high field and is usually SAR-limited due to high-power saturation pulses. While MT imaging can be deployed at 7T, there has been increased attention paid to quantitative MT (qMT) to derive physiological parameters of tissue independent of field strength and pulse sequence design. These techniques can benefit from using a combination of pTx, prolonged T_1 to allow for longer TR, or variable density saturation schemes as shown by Oh et al. (2018) for MT. However, further investigation is required, and both MT and qMT have yet to be applied to the SC at 7T.

More clinically relevant sequences, such as STIR, PSIR, or T_2-SPACE, have not been optimized at 7T and would require innovations to overcome SAR issues. However, the MP2RAGE may be a viable alternative to the STIR/PSIR sequences classically used at 3T for MS lesion detection, and the DESS sequence could be a promising method to visualize the nerve rootlets (Galley et al., 2021).

Nonproton MRI, which offers one of the main noninvasive techniques for studying metabolism in human tissue, has not been optimized for SC assessment at 7T. Specifically, sodium (^{23}Na) has shown potential in neuroimaging applications, and high fields are recommended to overcome challenges related to its low sensitivity, concentration, and short relaxation times (see Chapters 26 and 27). Custom coil considerations (such as dual-tuned), spectroscopic approaches, and adequate sequences with high spatial resolution overcoming PVE issues are ongoing opportunities for development.

Finally, implementation of UHF imaging for patients with surgical antecedents is also complicated by the presence of hardware and fixation apparatus (e.g., in cases of spinal fusion), and would require development of techniques robust to paramagnetic effects, as well as characterization of implanted materials' behavior at 7T, and guidelines for safe patient scanning (see Chapter 4).

19.4.4 Quantification tools

As 7T MR images present with different contrast and resolution, some of the tools traditionally used for 3T MR postprocessing may not be fully adequate for robust analyses. Cord/CSF or WM/GM segmentation algorithms may need to be improved to incorporate new knowledge and overcome issues linked to T_2^* signal dropout at the interface of the disks, root insertion in the dorsal GM horns, refined shape and cord contours, or new type of artifacts. In that perspective, preliminary work based on deep-learning approaches has been proposed (Medina et al., 2021). Meanwhile, the availability of very high-resolution multiparametric images also opens new perspectives to build probabilistic atlases of

SC substructures, especially within the GM where quantification in specific laminae or motor neuron clusters may be of great interest to study SCI or ALS, for instance, while avoiding contamination from central canal, septum, or anterior median fissure (Massire et al., 2020).

19.5 Conclusion

While there is no doubt that methodological developments dedicated to 7T SC MRI will be addressed in the near future and that anatomical MRI already helps visualizing cord abnormalities not seen at 3T, the added value of SC 7T quantitative MRI for diagnosis and prognosis remains to be demonstrated and validated. This will be addressed through multicentric initiatives, neuroradiologist involvement, and further implications from the vendors to make technical solutions fully available to the community. Nevertheless, the potential for 7T to change our perspective on diagnoses, clinical outcomes, and neuroscientific studies of the human SC continues to provide enthusiasm to the community.

References

Altman, J., Bayer, S.A., 2001. Development of the Human Spinal Cord. Oxford University Press, Oxford, NY.

Barry, R.L., Smith, S.A., Dula, A.N., Gore, J.C., 2014. Resting state functional connectivity in the human spinal cord. eLife 3, e02812. https://doi.org/10.7554/eLife.02812.

Barry, R.L., Rogers, B.P., Conrad, B.N., Smith, S.A., Gore, J.C., 2016. Reproducibility of resting state spinal cord networks in healthy volunteers at 7 tesla. NeuroImage 133, 31–40. https://doi.org/10.1016/j.neuroimage.2016.02.058.

Barry, R.L., Vannesjo, S.J., By, S., Gore, J.C., Smith, S.A., 2018. Spinal cord MRI at 7T. NeuroImage 168, 437–451. https://doi.org/10.1016/j.neuroimage.2017.07.003.

By, S., Barry, R.L., Smith, A.K., et al., 2018. Amide proton transfer CEST of the cervical spinal cord in multiple sclerosis patients at 3T. Magn. Reson. Med. 79, 806–814. https://doi.org/10.1002/mrm.26736.

Callot, V., Massire, A., Guye, M., Attarian, S., Verschueren, A., 2021. Visualization of gray matter atrophy and anterior corticospinal tract signal hyperintensity in amyotrophic lateral sclerosis using 7T MRI. Neurology 96, 1094–1095. https://doi.org/10.1212/WNL.0000000000012072.

Cohen-Adad, J., Zhao, W., Wald, L.L., Oaklander, A.L., 2012. 7T MRI of spinal cord injury. Neurology 79, 2217. https://doi.org/10.1212/WNL.0b013e31827597ae.

Cohen-Adad, J., Zhao, W., Keil, B., et al., 2013. 7-T MRI of the spinal cord can detect lateral corticospinal tract abnormality in amyotrophic lateral sclerosis. Muscle Nerve 47, 760–762. https://doi.org/10.1002/mus.23720.

Conrad, B.N., Barry, R.L., Rogers, B.P., et al., 2018. Multiple sclerosis lesions affect intrinsic functional connectivity of the spinal cord. Brain 141, 1650–1664. https://doi.org/10.1093/brain/awy083.

De Leener, B., et al., 2016. Segmentation of the human spinal cord. MAGMA 29 (2), 125–153. https://doi.org/10.1007/s10334-015-0507-2.

Destruel, A., Jin, J., Weber, E., et al., 2021. Integrated multi-modal antenna with coupled radiating structures (I-MARS) for 7T pTx body MRI. IEEE Trans. Med. Imaging. https://doi.org/10.1109/TMI.2021.3103654.

Dula, A.N., Pawate, S., Dethrage, L.M., et al., 2016a. Chemical exchange saturation transfer of the cervical spinal cord at 7 T: CEST of the cervical spinal cord AT 7 T. NMR Biomed. 29, 1249–1257. https://doi.org/10.1002/nbm.3581.

Dula, A.N., Pawate, S., Dortch, R.D., et al., 2016b. Magnetic resonance imaging of the cervical spinal cord in multiple sclerosis at 7T. Mult. Scler. 22, 320–328. https://doi.org/10.1177/1352458515591070.

Finsterbusch, J., Eippert, F., Büchel, C., 2012. Single, slice-specific z-shim gradient pulses improve T2*-weighted imaging of the spinal cord. NeuroImage 59, 2307–2315. https://doi.org/10.1016/j.neuroimage.2011.09.038.

Galley, J., Sutter, R., Germann, C., Wanivenhaus, F., Nanz, D., 2021. High-resolution in vivo MR imaging of intraspinal cervical nerve rootlets at 3 and 7 tesla. Eur. Radiol. https://doi.org/10.1007/s00330-020-07557-3.

Henning, A., Koning, W., Fuchs, A., et al., 2016. 1H MRS in the human spinal cord at 7 T using a dielectric waveguide transmitter, RF shimming and a high density receive array: spinal cord MRS 7 T. NMR Biomed. 29, 1231–1239. https://doi.org/10.1002/nbm.3541.

Kogan, F., Singh, A., Debrosse, C., et al., 2013. Imaging of glutamate in the spinal cord using GluCEST. NeuroImage 77, 262–267. https://doi.org/10.1016/j.neuroimage.2013.03.072.

Kraff, O., Bitz, A.K., Kruszona, S., et al., 2009. An eight-channel phased array RF coil for spine MR imaging at 7 T. Investig. Radiol. 44, 734–740. https://doi.org/10.1097/RLI.0b013e3181b24ab7.

Lefeuvre, J., Qi, J., de Zwart, J., et al., 2016. MRI of the thoracic spinal cord in multiple sclerosis at 7T. In: Proceedings of the Annual Meeting of ISMRM.

Lévy, S., Rapacchi, S., Massire, A., et al., 2020. Intravoxel incoherent motion at 7 tesla to quantify human spinal cord perfusion: limitations and promises. Magn. Reson. Med. 84, 1198–1217. https://doi.org/10.1002/mrm.28195.

Lévy, S., Roche, P., Guye, M., Callot, V., 2021. Feasibility of human spinal cord perfusion mapping using dynamic susceptibility contrast imaging at 7T: preliminary results and identified guidelines. Magn. Reson. Med. 85, 1183–1194. https://doi.org/10.1002/mrm.28559.

Lopez Rios, N., Topfer, R., Foias, A., et al., 2019. Integrated AC/DC coil and dipole Tx array for 7T MRI of the spinal cord. In: Proceedings of the Annual Meeting of ISMRM.

Marques, J.P., Kober, T., Krueger, G., van der Zwaag, W., Van de Moortele, P.-F., Gruetter, R., 2010. MP2RAGE, a self bias-field corrected sequence for improved segmentation and T1-mapping at high field. NeuroImage 49, 1271–1281. https://doi.org/10.1016/j.neuroimage.2009.10.002.

Massire, A., Taso, M., Besson, P., Guye, M., Ranjeva, J.-P., Callot, V., 2016. High-resolution multi-parametric quantitative magnetic resonance imaging of the human cervical spinal cord at 7T. NeuroImage 143, 58–69. https://doi.org/10.1016/j.neuroimage.2016.08.055.

Massire, A., Feiweier, T., Kober, T., et al., 2018a. MR imaging of the cervical spinal cord at 7T: a multiparametric portfolio. Magnetom Flash—Siemens Healthineers 8.

Massire, A., Rasoanandrianina, H., Taso, M., et al., 2018b. Feasibility of single-shot multi-level multi-angle diffusion tensor imaging of the human cervical spinal cord at 7T: transverse 7T DTI of the whole cervical spinal cord. Magn. Reson. Med. 80, 947–957. https://doi.org/10.1002/mrm.27087.

Massire, A., Demortière, S., Lehmann, P., et al., 2019. High-resolution multiparametric quantitative MRI of the cervical spinal cord at 7T: preliminary results at the early stage of multiple sclerosis. In: Proceedings of the Annual Meeting of ISMRM.

Massire, A., Rasoanandrianina, H., Guye, M., Callot, V., 2020. Anterior fissure, central canal, posterior septum and more: new insights into the cervical spinal cord gray and white matter regional organization using T1 mapping at 7T. NeuroImage 205, 116275. https://doi.org/10.1016/j.neuroimage.2019.116275.

May, M.W., Hansen, S.-L.J.D., Mahmutovic, M., et al., 2022. A patient-friendly 16-channel transmit/64-channel receive coil array for combined head–neck MRI at 7 tesla. Magn. Reson. Med. https://doi.org/10.1002/mrm.29288.

Medina, N.J.L., Gros, C., Cohen-Adad, J., Callot, V., Troter, A.L., 2021. 2D multi-class model for gray and white matter segmentation of the cervical spinal cord at 7T. ArXiv211006516 Cs Eess. Available from: http://arxiv.org/abs/2110.06516.

Oh, S.-H., Shin, W., Lee, J., Lowe, M.J., 2018. Variable density magnetization transfer (vdMT) imaging for 7T MR imaging. NeuroImage 168, 242–249. https://doi.org/10.1016/j.neuroimage.2016.09.009.

Ouellette, R., Treaba, C.A., Granberg, T., et al., 2020. 7 T imaging reveals a gradient in spinal cord lesion distribution in multiple sclerosis. Brain 143, 2973–2987. https://doi.org/10.1093/brain/awaa249.

Padormo, F., Beqiri, A., Hajnal, J.V., Malik, S.J., 2016. Parallel transmission for ultrahigh-field imaging. NMR Biomed. https://doi.org/10.1002/nbm.3313.

Raaijmakers, A.J.E., Italiaander, M., Voogt, I.J., et al., 2016. The fractionated dipole antenna: a new antenna for body imaging at 7 tesla. Magn. Reson. Med. https://doi.org/10.1002/mrm.25596.

Roussel, T., Le Fur, Y., Guye, M., Viout, P., Ranjeva, J.-P., Callot, V., 2022. Respiratory-gated quantitative MR spectroscopy of the human spinal cord at 7 T. Magn. Reson. Med. 87 (6), 2600–2612. https://doi.org/10.1002/mrm.29182.

Seifert, A.C., Kong, Y., Miller, K.L., Tracey, I., Vannesjo, S.J., 2019. Finger-tapping task fMRI in the human cervical spinal cord at 7T. In: Proceedings of the Annual Meeting of ISMRM.

Seifert, A.C., Vannesjo, S.J., 2020. Spatial specificity of BOLD signal in the spinal cord at 7T using a noxious thermal stimulus. In: Proceedings of the Annual Meeting of ISMRM.

Sigmund, E.E., Suero, G.A., Hu, C., et al., 2012. High-resolution human cervical spinal cord imaging at 7T. NMR Biomed. 25, 891–899. https://doi.org/10.1002/nbm.1809.

Topfer, R., Starewicz, P., Lo, K.-M., et al., 2016. A 24-channel shim array for the human spinal cord: design, evaluation, and application. Magn. Reson. Med. 76, 1604–1611. https://doi.org/10.1002/mrm.26354.

Vannesjo, S.J., Miller, K.L., Clare, S., Tracey, I., 2018. Spatiotemporal characterization of breathing-induced B0 field fluctuations in the cervical spinal cord at 7T. NeuroImage 167, 191–202. https://doi.org/10.1016/j.neuroimage.2017.11.031.

Vannesjo, S.J., Clare, S., Kasper, L., Tracey, I., Miller, K.L., 2019. A method for correcting breathing-induced field fluctuations in T2*-weighted spinal cord imaging using a respiratory trace. Magn. Reson. Med. 81, 3745–3753. https://doi.org/10.1002/mrm.27664.

Vossen, M., Teeuwisse, W., Reijnierse, M., Collins, C.M., Smith, N.B., Webb, A.G., 2011. A radiofrequency coil configuration for imaging the human vertebral column at 7T. J. Magn. Reson. 208, 291–297. https://doi.org/10.1016/j.jmr.2010.11.004.

Zhang, B., Seifert, A.C., Kim, J.-W., Borrello, J., Xu, J., 2017. 7 tesla 22-channel wrap-around coil array for cervical spinal cord and brainstem imaging. Magn. Reson. Med. 78, 1623–1634. https://doi.org/10.1002/mrm.26538.

Zhao, W., Cohen-Adad, J., Polimeni, J.R., et al., 2014. Nineteen-channel receive array and four-channel transmit array coil for cervical spinal cord imaging at 7T: RF coil for spinal cord MRI at 7T. Magn. Reson. Med. 72, 291–300. https://doi.org/10.1002/mrm.24911.

Diffusion and perfusion imaging at ultra-high field

Diffusion MRI at ultra-high field strengths

20

Markus Nilsson

Diagnostic Radiology, Department of Clinical Sciences Lund, Lund University, Lund, Sweden

Highlights

- Diffusion MRI (dMRI) benefits from the increased signal-to-noise ratio offered by ultra-high field (UHF) strengths, but only if the echo time can be kept short.
- The image-readout strategy needs special attention in UHF-dMRI due to the increased magnetic field inhomogeneities.
- Multiple methods have been developed for the acquisition of high-resolution dMRI.

20.1 Introduction

20.1.1 Why diffusion MRI and MRS?

The microstructure of tissue influences its function, but analysis of the microstructure requires dedicated tools. For example, the white matter of a dissected brain appears rather uniform to the naked eye. However, with a microscope and appropriate stains we can see cellular components appear such as axons and the myelin sheaths that wrap the axons. Furthermore, the direction and the path of the axon determine the brain areas that it connects to and its diameter determines how fast it transmits electrical impulses. MRI typically has a resolution of 1 mm isotropic or worse, although custom sequences and ultra-high field strengths can enable resolutions in the submillimeter regime. This is, however, still insufficient to resolve the microstructure as cell sizes are typically found in the range of 1–10 μm. A viable alternative is to use diffusion MRI (dMRI), which yields information about the tissue microstructure by probing thermally driven random molecular displacements of water molecules.

Diffusion MRI is a general technique that supports different use cases, each with unique and specific advantages. For example, diffusion-weighted imaging (DWI) can reveal stroke lesions minutes after onset. Mapping the apparent diffusion coefficient (ADC) provides a parameter associated with tumor cellularity. Diffusion tensor imaging (DTI) reveals the general direction of elongated microscopic structures such as axons. Together with more sophisticated methods for estimating fiber directions such as constrained spherical deconvolution (CSD), it can be used to map the connectivity of the brain. In addition, there are methods that in specific situations provide metrics associated with specific features of the tissue microstructure such as the axonal water fraction, the amount of elongated cellular structures, or the tissue heterogeneity in tumors. Some authors have crafted excellent reviews of such methods (Tournier et al., 2011; Novikov et al., 2019; Alexander et al., 2019; Szczepankiewicz et al., 2021), including their application at ultra-high field strengths (Gallichan, 2018). Here, we will

Advances in Magnetic Resonance Technology and Applications. Volume 10. ISSN 2666-9099. https://doi.org/10.1016/B978-0-323-99898-7.00036-5

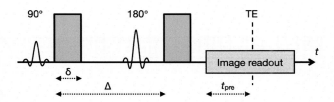

FIG. 20.1

Pulse sequence for spin echo diffusion MRI. A pair of diffusion-encoding magnetic field gradients (blue) is inserted into a spin echo, with a specified duration (δ) and time between their leading edges (Δ). The image readout is typically composed of a Cartesian echo-planar readout, but alternatives that reduce the time from the start of the image acquisition to the echo time (t_{pre}) are important to consider as this minimizes the echo time and thus improves the signal-to-noise ratio.

consider how dMRI can utilize the SNR benefits of higher field strengths to enhance our ability to non-invasively map the tissue microstructure of the living human body.

20.1.2 Basics of diffusion MRI

Diffusion MRI is enabled by the use of gradient waveforms that link molecular displacements to an attenuation of the MR signal. The attenuation is determined by the strength of the diffusion-weighting (b), defined as

$$b = \int q^2(t) \, dt \text{ with } q(t) = \gamma \int_0^t g(t')dt', \qquad (20.1)$$

where γ is the gyromagnetic ratio and $g(t)$ is the effective gradient waveform that takes effects of refocusing by radiofrequency pulses into account. Most commonly, the diffusion encoding is implemented by inserting a pair of pulsed gradients in a spin echo (SE) sequence and using echo-planar imaging (EPI) for the image readout (Fig. 20.1). In that case, the b-value is given by

$$b = \gamma^2 \delta^2 g^2 \left(\Delta - \frac{\delta}{3} \right), \qquad (20.2)$$

where δ is the duration of the gradient pulse, Δ is the separation between their leading edges, and g is the gradient amplitude. However, note that there are alternatives to the pulsed-gradient spin echo approach which are useful in specific situations (Alexander et al., 2019; Szczepankiewicz et al., 2021).

20.2 Diffusion MRI and SNR

Maps of parameters such as the ADC are produced by solving an inverse problem, where the parameter is estimated from a set of MR signals acquired with different gradient waveforms. The precision of the parameter estimate is ultimately determined by the signal-to-noise ratio (SNR) of the MR signal.

20.2.1 SNR and SNR efficiency

To analyze precision in dMRI at UHF, we must consider the factors that influence the signal-to-noise ratio (SNR) (Vaughan et al., 2001). For the spin echo (SE) case (Fig. 20.1), we will consider five factors:

$$SNR_{SE} \propto f(B_0) \cdot V \cdot A \cdot (1 - \exp(-TR/T_1)) \cdot \exp(-TE/T_2), \qquad (20.3)$$

where B_0 is the magnetic field strength, $f(\cdot)$ is a function mapping field strength to the base-rate SNR, V is the voxel volume, A is a factor that accounts for how the image is acquired and reconstructed, TR and TE are the repetition and echo times, respectively, and T_1 and T_2 are the longitudinal and transversal relaxation times, respectively. Note that this is the SNR per shot, meaning the SNR for a single repetition of the spin echo experiment. Apart from SNR, we also consider the SNR efficiency (ρ) defined as the SNR per unit time

$$\rho = SNR \sqrt{N_{DWI}/T}, \qquad (20.4)$$

where N_{DWI} is the number of acquired DWI volumes and T is the total scan time. A volume refers to the full stack of slices covering the target volume. The precision of microstructure estimates is also determined by the imaging protocol, including what b-values and encoding gradient waveforms are used (Alexander et al., 2019). However, the protocol influence is generally field-independent and will not be further considered here. Note that $T = TR \cdot N_{DWI}$ for single-shot image readouts such as EPI, where the full k-space of an image slice is acquired for each excitation.

20.2.2 Effects of the diffusion protocol on the SNR

There is much to learn already from Eq. 20.3. With all other factors equal and assuming a linear dependence of SNR on B_0, going from 3T to 7T would increase the SNR by approximately 230%. This could be used to reduce either the total scan time or the voxel size by approximately 60% with retained SNR. Note that this is a conservative estimate, as the SNR increase with field strength may be superlinear (Le Ster et al., 2022). On the downside, T_1 is longer and T_2 shorter at 7T compared with 3T (Uğurbil et al., 2013), which may partially or fully negates the SNR increase. The detrimental effect of longer T_1 could be addressed by prolonging TR. This would increase SNR per shot but reduce the number of acquisitions per time unit and thus reduce the SNR efficiency. In gradient echo-based imaging, this problem can be partially mitigated by reducing flip angles but this is not an option for dMRI as it is based on a spin echo. The detrimental effect of shorter T_2 could be addressed by reducing TE; however, for a given b-value, the minimal TE is determined by the maximal gradient amplitude available at the system (consider Eq. 20.2). Fig. 20.2 illustrates the difference in SNR between 3T and 7T for various TR and TE. It shows a situation assuming that an 80 mT/m gradient coil is available at both field strengths. In that case, the SNR is expected to be 40%–50% higher at 7T for b-values up to 1.0 ms/μm^2 (often written as 1000 s/mm^2). This is in line with experimental results (Polders et al., 2011). For higher b-values, the SNR advantage is smaller or absent as TE must increase to allow for longer diffusion encoding gradients to reach the desired b-value, and the acquired signal is reduced with TE due to the shorter T_2. Note that the SNR also depends on how duty cycle issues are handled. Using high b-values tends to demand more energy to be put into the gradient coil, which heats the coil more. If the heating power exceeds the cooling power, the duty cycle must be reduced to get them to balance again, meaning a longer TR is required. This reduces the SNR efficiency. Alternatively, the TE can be extended to allow for longer lasting but weaker gradients. This also produces less heating (Szczepankiewicz et al., 2021). At 7T, however, this strategy yields worse SNR and worse SNR efficiency compared with the strategy where TE is minimized and TR prolonged as much as needed for the heating and cooling to come into balance. This example serves to illustrate that details regarding both the hardware and software are important to understand in order to optimize the SNR.

Note that Fig. 20.2 shows the SNR typical for white matter. In more liquid tissue such as in white matter lesions and some types of tumors, we expect longer T_2 relaxation times which make the SNR

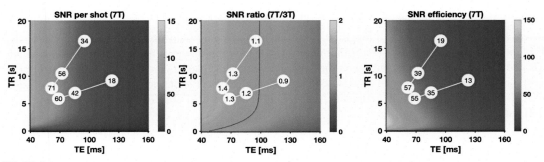

FIG. 20.2

Plots of SNR per shot for 7T, the ratio of the SNR per shot for 7T versus 3T, and the SNR efficiency per time unit for 7T. The calculation assumed values of the T_1/T_2 relaxation times typical of white matter: 800/70 ms for 3T and 1200/45 ms for 7T (Rydhög et al., 2014). White circles show examples of TE/TR combinations that could be achieved in a protocol where 60 slices are acquired and the b-value is 1.0, 2.5, or 10 ms/μm^2 with a system having a maximal gradient amplitude of 80 mT/m and a situation where the refocusing pulse is assumed to take 8 ms and t_{pre} in Fig. 20.1 is 15 ms. Higher TE/TR are associated with higher b-values. The two sets of lines indicate two different strategies for dealing with duty cycle requirements. The first (top line) represents a strategy that minimizes TE. This is energy-demanding and entails a penalty in terms of additional prolongation of TR to accommodate duty cycle requirements. The second (bottom line) represents a strategy that strives to minimize TR and thereby extends TE as well as the diffusion encoding time, which achieves more energy-efficient diffusion encoding. The red line in the middle panel follows the break-even point where the SNR ratio is 1. This means that 7T holds an advantage over 3T to the left of it and a disadvantage to the right of it.

more favorable for 7T than what is the case in white matter. The figure is also only relevant for diffusion encoding in a spin echo. Alternative sequence designs such as the diffusion-weighted stimulated-echo sequence trade some of the transversal relaxation for longitudinal relaxation by storing the magnetization in the longitudinal axis during the diffusion time (Schick, 1998). This means the sequence can be more favorable at 7T, in particular in tissues with exceptionally short T_2 such as the fixed postmortem brain (Harms et al., 2019). However, for the healthy in vivo brain, a detailed comparison of spin echo and stimulated echo diffusion-weighted preparations shows theoretical SNR benefits of the stimulated echo sequence only for very high b-values above 5 ms/μm^2 (Reischauer et al., 2012). This comes to no surprise as this is the weak spot for the diffusion-weighted spin echo sequence (Fig. 20.2).

20.2.3 Inhomogeneity

Diffusion MRI at ultra-high field strengths offers SNR benefits compared to lower fields, but as we saw in Fig. 20.2, this advantage can be squandered unless we address the challenges associated with the detrimental effects of shorter T_2 and longer T_1. Apart from such concerns, there are also challenges related to the image readout. These challenges are caused by larger B_1 and B_0 inhomogeneities, which are essential to address in order to realize the tentative SNR benefits of ultra-high field strengths (Choi et al., 2011).

20.2.3.1 B_1 inhomogeneity

The inhomogeneity in B_1 manifests when the Larmor frequency increases to a level where the associated radiofrequency wavelength starts to match the size of the object (see Chapter 7 for details). At 7T, the wavelength is approximately 1 m in air but only about 10 cm in the human body due to its dielectric properties (Schmitt et al., 2006). As a consequence, interference effects appear and the B_1 becomes inhomogeneous. This is problematic, as it can cause complete or partial loss of signal, in particular in the temporal lobes. Strategies to homogenize B_1 and partially mitigate this effect include the use of dielectric pads (Webb et al., 2022) and parallel transmission (Wu et al., 2018). Even so, these phenomena warrant careful pilot investigations in the setup of dMRI studies targeting the temporal lobe.

20.2.3.2 B_0 inhomogeneity

The effect of B_0 inhomogeneities on images acquired with an EPI-based readout—the most commonly used readout strategy in dMRI—is spatial distortions. It can also cause image blurring, which will be discussed later. The distortions occur as the Larmor frequency differs across the image, which translates to distortions in directions with long readout times, which for EPI is the phase encoding direction. Distortions can be corrected in postprocessing (Andersson et al., 2003), but should be minimized in the image acquisition setup if possible. Apart from advanced strategies to better homogenize (shim) the field (see Chapter 6), distortions can be minimized by traversing the k-space faster, using for example parallel imaging (Bammer et al., 2002) or techniques for reduced field-of-view imaging (von Morze et al., 2010). These techniques can also be combined to achieve image resolutions as high as 800 μm isotropic (Heidemann et al., 2012). However, faster traversal of the k-space (higher bandwidths) also reduces the SNR efficiency, as less time is spent listening to the signal. This is an issue of concern because in principle the B_0 inhomogeneities scale with field strength, meaning that the k-space must be traversed in less than half the time at 7T compared with 3T for the same levels of distortions. Fulfilling this condition reduces the SNR by approximately 35% at 7T compared with a situation where the readout strategies are identical on both field strengths. Another but related challenge is the shorter T_2^* at higher fields (Peters et al., 2007). A shorter T_2^* means that if all other things are equal, higher k-space frequencies are attenuated more, which leads to image blurring and reduced effective resolution (Constable and Gore, 1992). This can again be addressed by techniques that traverse the k-space faster, at the expense of the SNR. Methods for faster traversal of the k-space and their effects on SNR are covered in more detail in the next section.

20.2.4 Effects of excitation and image readout strategies on SNR

Traversing the k-space faster can be achieved by different means such as merely increasing the bandwidth of the EPI readout (by using stronger gradients during the readout), using parallel imaging techniques or reducing the resolution (increasing the distance between k-space lines). Regardless of what technique is used, traversing the k-space faster means a shorter time is used to acquire the signal, which reduces the SNR. This can be incorporated in the SNR analysis by considering the image-acquisition related factor (A) in Eq. 20.3. In general terms, this factor is given by

$$A \propto \sqrt{T_A} \cdot g, \tag{20.5}$$

where T_A is the time spent to acquire one k-space and g is here not the gradient amplitude but an error-propagation factor that depends on the k-space sampling method and image reconstruction algorithm

(Pruessmann et al., 1999). We will now consider how this factor is affected by image acquisition methods that go beyond just increasing the bandwidth.

20.2.4.1 Parallel imaging
Parallel imaging is an image acquisition and reconstruction technique where the k-space is subsampled by only acquiring every R-th line of k-space, where R is the acceleration factor (Pruessmann et al., 1999; Bammer et al., 2002). This would normally result in fold-over artifacts, but parallel imaging techniques utilize the local and unique sensitivity profiles of multiple receiver coils to reconstruct an image without such artifacts. By omitting the acquisition of k-space lines, the k-space is traversed faster in the phase encoding direction and thereby distortions are reduced. However, it causes two types of SNR penalties. One that is due to the shorter time during which the k-space data is acquired, and one due to the so-called g-factor (Eq. 20.5). This factor increases with the acceleration factor but is not uniform in space. It is close to one in regions where a single coil is dominantly sensitive and highest in regions far away from all coils where many coils have similar sensitivity. The g-factor is lower at higher fields (Wiesinger et al., 2004), however, which means that higher parallel acceleration factors can be used with less SNR penalty (Reischauer et al., 2012). High acceleration factors are desired in order to reduce distortions and blurring as discussed above but also in itself reduce the SNR. Balancing distortions and SNR is not trivial, and one may need to accept either lower SNR or higher distortions than desired (Reischauer et al., 2012).

20.2.4.2 Readout segmentation
Readout segmentation techniques can also be used to increase the speed of the readout in the phase direction. This is achieved by acquiring k-space lines in multiple shots, meaning each shot can emit some k-space lines. Compared with single-shot readouts, this increases the SNR of the reconstructed image by the square root of the number of segments but does not in itself change the SNR efficiency unless TE or TR is also changed. Readout segmentation tends to demand the use of navigators, however, in order to unwrap the near random low-frequency phase deviations seen in dMRI due to the pulsatile motion of the brain. The approach has been used to acquire diffusion-weighted images with submillimeter in-plane resolution (Heidemann et al., 2012; Jeong et al., 2013). Fig. 20.3 illustrates the benefits of readout segmentation for reduced distortions.

20.2.4.3 Slab and multislice readouts
A common factor of parallel imaging and readout segmentation is that they have a limited effect on TR but can slightly reduce TE. Thus, the minimal TR is still determined by the product between the number of slices and the time it takes to acquire one slice or segment of the k-space (a shot). This is different for acceleration techniques such as simultaneous multislice (Feinberg and Setsompop, 2013) or slab-based readouts (Wu et al., 2016; Setsompop et al., 2018). These have a limited effect on the time per shot but allow the acquisition of many slices per shot. Hence, they do not directly target issues such as distortions and blurring but they rather enable faster imaging. This can increase the SNR efficiency considerably, which is of particular relevance for high-resolution dMRI (Engström and Skare, 2013). Shortening TR improves the SNR efficiency until the detrimental effects of a slow saturation recovery outcompete that of increased number of averages (Vis et al., 2021). This can be analyzed by considering that the SNR efficiency is effectively proportional to

A. Single-shot EPI

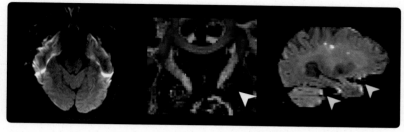

B. Readout-segmented EPI with simultaneous multi-slice

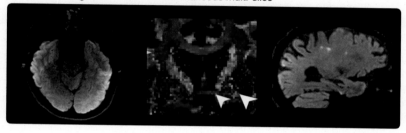

FIG. 20.3

Single-shot EPI versus readout-segmented EPI. The leftmost pair of images shows trace-weighted images in a region with strong distortions. The use of a multishot EPI sequence leads to reduced distortions. The middle pair shows a directional encoded FA map, where the anterior commissure is absent due to distortions with single-shot EPI but not multishot EPI (white arrows). Finally, the rightmost pair shows images from a lacunar stroke patient. Regions with signal pileup due to distortions appear similar to stroke lesions (yellow arrows). *Images adapted from Frost et al. (2015) (license: CC BY 4.0).*

$$\rho \propto \left(1 - \exp\left(-\frac{\text{TR}}{T_1}\right)\right)\sqrt{\frac{1}{\text{TR}}}, \tag{20.6}$$

which has a relatively flat optimum in the range where TR is between 100% and 150% of T_1. As T_1 increases with field strength, it means that the highest possible SNR efficiency is lower at higher fields as the optimal TR range is prolonged. This does not mean that techniques to reduce TR are not useful, however. On the contrary, imaging with thin slices, readout segmented methods, and SAR management all tends to increase TR considerably so that acceleration techniques are needed to even approach the optimal TR (Frost et al., 2015). Note that methods that work well on 3T such as simultaneous multislice imaging are not always immediately translatable to 7T due to issues concerning SAR and B_1 (Eichner et al., 2014). Fig. 20.4 illustrates the quality that can be obtained using a three-dimensional multislab acquisition.

20.2.5 Other aspects to consider

Apart from the previous topics concerning sequence timing, signal preparation, and image readout and their relationship to relaxation and SNR, there are other factors that also need to be considered in the

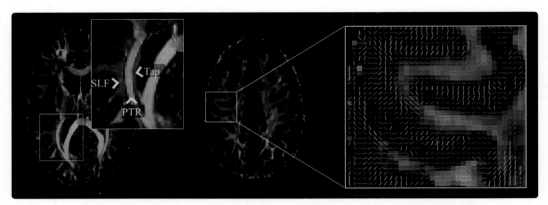

FIG. 20.4

DTI with 1 mm resolution. The left image shows a diffusion-encoded color map, with the inset illustrating how the high spatial resolution enables crisp disambiguation of structures such as the superior longitudinal fasciculus (SLF), posterior thalamic radiation (PTR), and the tapetum of the corpus callosum (Tap). These can be difficult to separate with 2 mm resolution. The rightmost set of images shows how cortical anisotropy is clearly detected with high-resolution DTI. The direction of the stripes shows the primary diffusion direction. It follows the fibers in white matter and is perpendicular to the cortical surface in the gray matter. *Images were adapted from Wu et al. (2016) (license: CC BY 4.0).*

context of dMRI at ultra-high field strengths. Such factors include fat suppression and SAR management, which we have only briefly mentioned before. Furthermore, we will touch briefly upon alternative diffusion encoding strategies and their application in ultra-high field strengths.

20.2.5.1 Fat suppression and SAR management

Fat suppression in dMRI is usually performed with a fat-selective saturation pulse prior to the main excitation pulse. However, such an approach performs poorly in situations where the B_0 inhomogeneity is large, as the fat no longer exhibits a sharp range of resonance frequencies. Alternative strategies involve the use of reversed polarities of the excitation and refocusing slice-selection gradients (Gomori and Grossman, 1987). This means that the fat resonance signals appear on opposite sides of the water peak during the excitation and refocusing pulses. Hence, the fat signal is not refocused. As the absolute chemical shift between water and fat increases with field strength, this method benefits from higher fields. A modification of this strategy has also been proposed, where the bandwidth of the two RF pulses is modulated instead, with the additional benefit of an SAR reduction (Ivanov et al., 2010). A detailed discussion on relative benefits of different fat suppression approaches at 7T can be found in Vu et al. (2015).

20.2.5.2 Diffusion-encoding strategies

Molecular diffusion is independent of field strength, and thus, there is no intrinsic benefit for dMRI at 7T compared with 3T, as opposed to the case of fMRI where the BOLD effect is amplified. However, there are other mechanisms that can be considered or exploited to improve dMRI analysis. First, the field-driven change in T_2 relaxation time can differ between different subcellular compartments.

This could be utilized by executing experiments at multiple field strengths to better probe microstructure or may in itself be beneficial for diffusion-relaxation experiments (Lampinen et al., 2020). Second, the longer T_1 relaxation time at higher field strengths could be useful for stimulated echo-based experiments mapping diffusion time dependence. For example, diffusion times as long as 2 s have been probed using a preclinical 7T scanner (Palombo et al., 2016). Third, there are also some unusual dMRI methods that benefit from higher field strengths. For example, the SNR of diffusion-weighted balanced steady-state free precession is nearly twice as high at 7T than at 3T (Foxley et al., 2014). Another example is the use of stimulated echoes to map both diffusion and T_1 relaxation (Fritz et al., 2021), which is an approach that leverages the benefits and addresses the drawbacks of ultra-high fields.

20.3 Conclusions and outlook

Diffusion MRI at ultra-high field strengths offers the benefit of a higher SNR, but only when drawbacks concerning relaxation times and inhomogeneities are properly managed. An analysis of the interplay between the diffusion encoding strength (b-value) and the shorter T_2 relaxation and longer T_1 relaxation times showed that the SNR benefit is present up to moderately high b-values. Stronger gradients are needed for the benefit to prevail to higher b-values. Magnetic field inhomogeneities increase with field strength, which must be taken into account in the choice of imaging strategy as the inhomogeneities tend to translate to image distortions. Multiple strategies are available, and the aim of the study determines which is the optimal one. Multishot strategies enable high-resolution imaging, at the cost of scan time. Single-shot strategies enable faster imaging but typically lead to higher levels of distortions. Apart from these factors, the design of an optimal dMRI protocol at 7T also needs to consider strategies for fat suppression and SAR management. Although many successful strategies have been developed over the last decade, there are still exciting opportunities for developing new methods to leverage the enhanced SNR afforded by ultra-high field dMRI. Notwithstanding such exciting opportunities, dMRI at 7T with commercially available read-out segmentation methods already offers clear benefits compared with dMRI at 1.5T and 3T for detection of small lesions (Unsgård et al., 2022).

References

Alexander, D.C., Dyrby, T.B., Nilsson, M., Zhang, H., 2019. Imaging brain microstructure with diffusion MRI: practicality and applications. NMR Biomed. 32 (4), e3841.

Andersson, J.L.R., Skare, S., Ashburner, J., 2003. How to correct susceptibility distortions in spin-echo echo-planar images: application to diffusion tensor imaging. Neuroimage 20 (2), 870–888.

Bammer, R., Auer, M., Keeling, S.L., et al., 2002. Diffusion tensor imaging using single-shot SENSE-EPI. Magn. Reson. Med. 48 (1), 128–136.

Choi, S., Cunningham, D.T., Aguila, F., et al., 2011. DTI at 7 and 3 T: systematic comparison of SNR and its influence on quantitative metrics. Magn. Reson. Imaging 29 (6), 739–751.

Constable, R.T., Gore, J.C., 1992. The loss of small objects in variable TE imaging: implications for FSE, RARE, and EPI. Magn. Reson. Med. 28 (1), 9–24.

Eichner, C., Setsompop, K., Koopmans, P.J., et al., 2014. Slice accelerated diffusion-weighted imaging at ultra-high field strength. Magn. Reson. Med. 71 (4), 1518–1525.

Engström, M., Skare, S., 2013. Diffusion-weighted 3D multislab echo planar imaging for high signal-to-noise ratio efficiency and isotropic image resolution. Magn. Reson. Med. 70 (6), 1507–1514.

Feinberg, D.A., Setsompop, K., 2013. Ultra-fast MRI of the human brain with simultaneous multi-slice imaging. J. Magn. Reson. 229, 90–100.

Foxley, S., Jbabdi, S., Clare, S., et al., 2014. Improving diffusion-weighted imaging of post-mortem human brains: SSFP at 7 T. Neuroimage 102 (Pt 2), 579–589.

Fritz, F.J., Poser, B.A., Roebroeck, A., 2021. MESMERISED: super-accelerating T1 relaxometry and diffusion MRI with STEAM at 7 T for quantitative multi-contrast and diffusion imaging. Neuroimage 239, 118285.

Frost, R., Jezzard, P., Douaud, G., Clare, S., Porter, D.A., Miller, K.L., 2015. Scan time reduction for readout-segmented EPI using simultaneous multislice acceleration: diffusion-weighted imaging at 3 and 7 tesla. Magn. Reson. Med. 74 (1), 136–149.

Gallichan, D., 2018. Diffusion MRI of the human brain at ultra-high field (UHF): a review. Neuroimage 168, 172–180.

Gomori, H., Grossman, 1987. Fat suppression by section-select gradient reversal on spin-Echo MR imaging. Radiology. https://inis.iaea.org/search/search.aspx?orig_q=RN:20003084.

Harms, R.L., Tse, D.H., Poser, B.A., Roebroeck, A., 2019. Ultra-high resolution and multi-shell diffusion MRI of intact ex vivo human brains using kT-dSTEAM at 9.4 T. Neuroimage. https://www.sciencedirect.com/science/article/pii/S1053811919306755.

Heidemann, R.M., Anwander, A., Feiweier, T., Knösche, T.R., Turner, R., 2012. K-space and Q-space: combining ultra-high spatial and angular resolution in diffusion imaging using ZOOPPA at 7 T. Neuroimage 60 (2), 967–978.

Ivanov, D., Schäfer, A., Streicher, M.N., Heidemann, R.M., Trampel, R., Turner, R., 2010. A simple low-SAR technique for chemical-shift selection with high-field spin-echo imaging. Magn. Reson. Med. 64 (2), 319–326.

Jeong, H.-K., Gore, J.C., Anderson, A.W., 2013. High-resolution human diffusion tensor imaging using 2-D navigated multishot SENSE EPI at 7 T. Magn. Reson. Med. 69 (3), 793–802.

Lampinen, B., Szczepankiewicz, F., Mårtensson, J., et al., 2020. Towards unconstrained compartment modeling in white matter using diffusion-relaxation MRI with tensor-valued diffusion encoding. Magn. Reson. Med. 84 (3), 1605–1623.

Le Ster, C., Grant, A., Van de Moortele, P.-F., et al., 2022. Magnetic field strength dependent SNR gain at the center of a spherical phantom and up to 11.7T. Magn. Reson. Med. doi:https://doi.org/10.1002/mrm.29391.

Novikov, D.S., Fieremans, E., Jespersen, S.N., Kiselev, V.G., 2019. Quantifying brain microstructure with diffusion MRI: theory and parameter estimation. NMR Biomed. 32 (4), e3998.

Palombo, M., Ligneul, C., Najac, C., et al., 2016. New paradigm to assess brain cell morphology by diffusion-weighted MR spectroscopy in vivo. Proc. Natl. Acad. Sci. U. S. A. 113 (24), 6671–6676.

Peters, A.M., Brookes, M.J., Hoogenraad, F.G., et al., 2007. T2* measurements in human brain at 1.5, 3 and 7 T. Magn. Reson. Chem. https://www.sciencedirect.com/science/article/pii/S0730725X07001701.

Polders, D.L., Leemans, A., Hendrikse, J., Donahue, M.J., Luijten, P.R., Hoogduin, J.M., 2011. Signal to noise ratio and uncertainty in diffusion tensor imaging at 1.5, 3.0, and 7.0 Tesla. J. Magn. Reson. Imaging 33 (6), 1456–1463.

Pruessmann, K.P., Weiger, M., Scheidegger, M.B., Boesiger, P., 1999. SENSE: sensitivity encoding for fast MRI. Magn. Reson. Med. 42 (5), 952–962.

Reischauer, C., et al., 2012. Optimizing signal-to-noise ratio of high-resolution parallel single-shot diffusion-weighted echo-planar imaging at ultrahigh field strengths. Magn. Reson. Med. 67 (3), 679–690.

Rydhög, A.S., van Osch, M.J.P., Lindgren, E., et al., 2014. Intravoxel incoherent motion (IVIM) imaging at different magnetic field strengths: what is feasible? Magn. Reson. Imaging 32 (10), 1247–1258.

Schick, F., 1998. Signal losses in diffusion preparation: comparison between spin-echo, stimulated echo and SEASON. MAGMA 6 (1), 53–61.

Schmitt, F., Potthast, A., Stoeckel, B., Triantafyllou, C., Wiggins, C.J., Wiggins, G., Wald, L.L., 2006. Aspects of clinical imaging at 7T. Ultra High Field Magn. Reson. Imaging 26, 59–104.

Setsompop, K., Fan, Q., Stockmann, J., 2018. High-resolution in vivo diffusion imaging of the human brain with generalized slice dithered enhanced resolution: simultaneous multislice (gSlider-SMS). Magn. Reson. Med. https://onlinelibrary.wiley.com/doi/abs/10.1002/mrm.26653.

Szczepankiewicz, F., Westin, C.-F., Nilsson, M., 2021. Gradient waveform design for tensor-valued encoding in diffusion MRI. J. Neurosci. Methods 348, 109007.

Tournier, J.-D., Mori, S., Leemans, A., 2011. Diffusion tensor imaging and beyond. Magn. Reson. Med. 65 (6), 1532–1556.

Uğurbil, K., Junqian, X., Auerbach, E.J., et al., 2013. Pushing spatial and temporal resolution for functional and diffusion MRI in the human connectome project. Neuroimage 80, 80–104.

Unsgård, R.G., Doan, T.P., Nordlid, K.K., Kvistad, K.A., Goa, P.E., Berntsen, E.M., 2022. Transient global amnesia: 7 Tesla MRI reveals more hippocampal lesions with diffusion restriction compared to 1.5 and 3 Tesla MRI. Neuroradiology, 1–10.

Vaughan, J.T., Garwood, M., Collins, C.M., et al., 2001. 7T vs. 4T: RF power, homogeneity, and signal-to-noise comparison in head images. Magn. Reson. Med. 46 (1), 24–30.

Vis, G., et al., 2021. Accuracy and precision in super-resolution MRI: enabling spherical tensor diffusion encoding at ultra-high b-values and high resolution. NeuroImage 245, 118673.

von Morze, C., Kelley, D.A.C., Shepherd, T.M., Banerjee, S., Duan, X., Hess, C.P., 2010. Reduced field-of-view diffusion-weighted imaging of the brain at 7 T. Magn. Reson. Imaging 28 (10), 1541–1545.

Vu, A.T., Auerbach, E., Lenglet, C., et al., 2015. High resolution whole brain diffusion imaging at 7T for the human connectome project. Neuroimage 122, 318–331.

Webb, A., Shchelokova, A., Slobozhanyuk, A., Zivkovic, I., Schmidt, R., 2022. Novel materials in magnetic resonance imaging: HIGH permittivity ceramics, metamaterials, metasurfaces and artificial dielectrics. MAGMA. doi:https://doi.org/10.1007/s10334-022-01007-5.

Wiesinger, F., Boesiger, P., Pruessmann, K.P., 2004. Electrodynamics and ultimate SNR in parallel MR imaging. Magn. Reson. Med. 52 (2), 376–390.

Wu, W., Poser, B.A., Douaud, G., et al., 2016. High-resolution diffusion MRI at 7T using a three-dimensional multi-slab acquisition. Neuroimage 143, 1–14.

Wu, X., Auerbach, E.J., Vu, A.T., et al., 2018. High-resolution whole-brain diffusion MRI at 7T using radiofrequency parallel transmission. Magn. Reson. Med. 80 (5), 1857–1870.

Ultra-high field brain perfusion MRI

21

Xingfeng Shao[a], William D. Rooney[b], and Danny J.J. Wang[a]

[a]*Laboratory of FMRI Technology (LOFT), USC Mark & Mary Stevens Neuroimaging and Informatics Institute, Keck School of Medicine, University of Southern California, Los Angeles, CA, United States* [b]*Advanced Imaging Research Center, Oregon Health and Science University, Portland, OR, United States*

Highlights
- UHF offers dual benefits for ASL with increased SNR and blood T_1.
- UHF offers increased sensitivity for dynamic contrast-based perfusion MRI.
- UHF perfusion MRI can be performed with (sub)millimeter resolution and high sensitivity.
- Strategies for mitigating B_1/B_0 field inhomogeneity and SAR limitations are being developed.

21.1 Introduction

Ultra-high field (UHF) MRI instruments offer substantial promise for use in applications that quantify cerebral vascular properties. There are several key features of UHF MRI that benefit perfusion imaging and cerebral vasculature phenotyping. Perhaps, the most important is increased signal strength, which delivers higher sensitivity and increased spatial and/or temporal resolution acquisitions in signal-limited techniques such as arterial spin labeling (ASL). Additionally, increased tissue and blood ^1H_2O T_1 values at UHF benefit both dynamic contrast-based techniques and ASL, with increased contrast agent detection sensitivity and increased lifetime of labeled blood water, respectively. Despite the considerable promise of perfusion MRI at ultra-high field, these applications are not yet routine, chiefly owing to B_1 homogeneity issues, increased susceptibility effects, increased specific absorption rate (SAR), reduced T_2^* which result in labeling inefficiency, image distortion and blurring, and decreased temporal stability in time series acquisitions. In this chapter, strategies for improved contrast and non-contrast UHF perfusion MRI of the brain which leverage advantages and mitigate limitations are discussed.

21.2 Potentials and challenges for ASL at UHF

Arterial spin labeling (ASL) is a noncontrast perfusion MRI technique that utilizes magnetically labeled arterial blood water as an endogenous tracer to measure cerebral blood flow (CBF). Common ASL techniques either use an adiabatic inversion pulse or a train of discrete RF pulses to label the blood water in inflowing arteries. Images are acquired following a postlabeling delay (PLD) that allows the labeled blood to flow into the brain tissue, and perfusion images are derived from the difference between control and label acquisitions where the only difference is whether spin labeling is applied. Compared to dynamic susceptibility contrast (DSC) perfusion MRI, ASL techniques have lower signal-to-noise ratio (SNR) and are limited by the T_1 relaxation of the labeled blood. Ultra-high field (UHF) benefits ASL with an increased intrinsic SNR of MRI signal ($B_0^{1.94\pm0.16}$ (Le Ster et al., 2022)) and a prolonged tracer half-life (blood T_1). Theoretical analysis has shown an approximate threefold SNR gain for 7T ASL versus 3T ASL without considering transverse relaxation effects (Zuo et al., 2013). However, considerable obstacles remain to reliably implement ASL sequences at UHF. The transmit B_1 (B_1^+) and B_0 field inhomogeneities may undermine the adiabatic inversion condition, leading to reduced labeling efficiency and/or residual static tissue signal due to imperfect profiles of inversion pulses. UHF ASL is further limited by the SAR of RF pulses that increase approximately quadratically with field strength. ASL sequences generally consist of three blocks of labeling, postlabeling delay (PLD), and image readout, each of which requires specific adaptation and optimization for UHF.

21.2.1 Considerations for labeling

Modern ASL techniques include pulsed ASL (PASL), continuous ASL (CASL), and pseudo-continuous ASL (pCASL). To date, CASL has been performed with separate neck labeling coils at 7T. This was found to be challenging due to the variability of individual anatomy and the difficulty for B_0 shimming in the neck region (Stafford et al., 2016). Both PASL and pCASL at UHF were performed using head coil with spin labeling applied inferior to the imaging slices. For PASL, the existing efforts have been focused on designing and optimizing adiabatic inversion pulses resilient to B_1^+ and B_0 field variations at UHF. The time-resampled frequency-offset-correction-inversion (trFOCI) pulse was designed to overcome the B_1^+ field inhomogeneities at UHF with a genetic algorithm (Hurley et al., 2010). Although B_0 offset was not considered in the design process, the trFOCI pulse has shown resilience to B_1^+ field variations and has been applied in PASL studies at 7T and 9.4T (Bause et al., 2016; Kashyap et al., 2021). A recent study optimized and evaluated four common adiabatic inversion pulses, including hyperbolic-secant (HS), wideband-uniform-rate-smooth-truncation (WURST), FOCI, and trFOCI pulses for flow-sensitive alternating inversion recovery (FAIR) PASL at 7T (Wang et al., 2021a) (Fig. 21.1). Both B_1^+ and B_0 field inhomogeneities were considered in the optimization, and the optimized WURST pulse achieved a good balance between labeling efficiency and residual tissue signal, and it was therefore recommended for 7T PASL. In summary, existing data suggest that trFOCI performs well when B_0 field variation is not large (e.g., for an imaging slab of 40 mm covering the cortex), while WURST may be more suitable for wider coverage of PASL at UHF. In addition, dielectric pads were used to improve the labeling efficiency in PASL studies at UHF (Kashyap et al., 2021).

For pCASL, several strategies have been applied to overcome the B_1^+ and B_0 field inhomogeneities at the labeling plane: (1) dielectric pads and adjustment of labeling location; (2) precalibration for B_0 offset; (3) parallel transmission (pTx) B_1^+ shimming; and (4) optimization of labeling parameters. Earlier 7T pCASL studies used dielectric pads at the neck region to increase B_1^+ field and pCASL labeling efficiency at 7T (Wang et al., 2015). Due to the limited coverage of head coils at UHF, the labeling plane needs to be raised from the neck to the bottom of the cerebrum (at the C1 segment

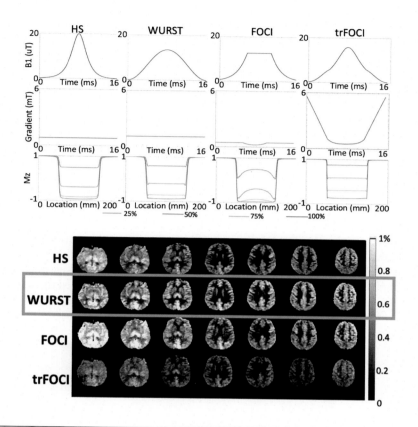

FIG. 21.1

RF and gradient waveforms and inversion profiles of HS, FOCI, trFOCI, and WURST pulses. The peak B_1 amplitude of HS was set to $20\,\mu T$, and the other three pulses were then scaled to have the same SAR as HS. Inversion profiles were simulated with targeted B_1 scaled by 25%, 50%, 75%, and 100% for each pulse. It is seen that trFOCI has a more uniform inversion band but lower labeling efficiency compared with HS and WURST. In vivo results verified simulation results with WURST pulse outperforming HS, FOCI, and trFOCI pulses in terms of labeling efficiency (i.e., signal intensity of center slice) and residual tissue signal (i.e., signal homogeneity across slices, right figure). *Reproduced from Meixner et al. (2021).*

of internal carotid arteries based on Bouthillier classification) to take advantage of the higher B_1^+ amplitude there (Zuo et al., 2013). The pCASL labeling consists of a train of short RF pulses to emulate continuous flow-driven adiabatic inversion. The B_0 offset at inflowing arteries will cause phase errors in pCASL pulse train resulting in a low labeling efficiency. This B_0 offset can be measured by a prescan and compensated by adding an extra RF phase increment and transverse gradient blips into the pCASL RF pulse train (Luh et al., 2013). Parallel transmission (pTx) B_1^+ shimming can be performed to increase the B_1^+ field (with homogeneous distribution) at inflowing arteries within the labeling plane (Wang et al., 2021b; Tong et al., 2020; Meixner et al., 2021). The cost function for B_1^+ shimming optimization included an efficiency term to maximize B_1^+ with the option for including a homogeneity term. PTx B_1^+ shimming has been shown to increase the mean B_1^+ amplitude by 15% (Wang et al., 2021b), 24% (Meixner et al., 2021), and 90% (Tong et al., 2020) compared to the circular polarized (CP) mode, depending on the specific cost function employed. Inspired by the concept of universal pulse for pTx (Gras et al., 2017), a "universal weight" approach has been developed for pTx pCASL based on optimization results from a cohort of subjects, without the need for adjustments for individual subjects during pTx pCASL scans (Fig. 21.2) (Wang et al., 2021b).

Alternatively, pCASL parameters (e.g., RF pulse duration and gap, mean and maximum gradient) can be optimized to achieve a reliable labeling efficiency in the presence of B_1^+ and B_0 field inhomogeneities at 7T. In general, shorter RF pulse duration and gap benefit the resilience of pCASL to B_0 off-resonance. A recent study recommended an optimized pCASL parameter set (RF duration/gap = 300/250 μs, $G_{average}$ = 0.6 mT/m, G_{max} = 6 mT/m) to achieve robust perfusion measurement at 7T without any special B_1^+/B_0 field calibration or shimming (Fig. 21.2). This approach achieved good test-retest repeatability for repeated 7T pCASL scans 1 day apart (intraclass correlation or ICC = 0.66), and the spatial SNR was 78% higher compared to a matched pCASL sequence at 3T (Wang et al., 2021b). This approach may make 7T pCASL applicable to clinical applications without sophisticated and time-consuming calibrations, although the optimized pCASL parameter set may be further improved. For specific applications such as zoomed laminar perfusion imaging, pCASL can also be applied to intracranial arteries with optimized labeling parameters (e.g., reduced flip angle) to achieve a high labeling efficiency (Shao et al., 2020a).

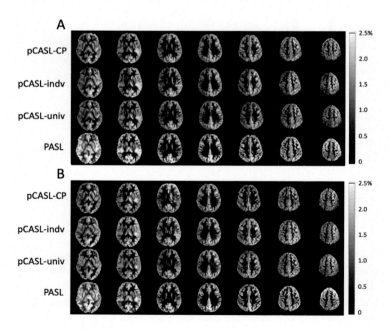

FIG. 21.2

7 T pCASL and PASL perfusion maps of one representative subject at visit 1 (A) and visit 2 (B). Consistent and high-quality perfusion maps were obtained with optimized pCASL sequences with circular polarized (CP) B_1 transmission, individualized, and universal B_1 shimming. Good repeatability was achieved between visit 1 and visit 2. *Reproduced from Alsop et al. (2015).*

21.2.2 Considerations for background suppression

Background suppression (BS) was recommended by the ASL white paper to suppress physiological noise and improve temporal SNR of ASL. Adiabatic inversion pulses are generally applied for BS, the performance of which is susceptible to B_1^+/B_0 field inhomogeneities as well as the short T_2 relaxation times at 7T. Based on our testing (unpublished data), the BS efficiency of optimized HS and WURST pulses is around 90% which is lower than that at 3T. Nevertheless, a recent study showed benefits of BS in improving the temporal SNR of pTx pCASL with 2D echo-planar imaging (EPI) readout at 7T (Meixner et al., 2021). At UHF, the potential benefit of BS needs to be weighed against the potential loss of ASL signals, and the BS pulse needs to be carefully optimized for B_1^+ and B_0 field distributions and short T_2 relaxation times.

21.2.3 Common readout sequences for ASL at UHF

A segmented 3D readout such as gradient and spin echo (GRASE) is optimal for background suppression and is SNR efficient as compared to 2D readouts (Alsop et al., 2015). It also has dual benefits of reduced T_2^* sensitivity and time efficiency and thus has been recommended as the preferred ASL readout at 3T. The shortened transverse relaxation times (T_2 and T_2^*) at 7T may lead to severe blurring. This can be compensated for by increasing the number of segments at the cost of prolonged scan time and additional motion sensitivity. To keep the number of segments and scan time low, it is necessary to apply accelerated image acquisition with constrained reconstruction. For instance, a recent study acquired 3D GRASE pCASL images with isotropic 2 mm resolution at 7T with 12-fold acceleration using 2D Controlled Aliasing in Parallel Imaging (CAIPI) undersampling and total-generalized-variation (TGV) regularized reconstruction (Shao et al., 2020b) (Fig. 21.3A, B). Alternatively, zoomed GRASE imaging can be achieved by switching the directions of excitation and refocusing gradients (Beckett et al., 2020). This has been applied to acquire high-resolution ASL and obtain laminar profiles of resting state and task activation CBF in a selected imaging volume such as the motor and visual cortex (Shao et al., 2020a; Shao et al., 2021).

Single-shot 2D or 3D EPI (Poser et al., 2010) is less sensitive to motion artifacts and has been utilized to obtain ASL images with high temporal resolution and submillimeter spatial resolution. A drawback of the EPI readout is that it is sensitive to susceptibility effects and fast T_2^* decay, two effects that are more pronounced at ultra-high field strengths (Poser & Setsompop, 2018). Thus, advanced B_0-shimming and/or manual shimming adjustments are recommended. However, it still remains challenging to achieve a homogeneous B_0 field across the whole brain ($\sim$1-ppm variation), and postprocessing steps including distortion correction (e.g., TOPUP) and advanced coregistration algorithms (i.e., boundary-based method) (Saad et al., 2009) are necessary. 2D Turbo-FLASH (Fast Low Angle Shot, TFL) is an alternative approach for fast imaging at ultra-high fields due to its relatively low SAR and short TE that minimizes susceptibility artifacts. Zuo et al. (Zuo et al., 2013) demonstrated that TFL-based ASL yielded approximately four times SNR gain at 7T compared to 3T, and TFL has been utilized in two recent PASL and pCASL optimization studies at 7T (Wang et al., 2021a; Wang et al., 2021b). A major drawback of TFL is the relatively long acquisition time. This can be addressed by using simultaneous-multislice (SMS) acceleration (Fig. 21.3C, D) (Wang et al., 2015). SMS techniques can also be applied to EPI and other readout sequences to accelerate ASL scans and reduce T_1 relaxation of the label.

A. Time dependent 2D CAIPI k-space under-sampling pattern for 3D GRASE pCASL

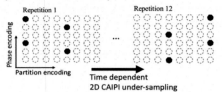

B. Whole-brain CBF maps with 12-fold acceleration and spatial-temporal TGV reconstruction

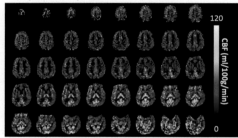

2×2×2 mm³ isotropic spatial resolution

C. Schematic diagram of 2D SMS-TFL pCASL

D. Perfusion images with SB, MB-3 and MB-5 slice acceleration

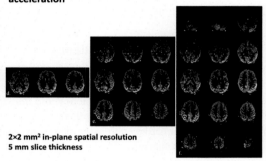

2×2 mm² in-plane spatial resolution
5 mm slice thickness

FIG. 21.3

Acceleration strategies for 2D and 3D pCASL at 7T. (A) Implementation of a time-dependent 2D CAIPI *k*-space undersampling pattern for 3D GRASE pCASL. The total acceleration factor is 12 (3/4 along phase/partition encoding direction). The undersampling pattern is shifted between repetitions to increase the temporal incoherence, which benefits the spatial-temporal TGV regularized reconstruction. (B) The corresponding whole brain CBF maps with spatial-temporal TGV reconstruction with 2 mm isotropic spatial resolution. (C) Schematic diagram of 2D SMS-TFL pCASL. Blue, red, and green lines indicate simultaneously excited image slices for single-band (SB), multiband (MB)-3, and MB-5 slice acceleration. (D) The corresponding example axial perfusion images from the SMS-TFL readout with SB (left), MB-3 (middle), and MB-5 (right) with 2 mm in plane spatial resolution and 5 mm slice thickness. *Panel A and B were adapted from Wang et al. (2015). Panel C and D were adapted from Shao et al. (2020b). Permissions obtained.*

PTx B_1 shimming may be applied in the imaging volume to improve B_1 field homogeneity for image acquisition. To increase B_1 at the labeling plane and increase labeling efficiency (Wang et al., 2021b; Tong et al., 2020; Meixner et al., 2021), dynamic pTx B_1 shimming with two different cost functions for pCASL labeling and image acquisition respectively may be useful, but this approach needs further investigation.

21.2.4 SAR considerations

The SAR of RF power deposition scales quadratically with field strength and becomes a major challenge at 7T. This is especially true for pCASL that uses a long train of RF pulses for labeling. SAR can be reduced by shortening the labeling duration or increasing TR at the cost of SNR efficiency (Wang et al., 2015). Variable-Rate Selective Excitation (VERSE) RF is a promising technique to reduce SAR for pCASL at 7T. VERSE reduces the sampling bandwidth for the RF period with peak B_1 (Tong et al., 2020; Meixner et al., 2021). However, VERSE pulses generally require a longer pulse duration which may affect the robustness of pCASL to B_0 off-resonance effects. Alternatively, the SAR limit can be included in the optimization of pTx B_1 shimming (Tong et al., 2020). The calculation of local SAR requires the virtual observation point (VOP) matrix which needs to be supplied by the coil manufacturer (Eichfelder & Gebhardt, 2011).

21.2.5 Quantification issues

Faster T_2 and T_2^* decay of brain tissue at higher field strength will attenuate the tissue contribution to the ASL signal and may complicate the CBF quantification when the ASL data are analyzed with the single-compartment Kety model (Wang et al., 2002). St Lawrence and Wang (St Lawrence & Wang, 2005) proposed a tracer kinetic model that includes T_2^* differences between capillary blood and tissue. Both theoretical simulations and experimental data showed around 20% decrease in resting state gray matter CBF when TE increased from 19 to 58 ms at 4T (St Lawrence & Wang, 2005). This model also predicted a 24% underestimation of activation-induced CBF increase at 4T and even greater underestimation at 7T. These results suggest that at UHF, ASL data should be carefully analyzed with two-compartment models that take the T_1 and T_2/T_2^* difference between capillaries and tissue into account, unless the data are acquired with sequences insensitive to susceptibility effects (e.g., Turbo-FLASH).

21.2.6 Pushing the limits of spatial resolution

ASL perfusion maps are usually acquired with a moderate spatial resolution of 3–5 mm at 3T or lower field strength. UHF ASL may overcome the limitation of low SNR and achieve high spatial resolutions. FAIR PASL with a 3D EPI readout has been proposed to measure brain perfusion with submillimeter spatial resolution at 7T (Kashyap et al., 2021; Ivanov et al., 2018) (Fig. 21.4A). Kashyap et al. (Kashyap et al., 2021) applied a 3D-EPI-based FAIR PASL which allowed fast acquisition with a volume TR of a few seconds to capture the dynamic CBF changes in response to functional stimuli across cortical layers in human visual cortex. The T_2^*/BOLD contribution to CBF activation was mitigated by dividing the ASL signal by the mean EPI signal (Fig. 21.4B, C).

Shao et al. (Shao et al., 2020a; Shao et al., 2021) proposed to label intracranial arteries with pCASL and acquire 1 mm^3 isotropic volume with 3D zoomed GRASE (Fig. 21.4D). The pCASL parameters were optimized to achieve >80% labeling efficiency and low SAR. With multidelay resting state pCASL, they found that the arterial transit time in superficial layers is $\sim$100 ms shorter than in middle/deep layers, revealing the time course of labeled blood flowing from pial arteries to downstream microvasculature. Resting state CBF peaked in the middle layers which is highly consistent with microvascular density measured from human cortex specimens (Fig. 21.4E). They also observed that finger tapping induced a two-peak laminar profile of CBF increases in the primary motor cortex (M1), and visuospatial attention induced a predominant CBF increase in deep layers and a smaller CBF increase on top of the lower baseline CBF in superficial layers of the primary visual cortex (V1) (Fig. 21.4E). Relatively long volume TR and limited spatial coverage are two major limitations of zoomed GRASE pCASL and can be potentially mitigated by accelerated image acquisition and stimulus-dithering methods (Kim et al., 2020).

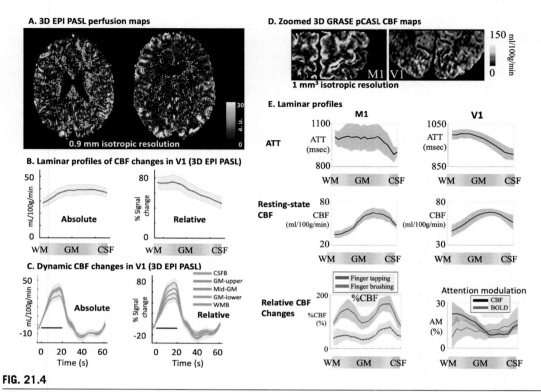

FIG. 21.4

Acquisition strategies for laminar ASL at 7T. (A) A superior (left) and an inferior (right) slice of baseline 3D EPI PASL perfusion maps overlaid on the T_1-weighted anatomical image. 3D-EPI allows fast acquisition with a volume TR of a few seconds and 0.9 mm isotropic spatial resolution. (B) and (C) show the absolute (left) and relative (right) laminar profiles CBF changes and dynamic CBF changes in response to functional stimuli across cortical layers in human visual cortex. (D) The zoomed 3D GRASE pCASL CBF maps in M1 (left) and V1 (right). (E) The laminar profiles of resting state ATT (first row), CBF (second row) in M1 (left column), and V1 (right column). The bottom left panel of (E) shows the laminar profiles relative CBF changes evoked by finger tapping and finger brushing tasks in M1. The bottom right panel of (E) shows the laminar profiles of CBF and BOLD evoked by attention modulation in V1. *Panels A–C were adapted from Kashyap et al. (2021). Panels D and E were adapted from Shao et al. (2021). Permissions obtained.*

21.3 Contrast-enhanced MRI at ultra-high field: Challenges and solutions

Contrast agents (CA) have been utilized since the earliest days of MRI and continue to find widespread use in research and clinical applications. Although, minimally invasive, these agents offer unique advantages for characterizing cerebral vascular properties including blood volume, blood flow, transit times, and blood–brain barrier permeabilities (Sourbron & Buckley, 2012). They complement ASL-based techniques (Weber et al., 2003), particularly for tissue with long transit times that are difficult to investigate using ASL. Although most clinical studies are currently performed at 3T and below, UHF MRI instruments are becoming more common as these provide increased SNR and enhanced image contrast which together can be used to generate high spatial resolution images with remarkable feature conspicuity. An important consideration in UHF MRI relates to contrast-enhanced techniques and the specific challenges and opportunities these techniques present. These techniques involve the intravenous administration of a paramagnetic MRI CA which is detected indirectly via a concentration dependent catalysis of ^1H_2O MRI relaxation (Rooney et al., 2007).

21.3.1 Contrast agent detection sensitivity and UHF

The variation in tissue ^1H_2O R_1 values at any given B_0 can be empirically modeled using Eq. 21.1, where R_I' is the value for pure saline (at physiological temperature), r_{1M} and r_{1CA} are the respective macromolecular site and CA longitudinal relaxivities (a scaling factor that relates a site's potency to catalyze the relaxation rate constant), each of which has a characteristic field dependence

$$R_1 = R_I' + r_{1M}f_M + r_{1CA}[\text{CA}] = R_{10} + r_{1CA}[\text{CA}]. \tag{21.1}$$

In principle, each relaxivity could be further indexed for brain region or tissue subtype. The concentration of macromolecular sites is proportional to the macromolecular mass fraction, f_M (the macromolecular volume fraction, if the density is taken as unity (Rooney et al., 2007)). Thus, we can define r_{1M} as the relaxivity per unit macromolecular mass fraction and [CA] as the local tissue CA concentration. An assumption inherent in Eq. 21.1 is that fast-exchange-limit conditions (on the T_1 timescale) apply for water interchange between all sites. That is, within a given measurement volume, water can sample all possible equivalent sites with exchange rate constants that are much greater than the difference in site-associated R_1 values.

It is well known that longitudinal relaxivities of low molecular weight gadolinium-based contrast agents (GBCA) decrease with increasing B_0, which by itself leads to reduced detection sensitivity. However, intrinsic tissue longitudinal macromolecular relaxivity (r_{1M}, principally due to the macromolecular volume fraction) also decreases with increasing B_0 and to an even greater extent than r_{1CA} in the clinically relevant field B_0 range (Rooney et al., 2007). Taken together, these competing effects result in CA detectability increasing with B_0 due to relaxivity considerations alone. Based on literature values for the field dependence of tissue longitudinal and cell-free GdDTPA^{2-} relaxivities, the expected B_0-dependence of CA detection sensitivity (which is proportional to r_{1CA}/R_{10}, R_{10} is nominal tissue ^1H_2O R_1) is plotted in Fig. 21.5A.

To validate the CA detection sensitivities predicted in Fig. 21.5A, we compared real-world changes in tissue ^1H_2O R_1 following CA administration. The results are summarized in Fig. 21.5B, C, showing the normalized difference plots for ^1H_2O R_1 (i.e., $\Delta R_1/R_{10} = (R_1 - R_{10})/R_{10} = r_{1CA}[\text{CA}]/R_{10}$; R_{10} is the pre-contrast tissue R_1) in the temporalis muscle and white matter (WM), tissues with blood vessels which differ markedly in CA extravasation behavior. The blue bars and the red bars measure the group-average-normalized ΔR_1 values at 3T and 7T, respectively, and for the same individuals. For muscle tissue (Fig. 21.5B), the 7T $\Delta R_1/R_{10}$ value exceeds the paired 3T value ($p < 0.001$) by an amount increasing by dose. The improved sensitivity of CA tissue detection at increasing magnetic field strength is in agreement with observations from other groups (Trattnig et al., 2006). The analysis of large WM ROIs located bilaterally in the centrum semiovale (CSO) WM (Fig. 21.5C) also shows

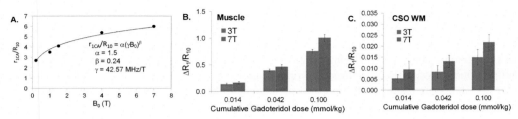

FIG. 21.5

The magnetic field dependence for relative detection sensitivity of gadoteridol, a low molecular weight GBCA, is plotted in panel A. Although gadoteridol's r_{1CA} decreases with B_0, the decrease of nominal tissue ^1H_2O R_1 (R_{10}) through the field dependence of r_{1m} more than compensates for this decrease. The resulting behavior is therefore predicted to increase GBCA detection sensitivity with increasing B_0. To validate the predicted behavior, ^1H_2O R_1 data were collected from 12 subjects before and after three fractional doses of gadoteridol administration (for a total dose of 0.1 mmol/kg) at 3T and 7T for each subject with repeated measurements occurring typically within 1 week. Quantitative R_1 maps were acquired using a four inversion time MPRAGE series with R_1 values calculated using Bloch formalism. Group average results for two tissue types, temporalis muscle and centrum semiovale white matter (CSO WM), across the three gadoteridol injections are plotted in panels B and C, respectively. The CA detection sensitivity index, r_{1CA}/R_{10}, of panel A indicates a ~25% increase for 7T compared to 3T. This is in good agreement with average $\Delta R_1/R_{10}$ values across three injection and two tissue classes with large dynamic range difference (50×) in tissue CA uptake.

greater CA detection sensitivity at 7T compared to 3T ($p < 0.003$). It is important to appreciate that the total sensitivity increase includes not only relaxation property differences, which we demonstrate are significantly improved at 7T compared to 3T, but also increased signal-to-noise ratio (SNR) of the base images.

Increased 7T SNR improves precision of individual tissue R_1 determinations compared to 3T by approximately a factor of 1.6. It is important to note that the error bars in Fig. 21.5 are largely determined by interindividual differences. Our results show improved precision of R_1 determination for individuals, although coverage was superior at 3T with the RF coil configurations used in this study.

In summary, our results support the view that CA detection improves at 7T compared to 3T. This finding is important for several reasons. First, it allows lower CA doses to be used to achieve the same blood vessel or lesion conspicuity which improves the CA administration safety margin. Also, it allows more precise characterization of blood flow, blood volume, transit time, and blood-brain barrier permeability to CA in normal appearing brain regions.

21.3.2 Characterizing perfusion and blood vessel permeability

MRI offers a wide range of techniques to quantify tissue perfusion and blood vessel properties. Contrast agent approaches provide a strong complement to noninvasive techniques such as ASL and time-of-flight measurements. One of the major challenges in UHF quantitative MRI studies, such as dynamic contrast MRI studies, is effective strategies for dealing with heterogeneity in B_0 and B_1^+ fields. Spatial variation in magnetic field homogeneity degrades the quality of EPI-based images, which are frequently used in dynamic susceptibility contrast (DSC) measurements, by inducing regional distortions, reducing signal intensity due to intravoxel destructive interference, increasing off-resonance effects and modifying contrast realized due to limited bandwidth of radiofrequency pulses. Truncating total EPI readout time through segmented acquisition, increasing spatial resolution, and advanced shimming approaches all help to mitigate B_0 effects. Designing radiofrequency pulses of increased bandwidth with tolerance to B_0 inhomogeneity can markedly improve image quality (He & Blamire, 2010; Ordidge et al., 2021).

21.3.3 Dynamic contrast-enhanced MRI

Dynamic contrast-enhanced (DCE) MRI data, which at its core represents a time series R_1 measurement technique, typically are acquired using one of two general approaches (Schabel, 2012; Anderson et al., 2021; Tagge et al., 2021). The first is a progressive saturation approach, which offers substantial advantage in spatial and temporal resolution flexibility and also provides excellent coverage. The progressive saturation class of technique often relies on gradient echo (GE) sequences, which work well at UHF with minimal spatial distortion and low SAR. A downside is that spatially inhomogeneous radiofrequency (RF) transmit fields (B_1^+), which typically are more problematic at UHF, must be considered. Incorporating B_1^+-tolerant RF pulses in the DCE-MRI sequence is a useful strategy, though it often comes with some trade-offs including prolonged minimum echo time and increased SAR (He & Blamire, 2010; Ordidge et al., 2021). More common are techniques to correct for spatially variant B_1^+ on the processing side, usually accomplished by incorporating an independent B_1 mapping measurement in the data acquisition.

A second strategy is to collect DCE-MRI data based on inversion recovery sequences. This approach typically is tolerant of B_1 inhomogeneity since R_1 weighting is achieved based on sampling time variation postinversion and efficiency of inversion. Accurate postinversion timing is readily controlled on MRI instruments at any field, and the T_1 timescale allows selection of an inversion radiofrequency pulse tolerant to B_1 and B_0 spatial variations. The downside of the IR-based technique is acquisition efficiency which results in some compromises in total coverage, temporal resolution, spatial resolution, or a combination of the above.

An example of a 7T blood-volume mapping is presented in Fig. 21.6. Here, the DCE time series scans were motion-corrected with AFNI (3dvolreg; (Cox & Jesmanowicz, 1999)), and spatially coregistered to PDw GE MRI, and B_1 maps. R_1 maps were calculated from DCE images on a voxel-wise basis by fitting a two-parameter single-exponential saturation recovery equation,

$$S_i(t) = S_{0i} \frac{\sin(B_{1i} \cdot \alpha)\left(1 - e^{(-TR \cdot R_{1i}(t))}\right)}{\left(1 - \cos(B_{1i} \cdot \alpha)e^{(-TR \cdot R_{1i}(t))}\right)}, \tag{21.2}$$

where B_{1i} is the flip angle (FA) correction factor from a B_1 map for the ith voxel, α is the nominal flip angle, S_{0i} is the voxel signal intensity in the PDw GE image, and $S_i(t)$ is the voxel signal intensity at a given time point in the DCE series.

Concentration of contrast agent in the blood plasma is denoted by $[CA_p]$, where R_{1b0} is the pre-CA blood relaxation rate constant, and r_{1CA} used was 3.2 s^{-1}/mM. Since CA in blood is restricted to the plasma, the equation is modified from Eq. 21.1 to account for the hematocrit (h):

$$R_{1b}(t) = R_{1b0} + r_{1CA} \cdot (1 - h) \cdot [CA_p](t), \tag{21.3}$$

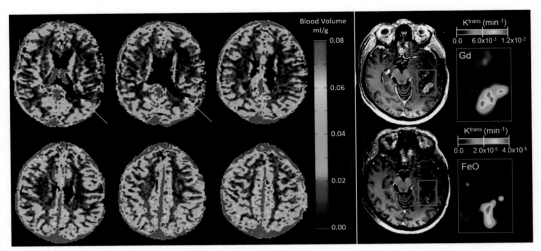

FIG. 21.6

The left panel shows brain blood volume maps for a 42-year F person with MS shown in an axial slice orientation. 7T DCE-MRI data were collected with 2 mm isotropic resolution and 2.7 s temporal resolution. This accelerated 3D gradient echo sequence provides excellent coverage and spatiotemporal resolution. Absolute blood volume (v_b) maps (from 0% to 8%) show values of ~1.5% in NAWM and 3.5% in NAGM. The regions with red areas represent highly macrovascularized areas including cortical veins and choroid plexus. Interestingly, we find greatly reduced blood volume values (~0.6%) in chronic MS periventricular lesions (arrow). The right panel shows a 7T T_1w MPRAGE from a 57-year male with glioblastoma multiforme (GBM). The panel insets map the spatial distribution of first order rate constants, K^{trans}, for blood-brain barrier extravasation of gadoteridol (Gd; upper right) and ferumoxytol (FeO; lower right) calculated from a sparse temporally sampled quantitative R_1 time series. The K^{trans} maps have differing spatial properties and also magnitudes, the scale for the gadoteridol K^{trans} map is 300× larger than the scale for the ferumoxytol map, and provide different information regarding underlying pathophysiology. MRI data were acquired at 7T (Siemens) using a 24-channel phased array T/R head RF coil

where R_{1b} is the longitudinal relaxation rate constant of blood ^1H_2O. The longitudinal relaxation time series behavior was fitted using a two-site exchange (2SX) formalism (Tagge et al., 2021; Li et al., 2005; Li et al., 2010). Ferumoxytol, a high molecular weight iron-based agent (FDA-approved for iron replacement), maintains a high plasma concentration for prolonged periods ($t_{1/2} \sim 15$ h), can be used for blood volume mapping at very high spatial resolution using an R_2^* contrast approach (Varallyay et al., 2013), and with delayed T_1w acquisitions of 24–72 h shows areas of BBB defect (Fig. 21.6, bottom right).

An important consideration, and challenge, in DCE and DSC measurements is determination of arterial input functions (AIF) and vascular output functions (VOF). These functions typically are determined from MRI regions of interest selected to represent the appropriate blood vessel class and are used as independent variables from which [CA_p] is estimated in dynamic time series modeling (see Eq. 21.3). Partial volume effects almost always represent a challenge for accurate AIF/VOF determination, and these effects are somewhat mitigated by higher spatial resolution acquisitions achieved at UHF. Another challenge is chemical shift offset of blood vessel water signal induced by bulk magnetic susceptibility effects during contrast agent first passage, when [CA_p] values are high. The magnitude of the susceptibility-induced shift depends on acquisition parameters, the orientation between the blood vessel and B_0, and increases with magnetic field strength. For EPI-based readout in a dynamic series at UHF, the induced shift can be quite large with AIF/VOF from some vessels often obscured by contamination with other tissue signal.

In the right panel of Fig. 21.6, results from an IR DCE-MRI time series for blood-brain barrier (BBB) permeability measures are shown. The R_1 maps were collected using inversion prepared GE with full-brain coverage 2 mm isotropic resolution and four separate inversion times sampled using a sparse temporal sampling DCE-MRI approach. R_1 maps across the time series were calculated using a full Bloch estimation approach and results in high-fidelity R_1 measurements. The first-order volume transfer constants of CA (gadoteridol and ferumoxytol) across the BBB, K^{trans}, were calculated as described by Li and colleagues (Li et al., 2005). Two compartment models, which account for equilibrium intercompartmental water molecule exchange, were used (Li et al., 2005). Prior to multiparametric fitting, R_1 time series were spatially coregistered to a common reference image set using a rigid-body transformation technique.

21.4 Summary

The high sensitivity and increased tissue and blood T_1 values of UHF MRI benefit both dynamic contrast-based and noncontrast ASL perfusion imaging. It is feasible to perform UHF perfusion MRI of the brain with (sub)millimeter spatial resolution and high sensitivity. New strategies are being developed for addressing challenges of UHF perfusion MRI, including B_1/B_0 field inhomogeneity, SAR limitations, and image distortions. With increasing availability of clinically approved UHF MR systems, we expect the applications for UHF perfusion imaging to grow in the coming years.

Acknowledgments

This work was supported by the National Institute of Health (NIH) grant S10-OD025312, R01-NS114382, R01-EB032169, R01-EB028297, R01NS40801, S10OD018224 and C.N. Hilton Foundation.

References

Alsop, D.C., Detre, J.A., Golay, X., et al., 2015. Recommended implementation of arterial spin-labeled perfusion MRI for clinical applications: a consensus of the ISMRM perfusion study group and the European consortium for ASL in dementia. Magn. Reson. Med. 73 (1), 102–116.

Anderson, V.C., Tagge, I.J., Doud, A., et al., 2021. DCE-MRI of brain fluid barriers: *in vivo* water cycling at the human choroid plexus. Tissue Barriers, 1963143. https://doi.org/10.1080/21688370.2021.1963143. Epub ahead of print. PMID: 34542012.

Bause, J., Ehses, P., Mirkes, C., Shajan, G., Scheffler, K., Pohmann, R., 2016. Quantitative and functional pulsed arterial spin labeling in the human brain at 9.4 T. Magn. Reson. Med. 75 (3), 1054–1063.

Beckett, A.J.S., Dadakova, T., Townsend, J., Huber, L., Park, S., Feinberg, D.A., 2020. Comparison of BOLD and CBV using 3D EPI and 3D GRASE for cortical layer functional MRI at 7 T. Magn. Reson. Med. 84 (6), 3128–3145.

Cox, R.W., Jesmanowicz, A., 1999. Real-time 3D image registration for functional MRI. Magn. Reson. Med. 42 (6), 1014–1018. https://doi.org/10.1002/(sici)1522-2594(199912)42:6<1014::aid-mrm4>3.0.co;2-f. PMID: 10571921.

Eichfelder, G., Gebhardt, M., 2011. Local specific absorption rate control for parallel transmission by virtual observation points. Magn. Reson. Med. 66 (5), 1468–1476.

Gras, V., Vignaud, A., Amadon, A., Le Bihan, D., Boulant, N., 2017. Universal pulses: a new concept for calibration-free parallel transmission. Magn. Reson. Med. 77 (2), 635–643.

He, J., Blamire, A.M., 2010. Application of variable-rate selective excitation pulses for spin labeling in perfusion MRI. Magn. Reson. Med. 63 (3), 842–847. https://doi.org/10.1002/mrm.22251. PMID: 20146373.

Hurley, A.C., Al-Radaideh, A., Bai, L., et al., 2010. Tailored RF pulse for magnetization inversion at ultrahigh field. Magn. Reson. Med. 63 (1), 51–58.

Ivanov, D., Kashyap, S., Haast, R.A., et al., 2018. Human Whole-Brain Sub-Millimeter Cerebral Blood Flow Map Using 7T ASL.

Kashyap, S., Ivanov, D., Havlicek, M., Huber, L., Poser, B.A., Uludağ, K., 2021. Sub-millimetre resolution laminar fMRI using arterial spin labelling in humans at 7 T. PloS One 16 (4), e0250504.

Kim, J.H., Taylor, A.J., Wang, D.J., Zou, X., Ress, D., 2020. Dynamics of the cerebral blood flow response to brief neural activity in human visual cortex. J. Cereb. Blood Flow Metab. 40, 1823–1837. 271678x19869034.

Le Ster, C., Grant, A., Van de Moortele, P.F., et al., 2022. Magnetic field strength dependent SNR gain at the center of a spherical phantom and up to 11.7T. Magn. Reson. Med. 88 (5), 2131–2138.

Li, X., Rooney, W.D., Springer C.S., Jr., 2005. A unified magnetic resonance imaging pharmacokinetic theory: intravascular and extracellular contrast reagents. Magn. Reson. Med. 54 (6), 1351–1359. https://doi.org/10.1002/mrm.20684. Erratum in: Magn Reson Med. 2006 May;55(5):1217. PMID: 16247739.

Li, X., Rooney, W.D., Várallyay, C.G., et al., 2010. Dynamic-contrast-enhanced- MRI with extravasating contrast reagent: rat cerebral glioma blood volume determination. J. Magn. Reson. 206 (2), 190–199. https://doi.org/10.1016/j.jmr.2010.07.004. PMID: 20674422. PMCID: PMC2946221. Epub 2010 Jul 31.

Luh, W.M., Talagala, S.L., Li, T.Q., Bandettini, P.A., 2013. Pseudo-continuous arterial spin labeling at 7 T for human brain: estimation and correction for off-resonance effects using a Prescan. Magn. Reson. Med. 69 (2), 402–410.

Meixner, C.R., Eisen, C.K., Schmitter, S., et al., 2021. Hybrid B1+ -shimming and gradient adaptions for improved pseudo-continuous arterial spin labeling at 7 Tesla. Magn. Reson. Med. 87, 207–219.

Ordidge, R., Cleary, J., Glarin, R., Blunck, Y., Farquharson, S., Moffat, B., 2021. Ultra-high- field MRI using composite RF (STEP) pulses. NMR Biomed. 34 (2), e4445. https://doi.org/10.1002/nbm.4445. Epub 2020 Nov 17. PMID: 33205505.

Poser, B.A., Setsompop, K., 2018. Pulse sequences and parallel imaging for high spatiotemporal resolution MRI at ultra-high field. Neuroimage 168, 101–118.

Poser, B.A., Koopmans, P.J., Witzel, T., Wald, L.L., Barth, M., 2010. Three dimensional echo-planar imaging at 7 Tesla. Neuroimage 51 (1), 261–266.

Rooney, W.D., Johnson, G., Li, X., et al., 2007. Magnetic field and tissue dependencies of human brain longitudinal 1H2O relaxation in vivo. Magn. Reson. Med. 57 (2), 308–318. https://doi.org/10.1002/mrm.21122. PMID: 17260370.

Saad, Z.S., Glen, D.R., Chen, G., Beauchamp, M.S., Desai, R., Cox, R.W., 2009. A new method for improving functional-to-structural MRI alignment using local Pearson correlation. Neuroimage 44 (3), 839–848.

Schabel, M.C., 2012. A unified impulse response model for DCE-MRI. Magn. Reson. Med. 68 (5), 1632–1646. https://doi.org/10.1002/mrm.24162. Epub 2012 Jan 31. PMID: 22294448.

Shao, X., Jann, K., Wang, K., Guo, F., Zhang, P., Wang, D.J., 2020a. In-vivo laminar CBF fMRI using high-resolution pseudo-continuous arterial spin labeling at 7T. Proc ISMRM 28, 1232.

Shao, X., Spann, S., Wang, K., Yan, L., Rudolf, S., Wang, D.J., 2020b. High-resolution whole brain ASL perfusion imaging at 7T with 12-fold acceleration and spatial-temporal regularized reconstruction. Proc ISMRM 28, 23.

Shao, X., Guo, F., Shou, Q., Wang, K., Jann, K., Yan, L., Toga, A.W., Zhang, P., Wang, D.J., 2021. Laminar perfusion imaging with zoomed arterial spin labeling at 7 Tesla. Neuroimage 245, 118724.

Sourbron, S.P., Buckley, D.L., 2012. Tracer kinetic modelling in MRI: estimating perfusion and capillary permeability. Phys. Med. Biol. 57 (2), R1–33. https://doi.org/10.1088/0031-9155/57/2/R1. Epub 2011 Dec 15. PMID: 22173205.

St Lawrence, K.S., Wang, J., 2005. Effects of the apparent transverse relaxation time on cerebral blood flow measurements obtained by arterial spin labeling. Magn. Reson. Med. 53 (2), 425–433.

Stafford, R.B., Woo, M.K., Oh, S.H., et al., 2016. An actively decoupled dual transceiver coil system for continuous ASL at 7 T. Int. J. Imaging Syst. Technol. 26 (2), 106–115.

Tagge, I.J., Anderson, V.C., Springer C.S., Jr., et al., 2021. Gray matter blood-brain barrier water exchange dynamics are reduced in progressive multiple sclerosis. J. Neuroimaging. https://doi.org/10.1111/jon.12912. Epub ahead of print. PMID: 34355458.

Tong, Y., Jezzard, P., Okell, T.W., Clarke, W.T., 2020. Improving PCASL at ultra-high field using a VERSE-guided parallel transmission strategy. Magn. Reson. Med. 84 (2), 777–786.

Trattnig, S., Pinker, K., Ba-Ssalamah, A., Nöbauer-Huhmann, I.M., 2006. The optimal use of contrast agents at high field MRI. Eur. Radiol. 16 (6), 1280–1287. https://doi.org/10.1007/s00330-006-0154-0. Epub 2006 Mar 1. PMID: 16508769.

Varallyay, C.G., Nesbit, E., Fu, R., et al., 2013. High-resolution steady-state cerebral blood volume maps in patients with central nervous system neoplasms using ferumoxytol, a superparamagnetic iron oxide nanoparticle. J. Cereb. Blood Flow Metab. 33 (5), 780–786. https://doi.org/10.1038/jcbfm.2013.36. Epub 2013 Mar 13. PMID: 23486297. PMCID: PMC3653563.

Wang, J.J., Alsop, D.C., Li, L., et al., 2002. Comparison of quantitative perfusion imaging using arterial spin labeling at 1.5 and 4.0 tesla. Magn. Reson. Med. 48 (2), 242–254.

Wang, Y., Moeller, S., Li, X., et al., 2015. Simultaneous multi-slice Turbo-FLASH imaging with CAIPIRINHA for whole brain distortion-free pseudo-continuous arterial spin labeling at 3 and 7 T. Neuroimage 113, 279–288.

Wang, K., Shao, X., Yan, L., Ma, S.J., Jin, J., Wang, D.J.J., 2021a. Optimization of adiabatic pulses for pulsed arterial spin labeling at 7 tesla: comparison with pseudo-continuous arterial spin labeling. Magn. Reson. Med. 85 (6), 3227–3240.

Wang, K., Ma, S.J., Shao, X., et al., 2021b. Optimization of pseudo-continuous arterial spin labeling at 7T with parallel transmission B1 shimming. Magn. Reson. Med. 87, 249–262.

Weber, M.A., Günther, M., Lichy, M.P., et al., 2003. Comparison of arterial spin-labeling techniques and dynamic susceptibility-weighted contrast-enhanced MRI in perfusion imaging of normal brain tissue. Invest. Radiol. 38 (11), 712–718. https://doi.org/10.1097/01.rli.0000084890.57197.54. PMID: 14566181.

Zuo, Z., Wang, R., Zhuo, Y., Xue, R., St Lawrence, K.S., Wang, D.J., 2013. Turbo-FLASH based arterial spin labeled perfusion MRI at 7 T. PloS One 8 (6), e66612.

Ultra-high field functional imaging

BOLD fMRI: Physiology and acquisition strategies

Kâmil Uludağ[a,b,c] and Lars Kasper[a]
[a]*Techna Institute to Krembil Brain Institute, University Health Network Toronto, Toronto, ON, Canada* [b]*Department of Medical Biophysics, University of Toronto, Toronto, ON, Canada* [c]*Center for Neuroscience Imaging Research, Institute for Basic Science & Department of Biomedical Engineering, Sungkyunkwan University, Suwon, Republic of Korea*

Highlights

- BOLD is an indirect measure of neuronal activity.
- Gradient echo BOLD signal has higher sensitivity to brain activation than SE BOLD signal but lower spatial specificity.
- Hemodynamic biophysical modeling considers draining vein-related spatial bias in laminar fMRI and can recover cortical depth-resolved neuronal activity through Bayesian model inversion.
- SMS and 3D EPI are the standard approaches for UHF fMRI with advantages for whole-brain and laminar fMRI, respectively.
- Spiral, 3D GRASE and bSSFP MRI acquisitions are promising alternatives to 2D and 3D EPI for laminar fMRI.

22.1 BOLD physiology and biophysical models

The fMRI signal acquired with T_2^* or T_2 contrast has complex physiological and physical underpinnings. Importantly, the properties of BOLD physiology (Sections 22.1–22.3) dictate the MRI acquisition requirements for both contrast selection and spatial encoding in ultra-high field (UHF) fMRI (Sections 22.4–22.6).

The functional MRI signal detected with gradient or spin echo (GE or SE) acquisitions is primarily sensitive to changes in blood oxygenation (Buxton et al., 2004 and references therein). However, as the intra- and extravascular relaxation rates are typically different (see Section 22.2), a change in cerebral blood volume (CBV) corresponds to a change in apparent proton density and, thus, also evokes a change in the fMRI signal (Uludağ et al., 2009). This effect is small compared to the effect from blood oxygenation, and therefore, the GE or SE fMRI signal change following neuronal activation has been termed the blood oxygenation level-dependent (BOLD) signal. Nevertheless, the CBV-related changes in GE BOLD signal have been hypothesized as a possible explanation for, for example, the initial dip detected at ultra-high field (UHF) strengths (Uludağ, 2010).

The BOLD signal stems from the vasculature and, thus, is an indirect reflection of neuronal activity. Activation in neurons and astrocytes is associated with changes in oxidative (and nonoxidative) metabolism (i.e., cerebral metabolic rate of oxygen, $CMRO_2$), leading to an increase in oxygen extraction fraction from the blood and a decrease in blood oxygenation and, hence, a decrease in the BOLD signal.

Advances in Magnetic Resonance Technology and Applications. Volume 10. ISSN 2666-9099. https://doi.org/10.1016/B978-0-323-99898-7.00027-4

CBV changes of blood vessels containing deoxygenated hemoglobin increase magnetic susceptibility and also decrease the BOLD signal. However, these decreases are overcompensated by the inflow of oxygenated blood from the arteries due to an increase in cerebral blood flow (CBF). Therefore, the combined effect of $CMRO_2$, CBV, and CBF results in an increase in the BOLD signal (Buxton et al., 2004) (see Fig. 22.1).

The so-called neurovascular coupling describes the changes in CBF and CBV associated with neuronal activation. It is currently not thought to be driven by metabolic demands, such as drop in partial pressure of oxygen in the tissue, but by the release of vasoactive substances from neurons and astrocytes. However, the role of the neurovascular coupling is to ensure the homeostasis of the brain tissue (i.e., delivery of nutrients such as oxygen and glucose and clearance of metabolic products of neuronal and astrocytic processes such as CO_2). Therefore, CBF changes, even though not casually linked, are tightly correlated with oxidative metabolism changes.

Physiological processes in the brain tissue during activation can be described at many levels, ranging from molecular genetic to mean electrical or magnetic fields generated. In the context of fMRI, multi-unit activity (MUA) and local field potentials (LFPs) are most discussed and investigated as neuronal correlates of the hemodynamic changes. MUA corresponds to the average of action potentials of multiple neurons weighted by their distance to the electrode tip; LFP is the electric field generated by, among other processes, the slower ionic currents through the membrane and membrane potential changes. Usually, MUA and LFP are highly correlated, but they can also be dissociated in some experiments. In such cases, it is thought that LFP represents more the input and MUA the processing and output of the local neuronal population. It has been experimentally found that LFP is a better correlate of the GE BOLD signal than MUA, albeit this correlation can be nonlinear, in particular, for small and

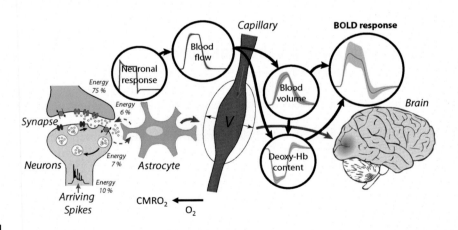

FIG. 22.1

Physiological processes leading to the BOLD signal. Neurons and astrocytes change their activity following external stimulation or spontaneously and extract oxygen from the blood vessels. Neurovascular coupling leads to increase in cerebral blood flow (CBF), which in turn changes the cerebral blood volume (CBV) and paramagnetic deoxyhemoglobin content in the blood. The change in blood oxygenation and, to a lesser extent, CBV lead to a detectable fMRI signal, termed the blood oxygenation level-dependent (BOLD) response.

large neuronal activations (Logothetis et al., 2001). LFP is also metabolically more intensive than MUA as restoring membrane potentials is a thermodynamic uphill process, whereas action potentials consume less energy due to being a thermodynamic downhill process. Thus, expressed in a simplified way, the fMRI signal is not primarily a marker for information processing (i.e., represented by MUA) but a metabolic marker of neuronal activity (i.e., represented by LFP).

The relationship of LFP and MUA to the underlying neural micro-circuitry is complex. The so-called canonical micro-circuit is often utilized to describe the relationship of excitatory and inhibitory neuronal activity distributed over the cortical depths (usually labeled from I to VI) and mesoscopic and macroscopic measures of population activity, such as LFP and MUA (Douglas and Martin, 2004). The input to a brain area arrives predominantly to layers IV and VI, and the output is projected from and feedback received in layers II and V. However, it must be kept in mind that this is a simplistic view of the distributions of activation across cortical depth, which currently nevertheless serves as an interpretation framework for both depth-resolved electrophysiology and laminar fMRI.

Neuronal activity is related to hemodynamic changes in a highly spatially specific manner. The precise level of control of CBF changes is still under investigation, i.e., whether it occurs on the level of arterioles or capillaries, but certainly below the currently achievable spatial resolution of fMRI in humans. The spatial specificity of fMRI is therefore not limited by the nominal spatial resolution of the fMRI technique used, but by the spatial sensitivity of the vascular changes they are correlated to (i.e., to blood oxygenation, to blood volume, or to flow changes) (Huber et al., 2019). Currently, CBF as measured with ASL—measuring the delivery of water from arteries to the capillaries—is thought to be most spatially specific as capillary flow changes are most proximal vascular changes relative to neuronal activity. CBV techniques also have high specificity as the highest CBV change is thought to be colocalized to the neuronal activity with some changes in CBV also present in penetrating arteries and draining intracortical veins and not much change in pial veins (Uludağ and Blinder, 2018). This blurs the CBV activation locus toward the surface of the brain but much less so compared to the GE BOLD signal.

In the recent physiologically inspired dynamic causal modeling (P-DCM) (Havlicek et al., 2015, 2017), (i) local neuronal population consists of excitatory and adaptive inhibitory neuronal subpopulations, (ii) the neurovascular coupling is feed-forward, (iii) the hemodynamics is described by the original balloon model (Buxton et al., 2004) (see Fig. 22.1), and (iv) the BOLD signal equation translating these physiological changes to the GE fMRI signal has been updated. For depth-resolved fMRI studies, the draining of deoxyhemoglobin via intracortical veins has to be accounted for. Havlicek and Uludag proposed a new model based on mass-balance principle modeling the depth-specific vasculature and the draining vein effect (see Fig. 22.2) (Havlicek and Uludağ, 2020).

This study showed that the commonly observed BOLD signal amplitude increase toward the brain surface during steady state can be explained by the increase in baseline CBV. In addition, the so-called bump in the middle layers observed in some studies using stimuli with strong feed-forward neuronal activation pattern is most likely correlated with neuronal activation and not a bias representation due to the vasculature. Finally, it showed that the intracortical draining vein effect causes an increase in the delay of the hemodynamic response function toward the surface of the brain.

The laminar hemodynamic BOLD signal model has recently been extended to model neuronal activity by adding the excitatory-inhibitory neuronal populations component of P-DCM (Uludag and Havlicek, 2021). In addition, this model included modeling of the finite voxel resolution and angular dependence of the BOLD signal. Using this laminar DCM approach, it has been found that: (i) laminar

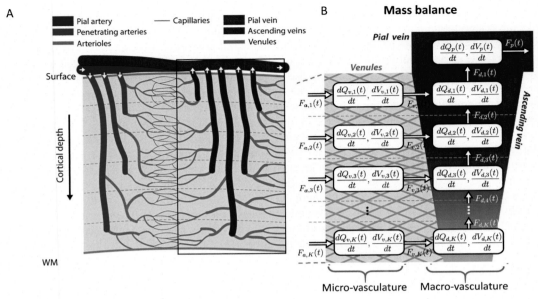

FIG. 22.2

(A) Scheme of the vascular architecture of the cortex. Oxygenated blood is delivered to the cortical tissue via surface arteries and delivered to the different cortical layers via penetrating arteries, arterioles, and capillaries. Oxygen extraction occurs predominantly on the capillary level, and the partially deoxygenated blood is drained to pial vein via venules and ascending veins. (B) The laminar BOLD signal model is based on mass principles, accounting for sources and sinks of deoxygenated hemoglobin (symbolized by "Q") and CBV (symbolized with "V") changes in the local micro-vasculature and nonlocal macro-vasculature.

neuronal activity differences between conditions are better reflected by the GE BOLD signal than single condition neuronal laminar profiles; (ii) angular dependence of the GE BOLD signal can significantly add signal variability and therefore should be corrected in laminar fMRI studies; and (iii) it is recommended that, even if few neuronal depths are distinguished, more BOLD signal depths are calculated from the original data. Finally, this paper demonstrated that, analogous to the original DCM framework, Bayesian model inversion can be performed to determine neuronal activity spatial profiles from high-resolution GE BOLD data. One important limitation is that the laminar DCM uses independent excitatory-inhibitory neuronal models for each depth considered, a simplification over the canonical micro-circuit model (see above).

22.2 BOLD contrast contributions

The GE and SE BOLD signal are determined by changes in dOHb and CBV from all intracortical and pial vessels. The intravascular susceptibility changes induced by the paramagnetic dOHb induces proton dephasing in and around blood vessels. Thus, the MRI signal with T_2 or T_2^*-contrast is composed of intra- and extravascular signal changes from arteries, arterioles, capillaries, venules and veins weighted by their respective blood volumes (Uludağ et al., 2009, and references therein):

$$S_{tot} = (1 - CBV) * S_{ex} + \sum_i CBV_i * S_{in,i}. \tag{22.1}$$

The terms S_{ex} and S_{in} are the extravascular and intravascular signals, respectively. The index i denotes the specific vascular compartment within the voxel (artery, vein, etc.). They are typically well-described as monoexponentials to the power of the negative echo time multiplied by the transverse relaxation rate (R_2^* or R_2), the inverse of T_2^* and T_2 (Yablonskiy and Haacke, 1994). As shown in Eq. 22.1, separate signal exponentials are added together for each vascular compartment (artery, vein, etc.) within a voxel for S_{in}. In contrast, as the dephasing in the extravascular space is linear for each component, extravascular relaxation rates are added from each vascular compartment within a single exponential for S_{ex}. The signal components for GE BOLD signal can be written as:

$$S_{ex} = e^{-TE*\left(R_{2,0,ex}^* + R_{2,Hb,ex}^*\right)}, \tag{22.2}$$

$$S_{in} = e^{-TE*\left(R_{2,0,in}^* + R_{2,Hb,in}^*\right)}. \tag{22.3}$$

Here, $R_{2,0,ex}^*$ and $R_{2,0,in}^*$ are the intrinsic magnetic relaxation rates for extravascular and intravascular space without any dOHb present, respectively. $R_{2,Hb,ex}^*$ and $R_{2,Hb,in}^*$ are the corresponding relaxation rates as a function of dOHb concentration. (For SE BOLD, R_{2s} have to be used instead of R_{2s}^*.)

As the BOLD signal change is only in the order of few percent, the relaxation rate in a typical brain gray matter voxel is dominated by the intrinsic extravascular relaxation rate. A literature review found that the tissue relaxation rates are linearly dependent on the magnetic field strength:

$$R_{2,0,ex}^* = 2.71 \frac{1}{Ts} B_0 + 10.96 \frac{1}{s}, \tag{22.4}$$

$$R_{2,0,ex} = 1.74 \frac{1}{Ts} B_0 + 7.77 \frac{1}{s}. \tag{22.5}$$

That is, as the signal decay occurs faster with field strength, the acquisition speed has to increase (i.e., shorter TE and readout duration). For the intrinsic intravascular relaxation rate for SE also a linear dependency has been found in blood phantom measurements:

$$R_{2,0,in} = 2.74 \frac{1}{Ts} B_0 - 0.6 \frac{1}{s}. \tag{22.6}$$

For T_2^* contrast, the intravascular signal is small at UHF and can be set to zero for practical purposes at standard TE values and therefore no equation is needed.

These intrinsic relaxation rates do not include the effect of blood oxygenation and therefore correspond to the relaxation rate in and around arteries. The SE relaxation rate as a function of blood oxygenation is quadratically dependent on B_0:

$$R_{2,Hb,in} = 12.67 \frac{1}{T^2 s} B_0^2 \cdot (1 - Y)^2. \tag{22.7}$$

No equation is needed for $R_{2,Hb,in}^*$, as the intravascular signal for GE images is very low. Finally, in Uludağ et al. (2009), quantitative expressions for $R_{2,Hb,ex}^*$ and $R_{2,Hb,ex}$ up to 16.4T were given for

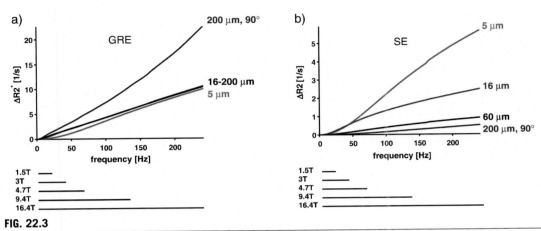

FIG. 22.3

Extravascular relaxation rates as a function of surface frequency induced by a paramagnetic agent such as dOHb or gadolinium, for(A) GE and (B) SE at different vessel diameters. The typical frequency shift associated with dOHb is shown in the bottom for different magnetic field strengths.

different vessel diameters and orientations, fitting the curves shown in Fig. 22.3. Equipped with these equations, GE and SE BOLD signal for any tissue composition at any field strength for arbitrary blood oxygenation and CBV changes can be calculated.

The faster relaxation at higher fields necessitates faster acquisition. In particular, the intravascular signal for T_2^* contrast is negligible at UHF, and the extra vascular relaxation rate becomes vessel size independent. Therefore, R_2^* changes using contrast agents (i.e., same susceptibility change in all vessels) are thought to be proportional to CBV for randomly oriented blood vessels (see Fig. 22.3). However, dOHb changes are largest in the veins, resulting in a GE BOLD signal that is weighted toward the pial veins. For this reason, in low-resolution studies, GE BOLD signal is dominated by the signal from pial veins. In high-resolution studies, it leads to the further observation of an increase of the BOLD signal toward the surface of the cortex due to the increase in baseline CBV in the intracortical ascending veins.

For T_2 contrast, the 180 degree refocusing pulse recovers much of the extravascular signal around large vessels and therefore reduces the SE BOLD signal sensitivity to large veins. However, intravascular signal persists in T_2 contrast even at UHF. Since the largest blood oxygenation change is in the veins, a nonnegligible sensitivity to the veins remains even for SE BOLD acquisition.

22.3 BOLD sensitivity and specificity at UHF

For high-resolution BOLD studies, an often-made distinction is between macro- and micro-vasculatures (Uludağ et al., 2009). Macro-vasculature refers to the intracortical ascending and pial veins. Micro-vasculature is defined as the local vasculature in close spatial proximity to the neuronal activation. Depending on spatial resolution, both can be present in an imaging voxel. The ratio of micro- to macro-vasculature BOLD signal is a marker for laminar specificity. Through numerical simulations, the GE BOLD signal has been found to have low laminar specificity at all magnetic field strengths. In contrast, the SE BOLD signal has high laminar specificity above 4T, but with still substantial macro-vasculature contribution (Uludağ et al., 2009).

The field strength dependence of GE BOLD also provides a window for investigating the physiological basis of the fMRI signal. As discussed above, the locus of the largest CBV changes is still under discussion. The general consensus is that relative CBV changes in the pial vessels are small compared to those in the tissue. However, there is conflicting data whether the CBV changes are predominantly in the precapillary arteries, in the capillaries, or in the intracortical ascending veins. These conflicting findings may be reconciled by considering the different conditions under which the data were acquired (i.e., animal vs humans, anesthesia vs awake, short vs long stimulation, optical imaging vs MRI) (Uludağ and Blinder, 2018). Venous CBV changes with its slow rise to steady state and slow recovery to baseline may only be observable for long stimulus durations. As short stimulus paradigms are typically employed in animal studies, this may explain why significant venous CBV changes remain undetected.

As shown in Fig. 22.3D (Uludağ et al., 2009), for illustration purposes, it was assumed that macro-vasculature has twice the CBV than the micro-vasculature, resulting in a SE signal amplitude of the macro-vasculature at 7T to be approximately half of that of the micro-vasculature. Thus, SE BOLD signal has much higher spatial specificity than the GE BOLD signal (see Fig. 22.4). Interestingly, the micro-vasculature signal in SE and GE is of similar magnitude (see black lines in 3d and 5b in Uludağ et al., 2009). That is, the reduced amplitude of the SE BOLD signal and the loss of sensitivity relative to the GE BOLD signal come at the expense of the macro-vasculature.

Recently, a new method was proposed to combine SE and GE BOLD signal using filters based on relative signal changes (Han et al., 2021). These filters are inspired by vessel size imaging: the larger the vessel diameter the larger is the ratio of the GE to SE BOLD relaxation rates in the same voxel. As the average vessel diameter is smaller in the micro-vasculature, choosing appropriate scaling of the

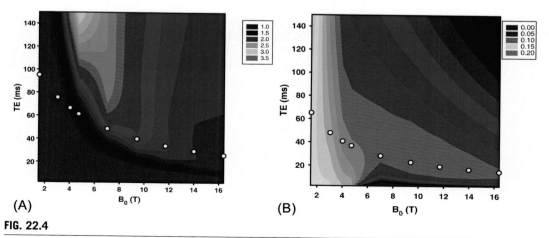

FIG. 22.4

Ratio of simulated micro- to macro-vascular SE and GE signal; (A) and (B), respectively, for different field strength and TEs. Note the scaling is much smaller for GE.

GE BOLD signal as a function to this ratio and then multiplying with the SE BOLD signal can achieve suppressing of large vessels and enhancing micro-vasculature. It was demonstrated that the laminar profile of this combined BOLD signal peaks in the middle layers (as expected from electrophysiology and the SE BOLD signal) and has higher SNR compared to the SE BOLD signal across all cortical depths.

The above biophysical model of the GE and SE fMRI signals (see Section 22.2) does not include some important effects relevant to depth-resolved BOLD studies (see Uludag and Havlicek, 2021 for details, and references therein). Most important are as follows: (i) blooming effect; (ii) angular dependence; and (iii) effect of readout window on the resolution and specificity.

22.4 Common acquisition sequences

22.4.1 BOLD sensitivity implications on TE and acquisition window

To optimize contrast-related sequence parameters, such as TE or total readout acquisition duration (TAQ), BOLD sensitivity (Deichmann et al., 2002) is used to formalize the notion of contrast, defined as the BOLD signal ΔS induced by changes in T_2^*, relative to the respective baseline value of tissue

$$\Delta S(\text{TE}, T_2^*, \Delta T_2^*) = S(\text{TE}, T_2^* + \Delta T_2^*) - S(\text{TE}, T_2^*) \approx \Delta T_2^* \cdot \frac{dS(\text{TE}, T_2^*)}{dT_2^*} = \Delta T_2^* \frac{d}{dT_2^*} \left(M_0 \exp\left(-\frac{\text{TE}}{T_2^*} \right) \right)$$

$$= \Delta T_2^* \cdot \left(M_0 \frac{\text{TE}}{T_2^{*2}} \exp\left(-\frac{\text{TE}}{T_2^*} \right) \right) = \frac{\Delta T_2^*}{T_2^{*2}} \cdot \text{TE} \cdot S. \tag{22.8}$$

In addition to the general gain in baseline signal (M_0) at UHF, the difference in T_2^* between activated and deactivated tissues increases (van der Zwaag et al., 2009), leading to an overall enhanced BOLD sensitivity (Fig. 22.5A).

BOLD sensitivity as a function of TE resembles an inverse U-shape, with a maximum at $\text{TE} = T_2^*$ and a prolonged tail for longer echo times. The signal change relative to the baseline signal, $\Delta S/S$, increases with TE, but in practice is limited by the noise floor. Maintaining at least 80% of maximum BOLD sensitivity throughout the readout allows for acquisition windows TAQ of about 90 ms for cortical gray matter at 3T, but only about 45 ms (15–60 ms) at 7T (Fig. 22.5B). Static B_0 inhomogeneity at UHF imposes similar restrictions on TAQ by inducing geometric distortions proportional to the readout duration (see Chapter 6 for causes and coping strategies), as does the T_2^* blurring of the point-spread function (PSF) that occurs for any extended readout.

22.4.1.1 2D echo-planar imaging (EPI)

For BOLD fMRI, the prepared contrast is typically a T_2^*-weighting of a gradient-recalled echo (GE) after selective excitation of the whole imaging slice (Fig. 22.6A).

Alternatively, T_2-weighting is accomplished in spin echo (SE) contrast through a refocusing module, which takes tens of milliseconds and reduces acquisition efficiency. Following contrast preparation, EPI is the predominant sampling scheme for BOLD acquisition. It allows capturing a full 2D slice at targeted fMRI resolutions within a single shot lasting a few tens of milliseconds (Fig. 22.6B). In 2D EPI, k-space is traversed line by line (readout direction k_{read}) using trapezoidal gradients (G_{read}), with equidistant phase "blips" between lines induced by triangular gradients (phase-encoding direction k_{phase}).

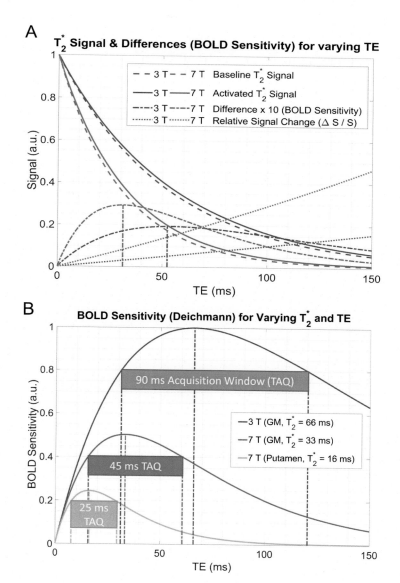

FIG. 22.5

BOLD sensitivity and its impact on acquisition parameters. (A) Signal differences between activated and baseline gray matter T_2^* decay (van der Zwaag et al., 2009) determine BOLD contrast-to-noise, with a maximum at $TE = T_2^*$, while relative signal changes $\Delta S/S$ continue to increase with TE. (B) The favorable acquisition window for BOLD fMRI after excitation (80% of max BOLD sensitivity, scaled by T_2^{*2} here, as in Deichmann et al., 2002) shrinks with higher field strength (shorter T_2^*) and for subcortical gray matter.

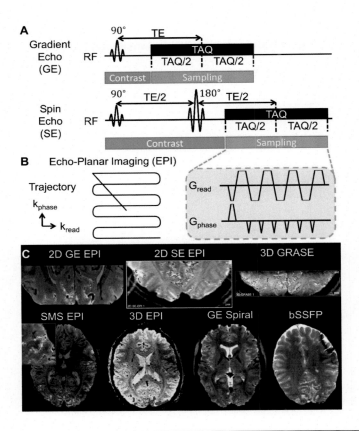

FIG. 22.6

Pulse sequences for BOLD acquisition. (A) BOLD contrast formation. Every BOLD fMRI sequence consists at least of a contrast preparation and sampling part. For gradient echo (GE) BOLD, a slice- (or slab-) selective excitation pulse prepares contrast. For spin echo (SE) BOLD, this excitation is followed by a refocusing pulse (centered between excitation and sampling of the k-space origin), considerably prolonging contrast preparation compared to GE. In both cases, the subsequent signal decay (T_2^* or T_2, respectively) is acquired with the same sampling module. (B) Echo-planar imaging (EPI) is the most common sampling scheme (*left*: k-space trajectory, *right*: gradient waveform) for BOLD acquisition, and can be combined with 2D/3D/SMS encoding in slice direction. (C) Example BOLD activation maps for GE and SE EPI, as well as specialized acquisition sequences (see "Specialized acquisition sequences" section). All fMRI studies were performed at UHF (7T, except bSSFP, 9.4T), presented are color-coded and thresholded statistical maps of a task contrast (visual stimulation, SMS-EPI: also motor response), overlaid on (mean) images of the same sequence. *Brain images used with permission from Heidemann et al. (2012), Huber et al. (2016), Kasper et al. (2022), Kemper et al. (2015), Poser et al. (2010), and Scheffler and Ehses (2016).*

Overall image contrast is determined by the echo time TE—i.e., when k-space center is traversed—and traditional EPI readouts are centered around TE (but see Fig. 22.4B).

For a transverse brain FOV (e.g., 220 mm) and the identified TAQ = 50 ms at 7T (Fig. 22.5B), EPI allows to fully sample a slice with up to 2-mm in-plane resolution without acceleration (Fig. 22.7A, black line), given a contemporary whole-body gradient system. Dedicated head-insert gradients push this limit to 1.3 mm due to much higher slew rates and gradient strengths (Fig. 22.7A, blue and red line, Feinberg et al., 2021; Weiger et al., 2018). Nevertheless, targeted submillimeter UHF BOLD applications, for example laminar fMRI (see Chapter 24), require acceleration beyond what is available by improved imaging hardware.

22.4.2 Acceleration by partial Fourier imaging

By introducing prior information, images can be reconstructed from less data, enabling higher resolution within the same TAQ. In widely used partial Fourier imaging (Feinberg et al., 1986), the constraint of a real-valued brain image is used, implying Hermitian symmetry of k-space data: $s(k_{read}, k_{phase})^* = s(-k_{read}, -k_{phase})$. Ideally, measuring half of k-space suffices, and the EPI trajectory starts/stops after reaching k-space center. At UHF in particular, this assumption is violated by Tx/Rx or B_0 off-resonance phase imprinted on the sampled object. A partial Fourier factor of k-space greater than ½ is typically acquired, representing a relaxed constraint (low-resolution phase image). This allows for asymmetric EPI readouts with echo times shorter than TAQ/2.

22.4.3 Acceleration by parallel imaging

Parallel imaging (Chapter 9), which employs receiver coils' spatial-encoding capability, can further accelerate BOLD acquisition. For EPI, parallel imaging reduces the number of acquired k-space lines by a factor R, spacing them further apart and thus decreasing FOV. Acquisition time and samples are reduced by R as well, inducing an SNR loss by a factor $\sqrt{R}$. The nonorthogonality of coil sensitivity profiles incurs further noise amplification by a spatially dependent geometry factor g (Pruessmann et al., 1999). Thus, parallel imaging SNR compared to a fully sampled dataset reads as follows:

$$SNR_{PI}(r) = \frac{SNR_{full}(r)}{g(r) \cdot \sqrt{R}}. \tag{22.9}$$

Acceleration factors of $R = 3$ or 4 are chosen for most UHF fMRI studies (Heidemann et al., 2012; Polimeni et al., 2010), since g increases exponentially beyond that (Wiesinger et al., 2004). This enables single-shot EPI resolving brain slices of up to 0.8 mm in-plane resolution within TAQ = 50 ms for a whole-body gradient system, and 0.5 mm for a head-insert gradient (Fig. 22.7A, black/red lines with x markers).

22.4.4 Extending parallel imaging to 3D

For the 2D imaging considered so far, submillimeter resolution of the whole brain with a typical head-foot FOV (120 mm) requires sampling for 7.5 s (150 slices). The addition of a second-phase-encoding dimension provides new degrees of freedom for parallel imaging, enabling TRs of a few seconds. Utilizing through-plane spatial-encoding capabilities of the coil array also overcomes the one-dimensional g-factor limit of $R = 4$ (Wiesinger et al., 2004).

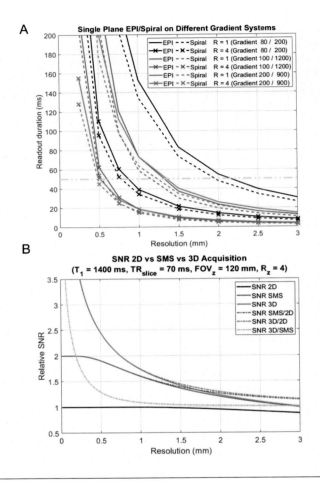

FIG. 22.7

Acceleration constraints for whole-brain BOLD fMRI acquisition. (A) Readout durations of single-shot 2D trajectories (rectilinear EPI and spiral) for different gradient systems. A favorable acquisition window of 50 ms at 7T (*horizontal yellow line*) allows fully sampled trajectories of about 2-mm resolution using whole-body gradients (80/200), and 1.3 mm using head-insert gradients (100/1200 or 200/900). Parallel imaging acceleration with reduction factors of $R = 4$ enables single-shot submillimeter fMRI (0.8 mm) at UHF on conventional gradient systems, with 0.5 mm being the limit for modern-insert gradients. (B) Steady-state thermal SNR for 2D, 3D, and SMS acquisitions at different resolutions. Both 3D and SMS acceleration outperform 2D SNR at ultra-high field. Between each other, they deliver similar SNR for typical high resolutions (1 mm), with 3D excelling over SMS for even smaller voxel sizes. For higher resolutions with in-plane segmentation, because of multiple excitations of the same voxel, the resulting SNR gain is found at the "lower" resolution $N_{segments} \cdot \Delta x$. Simulated gradient systems, specified by their maximum gradient strength (in mT/m) and slew rate (in mT/m/ms): (1) Gradient 80/200: conventional whole-body gradient (e.g., Siemens Prisma), (2) Gradient 100/1200: head-insert gradient with highest available slew rate (Weiger et al., 2018), and (3) Gradient 200/900: head-insert gradient with highest available gradient strength at high slew rate (Feinberg et al., 2021).

For echo-planar acquisition, there are two ways of extending to 3D and enabling hexagonal sampling, which is more efficient than rectangular sampling due to the circular coil and brain geometry (Mersereau, 1979, CAIPIRINHA (Breuer et al., 2006)). First, multi-shot 3D EPI (Poser et al., 2010) can be performed, exciting the whole-volume FOV at every slice TR, but only acquiring one k-space plane at a given k_{slice} per shot. Between shots, EPI planes are shifted in phase-encoding direction via additional prephasers to form the hexagonal pattern (see Chapter 9). Alternatively, simultaneous multi-slice (SMS) imaging (Larkman et al., 2001) enables excitation and acquisition of several slices at the same time. The hexagonal sampling is accomplished by additional triangular gradient blips in slice direction between readout lines ("blipped CAIPIRINHA," (Setsompop et al., 2012)) that zigzag between different k_{slice} planes.

Unlike parallel imaging within a slice, acquisition time per slice is unaltered in SMS, avoiding the $\sqrt{R}$ factor SNR penalty as in Eq. 22.9. However, the exact SNR relation for an fMRI time *series* is more intricate.

22.4.5 Signal-to-noise comparison of 2D, 3D, and SMS imaging

While 2D, 3D, and SMS EPI sequences can be performed with near-identical sequence timing (only differing in the employed RF pulses and gradient blips for k_{slice}), they differ in terms of the available (thermal) SNR. Targeting whole-brain coverage, both SMS and 3D outperform 2D encoding, because they excite and thus average the signal of each voxel multiple times (number of simultaneously excited slices R_{slice} for SMS, total number of slices N_{slices} for 3D) within the volume repetition time of the 2D scan. This outweighs the reduction in steady-state magnetization signal due to the shorter TR between voxel re-excitations. We can quantify by considering the steady-state magnetization in a spoilt GE sequence excited with the Ernst angle (Fig. 22.7B, see Poser et al. (2010) and online material for a full derivation):

$$SNR_{2D|SMS|3D} = SNR_0 \cdot \sqrt{N_{averages,2D|SMS|3D}} \cdot \sqrt{\tanh \frac{TR_{2D|SMS|3D}}{2T_1}}, \tag{22.10}$$

with

$$N_{averages,s} = \begin{cases} 1, & s = 2D \\ R_{slice}, & s = SMS \\ N_{slices}, & s = 3D \end{cases} \quad \text{and} \quad TR_s = \begin{cases} R_{slice} \cdot TR_{vol}, & s = 2D \\ TR_{vol}, & s = SMS \\ \dfrac{R_{slice}}{N_{slices}} \cdot TR_{vol}, & s = 3D \end{cases}. \tag{22.11}$$

Both SMS and 3D outperform 2D imaging and deliver similar thermal SNR for resolutions up to 1 mm at UHF (Fig. 22.7B). At submillimeter voxel size, 3D SNR surpasses SMS, by 13% at 0.8 mm and 29% at 0.5-mm resolution, the respective limits of single-plane acquisitions with whole-body and head-insert gradients (see Fig. 22.7A).

Besides thermal noise, physiological fluctuations (induced by motion, the cardiac or respiratory cycle) influence effective SNR of 2D, SMS, and 3D imaging. Here, SMS and 2D benefit from being conceptually single-shot techniques, while 3D EPI suffers from phase inconsistencies between shots and ghosting artifacts, for example, induced by magnetic field changes due to breathing, which are exacerbated at UHF. Physiological noise correction can typically recover the SNR advantage of 3D EPI (Stirnberg et al., 2017).

Higher acquisition efficiency, on the other hand, benefits the SNR of 3D EPI compared to SMS: Excitation pulses are shorter, and fat suppression can be accomplished by spatially selective water excitation instead of slice-specific saturation (Stirnberg et al., 2017). The increased SAR levels for SMS can limit minimum TR_{vol} and thus, acquisition efficiency, in particular in combination with SE EPI.

Overall, both 3D and SMS EPI have been successfully applied for UHF BOLD acquisition, and their several-fold increased acquisition efficiency compared to 2D EPI due to slice acceleration (see next section and Fig. 22.8A) makes them the method of choice for high-resolution whole-brain fMRI applications (Huber et al., 2016; Poser et al., 2010 and references in Fig. 22.8A).

22.5 Specialized acquisition sequences

22.5.1 Spiral acquisition

In spiral fMRI (Glover, 2012; Noll et al., 1995), k-space sampling is achieved by sinusoidal gradient waveforms in G_{read} and G_{phase} that parameterize an Archimedean spiral with equidistant revolutions. Most commonly, spiral trajectories traverse k-space from the center out (spiral-out), placing nominal TE right at the beginning of the readout. Spirals are compatible with GE and SE contrast, SMS, and 3D encoding, as well as CAIPIRINHA-like sampling via tilted hexagonal k-space grids (t-Hex, Engel et al., 2021).

The key advantage of spirals is their high acquisition efficiency, because the steady rotation along the trajectory maximizes the average speed of k-space traversal. Spirals are 15%–20% faster than EPIs for typical fMRI resolutions (see Fig. 22.7A, dashed lines, and Fig. 22.8A). The flexible choice of TE is another key benefit at UHF for high spatial resolution, where $TE = T_2^*$ cannot be reached by a long EPI readout. Furthermore, g factor noise is reduced for spirals due to the symmetric use of in-plane coil sensitivities (Lee et al., 2021).

Despite these benefits, there are substantial challenges for spiral imaging (see full discussion in Kasper et al., 2022 and references therein). At UHF in particular, the stronger static B_0 off-resonance effects lead to enhanced blurring and local ringing artifacts at magnetic susceptibility gradients. The nonlocal point-spread function (PSF) of spirals typically requires correction via incorporation of the B_0 map into the signal model. Image reconstruction becomes more involved with re-gridding as well as iterative reconstruction algorithms for parallel imaging, such as cg-SENSE (Pruessmann et al., 2001) that are—at the time of writing—not available on vendor systems. Finally, most gradient systems are not optimized for the broad-band sinusoidal waveform of spirals, leading to low-pass filtering and subsequent gradient delays (rotations) and amplitude scaling. Calibration measurements of the actual k-space trajectory can mitigate ensuing artifacts.

2D spirals have been used successfully for submillimeter UHF fMRI at 7T (Kasper et al., 2022) (Fig. 22.7C). First reports of fMRI-capable 3D spiral t-Hex trajectories at UHF (Engel et al., 2021) include some of the highest acquisition efficiencies achieved so far (Fig. 22.8A), but have not been utilized for BOLD fMRI studies yet.

22.5.2 GRASE

GRASE stands for "*GR*adient *A*nd *S*pin *E*cho" imaging and combines the GE EPI and SE EPI sampling (Oshio and Feinberg, 1991). In essence, GRASE is an in-plane segmented SE EPI, where the different segments are acquired as spin echoes between a train of refocusing pulses following a single excitation.

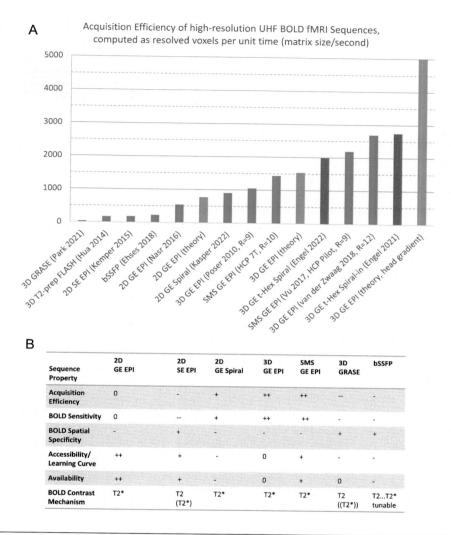

FIG. 22.8

Comparison of properties for different BOLD acquisition sequences. (A) Acquisition efficiency of different sequences used in the UHF literature for whole-brain fMRI, computed as resolved voxels per unit time (matrix size/second). Values were extracted from the referenced publications. Bar colors: (*blue*) studies with fMRI data reported; (*gray*) fMRI-compatible in vivo data reported, no time series analysis; (*orange*) theoretical computations, based on gradient waveform simulations in (A) with 50 ms max readout duration, 20 ms sequence overhead per plane (excitation, contrast formation, fat suppression, spoiling), and for whole-body as well as 200/900 head-insert gradient system (Feinberg et al., 2021). Common selection criteria (deviations mentioned in the labels): single-shot sequence per slice or k-space plane (no in-plane segmentation), maximum in-plane acceleration $R=4$, maximum total acceleration $R=8$, no partial Fourier acceleration, no nonlinear reconstruction (e.g., spatiotemporal prior information). (B) Qualitative assessment of performance criteria for BOLD fMRI sequences mentioned in this chapter in a 5-point scale (++ = key advantage, 0 = average, − = key challenge). While acquisition efficiency can be compared quantitatively with the data in (A), other criteria have not been standardized by the field yet, and are based on assessments relative to the competing sequences here; thus, they depend on site-/vendor-specific expertise and specialization. See the text for definition of the criteria.

The main application of GRASE in fMRI is reduced FOV acquisition with smaller matrix sizes, enabled by orthogonal slice selection of excitation and refocusing pulses. While SE EPI shares this benefit, GRASE exhibits a reduced T_2^*-weighting, because the multiple refocusing pulses provide several k-space lines with pure T_2-weighting, while the shorter interleaved EPI readout segments reduce the remaining T_2^*-weighting and also reduce the distortions due to static B_0 off-resonance. Taken together, this leads to a higher spatial specificity of GRASE than SE EPI in practice.

The main drawback of GRASE is its low acquisition efficiency (Fig. 22.8A) and high SAR levels due to the multiple refocusing pulses. The spatial specificity of GRASE is constrained by a complex mix of GE and SE contrasts, and methods to increase acquisition efficiency (variable flip angle imaging, extended EPI trains) directly compromise it by increasing large-vessel contributions (Scheffler et al., 2021).

22.5.3 Balanced steady-state free precession (bSSFP)

Balanced steady-state free-precession (bSSFP) differs from the BOLD acquisitions considered so far, in that its functional contrast is generated from the frequency sensitivity of the sequence (Scheffler et al., 2001). Susceptibility differences between oxygenated and de-oxygenated blood create off-resonances of more than 10 Hz at 7T, resulting in BOLD effects on bSSFP signal intensity.

The sequence consists of a 3D FLASH sampling module where, after each low flip angle excitation and single k-space line readout, the gradients of every axis are *balanced* (net integral of zero per TR), leading to a single steady-state magnetization vector (instead of superpositions). Furthermore, the phase of consecutive excitation pulses alternates (α_{+x}, α_{-x}, α_{+x}, ...), maximizing signal amplitude by restoring longitudinal magnetization from the remaining on-resonant transverse one. Off-resonant magnetization is not fully restored, and an intensity minimum (banding artifact) occurs, if magnetization is out of phase at the time of the next excitation. This leads to a magnitude profile of bSSFP that depends on the off-resonance frequency and is periodic with TR^{-1} [Hz]. Intensity changes are small within 75% of this range (the passband), with steep magnitude changes in the remaining 25% (the transition band), including banding artifacts.

bSSFP for BOLD is mostly performed within the passband, whose larger extent offers higher robustness to static B_0 off-resonance, which is particularly relevant at UHF. The resulting contrast is mainly T_2-weighted due to spin diffusion around micro-vasculature (see review by Miller, 2012 for details).

Passband bSSFP has accomplished high-quality whole-brain imaging, with few banding artifacts, and convincing BOLD contrast at 9.4T (Fig. 22.7C, Scheffler and Ehses, 2016). The main advantages of bSSFP are high spatial specificity due to its T_2-weighting, in combination with the distortion-free geometry of the FLASH readout. Taken together, bSSFP is slightly less specific and BOLD-sensitive than SE EPI. A unique feature of bSSFP is that T_2^*-weighting can be tuned by longer TRs. Acquisition efficiency is comparable to SE EPI (Fig. 22.8A), while SAR is lower, but remains a limiting factor for bSSFP at UHF, necessitating concessions to sensitivity (lower flip angle) or acquisition efficiency (less selective slab excitation). Finally, banding artifacts remain a practical challenge to whole-brain image quality at UHF.

22.5.4 What is the best sequence for BOLD acquisition?

To conclude, we compare all the introduced sequences for BOLD acquisitions at UHF along five criteria that are important for research application (Fig. 22.8B), namely:

1. Acquisition efficiency: How many voxels are acquired per unit time?
2. BOLD sensitivity: How much signal change relative to noise is induced in the image by neuronal activation (contrast-to-noise ratio)?
3. Spatial specificity: How localized is the point-spread function of the induced BOLD response in the image depiction?
4. Accessibility/learning curve: How much familiarity with the sequence is required to adjust parameters, detect artifacts for optimal CNR, and reconstruct and preprocess the data?
5. Availability: How available is the sequence on commercial scanners or via standardized research collaboration channels? Are there open-source implementations, and is there a fast or online image reconstruction at the scanner?

While such a tabular comparison is by nature simplistic, it may provide some intuitive understanding about the fundamental properties of different sequences, for example, the high acquisition efficiency and availability of GE EPI that led to its widespread use. The multi-dimensional variability within this comparison may also emphasize the universal truth that the best sequence for BOLD acquisition is the one that is available and well tested on the MRI system one is working with.

22.6 Code and data availability

Code to recreate the modeling figures on BOLD acquisition is available on GitHub https://github.com/BRAIN-TO/book-chapter-uhf-neuro-mri (citable version at https://doi.org/10.5281/zenodo.6359931), with the flexibility to adjust own parameters (gradient specifications, tissue and sequence parameters, etc.) for future comparisons.

Acknowledgments

We thank Saskia Bollmann, Maria Engel, Jakob Heinzle, and S. Johanna Vannesjo for helpful discussions about BOLD acquisition, and Ruediger Stirnberg for his educational talk at ISMRM 2020 and subsequent discussions on 2D/3D/SMS SNR that sparked Section 22.4.5. We also thank Renzo Huber for discussions on how (not) to compare fMRI sequences that inspired Fig. 22.8.

References

Breuer, F.A., Blaimer, M., Mueller, M.F., et al., 2006. Controlled aliasing in volumetric parallel imaging (2D CAIPIRINHA). Magn. Reson. Med. 55, 549–556. https://doi.org/10.1002/mrm.20787.

Buxton, R.B., Uludağ, K., Dubowitz, D.J., Liu, T.T., 2004. Modeling the hemodynamic response to brain activation. NeuroImage 23, S220–S233. https://doi.org/10.1016/j.neuroimage.2004.07.013.

Deichmann, R., Josephs, O., Hutton, C., Corfield, D.R., Turner, R., 2002. Compensation of susceptibility-induced BOLD sensitivity losses in echo-planar fMRI imaging. NeuroImage 15, 120–135. https://doi.org/10.1006/nimg.2001.0985.

Douglas, R.J., Martin, K.A.C., 2004. Neuronal circuits of the neocortex. Annu. Rev. Neurosci. 27, 419–451. https://doi.org/10.1146/annurev.neuro.27.070203.144152.

Engel, M., Kasper, L., Wilm, B., et al., 2021. T-hex: Tilted hexagonal grids for rapid 3D imaging. Magn. Reson. Med. 85, 2507–2523. https://doi.org/10.1002/mrm.28600.

Feinberg, D.A., Hale, J.D., Watts, J.C., Kaufman, L., Mark, A., 1986. Halving MR imaging time by conjugation: demonstration at 3.5 kG. Radiology 161, 527–531. https://doi.org/10.1148/radiology.161.2.3763926.

Feinberg, D.A., Dietz, P., Liu, C., et al., 2021. Design and development of a next-generation 7T human brain scanner with high-performance gradient coil and dense RF arrays. In: Proc. Intl. Soc. Mag. Reson. Med. vol. 29. Presented at the ISMRM 2021, p. 562.

Glover, G.H., 2012. Spiral imaging in fMRI. NeuroImage 62, 706–712. https://doi.org/10.1016/j.neuroimage.2011.10.039.

Han, S., Eun, S., Cho, H., Uludağ, K., Kim, S.-G., 2021. Improvement of sensitivity and specificity for laminar BOLD fMRI with double spin-echo EPI in humans at 7 T. NeuroImage 241, 118435. https://doi.org/10.1016/j.neuroimage.2021.118435.

Havlicek, M., Uludağ, K., 2020. A dynamical model of the laminar BOLD response. NeuroImage 204, 116209. https://doi.org/10.1016/j.neuroimage.2019.116209.

Havlicek, M., Roebroeck, A., Friston, K., Gardumi, A., Ivanov, D., Uludag, K., 2015. Physiologically informed dynamic causal modeling of fMRI data. NeuroImage 122, 355–372. https://doi.org/10.1016/j.neuroimage.2015.07.078.

Havlicek, M., Roebroeck, A., Friston, K.J., Gardumi, A., Ivanov, D., Uludag, K., 2017. On the importance of modeling fMRI transients when estimating effective connectivity: A dynamic causal modeling study using ASL data. NeuroImage 155, 217–233. https://doi.org/10.1016/j.neuroimage.2017.03.017.

Heidemann, R.M., Ivanov, D., Trampel, R., et al., 2012. Isotropic submillimeter fMRI in the human brain at 7 T: combining reduced field-of-view imaging and partially parallel acquisitions. Magn. Reson. Med. 68, 1506–1516. https://doi.org/10.1002/mrm.24156.

Huber, L., Ivanov, D., Guidi, M., et al., 2016. Functional cerebral blood volume mapping with simultaneous multi-slice acquisition. NeuroImage 125, 1159–1168. https://doi.org/10.1016/j.neuroimage.2015.10.082.

Huber, L., Uludağ, K., Möller, H.E., 2019. Non-BOLD contrast for laminar fMRI in humans: CBF, CBV, and CMRO2. NeuroImage 197, 742–760. https://doi.org/10.1016/j.neuroimage.2017.07.041.

Kasper, L., Engel, M., Heinzle, J., et al., 2022. Advances in spiral fMRI: a high-resolution study with single-shot acquisition. NeuroImage 246, 118738. https://doi.org/10.1016/j.neuroimage.2021.118738.

Kemper, V.G., De Martino, F., Vu, A.T., et al., 2015. Sub-millimeter T2 weighted fMRI at 7 T: comparison of 3D-GRASE and 2D SE-EPI. Front. Neurosci. https://doi.org/10.3389/fnins.2015.00163.

Larkman, D.J., Hajnal, J.V., Herlihy, A.H., Coutts, G.A., Young, I.R., Ehnholm, G., 2001. Use of multicoil arrays for separation of signal from multiple slices simultaneously excited. J. Magn. Reson. Imaging 13, 313–317. https://doi.org/10.1002/1522-2586(200102)13:2<313::AID-JMRI1045>3.0.CO;2-W.

Lee, Y., Wilm, B.J., Brunner, D.O., et al., 2021. On the signal-to-noise ratio benefit of spiral acquisition in diffusion MRI. Magn. Reson. Med. 85, 1924–1937. https://doi.org/10.1002/mrm.28554.

Logothetis, N.K., Pauls, J., Augath, M., Trinath, T., Oeltermann, A., 2001. Neurophysiological investigation of the basis of the fMRI signal. Nature 412, 150–157. https://doi.org/10.1038/35084005.

Mersereau, R.M., 1979. The processing of hexagonally sampled two-dimensional signals. Proc. IEEE 67, 930–949. https://doi.org/10.1109/PROC.1979.11356.

Miller, K.L., 2012. FMRI using balanced steady-state free precession (SSFP). NeuroImage 62, 713–719. https://doi.org/10.1016/j.neuroimage.2011.10.040.

Noll, D.C., Cohen, J.D., Meyer, C.H., Schneider, W., 1995. Spiral K-space MR imaging of cortical activation. J. Magn. Reson. Imaging 5, 49–56. https://doi.org/10.1002/jmri.1880050112.

Oshio, K., Feinberg, D.A., 1991. GRASE (gradient-and spin-echo) imaging: a novel fast MRI technique. Magn. Reson. Med. 20, 344–349. https://doi.org/10.1002/mrm.1910200219.

Polimeni, J.R., Fischl, B., Greve, D.N., Wald, L.L., 2010. Laminar analysis of 7T BOLD using an imposed spatial activation pattern in human V1. NeuroImage 52, 1334–1346. https://doi.org/10.1016/j.neuroimage.2010.05.005.

Poser, B.A., Koopmans, P.J., Witzel, T., Wald, L.L., Barth, M., 2010. Three dimensional echo-planar imaging at 7 tesla. NeuroImage 51, 261–266. https://doi.org/10.1016/j.neuroimage.2010.01.108.

Pruessmann, K.P., Weiger, M., Scheidegger, M.B., Boesiger, P., 1999. SENSE: Sensitivity encoding for fast MRI. Magn. Reson. Med. 42, 952–962. https://doi.org/10.1002/(SICI)1522-2594(199911)42:5<952::AID-MRM16>3.0.CO;2-S.

Pruessmann, K.P., Weiger, M., Börnert, P., Boesiger, P., 2001. Advances in sensitivity encoding with arbitrary k-space trajectories. Magn. Reson. Med. 46, 638–651. https://doi.org/10.1002/mrm.1241.

Scheffler, K., Ehses, P., 2016. High-resolution mapping of neuronal activation with balanced SSFP at 9.4 tesla. Magn. Reson. Med. 76, 163–171. https://doi.org/10.1002/mrm.25890.

Scheffler, K., Seifritz, E., Bilecen, D., et al., 2001. Detection of BOLD changes by means of a frequency-sensitive trueFISP technique: preliminary results. NMR Biomed. 14, 490–496. https://doi.org/10.1002/nbm.726.

Scheffler, K., Engelmann, J., Heule, R., 2021. BOLD sensitivity and vessel size specificity along CPMG and GRASE echo trains. Magn. Reson. Med. 86, 2076–2083. https://doi.org/10.1002/mrm.28871.

Setsompop, K., Gagoski, B.A., Polimeni, J.R., Witzel, T., Wedeen, V.J., Wald, L.L., 2012. Blipped-controlled aliasing in parallel imaging for simultaneous multislice echo planar imaging with reduced g-factor penalty. Magn. Reson. Med. 67, 1210–1224. https://doi.org/10.1002/mrm.23097.

Stirnberg, R., Huijbers, W., Brenner, D., Poser, B.A., Breteler, M., Stöcker, T., 2017. Rapid whole-brain resting-state fMRI at 3 T: efficiency-optimized three-dimensional EPI versus repetition time-matched simultaneous-multi-slice EPI. NeuroImage 163, 81–92. https://doi.org/10.1016/j.neuroimage.2017.08.031.

Uludağ, K., 2010. To dip or not to dip: Reconciling optical imaging and fMRI data. Proc. Natl. Acad. Sci. U. S. A. 107, E23. https://doi.org/10.1073/pnas.0914194107.

Uludağ, K., Blinder, P., 2018. Linking brain vascular physiology to hemodynamic response in ultra-high field MRI. NeuroImage 168, 279–295. https://doi.org/10.1016/j.neuroimage.2017.02.063.

Uludağ, K., Havlicek, M., 2021. Determining laminar neuronal activity from BOLD fMRI using a generative model. Prog. Neurobiol., 102055. https://doi.org/10.1016/j.pneurobio.2021.102055.

Uludağ, K., Müller-Bierl, B., Uğurbil, K., 2009. An integrative model for neuronal activity-induced signal changes for gradient and spin echo functional imaging. NeuroImage 48, 150–165. https://doi.org/10.1016/j.neuroimage.2009.05.051.

van der Zwaag, W., Francis, S., Head, K., et al., 2009. fMRI at 1.5, 3 and 7 T: Characterising BOLD signal changes. NeuroImage 47, 1425–1434. https://doi.org/10.1016/j.neuroimage.2009.05.015.

Weiger, M., Overweg, J., Rösler, M.B., et al., 2018. A high-performance gradient insert for rapid and short-T2 imaging at full duty cycle. Magn. Reson. Med. 79, 3256–3266. https://doi.org/10.1002/mrm.26954.

Wiesinger, F., Boesiger, P., Pruessmann, K.P., 2004. Electrodynamics and ultimate SNR in parallel MR imaging. Magn. Reson. Med. 52, 376–390. https://doi.org/10.1002/mrm.20183.

Yablonskiy, D.A., Haacke, E.M., 1994. Theory of NMR signal behavior in magnetically inhomogenous tissues: the static dephasing regime. Magn. Reson. Med 32, 749–763.

Sequences and contrasts for non-BOLD fMRI

Nils Nothnagel[a], Laurentius Huber[b], and Jozien Goense[c,d,e,f]

[a]*School of Psychology and Neuroscience, University of Glasgow, Glasgow, United Kingdom* [b]*Functional Magnetic Resonance Imaging Facility, National Institute of Mental Health, National Institutes of Health, Bethesda, MD, United States* [c]*Department of Psychology, University of Illinois Urbana-Champaign, Champaign, IL, United States* [d]*Department of Bioengineering, University of Illinois Urbana-Champaign, Urbana, IL, United States* [e]*Beckman Institute for Advance Science and Technology, University of Illinois Urbana-Champaign, Urbana, IL, United States* [f]*Neuroscience Program, University of Illinois Urbana-Champaign, Urbana, IL, United States*

Highlights

- Non-BOLD fMRI sequences measure a single brain physiology parameter, such as cerebral blood flow (CBF) or cerebral blood volume (CBV).
- Non-BOLD fMRI sequences measure brain activity with higher specificity and potential quantifiability.
- Higher specificity is needed to better separate neural activity across cortical layers and columns.
- Non-BOLD sequences may enable a better interpretation of conventional BOLD fMRI at UHF.
- A low SNR/CNR imposes additional challenges to the implementation of non-BOLD fMRI sequences and requires technical solutions.

23.1 Introduction

Technical advances in ultra-high field (UHF) MRI technology have allowed us to study brain activity at high spatial resolution. BOLD has been the dominant functional contrast in brain fMRI experiments for more than 30 years. However, our understanding of the BOLD response remains incomplete, in particular at resolutions that are accessible at UHF. One of the drawbacks of BOLD is that it is not directly related to a single physiological parameter but it is a combination of metabolism and blood flow. Other methods such as fCBV, fCBF, and $fCMRO_2$ have been used and have advantages for certain applications. In this chapter, we give an overview of alternative fMRI techniques and highlight their strengths and challenges at ultra-high field.

Neuronal activity causes a hemodynamic response that depends on the local vasculature as deoxygenated blood is rapidly drained by veins to the pial surface. The cortical vasculature is heterogeneous, consisting of radially penetrating venules and arterioles, as well as large superficial draining veins (Fig. 23.1A). Since BOLD is sensitive to deoxygenated blood, primarily in capillaries and veins, BOLD activity recorded with submillimeter spatial resolution will be detected not only in voxels with neural activity but also in voxels downstream. This lack of specificity may challenge the interpretation

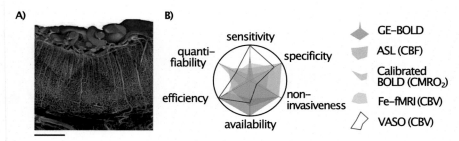

FIG. 23.1

(A) Corrosion cast of the macaque visual cortex. The image shows the cortical blood supply, with arterial blood reaching the cortex and the capillaries through radially penetrating arterioles (*red*). Deoxygenated blood leaves the brain tissue by venules (*blue*) and gets drained via large veins on the cortical surface back to the lungs (bar is 1 mm). (B) Summary of available methods: GE BOLD originates from oxygenation changes in downstream veins and venules, non-BOLD fMRI responses are believed to arise predominantly from arterioles and capillaries (CBF), tissues ($CMRO_2$), and arterioles (CBV). Each method has a trade-off between various quality features, including detection sensitivity, localization specificity, invasiveness, availability, sampling efficiency, and quantifiability. *Taken from Hirsch et al. (2012), with permission under STM guidelines.*

of high-resolution fMRI, and it can be therefore desirable, particularly at ultra-high field, to study parameters more directly related to brain physiology. Examples of such parameters are as follows:

- Brain tissue perfusion or cerebral blood flow (CBF) (mL/g/min): a local increase in blood flow in response to neuronal activity measured using arterial spin labeling (ASL).
- Changes in the cerebral blood volume (CBV) (mL) either using an Fe-based contrast agent or vascular space occupancy (VASO).
- The cerebral metabolic consumption of O_2 (mL O_2/min) employing gradient echo (GE) BOLD and ASL/VASO sequences.

BOLD is a combination of blood flow and metabolism and reflects a combination of $CMRO_2$, CBF, and CBV changes (see Fig. 22.1). The BOLD response can be difficult to interpret, especially in cases where the relationship between $CMRO_2$, CBF, and CBV is variable or not clearly defined (for instance, in disease). The differences between laminar profiles of CBV, CBF, and BOLD show that non-BOLD methods clearly measure different aspects of the functional response (Jin and Kim, 2008). A close correspondence of functional activation to physiological parameters is important for quantitative fMRI, to have clinical potential, but at high resolution, there may be differences in neurovascular coupling in different structures (Goense et al., 2012). Furthermore, a quantitative measure of brain activity may lead to a more straightforward interpretation than changes in BOLD activity. The main disadvantage of non-BOLD sequences at UHF is a relatively premature state of development and the lack of a gold standard for their implementation in human scanners compared with non-BOLD imaging in animals with less restrictions for RF pulses and gradients. Most of these sequences also suffer a lower SNR than BOLD fMRI and have worse temporal precision and efficiency due to the need for additional RF pulses for labeling or inverting the signal. Moreover, they are less streamlined than GE BOLD sequences because they are more difficult to set up and apply. Additionally, these sequences are not always directly available at each research site. A comparison of the strength and weaknesses of the most commonly used non-BOLD sequences is visualized in Fig. 23.1B. In spite of these individual challenges, fMRI using non-BOLD sequences is gaining traction at UHF because of the requirement of a highly specific signal that is needed for high-resolution fMRI and because UHF is making non-BOLD methods feasible as a result of the improved SNR at UHF.

There are several fMRI sequences that are commonly used at UHF. They are briefly introduced here, with more in-depth discussion in later sections of this chapter.

(1) GE BOLD, the standard, has high SNR, good CNR, and high temporal resolution.

GE BOLD is a highly efficient sequence and the most straightforward to implement, making it very popular for UHF fMRI. GE BOLD is most sensitive to venous blood.

(2) BOLD-based sequences and hybrid/other techniques (SE BOLD, 3D GRASE, MT, DW fMRI, etc.)

SE BOLD, 3D GRASE, etc., are based on spin echo, and at UHF, they are highly specific to small vessels such as capillaries. These sequences are harder to implement because of the refocusing pulse, the associated RF power deposition, and large flip angle variations due to B_1 inhomogeneity. There has been much discussion about whether SE BOLD methods are better for high-resolution fMRI, which is not fully resolved within the field. One potential reason why there is no clear consensus on SE BOLD might be the complication that SE BOLD has a lower SNR and CNR, thus making it difficult to separate specificity from SNR/CNR effects. Furthermore, SE-based sequences are almost always a mixture of multiple static and dynamic dephasing processes and have some sensitivity to GE contrast by virtue of their readout window and the need to acquire it with a practical sequence. Hence, SE BOLD is quite sensitive to its specific implementation choices. For a discussion of GE BOLD and other BOLD-based sequences, see Chapter 22 "BOLD fMRI: Physiology and acquisition strategies" by Uludag and Kasper.

(3) CBV measured with Fe-based contrast agents or VASO

There are two mainstream fMRI methods that measure CBV changes: contrast agent-based methods, which are mostly used in animals, and the more recent VASO fMRI methods, which have been successfully applied to human high-resolution fMRI. Contrast agent-based fCBV and VASO fMRI have shown good correspondence (Goense et al., 2012). CBV methods are more specific, even though the contrast agent based CBV uses the same sequence as GE BOLD. VASO has a lower temporal sampling efficiency as it is based on a "labeling" approach. VASO CBV data can be quantifiable to some degree.

(4) CBF measured with ASL

CBF is measured using various arterial spin labeling methods, where spins are labeled and inflow into a target slice is measured. Since the ASL-signal consists of the subtraction of a label- and control-image, it has lower temporal resolution, but it has the advantage of being quantifiable. While other non-BOLD fMRI methods also refer to clearly defined physiological parameters, the relationship between ASL and CBF is more widely established.

(5) $CMRO_2$ measured using calibrated BOLD

$CMRO_2$ reflects the cerebral oxygen consumption, and thus measures an important biological variable of brain metabolism. However, its application is complicated by its experimental setup. It is calculated from BOLD and CBF or CBV scans during vascular calibration (using CO_2, O_2, or carbogen), as well as during functional tasks. It relies on the difference of these signals and is based on an oxygenation-dilution model. Due to the nonlinear nature of the model and because of respective error propagations, it is limited by the SNR/CNR. Calibrated BOLD methods are still under development and not widely applied at UHF.

This chapter on non-BOLD fMRI focuses on vascular-based contrasts. For nonvascular non-BOLD fMRI such as diffusion-weighted layer fMRI, see Truong and Song (2009), or for $T_{1\rho}$-based non-BOLD fMRI at UHF, see Jin and Kim (2010).

23.2 Motivation for using non-BOLD fMRI

23.2.1 Non-BOLD fMRI is more closely related to neural activity than BOLD fMRI

BOLD is a combination of metabolism and blood flow, and the mismatch between them, i.e., the BOLD signal, is related to the excess blood flow upon stimulation. Upon stimulation, CBF increases, metabolism increases, and CBV increases. BOLD measures the amount of deoxy-hemoglobin, which makes it mostly sensitive to downstream vascular compartments of capillaries and veins. Metabolism, flow, and volume changes, however, are heterogeneous across the cortex, and one can model them as different compartments. Voxels that have different compositions of veins, arteries, gray matter, and white matter will have different hemodynamic properties. The vascular density and anatomy of the vascular system also play a role in all this. This is not much of an issue at lower resolutions; however, these effects become more relevant at the submillimeter scale. Additionally, within the cortex across layers, there are differences in vascular density and possibly neurovascular coupling (Hirsch et al., 2012). Since BOLD is a combination of all these factors, using non-BOLD methods allows researchers to separate some of these contributions.

23.2.2 Non-BOLD fMRI has higher localization specificity than BOLD fMRI

Specificity is a term that refers to how closely the fMRI signal is related to the underlying neural phenomena, and especially how closely the fMRI response reflects the neural signal in spatial terms. The ideal is that the fMRI signal increases very closely to the location of the neural activity. This is generally the case if one can measure capillary responses. In the field of optical imaging, it has been shown that the vascular response is regulated at capillary scales (Blinder et al., 2013). However, whether the total blood volume or deoxygenated blood are measured, and the time point of the measurement affect the specificity of the response (in both optical imaging and fMRI).

Summary of current theory of the location within the vasculature where the BOLD, fCBV, fCBF, and fCMRO2 signals originate:

- GE BOLD is sensitive to venules and larger veins because it measures spins within susceptibility gradients.
- SE BOLD is sensitive to capillaries because it only measures spins that move within the susceptibility gradients.
- fCBV measures blood volume changes, which occur mostly in arterioles (Yu et al., 2016).
- fCBF measures flow, and depending on the labeling delay, it is more sensitive to arteries and arterioles vs capillaries (at short vs long labeling delays respectively) (Kim and Ogawa, 2012).

- CMRO2 is calculated using a biophysical model, the calibrated BOLD model, and is a mixture signal as typically BOLD and CBF are used to estimate the local metabolism (Davis et al., 1998). Little is known about its specificity, as it depends on the component sequences (typically BOLD and CBF) and the applied model, but it is thought to be quite specific.

The specificity and sensitivity of all methods depends on sequence parameters, either the sequence's imaging module and/or the labeling period and its parameter choices.

23.3 Functional CBV

Neuronal activity leads to an increase in the local oxygen demand. This need is accommodated by dilation of arterioles and capillaries in the brain, which leads to a local increase in the blood volume in the activated area. In contrast to BOLD fMRI, which is biased toward veins, CBV fMRI is sensitive to changes in the blood volume, predominantly in arterioles and capillaries, and is therefore a more precise measure of brain activity. A major advantage of CBV fMRI is that it has a higher localization specificity than GE BOLD. The functional change can be measured as a relative change (ranging from a few % signal change to $\sim$20%) or as an absolute change (in units of mL). Small changes make the signal more sensitive to physiological and thermal noise.

Most CBV fMRI sequences use EPI-based readouts. Since most applications at UHF are aiming for high spatial resolution, the respective sequence readout modules consist of correspondingly long echo trains and often long TEs. This means that the functional signal can be contaminated by unwanted BOLD weighting, which needs to be accounted for. Common BOLD correction methods consist of additional acquisitions of BOLD-only reference data, which allow the quantification and retrospective removal of the BOLD signal from the CBV-weighted images.

23.3.1 Contrast agent-based functional CBV

Iron oxide-based fMRI experiments are based on contrast agent injections with ultra-small superparamagnetic iron particles (USPIO) or iron nanoparticles (with particle sizes <20 nm, e.g., ferumoxytol and MION) (Mandeville and Marota, 1999). The particles stay within the vasculature and dramatically shorten the T_2/T_2^* of the blood. An increase in the blood volume due to functional activation increases the concentration of the contrast agent in a voxel and shortens its T_2^*, leading to a signal reduction proportional to the CBV change. Iron oxide-based (or Fe-based) functional CBV changes can be on the order of 20%, thus representing strong functional signals and a high CNR. Any sequence that can be used for BOLD can be used for Fe-based functional CBV. Similar to BOLD, a higher specificity has been observed in SE-based CBV fMRI than in GE-based CBV fMRI (Kim et al., 2013).

Contrast agent-based fMRI has been mostly limited to animal work as there are currently no iron oxides approved for MRI in human subjects outside clinical use or studies. (Ferumoxytol has been approved in the United States for the treatment of iron deficiency anemia in patients with chronic kidney disease.)

Due to their high CNR, iron oxide-based methods are highly suitable for high-resolution fMRI, and studies of cortical columns and layers have shown that the CBV signal is highly specific to small vessels (capillaries and small arterioles) (Yu et al., 2016). Another common application of contrast agent-based functional CBV is in fMRI of awake behaving monkeys (Leite et al., 2002).

23.3.2 **VASO functional CBV**

VASO is a noninvasive CBV method (Lu et al., 2003) that is now widely applied in humans (Huber et al., 2021) at UHF as well as at more common clinical field strengths. The VASO sequence takes advantage of the T_1 difference between the blood and the surrounding tissue by using an inversion recovery sequence to specifically null the blood signal, while maintaining part of the tissue signal (see Fig. 23.2). The (relative) VASO signal intensity can thus be considered to be proportional to $1 - CBV$ (if no BOLD contamination is present). When neural activation causes CBV to increase, the VASO signal will decrease, allowing the detection of activated regions. Since VASO is an inversion recovery-based sequence, it can suffer from the wellknown B_1-inhomogeneities and SAR constraints at UHF, which is usually mitigated by means of numerically optimized adiabatic inversion pulses (e.g., TR-FOCI).

After VASO had first been applied in human UHF MRI (Hua et al., 2013), it quickly became the most popular non-BOLD fMRI method in the human UHF community. Currently with 27 peer-reviewed UHF VASO journal publications, it constitutes 20% of all human high-resolution fMRI papers (source: https://layerfmri.com/vasoworldwide/). By comparison, there are only 2.1% human ASL studies and 1% calibrated BOLD studies with comparable spatial resolution. While VASO is noisier than GE BOLD, it has the highest detection sensitivity among non-BOLD fMRI methods that are applicable in humans. Due to the inversion recovery-based contrast generation and respective inversion delays (sequence dead times), VASO generally has a lower effective temporal resolution than BOLD. For common UHF applications with submillimeter resolutions, VASO protocols with TRs of 2–5 s are used. However, faster VASO imaging approaches with sampling rates in the subsecond regime are being developed (Huber et al., 2020).

While BOLD and ASL sequences are usually provided by the MRI vendors, VASO sequences are not (yet) distributed as a commercial product. Thus, UHF VASO users are sometimes constrained by limited access to proprietary sequence code and have to rely on cross-site research agreements and local MRI developer expertise to use custom VASO sequences. Currently, approximately 45 MRI labs actively use VASO at UHF with custom sequences on various vendor systems.

Since animal fCBV work typically uses iron oxide-based contrast agents and human work employs VASO, translatability is a potential issue. Fortunately, comparative work in animals using VASO and contrast agent-based functional CBV have shown the same results for all comparisons made so far (see also Fig. 23.2) (Huber et al., 2015; Goense et al., 2012).

23.4 **Functional CBF**

As the BOLD response relies on an increase in CBF over the metabolic need, it should be no surprise that one can also measure a CBF increase upon stimulation. Baseline and functional CBF can be measured using arterial spin labeling (ASL) methods. CBF sequences follow the basic labeling protocol, where images acquired after labeling are compared with control images. This makes the CBF signal a difference signal and more sensitive to noise. Furthermore, CBF is also a rather small signal with a correspondingly limited perfusion CNR (Huber et al., 2019). Functional CBF arises when CBF measurements are combined with a functional stimulation protocol. These changes are comparatively large, typically 20%–100%, depending on the stimulus. Here, we review the work on functional CBF or functional ASL (fASL). The CBF contrast as measured with ASL has its origin in water exchange

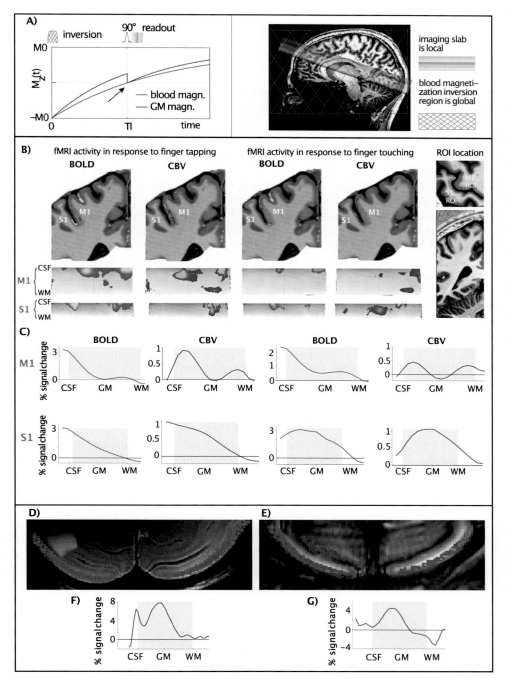

FIG. 23.2

CBV applications at UHF. (A) Schematic of VASO showing the blood nulling (*left*) and the location of the imaging and inversion slab. (B) Human BOLD and VASO maps (coronal slice) in response to finger tapping/touching in the primary motor (M1) and sensory cortex (S1). Resolution 0.78×0.78 mm^2. (C) Cortical profile for the VASO and BOLD signals in M1 and S1. (D) Fe-contrast agent-based CBV map in response to a full-field rotating checkerboard stimulus in the primary visual cortex (V1) of an anesthetized macaque. SE-CBV, 4.7T, resolution 250×180 μm^2. (E) VASO map in V1 of an anesthetized macaque in response to a full-field rotating checkerboard stimulus. 4.7T, resolution 500×333 μm^2, (F) cortical profiles for the Fe-based CBV map in (D), and for the VASO-based CBV map in (E).

between vessels and tissue, as well as in the intravascular (mostly arterial) signal. Depending on the labeling times, the signal is weighted toward arteries, arterioles, or capillaries. At shorter labeling times, the response is more arterial weighted, while at longer labeling times, the capillary signal becomes more important (Zappe et al., 2008a). Longer labeling times tend to have a reduced baseline perfusion CNR. There are many different CBF sequences that differ in how labeling is performed, provide more efficient and precise labeling, and differ in how artifacts and spurious (background) signals are controlled. Perfusion techniques and their challenges and solutions at UHF are covered in more detail in Chapter 21: "Ultra-high field brain perfusion MRI" by Wang et al.

fCBF has been measured in rats, cats, and monkeys and is recently starting to be applied in humans at UHF. Numerous studies have compared different fMRI methods in animals, particularly comparisons between BOLD and non-BOLD methods (Duong et al., 2002; Kim and Ogawa, 2012; Goense et al., 2016). The questions have focused on localization specificity and neurovascular coupling mechanisms. These studies showed that the fCBF signal is localized in gray matter (and shown to be highest in layer IV in the sensory cortex) (Fig. 23.3), while laminar and olfactory work has shown the promise of fCBF for high-resolution applications (Poplawsky et al., 2015). Compared with GE BOLD or VASO studies, there are relatively few fCBF (or fASL) studies at UHF in humans that go beyond the common resolution of lower field strengths, which is largely related to the lower SNR of ASL and the challenges associated with its implementation (see references in Chapter 21).

fCBF has the potential advantage that it is more specific and more accurately reflects the site of neural activation. It is also less sensitive to large veins, so it produces more accurate localization, and it directly measures a physiological variable. This might be a key factor for studying pathologies using fCBF in a clinical setting. Another advantage is its potential for quantification (its unit is mL/100 g/min). Comparison of MRI- and PET-based CBF methods and their respective response magnitudes evoked by neural tasks showed good agreement. Initial results on reproducibility suggest that fCBF is slightly more reproducible (intra-individual) than BOLD. This is despite the much lower SNR of the fCBF method. fCBF is a promising method but has been so for a very long time. It has been mostly hampered by a low SNR. UHF may have a role here, although SAR limitations and reduced B_1 homogeneity pose challenges.

One of the disadvantages of fCBF is its sensitivity to physiological noise. In particular, B_0 changes during respiration are a common source of error and require an additional correction step during analysis to mitigate the effect. Although other CBF methods have the advantage of more precise labeling, the most common sequence at UHF in humans is FAIR ASL due to its lower SAR and easier implementation. A potential way to mitigate this issue is to use dedicated labeling coils or pTx pulses. However, this makes the implementation more difficult and requires specialized hardware).

23.5 Functional CMRO$_2$

Although there are several methods to measure the cerebral metabolic rate of oxygen consumption (CMRO$_2$), here, we focus on the most commonly used calibrated BOLD method. It is currently not possible to directly measure CMRO$_2$ changes with MRI, but they can be calculated from the BOLD response and the CBF response using appropriate models. While BOLD is a combination of blood flow and metabolism, it is possible to disentangle the two, and it can provide access to estimates of functional CMRO$_2$ change. This idea underlies the calibrated BOLD method, which is the most

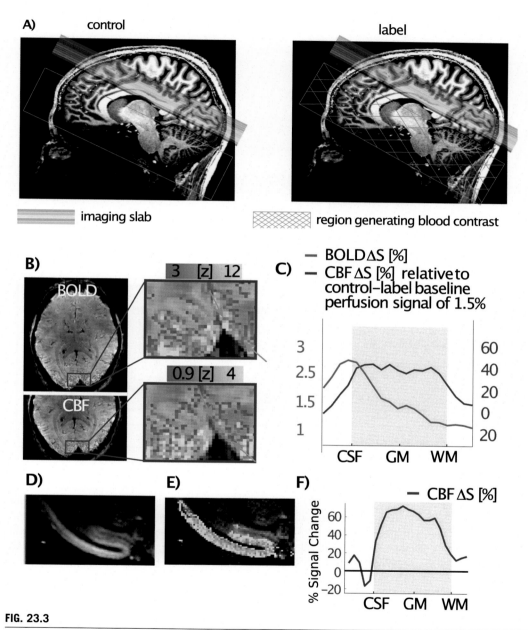

FIG. 23.3

CBF applications at UHF. (A) Schematic of a CBF experiment showing the imaging and inversion slab in the "control" and the "label" condition. (B) Human BOLD and fCBF in visual cortex (resolution 0.8×0.8 mm^2). (C) Cortical fCBF profile in human V1 (Huber et al., 2019, using data from Ivanov et al., 2016, with permission). (D) Baseline CBF map acquired in V1 of an anesthetized macaque using CASL (Zappe et al., 2008a). 4.7T, resolution 375×333 μm^2. (E) Functional CBF in response to a rotating checkerboard stimulus. (F) Cortical profile of the functional CBF in (E). *Panel B: Data from Ivanov et al. (2016).*

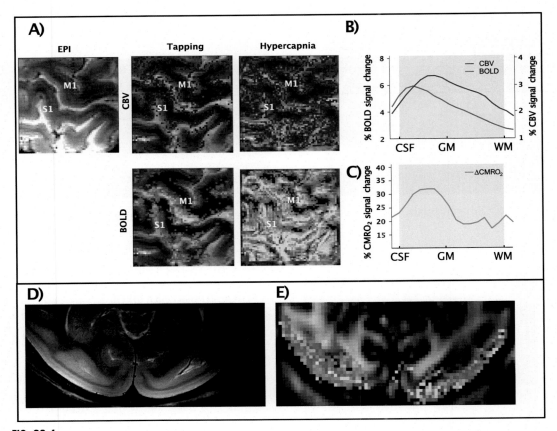

FIG. 23.4

$CMRO_2$ applications at UHF. (A) The Calibrated BOLD method uses functional images acquired under stimulation (here, finger tapping, middle panels) and respiratory (CO_2) challenge (*right*). VASO-CBV (*top row*) and BOLD (*bottom row*) are acquired in the stimulation and hypercapnic runs. An anatomical reference (left panel) shows the somatosensory and motor cortex. (B) Cortical profiles for the BOLD and VASO responses after finger tapping. (C) $CMRO_2$ profile in human M1. (D) Anatomical reference image of the early visual cortex in the macaque (RARE, 7T, 250×250 μm^2). (E) $CMRO_2$ map using calibrated BOLD in an anesthetized macaque. Activation in response to a full-field rotating checkerboard can be seen in V1 and V2. Calibrated BOLD using BOLD, CBF, and hypercapnic challenge, 7T, 750×750 μm^2. *Panel C: Adapted from Guidi et al. (2016).*

common method for assessing $CMRO_2$. In this method, BOLD and CBF measurements are performed, once in presence of a stimulus and once during a respiratory challenge, usually a CO_2 challenge (Fig. 23.4). The underlying assumption is that the respiratory challenge changes blood flow but does not change metabolism, while the stimulus presentation changes both flow and metabolism. $CMRO_2$ can then be calculated using the Davis model (Davis et al., 1998), as follows:

$$\frac{CMRO_2}{CMRO_{2,0}} = \left(1 - \frac{\frac{\Delta BOLD}{BOLD_0}}{M}\right)^{\frac{1}{\beta}} \left(\frac{CBF}{CBF_0}\right)^{1-\frac{\alpha}{\beta}}, \tag{23.1}$$

where the subscript "0" denotes the baseline condition, no subscript denotes the activated condition, α is derived from the Grubb relation, and β is a field-dependent and TE-dependent constant, which depends on the average blood volume in the tissue, and is assumed to be 1 at 7T. α was measured with PET to be 0.38, representing total CBV, but for the purpose of BOLD-relevant CBV, it is generally taken as 0.2, although there is still discussion about its most suitable value (Griffeth and Buxton, 2011).

From the respiratory challenge, the constant M is calculated:

$$M = \frac{\frac{\Delta BOLD}{BOLD_0}}{1 - \left(\frac{CBF}{CBF_0}\right)^{\alpha-\beta}}, \tag{23.2}$$

where $\Delta BOLD$ and CBF refer to the activation responses during the respiratory challenge. M has the biological interpretation as the maximum possible BOLD response. Using M, CMRO$_2$ during stimulus presentation can then be calculated. This model framework relies on the assumption that CBF and CBV are tightly coupled (as described in the form of the Grubb relation α), and the assumption that the respiratory challenge does not affect metabolism, which is valid for mild respiratory challenges (Zappe et al., 2008b).

There are numerous variations in the CMRO$_2$ measurement: using different respiratory challenges, e.g., O$_2$ or carbogen; using models to determine M; and using different sequences, not only different CBF or BOLD sequences but also CBV/VASO implementations are possible.

Functional CMRO$_2$ uses the calibrated BOLD method as a relative parameter and is expressed as a % change. There are also approaches to quantify the absolute CMRO$_2$ during baseline and activation separately (Germuska and Wise, 2019). Absolute CMRO$_2$ can be calculated using a calibrated BOLD method using two gas challenges, or by calculating the OEF from a measurement of R_2^* by quantitative susceptibility mapping (QSM) and applying it in the CMRO$_2$ model. Calibration-free CMRO$_2$ models are currently under development for layer fMRI applications at UHF in animals and humans (Shao et al., 2022; Herman et al., 2013).

CMRO$_2$ and CBF are related through the OEF, and generally, CMRO$_2$ = CBF*OEF*Ca with Ca the arterial O$_2$ concentration. OEF is a stable/preserved parameter in the brain and measured as 0.42 (Fan et al., 2020) at relatively coarse resolution. However, due to a low SNR and error propagation, quantitative functional CMRO$_2$ is still uncommon, even at UHF. Calibrated BOLD has shown good correspondence with CMRO$_2$ calculated using PET at low resolution (Fan et al., 2020).

Some of the most important current challenges to CMRO$_2$ quantification are its low SNR, the error propagation/amplification in (the nonlinear) models, a complicated experimental gas delivery setup with time-consuming measurement, and the validity of model assumptions. While a lot of studies investigated the latter issues (setup and model validation, alternate models), the limiting factor of nonlinear noise amplification remains challenging, even at UHF.

For high-resolution CMRO$_2$ measurements, there is the additional complication that when one calculates CMRO$_2$ from the BOLD and CBF measurements, there is the assumption that functional activation in BOLD and CBF maps are all spatially in the same location. This is based on Fick's principle—a central building block of the Davis model—which assumes that all oxygen delivered by CBF is either consumed ($CMRO_2$) or drained away in the veins (BOLD). While this assumption is valid for individual voxels at conventional fMRI resolutions, or for ROI-based $CMRO_2$ calculations, it does necessarily hold for high-resolution $CMRO_2$ mapping, where each of the parameters is measured in voxels with different vascular compositions; e.g., the deoxygenated blood that drives the BOLD signal arise mostly from draining veins, whereas CBF or CBV estimates arise mainly from arterioles and capillaries. Thus, at high resolutions, when different vascular compartments are captured in different voxels, the application of Fick's principle is challenged. For example, in superficial voxels that are dominated by large veins, large BOLD signal changes may not be accompanied with comparably large signal changes in ASL and VASO. As a result, the Davis model can provide $CMRO_2$ estimates that are physiologically unreasonable.

23.6 Discussion

23.6.1 Prospects of and challenges to non-BOLD methods

23.6.1.1 Challenges posed by the need for efficient non-BOLD signal readouts

Similar to conventional GE BOLD, non-BOLD fMRI is usually conducted in combination with EPI based readouts. The functional contrast of VASO and ASL is generated during separate T_1-based contrast-encoding sequence modules, which are different from the spatial encoding module (EPI). The addition of the contrast encoding module to the regular EPI modules means that non-BOLD methods are susceptible to the same EPI constraints at UHF as conventional BOLD. These include

- challengingly long echo-train lengths at high resolution,
- B_1 inhomogeneities, and
- heterogeneous CNR across brain areas.

Potential mitigation approaches usually consist of advanced sequence strategies, including pTx, readout segmentation, and advanced undersampling trajectories in 2D and 3D, as well as high-performance RF and gradient hardware. For technical details of these challenges and respective solutions, see the review article by Bollmann and Barth (2021).

As long as non-BOLD acquisition methods rely on additional sequence modules for contrast generation, non-BOLD imaging will always suffer from a reduced sampling efficiency, with and without applying the aforementioned advanced acquisition strategies.

23.6.1.2 Current and future trends: Non-BOLD as quantitative contrast and non-BOLD vein-free fMRI signals

While BOLD suffers from the drawback that it is a composite signal of multiple physiological parameters, non-BOLD methods have the advantage that they capture singular physiological parameters that are quantifiable in physical units. As such, there are established signal models that allow researchers to convert the ASL signal, VASO signal, and calibrated BOLD signal to estimates of fCBF, fCBV, and $fCMRO_2$.

However, these non-BOLD signal models can be quite complicated and have been originally developed for low magnetic field strengths and large voxel sizes. Thus, they partly rely on assumptions of average physiological processes that are not entirely valid for UHF and high resolutions. Refinements of quantification models are helpful for clinical applications and are subject to development.

However, despite the advantage in estimating the magnitude of physiological parameters, currently, the majority of non-BOLD fMRI studies are not taking full advantage of the quantifiability of their signal.

Because of its advantages over non-BOLD sequences, we believe that GE BOLD will be a mainstay of fMRI for the foreseeable future. Non-BOLD sequences will continue to find their use not necessarily as a competitor sequence to GE BOLD but for those research questions where higher specificity of the functional activation is required, or the ability to quantify activation, to understand neurovascular processes and/or to provide additional information to control for venous biases.

23.6.2 Applications of non-BOLD fMRI at UHF

23.6.2.1 Investigating mechanisms of neurovascular coupling

fMRI at conventional resolutions and field strengths is mostly conducted with GE BOLD sequences. While we believe that this will not change in the foreseeable future, we anticipate that non-BOLD applications at UHF will have an impact on conventional studies by providing information to refine BOLD models, i.e., non-BOLD fMRI will be helpful to interpret conventional BOLD signals despite the fact that the composite BOLD contrast generation mechanism is elusive and affected by many confounds:

- BOLD signals are hard to interpret across different pathological states.
- BOLD signals are hard to interpret for pharmacological interventions.
- BOLD signals are hard to interpret for voxels that contain different compartments of the vascular tree; e.g., at high spatial resolution.
- BOLD signals are hard to interpret when vascular plumbing effects might contaminate the signal; e.g., vascular steal and negative BOLD.

In those cases, non-BOLD contrasts can be helpful to characterize neurovascular processes and help inform case-specific BOLD models.

23.6.2.2 Laminar/high-resolution fMRI

Submillimeter non-BOLD fMRI and high-resolution fMRI, in general, are important drivers of UHF MRI technology. A large number of the ∼100 human UHF scanners around the globe have been installed with the aim of performing high-resolution functional neuroimaging. Submillimeter resolutions can potentially resolve fine-scale structures such as cortical layers and columns. However, due to the draining vein bias in conventional GE BOLD data, non-BOLD contrasts became more popular. In fact, while VASO methods had been originally developed for the purpose of quantitative clinical applications, they are currently almost exclusively used for high-specificity laminar fMRI. In the application of laminar fMRI, non-BOLD sequences/contrasts are popular because the sensitivity limitations of non-BOLD imaging are counterbalanced by their high localization specificity (Fig. 23.5). Examples include investigations of neural circuitry in the prefrontal cortex during working memory tasks (Finn et al., 2019) and mental imagery of hand movements (Persichetti et al., 2020).

For further discussion of applications at UHF, see Chapter 25 "The power of gray-matter optimized fMRI at UHF for cognitive neuroscience" by Dumoulin and Knapen in this book. For a more in-depth

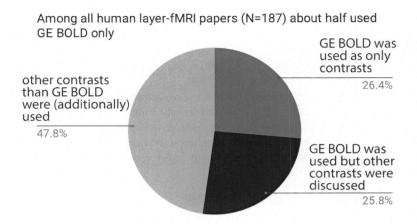

Among all human layer-fMRI papers (N=187) about half used GE BOLD only

GE BOLD was used as only contrasts
26.4%

other contrasts than GE BOLD were (additionally) used
47.8%

GE BOLD was used but other contrasts were discussed
25.8%

FIG. 23.5

Distribution of applied fMRI contrasts among all human layer fMRI papers published as of March 2022. About half of the published layer fMRI studies solely used GE BOLD. The other half also exploited other fMRI sequences. Almost all studies that used an additional fMRI contrast based their neuroscientific conclusion on a combination of contrasts; i.e., most studies use the superior sensitivity of GE BOLD to define the ROI and then later investigate the layer-specific responses within this ROI with non-BOLD signals. For a complete list of all human layer fMRI papers and a continuously updated version of this graph, visit www.layerfmri.com/papers.

discussion of layer fMRI, see Chapter 24 "Laminar and columnar imaging at UHF: considerations for mesoscopic scale imaging with fMRI" by Vizioli et al.

Acknowledgment

NN and JG were supported by the Medical Research Council (grant MR/N005745/1).

References

Blinder, P., Tsai, P.S., Kaufhold, J.P., Knutsen, P.M., Suhl, H., Kleinfeld, D., 2013. The cortical angiome: an interconnected vascular network with noncolumnar patterns of blood flow. Nat. Neurosci. 16. https://doi.org/10.1038/nn.3426.

Bollmann, S., Barth, M., 2021. New acquisition techniques and their prospects for the achievable resolution of fMRI. Prog. Neurobiol. https://doi.org/10.1016/j.pneurobio.2020.101936.

Davis, T.L., Kwong, K.K., Weisskoff, R.M., Rosen, B.R., 1998. Calibrated functional MRI: mapping the dynamics of oxidative metabolism. Proc. Natl. Acad. Sci. U. S. A. 95. https://doi.org/10.1073/pnas.95.4.1834.

Duong, T.Q., Yacoub, E., Adriany, G., et al., 2002. High-resolution, spin-echo BOLD, and CBF fMRI at 4 and 7 T. Magn. Reson. Med. 48. https://doi.org/10.1002/mrm.10252.

Fan, A.P., An, H., Moradi, F., et al., 2020. Quantification of brain oxygen extraction and metabolism with [15O]-gas PET: a technical review in the era of PET/MRI. NeuroImage. https://doi.org/10.1016/j.neuroimage.2020.117136.

Finn, E.S., Huber, L., Jangraw, D.C., Molfese, P.J., Bandettini, P.A., 2019. Layer-dependent activity in human prefrontal cortex during working memory. Nat. Neurosci. 22. https://doi.org/10.1038/s41593-019-0487-z.

Germuska, M., Wise, R.G., 2019. Calibrated fMRI for mapping absolute CMRO2: practicalities and prospects. NeuroImage 187. https://doi.org/10.1016/j.neuroimage.2018.03.068.

Goense, J., Merkle, H., Logothetis, N.K., 2012. High-resolution fMRI reveals laminar differences in neurovascular coupling between positive and negative BOLD responses. Neuron 76. https://doi.org/10.1016/j.neuron.2012.09.019.

Goense, J., Bohraus, Y., Logothetis, N.K., 2016. fMRI at high spatial resolution implications for BOLD-models. Front. Comput. Neurosci. 10. https://doi.org/10.3389/fncom.2016.00066.

Griffeth, V.E.M., Buxton, R.B., 2011. A theoretical framework for estimating cerebral oxygen metabolism changes using the calibrated-BOLD method: modeling the effects of blood volume distribution, hematocrit, oxygen extraction fraction, and tissue signal properties on the BOLD signal. NeuroImage 58. https://doi.org/10.1016/j.neuroimage.2011.05.077.

Guidi, M., Huber, L., Lampe, L., Gauthier, C.J., Möller, H.E., 2016. Lamina-dependent calibrated BOLD response in human primary motor cortex. NeuroImage 141. https://doi.org/10.1016/j.neuroimage.2016.06.030.

Herman, P., Sanganahalli, B.G., Blumenfeld, H., Rothman, D.L., Hyder, F., 2013. Quantitative basis for neuroimaging of cortical laminae with calibrated functional MRI. Proc. Natl. Acad. Sci. U. S. A. 110. https://doi.org/10.1073/pnas.1307154110.

Hirsch, S., Reichold, J., Schneider, M., Székely, G., Weber, B., 2012. Topology and hemodynamics of the cortical cerebrovascular system. J. Cereb. Blood Flow Metab. https://doi.org/10.1038/jcbfm.2012.39.

Hua, J., Jones, C.K., Qin, Q., van Zijl, P.C.M., 2013. Implementation of vascular-space-occupancy MRI at 7T. Magn. Reson. Med. 69. https://doi.org/10.1002/mrm.24334.

Huber, L., Goense, J., Kennerley, A.J., et al., 2015. Cortical lamina-dependent blood volume changes in human brain at 7T. NeuroImage 107. https://doi.org/10.1016/j.neuroimage.2014.11.046.

Huber, L., Uludağ, K., Möller, H.E., 2019. Non-BOLD contrast for laminar fMRI in humans: CBF, CBV, and CMRO2. NeuroImage. https://doi.org/10.1016/j.neuroimage.2017.07.041.

Huber, L., Chai, Y., Stirnberg, R., et al., 2020. Beyond the limits of layer-dependent CBV fMRI in humans: strategies towards whole brain coverage, sub-second TR, and very high 0.5 mm resolutions. Proc. Int. Soc. Magn. Reson. Med. abstract #3864.

Huber, L., Finn, E.S., Chai, Y., et al., 2021. Layer-dependent functional connectivity methods. Prog. Neurobiol. 207. https://doi.org/10.1016/j.pneurobio.2020.101835.

Ivanov, D., Poser, B.A., Kashyap, S., Gardumi, A., Huber, L., Uludag, K., 2016. Sub-millimeter human brain perfusion imaging using arterial spin labelling at 3 and 7 Tesla. In: ISMRM Workshop on Ultra High Field MRI.

Jin, T., Kim, S.G., 2008. Cortical layer-dependent dynamic blood oxygenation, cerebral blood flow and cerebral blood volume responses during visual stimulation. NeuroImage 43. https://doi.org/10.1016/j.neuroimage.2008.06.029.

Jin, T., Kim, S.G., 2010. Change of the cerebrospinal fluid volume during brain activation investigated by T1ρ-weighted fMRI. NeuroImage 51. https://doi.org/10.1016/j.neuroimage.2010.03.047.

Kim, S.G., Ogawa, S., 2012. Biophysical and physiological origins of blood oxygenation level-dependent fMRI signals. J. Cereb. Blood Flow Metab. https://doi.org/10.1038/jcbfm.2012.23.

Kim, S.G., Harel, N., Jin, T., Kim, T., Lee, P., Zhao, F., 2013. Cerebral blood volume MRI with intravascular superparamagnetic iron oxide nanoparticles. NMR Biomed. 26. https://doi.org/10.1002/nbm.2885.

Leite, F.P., Tsao, D., Vanduffel, W., et al., 2002. Repeated fMRI using iron oxide contrast agent in awake, behaving macaques at 3 Tesla. NeuroImage 16. https://doi.org/10.1006/nimg.2002.1110.

Lu, H., Golay, X., Pekar, J.J., van Zijl, P.C.M., 2003. Functional magnetic resonance imaging based on changes in vascular space occupancy. Magn. Reson. Med. 50. https://doi.org/10.1002/mrm.10519.

Mandeville, J.B., Marota, J.J.A., 1999. Vascular filters of functional MRI: spatial localization using BOLD and CBV contrast. Magn. Reson. Med. 42. https://doi.org/10.1002/(SICI)1522-2594(199909)42:3<591::AID-MRM23>3.0.CO;2-8.

Persichetti, A.S., Avery, J.A., Huber, L., Merriam, E.P., Martin, A., 2020. Layer-specific contributions to imagined and executed hand movements in human primary motor cortex. Curr. Biol. 30. https://doi.org/10.1016/j.cub.2020.02.046.

Poplawsky, A.J., Fukuda, M., Murphy, M., Kim, S.G., 2015. Layer-specific fMRI responses to excitatory and inhibitory neuronal activities in the olfactory bulb. J. Neurosci. 35. https://doi.org/10.1523/JNEUROSCI.1015-15.2015.

Shao, X., Hua, J., Wang, D.J.J., 2022. Concurrent laminar CBF, CBV, T2 BOLD and CMRO2 fMRI at 7T in human primary motor cortex. Proc. Int. Soc. Magn. Reson. Med. abstract #0404.

Truong, T.K., Song, A.W., 2009. Cortical depth dependence and implications on the neuronal specificity of the functional apparent diffusion coefficient contrast. NeuroImage 47. https://doi.org/10.1016/j.neuroimage.2009.04.045.

Yu, X., He, Y., Wang, M., et al., 2016. Sensory and optogenetically driven single-vessel fMRI. Nat. Methods 13. https://doi.org/10.1038/nmeth.3765.

Zappe, A.C., Pfeuffer, J., Merkle, H., Logothetis, N.K., Goense, J.B.M., 2008a. The effect of labeling parameters on perfusion-based fMRI in nonhuman primates. J. Cereb. Blood Flow Metab. 28. https://doi.org/10.1038/sj.jcbfm.9600564.

Zappe, A.C., Uludağ, K., Oeltermann, A., Uğurbil, K., Logothetis, N.K., 2008b. The influence of moderate hypercapnia on neural activity in the anesthetized nonhuman primate. Cereb. Cortex 18. https://doi.org/10.1093/cercor/bhn023.

Laminar and columnar imaging at UHF: Considerations for mesoscopic-scale imaging with fMRI

24

Luca Vizioli[a], Laurentius Huber[b], and Essa Yacoub[a]

[a]*Center for Magnetic Resonance Research (CMRR), University of Minnesota, Minneapolis, MN, United States*
[b]*Maastricht Brain Imaging Centre, Faculty of Psychology and Neuroscience, Maastricht University, Maastricht, Netherlands*

Highlights

- Submillimeter resolutions at UHF allow studying the human brain at the mesoscale level and targeting layers and columns.
- Laminar fMRI is growing in popularity.
- Laminar fMRI remains very challenging, requiring tailored acquisition, analyses, and manual intervention.
- Continued technological developments and increased field strengths allow achieving unprecedented spatial resolutions.
- These ultra-high resolutions, paired with tailored analytical approaches, can help bridge the gap between fMRI and invasive electrophysiology and study the human brain with unprecedented precision.

24.1 Introduction

Since the early 1990s, with the introduction of the blood oxygen level-dependent contrast (BOLD, Ogawa et al., 1992), functional MRI (fMRI) has become a primary tool to noninvasively investigate the human brain. The growing availability of ultra-high field scanners (UHF; i.e., ≥ 7 Tesla) and the development of highly efficient hardware and accelerated acquisition protocols for fMRI have led to significant gains in the signal-to-noise ratio (SNR). Recently, researchers have begun to trade the gains in the SNR for recording functional images with unparalleled spatial precision, spanning the submillimeter range. These spatial resolutions allow, at least in principle, neurofunctional organization to be studied at the mesoscopic scale, accessing fundamental units of neural computations, such as *layers* and "*columns.*"

The increasing number of publications on this topic (see Fig. 24.1) reflects the momentous excitement surrounding laminar and columnar fMRI. It has the potential to revolutionize the landscape of cognitive neuroscience by unlocking new horizons into human neurofunctional organization and bridging the gap with invasive animal electrophysiology and optical imaging.

The field of human layer fMRI is built on decades of animal research. The first decade of layer-specific localization and specificity of various fMRI contrasts, quantitative hemodynamics, and

Timeline of layer-fMRI papers

Ever since 2015, the field of layer-fMRI is continuously increasing.

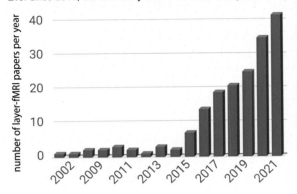

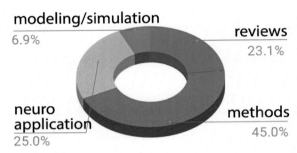

FIG. 24.1

Popularity of human layer fMRI. A source and continuously updated list of papers can be found at https://layerfmri.com/papers.

metabolic imaging modalities was largely influenced by previous nonhuman layer fMRI studies in rats, cats, and monkeys (see Chapter 23 on non-BOLD fMRI). Spatial resolution in nonhuman animal fMRI has always been several factors higher than that in human layer fMRI, and as such, many of the transformative innovations in MRI methods in the last decades were motivated by the goal of efficient high-resolution functional imaging in humans. Examples are ultra-high field MRI, highly parallel acquisitions with array coils (Chapter 8), high-performance head gradients, and pulse sequence developments for fMRI with controlled aliasing (CAIPIRINHA) that enable efficient 2D multiband (MB) EPI and 3D EPI acquisition (discussed in Chapter 9). Arguably, the developments of efficient high-resolution fMRI in humans helped propel 7T MRI into a clinically approved system.

Thus, while layer fMRI is still a relatively small subdiscipline within the MR neuroimaging community and has not yet hugely impacted the understanding of the brain's information processing across the mesoscopic circuitry, its indirect impact as a technology driver cannot be underestimated as methodological advancements, such as MB fMRI, originally developed for high-resolution applications have found their way into standard clinical and neuroscience routine protocols using conventional imaging resolutions. In addition, layer fMRI methods have reached a level of maturity at which we have begun to experience a shift from methodologically focused work to neuroscience applications studies (see Section 24.5).

Despite its growing popularity, fMRI to study the human brain's functional organization at the mesoscopic scale does not come without its own set of arduous challenges. These need to be appropriately addressed if this technique is to blossom into a routinely applicable tool.

In this chapter, we aim to give an overview of *layer* and *columnar* fMRI, briefly touching upon the history of the cortical layer and "columns," the challenges of laminar and columnar fMRI, and some of their applications.

24.2 Layers and "columns": A brief historical overview

Almost 200 years ago, Baillarger (1840) was the first physician to observe, without a microscope, thin sections of postmortem tissue, where the cortex is divided into six layers characterized by different cell types and concentrations (Fig. 24.2). This observation, together with the development of cell staining techniques, led to a boom in the number of studies in the 1900s focusing on this peculiar cortical laminar architecture. Early work primarily focused on describing the structure of the cerebral cortex as a laminar structure based on the cytoarchitecture. This endeavor peaked in the first half of the 20th century (DeFelipe and Jones, 1988) and led to detailed descriptions of the precise laminar configuration of cells and axons.

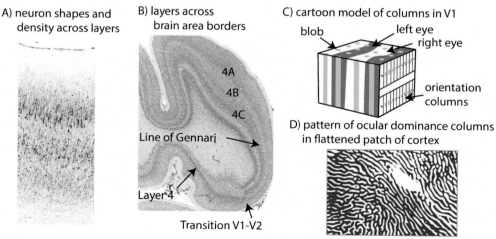

FIG. 24.2

Layer and column examples. Panel (A): Ex vivo histology cross-sections of the cortex showing the individual layers by means of cell size, shape, and density. (B) Histology section showing the border between V1 and V2. (C) Schematic cartoon model displaying orientation and ocular dominance "columns." (D) Pattern of ocular dominance "columns" as known from autoradiograph-prepared sections.

This peculiar cytoarchitecture sparked curiosity regarding a potential functional differentiation of cortical laminae, which could only be addressed with recording of neural activity at the cell site in the second half of the 1900s (Hubel and Wiesel, 1962; Mountcastle, 1978). With the ability to measure cellular responses, paired with the development of techniques that allowed mapping cell tracts, the emphasis shifted from a simple anatomical description to studying laminar organization and connectivity. Contemporary theories regarding the computational roles of different layers are rooted in studies that precisely traced layer-specific connectivity patterns across the cortex (for a review see Kobbert et al., 2000).

One of the earlier, yet still relevant, models of laminar connectivity, with specific bearings on layers' functional roles, was postulated by Felleman and Van Essen (1991) through careful analysis of connectional patterns. They reported different types of layer connectivity, which described hierarchical information flow across the cortex. In short, feedforward, or bottom-up, connections primarily originate from supragranular layers (*II/III*) and project to granular layer IV of a hierarchically higher target region. Feedback, or top-down, connections from higher to lower areas instead originate from and terminate in extragranular layers (i.e., outside layer IV).

This model formed the basis of many prominent accounts of the computational roles of cortical layers that are still relevant today. Moreover, within a cortical area, the local circuitry suggests a columnar flow of information across layers. While many have reported a vertical column-like arrays of cells that are arranged orthogonally to the laminae, Mountcastle (1957) was the first to propose this columnar organization as a fundamental organizing principle, key to neuronal computations. His postulation stemmed from the observation in the somatosensory cortex of the cat that cells in a vertical electrode responded to both superficial and deep stimulations. The author reported that for a common receptive field location, cells arranged perpendicularly to the cortical ribbon could be separated into specific domains representing different sensory modalities. These "columns" were discrete modules, 200–1000 µm apart, arranged in a "periodic" fashion and contained neurons whose physiological properties were identical (therefore encoding the same features). Columnar organization has, for example, been observed for ocular dominance and orientation preference in the visual cortex, frequency preference in the auditory cortex, and digit representation in the somatosensory cortex. No consensus has however been reached with regard to the functional role of cortical "columns," and it is yet to be fully understood whether this columnar organization extends beyond early cortices. These questions, however, can now be addressed in humans using fMRI. Albeit spatially and temporally coarser than electrophysiology, it allows assessing larger cortical areas and regions that may be difficult to reach with electrodes or optical imaging.

24.3 **fMRI**

If we consider that the thickness of the cortical ribbon ranges from 1.5 to 5 mm and that cortical "columns" are roughly 200–1000 µm apart, it is unsurprising that the functional properties of these potentially fundamental units of neural computations have remained largely unstudied in humans. While submillimeter fMRI cannot reach the spatial and temporal resolutions achievable with invasive animal techniques, recent technological advances at UHF do allow acquiring functional images with nominal resolutions, which would be compatible with those required to tackle laminar and columnar

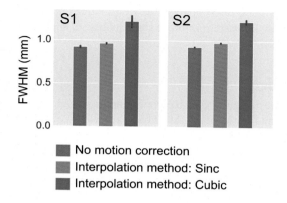

FIG. 24.3

Example of the impact of different motion correction algorithms on spatial precision. The plots depict two exemplary subjects (S1 and S2). The bar plots show the spatial precision of functional images (measured by means spatial autocorrelation among voxels computed using Gaussian + monoexponential decay mixed model) before motion correction (*blue bar*), after motion correction with sinc interpolation (*green bar*), and after motion correction with cubic interpolation. Spatial precision generally decreases after motion correction, but more so for cubic than for sinc interpolation. *Figure courtesy of Logan Dowdle.*

investigations (see, e.g., Fig. 24.3). This would allow not only replication of animal studies but also studying processes that are unique to humans (e.g., higher level cognitions), while targeting much larger portions of the cortex than has been possible with invasive animal approaches.

However, even though implemented with some degrees of success (see Section 24.5), laminar and columnar fMRI in humans remain relatively challenging.

24.4 Challenges of mesoscale imaging

24.4.1 Less tolerant to errors

SNR gains that accompany UHF applications are traded to achieve nominal resolution as high as possible, putting us back into an SNR-starved regime. The choice of acquisition protocol, which impacts the SNR and the precision of functional measurements, along with the true resolution, is therefore of paramount importance in understanding the feasibility of studying human mesoscopic-scale cortical organization with fMRI.

Unlike standard supramillimeter fMRI, submillimeter fMRI is much less tolerant to error. Standard preprocessing steps like correcting for subject motion, run-to-run alignment, geometric distortion corrections, coregistration between functional and structural images, and cortical segmentation become critical. With many laminar and columnar fMRI studies carried out with 0.8-mm resolutions, a single voxel in these studies can span several layers. Misalignment across modalities, volumes, or runs of even a single voxel may have catastrophic repercussions on the interpretation of functional results.

The low-SNR regime further renders analyses of BOLD time courses even more arduous. Spatial smoothing, which is traditionally used to improve data quality, is undesirable as the resolution of the final image is paramount.

24.4.2 Motion correction

Correcting for motion is more difficult but also more important at high spatial resolutions. For example, a small 1-mm head movement may be negligible when the voxel size is around 2-mm isotropic voxels. Even at the lower end of submillimeter resolutions (e.g., 0.8-mm isotropic), head movement of just a millimeter has the potential to misassign a voxel by 1 or even more layers. Moreover, the choice of interpolation algorithm is also crucial in preserving the spatial precision of the images. Any type of spatial interpolation will introduce a degree of spatial autocorrelation, the extent of which will depend on the interpolation algorithm. This blurs the data, potentially compromising the spatial precision of functional maps. It would therefore be important to minimize the number of interpolation steps during preprocessing, as well as to choose algorithms that minimally impact the data. For the example of motion correction, Fig. 24.4 shows the differential impact of cubic versus sinc interpolation on spatial autocorrelation (expressed in millimeters), a metric which is indicative of the spatial precision of the functional images. It is evident how the estimated precision of the images is significantly more preserved by sinc (which yields comparable estimates to those computed before applying motion correction) than by cubic interpolation. Moreover, the limited coverage employed in submillimeter imaging represents a further challenge in performing accurate motion correction.

24.4.3 Coregistration and segmentation

Cortical segmentation and cross-modality coregistration are also critical for performing mesoscopic-scale fMRI (e.g., see Fig. 24.3). Traditionally, due to relatively weak structural contrast in functional images generated with EPI, we tend to acquire one or more T_1-weighted images that are used to perform white-gray matter segmentation, as well as parcellation of the cortical ribbon into cortical depths or layers. Segmentation needs to be very precise to avoid misrepresentation of the cortical ribbons and its layers. As such, unlike standard fMRI, where automated segmentation algorithms can suffice, for high-spatial-resolution fMRI, segmentation generally requires a considerable number of manual adjustments to maximize precision.

Once an acceptable gray-white matter segmentation has been achieved, the cortical ribbon has to be parcellated into three or more "cortical depths." This can be achieved by parcellating the cortex into equidistant depths (each of a given distance from the outer pial surface; i.e., the equidistant approach) or in an equivolume fashion (i.e., with each depth having the same volume as all others; e.g., see Bok, 1929; Kemper et al., 2018; Waehnert et al., 2014 and references therein). While equivolume layering has been suggested to be more precise in its correspondence with anatomical laminae, a number of studies suggest no meaningful differences between the approaches (Huber et al., 2021; Kemper et al., 2018; Vizioli et al., 2020).

The common nomenclature "cortical depths" stems from the fact that layer parcellation is imprecise. It is difficult, if not impossible, to confidently equate a specific cortical depth to corresponding lamina. This is related to the imprecision during segmentation and to the fashion in which cortical depth parcellation is implemented. For example, while some software packages allow cortical depth

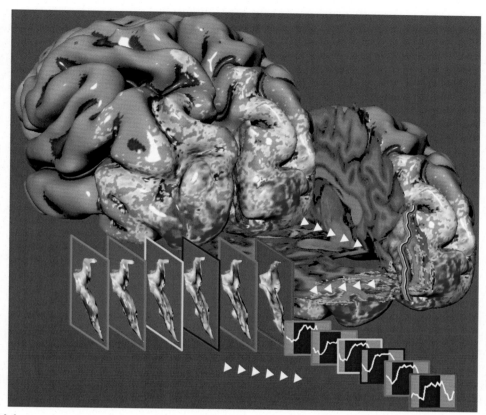

FIG. 24.4

Example of cortical depth activation and time courses. 7T submillimeter (0.8-mm isotropic voxels) BOLD activation map computed by contrasting two visual conditions consisting of flickering gratings (as those shown in Fig. 24.7). The map is superimposed on an occipital view of an inflated cortical mesh (*upper left*) and on cortical depths (*lower left*), with related activation time courses (*bottom right*). Cortical depths are also portrayed as meshes in the image slicing through the brain (*mid-right*), which shows the same activation map on a structural (T_1-weighted) image. The edges of the cortical depths and related time courses are color-coded according to location (*red*, innermost; *cyan*, outermost). Cover figure from the special issue "How high spatiotemporal resolution fMRI can advance neuroscience," published in Progress in Neurobiology in 2021.

parcellations to be carried out directly on the functional images (e.g., LayNii, Huber et al., 2021), this process is more commonly carried out with T_1-weighted images, which has superior gray-white matter contrast. If cortical depths are estimated on functional images directly, the paucity of tissue contrast makes it difficult to establish precise correspondence between these depths and their anatomical counterpart. Establishing this correspondence is also challenging for cortical depths computed on the higher contrast coregistered T_1 image. At typical high-resolution fMRI voxel sizes (i.e., 0.8-mm isotropic voxels), the images still lack enough fine-grained details to accurately identify anatomical landmarks (like, e.g., the stria of Gennari), which would help in establishing this correspondence. When cortical depths are computed on T_1-weighted images, the regions of interest are then projected to EPI images, increasing the importance of coregistration across modalities.

In light of the geometric distortions present in echo-planar images at UHF, there is a large difference in distortion between a standard T_1-weighted and EPI-based functional images. Optimally correcting for distortion is critical and can ameliorate the quality of coregistration across the different images. While distortion correction can lead to reasonable results, unwarping can still be imperfect and can represent an additional interpolation step, which could even be counterproductive in that it may further reduce the spatial precision of the images.

T_1-weighted images, which use a gradient echo readout, also suffer from spatial distortion, which can also be corrected, albeit it is a much smaller effect. Ultimately, after compensating for these distortions, coregistration does tend to be more optimized in specific portions of the cortex but, in general, remains imperfect.

Another approach proposes to use a distortion matched T_1-weighted EPI image (see van der Zwaag et al., 2018 and references therein). The matched distortion between the T_1-weighted EPI and the functional images permits a more efficient coregistration of functional data onto the cortical ribbon, thus significantly enhancing the precision and quality of the assignment of voxels to specific cortical depths.

24.4.4 Living in an SNR-starved regime

Submillimeter fMRI is undeniably highly SNR starved. Spatial smoothing by means of a Gaussian convolution of the activation pattern with a kernel of a given size is often implemented to improve SNR in conventional fMRI. Gaussian smoothing, however, can be an issue as it blurs the data and dilutes spatial precision. Moreover, smoothing can alter the spatial structure of a map, for example, by displacing the center of activation. As such, smoothing is also undesirable even when using multi-voxel pattern analyses as it exploits the structure of the spatial pattern of activation, which has been shown to be sensitive to fine-grained patterns of information in voxel subpopulations (e.g., Vizioli et al., 2020).

Tailored smoothing strategies, designed to minimize the loss of spatial precision, have also been proposed (e.g., see Blazejewska et al., 2019). For example, smoothing within layers to blur the pattern of activation within a given layer, but it should preserve the spatial precision across layers.

Postprocessing denoising strategies can be implemented to boost the SNR. While a plethora of excellent denoising algorithms exist, most of these target structured noise and can blur the spatial precision of functional maps (e.g., Caballero-Gaudes and Reynolds, 2017; Murphy et al., 2013 and references there in). Recently, a denoising algorithm (NORDIC) that specifically targets unstructured thermal noise, a dominant noise source in submillimeter images in fMRI, has been proposed (see also DWI Denoise). NORDIC has been shown to effectively increase the SNR while preserving the spatial precision of functional maps (Fig. 24.5).

Different layers are characterized by different venous architectures and thus have different hemo-dynamic response functions (HRFs). Using the same canonical HRF model for each layer can therefore be undesirable when directly comparing the activation profile across layers. Using an HRF derived per each layer and/or region would therefore be desirable. The choice of HRF may be less of an issue if comparing, for example, the activation elicited by different cognitive tasks or conditions within each layer. However, this will result in nosier response estimates and may fail to allow the detection of potential differences across conditions or tasks.

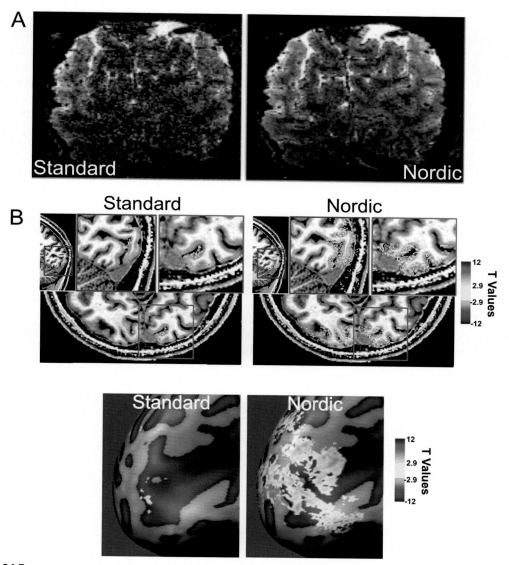

FIG. 24.5

Example of NORDIC denoising on 0.5-mm isotropic functional images and resulting activation maps. Panel (A) shows a single slice from a single fMRI image for standard (*left*) and NORDIC (*right*) images. Panel (B) shows functional maps (for the contrast target > surround) on a T_1-weighted anatomical image for standard (*left*) and NORDIC (*right*) reconstructions for a sagittal and an axial slice [with related zoom-ins on the sagittal (*blue*) and axial (*red*) planes].

24.4.5 Sensitivity vs. specificity

Different acquisition protocols result in different tradeoffs in specificity versus sensitivity. Sensitivity refers to the ability to detect signal changes from baseline and is therefore related to the concept of the SNR since the noisier the data, the more difficult it is to detect signal changes. Spatial specificity refers to the spatial precision of functional maps and depends on the sensitivity of the images to the different vascular compartments.

This sensitivity-specificity tradeoff for some of the most widely used acquisition protocols is quantitatively summarized in Fig. 24.6.

24.4.6 Nominal vs functional resolution

Before delving into the pros and cons of different acquisition contrasts, it would be useful to differentiate between image nominal resolution, image effective resolution, and functional resolution. While these three concepts are tightly linked, nominal resolution refers to the achievable resolution with which fMRI images can be recorded. Then, this is what we refer to as sequence resolution, which takes into account issues like blurring in the phase encode direction and the spatial correlation in the noise of the image and therefore is less precise than its nominal counterpart. Functional resolution (which will be further discussed later) refers to the spatial precision of the functional signals and is perhaps the limiting factor in the feasibility of imaging layers and "columns."

24.4.6.1 Gradient echo BOLD and spin echo BOLD

In the section, we discuss gradient echo (GE)- and spin echo (SE)-based BOLD contrasts to illustrate sensitivity vs. specificity considerations. A growing number of alternative contrasts have been proposed, and for a more complete overview, the reader is referred to Chapters 22 and 23.

GE BOLD is perhaps one of, if not the most, the widely used contrast mechanism for submillimeter fMRI. GE BOLD images possess a high SNR but can be limited in their spatial precision.

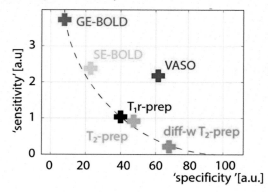

FIG. 24.6

Specificity vs. sensitivity tradeoff across acquisition protocols. Data shown here refer to the specific experimental setup of a 12-min block-designed, single-contrast motor task of a study that was designed for applications with VASO and GE BOLD (Huber et al., 2017). The generalizability of such comparison studies might be limited, as explained here: https://layerfmri.com/the-best-sequence/.

Conversely, SE BOLD images can instead produce more spatially precise functional maps, but their SNR is significantly lower.

In SE (or T_2-weighted images), refocusing pulses refocus some of the T_2^* dephasing, leading to a lower contribution from undesirable large draining vessels (Uludag et al., 2009).

In GE (or T_2^*-weighted images), large vessels contribute large (in terms of magnitude) BOLD response amplitudes (Uludag et al., 2009; Yacoub et al., 2005). The neuronal information contained within these responses are sluggish in time and coarse in space, making depth-dependent fMRI challenging if these responses are not adequately accounted for (e.g., see Muckli et al., 2015).

Relative to SE, GE acquisitions are characterized by higher sensitivity and temporal efficiency because susceptibility-based functional contrast from changes in T_2^* are much larger and evolve over much shorter echo times, albeit arising from significant contributions from both large and small vessels. SE images, on the contrary, are more spatially precise; however, the images take much longer to acquire due to both the power deposition limits imposed by the required refocusing pulses and the longer echo times required to generate the functional contrast, which is weighted by relatively much smaller T_2 changes than T_2^* changes. This reduced encoding efficiency, along with the reduced overall sensitivity and sensitivity to larger vessels, results in an overall significantly lower contrast-to-noise ratio (CNR) and SNR efficiency than GE BOLD images (see Fig. 24.6).

24.4.6.2 Functional point spread function

A critical component of the feasibility of high-spatial-resolution fMRI is the functional point spread function (PSF, Fig. 24.7; e.g., Shmuel et al., 2007). In vision, for example, PSF builds on retinotopic properties to estimate the spatial precision of functional maps for the acquisition contrast of choice. For example, by exploiting the retinotopic properties of V1, we can estimate the precise location of a hard edge between two concentric gratings, by computing the differential map of the activity elicited by one minus that elicited by the other. We can then superimpose the activity only elicited by one of the two gratings and superimpose the obtained functional map to the previously computed empirical edge of the visual stimulus. With very fine functional spatial precision, we would expect the activity elicited by one of the visual conditions to sharply cease once we reach the outer edge of the stimulus. The fashion in which the amplitude of the BOLD responses decreases as a function of distance from the stimulus edge conveys information about the spatial precision of the signal. The PSF along the cortical ribbon can be quantified empirically by fitting to the BOLD map a point spread function, consisting of a step function (reflecting infinite spatial precision), with the "step" representing the edge of the visual stimulus; and a Gaussian PSF (the standard deviation of the full-width half max of the Gaussian reflecting the functional PSF, see Shmuel et al., 2007). More discussion of the PSF with specific focus of signal leakage across cortical depths, and the respective correction thereof can be found in Chapter 22 by Uludag and Kasper.

24.4.6.3 Strategies to account for venous bias in GE BOLD

Together with spatially coarser activation maps, GE data display a ubiquitous ramping profile of increasingly larger BOLD responses when approaching the pial surface (Goense and Logothetis, 2006). This profile would be observable even when the true underlying neuronal response would be largest in the mid layers, as, for example, during pure feedforward stimulation. The GE amplitude differences across cortical depths reflect, in fact, the cortical vascular architecture, where a larger draining vessel concentration is prominent toward the surface, rather than neuronal mechanisms (Goense and Logothetis, 2006). Conversely, non-GE BOLD acquisitions, albeit noisier, can reflect

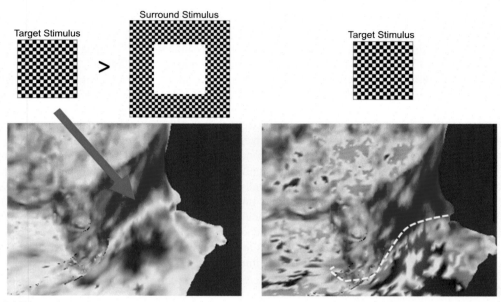

FIG. 24.7

Quantification of functional spatial precision by point-spread function (PSF). Shown are the percent signal change (PSC) maps for the differential mapping target (in *red*) > surround (in *blue, left*), and the target only (*right*) superimposed on a flattened cortical mesh. The empirical medial boundary between the target and surround stimuli (shown at the *top*) is computed on the differential image (indicated by the *blue arrow* on the left panel). This boundary is superimposed (*white dotted line*) on the target-only PSC map, where PSC amplitudes are greater than zero but decreasing in magnitude progressively away from this "boundary." The functional PSF is calculated from this spread in PSC beyond the empirical "boundary."

neuronal responses more locally and thus show BOLD peak amplitudes in layers other than the outer (e.g., Zhao et al., 2006).

There is a long list of alternative strategies or fMRI contrasts other than the conventional GE BOLD response. This list includes SE EPI (Goense and Logothetis, 2006), steady-state contrasts, ASL, diffusion fMRI, 3D-GRASE (Feinberg and Oshio, 1991), calibrated BOLD aka $CMRO_2$ mapping, VASO, phase regression, initial dip, onset-time imaging (see https://layerfmri.com/the-best-sequence/ for references), depth-dependent deconvolution (Markuerkiaga et al., 2021), physiological models of blood flow (e.g., Uludag and Havlicek, 2021), CVR calibration (Guidi et al., 2016), and many more. The field of layer fMRI has dedicated a large portion of its resources and a lot of its public discussion on comparison studies that investigate which contrast and analysis method is best suited for laminar fMRI and the mitigation of draining vein effects.

Despite the large number of comparison studies conducted over the years, no consensus has been reached as to which is the optimal approach to image the mesoscale functional organization. This is probably due to the fact that results of sequence comparisons are difficult to generalize beyond the specific test case that was used for benchmarking of the methods (Yacoub et al., 2007). A claimed superiority of one method over another method was usually confined to the specifics such as investigated SNR constraints, experimental duration, task strengths, imaging coverage, SAR limits, or analysis choices.

A combination of BOLD and non-BOLD acquisitions can, in fact, be advantageous for the interpretation of layer fMRI results in the sense that it provides a more comprehensive understanding of potential contamination of the biophysical contrast generation of the fMRI signal. The contrast mechanisms and additional information of those sequences are discussed in Chapter 23 on non-BOLD fMRI at UHF by Nothnagel, Huber, and Goense (in this book).

The larger sensitivity of GE BOLD data will also be a highly attractive option at high fields and is the most widely used technique when studying mesoscopic-level functional organization.

Alternatively, tailored analytical strategies can be implemented, for example, in an attempt to filter out spatially nonspecific signals. For example, if a higher SNR is the most desirable feature, it is possible to acquire high-resolution data using GE EPI protocols and contrast different computational models, tasks, or conditions across cortical depths (e.g., Lawrence et al., 2019). Moreover, spurious venous contribution can be modeled out using vascular flow models (such as the linear-offset model, scaling model, and leakage model; see for references Huber et al., 2021) to account for and remove the venous-driven increases in the magnitude of BOLD responses as a function of proximity toward the surface.

It has also been shown that it is possible to retrieve some specificity using multivoxel pattern analyses, which can be sensitive to fine-grained pattern of activation across the voxel subpopulation in GE EPI data (Vizioli et al., 2020).

In summary, while a plethora of different acquisition protocols and analytical strategies are available to neuroscientists willing to image cortical layers, we believe that no "one-solution-fits-all" exists. The choice of acquisition protocol and analytical strategy rather depends highly on the context, including experimental design, target population, and target area.

24.5 Applications of high-resolution fMRI in cognitive neuroscience

The interest and applications of layer fMRI have grown over the last years. Some of the earliest attempts to layer fMRI in humans started in the 1990s as an auxiliary method to capture perpendicularly aligned columnar structures (Menon et al., 1997). Despite this early work and many influential highly publicized studies in the following years, it took until 2015 for the field of laminar fMRI to become more widely used beyond a small number of selected research centers with specialized hardware (see sudden slope change in Fig. 24.1A after 2015). At the time of the writing of this chapter, layer fMRI is used by more than 30 research laboratories around the globe. Recent years have marked a shift in the literature from traditional methodologically focused work toward a domination by neuroscientific application studies. In this paragraph, we provide a few examples to illustrate how fMRI has been successfully applied to gain insights into human mesoscale functional organization.

Yacoub et al. (2008) used submillimeter UHF fMRI to image orientation-selective "columns" in humans, with striking similarities to those observed in animal models by means of invasive optical imaging and electrophysiology.

In accordance with animal results, Nasr et al. (2016) reported fine-scale representation of color- and disparity-selective columnar stripes (characterized by different widths and thicknesses) in human V2 and V3.

Using MVPA at UHF, Muckli et al. (2015) showed that contextual feedback information arrived in the outer layers of human V1, V2, and V3, confirming what was known about laminar circuitry from animal studies, but using high-level meaningful scenes of everyday life. They thus provided empirical support for theoretical feedback models such as predictive coding in the human cortex.

Jia et al. (2020) also showed that the superficial layers of human V1 are involved in processing feedback signal. Consistent with recurrent plasticity mechanisms via horizontal connections, the authors demonstrated that learning and the ensuing experience-dependent plasticity modulate orientation specific representations in the outer layers of the primary visual cortex. They also reported that learning increases feedforward connectivity in occipito-parietal regions.

Lawrence et al. (2019) also successfully discerned bottom-up and top-down signals across layers in V1. They implemented orthogonal manipulations of stimulus contrast and feature-based attention to show that bottom-up modulations of BOLD responses were strongest in the middle layers, while top-down modulations were strongest in the superficial layers. As such, they demonstrate that laminar activity profiles can discriminate between concurrent top-down and bottom-up processing.

Further demonstrating the ability of laminar fMRI to gain insights into the role of top-down signals during perceptual processing, Kok et al. (2016) showed that feedback signals evoked by a visual illusion selectively activate the deep layers of the primary visual cortex.

The work described thus far primarily focuses on early visual cortices and using almost exclusively GE EPI acquisition protocols. However, Yacoub et al. (2008) used SE EPI and Muckli et al. (2015) validated their results with 3D GRASE.

Several application studies have begun using other acquisition contrast mechanisms and/or focusing on areas other than early visual cortices.

Liu et al. (2021) employed different acquisition methods (specifically, GE EPI and balanced steady-state free precession bSSFP), illustrating the distinct properties and advantages of each method for addressing questions in cognitive neuroscience. Liu et al. showed that top-down spatial attention differentially modulated different cortical depths in human V1. They observed that attention modulations were stronger in the superficial and deep depths of V1.

Zimmermann et al. (2011) used 3D GRASE to show that the axis of motion selectivity in the middle temporal area (MT) is arranged in a columnar fashion, reproducing topographical organization observed in monkeys.

De Martino et al. (2015) explored the functional organization primary auditory cortex (A1) in humans, reporting that the frequency preference is stable through cortical depth in a columnar-like fashion and that task demands sharpen frequency tuning primarily in superficial layers. Their findings provided some of the first insights into the organization and flow of information in the human auditory cortex.

Huber et al. (2017) used a CBV-based VASO acquisition protocol to show that in agreement with animal studies, it was possible to discriminate different tasks in the human motor cortex (M1); the authors reported evidence for somatosensory and premotor inputs in superficial layers of M1, and for cortico-spinal motor-output in deep layers.

Finn et al. (2019) also used VASO to provide one of the first pieces of evidence for mapping laminar profiles in higher level cortical areas. They showed that layers in the human dorsolateral prefrontal cortex are differentially activated during working memory storing, retrieval, and manipulation of previously encoded information. The application listed before and the ensuing findings demonstrate the feasibility of laminar and columnar fMRI. They further represent a promising step toward *bridging the gap between micro- and macro-circuits in the human cortex,* allowing investigations of information flow between brain regions with unprecedented precision (Fig. 24.8).

For more discussions on neuroscience applications of high-resolution fMRI, see Chapter 25 by Knapen and Dumoulin.

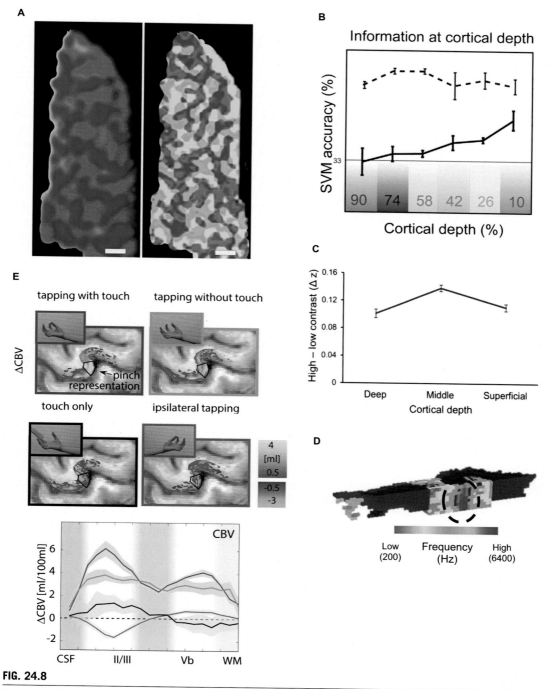

FIG. 24.8

Example of laminar and columnar fMRI applications. (A) Human ocular dominance (*left*) and orientation preference "columns" measure with SE EPI (Yacoub et al., 2008). (B) Different layer information content across human cortical depths for feedforward (*dotted line*) and feedback (*solid line*) computed using MVPA with GE EPI data (Muckli et al., 2015). (C) Example of differences in bottom-up signal amplitude across cortical depths in humans using a differential mapping approach with GE EPI data. (D) Example of differential layer activation in the human motor cortex during motor tasks using VASO (Huber et al., 2017). (E) Example of tonotopic columnar organization in the human auditory cortex (e.g., tuning to high frequency shown in *dotted circles*) using GRASE (De Martino et al., 2015).

24.6 Conclusion

The growing availability of UHF MRI scanners and the optimization of highly accelerated acquisition protocols have transformed fMRI, allowing acquisition of functional images with unprecedented resolutions and with unprecedented SNR efficiency. As we have seen throughout this chapter, this enables us to study the functional organization of human cortical layers and "columns," a feat previously achievable only in animals by means of invasive techniques. However, as the horizon of possible applications widens, the challenges also increase.

While many groups have begun to characterize the functional profile of layers and "columns," the with some degree of success, the employed 0.8-mm resolution can be barely sufficient to image layers and "columns." If we consider, for example, that the cortical ribbon spans a thickness of approximately 2.5–5 mm and that a number of factors further blur the functional precision of these submillimeter images, it becomes evident how 0.8-mm isotropic voxels may not suffice to accurately and exhaustively image the six laminae, especially in areas where the cortex is at its thinnest. This observation may account for some of the inconsistencies in the literature and is reflected in the Brain Initiative Working Group goals, which challenged the MR community to achieve functional resolutions of $\leq$0.1-μL voxels initially and 0.01-μL voxels subsequently.

Using a combination of state-of-the-art hardware (such as high-channel-count coil arrays and high-performance head gradients or ultra-high field magnets, i.e., >7T), efficiently accelerated acquisition protocols and denoising strategies and parallel efforts to achieve higher resolutions are taking place.

Currently, the highest reported resolutions in humans range in isotropic voxels from 0.39 mm ($\sim$0.059 μL) to 0.35 mm (0.049 μL) at 7T and 10.5T shown by the Feinberg and Ugurbil groups at ISMRM 2022, where differences in gradients and receiver arrays can affect actual resolution (PSF) and FOV, with expected improvements as technology develops.

At these ultra-high resolutions, a single voxel only contains a few thousand cells, further bridging the gap between fMRI and invasive optical imaging. In future, these ultra-high resolutions will allow reducing or even eliminating partial voluming across layers, and thus deriving a unique set of voxels per layer, further promoting the precision with which we can image human functional mesoscale organization.

With the continued growth and development in acquisition protocols, field strengths, and denoising methods, we can keep pushing the resolutions and continue bridging the gap with invasive animal electrophysiology. While arduous and not without limits, we see the glass as half full: great innovation comes with great challenges, and challenges are the engine that spark progress. We believe that innovations toward even more optimal submillimeter fMRI acquisitions can bring about a qualitative change in the way we study the human brain.

Acknowledgments

The authors thank Logan Dowdle for generating Fig. 24.3. Essa Yacoub was supported by the NIH grant RF1 MH116978. Renzo Huber was funded by the NWO VENI project 016.Veni.198.032.

References

The number of references listed below is limited by editorial constraints. Thus, please consider these references to represent a sparse cross section of a much larger literature.

Baillarger, J., 1840. Recherches sur la structure de la couche corticale des circonvolutions du cerveau. Mém. Acad. roy. de méd.

Blazejewska, A.I., Fischl, B., Wald, L.L., Polimeni, J.R., 2019. Intracortical smoothing of small-voxel fMRI data can provide increased detection power without spatial resolution losses compared to conventional large-voxel fMRI data. NeuroImage 189, 601–614. https://doi.org/10.1016/j.neuroimage.2019.01.054.

Bok, S., 1929. Der Einfluß der in den Furchen und Windungen auftretenden Krümmungen der Großhirnrinde auf die Rindenarchitektur. Z. Gesamte Neurol. Psychiatr. 12, 682–750.

Caballero-Gaudes, C., Reynolds, R.C., 2017. Methods for cleaning the BOLD fMRI signal. NeuroImage 154, 128–149. https://doi.org/10.1016/j.neuroimage.2016.12.018.

De Martino, F., Moerel, M., Ugurbil, K., Goebel, R., Yacoub, E., Formisano, E., 2015. Frequency preference and attention effects across cortical depths in the human primary auditory cortex. Proc. Natl. Acad. Sci. U. S. A. 112 (52), 16036–16041. https://doi.org/10.1073/pnas.1507552112.

DeFelipe, J., Jones, E.G., 1988. Cajal on the Cerebral Cortex. An Annotated Translation of the Complete Writings. Oxford University Press, Oxford.

Feinberg, D.A., Oshio, K., 1991. GRASE (gradient- and spin-echo) MR imaging: a new fast clinical imaging technique. Radiology 181 (2), 597–602. https://doi.org/10.1148/radiology.181.2.1924811.

Felleman, D.J., Van Essen, D.C., 1991. Distributed hierarchical processing in the primate cerebral cortex. Cereb. Cortex 1 (1), 1–47. https://doi.org/10.1093/cercor/1.1.1-a.

Finn, E.S., Huber, L., Jangraw, D.C., Molfese, P.J., Bandettini, P.A., 2019. Layer-dependent activity in human prefrontal cortex during working memory. Nat. Neurosci. 22 (10), 1687–1695. https://doi.org/10.1038/s41593-019-0487-z.

Goense, J.B., Logothetis, N.K., 2006. Laminar specificity in monkey V1 using high-resolution SE-fMRI. Magn. Reson. Imaging 24 (4), 381–392. https://doi.org/10.1016/j.mri.2005.12.032.

Guidi, M., Huber, L., Lampe, L., Gauthier, C.J., Moller, H.E., 2016. Lamina-dependent calibrated BOLD response in human primary motor cortex. NeuroImage 141, 250–261. https://doi.org/10.1016/j.neuroimage.2016.06.030.

Hubel, D.H., Wiesel, T.N., 1962. Receptive fields, binocular interaction and functional architecture in the cat's visual cortex. J. Physiol. 160, 106–154. https://doi.org/10.1113/jphysiol.1962.sp006837.

Huber, L., Handwerker, D.A., Jangraw, D.C., et al., 2017. High-resolution CBV-fMRI allows mapping of laminar activity and connectivity of cortical input and output in human M1. Neuron 96 (6), 1253–1263. e1257. https://doi.org/10.1016/j.neuron.2017.11.005.

Huber, L.R., Poser, B.A., Bandettini, P.A., et al., 2021. LayNii: a software suite for layer-fMRI. NeuroImage 237, 118091. https://doi.org/10.1016/j.neuroimage.2021.118091.

Jia, K., Zamboni, E., Kemper, V., et al., 2020. Recurrent processing drives perceptual plasticity. Curr. Biol. 30 (21), 4177–4187. e4174. https://doi.org/10.1016/j.cub.2020.08.016.

Kemper, V.G., De Martino, F., Emmerling, T.C., Yacoub, E., Goebel, R., 2018. High resolution data analysis strategies for mesoscale human functional MRI at 7 and 9.4T. NeuroImage 164, 48–58. https://doi.org/10.1016/j.neuroimage.2017.03.058.

Kobbert, C., Apps, R., Bechmann, I., Lanciego, J.L., Mey, J., Thanos, S., 2000. Current concepts in neuroanatomical tracing. Prog. Neurobiol. 62 (4), 327–351. https://doi.org/10.1016/s0301-0082(00)00019-8.

Kok, P., Bains, L.J., van Mourik, T., Norris, D.G., de Lange, F.P., 2016. Selective activation of the deep layers of the human primary visual cortex by top-down feedback. Curr. Biol. 26 (3), 371–376. https://doi.org/10.1016/j.cub.2015.12.038.

Lawrence, S.J., Norris, D.G., de Lange, F.P., 2019. Dissociable laminar profiles of concurrent bottom-up and top-down modulation in the human visual cortex. elife 8, e44422. https://doi.org/10.7554/eLife.44422.

Liu, C., Guo, F., Qian, C., et al., 2021. Layer-dependent multiplicative effects of spatial attention on contrast responses in human early visual cortex. Prog. Neurobiol. 207, 101897. https://doi.org/10.1016/j.pneurobio.2020.101897.

Markuerkiaga, I., Marques, J.P., Gallagher, T.E., Norris, D.G., 2021. Estimation of laminar BOLD activation profiles using deconvolution with a physiological point spread function. J. Neurosci. Methods 353, 109095. https://doi.org/10.1016/j.jneumeth.2021.109095.

Menon, R.S., Ogawa, S., Strupp, J.P., Ugurbil, K., 1997. Ocular dominance in human V1 demonstrated by functional magnetic resonance imaging. J. Neurophysiol. 77 (5), 2780–2787. https://doi.org/10.1152/jn.1997.77.5.2780.

Mountcastle, V.B., 1957. Modality and topographic properties of single neurons of cat's somatic sensory cortex. J. Neurophysiol. 20 (4), 408–434. https://doi.org/10.1152/jn.1957.20.4.408.

Mountcastle, V.B., 1978. Brain mechanisms for directed attention. J. R. Soc. Med. 71 (1), 14–28. https://www.ncbi.nlm.nih.gov/pubmed/416210.

Muckli, L., De Martino, F., Vizioli, L., et al., 2015. Contextual feedback to superficial layers of V1. Curr. Biol. 25 (20), 2690–2695. https://doi.org/10.1016/j.cub.2015.08.057.

Murphy, K., Birn, R.M., Bandettini, P.A., 2013. Resting-state fMRI confounds and cleanup. NeuroImage 80, 349–359. https://doi.org/10.1016/j.neuroimage.2013.04.001.

Nasr, S., Polimeni, J.R., Tootell, R.B., 2016. Interdigitated color- and disparity-selective columns within human visual cortical areas V2 and V3. J. Neurosci. 36 (6), 1841–1857. https://doi.org/10.1523/JNEUROSCI.3518-15.2016.

Ogawa, S., Tank, D.W., Menon, R., et al., 1992. Intrinsic signal changes accompanying sensory stimulation: functional brain mapping with magnetic resonance imaging. Proc. Natl. Acad. Sci. U. S. A. 89 (13), 5951–5955. https://doi.org/10.1073/pnas.89.13.5951.

Shmuel, A., Yacoub, E., Chaimow, D., Logothetis, N.K., Ugurbil, K., 2007. Spatio-temporal point-spread function of fMRI signal in human gray matter at 7 Tesla. NeuroImage 35 (2), 539–552. https://doi.org/10.1016/j.neuroimage.2006.12.030.

Uludag, K., Havlicek, M., 2021. Determining laminar neuronal activity from BOLD fMRI using a generative model. Prog. Neurobiol. 207, 102055. https://doi.org/10.1016/j.pneurobio.2021.102055.

Uludag, K., Muller-Bierl, B., Ugurbil, K., 2009. An integrative model for neuronal activity-induced signal changes for gradient and spin echo functional imaging. NeuroImage 48 (1), 150–165. https://doi.org/10.1016/j.neuroimage.2009.05.051.

van der Zwaag, W., Buur, P.F., Fracasso, A., et al., 2018. Distortion-matched T1 maps and unbiased T1-weighted images as anatomical reference for high-resolution fMRI. NeuroImage 176, 41–55. https://doi.org/10.1016/j.neuroimage.2018.04.026.

Vizioli, L., De Martino, F., Petro, L.S., et al., 2020. Multivoxel pattern of blood oxygen level dependent activity can be sensitive to stimulus specific fine scale responses. Sci. Rep. 10 (1), 7565. https://doi.org/10.1038/s41598-020-64044-x.

Waehnert, M.D., Dinse, J., Weiss, M., et al., 2014. Anatomically motivated modeling of cortical laminae. NeuroImage 93 Pt 2, 210–220. https://doi.org/10.1016/j.neuroimage.2013.03.078.

Yacoub, E., Van De Moortele, P.F., Shmuel, A., Ugurbil, K., 2005. Signal and noise characteristics of Hahn SE and GE BOLD fMRI at 7 T in humans. NeuroImage 24 (3), 738–750. https://doi.org/10.1016/j.neuroimage.2004.09.002.

Yacoub, E., Shmuel, A., Logothetis, N., Ugurbil, K., 2007. Robust detection of ocular dominance columns in humans using Hahn Spin Echo BOLD functional MRI at 7 Tesla. NeuroImage 37 (4), 1161–1177. https://doi.org/10.1016/j.neuroimage.2007.05.020.

Yacoub, E., Harel, M., Ugurbil, K., 2008. High-field fMRI unveils orientation columns in humans. Proc. Natl. Acad. Sci. U. S. A. 105, 10607–10612. https://doi.org/10.1073/pnas.0804110105.

Zhao, F., Wang, P., Hendrich, K., Ugurbil, K., Kim, S.G., 2006. Cortical layer-dependent BOLD and CBV responses measured by spin-echo and gradient-echo fMRI: insights into hemodynamic regulation. NeuroImage 30 (4), 1149–1160. https://doi.org/10.1016/j.neuroimage.2005.11.013.

Zimmermann, J., Goebel, R., De Martino, F., et al., 2011. Mapping the organization of axis of motion selective features in human area MT using high-field fMRI. PLoS One 6 (12), e28716. https://doi.org/10.1371/journal.pone.0028716.

Further reading

Vizioli, L., Moeller, S., Dowdle, L., Akçakaya, M., De Martino, F., Yacoub, E., Uğurbil, K., 2021. Lowering the thermal noise barrier in functional brain mapping with magnetic resonance imaging. Nat. Commun. 12. https://doi.org/10.1038/s41467-021-25431-8.

The power of ultra-high field for cognitive neuroscience: Gray-matter optimized fMRI

25

Serge O. Dumoulin[a,b,c,d] **and Tomas Knapen**[a,b,c]

[a]*Spinoza Centre for Neuroimaging, Amsterdam, The Netherlands* [b]*Computational Cognitive Neuroscience and Neuroimaging, Netherlands Institute for Neuroscience, Amsterdam, The Netherlands* [c]*Experimental and Applied Psychology, Vrije Universiteit Amsterdam, Amsterdam, The Netherlands* [d]*Experimental Psychology, Utrecht University, Utrecht, The Netherlands*

Highlights

- 7T MRI has greatly improved sensitivity and specificity.
- Gray-matter optimized (GMO) fMRI balances sensitivity and specificity at UHF.
- GMO fMRI confronts traditional data-analysis assumptions.
- GMO fMRI reorients experiments toward individuals and local neural computations.
- UHF forces a paradigm shift toward high-SNR measurements in single individuals.

25.1 Introduction

The human brain holds the key to who we are, our memories, thoughts, and perception of the world around us. The goal of cognitive neuroscience is to explain how these mental processes arise from neural computations. Since the discovery of functional MRI more than 30 years ago, the promise has been its ability to measure the response properties of populations of neurons inside the living human brain. As such, it has powered a revolution in cognitive neuroscience. Even in popular culture, the concept of localized brain function has placed our minds firmly inside our heads. Ultra-high field (UHF) MRI imaging at magnetic field strengths of 7 Tesla or more stands to push the envelope in terms of our measurement capabilities. But these more powerful measurements at UHF also reveal limitations of engrained paradigms of experimentation and analyses. So, how should we as cognitive neuroscientists wield this new, powerful tool? In this chapter, we outline how ongoing developments in the field of UHF imaging may prompt a paradigm change in cognitive neuroscience.

The most basic advantage of increased field strengths is increased signal-to-noise ratios (SNRs). The MRI signal and fMRI response scale superlinearly with field strength (Yacoub et al., 2001; Uludağ et al., 2009). This means that when cognitive neuroscientists move to UHF from standard field strengths such as 3 Tesla, they can expect a rough fourfold improvement in the efficacy of their measurements (Cai et al., 2021). Moreover, the spatial point-spread function is more narrow at UHF, meaning that our measurements are not only more sensitive, but also inherently more spatially specific than at lower field strengths. One popular avenue of research is to let the improvements in sensitivity go toward higher spatial resolutions and to bring the mesoscopic scale of cortical columns and layers into view (as discussed in Chapter 24). Here in this chapter, however, we assert a much more readily available and more powerful gain for cognitive neuroscience: whole-brain fMRI experiments of the type that are now customarily conducted at a field strength of 3 Tesla. This assertion is supported by the fact that an impressive wave of impactful recent findings has resulted from this specific use of UHF fMRI, an observation we draw from in this chapter.

We focus on whole-brain functional MRI in this chapter because (1) it is the most readily available tool for cognitive neuroscientists and (2) it has proven to be the most productive tool in the last few years. In separate boxes, we highlight the unique potential of UHF for in-vivo histology (Box 25.1), laminar and columnar fMRI (Box 25.2), and functional spectroscopy (Box 25.3). However, all of these applications have several significant still-unresolved challenges that limit, for now, their usefulness for the cognitive neuroscience community at large.

25.2 What is the optimal spatial resolution from a cognitive neuroscience perspective?

If the goal of the fMRI experiment is not to image cortical columns or layers, but to examine whole-brain responses to certain stimuli and tasks, what is the optimal resolution? From an MR physics perspective, it is common to describe signal quality in terms of a trade-off between thermal noise and physiological noise. The chosen resolution determines which of the two noise sources is dominant, with smaller voxels being dominated by thermal noise whereas larger voxels are physiological-noise-dominated. The optimal resolution is then where the two are balanced. However, when reasoning about the optimal fMRI resolution from a cognitive neuroscientist's perspective, a similar trade-off along the dimension of voxel size exists—but it is defined by different factors. As shown in Fig. 25.1, these factors are *spatial specificity* and *effective SNR*. By sampling smaller tissue volumes, higher resolutions

---

BOX 25.1 PUSHING ANATOMICAL MRI TOWARD INDIVIDUAL-LEVEL IN-VIVO HISTOLOGY

The cortex consists of different layers or laminae that differ in cyto- and myeloarchitecture. These laminar differences were the basis of the well-known cortical area parcellations of Brodmann based on post-mortem histology (Brodmann, 1909). Whereas the Brodmann areas were based on differences in cytoarchitecture, contemporaries Vogt and Vogt based their area definitions on histological differences in myeloarchitecture (Vogt and Vogt, 1919). Beyond the cortex, also subcortical nuclei and cerebellum contain subdivisions differencing in cyto- and myeloarchitecture. These structural differences support different functions of the brain. The Brodmann areas are still used today, though the laminar organizations that define the Brodmann areas are not visible on conventional MRI.

The resolution of anatomical images at UHF is high enough to start resolving these laminar differences. Furthermore, together with recent developments toward the efficient and often simultaneous collection of multiple MRI contrasts (see also Chapter 14) provides different clues about the underlying laminar architecture (Caan et al., 2018; Fracasso et al., 2016; Weiskopf et al., 2013). The higher resolution thus affords researchers the possibility to sample tissue properties at different cortical depths, providing diverse clues regarding local histological organization, i.e., in-vivo histology.

In-vivo histology has the potential to define cortical areas in individuals providing a new anatomical reference frame for function, inter-participant alignment, or disease biomarkers. For instance, localization of the stria of Gennari allows the anatomical delineation of the primary visual cortex even in the blind (Trampel et al., 2011). Though there is a lot of potential in in-vivo histology, there are several strides to be made in data-acquisition and data-analysis strategies. This makes in-vivo histology not an off-the-shelf technique for cognitive neuroscientists, but certainly a promising avenue.

BOX 25.2 IMAGING A NEW ORGANIZATION SCALE: LAMINAR AND COLUMNAR FMRI

Laminae: The laminae of the cortex differ in their connectivity and function. For example, thalamocortical connections arrive primarily in central (granular) layers (Felleman and Essen, 1991). Hence, the granular layers are most prominent in primary sensory cortices and nearly absent in motor cortices. Likewise, supra- and infragranular layers are thought to contain predominantly corticocortical and subcortical/corticospinal connections, respectively. Cortical laminae therefore contain unique information on the information flow in the brain.

Columns: In a cortical column, neurons with similar functions are grouped together across cortical depth. Columns are well established in early visual cortex and somatosensory cortices. In the primary visual cortex, different columnar structures (such as ocular dominance and orientation) are organized in such a way that all combinations repeat themselves. This has led to the notion of a hypercolumn or cortical processing unit (Hubel and Wiesel, 1977; Mountcastle et al., 1957). Moreover, between-area connections are often columnar (Jones et al., 1975). Columns are often hypothesized to exist across the brain, although the generality of this principle is uncertain (Horton and Adams, 2005). For example, the columnar structure of the primary visual cortex is not always present across species.

The resolution of functional images at UHF is high enough to start to resolve these laminar columnar functional structures (see also Chapter 24). Ultimately, this could provide a window into the information flow within the cortex and the hypothesized cortical processing unit. Although there is a lot of effort and interest in laminar and columnar imaging, there are passionate debates in the field on the different data-acquisition techniques (see Chapter 23), different data-analysis strategies, fine-scale link of the fMRI signal to the underlying physiology, and the correct interpretation of the results. This makes laminar and columnar fMRI not an off-the-shelf technique for cognitive neuroscientists, but certainly a promising avenue.

BOX 25.3 TOWARD DIRECT MEASURES OF BRAIN ACTIVITY: FUNCTIONAL MR SPECTROSCOPY

Magnetic resonance spectroscopy (MRS) quantifies the regional biochemistry composition in the living human brain (see also Chapter 26). In most studies, MRS is a steady-state measurement that reflects the concentrations of various compounds, for example, the neurotransmitter glutamate or GABA. The increased SNR of UHF enables not only steady-state measures, but also tracking, for example, glutamate modulations over time as a function of cognitive tasks, i.e., functional MRS (Stanley and Raz, 2018). Unlike functional MRI, functional spectroscopy may yield a more direct measure of neural activity and likely less sensitivity to vascular changes. Although there is a lot of potential in functional MRS, there are still several strides to be made in the development of robust data acquisition techniques and data-quantification methods. Furthermore, a lot is currently unknown about the nature of the glutamate changes over time and how these changes should be interpreted, necessitating work into the exact underlying mechanisms that are verified by direct neurophysiological measurements in animal models.

increase the specificity of the neural populations sampled by our voxels, i.e., sampling only gray matter as opposed to a mix of gray matter, white matter, and CSF. The latter of these two factors, effective SNR, more akin to contrast-to-noise than signal-to-noise in classical MR terms, can be seen as related to the amount of explainable variance in the fMRI signal time course, or its *noise ceiling*. These two factors compete, since any increase in spatial resolution increases spatial specificity but decreases effective SNR roughly as a function of voxel volume. We argue that for cognitive neuroscience experiments, the goal is to balance these two countervailing factors to optimize the detection of localized responses of neuronal populations in gray matter.

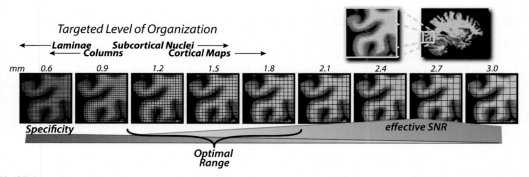

FIG. 25.1

Optimal resolution depends on the required spatial specificity and effective SNR. Pushing for higher resolution sacrifices effective SNR. We argue that for cognitive neuroscience, the optimal range for this trade-off is intermediate and advocates the use of voxel sizes that optimize sampling of BOLD responses from gray matter, i.e., gray-matter optimized fMRI. This approach capitalizes increases in both specificity and effective SNR at UHF relative to lower-field imaging. This measurement strategy has already proven highly effective in answering fundamental questions about brain organization by allowing the sampling of local neuronal population responses at UHF.

The inherent increase in fMRI signal sensitivity and specificity at UHF presents the possibility of increasing spatial resolution and moving leftward on the continuum depicted in Fig. 25.1. For typical cognitive neuroscience experiments, one should refrain from moving to submillimeter "laminar" resolution fMRI (see Box 25.2). These resolutions often yield lower effective sensitivity than traditional whole-brain 3T measurements. Instead, by moving to what we coin *gray-matter optimized (GMO) fMRI*, intermediate voxel sizes between 1 and 2 mm isotropic, one can already benefit greatly in a variety of mutually enhancing ways. Crucially, GMO resolutions are more likely to retain a marked improvement in BOLD sensitivity relative to 3T, not only in the cerebral cortex (van der Zwaag et al., 2009), but also in the cerebellar cortex and the subcortex (Colizoli et al., 2021). As its name implies, GMO sampling is more likely to draw BOLD signals specifically from gray matter than larger, traditional voxels. This resolution reduces partial voluming effects with white matter, veins, or cerebrospinal fluid (Viessmann and Polimeni, 2021). This resolution also decreases the probability that single voxels sample from the two opposite banks of a sulcus, improving the specificity of functional localization. Moreover, the co-registration of functional images with anatomy improves, due to the increased anatomical detail at GMO resolutions. GMO fMRI decreases distortions induced by B_0 inhomogeneity, while simultaneously improving their post-hoc correction. When GMO voxels are subsequently averaged across cortical depth, this further improves the BOLD sensitivity of the resulting surface-based functional data. Last, this approach still allows whole-brain coverage, including the cerebellum, at a reasonable sample rate of at least every two seconds (0.5 Hz). This temporal resolution improves the ability to perform nuisance regression, further enhancing effective sensitivity relative to the low temporal resolutions (<0.5 Hz) often used in higher resolutions.

In addition to these technical reasons for GMO sampling, there is a fundamental neuroscientific reason for the focus of GMO fMRI on the organization of the brain along the cortical surface. Because the cerebral cortex consists of intertwined hierarchies of maps on the surface of the cerebral cortex, this surface, sampled at the millimeter scale, constitutes a naturally appropriate level of detail for the study of cognitive brain function. The fact that GMO fMRI at UHF can sample the entire brain without sacrificing coverage accords well with this focus. The high-fidelity sampling of local neuronal population activations can thus be achieved while researchers need to adopt only minor changes to their traditional preprocessing and analysis approaches. We argue that for cognitive neuroscience, gray-matter optimized sampling represents a perfect combination of the desired precision and the precision that is practically attainable.

25.3 Moving toward individualized cognitive neuroscience

To highlight the promise of UHF for cognitive neuroscience experiments, we will first sketch the approach taken by the majority of current cognitive neuroimaging studies. Standard practice for functional MRI as it has evolved over the last two decades is to perform multiparticipant experiments. The typical 3T fMRI sequence scans the entire brain using about 2–4 mm isotropic voxels every 1–2 s or so (TR) for roughly 5–10 several minutes. This fMRI sequence is repeated multiple times for about an hour, in which participants perform cognitive tasks. These functional acquisitions are supplemented by a T_1-weighted anatomy at $\sim$1-mm resolution, and possibly several types of scans intended to aid in preprocessing of the data. During preprocessing, the functional data are registered to the anatomy, often smoothed spatially, and the anatomy is coregistered to a volumetric standard-brain atlas (Collins et al., 1994). A more sophisticated way of alignment across participants is to reconstruct the cortical surfaces from the anatomy. Sampling the functional data to these surfaces honors the sheet-like anatomical structure of the cerebral cortex. The surfaces can be aligned to a surface-defined atlas. Both volumetric and surface-based atlases provide a common spatial reference frame for all participants in a given study, and also allow cross-experiment comparison of results. These results are often displayed as clusters of across-participants, mixed-effects statistical values, for example, of a GLM analysis contrast comparing experimental conditions.

There are a number of assumptions in this general approach. First, that neural tissue responds homogeneously enough throughout a brain region so that fMRI results from clusters of voxels with identical responses. That is, larger clusters or regions—and not the local neural populations sampled by single voxels—are the assumed unit of function or measurement. This assumption may misguide researchers to think in quasi-phrenological structure–function relationships with limited focus on explicit computational mechanisms: "brain region X does Y." Moreover, this assumption is known to be false for virtually all well-described brain regions, such as primary visual and motor cortices. Second, this approach assumes that the alignment of individual participants' brains into a standard geometric space based on anatomical features aligns the participants' functional organization, such that fMRI responses can be averaged in this common space. This second assumption might be sensible for brain regions with low inter-individual variability such as primary sensory and motor regions in the cerebral cortex, or subcortical regions that are precisely localizable based on anatomical details. However, inter-individual variability increases when moving from primary regions toward those regions responsible for higher-order cognitive processes, invalidating the practice of across-participant averaging. For example, one of the historically most studied nonprimary cortical areas, visual area V5 or MT, is about 1 by 2 cm in size, and its position is on average 1 cm in any direction along the cortex from an anatomical landmark based on sulcal folding patterns (Dumoulin et al., 2000). The variation in position after perfect anatomical alignment is thus as large as the area itself. Last, the likelihood of these assumptions to be valid may be even worse if we move toward psychiatric and neurological disorders, and it is likely that the problems with these assumptions stand in the way of productive applications of fMRI in the clinical domain.

Recently, several investigators have called for the averaging of more participants in order to increase statistical power and, ultimately, replicability. However, statistical power depends not only on the number of participants but also on both the number of participants and the number of measurements (and their quality) per participant (Baker et al., 2020). The latter is often ignored but equally important. UHF fMRI increases the measurement power at the participant level, thereby shifting the balance toward within-participant experimentation. As within-participant results improve, the across-participant variance is likely not dominated by variations in function, but by limitations of volumetric and surface-based alignment. That is, individuals differ and likewise brains differ. A clear example for this is the visual system. The primary visual cortex varies in size by a factor 2–3 with relatively minor perceptual consequences.

We argue that in order to harness the power of UHF, either more sophisticated alignment methods are needed that respect the functional anatomy, or alignment is circumvented altogether. The latter can be achieved by the use of ROI-based averaging, or not averaging at all if signals are strong enough to reach statistical significance per participant. UHF provides the power to achieve statistical significance per participant, using multiple participants as replication units rather than measurement units.

An example of more sophisticated alignment is the open resource of the human connectome project (HCP) 7T fMRI dataset of 181 individual participants (Essen et al., 2013). The surface-based alignment is based upon cortical folding, cortical myelin distribution, functional resting state connectivity, and mapping data. This experiment resulted in high-quality maps of visual space in early visual cortex, visual thalamus and superior colliculus (Benson et al., 2018), and tonotopic maps in early auditory cortex (Hedger and Knapen, 2021), but has also lead to discoveries of maps of visual space outside the traditional visual cortex: in the hippocampus (Knapen, 2021; Silson et al., 2021), default mode network (Szinte and Knapen, 2020), and cerebellum (van Es et al., 2019) (see Fig. 25.2, cf. (Groen et al., 2021)). At brain locations that are less consistent across individuals, such as is the case in higher-level visual regions in occipital, parietal, and frontal cortex, this across-participant averaging is problematic. Specifically, for maps of visual space, it is likely to lead to (a) an under-estimation of the strength of visually tuned responses because we will average out relevant signals instead of noise and (b) an unpredictable effects on the precise tuning that is found, making these results hard to interpret. We note that this is not a problem specific to visual processing. Rather, it is a specific instance of the above-mentioned problem that alignment across individuals based on anatomical landmarks does not guarantee alignment of functional organization. In regions with appreciable across-individual variability (the better part of the cerebral cortex), we are therefore forced to go to the level of the single individual.

UHF fMRI compels us to confront the above-mentioned assumptions and allows us to challenge them. Its increased sensitivity and specificity allow UHF fMRI to fulfill its promise as a tool for the measurement of local neural population activity, and as a tool for a cognitive neuroscience that rightfully values the uniqueness of individuals' brain structure and function, thereby encouraging researchers to focus on individual participants and local neural computations.

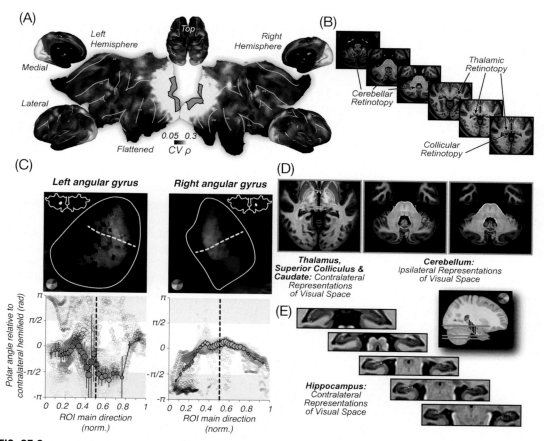

FIG. 25.2

GMO fMRI has revealed tuning for visual location for beyond the occipital lobe, i.e., visual population receptive fields and connective fields. (A) Distribution of cross-validated variance explained by connective fields on the flattened cerebral cortex. (B) Distribution of variance explained in the subcortex, same quantification as in (A). (C) Map-like structure of population receptive fields in the default mode network. Color denotes preferred polar angle: the direction in the visual field independent of visual eccentricity. These regions represent contralateral visual space. (D) Population receptive field polar angle position throughout the subcortex, in thalamus, superior colliculus, caudate nucleus, and cerebellum. As in the traditional visual system and default mode network, subcortical visual responses in these regions reflect contralateral visual space except cerebellum. Cerebellum features ipsilateral visual field representations, in line with its ipsilateral somatotopic maps. (E) Polar angle distribution in hippocampus, showing a detailed pattern of contralateral visual field preference. *Based on Groen et al. (2021).*

25.4 **Respecting local neural populations: Human systems neuroscience at UHF**

One of the previously considered assumptions is that neural tissue responds homogeneously enough throughout a brain region, so that fMRI results from clusters of voxels with identical responses. However, none of the most well-described cortical regions have homogeneous responses throughout what is considered a homogeneous area. For example, within the primary visual cortex (V1), different parts respond to different locations in the visual field, and V1 function differs drastically between central and peripheral visions. Despite these differences, V1 is indeed homogenous in its implementation of fixed computational principles. The same holds for early visual cortex in general, and other sensory and motor cortices: Although exact tuning varies drastically within regions, computational principles do not. We contend that this is likely the case for the brain in general; therefore, we suggest that the underlying assumption should not be that an area responds homogeneously, but that responses in an area reflect coherent computational principles.

There are several types of analysis that respect local neural populations as reflected in single time courses of individual voxels, for example, multivoxel pattern analysis and single-time-course modeling. For example, single-time-course modeling has been used to great effect even at 3T, with encoding-model analysis capturing receptive field properties of the sampled neuronal population (Dumoulin and Wandell, 2008; Kay et al., 2008) and, for example, revealing the brain's semantic organization (Huth et al., 2016). These types of experiments can readily benefit from UHF as they already focus on high SNR measurements on individual participants (Gratton

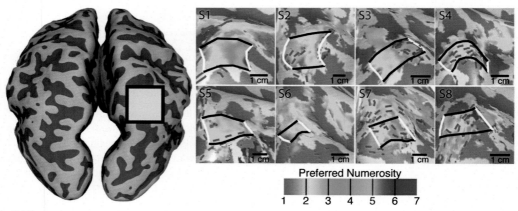

FIG. 25.3

Example of across-participant variability of cortical organization in the cerebral cortex. Topographic maps of numerosity preference are shown for eight participants, zoomed into the portion of the brain highlighted on the left. There is a topographic map in each of the participants at the same approximate location and approximate orientation, but the exact tuning at each location varies widely. Averaging this tuning across participants in a common anatomical space would drastically dilute this information tuning. *Based on Harvey et al. (2013).*

et al., 2022). A recent initiative, the natural scenes dataset (Allen et al., 2021), provides a beautiful example of how GMO UHF fMRI can be leveraged at the unique individual level. In this project, 8 participants were scanned for 30–40 sessions each while viewing up to 10,000 natural images on which they performed an image-recognition task. With GMO single-voxel responses to this amount of stimuli, this is an invaluable resource with a unique focus on high-SNR measurements in individual participants.

One of the earliest discoveries using UHF in the field of cognitive neuroscience was the topographic maps that represent dimensions of numerical cognition. First, the discovery of maps that systematically represents numerosity akin to a mental number line (Harvey et al., 2013), followed by cognitive topographic maps that represent object size (Harvey et al., 2015), time duration (Protopapa et al., 2018), and haptic numerosity (Hofstetter et al., 2021). These discoveries suggest that topographic principles common in primary sensory and motor cortices may also be an organizing principle of cognitive functions in association cortex. Fig. 25.3 demonstrates that these human numerosity maps vary strongly between individuals in terms of their precise location and orientation—again highlighting the necessity of performing these analyses at the single-participant level.

These numerosity maps have been used to showcase the strength of UHF relative to standard field strength acquisitions. We compared the relative efficacy of 3T and 7T acquisitions in charting these numerosity maps in single individuals (Cai et al., 2021), and showed that for every run acquired at 7T, one would need to acquire approximately four runs at 3T to attain the same variance explained or effective SNR (see Fig. 25.4).

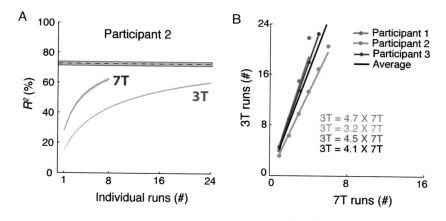

FIG. 25.4

The amount of data needed for a given variance explained (R2) at 3T is roughly four times the amount of data needed at 7T. (A). Test–retest reliability as a function of number of runs averaged, expressed as cross-validated R2. These data were acquired in a numerosity-mapping experiment (Fig. 25.3). Curves show the amount of runs needed to approach the noise ceiling for a single participant. 8 runs of 7T data have higher cross-validated R2 than 24 runs of 3T data. (B). The amount of 3T runs that equal the amount of 7T runs for 3 participants: Only about a quarter of the data is needed at 7T to reach the same variance explained as at 3T. *Based on Cai et al. (2021).*

25.5 Outlook

UHF fMRI optimized to sample gray-matter responses can be performed with whole-brain coverage, and analyzed using well-established analytical tools. This high degree of accessibility combined with the very high level of attainable data quality makes GMO fMRI a very compelling strategy for cognitive neuroscience. GMO fMRI's specific sampling of local neuronal population activations allows it to probe computational principles at work in the living human brain. This allows UHF fMRI to bridge cognitive neuroscience, neurophysiology in animal models, and computational neuroscience, with a unique focus on high-SNR measurements in individual participants. Since specific deficits in computational processes characterize many psychiatric disorders, GMO fMRI also holds promise for the eventual use of fMRI for clinical purposes.

References

Allen, E.J., St-Yves, G., Wu, Y., et al., 2021. A massive 7T fMRI dataset to bridge cognitive neuroscience and artificial intelligence. Nat. Neurosci. 1–11. https://doi.org/10.1038/s41593-021-00962-x.

Baker, D.H., Vilidaite, G., Lygo, F.A., et al., 2020. Power contours: optimising sample size and precision in experimental psychology and human neuroscience. Psychol. Methods 26, 295–314. https://doi.org/10.1037/met0000337.

Benson, N.C., Jamison, K.W., Arcaro, M.J., et al., 2018. The Human Connectome Project 7 Tesla retinotopy dataset: description and population receptive field analysis. J. Vis. 18, 23. https://doi.org/10.1167/18.13.23.

Brodmann, K., 1909. In: Brodmann, K. (Ed.), Vergleichende Lokalisationslehre der Grosshirnrinde in ihren Prinzipien dargestellt auf Grund des Zellenbaues von Dr. J.A. Barth.

Caan, M.W.A., Bazin, P., Marques, J.P., Hollander, G., Dumoulin, S.O., Zwaag, W., 2018. MP2RAGEME: T1, T2*, and QSM mapping in one sequence at 7 tesla. Hum. Brain Mapp. https://doi.org/10.1002/hbm.24490.

Cai, Y., Hofstetter, S., van der Zwaag, W., Zuiderbaan, W., Dumoulin, S.O., 2021. Individualized cognitive neuroscience needs 7T: Comparing numerosity maps at 3T and 7T MRI. Neuroimage 237, 118184. https://doi.org/10.1016/j.neuroimage.2021.118184.

Colizoli, O., de Gee, J.W., van der Zwaag, W., Donner, T.H., 2021. Functional magnetic resonance imaging responses during perceptual decision-making at 3 and 7 T in human cortex, striatum, and brainstem. Hum. Brain Mapp. 43, 1265–1279. https://doi.org/10.1002/hbm.25719.

Collins, D.L., Neelin, P., Peters, T.M., Evans, A.C., 1994. Automatic 3D intersubject registration of MR volumetric data in standardized talairach space. J. Comput. Assist. Tomogr. 18, 192–205. https://doi.org/10.1097/00004728-199403000-00005.

Dumoulin, S.O., Wandell, B.A., 2008. Population receptive field estimates in human visual cortex. Neuroimage 39, 647–660.

Dumoulin, S.O., Bittar, R.G., Kabani, N.J., et al., 2000. A new anatomical landmark for reliable identification of human area V5/MT: a quantitative analysis of sulcal patterning. Cereb. Cortex 10, 454–463. https://doi.org/10.1093/cercor/10.5.454.

Essen, D.C.V., Smith, S.M., Barch, D.M., Behrens, T.E.J., Yacoub, E., Ugurbil, K., 2013. The WU-Minn human connectome project: an overview. Neuroimage 80 (62), 79. https://doi.org/10.1016/j.neuroimage.2013.05.041.

Felleman, D.J., Essen, D.C.V., 1991. Distributed hierarchical processing in the primate cerebral cortex. Cereb. Cortex 1 (1), 47. https://doi.org/10.1093/cercor/1.1.1.

Fracasso, A., van Veluw, S.J., Visser, F., et al., 2016. Lines of Baillarger in vivo and ex vivo: Myelin contrast across lamina at 7T MRI and histology. Neuroimage 133, 163–175. https://doi.org/10.1016/j.neuroimage. 2016.02.072.

Gratton, C., Nelson, S.M., Gordon, E.M., 2022. Brain-behavior correlations: two paths toward reliability. Neuron 110, 1446–1449. https://doi.org/10.1016/j.neuron.2022.04.018.

Groen, I.I.A., Dekker, T.M., Knapen, T., Silson, E.H., 2021. Visuospatial coding as ubiquitous scaffolding for human cognition. Trends Cogn. Sci. https://doi.org/10.1016/j.tics.2021.10.011.

Harvey, B.M., Klein, B.P., Petridou, N., Dumoulin, S.O., 2013. Topographic representation of numerosity in the human parietal cortex. Science (New York, NY) 341, 1123–1126. https://doi.org/10.1126/science.1239052.

Harvey, B.M., Fracasso, A., Petridou, N., Dumoulin, S.O., 2015. Topographic representations of object size and relationships with numerosity reveal generalized quantity processing in human parietal cortex. Proc. Nat. Acad. Sci. 112, 13530. https://doi.org/10.1073/pnas.1515414112.

Hedger, N., Knapen, T., 2021. Naturalistic audiovisual stimulation reveals the topographic organization of human auditory cortex. Biorxiv. https://doi.org/10.1101/2021.07.05.447566.

Hofstetter, S., Cai, Y., Harvey, B.M., Dumoulin, S.O., 2021. Topographic maps representing haptic numerosity reveals distinct sensory representations in supramodal networks. Nat. Commun. 12, 221. https://doi.org/10.1038/s41467-020-20567-5.

Horton, J.C., Adams, D.L., 2005. The cortical column: a structure without a function. Philos. Trans. Roy. Soc. B Biol. Sci. 360, 837–862. https://doi.org/10.1098/rstb.2005.1623.

Hubel, D.H., Wiesel, T.N., 1977. Ferrier lecture—functional architecture of macaque monkey visual cortex. Proc. R. Soc. Lond. B Biol. Sci. 198, 1–59. https://doi.org/10.1098/rspb.1977.0085.

Huth, A.G., de Heer, W.A., Griffiths, T.L., Theunissen, F.E., Gallant, J.L., 2016. Natural speech reveals the semantic maps that tile human cerebral cortex. Nature 532 (453), 458. https://doi.org/10.1038/nature17637.

Jones, E.G., Burton, H., Porter, R., 1975. Commissural and cortico-cortical "Columns" in the somatic sensory cortex of primates. Science 190, 572–574. https://doi.org/10.1126/science.810887.

Kay, K.N., Naselaris, T., Prenger, R.J., Gallant, J.L., 2008. Identifying natural images from human brain activity. Nature 452, 352–355.

Knapen, T., 2021. Topographic connectivity reveals task-dependent retinotopic processing throughout the human brain. Proc. Nat. Acad. Sci. 118, e2017032118. https://doi.org/10.1073/pnas.2017032118.

Mountcastle, V.B., Davies, P.W., Berman, A.L., 1957. Response properties of neurons of cat's somatic sensory cortex to peripheral stimuli. J. Neurophysiol. 20, 374–407. https://doi.org/10.1152/jn.1957.20.4.374.

Protopapa, F., Hayashi, M., Kulashekhar, S., et al., 2018. Chronotopic maps in human medial premotor cortex. Biorxiv. https://doi.org/10.1101/399857.

Silson, E.H., Zeidman, P., Knapen, T., Baker, C.I., 2021. Representation of contralateral visual space in the human hippocampus. J. Neurosci. 41, 2382–2392. https://doi.org/10.1523/jneurosci.1990-20.2020.

Stanley, J.A., Raz, N., 2018. Functional magnetic resonance spectroscopy: the "New" MRS for cognitive neuroscience and psychiatry research. Front. Psych. 9, 76. https://doi.org/10.3389/fpsyt.2018.00076.

Szinte, M., Knapen, T., 2020. Visual organization of the default network. Cereb Cortex New York N Y 1991 (30), 3518–3527. https://doi.org/10.1093/cercor/bhz323.

Trampel, R., Ott, D.V.M., Turner, R., 2011. Do the congenitally blind have a stria of Gennari? First intracortical insights in vivo. Cereb. Cortex 21, 2075–2081. https://doi.org/10.1093/cercor/bhq282.

Uludağ, K., Müller-Bierl, B., Uğurbil, K., 2009. An integrative model for neuronal activity-induced signal changes for gradient and spin echo functional imaging. Neuroimage 48, 150–165.

van der Zwaag, W., Francis, S., Head, K., et al., 2009. fMRI at 1.5, 3 and 7 T: characterising BOLD signal changes. Neuroimage 47, 1425–1434. https://doi.org/10.1016/j.neuroimage.2009.05.015.

van Es, D.M., van der Zwaag, W., Knapen, T., 2019. Topographic maps of visual space in the human cerebellum. Curr. Biol. 29, 1689–1694.e3. https://doi.org/10.1016/j.cub.2019.04.012.

Viessmann, O., Polimeni, J.R., 2021. High-resolution fMRI at 7Tesla: challenges, promises and recent developments for individual-focused fMRI studies. Curr. Opin. Behav. Sci. 40, 96–104. https://doi.org/10.1016/j.cobeha.2021.01.011.

Vogt, C., Vogt, O., 1919. Allgemeine Ergebnisse unserer Hirnforschung. J. Psych. Neurol. 25 (J.A. Barth).

Weiskopf, N., Suckling, J., Williams, G., et al., 2013. Quantitative multi-parameter mapping of R1, PD*, MT, and R2* at 3T: a multi-center validation. Front. Neurosci. 7, 95. https://doi.org/10.3389/fnins.2013.00095.

Yacoub, E., Shmuel, A., Pfeuffer, J., et al., 2001. Imaging brain function in humans at 7 Tesla. Magn. Reson. Med. 45, 588–594. https://doi.org/10.1002/mrm.1080.

Techniques for ultra-high field metabolic imaging and spectroscopy

8

MR spectroscopy and spectroscopic imaging

26

Kimberly L. Chan[a], Loreen Ruhm[a,b], and Anke Henning[a,b]

[a]*Advanced Imaging Research Center, University of Texas Southwestern Medical Center, Dallas, TX, United States* [b]*Max Planck Institute for Biological Cybernetics, Tübingen, Germany*

Highlights

- Magnetic resonance spectroscopy benefits from increased signal-to-noise ratio and spectral dispersion from ultra-high field.
- Technical challenges include static and radiofrequency magnetic field inhomogeneity, stricter specific absorption rates, and altered relaxation times.
- Improved spectral resolution enables better distinction of metabolite peaks and upfield and downfield resonances for proton magnetic resonance spectroscopy.
- Increased signal-to-noise ratio is especially beneficial for X-nuclei magnetic resonance spectroscopy which has low sensitivity.

26.1 Introduction

The aim of this chapter is to give a comprehensive overview of the advantages, challenges, and advances of ultra-high field magnetic resonance spectroscopy (MRS) and magnetic resonance spectroscopic imaging (MRSI) with regard to methodological development, discoveries, and applications. It is limited to human whole-body MRI scanners with field strength >7 T and includes four relevant nuclei ^{1}H, ^{31}P, ^{13}C, and ^{2}H.

26.1.1 The promise

MRS and MRSI benefit threefold from ultra-high field strengths: (i) a gain in signal-to-noise ratio (SNR), (ii) a larger frequency dispersion, and (iii) a reduction in J-coupling for strongly coupled spin systems. These advantages can be traded against higher spatial and temporal resolution at shorter scan times and allow for the detection, better distinction, and more accurate and precise quantification of a larger number of metabolites.

26.1.1.1 Signal-to-noise ratio

Due to the low tissue concentration of metabolites (on the order of mmol/kg) compared to water (55 mol/kg), ^{1}H MRS is approximately 10,000 times less sensitive than anatomical MR imaging (MRI). Hence, ^{1}H MRS benefits substantially from the gain in SNR that ultra-high field MR offers.

Advances in Magnetic Resonance Technology and Applications. Volume 10. ISSN 2666-9099. https://doi.org/10.1016/B978-0-323-99898-7.00035-3

X-nuclei MRS has even lower sensitivity compared to ^1H MRS due to the lower gyromagnetic ratios, concentrations, and natural abundance of the X-nucleus (see Table 1, Chapter 26). The increased SNR provided by ultra-high field (UHF) MR systems ($B_0 \geq 7T$) is therefore an enabling factor of X-nuclei MRS and MRSI.

Classical theory predicts an all-over linear increase in SNR with field strength based on a linear increase in spin polarization. In data acquisition, the induction also increases with field strength, but this effect has no net contribution to the SNR gain because both the signal- and noise-induced voltages increase linearly. In recent years, it has been shown that the characteristics of the receive coil arrays in combination with shorter electromagnetic wavelength lead to a spatially inhomogeneous increase in SNR with field strength. In central parts of the human brain and body, an almost quadratic gain in SNR can be achieved with optimal coil designs, while only a linear increase can be expected in the periphery.

Experimentally, an average SNR gain with field strength is estimated to be

$$ \text{SNR} \sim B_0^{+1.65} $$

This relationship has been reported for ^1H MRI and MRS across different regions of the human brain (Pohmann et al., 2016); similar values have been measured for different X-nuclei as well.

Following this result, SNR is approximately four times higher at 7T than at 3T. However, the exact experimental SNR for a given region inside the human brain or body is determined not only by tissue type and field strength but also by additional factors such as the relaxation times of the detectable resonances, the spectroscopy sequence, and the radiofrequency coil used.

The combination of improved SNR and increased spectral resolution at UHF generally enables quantification of a higher number of ^1H, ^{31}P, and ^{13}C MRS resonances and can be translated to improved spatial resolution for ^1H, ^{31}P, and ^2H MRSI. The SNR in ^{31}P and ^{13}C MRS can be further improved by making use of the nuclear Overhauser effect (nOe), proton decoupling, or polarization transfer, which yield additional SNR enhancement factors between 1.2 and 4 for each of these methods, and which can also be combined (De Graaf, 2019).

26.1.1.2 Spectral resolution

Spectral resolution generally benefits from a larger frequency dispersion combined with weaker J-coupling at UHF, and frequency dispersion increases linearly with field strength. This is illustrated in Fig. 26.1A which shows the same resonance lines of an upfield proton brain spectrum between 0 and 4 ppm which are distributed over a frequency range of ~ 250 Hz at 1.5T and ~ 1200 Hz at 7T. This moves overlapping resonance lines further apart from each other and thus improves the spectral resolution of 1D spectra. In addition, the resonance lines of J-coupled spin systems are moved further apart, which introduces a shift from strong to weak(er) J-coupling and a respective simplification of spectral patterns and their phase and amplitude evolution with TE. This also enhances the effective spectral resolution.

However, the stronger local B_0 inhomogeneity and shorter T_2 relaxation times at UHF result in broader linewidths which reduce the spectral resolution of ^1H and ^{31}P MRS. The negative effect caused by B_0 inhomogeneity is partly compensated by good B_0 shimming (Fig. 26.1B; Juchem et al., 2021). Excellent B_0 shimming combined with short-TE single-voxel MRS sequences enables the distinction of a large number of metabolites. In this context, it is important to note that smaller voxel sizes usually lead to a smaller intravoxel B_0 inhomogeneity and hence, using small voxel sizes is a favorable strategy at UHF.

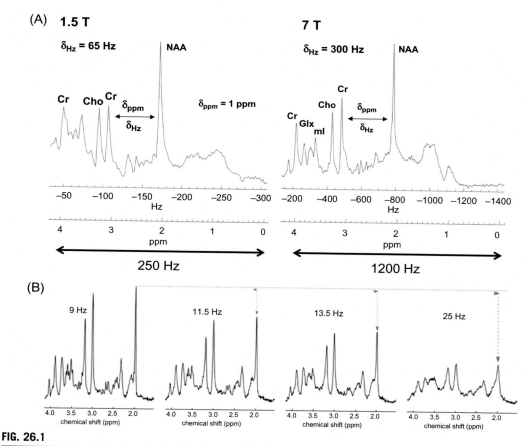

FIG. 26.1

(A) Spectral resolution comparison between ^{1}H MRS spectra acquired at 1.5 and 7 T. The frequency dispersion increases substantially with field strength with the frequency range at 1 ppm increasing from 65 to 300 Hz. Consequently, the frequency range of the upfield proton brain spectrum at 0 to 4 ppm increases from 250 to 1200 Hz. (B) Impact of B_0 shimming on effective spectral resolution in ^{1}H MRS of the human brain at 7 T. The narrower the linewidth, the more metabolite-specific resonance lines can be distinguished. *Reproduced from Juchem et al. (2021).*

The higher spectral dispersion provided by UHF combined with quasi-field-independent relaxation times and linewidths in ^{2}H MRS results in an improved spectral resolution for ^{2}H MRS at UHF. Although the number of detectable resonances does not increase with field strength for ^{2}H MRS, both the accuracy and precision of their quantification improve.

At lower field strengths, ^{13}C spectra already cover a very large frequency range; hence the benefit of the improved frequency dispersion at UHF for ^{13}C MRS is less substantial compared to ^{1}H MRS.

26.1.2 **The challenge**

To take advantage of the benefits provided by UHF, several technical challenges need to be overcome: (i) strong inhomogeneity and instability of the static magnetic field (B_0), (ii) inhomogeneous transmit (B_1^+) and receive (B_1^-) fields, (iii) radiofrequency pulse bandwidth limitations, (iv) specific absorption rate (SAR) constraints, and (v) altered T_1 and T_2 relaxation rates.

26.1.2.1 Static magnetic field B_0 inhomogeneity and instability

Static magnetic field (B_0) inhomogeneity is a major limitation of whole-brain ^{1}H MRSI at UHF. Inhomogeneities are induced by magnetic susceptibility differences between water-rich tissue and air, and between different tissue types (see Chapter 6). The most problematic areas, regardless of field strength, are in proximity to the frontal sinus and ear canals (Boer et al., 2012). The shape of the B_0 inhomogeneity is independent of the B_0 field strength, but its magnitude is proportional to B_0. If not corrected properly, the resultant detrimental effects on MRS data quality are magnified accordingly (Juchem et al., 2021). In addition, patient and physiological motion introduce temporal instabilities of the static magnetic field, which are also magnified at UHF (Giapitzakis et al., 2018). Altogether, B_0 shimming is a major concern for ^{1}H MRS and MRSI at UHF, while X-nuclei MRS is less affected due to the lower resonant frequencies.

B_0 homogenization (shimming) is usually performed by adjusting the currents in a set of dedicated B_0 shim coils which are integrated into commercial MRI scanners. These coils produce complementary shim fields mimicking the spherical harmonic functions. Projection-based B_0 shim techniques such as FASTMAP, FASTERMAP, or FASTESTMAP (De Graaf, 2019; Juchem et al., 2021) yield excellent homogeneity corrections for single-voxel spectroscopy (SVS) in the human brain at high magnetic field strengths. However, in the case of MRSI with large volume coverage, complex geometries, or strong local inhomogeneities, image-based B_0 shimming is recommended. This method requires the acquisition of a full 3D B_0 map (Juchem et al., 2021). For optimal B_0 shim results, actual shim field constraints and shim field imperfections have to be considered in the shim algorithm, and sufficiently high shim currents should be available. Prototypes of hardware-based approaches including very high-order and degree spherical harmonic B_0 shimming, matrix coil shimming, and slice-wise dynamic B_0 shimming have been implemented and tested for ^{1}H MRSI but are not widely available. While moderate improvements of B_0 shimming in the human brain have been reported, none of these hardware methods have fully solved the problem of the strong local B_0 inhomogeneities.

Recent work has shown that in case of single-voxel spectroscopy, second-order spherical harmonic B_0 shimming is sufficient and higher-order spherical harmonics contribute little (Nassirpour et al., 2018). If sufficiently well shimmed, linewidths for single-voxel spectroscopy in the brain range from 9 to 19 Hz (Table 1 of reference Juchem et al. (2021)).

The choice of a small voxel size, stack-wise or slice-wise B_0 shimming optimization, the use of vendor-provided third-order shim terms, and the inclusion of the skull lipid area into the B_0 shim optimization are practical solutions to improve the quality and coverage of brain ^{1}H MRSI (Juchem et al., 2021; Boer et al., 2012).

The temporal instability of the B_0 field is typically compensated for by retrospective frequency alignment. Prospective B_0 field drift correction methods using either interleaved water measurements or the metabolite cycling method, which enables simultaneous acquisition of water and metabolites, have been suggested for single-voxel ^{1}H MRS (Giapitzakis et al., 2018; Chan et al., 2021).

26.1.2.2 *Radiofrequency power amplifiers, coils, and pulse bandwidth limits*

Commercial 7 T systems are typically equipped with 8 kW proton radiofrequency (RF) amplifier power (a clinical MRI system amplifier has about 35 kW), and 4–8 kW broadband amplifier power is used for X-nuclei MRI/S. The first 7 T MRI scanners only had 4 kW proton amplifier power, while the most recent UHF human MRI scanners are equipped with up to 16 kW. Furthermore, about 50% of this power is lost due to cable losses between amplifier and radiofrequency coil. UHF human MRI systems do not have a body transmit coil and the amplifier power is used for local transmission coils instead.

The majority of the human brain 7 T ^{1}H MRS studies use the same commercial RF coil (Nova Medical), which typically consists of a head transmit birdcage volume coil combined with a separate helmet-shaped 16 or 32 channel receive array insert. This widespread RF coil design has limited coverage in z-direction, especially of the brain stem and cerebellum. More recently, commercial transmit coil arrays became available, which offer the possibility to shape or focus the transmit field. Close-fitting transceiver coil arrays produce higher transmit field and SAR efficiency in comparison to separate transmit and receive coils and also offer a better longitudinal coverage. Both are potentially beneficial for UHF MRS. However, the vast majority of transmit arrays, transceiver arrays, nonproton coils or coil arrays, and surface coils as well as all coils used at 9.4 or 10.5 T were custom built, mostly by the research groups themselves or in few cases by specialized RF coil vendors. This demonstrates that RF coil availability is an enabling factor for more widespread use of UHF brain MRS in scientific and clinical studies and is certainly the most important limiting factor for human nonproton and body MRS applications at UHF (see Chapter 8).

Altogether the technical specifications of the amplifiers and RF coils pose strict limits of the transmit field B_1 amplitude and in consequence also the bandwidth and fidelity of radiofrequency pulses. This problem translates into large chemical shift displacement artifacts for ^{1}H MRS and ^{1}H MRSI, especially when using sequences such as PRESS that rely on refocusing pulses as commonly used at 1.5 and 3 T (Fig. 26.2A). At 3 T, the chemical shift displacement error for resonances 3 ppm apart using the PRESS sequence is large at ~35% but is reduced to 6% with a sLASER sequence when using typical refocusing pulses with a bandwidth of 1.06 kHz for PRESS and 6.3 kHz for sLASER. Since frequency dispersion increases linearly with field strength, this chemical shift displacement error becomes even more profound at an UHF strength of 7 T and increases to 84% for the PRESS sequence and 14% for the sLASER sequence when using the same refocusing pulses. Thus, dedicated sequences have been developed to overcome this problem (see Single voxel ^{1}H MRS and ^{1}H MRSI).

Due to the larger frequency dispersion in ^{31}P MRS, not only does the chemical shift displacement problem persist, but it is even difficult to design frequency selective pulses with the required excitation bandwidth to include all relevant metabolites from phosphorylethanolamine (PE) to β-adenosine triphosphate (ATP). The chemical shift difference between PE and β-ATP is 23.1 ppm, which translates to a large frequency difference of approximately 3700 Hz at 9.4 T.

The relevant ppm-range in ^{2}H MRSI at UHF is narrow compared to ^{31}P MRS and similar to ^{1}H MRS at clinical field strength. Therefore, pulse bandwidth is not a major concern for ^{2}H MRSI at UHF.

The very large frequency range in ^{13}C MRS at UHF makes it practically impossible to design respective localization sequences at low and high fields. Alternatives include nonlocalized direct ^{13}C acquisition, proton-localized carbon-detected sequences, or proton-detected carbon-edited sequences (see Single voxel ^{13}C MRS and ^{13}C MRSI).

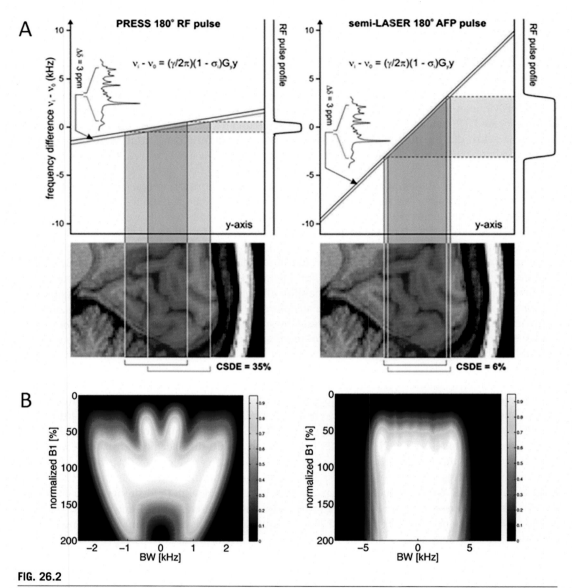

FIG. 26.2

(A) Chemical shift displacement at 3T in ^{1}H MRS for two resonances 3 ppm apart in the x and y refocusing pulse directions for both the PRESS and sLASER pulse sequences. Even at 3T, the PRESS pulse sequence yields a large 35% chemical shift displacement artifact when using a typical refocusing pulse bandwidth of 1.06 kHz. With the sLASER sequence, however, this chemical shift displacement error (CSDE) decreases to 6% with an adiabatic full-passage refocusing pulse bandwidth of 6.3 kHz. (B) RF pulse profiles for nonadiabatic (top) and adiabatic (bottom) refocusing pulses and their dependence of B_1^+ variation at 7T. Only the adiabatic refocusing pulse is robust against the B_1^+ inhomogeneity occurring at UHF. *(A) Reproduced from Oz et al. (2020) (B) Reproduced from Fuchs et al. (2013).*

26.1.2.3 Radiofrequency field B_1 inhomogeneity

With increasing field strength, the electromagnetic wavelength shortens, which leads to strong inhomogeneity of the transmit B_1^+ and receive B_1^- fields (see Chapter 7). This problem is most pronounced for ^{1}H MRS as it has the highest Larmor frequency among all nuclei but still needs consideration for ^{31}P, ^{2}H, and ^{13}C MRS.

For ^{1}H and ^{31}P single-voxel spectroscopy, volume-based power optimization can give accurate flip angle calibration at the spectroscopy voxel location (Versluis et al., 2010). With advances in RF transceiver array design allowing for multiple transmission channels, RF shimming has been demonstrated to focus the field in the target region to yield an adequate power level for single-voxel spectroscopy at UHF. Localization and suppression sequences have to be robust against B_1^+ inhomogeneity, which can be achieved by adiabatic RF pulses (Fig. 26.2B) (Fuchs et al., 2013) or numerically optimized pulse trains. A practical solution for ^{1}H MRSI is the use of low flip angle pulses, which yields a sequence that is insensitive to transmit field inhomogeneity (Henning et al., 2009; Bogner et al., 2021). While RF shimming using different RF shims for skull lipid suppression and brain metabolite excitation has been demonstrated for ^{1}H MRSI at UHF (Boer et al., 2012), it is not yet widely available. Parallel transmission pulses have so far not gained any practical relevance for UHF MRS or MRSI studies.

Receive field inhomogeneity is usually considered by internal reference standards such as water in case of ^{1}H and ^{2}H MRS or ATP in case of ^{31}P MRS.

26.1.2.4 Specific absorption rate

Due to shortening of the electromagnetic wavelength at UHF, tissue is heated more efficiently. In addition, the absorption of energy is spatially inhomogeneous with local hotspots, which requires the consideration of local SAR instead of a global average SAR as typically used at low fields. The resulting strict SAR limitations are in conflict with the need of SAR intense adiabatic pulses, multipulse suppression sequences, and SNR enhancement methods for X-nucleus MRS that are based on pulse trains. This reduces the SNR efficiency, and in order to gain SNR over time in comparison to low-field MRS, pulse sequences have to be optimized to minimize SAR (see nucleus-specific sections).

26.1.2.5 Relaxation times

For ^{1}H MRS metabolites, T_1 relaxation times slightly increase with field strength, while T_2 relaxation times decrease substantially. Both effects counteract the potential UHF-induced SNR gain. Especially sequences with short echo time (TE) and Ernst-angle excitation yield high SNR efficiency, while long TE sequences can have equal or even lower SNR in comparison to 1.5 and 3 T and thus have to be avoided (Fig. 26.3).

^{31}P T_1 relaxation times are typically much longer and T_2 relaxation times are significantly shorter than in ^{1}H MRS (Fig. 26.3), both of which negatively influence SNR. The relaxation times for ^{31}P resonances are influenced by two effects with opposite behaviors at different field strengths: dipolar relaxation and chemical shift anisotropy (CSA) relaxation. A higher contribution of CSA relaxation leads to decreased T_1 relaxation times and therefore to an improved experimental sensitivity at ultra-high field strengths. However, a meta-analysis of PCr T_1 measurements acquired at the human brain showed no dependence on the static magnetic field (Fig. 26.1; Peeters et al., 2021).

The relaxation times and linewidths of the ^{2}H resonances appear to be field-independent (Ruhm et al., 2021). Overall, the T_1 relaxations of most ^{2}H resonances are relatively short (around 350 ms for natural abundant deuterated water) which benefits the SNR efficiency of ^{2}H MRSI.

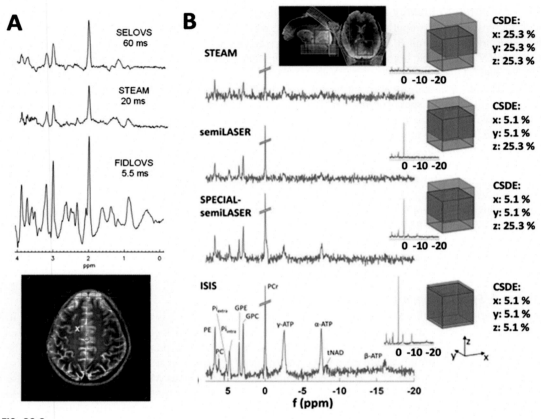

FIG. 26.3

(A) SNR comparison for non-apodized spectra from a $1\,cm^3$ voxel inside white matter (position marked with a white "x" on the anatomical image) using ^{1}H FID-MRSI Localized by Outer Volume Suppression (FIDLOVS), STEAM MRSI and Spin-Echo MRSI Localized by Outer Volume Suppression at 7T (SELOVS). Spectra are scaled to the same noise level; shim and receiver gain settings were equal for all three measurements performed in the same subject. The highest number of metabolite peaks is clearly visible in the FIDLOVS spectrum, whereas STEAM and even more SELOVS spectra suffer from loss of information content due to T_2 relaxation. (B) SNR comparison between different ^{31}P single-voxel localization methods: STEAM (TE=10ms), semiLASER (TE=30ms), SPECIAL-semiLASER (TE=17ms), and ISIS (TE=0.425ms) at 9.4T. The red and blue cubes represent the chemical shift displacement error between phosphocreatine and phosphoethanolamine. Of the four methods, ISIS has the highest localization accuracy, the lowest chemical shift displacement and the highest SNR per time due to minimization of T_2 relaxation. *(A) Reproduced from Henning et al., (2009) (B) Reproduced from Dorst et al., (2021).*

In ^{13}C MRS, the relaxation is primarily due to '^{1}H-'^{13}C dipole-dipole interaction if ^{13}C is bonded directly to one or more protons. Spin rotation can be expected to contribute in small molecules and to be a dominant relaxation mechanism for CH_3 groups due to the free internal rotation. Chemical shift anisotropy and scalar relaxation are negligible relaxation mechanisms in case of ^{13}C MRS. Altogether T_1 and T_2 relaxation times are longer than in ^{1}H MRS, which even allows for the detection of large and immobile metabolites such as glygogen (T_1: 300 ± 10 ms at 8.4 T, T_2: 9.5 ± 1 ms at 8.4 T).

26.2 Single voxel ^{1}H MRS and ^{1}H MRSI
26.2.1 Single voxel ^{1}H MRS sequences and methods
26.2.1.1 Localization and suppression sequences for single voxel ^{1}H MRS

Due to the challenges present at ultra-high field strengths, conventional localization methods such as PRESS are not optimal. As T_2 relaxation times are shorter at higher fields, the TE needs to be shortened so as not to lose SNR. Because of the greater frequency dispersion, the nonadiabatic refocusing pulses typically used at clinical field strengths have insufficient bandwidth at ultra-high field strengths, which leads to greater chemical shift displacement errors (CSDE) (Fig. 26.2A). These amplitude-modulated refocusing pulses are also sensitive to B_1 inhomogeneity, making them unsuitable for ultra-high field use (Fig. 26.2B). As such, other sequences such as the STEAM, LASER, semi-LASER, and SPECIAL are used instead. These sequences and their advantages and disadvantages are elaborated below. Their pulse sequence diagrams are shown in Fig. 26.4 (Zhu and Barker, 2011). Fig. 26.4A shows the spatial localization achieved by each of the three slice-selective RF pulses in each direction.

The STEAM sequence consists of three slice-selective 90-degree pulses (Fig. 26.4B) as opposed to the PRESS sequence which consists of one slice-selective 90-degree excitation pulse and two 180-degree refocusing pulses (Fig. 26.4C). This results in a "stimulated echo" with STEAM rather than a "spin echo" with PRESS. Relative to the refocusing pulses, the 90-degree RF pulses have lower RF power requirements, better slice profiles, and a higher bandwidth, which results in reduced CSDE, and allow for shorter echo times. A major downside to STEAM, however, is the 50% reduction in SNR relative to PRESS. This can be partly compensated for by achieving very short echo times below 10 ms. STEAM is the method of choice in severely B_1^+ field strength constrained situations but requires excellent phase cycling and gradient spoiling schemes for sufficient artifact suppression.

One downside to both PRESS and STEAM, however, is the sensitivity of the RF pulses to B_1^+ inhomogeneity (Fig. 26.2B). As such, a uniform flip angle throughout the volume-of-interest (VOI) is difficult to achieve with these sequences at ultra-high field strengths and results in a loss in signal and a reduction in the selection efficiency. Consequently, pulse sequences using adiabatic refocusing pulses have often been implemented at ultra-high field strengths such as Localization by Adiabatic Selective REfocusing (LASER) (Fig. 26.4D) and its variant, semi-LASER (sLASER) (Fig. 26.4E). Of the two sequences, sLASER is more commonly used and consists of a nonadiabatic excitation pulse followed by two pairs of slice-selective adiabatic refocusing pulses for localization in each direction (Fig. 26.4E). The large bandwidth of the adiabatic pulses results in significantly more uniform flip angles and reduced CSDEs (Fig. 26.2B). A downside of this technique, however, is the large number of RF pulses which result in higher SAR and a longer TE relative to STEAM and PRESS. The latter can be

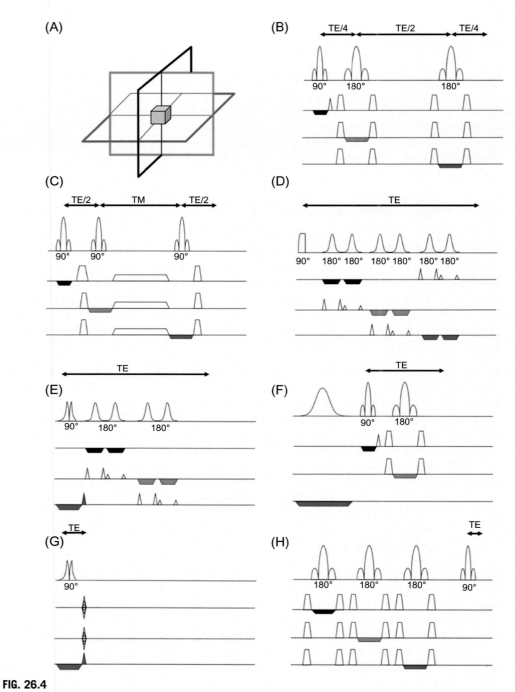

FIG. 26.4

(A) Spatial localization is achieved by collecting signals from the intersection of three slice-selective RF pulses applied in orthogonal directions for single-voxel MRS. Pulse sequences for single-voxel ^{1}H and ^{31}P MRS and MRSI: (B) PRESS, (C) STEAM, (D) LASER, (E) sLASER, (F) SPECIAL, (G) FID-MRSI, (H) ISIS. *Reproduced from Zhu and Barker (2011).*

partly overcome by the use of Offset-Independent Trapezoid (OIT), Frequency Offset-Corrected Inversion (FOCI), or Gradient-modulated Offset-Independent Adiabaticity (GOIA) adiabatic pulses, which all achieve large bandwidth at shorter pulse durations.

Another sequence used at ultra-high field strengths is the SPin-ECho full-Intensity Acquired Localized spectroscopy (SPECIAL) sequence. It consists of a slice-selective adiabatic broadband inversion pulse followed by two pulses: a 90-degree excitation pulse and a classical 180-degree refocusing pulse, which are slice-selective in different directions to allow for slice-based localization (Fig. 26.4F). The slice-selective inversion pulse is only applied at alternating TRs to allow for a full 3D spatial localization after applying an add-subtract scheme similar to ISIS. As such, SPECIAL combines the desirable features of both the full signal intensity of PRESS and the shorter TE of STEAM. Finally, the principles of SPECIAL and semi-LASER can be combined by substitution of the conventional refocusing pulse by an adiabatic pulse pair (SPECIAL-semi-LASER or sSPECIAL). The water suppression quality in SPECIAL may be somewhat worse in comparison to the other methods.

Finally, B_1^+ insensitive multipulse water suppression schemes with optimized flip angles and inter-pulse delays such as VAPOR have been developed for robust water suppression (Tkac et al., 2001). Alternatively, it has been demonstrated that the non-water-suppressed metabolite cycling method allows for simultaneous acquisition of high-quality ^{1}H metabolite spectra and the water reference signal at high field strength (Giapitzakis et al., 2018). This method is advantageous for prospective and retrospective frequency correction, simultaneous observation of the water BOLD effect in case of functional ^{1}H MRS, and measuring exchange rates in downfield resonances.

26.2.1.2 Detection of low-concentration metabolites

The spectral resolution improvement at UHF enables the distinction of a large number of metabolite peaks and the quantification of an extended neurochemical profile when using short TE ^{1}H single-voxel MRS. Several reports demonstrate that up to 17 metabolites can be quantified at 7 and 9.4 T in the human brain, while even with excellent B_0 shimming, a maximum of 12 metabolites can be distinguished at 3 T with short TE 1D MRS (Fig. 26.5A). The quantification precision for Glu, Gln, GABA, GSH, NAAG, Tau, Asp, sI, and Lac improves from 3 T/4 T to 7–9.4 T, while NAA, Cho, Cr, and mI can be detected with high precision at all field strengths (Pradhan et al., 2015). A clear benefit at ultra-high field strengths, however, is the better distinction of Glu and Gln, which are functionally distinct (Fig. 26.5B). At lower field strengths, Glu is often unresolved from glutamine (Gln) and is thus often measured as "Glx" (Glu+Gln). Even at high field strengths, the quantification precision of Glc, PE, Ace, and Asc from short TE 1D MRS data remains lower than for the other metabolites.

At clinical field strengths, specialized techniques such as TE optimization, J-difference editing, and 2D resolved MRS are needed to separate low-concentration metabolites with multiplet spectral patterns from larger singlets representing higher concentrated metabolites. Lac detection using long optimized TEs works very reliably at low field strength, especially in pathologies. J-difference editing is in widespread use due to its ability to reliably detect GABA and has been recently adopted by vendors in their commercial packages. MEGA-semi-LASER variants have been implemented successfully at 7 T for single-voxel MRS as well as MRSI (Fig. 26.9C). 2D J-resolved MRS enables the simultaneous quantification of up to 18 brain metabolites at 3 T including Glc but requires longer scan time and specialized analysis software (Fuchs et al., 2014). While at ultra-high field strengths, the increased spectral resolution allows for easier separation of metabolites with short TE 1D MRS methods, the short T_2 relaxation times reduces the SNR available at long TEs required by these specialized techniques.

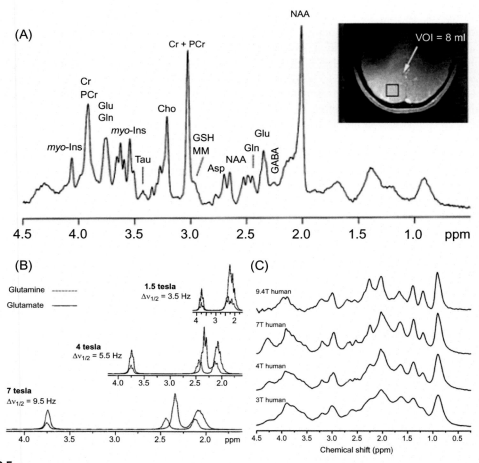

FIG. 26.5

(A) Example ^{1}H spectrum acquired using STEAM in the occipital lobe at 7T showing the range of detectable metabolites. (B) Typical linewidths and simulated ^{1}H spectra of Glu and Gln at different magnetic field strengths. (C) Macromolecular spectra at different field strengths. *(A,B) Reproduced from Tkac et al. (2001). (C) Reproduced from Cudalbu et al. (2021).*

As such, these specialized techniques may not be as beneficial they are at clinical field strengths. The extent of this benefit is also likely to differ depending on the target metabolite and (1) the echo time at which the multiplet is in-phase, (2) the T_2 relaxation of the metabolite-of-interest, and (3) the region-of-interest. To date, most studies that have sought to assess the benefits of these specialized techniques at UHF have focused on GABA, one of the most commonly measured metabolites which is typically detected with editing at clinical field strengths. These studies focused on single-voxel MRS and have produced inconsistent results, however, and further work is needed to determine the utility of J-difference editing, 2D MRS, and TE optimization at ultra-high field strengths.

26.2.1.3 Macromolecules and downfield MRS

UHF ¹H MRS enables the detection of a number of additional broader and low-intensity resonance lines upfield (right of the water peak) and downfield (left of the water peak) (Figs. 26.5C and 26.6). These are either not easily distinguishable at lower field strength or require a very large voxel size due to their very low SNR. The majority of these signals are assigned to macromolecules and more specifically amino acids in cytosolic proteins (Cudalbu et al., 2021).

Upfield metabolite signals with longer T_1 relaxation times can be suppressed by double-inversion recovery module prior to excitation by adjusting the delays between the inversion pulses and the excitation pulse such that the broader underlying macromolecular signal contributions with shorter T_1 can be retained. Recent advancements include the characterization of the relaxation times and exchange rates as well as the establishment of advanced spectral models of macromolecular resonances that consider relaxation correction or spectral pattern of amino acids. In addition, ¹H MRSI of macromolecular signals has been achieved and indicates different concentrations in gray versus white matter (Fig. 26.9B).

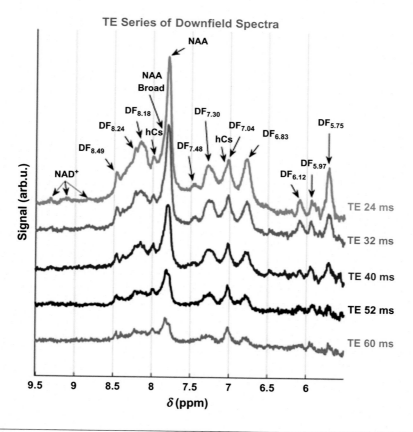

FIG. 26.6

Downfield metabolite spectra at different echo times (TE=24, 32, 40, 52, and 60 ms) at 9.4T. Each downfield resonance is labeled "DF" and the peak resonant frequency. *Adopted from Borbath (2021).*

Conventional spectroscopy localization sequences with a center frequency around 7 ppm can be used to detect the downfield macromolecular signals (Fig. 26.6). However, some of these resonance lines can only be quantified with non-water-suppressed metabolite cycled ^{1}H MRS due to exchange of their protons with water (Borbath et al., 2021). Downfield ^{1}H MRS enables the detection of several additional resonance lines, which relate to the metabolites NAA, Glc, homocarnosine (hCs), nicotinamine adenine dinucleotide (NAD$^+$), and adenosine triphosphate (ATP) with additional tentative assignments to GSH, Gln, NAAG, and urea. In case of elevated tissue concentrations, also histidine (Hist) and phenylalanine in phenylketonuria are detectable by downfield ^{1}H MRS.

26.2.1.4 Functional ^{1}H MRS

While typically considered a static measure of brain metabolism, ^{1}H MRS has been shown to be sensitive to dynamic changes. Neurochemical changes can be detected with repeated acquisitions, often measured in response to some kind of task or stimulus; this type of acquisition is known as functional MRS (or fMRS). Due to the small magnitude of the changes detected with fMRS, it has been an attractive application at ultra-high field strengths. As such, a large number of fMRS studies have been performed at ultra-high field strengths to assess changes in the excitation-inhibition balance and metabolism in response to a variety of stimuli including visual stimulation (Mangia et al., 2007). In these studies, several metabolites including Lac, Glu, and Asp have been reported to change dynamically (Mangia et al., 2007) (Fig. 26.7A). A consistently reported finding is an increase in Lac with stimulation. This is postulated to be due to transient increases in nonoxidative glycolysis due to a higher demand of substrate for the oxidative metabolism in response to prolonged stimulation. In line with this argument, Glu has also been found to increase with stimulation consistently across studies. In addition, Asp has been found to decrease with visual stimulation. These changes have been suggested to be indicative of increased activity of the malate–aspartate shuttle during glycolysis.

Another number of metabolites have also been reported to change with stimulation including NAA and Cr (Fig. 26.7B). These changes, however, are due to linewidth decreases caused by the blood oxygen level-dependent (BOLD) effect, which increases the T_2^* with stimulation which thus increases peak intensity and reduces the linewidth. This effect can be corrected in postprocessing by applying a linewidth correction factor to the transients acquired during stimulation before averaging (Fig. 26.7C) (Mangia et al., 2007).

26.2.1.5 Diffusion ^{1}H MRS

Diffusion-weighted ^{1}H MRS allows the local cellular environment to be probed through the measurement of the mobility of metabolites that are known to be confined to certain specific cell compartments. Mostly, NAA, Glu, Ins, and tCho have so far been investigated by diffusion weighted ^{1}H MRS. A difficulty in these types of measurements is the inherently low SNR due to the low concentration of metabolites, especially in the presence of high diffusion weightings. Ultra-high field strengths offer the promise to improve the sensitivity of diffusion MRS so that measurements can be extended to lower-concentration metabolites than are typically detected at clinical field strengths. However, the shortened T_2 relaxation times in combination with long diffusion gradients counteract the potential SNR gains. Only few studies have been performed at UHF so far, reporting diffusion-weighted ^{1}H MRS using PRESS to be feasible and have lower variability at 7 T relative to 3 T (Wood et al., 2015).

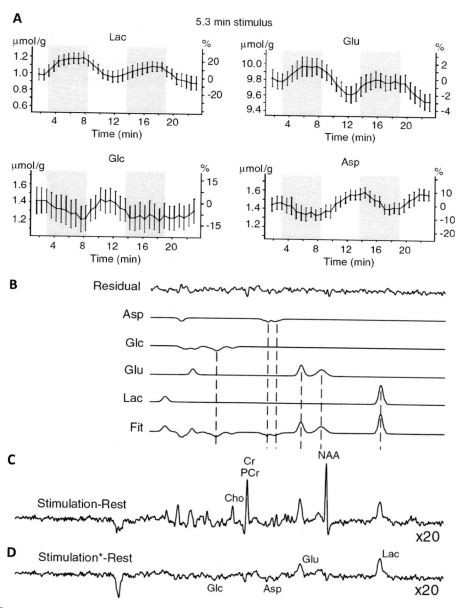

FIG. 26.7

fMRS study performed in the occipital lobe at 7 T in response to a radial red/black checkerboard visual stimulus. (A) Time courses of Lac, Glu, Glc, and Asp concentrations with alternating rest and 5.3 min stimulation blocks. (B) LCModel fit of the difference spectrum. (C) Difference spectrum between rest and stimulation without a BOLD correction. (D) Difference spectrum between rest and stimulation with an included BOLD linewidth correction. *Reproduced from Mangia et al. (2007).*

26.2.2 ^{1}H MRSI sequences and methods

26.2.2.1 Localization and suppression sequences for ^{1}H MRSI

In general, the same pulse sequences used for ultra-high field single-voxel acquisitions can be used for ^{1}H MRSI. A downside to these localization methods is the rectangular VOI. This limited VOI excludes much of the cortical areas of the brain, which are of interest for many clinical and research studies. To solve this, variants of these pulse sequences with just 2D localization combined with various lipid or outer volume suppression methods for slice-based acquisition are often used. Additional benefits of this approach include maximum signal retention due to very short echo time and no in-plane CSDE. The most widely used ultra-high field ^{1}H MRSI pulse sequence is the pulse-acquire or free induction decay (FID)-MRSI sequence (Henning et al., 2009; Fig. 26.4G). This sequence removes refocusing pulses all together so that ultra-short TEs can be achieved to further reduce the effects of T_2 relaxation and to maximize SNR (Fig. 26.3A). This increase in SNR and speed can then be traded off for a higher spatial resolution with 2D or 3D coverage (Fig. 26.8) and enables imaging of a comprehensive neurochemical profile (Fig. 26.9A).

Lipid suppression can be achieved by outer volume suppression using multiple saturation bands with optimized flip angles and interpulse delays, or by one or multiple frequency-selective lipid suppression pulses. The combination of a ring-shaped RF shim with lipid suppression has been demonstrated to specifically target the skull. However, lipid suppression methods contribute substantially to the SAR of the ^{1}H MRSI sequences and inhibit the use of very short repetitions times (TR). To enable high-resolution ^{1}H MRSI in a short scan time, lipid suppression methods are often omitted, and lipid signal-removal strategies during image reconstruction and processing have been developed instead (Bogner et al., 2021). In addition, short B_1^+ insensitive multipulse water suppression schemes have been developed to eventually allow TRs of 200–300 ms (Bogner et al., 2021).

A double-inversion ^{1}H FID MRSI pulse sequence has been developed for imaging the macromolecule distribution in the human brain at 7 T (Fig. 26.9B) (Cudalbu et al., 2021). Macromolecule-suppressed MEGA-semi-LASER ^{1}H MRSI yields high-resolution GABA maps of the human brain at 7 T (Fig. 26.9C) (Cudalbu et al., 2021).

26.2.2.2 Acceleration methods for ^{1}H MRSI

Due to the inherently long acquisition times, acceleration techniques are often applied to ^{1}H MRSI acquisitions. For a comprehensive review of these acceleration techniques, see Bogner et al. (2021). The higher SNR available at higher field strengths can be traded off for higher acceleration factors than that can normally be achieved at clinical field strengths. However, the acceleration techniques performed at clinical field strengths require alterations to better take advantage of the unique benefits and adapt to the disadvantages of higher field strengths. While short-TR sequences are an attractive option for ^{1}H MRSI acceleration, higher field strengths have more stringent SAR requirements, which places limits on the minimum TR and consequently increases scan times. As such, sequences that limit the number of pulses, such as the FID sequence without outer volume or lipid suppression, in combination with very short TRs of typically 200–300 ms, have been used in more than 50% of all UHF ^{1}H MRSI studies to allow for high acceleration factors (Chan et al., 2022; Bogner et al., 2021).

Efforts to accelerate ^{1}H MRSI at ultra-high field strengths have also included spatial-spectral encoding such as echo-planar readouts, concentric ring or rosette trajectories (Bogner et al., 2021), and k-space undersampling methods including compressed sensing and parallel imaging techniques such as SENSE, GRAPPA, or CAIPIRINHA (Chan et al., 2022; Bogner et al., 2021). Implementing spatial-spectral encoding methods at higher field strengths is more challenging than at clinical field strengths due to its limited spectral bandwidth. Despite this challenge, several implementations have

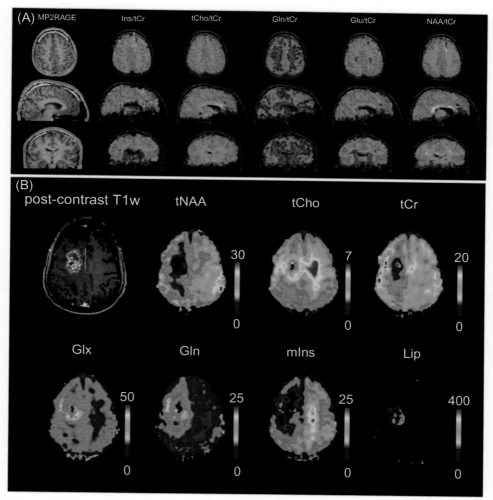

FIG. 26.8

Metabolic maps derived from 7 T ^{1}H MRSI data in healthy human brain (A) and in a patient with a brain tumor (anaplastic oligoastrocytoma) (B). (A) Whole-brain metabolic maps for Ins, tCho, Gln, Glu, and NAA referenced to tCr acquired with a ^{1}H FID-MRSI sequence and concentric-ring k-space sampling. (B) Postcontrast T_1-weighted MRI and tNAA, tCho, tCr, Glx, Gln, mIns, and Lip metabolic maps from a single-slice ^{1}H FID-MRSI acquisition at 7 T in a patient with an anaplastic oligoastrocytoma. Ins and Gln differences extend beyond the tumor region. *A and B reprinted from Maudsley et al. (2021).*

been achieved at 7 T with concentric rings and rosette trajectories being good choices. Parallel imaging techniques such as SENSE, GRAPPA, or CAIPIRINHA have also been implemented at ultra-high field strengths and generally allow for higher acceleration factors than at 1.5 or 3 T due to the increased spatial information content provided by the receive sensitivity profiles of array coil elements, yielding better g-factors (Wiesinger et al., 2004). An important research focus has been the reduction of spatial

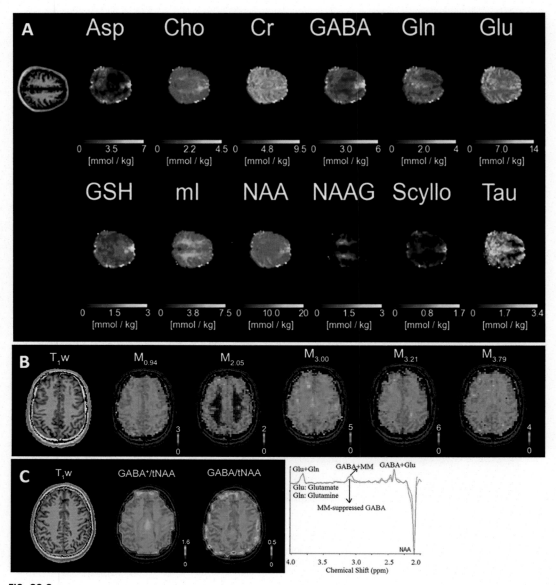

FIG. 26.9

(A) Quantitative metabolic maps of 12 human brain metabolites derived from 9.4T ^{1}H MRSI data illustrating the advantage of even higher field strength than 7T. (B) Maps reflecting the peak intensities of macromolecular resonance lines acquired with a double-inversion ^{1}H FID MRSI sequence at 7T. (C) GABA maps derived from MEGA-edited ^{1}H MRSI at 7T with and without macromolecular co-editing. *(A) Adopted from Wright and Henning (2021). (B, C) Reprinted from Maudsley et al. (2021).*

aliasing by adjusting undersampling and reconstruction methods. Classical methods result in significant lipid fold over artifacts from the scalp, especially when applied without skull lipid suppression as required by short TR sequences. The combination of neural networks for the reconstruction of undersampled data and retrospective lipid removal has yielded very promising results (Chan et al., 2022). Compressed sensing for ^{1}H MRSI was also found to be feasible provided that it was combined with sensitivity encoding (SENSE) (Bogner et al., 2021). Complimentary acceleration techniques such as short TR, k-space undersampling methods, and spectral-spatial encoding can also be combined.

26.2.3 Clinical and research applications

Due to the advantages of ultra-high field for MRS, there has been increasing interest in performing ^{1}H MRS and ^{1}H MRSI in the human brain at ultra-high field strengths for clinical and research applications. The vast majority of the published studies so far have used single-voxel ^{1}H MRS.

26.2.3.1 Brain tumors

Recently, there has been increasing attention on applying ^{1}H MRS and ^{1}H MRSI to study brain tumor metabolism at 7 T. Of these studies, the majority have focused on measuring 2-hydroxyglutarate (2HG), a biomarker of isocitrate dehydrogenase (IDH) mutation in gliomas, to aid in the diagnosis and treatment planning of glioma patients. Most of these studies focused on developing nonedited approaches such as long-TE sLASER or TE-optimized PRESS. Besides 2HG, other metabolites-of-interest in brain tumors have included NAA and Cho, which have been shown to be decreased and increased in tumors, respectively (Maudsley et al., 2021). This is hypothesized to be due to a loss in neuronal tissue (NAA) and increased membrane turnover (Cho), which is in agreement with prior studies at clinical field strengths. MRSI studies performed at 7 T have also shown differences in Ins and Gln that extend beyond the morphologically visible infiltration and reveal spatial variations in tumor metabolism (Maudsley et al., 2021) (Fig. 26.8B).

26.2.3.2 Neurodegenerative disorders

^{1}H MRS has been performed at 7 T to study various neurodegenerative disorders such as Alzheimer's, Huntington's, and Parkinson's disease. Several studies on Alzheimer's disease at 7 T have reported altered NAA and mI levels in the posterior cingulate relative to healthy normal controls (Schreiner et al., 2018), which is consistent with prior reports at clinical field strengths. In addition, a handful of ^{1}H MRS studies in Huntington's disease at 7 T have reported decreased NAA and Glu in the putamen (van den Bogaard et al., 2011), which is suggestive of neuronal death and disrupted glutamatergic signaling, respectively. This reported decrease in NAA is consistent with prior studies performed at clinical field strengths. There have also been several studies on amyotrophic lateral sclerosis (ALS) at 7 T that have reported decreases in NAA, which is consistent with studies at clinical field strengths (Cheong et al., 2017) and is suggested to be reflective of neuronal dysfunction or loss. While an increase in Glu is expected in ALS due to excitotoxicity being one of the pathophysiological mechanisms, studies at 7 T have reported inconsistent Glu results.

26.2.3.3 Psychiatric and neurodevelopmental disorders

To date, several ^{1}H single voxel MRS studies in psychiatric disorders have been performed at ultra-high field strengths. Of these studies, most have focused on schizophrenia. Studies of schizophrenia at 7 T have commonly reported reduced GABA and Glu levels in several areas across the brain including the prefrontal cortex (Wijtenburg et al., 2021). Although several studies on mood disorders have been published, none has been published on bipolar disorder and only four have been published on major depressive disorder (MDD) at 7 T with inconsistent results. Of these MDD studies, only one study appears to corroborate the findings of glutamatergic dysfunction found in prior ^{1}H MRS studies on MDD at clinical field strengths with findings of increased Glu with mindfulness-based cognitive therapy (Li et al., 2016). Even less common are studies on neurodevelopmental disorders. Only one study on autism spectrum disorder (ASD) has been published to date at 7 T (Harris et al., 2016). This study reported decreases in GABA in ASD relative to typically-developing children which agrees with prior MRS studies performed at clinical field strengths.

26.3 Single-voxel ^{31}P MRS and ^{31}P MRSI

26.3.1 Sequences and methods

To this point, ^{31}P MRS(I) studies at UHF with human volunteers were performed at 7T using nonlocalized pulse-acquire sequences, single-voxel sequences, and multivoxel acquisitions. Surface RF coils and birdcage RF coils are still most commonly used, but more and more complex coil designs with improved transmission and reception characteristics have been presented for ^{31}P MRS(I).

The Image Selected In vivo Spectroscopy (ISIS) localization sequence (Fig. 26.4H) was identified to be the most sensible choice for SVS ^{31}P MRS at the human brain at UHF compared to STEAM, semi-LASER, and SPECIAL due to a lower chemical shift displacement, a higher localization efficiency, and maximum signal retention in the presence of very short T_2 relaxation times (Fig. 26.3B; Dorst et al., 2021). ISIS combines three 180 degree adiabatic inversion pulses applied in an 8-step encoding scheme prior to a nonselective excitation pulse and requires a respective add-subtract scheme for 3D localization (Fig. 26.4H). GOIA pulses are preferable over hyperbolic secant adiabatic pulses. Potential disadvantages of ISIS are the sensitivity of a multishot method to motion and signal contribution from outside the volume of interest in case of long T_1 relaxation times as present in ^{31}P MRS in combination with short repetition times.

Due to the short T_2 relaxation times of some ^{31}P detectable metabolites, a short acquisition time or echo time (TE) is recommended as enabled by the ISIS sequence for ^{31}P single-voxel MRS acquisitions. For multivoxel ^{31}P acquisitions, FID-MRSI (Fig. 26.4G) is therefore the most favorable acquisition method at UHF (Ruhm et al., 2021) (Fig. 26.10C). To address short T_2^* and high B_1^+ inhomogeneities an adiabatic multiecho ^{31}P spectroscopic imaging (AMESING) sequence was presented at 7 T (van der Kemp et al., 2013). B_1^+ inhomogeneities at UHF were also addressed by a fully adiabatic GOIA-1D-ISIS/2D-CSI sequence which was tested for muscle, liver, and brain measurements at 7 T (Chmelík et al., 2013). A ^{31}P MRSI sequence including multiecho polarization transfer was successfully tested at 7 T (van der Kemp et al., 2014). The higher SNR at UHF potentially opens up the possibility for more advanced image reconstruction techniques for ^{31}P MRSI, such as low-rank reconstruction approaches (Ruhm et al., 2021).

For human brain ^{31}P MRS measurements at 7 T, nOe overall improved the repeatability of the ^{31}P MRS measurement (De Graaf, 2019). Due to different contributions of dipolar and chemical shift anisotrophy (CSA) relaxation in different tissue types and at different field strength, this result cannot be translated easily to ^{31}P MRS measurements at higher field strength and/or in different organs. The nOe

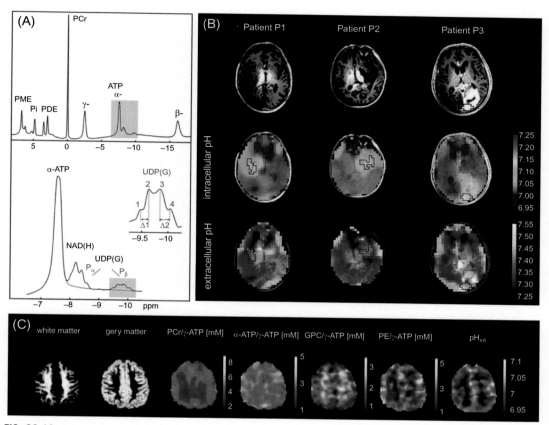

FIG. 26.10

(A) Nonlocalized ³¹P MRS spectrum acquired at 7 T, averaged over seven healthy human volunteer (top panel) and the enlarged region around α-ATP, NAD(H), and UDP(G) (bottom panel). (B) Anatomical images of glioma patients as well as intra- and extracellular pH images calculated from the chemical shift difference between pCr and Pi. The pH images show an alkaline pH in the tumor. (C) High-resolution ³¹P MRSI images from the healthy human brain acquired at 9.4 T demonstrate differences in metabolite concentrations in GM versus WM for PCr, ATP, GPC, and PE as well as in the intracellular pH. *(A) Reproduced from Ren et al. (2021). (B) Reproduced from Mirkes et al. (2016). (C) Reproduced from Ruhm et al. (2021).*

depends on the underlying relaxation mechanisms and is expected to decrease if the contribution of CSA relaxation increases. Polarization transfer on phosphomonoesters and diesters (PME/PDE) was successfully tested for measurements at 7 T (van der Kemp et al., 2014). Even though the increased SNR and spectral resolution improves the quantification of ³¹P MRS at UHF, additional application of polarization transfer, nOe, and proton decoupling can still improve the quantification of low SNR ³¹P resonances as NAHD/NAD+ and PDEs/PMEs. However, for all three methods, the additional power deposition and the resulting SNR efficiency need to be considered in any case.

The higher spectral dispersion at UHF also improves the selectivity in magnetization transfer ^{31}P MRS experiments and therefore the quantification of ATP-kinase flux and the creatine-kinase flux with ^{31}P MRS. In these techniques, a selective saturation or inversion of the γ-ATP resonance is performed, and saturation transfer effects to other metabolites such as PCr are observed.

The higher SNR at UHF can be exploited in dynamic (i.e., exercise/recovery) experiments, which require a temporal resolution of under 10 s. Frequency-selective ^{31}P MR imaging sequences for dynamic PCr and pH imaging benefit as well from the higher SNR and higher spatial dispersion at UHF.

26.3.2 Clinical and research applications

Applications of ^{31}P MRS and MRSI include the investigation of the energy metabolism, cell membrane turnover, pH, and Mg^{2+} content in different organs including the brain, liver, heart, calf muscle, breast, and prostate. The improved spectral resolution and the higher SNR at UHF improve the overall detectability of low signal resonances like NADH, NAD+, and UDP(G) (Fig. 26.10A) (Ren et al., 2021). It can also enable the separate detection of the intra- and extracellular pH and improves the separation of the individual PMEs and PDEs.

The additionally obtained information at UHF can improve clinical diagnostics as shown in several studies, including patients with brain tumors (Mirkes et al., 2016) and Parkinson's patients (Zhu et al., 2019). An altered energy metabolism was found during the aging process and in several brain pathologies and mental disorders including Alzheimer's disease, Parkinson's disease, Schizophrenia, and Huntington's diseases. The measurement of pH (Fig. 26.10B) and the alteration of PME and PDE concentrations and ratios as indicator of an altered cell membrane metabolism are of specific interest in brain cancer research (Mirkes et al., 2016).

^{31}P functional MRS was investigated in several studies at the human brain with highly varying results. Recent studies at UHF did not show significant effects within the presented achievable detection sensitivity (Bart et al., 2018).

26.4 Single-voxel ^{2}H MRS and ^{2}H MRSI
26.4.1 Sequences and methods

Deuterium (^{2}H) is a heavy isotope of hydrogen with spin 1 and a low natural abundance of 0.015% (see Table 1, Chapter 27). MRS-detectable natural abundant deuterium resonances are water and lipid resonances. For ^{2}H MRSI, also called deuterium metabolic imaging (DMI) (De Feyter et al., 2018), deuterium-labeled substrates are administered either orally or intravenously. The most commonly used substrate for ^{2}H MRSI is [6,6'-[2]H$_2$]-glucose. Other labeled substances that have been investigated include [1,2,3,4,5,6,6'-[2]H$_7$]-glucose, [2,3-[2]H$_2$]-fumarate, [[2]H$_9$]-choline chloride, [[2]H$_3$]-acetate, and D_2O. While highly spatially and temporally resolved mapping of the ^{2}H label incorporation into Glc, Glx, Lac, and deuterated water is possible at ultra-high field (Fig. 26.10) (Ruhm et al., 2021), the possibility to derive metabolic turnover rates from deuterium labeling experiments measured in the human brain is currently under investigation.

Deuterium imaging requires custom-designed dual-tune ^{2}H/^{1}H coil arrays and often a change in the configuration of the MRI scanner. For ^{2}H MRSI, 2D/3D FID-MRSI sequences are most favorable due to the short T_2 relaxation times of most ^{2}H metabolites. The use of k-space weighting can increase the

SNR at the cost of a compromised effective spatial resolution. The further investigation of advanced acquisition and reconstruction techniques will probably be an important part in future research for UHF ^{2}H MRSI acquisitions in humans. An emerging UHF method is the use of conventional ^{1}H MRS or ^{1}H MRSI to indirectly detect the exchange of ^{1}H by ^{2}H labeling by respective spectral pattern and peak intensity changes (Cember et al., 2022). This approach does not need specialized sequences or hardware and was demonstrated in the human brain at 7 and 9.4 T.

26.4.2 Clinical and research applications

Potential organs of interest for DMI include the brain, liver, skeletal muscle, heart, and eye. Depending on the applied deuterium-labeled substrate, different potential applications can be addressed with ^{2}H MRSI, including the investigation of perfusion, tumor malignancy, cellular proliferation, and lipid metabolism. Using [6,6$'$-^{2}H$_2$]-glucose, the metabolic fluxes of the TCA cycle can be investigated and the Warburg effect can be visualized in brain tumors (De Feyter et al., 2018) (Fig. 26.11C). The resulting ^{2}H label uptake in glutamate (Glu) and glutamine (Gln) can only be detected as a combined resonance (Glx), even for measurements at UHF (Ruhm et al., 2021) (Fig. 26.11 A and B). In the same way, the ^{2}H-labeled lactate resonance overlaps with natural abundant deuterated lipid signals.

The higher SNR and spectral resolution at UHF still improve the quantification of individual resonances in ^{2}H MRSI and can be used to improve the spatial and temporal resolution (Fig. 26.10A). Similar to ^{1}H MRS, the higher spatial resolution that can be achieved at UHF reduces the contamination from natural abundant deuterium signals from lipids surrounding the head due to an improved point-spread-function and thus allows for the investigation of deuterated Lac increase in brain tissue (Ruhm et al., 2021).

26.5 Single-voxel ^{13}C MRS and ^{13}C MRSI
26.5.1 Sequences and methods

Carbon-13 (^{13}C) is an MRI-detectable isotope of carbon with spin 1/2 and a low natural abundance of 1% (see Table 1, Chapter 27), whereas the most abundant carbon isotope (^{12}C) has no nuclear spin and is hence not MRI detectable. Natural abundant ^{13}C MRS-detectable resonances are from lipids and glycogen. Commonly, ^{13}C-labeled substrates are administered either orally or intravenously before or during ^{13}C MRS experiments in order to assess metabolic turnover rates (de Graaf et al., 2020). The most commonly used substrate for ^{13}C MRS is [1-^{13}C]-glucose. Other labeled substances that were investigated for human application include [U-^{13}C]-glucose, [2-^{13}C]-glucose, and [1-^{13}C]-acetate.

In spite of the SNR advantage of ultra-high field scanners, only very few UHF ^{13}C MRS studies in humans have been published so far. This can be assigned to the need of custom-built dual-tune ^{13}C/^{1}H RF coils, the technical challenges related to ^{13}C MRS sequence development under very strict SAR constraints, and the high cost of ^{13}C-labeled substrate of about 5000 US Dollars per subject in case of human studies.

So far, five human studies at 7 T were performed using a partial volume ^{13}C/^{1}H coil and a nonlocalized ^{13}C direct detection pulse acquire sequence. In brain applications, saturation bands were used to suppress the skull lipid signal. Either no proton decoupling was used or proton decoupling with narrow band, WALTZ-16, or low-power stochastic decoupling (Fig. 26.12A; Li et al., 2016). Only one study used nOe (Li et al., 2016). An emerging UHF method is the use of conventional ^{1}H MRS or ^{1}H MRSI to indirectly detect the incorporation of ^{13}C labeling by spectral pattern changes induced by the ^{13}C-^{1}H J-coupling (Ziegs et al., 2023). This approach does not need specialized sequences or hardware and was demonstrated in the human brain at 9.4 T (Fig. 26.11B and C). (See Fig. 26.12B and C.)

26.5.2 Clinical and research applications

Natural abundance direct detection ^{13}C MRS experiments are used to characterize lipids and glycogen in the brain, skeletal muscle, and liver to investigate energy storage in healthy and metabolic disorders such as the metabolic syndrome or glycogen storage disease.

Experiments with ^{13}C-labeled glucose administration aim at assessing metabolic turnover rates including the glycolytic rate, the tricarboxylic acid cycling rate, and neurotransmitter cycling rates. Related experiments have been applied in healthy human brain to study brain metabolism and to investigate alterations of energy metabolism in psychiatric disorders.

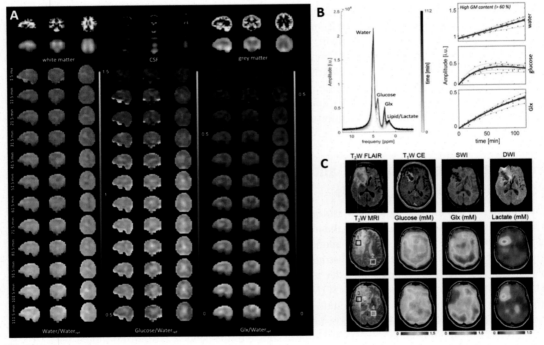

FIG. 26.11

(A). Tissue composition fractions in the brain (top 2 rows) without (top row) and with (2nd row) accounting for the point-spread function and temporally resolved deuterium metabolic images after ingestion of [6,6′-$^2H_2$]-glucose (bottom rows) for water, glucose, and Glx at 1.5, 11.5, 21.5, 31.5, 41.5, 51.5, 61.5, 71.5, 81.5, 91.5, 101.5, and 111.5 min. The amplitudes are in relative institutional units (i.u.) with [i.u.]/[i.u.] = 1. (B) Respective whole brain ^2H spectra and time courses. (C) Deuterium metabolic images from a brain cancer patient showing the Warburg effect after undergoing treatment on an experimental protocol involving nivolumab (2nd row) or placebo (3rd row). *(A, B) Reproduced from Ruhm et al. (2021). (C) Reproduced from De Feyter et al. (2018).*

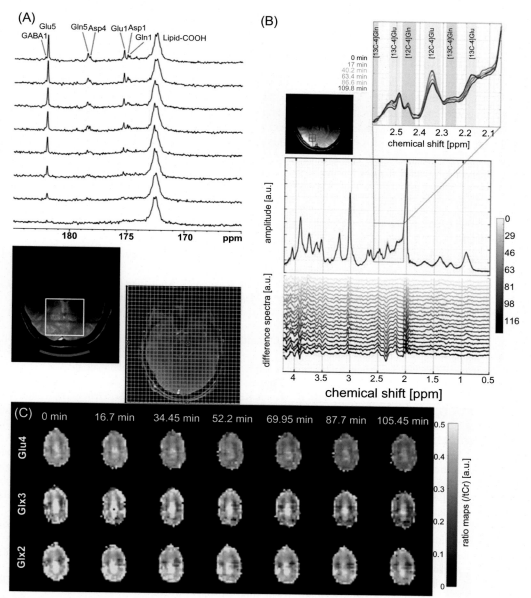

FIG. 26.12

(A) Nonlocalized ^{13}C MRS data acquired with nOe and stochastic proton decoupling at multiple time points after infusion of [2-^{13}C]D-glucose in the human brain at 7T (white box = B_0 shim volume, red line = position of surface coil). Each spectrum corresponds to a signal average over a 8.7-min time period. (B) Single-voxel ^1H MRS data and (C) ^1H FID MRSI data acquired from the human brain at multiple time points after oral intake of [1-^{13}C]D-glucose at 9.4T. Changes in the 12C-bonded H4-glutamatte and -glutamine signals are highlighted in the top zoomed figure at baseline (0min) and 17, 40.2, 63.4, 86.6, and 109.8min. While ^{13}C MRS offers a better spectral distinction of glutamate and glutamine resonances, ^1H MRS allows for the investigation of much smaller voxels and even imaging of the effects of ^{13}C label incorporation into glutamine and glutamate. *(A) Reproduced from Li et al. (2016). (B) Reproduced from Ziegs et al. (2023).*

26.6 Conclusions and outlook

The increased spectral resolution and SNR provided by UHF are highly advantageous for proton (^{1}H), carbon (^{13}C), phosphorous (^{31}P), and deuterium (^{2}H) MRS. To take full advantage of these benefits, however, technical challenges such as increased static and radiofrequency magnetic field inhomogeneity, stricter specific absorption rates, and altered relaxation times need to be addressed in order to allow for UHF MRS to reach its full potential. Despite these challenges, UHF proton and X-nuclei MRS are being increasingly used in clinical and research applications, and their usage will likely increase in the future with further technical development.

References

Bart, L., van de Bank, M.C.M., Bains, L.J., Heerschap, A., Scheenen, T.W.J., 2018. Is visual activation associated with changes in cerebral high-energy phosphate levels? Brain Struct. Funct. 223, 11.

Boer, V.O., Klomp, D.W., Juchem, C., Luijten, P.R., de Graaf, R.A., 2012. Multislice (1)H MRSI of the human brain at 7 T using dynamic B(0) and B(1) shimming. Magn. Reson. Med. 68 (3), 662–670.

Bogner, W., Otazo, R., Henning, A., 2021. Accelerated MR spectroscopic imaging-a review of current and emerging techniques. NMR Biomed. 34 (5), e4314.

Borbath, T., 2021. Magnetic Resonance Spectroscopy: Quantitative Analysis of Brain Metabolites and Macromolecules. Eberhard Karls Universität Tübingen.

Borbath, T., Murali-Manohar, S., Wright, A., Henning, A., 2021. In vivo characterization of downfield peaks at 9.4 T: T2 relaxation times, quantification, pH estimation, and assignments. Magn. Reson. Med. 85 (2), 587–600.

Cember, A.T.J., Wilson, N.E., Rich, L.J., Bagga, P., Nanga, R.P.R., Swago, S., Swain, A., Thakuri, D., Elliot, M., Schnall, M.D., Detre, J.A., Reddy, R., 2022. Integrating 1H MRS and deuterium labeled glucose for mapping the dynamics of neural metabolism in humans. Neuroimage 251, 118977. https://doi.org/10.1016/j.neuroimage.2022.118977. Epub 2022 Feb 7.

Chan, K.L., Hock, A., Edden, R.A.E., MacMillan, E.L., Henning, A., 2021. Improved prospective frequency correction for macromolecule-suppressed GABA editing with metabolite cycling at 3T. Magn. Reson. Med. 86 (6), 2945–2956.

Chan, K.L., Ziegs, T., Henning, A., 2022. Improved signal-to-noise performance of MultiNet GRAPPA (1) H FID MRSI reconstruction with semi-synthetic calibration data. Magn. Reson. Med.

Cheong, I., Marjanska, M., Deelchand, D.K., Eberly, L.E., Walk, D., Oz, G., 2017. Erratum to: ultra-high field proton MR spectroscopy in early-stage amyotrophic lateral sclerosis. Neurochem. Res. 42 (6), 1845–1846.

Chmelík, M., Just Kukurová, I., Gruber, S., et al., 2013. Fully adiabatic 31P 2D-CSI with reduced chemical shift displacement error at 7 T—GOIA-1D-ISIS/2D-CSI. Magn. Reson. Med. 69 (5), 1233–1244.

Cudalbu, C., Behar, K.L., Bhattacharyya, P.K., et al., 2021. Contribution of macromolecules to brain (1) H MR spectra: Experts' consensus recommendations. NMR Biomed. 34 (5), e4393.

De Feyter, H.M., Behar, K.L., Corbin, Z.A., et al., 2018. Deuterium metabolic imaging (DMI) for MRI-based 3D mapping of metabolism in vivo. Sci. Adv. 4 (8), eaat7314.

De Graaf, R.A., 2019. In Vivo NMR Spectroscopy: Principles and Techniques. Wiley.

de Graaf, R.A., Hendriks, A.D., Klomp, D.W.J., Kumaragamage, C., Welting, D., Arteaga de Castro, C.S., Brown, P.B., McIntyre, S., Nixon, T.W., Prompers, J.J., De Feyter, H.M., 2020. On the magnetic field dependence of deuterium metabolic imaging. NMR Biomed. 33 (3), e4235. https://doi.org/10.1002/nbm.4235. Epub 2019 Dec 26.

Dorst, J., Ruhm, L., Avdievich, N., Bogner, W., Henning, A., 2021. Comparison of four ^{31}P single-voxel MRS sequences in the human brain at 9.4 T. Magn. Reson. Med. 85 (6), 3010–3026.

Fuchs, A., Luttje, M., Boesiger, P., Henning, A., 2013. SPECIAL semi-LASER with lipid artifact compensation for (1) H MRS at 7 T. Magn. Reson. Med. 69 (3), 603–612.

Fuchs, A., Boesiger, P., Schulte, R.F., Henning, A., 2014. ProFit revisited. Magn. Reson. Med. 71 (2), 458–468.

Giapitzakis, I.A., Shao, T., Avdievich, N., Mekle, R., Kreis, R., Henning, A., 2018. Metabolite-cycled STEAM and semi-LASER localization for MR spectroscopy of the human brain at 9.4T. Magn. Reson. Med. 79 (4), 1841–1850.

Harris, A.D., Singer, H.S., Horska, A., et al., 2016. GABA and glutamate in children with primary complex motor stereotypies: an 1H-MRS study at 7T. AJNR Am. J. Neuroradiol. 37 (3), 552–557.

Henning, A., Fuchs, A., Murdoch, J.B., Boesiger, P., 2009. Slice-selective FID acquisition, localized by outer volume suppression (FIDLOVS) for (1)H-MRSI of the human brain at 7 T with minimal signal loss. NMR Biomed. 22 (7), 683–696.

Juchem, C., Cudalbu, C., de Graaf, R.A., et al., 2021. B0 shimming for in vivo magnetic resonance spectroscopy: experts' consensus recommendations. NMR Biomed. 34 (5), e4350.

Li, Y., Jakary, A., Gillung, E., et al., 2016. Evaluating metabolites in patients with major depressive disorder who received mindfulness-based cognitive therapy and healthy controls using short echo MRSI at 7 Tesla. MAGMA 29 (3), 523–533.

Mangia, S., Tkac, I., Gruetter, R., Van de Moortele, P.F., Maraviglia, B., Ugurbil, K., 2007. Sustained neuronal activation raises oxidative metabolism to a new steady-state level: evidence from 1H NMR spectroscopy in the human visual cortex. J. Cereb. Blood Flow Metab. 27 (5), 1055–1063.

Maudsley, A.A., Andronesi, O.C., Barker, P.B., et al., 2021. Advanced magnetic resonance spectroscopic neuro-imaging: experts' consensus recommendations. NMR Biomed. 34 (5), e4309.

Mirkes, C., Shajan, G., Chadzynski, G., Buckenmaier, K., Bender, B., Scheffler, K., 2016. (31)P CSI of the human brain in healthy subjects and tumor patients at 9.4 T with a three-layered multi-nuclear coil: initial results. MAGMA 29 (3), 579–589.

Nassirpour, S., Chang, P., Fillmer, A., Henning, A., 2018. A comparison of optimization algorithms for localized in vivo B0 shimming. Magn. Reson. Med. 79 (2), 1145–1156.

Oz, G., Deelchand, D.K., Wijnen, J.P., et al., 2020. Advanced single voxel (1) H magnetic resonance spectroscopy techniques in humans: experts' consensus recommendations. NMR Biomed. e4236.

Peeters, T.H., van Uden, M.J., Rijpma, A., Scheenen, T.W.J., Heerschap, A., 2021. 3D ^{31}P MR spectroscopic imaging of the human brain at 3 T with a ^{31}P receive array: an assessment of ^{1}H decoupling, T_1 relaxation times, ^{1}H-^{31}P nuclear overhauser effects and NAD+. NMR Biomed. e4169.

Pohmann, R., Speck, O., Scheffler, K., 2016. Signal-to-noise ratio and MR tissue parameters in human brain imaging at 3, 7, and 9.4 tesla using current receive coil arrays. Magn. Reson. Med. 75 (2), 801–809.

Pradhan, S., Bonekamp, S., Gillen, J.S., et al., 2015. Comparison of single voxel brain MRS AT 3T and 7T using 32-channel head coils. Magn. Reson. Imaging 33 (8), 1013–1018.

Ren, J., Malloy, C.R., Sherry, A.D., 2021. 31P-MRS of the healthy human brain at 7 T detects multiple hexose derivatives of uridine diphosphate glucose. NMR Biomed. 34 (7), e4511.

Ruhm, L., Avdievich, N., Ziegs, T., et al., 2021. Deuterium metabolic imaging in the human brain at 9.4 Tesla with high spatial and temporal resolution. Neuroimage 244, 118639.

Schreiner, S.J., Kirchner, T., Narkhede, A., et al., 2018. Brain amyloid burden and cerebrovascular disease are synergistically associated with neurometabolism in cognitively unimpaired older adults. Neurobiol. Aging 63, 152–161.

Tkac, I., Andersen, P., Adriany, G., Merkle, H., Ugurbil, K., Gruetter, R., 2001. In vivo 1H NMR spectroscopy of the human brain at 7 T. Magn. Reson. Med. 46 (3), 451–456.

van den Bogaard, S.J., Dumas, E.M., Teeuwisse, W.M., et al., 2011. Exploratory 7-Tesla magnetic resonance spectroscopy in Huntington's disease provides in vivo evidence for impaired energy metabolism. J. Neurol. 258 (12), 2230–2239.

van der Kemp, W.J.M., Boer, V.O., Luijten, P.R., Stehouwer, B.L., Veldhuis, W.B., Klomp, D.W.J., 2013. Adiabatic multi-echo 31P spectroscopic imaging (AMESING) at 7T for the measurement of transverse relaxation times and regaining of sensitivity in tissues with short T2* values. NMR Biomed. 26 (10), 1299–1307.

van der Kemp, W.J.M., Boer, V.O., Luijten, P.R., Klomp, D.W.J., 2014. Increased sensitivity of 31P MRSI using direct detection integrated with multi-echo polarization transfer (DIMEPT). NMR Biomed. 27 (10), 1248–1255.

Versluis, M.J., Kan, H.E., van Buchem, M.A., Webb, A., 2010. Improved signal to noise in proton spectroscopy of the human calf muscle at 7 T using localized B(1) calibration. Magn. Reson. Med. 63 (1), 207–211.

Wiesinger, F., Van de Moortele, P.F., Adriany, G., De Zanche, N., Ugurbil, K., Pruessmann, K.P., 2004. Parallel imaging performance as a function of field strength—an experimental investigation using electrodynamic scaling. Magn. Reson. Med. 52 (5), 953–964.

Wijtenburg, S.A., Wang, M., Korenic, S.A., Chen, S., Barker, P.B., Rowland, L.M., 2021. Metabolite alterations in adults with schizophrenia, first degree relatives, and healthy controls: a multi-region 7T MRS study. Front. Psych. 12, 656459.

Wood, E.T., Ercan, A.E., Branzoli, F., et al., 2015. Reproducibility and optimization of in vivo human diffusion-weighted MRS of the corpus callosum at 3 T and 7 T. NMR Biomed. 28 (8), 976–987.

Wright, A.M., Henning, A., 2021. Quantitative metabolite mapping of 12 metabolites in the human brain. In: Proceedings of the 30th Annual Scientific Meeting of ISMRM, May 7th–12th 2021, London, UK.

Zhu, H., Barker, P.B., 2011. MR spectroscopy and spectroscopic imaging of the brain. Methods Mol. Biol. 711, 203–226.

Zhu, X.-H., Lu, M., Chen, W., 2019. Quantitative imaging of brain energy metabolism and neuroenergetics using in vivo X-nuclear 2H. 17O and 31P MRS at ultra-high field. J. Magn. Reson. 292, 155–170.

Ziegs, T., Ruhm, L., Wright, A., Henning, A., 2023. Mapping of glutamate metabolism using 1H FID-MRSI after oral administration of [1-13C]Glc at 9.4 T. Neuroimage 270, 119940. https://doi.org/10.1016/j.neuroimage.2023.119940. Epub 2023 Feb 12.

Imaging with X-nuclei

27

Wafaa Zaaraoui[a] and Armin N. Nagel[b,c]

[a]CRMBM, CNRS, Aix-Marseille Université, Marseille, France [b]Institute of Radiology, Friedrich-Alexander-Universität Erlangen-Nürnberg (FAU), University Hospital Erlangen, Erlangen, Germany [c]Division of Medical Physics in Radiology, German Cancer Research Center (DKFZ), Heidelberg, Germany

Highlights

- X-nuclei MRI poses various physical and technical challenges to imaging techniques.
- X-nuclei MRI requires specific hardware and software that are typically not available on standard clinical MRI systems.
- Quadrupolar nuclei (i.e., nuclei with spin $>\frac{1}{2}$) such as ^2H, ^{17}O, ^{23}Na, ^{35}Cl, and ^{39}K strongly interact with local electric field gradients, which results in rapid transverse relaxation.
- To partially compensate the low SNR of X-nuclei MRI, voxel volumes are typically several orders of magnitude larger than those of ^1H MRI.
- Several in vivo studies highlighted the potential of sodium MRI as a promising biomarker for neuroinflammation and neurodegeneration in multiple sclerosis.

27.1 Introduction

Elements such as sodium, chloride, potassium, oxygen, and phosphorous play an important role in many physiological processes. In addition, isotopes such as deuterium (^2H), carbon (^{13}C), oxygen (^{17}O), and fluorine (^{19}F) can be used as tracers, for example, to analyze metabolic processes. Thus, in order to characterize various cellular processes, a noninvasive measurement via magnetic resonance imaging (MRI) of nuclei other than protons (^1H) is often desirable. Imaging of these elements is often called X-nuclei, nonproton, or multinuclear MRI.

Compared with ^1H, X-nuclei exhibit much lower in vivo abundance and reduced MR sensitivity. Thus, the SNR is the most limiting quantity in X-nuclei MRI. However, in the past decade, the increasing availability of ultra-high field (UHF) MRI systems ($B_0 \geq 7T$) largely extended the capabilities of X-nuclei MRI since the SNR increases at least linearly with magnetic field strength (Ladd et al., 2018). The increased SNR enables increased spatial resolutions and clinically feasible acquisition times. High-performance RF coils, dedicated pulse sequences, iterative image reconstruction techniques, and new postprocessing techniques have further improved the image quality and quantitative accuracy of X-nuclei MRI. In this chapter, the challenges to and principals of X-nuclei MRI will be explained, and clinical research applications in the field of neuroimaging will be discussed. This topic is also

Advances in Magnetic Resonance Technology and Applications. Volume 10. ISSN 2666-9099. https://doi.org/10.1016/B978-0-323-99898-7.00015-8

covered by several review articles (e.g., Hu et al., 2020; Huhn et al., 2019; Konstandin and Nagel, 2014; Madelin and Regatte, 2013; Niesporek et al., 2019; Shah et al., 2016; Wiggins et al., 2016).

27.2 Physics and technical aspects of X-nuclei MRI

X-nuclei MRI poses different physical and technical challenges to imaging techniques. First of all, only nuclei that have a nuclear magnetic spin (I) can be used for MRI. The requirement for a nonvanishing nuclear magnetic spin moment is an odd number of protons or an odd number of neutrons, which applies for approximately two-thirds of all isotopes. In most cases relevant for X-nuclei MRI in humans, noise is dominated by the sample. In this case, the SNR increases approximately linearly with field strength (B_0) (see Eq. 27.1, Fig. 27.1). The SNR also depends on the gyromagnetic ratio γ and the in vivo concentrations (c) (see Eq. 27.2). Thus, the in vivo SNR of X-nuclei MRI is several orders of magnitude lower than that of the SNR of ^{1}H MRI since in vivo concentrations of X-nuclei and also their MR sensitivities are typically much lower than those of ^{1}H (see Table 27.1). To compensate for the lower SNR, typically larger voxel volumes (Δx^3) are used. In addition, also the acquisition time (T_{Aq}) can be increased (see Eq. 27.3)

$$\text{SNR} \propto B_0, \tag{27.1}$$

$$\text{SNR} \propto c \cdot I \cdot (I+1)\, \gamma^2, \tag{27.2}$$

$$\text{SNR} \propto \Delta x^3 \cdot \sqrt{T_{Aq}}. \tag{27.3}$$

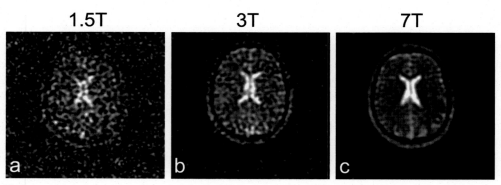

FIG. 27.1

Sodium (^{23}Na) MRI at different field strengths. Similar birdcage radiofrequency coils were used for image acquisition. For each field strength, a transversal slice of a 3D data set is shown. SNR increases approximately linearly with magnetic field strength. Acquisition parameters: nominal spatial resolution: (4 mm)^3; TE (1.5 and 3T) = 0.2 ms, TE(7T) = 0.5 ms, TR = 50 ms, flip angle $\alpha = 77°$, acquisition time: 10 min 50 s. *Figure reproduced with permission from Kraff et al. (2015).*

Table 27.1 Selected isotopes that can be used for X-nuclei MRI or X-nuclei spectroscopy.

Nucleus (spin I)	Gyromagnetic ratio γ (MHz/T)	Natural abundance (%)	Typical in vivo concentrations c (mol/L) of the isotope (in brain tissue)	Relative in vivo SNR (%)
^{1}H (1/2)	42.6	99.99	79	100
^{2}H (1)[a]	6.5	0.0115	≈ 0.01	$7.2 \cdot 10^{-4}$
^{13}C (1/2)[a]	10.7	1.07	≈ 0.005	$4.0 \cdot 10^{-4}$
^{17}O (5/2)[a]	-5.8	0.038	0.015	$4.1 \cdot 10^{-3}$
^{19}F (1/2)[a]	40.1	100	≈ 0.001	$1.1 \cdot 10^{-3}$
^{23}Na (3/2)	11.3	100	≈ 0.04	$1.8 \cdot 10^{-2}$
^{31}P (1/2)	17.3	100	≈ 0.003	$6.2 \cdot 10^{-4}$
^{35}Cl (3/2)	4.2	75.78	0.027	$2.2 \cdot 10^{-3}$
^{39}K (3/2)	2.0	93.26	0.108	$1.6 \cdot 10^{-3}$

Potential influences from differences in relaxation times were neglected. To calculate the relative SNR, Eq. 27.1 was used.
[a]These isotopes are typically used as tracers. So, the actual concentration depends on concentration of the used tracer substance.
Table adapted from Ladd et al. (2018).

X-nuclei MRI requires specific hardware and software that are typically not available on standard clinical MRI systems. First of all, MRI systems need to be equipped with a RF power amplifier that is able to transmit on the Larmor frequency of the desired X-nucleus.

In addition, specific transmit and receive RF coils are required. The design of RF coils for X-nuclei MRI presents several challenges. Often setups are desired that, in addition to X-nuclei MRI, enable transmission and reception on the ^{1}H frequency to facilitate B_0 shimming and to acquire data for anatomical reference. However, such dual-frequency designs are more complex and usually require trade-offs.

For brain imaging, often volume resonators are used (Choi et al., 2020; Wiggins et al., 2016). They provide homogeneous transmit and receive fields that facilitate quantitative measurements. To increase the SNR, the volume coils can be combined with receive array coils. However, this complicates post-processing in quantitative measurements since receive profiles have to be corrected for. More details about coil design for X-nuclei imaging can be found in review articles (Choi et al., 2020; Kraff and Quick, 2019; Wiggins et al., 2016).

In modern clinical MRI systems, the required adjustments such frequency calibration, transmitter voltage calibration, and B_0 shimming are normally performed automatically. These adjustment routines are usually not optimized or not available for X-nuclei MRI in commercially available MRI systems. Thus, typically frequency and transmitter voltage calibrations need to be performed manually. For double-tuned coils with a ^{1}H channel, B_0 shimming can be performed with the available routines for ^{1}H MRI. For X-nuclei RF coils without ^{1}H channel, custom solutions such as B_0 shimming based on ^{23}Na MRI can be used (Gast et al., 2020).

27.3 Acquisition techniques for X-nuclei MRI

Depending on the physical properties of the nucleus and the desired application, standard acquisition techniques that are available for ^{1}H MRI can be used. However, for most applications, acquisition techniques need to be specifically tailored to the X-nucleus of interest. In particular, quadrupolar nuclei (i.e., nuclei with spin $>\frac{1}{2}$) such as ^{2}H, ^{17}O, ^{23}Na, ^{35}Cl, and ^{39}K experience strong interactions with local electric field gradients, which result in rapid transverse relaxation. For example, transverse relaxation times in ^{23}Na MRI are typically in the order of a few milliseconds with short and long components of 0.2–5.0 ms and 10–64 ms, respectively. The measured relaxation times differ between various studies and depend on field strength (Nagel et al., 2016) and tissue type (Madelin and Regatte, 2013). Relaxation times of ^{17}O, ^{35}Cl, and ^{39}K are even shorter. Thus, quantitative MRI of these nuclei usually requires acquisition techniques with ultra-short echo (UTE) times (Konstandin and Nagel, 2014). For example, center-out radial k-space sampling techniques can be employed (Fig. 27.2). However, more sophisticated sampling schemes as density-adapted radial sampling or spiral techniques such as twisted projection imaging (TPI), acquisition-weighted stack of spirals (AWSOS), 3D CONES, or Fermat-looped orthogonally encoded trajectories (FLORET) can be employed to increase the SNR and sampling efficiency.

27.3.1 Partial volume effects

To partially compensate the low SNR of X-nuclei MRI, voxel volumes are typically several orders of magnitude larger than those of ^{1}H MRI. This results in partial volume effects, which can be caused by tissue fraction effects (i.e., one voxel contains two or more different types of tissue) or by signal spillover effects from neighboring voxels. For example, in ^{23}Na MRI of the human brain, fine structures such as sulci in combination with large concentration differences between cerebrospinal fluid and brain tissue cause partial volume effects that can bias quantitative measurements. Besides potential physiological variation, this might be one of the causes for the large variations in measured total sodium concentrations (TSC) that have been published. For example, literature values of sodium concentrations in brain white matter and gray matter range from 19 to 72 mmol/L and from 30 to 62 mmol/L, respectively. To reduce partial volume biases in quantitative measurements, high-resolution anatomical information and partial volume correction algorithms can be used. Here, it needs to be considered that the real (or effective spatial resolution) is typically lower than the nominal spatial resolution that is denoted in the imaging protocol. The real spatial resolution is influenced by the acquisition technique, applied postprocessing (e.g., filtering), and other factors such as T_2^* relaxation or patient motion. In X-nuclei MRI, often non-Cartesian UTE techniques that sample a spherical k-space volume are employed. Compared with acquisition techniques that sample a cuboid k-space volume, this results in an approximately 1.3-fold broader full-width-at-half maximum (FWHM) of the imaging point-spread function (PSF), which leads to a reduction of the spatial resolution by approximately the same factor. For common acquisition parameters as used in ^{23}Na MRI, the FWHM of the PSF is

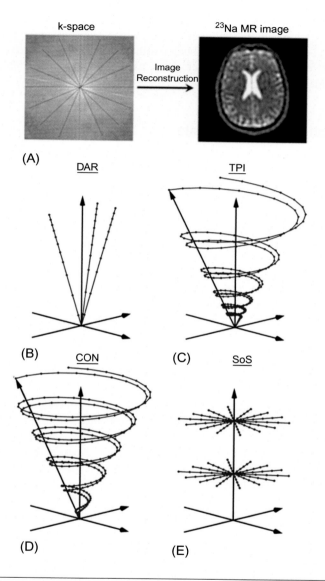

FIG. 27.2

2D visualization of center-out radial k-space sampling. Data acquisition starts directly in the center of k-space and, thus, can start immediately after excitation, which enables ultra-short echo times (TE < 0.5 ms) (A). Different types of k-space trajectories (B–E). *Reproduced with permission from Hu et al. (2020).*

$\approx$1.6–2.0 pixels and can be even larger if filters are applied. Considering the larger voxel sizes of ^{23}Na MRI ($\Delta x \approx$ 2–6 mm), this results in spillover effects, which even influence the signal intensity of voxels that can be $\gtrsim$ 1 cm away. For other nuclei with lower sensitivity such as ^{2}H, ^{17}O, ^{35}Cl, or ^{39}K, these spillover effects can be even larger. Thus, partial volume effects often result in a bias in quantitative measurements.

27.3.2 Quantification of ^{23}Na MRI data

Besides correction of relaxation and partial volume effects, quantitative measurements of sodium concentrations often require correction of transmit (B_1^+) and receive (B_1^-) profiles. To correct for transmit inhomogeneities, B_1^+ can be mapped (Lommen et al., 2016). For multichannel receive array coils, a correction of the B_1^- field is also mandatory (Lommen et al., 2016). Here, different intensity corrections methods are also available (Lachner et al., 2020). Quantification of sodium concentration requires the normalization of signal intensities to a known reference standard. Typically, external references with known sodium concentrations are used (Wilferth et al., 2022). However, for some dedicated head coils with integrated receive phased arrays, external references cannot be used due to the limit space. Thus, internal references such as cerebrospinal fluid have been used. However, this requires the application of partial volume corrections methods, and potential disease-related variations of sodium concentrations in cerebrospinal fluid might bias the quantification procedure.

27.3.3 Intra- and extracellular ^{23}Na concentrations

Quantitative measurements of ion concentrations such as the TSC also called tissue sodium concentration comprise a volume-weighted average of intra- and extracellular sodium concentrations. For many applications in clinical research, a separate quantification of intra- and extracellular sodium concentrations would be desirable. Although a separation between intra- and extracellular sodium has been a major goal in ^{23}Na MRI research in the past decades, this topic is still challenging and controversially discussed (Burstein and Springer, 2019). To enable a clear separation, paramagnetic shift reagents can be applied. These contrast agents do not penetrate the cell membrane and can selectively shift the resonance line of extracellular sodium and, thus, enable a separation between intra- and extracellular sodium. However, potential toxicity limits its application to preclinical studies only.

Noninvasive approaches, which can be applied in humans, are based on differences in the relaxation times between various sodium compartments. For instance, preclinical studies that employed shift reagents indicate that intracellular sodium exhibits shorter T_1 relaxations than extracellular sodium (Kline et al., 2000). Thus, inversion recovery techniques are often employed to suppress the sodium signal with long T_1 relaxation times such as in cerebrospinal fluid (see Fig. 27.3) and to achieve a weighting toward intracellular sodium (Nagel et al., 2011). Similarly, differences in T_2^* relaxation times can be exploited by applying multiecho imaging. Ridley and collaborators demonstrated that ^{23}Na relaxation components show substantial differences between

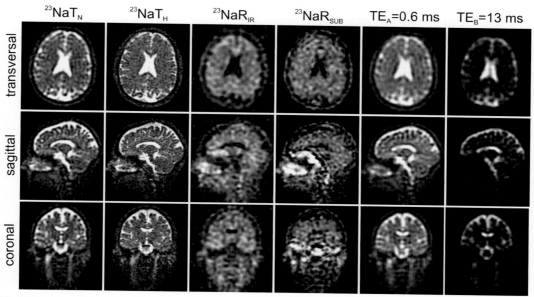

FIG. 27.3

Different image contrasts in ^{23}Na MRI. Transversal, sagittal, and coronal slices of 3D data sets acquired at 7T are shown. For the assessment of the total ^{23}Na signal, relaxation weighting was minimized by applying short TE (0.3 ms) and long repetition times (TR = 120 ms) (^{23}NaT$_N$ imaging; (4 mm)^3). If shorter repetition times are used and, thus, slight T_1-weighting is accepted, a higher SNR efficiency can be achieved and images with higher spatial resolution can be acquired (^{23}NaT$_H$ imaging; (2.5 mm)^3). Inversion recovery imaging allows suppression of sodium ions with long relaxation times such as in cerebrospinal fluid. However, this reduces the achievable spatial resolution (^{23}NaR$_{IR}$ imaging; (5.5 mm)^3). Relaxation weighting can also be achieved based on fast ^{23}Na multiecho imaging and the calculation of a weighted subtraction (^{23}NaR$_{SUB}$ imaging; (5 mm)^3) of images acquired at different TEs. *Images adapted and reproduced from permission from Nagel et al. (2011).*

brain regions of differing tissue composition, indicating sensitivity of multiecho ^{23}Na MRI toward features of tissue composition (Ridley et al., 2018). Moreover, multiquantum filtered techniques can be applied. These techniques are sensitive to the fluctuating electric field gradients, which can be caused by macromolecules in the vicinity of the ions. It is hypothesized that these techniques can also achieve a weighting toward intracellular sodium since macromolecules typically have high intracellular concentrations (Hu et al., 2020). However, extracellular sodium can also contribute to the multiquantum filtered signal. Similarly, multipulse sequences that are optimized in spin dynamics simulations can be applied to separate between different sodium compartments (Gilles et al., 2017). All these techniques have the potential to provide valuable information to TSC in biomedical research applications.

27.4 **Brain biomedical applications**

In addition to their NMR properties, several X-nuclei, such as ^{23}Na, ^{31}P, ^{39}K, and ^{35}Cl, play major roles in human biology. Among them, ^{23}Na is the most investigated X-nuclei by in vivo MRI. Sodium is the second most abundant element in vivo and is crucial in maintaining osmoregulation and cell physiology. Sodium is involved in the energy-consuming processes of membrane transport and as a counter ion for balancing charges of tissue anionic macromolecules (Thulborn, 2018). The sodium concentration is around 10–15 mmol/L in the intracellular space and 145 mmol/L in the extracellular space. The transmembrane concentration gradient is mainly supplied by the energy-dependent sodium-potassium pump (Na$^+$/K$^+$-ATPase), which transfers three sodium out of the cell in exchange of the influx of two potassium ions. Na$^+$/K$^+$-ATPase consumes 50% of the energy supply in the central nervous system. If ATP availability becomes insufficient to allow ion pumps to maintain the appropriate ion gradients, changes in electrical properties and excitability of cells occur. Thus, any injury to cell membrane integrity or disturbances of energy metabolism could alter the function of Na$^+$/K$^+$-ATPase and then lead to changes in transmembrane potential, increases in intracellular sodium concentration, and increases in the extracellular volume fraction, which could be responsible for cell death (Madelin and Regatte, 2013; Shah et al., 2016; Thulborn, 2018). The increasing availability of high-field and ultra-high field MR scanners as well as the improvements achieved in hardware and acquisition designs allowed several researchers to investigate the clinical applications of sodium MRI. This chapter will focus on brain sodium MRI studies performed in tumors, stroke, epilepsy, and multiple sclerosis (MS). These studies were mainly conducted at 3T. With an increasing number of 7T MRI scanners becoming accessible for clinical patients, higher magnetic fields will benefit further studies of these and other diseases.

27.4.1 **Brain tumors**

In brain tumors, several investigations have highlighted the added value of ^{23}Na MRI. Cell membrane depolarization and cell division in proliferating tissue lead to an increase in the TSC, which may be attributed to an increase in the intracellular sodium concentration, related to the increased energy demand arising from cell proliferation, and/or an increase in the extracellular volume space. Studies have shown differences in sodium MRI contrast among different tumor grades and between the active tumoral core and peritumoral related edema. These differences appear to reflect the general prognosis with higher TSC in areas of more aggressive tumor (review of (Thulborn, 2018)). Biller and collaborators demonstrated in human brain tumors that ^{23}Na MRI is a good prognostic marker, separating isocitrate dehydrogenase (IDH) mutant gliomas, known to predict a favorable disease outcome, from wild-type IDH gliomas. More importantly, sodium signal performed better than the IDH status to predict the patient's prognosis (Biller et al., 2016). Thus, sodium imaging may be considered a promising candidate for noninvasive tumor diagnosis and outcome prediction.

27.4.2 **Ischemic stroke**

Ischemic stroke occurs when a blood vessel supplying oxygen and glucose to a brain region is obstructed. Inadequate blood flow rapidly depletes tissue oxygen, inducing dysfunction of Na$^+$/K$^+$-ATPase and subsequent energy failure, leading to an increase in TSC. Several ^{23}Na MRI studies reported that TSC measurements may be considered a promising biomarker for assessing brain tissue viability and potentially for determining the stroke onset time, which is required to assess the eligibility for thrombolysis treatment (Hussain et al., 2009; Thulborn, 2018). Previous ^{23}Na MRI studies demonstrated that the sodium signal changes with early increases in the infarcted core tissue as early as 4h after the ischemic stroke onset. Interestingly, Hussain and collaborators explored 21 stroke patients and showed that the sodium signal in the core region increased about 10% (relative to the contralateral region) in the first 7h after the onset, followed by a more pronounced increase, which reached a plateau (69% of increase) at 48h (Hussain et al., 2009). An example of these sodium signal changes over time in a stroke patient is illustrated in Fig. 27.4. The authors suggested that the apparent linear increase in the sodium signal may be useful to determine the onset time, especially relevant for "wake-up" strokes

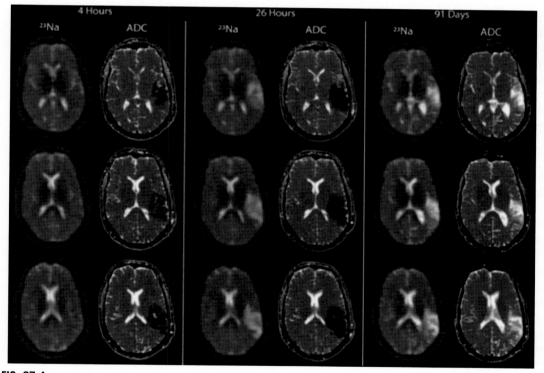

FIG. 27.4

^{23}Na images and ^{1}H apparent ADC maps from a patient with an ischemic stroke scanned at 4h, 26h, and 91 days. There is a dramatic increase in sodium signal intensity between the acute time point of 4h (no change over contralateral side) and the time point 22h later (45% increase over contralateral side). At 91 days, the sodium signal intensity increase persists (75% relative increase). *Figure reproduced with permission from Hussain et al. (2009).*

in which the exact time of the event is not known while crucial for selecting thrombolysis treatment. This hypothesis is still under investigation. Furthermore, findings also suggested that sodium imaging may better identify viable tissue in stroke patients, despite an unknown symptom onset time. Indeed, Tsang and collaborators calculated the sodium signal ratio between the signal intensity in the core (identified as hyperintense on diffusion imaging) and the putative penumbra (perfusion-diffusion mismatch) relative to the sodium signal in the contralateral region (Tsang et al., 2011). They found that the sodium signal cannot be predicted by the degree of hypoperfusion. Moreover, it was shown that in the critical perfusion-diffusion mismatch tissue, sodium intensity also remains unchanged, indicating preservation of ionic homeostasis.

27.4.3 Epilepsy

One study on epilepsy reported the use of in vivo sodium imaging to explore TSC changes in epileptogenic regions of patients, defined by intracranial stereo-electroencephalography (Ridley et al., 2017). Patients were explored during the interictal periods, except for one who had seizures during the MRI examination. This study provided the first evidence of a chronic TSC elevation in epileptogenic regions during the interictal period in human epilepsy and the possibility of reduced sodium concentration levels due to seizure. This result may be explained by an increase in the intra-cellular sodium concentration due to voltage-gated sodium channel mutations, leading to a persistent inward sodium current, in addition to an increase in the extracellular space due to cell loss and glial formation.

27.4.4 Neurodegeneration and neuroinflammation

Several in vivo studies highlighted the potential of sodium MRI as a promising biomarker for neuroinflammation and neurodegeneration in MS (Huhn et al., 2019; Inglese et al., 2013). While inflammation leads to mitochondrial dysfunction and decreases in energy production mainly due to nitric oxide and reactive oxygen species, demyelination, with the redistribution of sodium channels along the axon, increases energy requirements. These processes induce mitochondrial energy failure, which leads to axonal sodium accumulation and then to reversed activity of the Na^+/Ca^{2+} exchanger and, thus, axonal calcium import. This calcium overload stimulates several toxic Ca^{2+}-dependent enzymes, causing structural and functional axonal injury. In vivo alteration of sodium homeostasis in MS was evidenced by several studies that reported a TSC increase not only in MS lesions but also outside MS lesions, in the so-called normal-appearing brain tissues. The TSC increase was found in patients since the first stage of the disease, as illustrated in Fig. 27.5 which presents the topography of a TSC increase in early (1 year of disease duration) and advanced (13 years of disease duration) relapsing-remitting MS patients (Zaaraoui et al., 2012). In addition, the TSC increase was associated with physical and cognitive disability (Huhn et al., 2019; Inglese et al., 2013). All authors suggested that the TSC increase in MS was mainly related to the increased intracellular sodium concentration, but we cannot rule out the impact of the extracellular com-partment (atrophy, oedema) even if most studies tried to correct for atrophy. Thus, development of reliable sequences to better assess the intracellular sodium signal may lead to a better estimation of inflammation and neurodegeneration in MS.

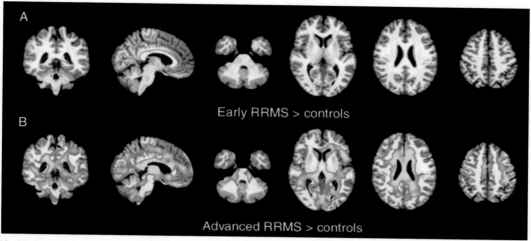

FIG. 27.5

Statistical maps of an abnormal increase in brain sodium concentrations in early and advanced relapsing-remitting multiple sclerosis (RRMS) patients. A local increase in the brain TSC is seen in (A) patients with early RRMS (1 year of disease duration) relative to control subjects and (B) patients with advanced RRMS (13 years of disease duration) relative to control subjects. *Figure reproduced with permission from Zaaraoui et al. (2012).*

Attempts to investigate sodium homeostasis changes in other neurodegenerative diseases such as Huntington's disease, Alzheimer's disease, Parkinson's disease, and amyotrophic lateral sclerosis were also performed (Shah et al., 2016; Thulborn, 2018; Grimaldi et al., 2021; Grapperon et al., 2019). While these pioneering studies evidenced a TSC increase in clinically relevant brain regions, the pathophysiological processes leading to sodium homeostasis changes are still poorly understood.

27.4.5 Applications with X-nuclei other than ^{23}Na

Other X-nuclei such as ^{31}P and ^{2}H are also subject to important interest in biomedical research and are mainly explored by MR spectroscopy or MR spectroscopic imaging (see Chapter 26). There is also an emerging interest for ^{19}F, which is mainly used in preclinical research (Modo, 2021). Due to the emergence of ultra-high magnetic field, pioneering studies became feasible to explore ^{35}Cl, ^{39}K, ^{7}Li, or even ^{17}O MRI, despite the very low sensitivity. ^{35}Cl MRI was used to evaluate tissue ion homeostasis changes in brain tumors and muscular diseases (Fig. 27.6) (Nagel et al., 2014). The feasibility of measuring ^{39}K, the most abundant intracellular ion, was demonstrated in healthy subjects (Umathum et al., 2013). Enriched ^{17}O gas can be applied to assess the cerebral metabolic rate of oxygen consumption ($CMRO_2$) in vivo in brain tumors (Fig. 27.6) (Hoffmann et al., 2014). Recently, accumulation of lithium was evidenced in the hippocampus of patients with bipolar disorder using ^{7}Li MRI (Stout et al., 2020).

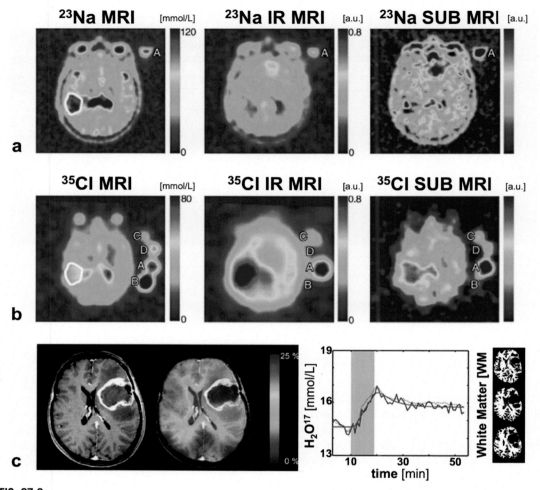

FIG. 27.6

(A) and (B) Illustrations of ^{23}Na and ^{35}Cl images from a patient with brain tumor. Note the different signal contrast mentioned in Fig. 27.3 of this chapter. (C) Anatomical ^{1}H image and colored overlay of the signal increase in ^{17}O MRI tumor. *(A and B) Reproduced with permission from Nagel et al. (2014). Adapted and reproduced with permission from Hoffmann et al. (2014). From the signal increase curve, the $CMRO_2$ can be calculated.*

27.5 Conclusion

In conclusion, there is still research required to better understand signal intensity changes of X-nuclei MRI in various pathologies. However, numerous biomedical research applications show that X-nuclei MRI at high and UHF strengths has a great potential to elucidate biological processes and disease mechanisms in vivo.

References

Biller, A., Badde, S., Nagel, A., et al., 2016. Improved brain tumor classification by sodium MR imaging: prediction of IDH mutation status and tumor progression. AJNR Am. J. Neuroradiol. 37, 66–73.

Burstein, D., Springer, C.S., 2019. Sodium MRI revisited. Magn. Reson. Med. 82, 521–524.

Choi, C.-H., Hong, S.-M., Felder, J., Shah, N.J., 2020. The state-of-the-art and emerging design approaches of double-tuned RF coils for X-nuclei, brain MR imaging and spectroscopy: a review. Magn. Reson. Imaging 72, 103–116.

Gast, L.V., Henning, A., Hensel, B., Uder, M., Nagel, A.M., 2020. Localized B_0 shimming based on 23 Na MRI at 7T. Magn. Reson. Med. 83, 1339–1347.

Gilles, A., Nagel, A.M., Madelin, G., 2017. Multipulse sodium magnetic resonance imaging for multicompartment quantification: proof-of-concept. Sci. Rep. 7, 17435.

Grapperon, A.-M., Ridley, B., Verschueren, A., et al., 2019. Quantitative brain sodium MRI depicts corticospinal impairment in amyotrophic lateral sclerosis. Radiology 292, 422–428.

Grimaldi, S., El Mendili, M.M., Zaaraoui, W., et al., 2021. Increased sodium concentration in substantia Nigra in early Parkinson's disease: a preliminary study with ultra-high field (7T) MRI. Front. Neurol. 12, 1610.

Hoffmann, S.H., Radbruch, A., Bock, M., Semmler, W., Nagel, A.M., 2014. Direct (17)O MRI with partial volume correction: first experiences in a glioblastoma patient. MAGMA 27, 579–587.

Hu, R., Kleimaier, D., Malzacher, M., Hoesl, M.A.U., Paschke, N.K., Schad, L.R., 2020. X-nuclei imaging: current state, technical challenges, and future directions. J. Magn. Reson. Imaging 51, 355–376.

Huhn, K., Engelhorn, T., Linker, R.A., Nagel, A.M., 2019. Potential of sodium MRI as a biomarker for neurodegeneration and neuroinflammation in multiple sclerosis. Front. Neurol. 10, 84.

Hussain, M.S., Stobbe, R.W., Bhagat, Y.A., et al., 2009. Sodium imaging intensity increases with time after human ischemic stroke. Ann. Neurol. 66, 55–62.

Inglese, M., Oesingmann, N., Zaaraoui, W., Ranjeva, J.P., Fleysher, L., 2013. Sodium imaging as a marker of tissue injury in patients with multiple sclerosis. Mult. Scler. Relat. Disord. 2, 263–269.

Kline, R.P., Wu, E.X., Petrylak, D.P., et al., 2000. Rapid in vivo monitoring of chemotherapeutic response using weighted sodium magnetic resonance imaging. Clin. Cancer Res. 6, 2146–2156.

Konstandin, S., Nagel, A.M., 2014. Measurement techniques for magnetic resonance imaging of fast relaxing nuclei. MAGMA 27, 5–19.

Kraff, O., Quick, H.H., 2019. Radiofrequency coils for 7 Tesla MRI. Top. Magn. Reson. Imaging 28, 145–158.

Kraff, O., Fischer, A., Nagel, A.M., Mönninghoff, C., Ladd, M.E., 2015. MRI at 7 Tesla and above: demonstrated and potential capabilities. J. Magn. Reson. Imaging 41, 13–33.

Lachner, S., Ruck, L., Niesporek, S.C., et al., 2020. Comparison of optimized intensity correction methods for ^{23}Na MRI of the human brain using a 32-channel phased array coil at 7 Tesla. Z. Med. Phys. 30, 104–115.

Ladd, M.E., Bachert, P., Meyerspeer, M., et al., 2018. Pros and cons of ultra-high-field MRI/MRS for human application. Prog. Nucl. Magn. Reson. Spectrosc. 109, 1–50.

Lommen, J., Konstandin, S., Krämer, P., Schad, L.R., 2016. Enhancing the quantification of tissue sodium content by MRI: time-efficient sodium B_1 mapping at clinical field strengths. NMR Biomed. 29, 129–136.

Madelin, G., Regatte, R.R., 2013. Biomedical applications of sodium MRI in vivo. J. Magn. Reson. Imaging 38, 511–529.

Modo, M., 2021. ^{19}F magnetic resonance imaging and spectroscopy in neuroscience. Neuroscience 474, 37–50.

Nagel, A.M., Bock, M., Hartmann, C., et al., 2011. The potential of relaxation-weighted sodium magnetic resonance imaging as demonstrated on brain tumors. Investig. Radiol. 46, 539–547.

Nagel, A.M., Lehmann-Horn, F., Weber, M.-A., et al., 2014. In vivo ^{35}Cl MR imaging in humans: a feasibility study. Radiology 271, 585–595.

Nagel, A.M., Umathum, R., Rösler, M.B., et al., 2016. ^{39}K and ^{23}Na relaxation times and MRI of rat head at 21.1 T. NMR Biomed. 29, 759–766.

Niesporek, S.C., Nagel, A.M., Platt, T., 2019. Multinuclear MRI at ultrahigh fields. Top. Magn. Reson. Imaging 28, 173–188.

Ridley, B., Marchi, A., Wirsich, J., et al., 2017. Brain sodium MRI in human epilepsy: disturbances of ionic homeostasis reflect the organization of pathological regions. NeuroImage 157, 173–183.

Ridley, B., Nagel, A.M., Bydder, M., et al., 2018. Distribution of brain sodium long and short relaxation times and concentrations: a multi-echo ultra-high field ^{23}Na MRI study. Sci. Rep. 8.

Shah, N.J., Worthoff, W.A., Langen, K.-J., 2016. Imaging of sodium in the brain: a brief review. NMR Biomed. 29, 162–174.

Stout, J., Hozer, F., Coste, A., et al., 2020. Accumulation of lithium in the hippocampus of patients with bipolar disorder: a lithium-7 magnetic resonance imaging study at 7 Tesla. Biol. Psychiatry 88, 426–433.

Thulborn, K.R., 2018. Quantitative sodium MR imaging: a review of its evolving role in medicine. NeuroImage 168, 250–268.

Tsang, A., Stobbe, R.W., Asdaghi, N., et al., 2011. Relationship between sodium intensity and perfusion deficits in acute ischemic stroke. J. Magn. Reson. Imaging 33, 41–47.

Umathum, R., Rösler, M.B., Nagel, A.M., 2013. In vivo ^{39}K MR imaging of human muscle and brain. Radiology 269, 569–576.

Wiggins, G.C., Brown, R., Lakshmanan, K., 2016. High-performance radiofrequency coils for ^{23}Na MRI: brain and musculoskeletal applications. NMR Biomed. 29, 96–106.

Wilferth, T., Mennecke, A., Gast, L.V., et al., 2022. Quantitative 7T sodium magnetic resonance imaging of the human brain using a 32-channel phased-array head coil: application to patients with secondary progressive multiple sclerosis. NMR Biomed., e4806.

Zaaraoui, W., Konstandin, S., Audoin, B., et al., 2012. Distribution of brain sodium accumulation correlates with disability in multiple sclerosis: a cross-sectional ^{23}Na MR imaging study. Radiology 264, 859–867.

Chemical exchange saturation transfer MRI in the human brain at ultra-high fields

28

Moritz Zaiss[a,b,c] and Angelika Mennecke[a]

[a]*Institute of Neuroradiology, Universitätsklinikum Erlangen, Friedrich-Alexander-Universität Erlangen-Nürnberg, Erlangen, Germany* [b]*Magnetic Resonance Center, Max-Planck-Institute for Biological Cybernetics, Tübingen, Germany* [c]*Department Artificial Intelligence in Biomedical Engineering, Friedrich-Alexander-Universität Erlangen-Nürnberg, Erlangen, Germany*

Highlights

- Understanding the CEST signal, including spillover dilution, labeling efficiency, and peak widths of CEST.
- Field inhomogeneities, their influence, and mitigation.
- In vivo examples from 3T to 21.1T in the normal and diseased brain.

28.1 The CEST experiment and imaging sequence

Standard MR imaging is typically MR imaging of water protons. Using MR spectroscopy, protons bound to other solute molecules, like proteins and metabolites, can as well be detected. However, these protons generate a very low signal due to their low concentration, which limits the spatial resolution of MR spectroscopy. The chemical exchange saturation transfer (CEST) experiment provides a way to measure this precious spectroscopic information with the high spatial resolution of water proton MRI. This is possible by utilizing the chemical exchange of protons between solute molecules and water for indirect detection of the protons of solutes. The basic CEST sequence (Fig. 28.1A) consists of a radiofrequency (RF) irradiation at the solute proton resonance frequency, after which indirect detection of the solute is possible by observing changes in the water magnetization due to transferred saturation. The CEST spectrum, or Z-spectrum, is created by subsequent RF irradiation at specific RF frequency offsets $\Delta\omega$ before each water proton MR acquisition (Fig. 28.1B). Depending on the chemically shifted resonance frequencies of solute protons, the water proton magnetization is affected differently. This is reflected in the Z-spectrum as peaks at the corresponding frequency offset $\Delta\omega$.

Before each repetition of preparation and acquisition, the magnetization has to be in a well-defined state, for example, a steady-state or a state after a certain relaxation delay. This brings us to the three main building blocks of a CEST sequence that are as follows: (i) a relaxation delay, (ii) an RF preparation period (at a different RF frequency offset $\Delta\omega$ relative to water), and (iii) an acquisition of the signal from the prepared water magnetization (Fig. 28.1A). Typically, after the preparation

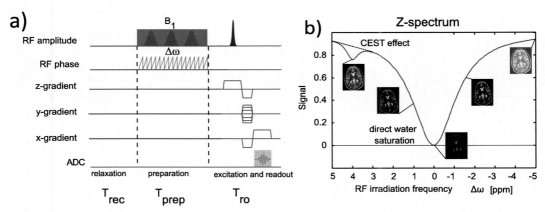

FIG. 28.1

(A) A typical CEST sequence with a relaxation delay (recovery time, T_{rec}) before CEST preparation. The CEST preparation consists of either continued or pulsed RF irradiation at a certain frequency offset $\Delta\omega$, with a certain RF amplitude B_1 or $B_{1,rms}$, for a certain duration T_{prep}. Subsequently, the prepared magnetization is excited, spatially encoded, and one or more k-space lines are acquired, in this example using a gradient echo readout of duration T_{ro}. This is repeated until the full k-space is sampled, if not acquired in a single shot. (B) To acquire a full Z-spectrum, the sequence of (A) is repeated for each offset frequency and/or B_1 level, leading to 4D data: an image for each offset $\Delta\omega$ or, equivalently, a Z-spectrum for each voxel. The Z-spectrum is further evaluated after normalization with an unsaturated image. Major characteristics are (B) direct water saturation, broad semi-solid magnetization transfer, and selective CEST effects.

period, a gradient crusher is applied; thus, all information of the preparation is only in the z-component of the water proton magnetization. This is why the resulting spectrum, sampled over a range of frequency offsets $\Delta\omega$, is also called the Z-spectrum (Fig. 28.1B). The Z-spectrum, consisting of different Z-values $Z(\Delta\omega)$, is typically normalized by an unsaturated scan. This Z-value is defined using the signal after preparation $S(\Delta\omega)$ and the signal without preparation S_0:

$$Z(\Delta\omega) = \frac{S_{sat}(\Delta\omega)}{S_0}. \tag{28.1}$$

The normalization has the benefit that the Z-spectrum is now largely independent from other system parameters, such as readout parameters and related contrast, or coil sensitivities.

To isolate a CEST effect at a certain offset, e.g., the **labeled value Z_{label}**, we need a **reference value Z_{ref}** that has minimal contribution of the exchange, which corresponds to the dashed line in Figs. 28.1B and 28.2A. Generating such a reference value using real data requires some efforts; methods such as asymmetry analysis, least-squares background fitting, or even other acquisition techniques are used. The CEST effect can then be isolated from the background, leading to the magnetization transfer ratio or CEST rate (CESTR), depicted in Fig. 28.2B:

$$\text{CESTR} = \frac{S_{ref}(\Delta\omega)}{S_0} - \frac{S_{label}(\Delta\omega)}{S_0} = Z_{ref} - Z_{label}. \tag{28.2}$$

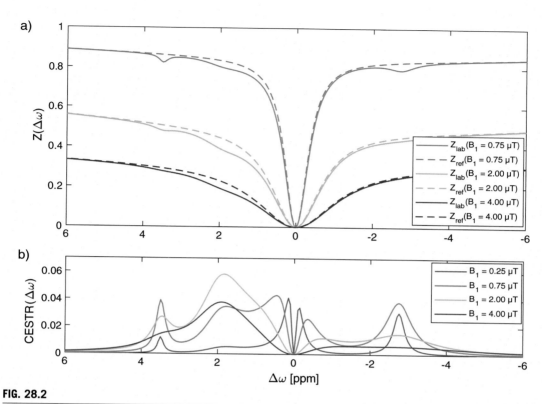

FIG. 28.2

(A) $B_0 = 7T$ simulation of a seven-pool Z-spectrum (*solid*), which is also the label scan here. The ideal reference Z-spectrum is a simulation with only water and MT contribution (*dashed*). These spectra are shown at low and high B_1 levels to depict the increased direct water and MT saturation and the concomitant dilution of CEST effects. (B) The CESTR generated by Eq. 28.2, but for different B_1 levels which shows the influence of B_1 on both CEST effect amplitudes and linewidths. Amplitudes first increase with B_1 due to better labeling (Eq. 28.4). Generating simulation codes available on https://github.com/cest-sources/Z-cw with water and MT pool mimicking white brain matter and five CEST pools: amide (3.5 ppm, $150\,s^{-1}$) guanidine (2 ppm, $1100\,s^{-1}$), amine (3 ppm, $5500\,s^{-1}$), hydroxyl (1.3 ppm, $3500\,s^{-1}$), rNOE (-2.75 ppm, $16\,s^{-1}$).

28.2 Understanding the CEST signal by equations

Using analytical solutions of the Bloch-McConnell equations (Zaiss et al., 2022), one can derive the theoretical value for this difference (Eq. 28.2) in the steady-state and on resonance of the CEST peak, leading to the **CEST signal equation in the steady-state or CEST rate**:

$$\text{CESTR} = \frac{f_s k_s}{R_1} \cdot \alpha(B_1) \cdot \sigma'(B_1), \tag{28.3}$$

where f_s is the solute proton fraction relative to the water proton concentration and k_s is the exchange rate to water. R_1 is the longitudinal relaxation rate of water, α is the so-called labeling efficiency, and

σ' forms the spillover dilution factor. The labeling efficiency is a factor between 0 and 1 and describes how well our RF labeling works for a given exchange rate k_s, preparation amplitude $\omega_1 = \gamma B_1$ and the transverse relaxation rate of the CEST pool R_{2s}. It is given by:

$$\alpha = \frac{\omega_1^2}{\omega_1^2 + k_s(R_{2s} + k_s)}. \tag{28.4}$$

The spillover dilution factor σ' was derived previously (Zaiss et al., 2022) to be given by the square of the Z-value

$$\sigma' \approx Z_{ref}^2. \tag{28.5}$$

Therefore, it also just takes values between 0 and 1. It can be viewed as the dilution of the saturation effects due to concomitant saturation of the water protons, via direct saturation or MT effects. It also reflects the fact that CESTR can never grow above 100% of the water magnetization, which is when all water proton magnetization is already depleted.

Moreover, the CEST peaks are actually Lorentzian peaks (see also Fig. 28.2) and have a B_1-dependent Lorentzian linewidth Γ given by

$$\Gamma = 2\sqrt{(R_{2s} + k_s)^2 + \frac{R_{2s} + k_s}{k_s}\omega_1^2}, \tag{28.6}$$

where R_{2s} is the transverse relaxation rate of the CEST protons. Thus, $R_{2s} + k_s$ is the natural linewidth of the solute protons, and the B_1-dependent term describes the increase in the CEST peak width due to saturation effects. For fixed relaxation and exchange parameters, both water and CEST linewidths in CEST scale with the B_1 amplitude. For a fixed B_1 amplitude, the width as a function of the B_0 field strength decreases on the ppm scale (while staying constant in Hz), leading to sharper peaks and less overlap at higher field strengths. With these equations for amplitude and width, most behavior in real CEST spectra can be understood. Fig. 28.2 shows both Z-spectra and CESTR-spectra for different B_1 amplitudes, showing first increase in CEST effects due to labeling and then reduction in CEST effects due to spillover dilution, as well as peak broadening at higher B_1.

Labeling efficiency and spillover dilution factors are again depicted as a function of B_1 in Fig. 28.3. Their competitive influence on the final signal is here directly visible: α grows with increasing B_1 (faster for slow exchange rates), and σ' shrinks with increasing B_1 (faster for peaks closer to water). Thus, optimal RF labeling is always a compromise between both factors.

The dispersion of the labeling efficiency allows the selection of a certain exchange regime. As seen in Fig. 28.3, higher exchange rate requires higher B_1, a helpful rule of thumb is that $\alpha \approx 50\%$ for $\omega_1 = k_s$. While α would further increase with B_1, the spillover dilution becomes also more dominant at higher B_1, counteracting the gain by α. Thus, the RF preparation amplitude $\omega_1 = \gamma B_1$ is a parameter that needs to be optimized carefully and requires simultaneous optimization of three variables: (i) maximizing the labeling efficiency α, higher exchange rate requires higher B_1, (ii) minimizing the spillover dilution factor σ', and (iii) minimizing width of the CEST peaks Γ.

Thus, using lower B_1 levels, higher selectivity is achieved. If the same system is now measured at higher static magnetic field strength B_0, also the selectivity on the ppm scale increases as depicted in the simulation in Fig. 28.4.

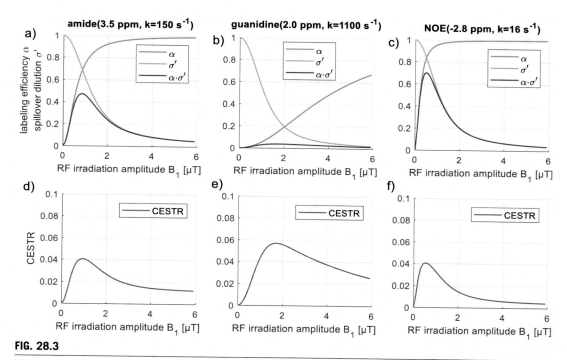

FIG. 28.3

Visualization of Eqs. 28.3–28.5. Individual labeling efficiencies and spillover dilution factors for the simulated CEST effects of (A) amides at 3.5 ppm and $k=150\,s^{-1}$, (B) guanidines at 2 ppm and $k=1100\,s^{-1}$, and (C) rNOEs at −2.75 ppm and $k=16\,s^{-1}$. Slower exchange rates are easier to label; faster exchange rates require high B_1 levels that also lead to strong spillover dilution. Be aware that in the signal (D–F) in Eq. 28.3, the term $\alpha \cdot \sigma'$ occurs with the exchange rate k_s as a factor, which means that the absolute effect size also scales with k_s, and thus, a high CESTR is also observed for guanidines, despite the low labeling and the high spillover dilution. Generating simulation codes available on https://github.com/cest-sources/Z-cw.

28.3 Field inhomogeneities and limitations

28.3.1 B_1 inhomogeneity and corrections

As seen above, the saturation amplitude B_1 is the governing factor for CEST labeling, selectivity, and spillover dilution. This makes CEST experiments prone to B_1 artifacts.

Thus, the appraisal of the benefits for CEST at UHF comes with the drawback of challenges related to the typically higher B_1 inhomogeneities at UHF scanners. Fig. 28.4 shows the direct impact of B_1 inhomogeneities on the emerging CEST contrast. As already described theoretically by Eqs. 28.3 and 28.4 and Fig. 28.3, this dependency is nonlinear and in addition depends on almost all Bloch-McConnell parameters. At 7T, the circular polarized mode (CP) shows high B_1 inhomogeneity as visible in Fig. 28.5A, which directly leads to inhomogeneous CEST maps (Fig. 28.5B). Thus, for homogeneity, as well as for reproducibility between different scans with different reference voltage or B_1 map, it is crucial to handle this B_1 inhomogeneity artifact.

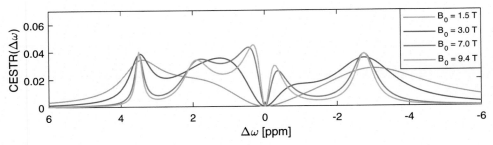

FIG. 28.4

Benefits of CEST at UHF are mostly linewidth dependent: the sharper CEST peaks allow for better separation, and the broader direct water saturation at lower field leads to more spillover dilution, thus larger effect sizes are measured at higher field. Especially peaks close to water, e.g., here guanidine at 2 ppm, can be resolved much better at 9.4T. The *red line* here corresponds to *red line* in Fig. 28.2. Compare with measured data depicted in Fig. 28.6. Generating simulation codes available on https://github.com/cest-sources/Z-cw.

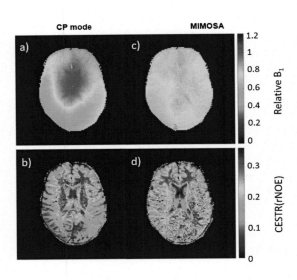

FIG. 28.5

B_1 dependency and inhomogeneity of 7T CEST effects are correlated to the B_1 mode. The relative B_1 map for CP mode at 7T in (A) shows inhomogeneities. The effects of these are directly visible in the CEST maps (rNOE CEST, B). Multiple interleaved mode saturation combines two modes to generate a more homogeneous B_1 distribution and therefore saturation (C), which leads to a more homogeneous CEST map (D). *Adapted from Liebert et al. (2019).*

For (i) B_1 inhomogeneity correction, the simplest, most accurate, but also but most time-consuming solution is to acquire the CEST data at more than one B_1 level and interpolate the data (Windschuh et al., 2015). Less time-consuming is to calibrate the B_1 dispersion of the final CEST contrast once and apply the calibrated curve as correction for single B_1 measurements. This approach is of course only valid for tissues with similar B_1 dispersion. Especially in pathologies with PD, T_1, T_2, or MT changes, approaches based on calibrations in healthy tissue can lead to erroneous B_1 corrections.

For (ii) B_1 inhomogeneity mitigation, parallel transmit system can be used to achieve a more homogeneous saturation, a Gaussian-spokes-pulse-based approach was shown by Tse et al. (2017) to yield more homogeneous CEST maps. A simpler approach only using two interleaved B_1 modes is the MIMOSA approach (Liebert et al., 2019), which lowers the residual B_1 inhomogeneity in the brain to similar levels as at 3T (see Fig. 28.5C and D).

At human scanners, the possible B_1 amplitudes are limited by SAR as well as coil-related restrictions. This leads to the fact that the B_1 level required by a certain exchange process cannot always be realized at UHF and a compromise must be found experimentally. Using shorter saturation pulse trains, lower duty-cycle, or pulses with smaller peak amplitude, allow for B_1 levels up to several µT also at UHF. However, for steady-state CEST, only B_1 levels around 1.5 µT are feasible at 7T and above. Still, too high spillover dilution effects due to direct water and MT saturation often constrain the experimental settings before SAR or hardware limits are reached.

To get quantitative results that are reproducible at different MRI systems, amplifier-dependent alterations due to the typically high duty-cycle of CEST saturation must be considered, mitigated, or corrected for (Voelker et al., 2021).

28.3.2 B_0 inhomogeneity and dynamic corrections

B_0 correction is an essential step in CEST imaging at all field strengths, as B_0 inhomogeneities lead to shifts in Z-spectra, which can lead to severe artifacts in final difference contrasts (Kim et al., 2009; Schuenke et al., 2017b; Singh et al., 2012; Sun et al., 2007). At UHF, B_0 inhomogeneities are generally larger, and these artifacts have to be handled with even more care. Moreover, the B_0 inhomogeneity can change during the CEST acquisition due to gradient heating (Windschuh et al., 2019) or subject motion (Zaiss et al., 2019b). Thus, dynamic B_0 acquisitions and dynamic B_0 corrections are needed. Such dynamic approaches are highly recommended for UHF applications, and additional navigator scans for each individual CEST offset measurement that measure subject motion, B_0, and B_1(+ and −) information would be the best solution.

28.4 Unique UHF CEST effects and applications

CEST acquisition at $B_0 > 3T$ leads to increased selectivity, and due to lower spillover dilution and longer T_1, also to increased sensitivity as shown in the field strength comparison in Figs. 28.4 and 28.6. However, amide and rNOE CEST effects at +3.5 and −3.5 ppm were shown to be detectable at 3T (Deshmane et al., 2019; Zhou et al., 2019) and due to the larger availability, many clinical benefits of CEST have already been shown at 3T.

A slow exchanging rNOE peak very close to water (−1.6 ppm) could until now only be extracted at 9.4T (Zaiss et al., 2018; Zhang et al., 2016) but might provide insights into dynamic substrate binding, e.g., the reversible binding of caffeine or other molecules to receptors, in the brain (Yadav et al., 2017). As also visible in Figs. 28.4 and 28.6, the faster exchanging protons like guanidines at 2 ppm, amines at 3 ppm, and hydroxyls at 1–2 ppm strongly benefit from UHF and some of them can only be extracted at high field strengths (Chung et al., 2017). This leads to a growing number of extractable different CEST contrast with higher B_0 field, as illustrated in Fig. 28.6. An important amine CEST effect originates from glutamate (Cai et al., 2012), and its detection clearly benefits from UHF. For labeled glucose hydroxyls in dynamic glucose-enhanced CEST imaging, up to a factor of two larger effects can be measured in brain tumors when going from 3T (Herz et al., 2019) to 7T (Schuenke et al., 2017a). At 21T, glucose uptake rates could also be

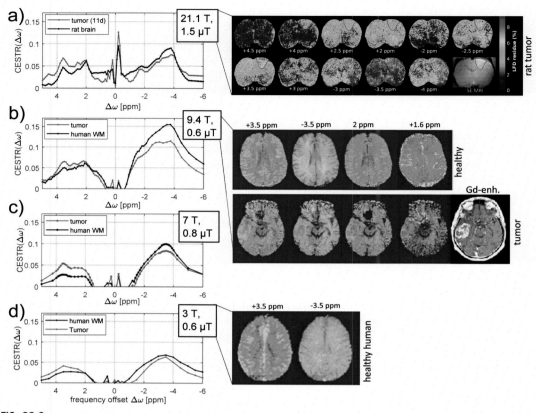

FIG. 28.6

In vivo CESTR-spectra for low B_1 amplitude at different B_0 fields between 21.1T (A) and 3T (D). The increasing spectral separation at higher B_0 and the decreased spillover dilution make it possible to extract more individual CEST peaks as separate image contrasts at higher field strengths. At 3T, only the coarse amide peak (3.5 ppm) and the rNOE peak (−3.5 ppm) can be extracted as images. At 7T (C) and 9.4T (B) more and more peaks are separable. At 21.1T, up to 11 different peaks can be evaluated as individual image contrast, which all show different features in brain tumors (B and D). *Panel A: 21.1T data from Roussel et al. (2018); panel B: 9.4T human data from Zaiss et al. (2018); panel C: 7T human data from Zaiss et al. (2017); and panel D: 3T human data from Deshmane et al. (2019). Figure reproduced from Zaiss et al. (2022).*

shown to be altered with neural activation (Roussel et al., 2019). Glucose CEST could thus form a novel neuroscientific tool and be an alternative to BOLD functional MRI.

Promising noninvasive applications of CEST at UHF in brain disease are more detailed tumor characterization (Heo et al., 2016; Paech et al., 2018), an alternative for gadolinium-enhanced imaging in tumors based on endogenous CEST (Zaiss et al., 2017) or glucose administration (Schuenke et al., 2017a; Xu et al., 2015), and early tumor therapy response monitoring via rNOE-CEST (Meissner et al., 2019). Glutamate CEST could lateralize nonlesional epilepsy (Hadar et al., 2021). 7T CEST can also serve as a biomarker for white-matter pathology (Dula et al., 2011, 2016), probably owed to the contribution of lipids to rNOE effects (Goerke et al., 2017b). The observed correlation of the rNOE-CEST effects with protein denaturation processes (Goerke et al., 2015, 2017a; Zaiss et al., 2013) also makes it a very interesting approach for investigating neurodegenerative disease, where first correlations were shown with Alzheimer's in mice (Chen et al., 2019). In the context of neurodegeneration, gray matter amide CEST signals of human brain scanned at 7T showed one of the most pronounced dependencies on the subject's age (Mennecke et al., 2022), as well the potential of early identification of Parkinson's disease. In animal studies, first 7T CEST signal changes in mitochondrial disease associated with lactate hydroxyl CEST effect could be found (Saito et al., 2019).

Finally, the high-field data provide insight into overlapping or unresolved peaks at lower field strengths, thus improving understanding and interpretation of, e.g., clinical 3T or 7T data, which is used to improve 3T fitting models (Goerke et al., 2019) or train predictive models (Zaiss et al., 2019a).

References

Cai, K., Haris, M., Singh, A., et al., 2012. Magnetic resonance imaging of glutamate. Nat. Med. 18, 302–306. https://doi.org/10.1038/nm.2615.

Chen, L., Wei, Z., Chan, K.W.Y., et al., 2019. Protein aggregation linked to Alzheimer's disease revealed by saturation transfer MRI. NeuroImage 188, 380–390. https://doi.org/10.1016/j.neuroimage.2018.12.018.

Chung, J.J., Choi, W., Jin, T., Lee, J.H., Kim, S.-G., 2017. Chemical-exchange-sensitive MRI of amide, amine and NOE at 9.4 T versus 15.2 T. NMR Biomed. 30. https://doi.org/10.1002/nbm.3740.

Deshmane, A., Zaiss, M., Lindig, T., et al., 2019. 3D gradient echo snapshot CEST MRI with low power saturation for human studies at 3T. Magn. Reson. Med. 81, 2412–2423. https://doi.org/10.1002/mrm.27569.

Dula, A.N., Asche, E.M., Landman, B.A., et al., 2011. Development of chemical exchange saturation transfer at 7T. Magn. Reson. Med. 66, 831–838. https://doi.org/10.1002/mrm.22862.

Dula, A.N., Pawate, S., Dethrage, L.M., et al., 2016. Chemical exchange saturation transfer of the cervical spinal cord at 7 T. NMR Biomed. 29, 1249–1257. https://doi.org/10.1002/nbm.3581.

Goerke, S., Zaiss, M., Kunz, P., et al., 2015. Signature of protein unfolding in chemical exchange saturation transfer imaging. NMR Biomed. 28, 906–913. https://doi.org/10.1002/nbm.3317.

Goerke, S., Milde, K.S., Bukowiecki, R., et al., 2017a. Aggregation-induced changes in the chemical exchange saturation transfer (CEST) signals of proteins. NMR Biomed. 30. https://doi.org/10.1002/nbm.3665.

Goerke, S., Zaiss, M., Longo, D., et al., 2017b. CEST signals of lipids. In: Proceeding of 25th Annual Meeting of ISMRM 2017, Honolulu 165.

Goerke, S., Soehngen, Y., Deshmane, A., et al., 2019. Relaxation-compensated APT and rNOE CEST-MRI of human brain tumors at 3 T. Magn. Reson. Med. 82, 622–632. https://doi.org/10.1002/mrm.27751.

Hadar, P.N., Kini, L.G., Nanga, R.P.R., et al., 2021. Volumetric glutamate imaging (GluCEST) using 7T MRI can lateralize nonlesional temporal lobe epilepsy: a preliminary study. Brain Behav. 11, e02134. https://doi.org/10.1002/brb3.2134.

Heo, H.-Y., Jones, C.K., Hua, J., et al., 2016. Whole-brain amide proton transfer (APT) and nuclear Overhauser enhancement (NOE) imaging in glioma patients using low-power steady-state pulsed chemical exchange saturation transfer (CEST) imaging at 7T. J. Magn. Reson. Imaging 44, 41–50. https://doi.org/10.1002/jmri.25108.

Herz, K., Lindig, T., Deshmane, A., et al., 2019. T1ρ-based dynamic glucose-enhanced (DGEρ) MRI at 3 T: method development and early clinical experience in the human brain. Magn. Reson. Med. 82, 1832–1847. https://doi.org/10.1002/mrm.27857.

Kim, M., Gillen, J., Landman, B.A., Zhou, J., van Zijl, P.C.M., 2009. Water saturation shift referencing (WASSR) for chemical exchange saturation transfer (CEST) experiments. Magn. Reson. Med. 61, 1441–1450. https://doi.org/10.1002/mrm.21873.

Liebert, A., Zaiss, M., Gumbrecht, R., et al., 2019. Multiple interleaved mode saturation (MIMOSA) for B 1+ inhomogeneity mitigation in chemical exchange saturation transfer. Magn. Reson. Med. 82, 693–705. https://doi.org/10.1002/mrm.27762.

Meissner, J.-E., Korzowski, A., Regnery, S., et al., 2019. Early response assessment of glioma patients to definitive chemoradiotherapy using chemical exchange saturation transfer imaging at 7 T. J. Magn. Reson. Imaging 50, 1268–1277. https://doi.org/10.1002/jmri.26702.

Mennecke, A., Khakzar, K.M., German, A., et al., 2022. 7 tricks for 7 T CEST: improving the reproducibility of multipool evaluation provides insights into the effects of age and the early stages of Parkinson's disease. NMR Biomed, e4717.

Paech, D., Windschuh, J., Oberhollenzer, J., et al., 2018. Assessing the predictability of IDH mutation and MGMT methylation status in glioma patients using relaxation-compensated multipool CEST MRI at 7.0 T. Neuro-Oncology 20, 1661–1671. https://doi.org/10.1093/neuonc/noy073.

Roussel, T., Rosenberg, J.T., Grant, S.C., Frydman, L., 2018. Brain investigations of rodent disease models by chemical exchange saturation transfer at 21.1 T. NMR Biomed. 31, e3995. https://doi.org/10.1002/nbm.3995.

Roussel, T., Frydman, L., Le Bihan, D., Ciobanu, L., 2019. Brain sugar consumption during neuronal activation detected by CEST functional MRI at ultra-high magnetic fields. Sci. Rep. 9, 4423. https://doi.org/10.1038/s41598-019-40986-9.

Saito, S., Takahashi, Y., Ohki, A., Shintani, Y., Higuchi, T., 2019. Early detection of elevated lactate levels in a mitochondrial disease model using chemical exchange saturation transfer (CEST) and magnetic resonance spectroscopy (MRS) at 7T-MRI. Radiol. Phys. Technol. 12, 46–54. https://doi.org/10.1007/s12194-018-0490-1.

Schuenke, P., Paech, D., Koehler, C., et al., 2017a. Fast and quantitative T1p-weighted dynamic glucose enhanced MRI. Sci. Rep. 7, 42093. https://doi.org/10.1038/srep42093.

Schuenke, P., Windschuh, J., Roeloffs, V., Ladd, M.E., Bachert, P., Zaiss, M., 2017b. Simultaneous mapping of water shift and B1(WASABI)—application to field-inhomogeneity correction of CEST MRI data. Magn. Reson. Med. 77, 571–580. https://doi.org/10.1002/mrm.26133.

Singh, A., Haris, M., Cai, K., et al., 2012. Chemical exchange saturation transfer magnetic resonance imaging of human knee cartilage at 3 T and 7 T. Magn. Reson. Med. 68, 588–594. https://doi.org/10.1002/mrm.23250.

Sun, P.Z., Farrar, C.T., Sorensen, A.G., 2007. Correction for artifacts induced by B(0) and B(1) field inhomogeneities in pH-sensitive chemical exchange saturation transfer (CEST) imaging. Magn. Reson. Med. 58, 1207–1215. https://doi.org/10.1002/mrm.21398.

Tse, D.H.Y., da Silva, N.A., Poser, B.A., Shah, N.J., 2017. B1+ inhomogeneity mitigation in CEST using parallel transmission. Magn. Reson. Med. 78, 2216–2225. https://doi.org/10.1002/mrm.26624.

Voelker, M.N., Kraff, O., Goerke, S., et al., 2021. The traveling heads 2.0: multicenter reproducibility of quantitative imaging methods at 7 Tesla. NeuroImage 232, 117910. https://doi.org/10.1016/j.neuroimage.2021.117910.

Windschuh, J., Zaiss, M., Meissner, J.-E., et al., 2015. Correction of B1-inhomogeneities for relaxation-compensated CEST imaging at 7T. NMR Biomed. 28, 529–537. https://doi.org/10.1002/nbm.3283.

Windschuh, J., Zaiss, M., Ehses, P., Lee, J.-S., Jerschow, A., Regatte, R.R., 2019. Assessment of frequency drift on CEST MRI and dynamic correction: application to gagCEST at 7 T. Magn. Reson. Med. 81, 573–582. https://doi.org/10.1002/mrm.27367.

Xu, X., Yadav, N.N., Knutsson, L., et al., 2015. Dynamic glucose-enhanced (DGE) MRI: translation to human scanning and first results in glioma patients. Tomography 1, 105–114. https://doi.org/10.18383/j.tom.2015.00175.

Yadav, N.N., Yang, X., Li, Y., Li, W., Liu, G., van Zijl, P.C.M., 2017. Detection of dynamic substrate binding using MRI. Sci. Rep. 7, 10138. https://doi.org/10.1038/s41598-017-10545-1.

Zaiss, M., Kunz, P., Goerke, S., Radbruch, A., Bachert, P., 2013. MR imaging of protein folding in vitro employing nuclear-Overhauser-mediated saturation transfer. NMR Biomed. 26, 1815–1822. https://doi.org/10.1002/nbm.3021.

Zaiss, M., Windschuh, J., Goerke, S., et al., 2017. Downfield-NOE-suppressed amide-CEST-MRI at 7 Tesla provides a unique contrast in human glioblastoma. Magn. Reson. Med. 77, 196–208. https://doi.org/10.1002/mrm.26100.

Zaiss, M., Schuppert, M., Deshmane, A., et al., 2018. Chemical exchange saturation transfer MRI contrast in the human brain at 9.4 T. NeuroImage 179, 144–155. https://doi.org/10.1016/j.neuroimage.2018.06.026.

Zaiss, M., Deshmane, A., Schuppert, M., et al., 2019a. DeepCEST: 9.4 T chemical exchange saturation transfer MRI contrast predicted from 3 T data—a proof of concept study. Magn. Reson. Med. 81, 3901–3914. https://doi.org/10.1002/mrm.27690.

Zaiss, M., Herz, K., Deshmane, A., et al., 2019b. Possible artifacts in dynamic CEST MRI due to motion and field alterations. J. Magn. Reson. 298, 16–22. https://doi.org/10.1016/j.jmr.2018.11.002.

Zaiss, M., Jin, T., Kim, S.-G., Gochberg, D.F., 2022. Theory of chemical exchange saturation transfer MRI in the context of different magnetic fields. NMR Biomed. 35, e4789. https://doi.org/10.1002/nbm.4789.

Zhang, X.-Y., Wang, F., Afzal, A., et al., 2016. A new NOE-mediated MT signal at around −1.6ppm for detecting ischemic stroke in rat brain. Magn. Reson. Imaging 34, 1100–1106. https://doi.org/10.1016/j.mri.2016.05.002.

Zhou, J., Heo, H.-Y., Knutsson, L., van Zijl, P.C.M., Jiang, S., 2019. APT-weighted MRI: techniques, current neuro applications, and challenging issues. J. Magn. Reson. Imaging 50, 347–364. https://doi.org/10.1002/jmri.26645.

Benefits of ultra-high field in clinical applications

Epilepsy

Gilbert Hangel[a,b], Karl Rössler[a], and Siegfried Trattnig[b]

[a]*Department of Neurosurgery, Medical University of Vienna, Vienna, Austria* [b]*High Field MR Centre, Medical University of Vienna, Vienna, Austria*

Highlights

- Ultra-high field imaging, specifically 7T MRI, allows higher resolution, enhanced contrast, and advanced MRI methods that can be utilized to identify epileptogenic lesions not visible at lower fields.
- Systematic reviews have confirmed that 7T MRI can identify lesions in a substantial number of such cases, but the total number of MR exams performed so far remains too low for precise estimations.
- To address this sparsity of data, there is now a consensus protocol for 7T epilepsy imaging that can guide the community toward a clearer definition of 7T benefits.
- Advanced techniques available at 7T that can image metabolism and function can add information on epileptogenicity beyond lesion morphology.

29.1 Background and clinical relevance

With at least 50 million cases worldwide (Ngugi et al., 2010), epilepsy is a major neurological disorder that causes seizures and associated cognitive, psychological, and social impairments (Holmes, 2015), as well as increased mortality (Sharma et al., 2015). After continuous refinements in classification since the 1960s, the International League Against Epilepsy (ILAE) (Scheffer et al., 2017) currently defines epilepsy diagnostics according to seizure type (focal, generalized, unknown) and epilepsy type (focal, generalized, combined generalized and focal, unknown) (Fig. 29.1). For this work, we will generally address focal epilepsy.

Focal epilepsy can be uni- or multifocal and includes seizures that involve localized regions or networks. While electroencephalography (EEG) in focal epilepsy mainly shows focal epileptiform discharges, a clinical diagnosis is generally achieved based on structural neuroimaging in the form of MRI. Epilepsy has a wide range of possible causes (Fig. 29.1), but focal epilepsy is mainly attributed to a structural etiology, more or less clearly visible on MRI, which can originate from stroke, trauma, infection, and cortical malformations during development (overlapping with genetic etiologies, such as tuberous sclerosis).

While the majority of cases are pharmaco-responsive, i.e., can be treated using pharmaceuticals, up to 40% of cases in which these measures fail to control seizures need to be classified as "pharmaco-resistant epilepsy," "drug-resistant focal epilepsy (DRFE)," or "refractory epilepsy" (Ryvlin et al., 2014). For refractory epilepsy, surgical resection or laser interstitial thermal therapy (LITT) of the

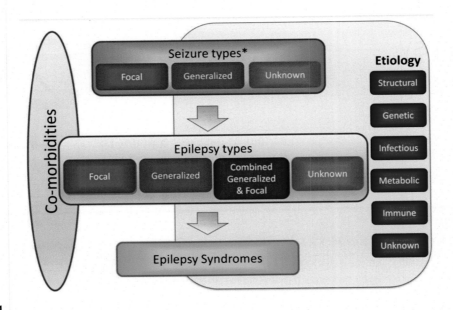

FIG. 29.1

Overview of the contemporary classification structure of etiology, seizure types, and epilepsy types. *Denotes the onset of seizure. *Reproduced with permission from Scheffer et al. (2017).*

epileptogenic zone has the highest chance for seizure relief (Wiebe et al., 2001), but these measures require information about the location of specific zones in the brain. MRI can supply this localization, but in approximately one-third of refractory epilepsy cases, called "MR-negative" (MRN), no such focus can be identified (Opheim et al., 2021). Even in the other two-thirds, MRI characterization can be complicated (Bernasconi et al., 2019), as a clear delineation of the epileptogenic zone is difficult due to many factors. One example is the definition of lesion boundaries, such as ganglioglioma margins in proximity to motor/sensory areas or the distinction of gray matter/white matter (GM/WM) in focal cortical dysplasia (FCD). Another example is the distribution of epileptogenic networks outside discernible zones (Laufs, 2012). Nonetheless, standards designed to achieve the best localization for clinical MRI at 1.5 Tesla (T) and 3T have been established (Bernasconi et al., 2019).

29.2 State-of-the-art imaging of patients with epilepsy

Modern MRI has the potential to identify even small anomalies in brain morphology based on the combination of different contrasts. The main target etiologies in focal pharmaco-resistant epilepsy are FCD, tumors (ganglioglioma, dysembryoplastic neuroepithelial tumor (DNET)), hippocampal sclerosis, and vascular malformations, such as arteriovenous malformations (AVM) and cavernomas. State-of-the-art protocols in radiology will include at least isometric T_1-weighted MRI (target parameters: cortical thickness; GM/WM-interface; aberrant gray matter), T_2-weighted MRI (target parameters: cortical and subcortical hyperintensities), T_2^*-weighted MRI (target parameters:

calcifications and hemosiderin rim), and fluid-attenuated inversion recovery (FLAIR) (target parameters: cortical and subcortical hyperintensities) imaging (Bernasconi et al., 2019).

For example, for FCDs, diagnostic parameters are the blurring in the subcortical GM/WM interface and trans-mantle signs. In contrast, cavernomas feature a T_2^*-hypointense zone, the hemosiderin rim. Hippocampal sclerosis is the most frequent cause of refractory epilepsy (Blumcke et al., 2013) and visible as one or more T_2-hyperintense lesions, shape alterations, and atrophy. Gangliogliomas are more difficult to discern due to highly variant T_1 hypointensity and T_2^* hyperintensity, which make them difficult to delineate and even to differentiate from other brain tumor types. This is summarized in Table 29.1. As stated above, two-thirds of structural abnormalities can be identified this way, but their extent often remains underestimated.

Additional MRI modalities have been found to be beneficial but have not yet become part of recognized standard protocols. This includes susceptibility-weighted imaging (SWI) (target parameters: hemosiderin rim, calcifications), diffusion tensor imaging (DTI) (target parameters: neuronal structure, brain connectivity), and functional MRI (fMRI) (target parameters: localization of motor, language, memory areas, postsurgical cognitive performance, functional connectivity) (Szaflarski et al., 2017). These advanced protocols go beyond a purely structural description and try to image epileptogenic zones and healthy brain function for better surgical planning and outcome evaluation.

29.3 **Relevance for neurosurgery**

Neurosurgical procedures, including resection, disconnection, invasive monitoring with intracranial electrodes combined with electrostimulation, as well as lesioning therapies, such as MR-guided LITT, are treatment options for focal pharmaco-resistant epilepsy. Neurosurgery does require a precise definition of epileptogenic zones and healthy brain matter in order to achieve the best seizure outcome and minimal side effects. But, as the performance of clinical MRI in this regard is limited (Scheffer et al., 2017), neurosurgical procedures based on clinical MRI have not yet reached their full potential. Postsurgical histopathology and seizure status remain the diagnostic gold standard, but are available only

Table 29.1 A summary of important etiologies of pharmaco-resistant epilepsy, their diagnostic parameters/underlying brain alterations, and corresponding radiological markers.

Category	Brain pathology	Diagnostic parameters	Radiology
Focal cortical dysplasia (FCD)	Malformed neuronal structures	Subcortical WM intensities, blurring of the GM/WM interface	Cortical thickness, blurring of the GM/WM interface, trans-mantle signs
Ganglioglioma	Slow-growing neoplasms, often located in the temporal lobes	Tumor margins	T_1 hypointensity and T_2^* hyperintensity
Cavernoma	Malformations of blood vessels into cavernous structures	Hemosiderin rim, developmental venous anomalies	T_2^* hypointensity
Hippocampal sclerosis	Loss of hippocampal neurons connected to TLE	Sclerosis and atrophy in the hippocampus	T_2 hyperintensity

after surgery, which requires challenging decision-making about resection targets by epilepsy boards for the one-third of MRN cases based only on EEG and positron-emission tomography (PET). In these MRN cases, the odds of a seizure-free outcome are reduced by at least a factor of two compared to patients with MRI-visible lesions (Bernasconi et al., 2019). However, delaying or even avoiding surgery in these MRN patients causes negative side effects that can include cognitive deficits and reduced life expectancy due to sudden unexpected death in epilepsy (SUDEP) (Bernasconi et al., 2019).

With their potentially higher spatial resolution and image contrast, 7T MRI scanners offer another chance for the identification and delineation of epileptic zones that cannot be discerned at lower fields. Promising imaging techniques have been introduced, and studies have identified the potential benefits of 7T MRI for epilepsy imaging.

29.4 7T state-of-the-art neuroimaging

After over a decade of research with ultra-high field human MRI scanners, which are mostly 7T devices, the theoretical benefits of 7T MRI have been applied to concrete clinical questions in neuroimaging (Trattnig et al., 2018). This ranges from better delineation of hippocampal sclerosis, due to higher resolution, to better visibility of vascular malformations using SWI. As detailed in previous chapters, and briefly summarized here, the increased field strength compared to 3T or 1.5T increases the signal-to-noise ratio, supralinearly from 3T to 7T which allows higher resolution and/or faster scans while comparatively longer T_1s and shorter T_2s and T_2^*s alter contrast behavior, which is inherently beneficial for SWI and blood oxygen level-dependent (BOLD) MRI. Magnetic resonance spectroscopy (MRS) benefits from increased spectral separation of resonances and increased SNR as well. Specific improvements for contrast and acquisition methodologies have been described abundantly in previous chapters. For the common disadvantages of increased B_0 and B_1 inhomogeneity, increased specific absorption rate (SAR), and susceptibility artifacts, solutions including parallel transmit systems, RF shimming, dedicated local shim coils, and other methods have been introduced.

Specifically for epilepsy imaging, the expectation of reduced MRN diagnoses compared to lower fields has driven 7T research and studies (Fig. 29.2). This year (2021) alone has seen thus far two metaanalyses of 7T epilepsy imaging (Park et al., 2021; van Lanen et al., 2021) and a consensus protocol paper (Opheim et al., 2021).

Overall, the initial imaging studies in epilepsy using 7T MRI have already identified benefits that range from the improved delineation of cavernomas (Frischer et al., 2012) to better detection of FCDs (Colon et al., 2016) and more detailed resolution of the different hippocampal scleroses (Stefanits et al., 2017). Studies with surgical sampling and histology have confirmed 7T-defined epileptogenic zones (Feldman et al., 2019) and found zones in one-third of 3T MRN patients (Colon et al., 2016). Two recent systematic reviews have now established a far more thorough understanding of the current state of 7T epilepsy imaging.

van Lanen et al. (2021) analyzed 16 studies, with diagnostic benefits of 7T imaging from 8% up to 67% in individual studies and a pooled identification of pathologies in 3T MRN cases of 31% of all patients. Freedom from seizures (i.e., Engel class I) was reported in 73% of all patients who received surgery, but no study has compared the outcomes between 7T MRN, 7T with identified zones, and 3T with identified zones. Therefore, effective treatment improvement due to the inclusion of 7T MRI has not been established as yet. FCD (54%), hippocampal sclerosis (12%), and gliosis (8.1%) were

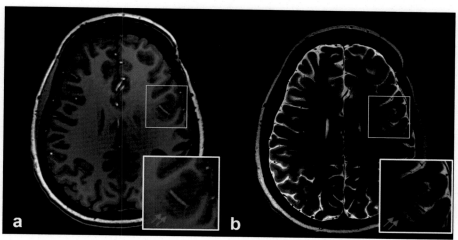

FIG. 29.2

7T visibility of FCD on T_1-weighted and T_2-weighted 7T MRI. Blurring of the gray-white matter junction *(double arrows)*, abnormally thick malformed cortex, an indistinct cortical ribbon in the left inferior frontal gyrus, and T_2 hyperintensity in the subjacent white matter are visible. *Reproduced under Creative Commons Attribution 4.0 International License from Vachha and Huang (2021).*

identified as the most common etiologies, with T_2^*-weighted imaging as the overall most useful modality. For FCD, FLAIR and T_2^*w imaging best defined lesion extent. For temporal lobe epilepsy, T_1-weighted MP2RAGE and T_2-weighted TSE performed best. In hippocampal sclerosis, it was T_2-weighted TSE and SWI, which also performed best in vascular abnormalities. One such vascular abnormality case, a cavernoma with an associated developmental venous anomaly, is presented in Fig. 29.3.

In a second systematic review, Park et al. (2021) evaluated 25 studies with 467 patients and 167 healthy control subjects overall. Nine of these studies, which compared 7T to lower fields, found a detection rate of 65% versus 22%. In particular, 7T MRI of the hippocampus was found to be beneficial. In summary, both systematic reviews agree that 7T MRI can supply diagnostic information in at least one-third of cases that are MRN at lower fields.

Still, due to the limited number of studies and subjects spread over different protocols and etiologies, the role of 7T MRI in epilepsy is still evolving. In order to support this process, the 7T Epilepsy Task Force, an international consortium of twenty-one 7T sites, has proposed a consensus protocol that defines a standard for further research (Opheim et al., 2021). Beyond advice on 7T safety, patient recruitment criteria, and clinical reference, the guidelines suggest the following protocol to utilize 7T resolution and contrast benefits: 3D sequences with submillimeter resolution for T_1w-MRI (MPRAGE or MP2RAGE); T_2w-MRI (TSE) and FLAIR with added T_2^*w-MRI (such as SWI); and T_2w-MRI of the hippocampus with 0.25–0.5 mm resolution. A possible extension is white matter-suppressed imaging (WMS) for the visualization of gray matter aberrations. Fig. 29.4 presents results from such a scan protocol, highlighting the imaging benefits, as well as the limitations of 7T, such as

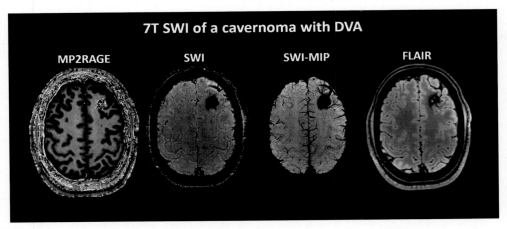

FIG. 29.3

7T SWI of a cavernoma with adjacent developmental venous anomaly (31-year-old male patient) compared to MP2RAGE and FLAIR imaging.

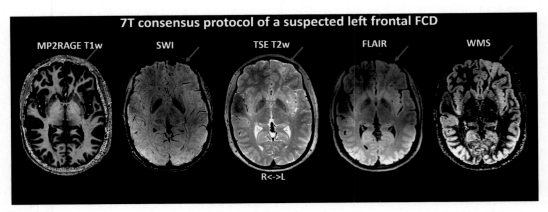

FIG. 29.4

7T consensus protocol results in a patient with suspected FCD (30-year-old female). The lesion is visible on all scans.

susceptibility artifacts and field inhomogeneities. The task force further identified specific lesion types of focal pharmaco-resistant epilepsy of interest beyond FCD, namely, tuberous sclerosis, ganglioglioma, DNET, vascular malformations, mesial temporal sclerosis, and polymicrogyria.

While these studies have focused heavily on morphological delineation of lesions, 7T scanners also allow advanced metabolic and functional imaging beyond the possible scope of clinical 1.5T and 3T systems.

29.5 Advanced epilepsy imaging at 7T

While the evaluation of morphological benefits of 7T compared to 3T is a good start, advanced 7T MRI methods can add new information that could further improve diagnostics and delineation through the use of metabolic imaging (MRSI, CEST), nonproton MRI (sodium), functional MRI, and quantitative MRI (QSM, MRF).

Magnetic resonance spectroscopy (MRS), consisting of single-voxel spectroscopy (SVS) and MR spectroscopic imaging (MRSI), is an established methodology that has seen limited clinical use, mainly in brain tumor grading and definition of tumor borders. Limitations, such as low resolution, long scan times, and reliance on selection boxes, have limited its utility, especially in MRN epilepsy where explorative brain coverage would be necessary. Instead, PET is used to boost the identification of lesions and epileptogenic networks. Nonetheless, MRS studies at lower fields have identified metabolic changes, mainly in the form of increased choline/*N*-acetylaspartate and creatine/*N*-acetylaspartate ratios (Mueller et al., 2005). 7T SVS studies have confirmed these findings and could further quantify the neurotransmitters, glutamate, and γ-aminobutyric acid (Gonen et al., 2020). As respective excitatory and inhibitory neurotransmitters, their importance to epileptogenesis has been demonstrated, for example, by excitotoxicity (Nicolo et al., 2019). Initial findings for glutamate and other compounds, such as glutathione, hint at the possibilities to identify epileptic activity and postresection seizure outcome (Gonen et al., 2020). 7T MRSI studies have been even more limited in scope thus far but could offer insight into spatial metabolic distributions necessary for future planning of resection extent. In the first 7T MRSI study published, increased creatine/*N*-acetylaspartate in hippocampal lesions correlated with postsurgical patient outcomes (Pan et al., 2013). Another study found correlation networks for glutamate and γ-aminobutyric acid using semi-LASER-based MRSI (van Veenendaal et al., 2018). Both were limited in resolution and brain coverage, but recent progress in 7T MRSI acquisition using spatial-spectral encoding (Hingerl et al., 2020) is a promising candidate with initial results in epilepsy patients shown at the ISMRM 2021 (Hangel et al., 2021). Fig. 29.5 demonstrates such high-resolution metabolic imaging in FCD and its correspondence to surgical resection. This approach also demonstrated the separation of glutamate and glutamine resonances (Hingerl et al., 2020), which could potentially improve studies of the role of glutamate in epilepsy.

Next to MRSI, chemical exchange saturation transfer imaging (CEST), with its ability to selectively image certain neurochemicals, has been developed for 7T metabolic imaging. For epilepsy, early studies have applied glutamate CEST (Neal et al., 2019; Nicolo et al., 2019) and found increased peritumoral contrast to correlate with seizures. Beyond proton MRI methods, other nuclei can be detected using dedicated coils. While phosphorous MRS has been the most prevalent of these so-called "X-nuclei" methods due to its ability to directly measure metabolism, for epilepsy, sodium ($_{23}$Na) has been the main focus of investigation using 7T MRI, due to the role of sodium channels of cell membranes in ionic homeostasis and cell viability (Opheim et al., 2021; Ridley et al., 2017). One possible sodium MRI-derived biomarker could be variations of T_2^* relaxation time parameters (Kolbe et al., 2020). Another nuclei, deuterium, which can be applied as a tracer in molecules like glucose, has recently been demonstrated to allow deuterium metabolic imaging (DMI) in volunteers and glioma patients (De Feyter et al., 2018). While DMI has not been applied to epilepsy as yet, it could be used to image the relation of glucose to glutamate in epileptogenic networks.

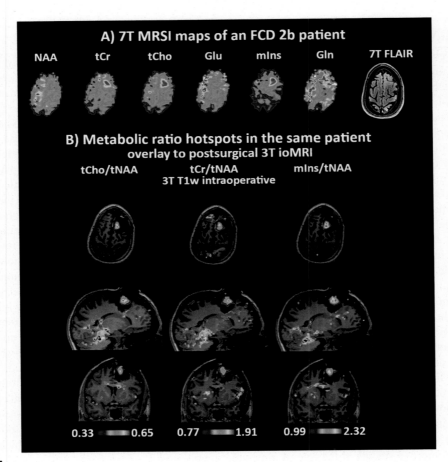

FIG. 29.5

High-resolution MRSI of a histologically verified FCD 2b patient (31-year-old male) compared to intraoperative MRI. Eventual surgical resection shows a good correspondence of choline and myo-inositol to N-acetylaspartate ratios to the resected volume. Surgery was not based on or influenced by MRSI data. The underlying MRSI method (Hingerl et al., 2020) used free induction decay and concentric ring trajectories to acquire full cerebrum metabolic maps with 3.4 mm nominal isotropic resolution in 15 min.

Functional MRI is a staple of neuroscientific research and benefits from the increased BOLD contrast between rest and activation due to shorter T_2^* times at 7T (Moser et al., 2012). A study by Shah et al. (2019) investigated changes in the temporal lobe/hippocampus networks of patients with temporal lobe epilepsy, using fMRI and MRI. Next to volumetric differences, they identified significant differences for functional network asymmetry between patients with visible lesions and no detectable lesions.

Quantitative 7T MRI applications for epilepsy have not yet been explored, but based on the findings in conventional epilepsy MRI and lower-field research, quantitative susceptibility imaging (QSM) (Lorio et al., 2021) and magnetic resonance fingerprinting (MRF) (Ma et al., 2019) seem to be promising tools. A recent multicenter study has confirmed a higher reproducibility for χ and R_2^* at 7T compared to 3T, which could be beneficial when progressing from SWI to QSM for the evaluation of epileptogenic lesions (Rua et al., 2020). MRF would be attractive as a source of T_2 maps, but for human brain 7T MRI, there is, to date, only a single exploratory study only (Yu et al., 2020).

29.6 Summary and conclusions: UHF MRI—Why do we want it?
29.6.1 Summary

Around 30%–40% of epilepsy cases are pharmaco-resistant. Focal epilepsy often is linked to a structural etiology that may be visualized on MRI (with T_2- and T_2^*-weighted imaging as the most important clinical modalities). In these cases, freedom from seizures with surgery can reach 70%–80% but requires satisfactory lesion delineation. At least one-third of focal epilepsy cases are MRN, significantly reducing the patient's odds of a seizure-free outcome. Any delay to surgery exacerbates cognitive deficits and reduces life expectancy due to SUDEP.

7T MRI offers a greater signal-to-noise ratio and different relaxation times that can be translated into higher spatial resolution within the same scan time as 3T and increased tissue contrast, especially for T_2^*w-MRI, such as SWI and fMRI. Disadvantages, such as SAR and B_0/B_1-inhomogeneities, can be minimized using specific software and hardware that have been developed over the last decade. Systematic reviews (Park et al., 2021; van Lanen et al., 2021) have found that 7T MRI can identify lesions in a substantial number of 3T MRN cases, with FCD and hippocampal sclerosis benefitting the most. Depending on the etiology, T_2w- and T_2^*w-MRI (FCD), T_2w-MRI and SWI (temporal lobe epilepsy and hippocampal sclerosis), or SWI (vascular abnormalities) provided the highest contributions to sensitivity.

Despite these studies, an overall lack of patient examinations at 7T and nonstandardized protocols limits our current knowledge. To address this, the 7T Epilepsy Task Force proposed a consensus protocol that could standardize further studies. The task force advises 3D T_1w-MRI, T_2w-MRI, and FLAIR with submillimeter resolution, T_2^*w-MRI such as SWI and T_2w-MRI of the hippocampus, with possible additions, such as WMS imaging.

Advanced MRI modalities could add more information that extends from morphology to metabolism (MRSI, CEST, X-nuclei) and functional connectivity (fMRI), but it is still in early phase of clinical research. There have only been first explorative studies in epilepsy patients. Quantitative MRI (QSM, MRF) could enhance protocols even further with regard to comparability.

29.6.2 Conclusions

Ongoing research has already clearly established that there are benefits with the use of 7T MRI for the imaging of focal epilepsy allowing for the better delineation of epileptogenic zones and potentially improved surgery planning. No applications in humans in vivo at even higher fields are currently available. For advanced 7T methods, despite their early application stages, we foresee a key role for metabolic and functional imaging to enhance morphological protocols. One of the key points could be the role of glutamate as a neurotransmitter in epileptogenesis (Nicolo et al., 2019).

Further progress will require greater efforts, such as randomized control trials, multicenter studies, the evaluation of 7T-guided surgery, the creation of comprehensive data banks, and radiomics to analyze the expected cornucopia of imaging data. The recent consensus protocol will hopefully be the basis for such renewed efforts, offering an array of contrasts that have been proven beneficial for the localization of the most difficult focal epilepsy cases. Such efforts will also require substantial funding, necessitating a strong advocacy for UHF imaging for epilepsy. Neither can be considered independently, and a clear analysis of expected gains beyond existing data is required. Only a positive feedback loop of ever more comprehensive studies will accomplish this.

Yet, we should not forget the long-term goals of our community beyond just developing better imaging techniques: the greater understanding of the complexities inherent to epileptogenesis and improved patient seizure outcome that will result from better surgical treatment based on enhanced lesion detection and definition. Our quest for these lofty goals has really just begun.

References

Bernasconi, A., Cendes, F., Theodore, W.H., et al., 2019. Recommendations for the use of structural magnetic resonance imaging in the care of patients with epilepsy: a consensus report from the International League Against Epilepsy Neuroimaging Task Force. Epilepsia 60, epi.15612.

Blumcke, I., Cross, J.H., Spreafico, R., 2013. The international consensus classification for hippocampal sclerosis: an important step towards accurate prognosis. Lancet Neurol. 12, 844–846.

Colon, A.J., van Osch, M.J.P., Buijs, M., et al., 2016. Detection superiority of 7 T MRI protocol in patients with epilepsy and suspected focal cortical dysplasia. Acta Neurol. Belg. 116, 259–269.

De Feyter, H.M., Behar, K.L., Corbin, Z.A., et al., 2018. Deuterium metabolic imaging (DMI) for MRI-based 3D mapping of metabolism in vivo. Sci. Adv. 4, eaat7314.

Feldman, R.E., Delman, B.N., Pawha, P.S., et al., 2019. 7T MRI in epilepsy patients with previously normal clinical MRI exams compared against healthy controls. PLoS One 14, e0213642.

Frischer, J.M., Göd, S., Gruber, A., et al., 2012. Susceptibility-weighted imaging at 7 T: improved diagnosis of cerebral cavernous malformations and associated developmental venous anomalies. NeuroImage Clin. 1, 116–120.

Gonen, O.M., Moffat, B.A., Desmond, P.M., Lui, E., Kwan, P., O'Brien, T.J., 2020. Seven-tesla quantitative magnetic resonance spectroscopy of glutamate, γ-aminobutyric acid, and glutathione in the posterior cingulate cortex/precuneus in patients with epilepsy. Epilepsia 61 (12), 2785–2794.

Hangel, G., Lazen, P., Tomschik, M., et al., 2021. CRT-FID-MRSI at 7T for the high-resolution metabolic imaging of epilepsy: preliminary results. In: Proceedings of the International Society for Magnetic Resonance in Medicine 29th Annual Meeting, p. 0723.

Hingerl, L., Strasser, B., Moser, P., et al., 2020. Clinical high-resolution 3D-MR spectroscopic imaging of the human brain at 7 T. Investig. Radiol. 55, 239–248.

Holmes, G.L., 2015. Cognitive impairment in epilepsy: the role of network abnormalities. Epileptic Disord. 17, 101–116.

Kolbe, S.C., Syeda, W., Blunck, Y., et al., 2020. Microstructural correlates of 23Na relaxation in human brain at 7 Tesla. NeuroImage 211, 116609.

Laufs, H., 2012. Functional imaging of seizures and epilepsy. Curr. Opin. Neurol. 25, 194–200.

Lorio, S., Sedlacik, J., So, P.-W., et al., 2021. Quantitative MRI susceptibility mapping reveals cortical signatures of changes in iron, calcium and zinc in malformations of cortical development in children with drug-resistant epilepsy. NeuroImage 238, 118102.

Ma, D., Jones, S.E., Deshmane, A., et al., 2019. Development of high-resolution 3D MR fingerprinting for detection and characterization of epileptic lesions. J. Magn. Reson. Imaging 49, 1333–1346.

Moser, E., Stahlberg, F., Ladd, M.E., Trattnig, S., 2012. 7-T MR-from research to clinical applications? NMR Biomed. 25, 695–716.

Mueller, S.G., Laxer, K.D., Barakos, J.A., et al., 2005. Metabolic characteristics of cortical malformations causing epilepsy. J. Neurol. 252, 1082–1092.

Neal, A., Moffat, B.A., Stein, J.M., et al., 2019. Glutamate weighted imaging contrast in gliomas with 7 Tesla magnetic resonance imaging. NeuroImage Clin. 22, 101694.

Ngugi, A.K., Bottomley, C., Kleinschmidt, I., Sander, J.W., Newton, C.R., 2010. Estimation of the burden of active and life-time epilepsy: a meta-analytic approach. Epilepsia 51, 883–890.

Nicolo, J.-P., O'Brien, T.J., Kwan, P., 2019. Role of cerebral glutamate in post-stroke epileptogenesis. NeuroImage Clin. 24, 102069.

Opheim, G., van der Kolk, A., Bloch, K.M., et al., 2021. 7T epilepsy task force consensus recommendations on the use of 7T in clinical practice. Neurology 96. https://doi.org/10.1212/WNL.0000000000011413.

Pan, J.W., Duckrow, R.B., Gerrard, J., et al., 2013. 7T MR spectroscopic imaging in the localization of surgical epilepsy. Epilepsia 54, 1668–1678.

Park, J.E., Cheong, E.-N., Jung, D.E., Shim, W.H., Lee, J.S., 2021. Utility of 7 Tesla magnetic resonance imaging in patients with epilepsy: a systematic review and meta-analysis. Front. Neurol. 12, 621936.

Ridley, B., Marchi, A., Wirsich, J., et al., 2017. Brain sodium MRI in human epilepsy: disturbances of ionic homeostasis reflect the organization of pathological regions. NeuroImage 157, 173–183.

Rua, C., Clarke, W.T., Driver, I.D., et al., 2020. Multi-centre, multi-vendor reproducibility of 7T QSM and R2* in the human brain: results from the UK7T study. NeuroImage 223, 117358.

Ryvlin, P., Cross, J.H., Rheims, S., 2014. Epilepsy surgery in children and adults. Lancet Neurol. 13, 1114–1126.

Scheffer, I.E., Berkovic, S., Capovilla, G., et al., 2017. ILAE classification of the epilepsies: position paper of the ILAE Commission for Classification and Terminology. Epilepsia 58, 512–521.

Shah, P., Bassett, D.S., Wisse, L.E.M., et al., 2019. Structural and functional asymmetry of medial temporal subregions in unilateral temporal lobe epilepsy: a 7T MRI study. Hum. Brain Mapp. 40, 2390–2398.

Sharma, A.K., Rani, E., Waheed, A., Rajput, S.K., 2015. Pharmacoresistant epilepsy: a current update on non-conventional pharmacological and non-pharmacological interventions. J. Epilepsy Res. 5, 1–8.

Stefanits, H., Springer, E., Pataraia, E., et al., 2017. Seven-tesla MRI of hippocampal sclerosis: an in vivo feasibility study with histological correlations. Investig. Radiol. 52, 666–671.

Szaflarski, J.P., Gloss, D., Binder, J.R., et al., 2017. Practice guideline summary: use of fMRI in the presurgical evaluation of patients with epilepsy. Neurology 88, 395–402.

Trattnig, S., Springer, E., Bogner, W., et al., 2018. Key clinical benefits of neuroimaging at 7 T. NeuroImage 168, 477–489.

Vachha, B., Huang, S.Y., 2021. MRI with ultrahigh field strength and high-performance gradients: challenges and opportunities for clinical neuroimaging at 7T and beyond. Eur. Radiol. Exp. 5, 35.

van Lanen, R.H.G.J., Colon, A.J., Wiggins, C.J., et al., 2021. Ultra-high field magnetic resonance imaging in human epilepsy: a systematic review. NeuroImage Clin. 30, 102602.

van Veenendaal, T.M., Backes, W.H., Tse, D.H.Y., et al., 2018. High field imaging of large-scale neurotransmitter networks: proof of concept and initial application to epilepsy. NeuroImage Clin. 19, 47–55.

Wiebe, S., Blume, W.T., Girvin, J.P., Eliasziw, M., 2001. A randomized, controlled trial of surgery for temporal-lobe epilepsy. N. Engl. J. Med. 345, 311–318.

Yu, Z., Madelin, G., Sodickson, D.K., Cloos, M.A., 2020. Simultaneous proton magnetic resonance fingerprinting and sodium MRI. Magn. Reson. Med. 83, 2232–2242.

Multiple sclerosis

30

Caterina Mainero[a,b] and Constantina A. Treaba[a,b]

[a]*Athinoula A. Martinos Center for Biomedical Imaging, Department of Radiology, Massachusetts General Hospital, Boston, MA, United States* [b]*Harvard Medical School, Boston, MA, United States*

Highlights

- The sensitivity of cortical lesion detection and specifically of the most frequent subtype subpial lesions is increased at 7T relative to lower field strength MRI.
- At 7T, the quantitative imaging approaches allow the estimation of the microstructural changes that extend beyond the visible limits of the lesions.
- 7T MRI provides enhanced lesion details that favor the identification of new radiological biomarkers (such as the central vein sign and the presence of a paramagnetic rim) that may play a decisive role in diagnosing and predicting the severity of the disease.
- The multiple sclerosis lesions located in the thalamus, cerebellum, and spinal cord can be more clearly defined at ultra-high field MRI than at lower field MR strength.

30.1 Introduction

Multiple sclerosis (MS) is a chronic inflammatory demyelinating and neurodegenerative disorder of the CNS and the leading cause of nontraumatic neurological disability in young adults in Western countries. Although traditionally considered the prototypical white matter CNS disease, MS often and extensively involves the gray matter at all disease stages.

Magnetic resonance imaging is pivotal for early MS diagnosis, investigating disease pathophysiology, and monitoring treatment response in clinical practice and experimental trials.

Ultra-high field MRI (7T) has gained a crucial role in MS, demonstrated by considerable research work, identifying novel radiological signs that can aid disease diagnosis and monitoring. Despite presenting some challenges related to B_0 and B_1 field inhomogeneities and higher energy deposition, ultra-high field systems show a significant increase in signal-to-noise ratio and, consequently, an increase in spatial resolution compared with 1.5T–3T MRI, allowing the detection of tissue abnormalities otherwise not visible at lower field strength. The use of susceptibility-weighted images at 7T has also been shown to improve gray/white matter contrast, better identifying the lesion territory. Furthermore, the availability of quantitative and metabolic imaging approaches that can investigate CNS tissue microstructure has improved our understanding of MS pathology beyond macroscopically visible lesions.

In this chapter, we will review the main advantages of ultra-high field systems (mainly 7T MRI) relative to lower field MRI for studying MS, which focus on an increased ability to detect and characterize lesioned tissue in the brain and spinal cord and to assess diffuse microstructural damage (Fig. 30.1).

We will then discuss how these achievements could be relevant for improving MS diagnosis, aid in the differential diagnosis, and assist in monitoring the disease outcome and, potentially, the effects of therapeutic approaches.

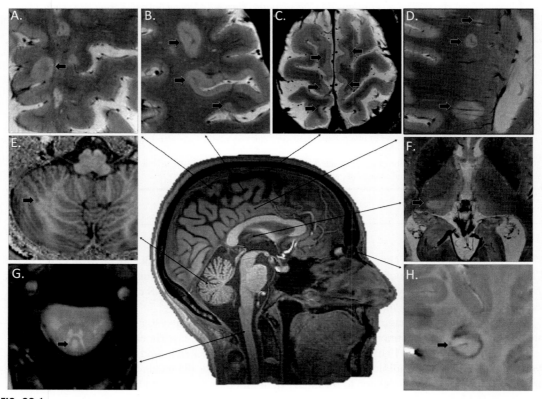

FIG. 30.1

7T MRI in detecting, delineating, and characterization of MS lesions. Examples of leukocortical (A) intracortical, and subpial lesions (B and C) on an axial T_2^* sequence at 7T in a patient with relapsing-remitting MS. The central vessel sign is present in most white matter lesions on T_2^* imaging at 7T (D). MP2RAGE acquisition shows its usefulness in cerebellar leukocortical lesion delineation (E). Thalamic lesion details (arrow to central vein) are well depicted by 7T MRI (F). Hyperintense T_2^* spinal cord lesion involving the white matter dorsal columns (G) as detected by ultra-high field MRI. The phase sequence at 7T identifies the hypointense paramagnetic rim that delineates the periphery of a white matter lesion (H).

30.2 Increased lesion detection
30.2.1 Cortex

Histopathological observations demonstrate that cortical demyelination is frequent and extensive during MS, particularly in patients with progressive disease. Cortical demyelinating lesions can develop from the earliest MS stages and are associated with neurological disability and disease progression.

The increase in signal-to-noise ratio achieved at 7T can be translated into a spatial image resolution in the submillimeter range and exquisite contrast for visualizing details within both the gray and the white matter. Cortical lesion visualization benefits from these advantages the most. Although we are still far from revealing the true number of cortical lesions in vivo, ultra-high field MRI can detect more than twice as many cortical lesions as 3T strength systems (Kilsdonk et al., 2016).

The gain in resolution and delineation across cortical layers allows the in vivo identification at 7T of the same cortical lesion subtypes (Mainero et al., 2009; Pitt et al., 2010) observed in histopathological studies: the type I leukocortical lesions located at the cortical-subcortical junction; type II intracortical plaques, wholly enclosed in the cortex without reaching its margins; type III-IV subpial lesions, extending downward from the juxtameningeal pial surface through different depths (layer III) or across the entire width of the cortex (layer IV), often extending along several gyri.

Different pulse sequences have been applied at 7T and optimized over time [T_2^*-weighted gradient echo, T_2-weighted, fluid-attenuated inversion recovery (FLAIR), double inversion recovery (DIR), T_1-weighted magnetization prepared rapid acquisition gradient echo (MPRAGE/MP2RAGE)] in efforts to determine which one might have the highest value for clinical use (Mainero et al., 2009; Pitt et al., 2010; Kilsdonk et al., 2016; Beck et al., 2018).

As different techniques seem to favor the identification of different subtypes of cortical lesions, the information offered by different contrasts is frequently complementary and, jointly, can only increase the definition of cortical lesions. Cortical lesion identification and segmentation, however, strongly rely on readers' training and experience, and the attempts to automatize these processes are still far from clinically acceptable performance.

30.2.2 White matter

The gain in sensitivity associated with 7T field strength for white matter lesion detection is less striking than for the cortical lesions. Nevertheless, the 7T MPRAGE sequence detects lesions in regions identified as normal-appearing white matter by standard clinical 3T FLAIR (Mistry et al., 2011).

30.2.3 Cerebellum

In the cerebellum, demyelination involves cerebellar white matter and the cortex, where it can be abundant. In the cerebellar cortex, MS lesions could present as subpial "band-like," purely intracortical arising around inflamed vessels or as leukocortical lesions involving both gray and white matter.

However, the complex cerebellar structure, with deeply convoluted cortical folds supported by an inner-branched white matter core, and the low MRI contrast between the normal-appearing gray matter and cortical lesions have made the visualization of cerebellar cortical lesions difficult. In the cerebellum, the MP2RAGE sequence augments the definition between the normal cortex and lesions, provides a spatial resolution that increases lesion detection, and allows a more accurate anatomical lesion localization and classification than the one obtained at 3T (Fartaria et al., 2017).

30.2.4 **Spinal cord**

Spinal cord lesions are present in all MS stages and are less frequent in other neurological disorders or healthy aging; therefore, they are included in the MS diagnostic criteria.

Spinal cord MRI at 1.5–3T is a powerful tool in MS assessment but may be insensitive to small lesions detection.

Cervical spinal cord lesions are more likely (by 50%) to be visualized by axial T_2^*-weighted imaging at 7T than at 3T (Dula et al., 2016). The high signal-to-noise ratio enables a stunning anatomical resolution visualization of spinal nerve roots, blood vessels, and dentate ligaments. At the same time, the superior contrast between white and gray matter ensures better gray-white matter segmentation and lesion mapping at 7T (Eden et al., 2019). At 7T, the location of MS lesions in the spinal cord shows a distinct pattern according to the MS subtype (close to the subpial surface in relapsing-remitting patients and near the central cerebrospinal fluid canal surface in the progressive form of the disease), supporting an inflammatory cerebrospinal fluid-mediated lesion pathogenesis of those lesions (Ouellette et al., 2020).

30.3 **Improved lesion characterization**

30.3.1 **Central vein sign**

Although the presence of a central parenchymal vein within white matter lesions has been acknowledged for more than a century by histologic reports, the first in vivo demonstration of the perivenular distribution of focal white matter lesions was achieved only with the development of contrast-based MR venography at 1.5T in the late-90s. In vivo confirmation of this finding has recently been reported with the use of susceptibility-based MRI sequences at 7T, taking advantage of local T_2^* shortening effects induced by the presence of deoxyhemoglobin molecules in venous blood. On T_2^*-weighted images, the vein thus appears as a dot or thin line, hypointense relative to the surrounding lesion, which crosses either the whole lesion or only a part of it.

Present mainly in white matter lesions, the "central vein" radiological sign can also be identified in vivo at 7T in some thalamic, cerebellar, pontine, and even cortical lesions.

Although documented by pathologic reports, the venocentric distribution of the MS lesions in the spinal cord has not yet been demonstrated in vivo.

The sensitivity of the central vein sign increases with the strength of the magnetic field (Tallantyre et al., 2009), and at 7T, a visible vein can be identified within 87% (Tallantyre et al., 2009) up to 92% (Wuerfel et al., 2012) of white matter lesions.

The central vein sign can be detected in all clinical MS phenotypes and is relatively uncommon in MS mimickers, including inflammatory vasculopathies, neuromyelitis optica spectrum disorder, and small vessel disease. It is believed that the demonstration of a central vein within 40%–50% of white matter lesions can adequately differentiate between MS and non-MS pathology. The "central vein" radiological sign assessment has been proposed as a component of the MS diagnosis workup, and guidelines for its evaluation have been created (Sati et al., 2016).

In the thalamus, the morphological details of lesions provided by 7T could potentially explain the mechanisms underlying the pathogenesis of focal demyelination. As such, most (78%) of the nodular/ovoidal lesions display a central venule hence cluing toward a common pathological source with white matter lesions, while diffuse confluent periventricular thalamic lesions have similarities with subpial cortical pathology suggesting a possible interaction with factors present within the adjoining cerebrospinal fluid (Mehndiratta et al., 2021).

30.3.2 Rim lesions

Susceptibility-weighted imaging at 7T may be especially sensitive to a particular pathologic feature, a persistent susceptibility rim (Hammond et al., 2008), observed in a subset of chronic white matter MS lesions. Since radiological-pathological correlative studies have demonstrated the presence of activated iron-enriched microglia content within this border, lesions with a susceptibility rim are considered the radiological correspondent of the "chronic active lesions" described by pathologists (Bagnato et al., 2011; Absinta et al., 2016; Kaunzner et al., 2019). Rim lesions tend to persist and are more likely to expand over time than rimless plaques (Dal-Bianco et al., 2017; Absinta et al., 2019). It has been suggested that the presence of multiple rim "chronic active lesions" (≥ 4) could bear a prognostic significance being linked to earlier disability progression and decreased brain volume (Absinta et al., 2019). Subsequent findings have, however, demonstrated that it is the volume of rim lesions rather than the count that matters most in predicting disability progression, and its evaluation, together with the assessment of leukocortical lesion load, could increase the ability to distinguish MS patients susceptible to experiencing a progression of the neurological disability (Treaba et al., 2021).

Interestingly, rim lesions appear to be specific to MS, being less noticed in MS mimickers, including neuromyelitis optica spectrum disorder (Maggi et al., 2020).

Rim detection and characterization can be further improved using quantitative susceptibility mapping (Kaunzner et al., 2019), which is now feasible at 7T. Since this technique is neither influenced by lesion orientation and geometry nor by the susceptibility of the surrounding tissues, it could reduce false-positive rim identifications.

30.3.3 Leptomeningeal enhancement

Histopathological studies have linked cortical demyelination and degeneration to meningeal inflammation and the presence of leptomeningeal inflammatory infiltrates organized in lymphoid follicle-like structures.

In MS, postcontrast T_2 FLAIR MRI with delayed image acquisition has shown usefulness in detecting inflammation in the leptomeningeal compartment (Absinta et al., 2015). This technique, however, does not directly detect the leptomeningeal inflammation but rather the vascular leakage induced by the increased vascular permeability within the leptomeningeal vessels secondary to meningeal inflammation. The small amounts of contrast material leaked are subsequently trapped within the subarachnoid space in the form of leptomeningeal enhancement, possibly due to meningeal inflammation-associated reactive fibrosis. At 7T, the prevalence of leptomeningeal enhancement has reached frequencies considerably higher than reports at 3T and closer to histopathologic data (90% of patients) (Harrison et al., 2017). However, the specificity of leptomeningeal enhancement to MS is controversial, as it has been reported in other conditions such as infectious and vascular diseases.

Yet, no in vivo study has investigated whether there is a spatial link between leptomeningeal enhancement and focal cortical demyelination, even though the aspect of adjacent cortical lesions across both sides of a sulcus showing linear leptomeningeal contrast enhancement ("kissing lesions") has been described at 7T in one case report (Kolber et al., 2017).

30.4 The damage beyond visible focal lesions

The use of quantitative MRI techniques at 7T could provide insights into the full extent of the disease, improve the pathological substrates characterization, and identify reliable and reproducible markers of disease burden.

Quantitative mapping of subpial pathology can be achieved in vivo by combining T_2^*-quantitative mapping at 7T with a surface-based analysis of the cortex to measure microstructural cortical integrity related to myelin and iron content (Cohen-Adad et al., 2011; Mainero et al., 2015).

This analysis has evidenced an abnormal increase in cortical quantitative T_2^* with a greater distribution in sulci than in gyri, which possibly reflects local myelin and iron loss (Cohen-Adad et al., 2011; Mainero et al., 2015). Intriguingly, in early MS, the quantitative T_2^* changes were confined to the outer cortical layers, while in later stages, they also involved deeper cortical layers and more of the gyri, supporting the hypothesis that cortical pathology is a pathological process likely driven from the pial surface, as suggested by neuropathological observations. Moreover, the increase in 7T quantitative T_2^* generated by cortical demyelination extended within the perilesional cortex, contributing to diffuse subpial pathology (Louapre et al., 2015). Similarly, increased T_2^* values were detected across the entire thalamus in advanced disease stages, partly independent of the visible thalamic lesions located mainly in the third ventricle proximity (Louapre et al., 2018).

In the cerebellum, quantitative T1 mapping with MP2RAGE at ultra-high field MRI has demonstrated alterations of the myelin content in the most external layers of the normal-appearing cortex consistent with widespread subpial microstructural damage (Galbusera et al., 2020).

Several imaging approaches have been tested at 7T to provide a marker of remyelination that would allow a high-resolution assessment of changes in both white matter and gray matter structures. Among these, the semiquantitative magnetization transfer ratio at 7T demonstrated a good sensitivity to regional variations in white matter myelin content and was histologically validated (Bagnato et al., 2018). Another technique uses the MP2RAGE sequence to calculate the approximate T_1 times, as they are mainly influenced by the myelin content (Kolb et al., 2021). At high resolution, the chronic white matter lesions have a range of hypointensity on MP2RAGE T_1-weighted images, potentially allowing for rating the myelin content by visual assessment (Kolb et al., 2021).

Finally, multivariate statistical approaches that combine multiple MRI contrast sensitive to myelin could increase confidence in assessing the degree of myelination. Obtained from quantitative 7T ultra-high resolution T_2^* and T_1 maps, the combined myelin estimation model has been used to probe and monitor cortical microstructural changes that are thought to reflect demyelination, incomplete demyelination, and remyelination (Barletta et al., 2021).

The potential of quantitative 7T MRI measures to enable a distinction between axonal loss, demyelination, and remyelination was also assessed in the postmortem spinal cord of patients with MS (Mottershead et al., 2003). Even if further studies are warranted, the results were promising as they reveal a strong correlation between the T_1, proton density, magnetization transfer ratio, diffusion anisotropy maps, and quantitative myelin content and axonal density measures.

The increase in accuracy of cortical lesion detection at 7T could also be used to guide the selective assessment of pathogenic mechanisms underlying the cortical pathology through complementary quantitative imaging techniques such as positron emission tomography. In that perspective, a combination of 7T MRI and positron emission tomography studies has suggested that widespread cortical demyelination is associated with diffuse glial activation not only within cortical lesions normal-appearing gray matter, linking the degree of cortical neuroinflammation with poor clinical outcomes (Herranz et al., 2016).

The low concentrations of some brain metabolites make their spectroscopic detection very challenging at lower field strengths. The increase in the magnetic field strength improves detection sensitivity and enhances spectral dispersion, allowing separation and individual quantification of the metabolites with overlapping resonances. One of the most promising ultra-high field MR spectroscopy applications is the assessment of glutathione concentration, a metabolite thought to exert a neuroprotective role. In MS patients, the glutathione concentration in the cortex and white matter is significantly reduced relative to healthy controls (Srinivasan et al., 2010). Alterations in glutathione levels and other metabolites could also predict lesion development as they can be detected even beyond the visible limits of white matter lesions (Srinivasan et al., 2010). These findings suggest that glutathione levels could probe disease progression and as a therapeutic target.

At ultra-high field simultaneous, multislice functional MRI could highlight subtle and focal activation differences between minimally disabled MS patients and healthy controls that are otherwise undetectable at lower field strength (Strik et al., 2021).

30.5 Clinical implications

30.5.1 The impact on MS diagnosis

The MRI-detectable "central vein" sign within white matter lesions has recently been proposed as a reliable diagnostic marker with high specificity for MS lesions. Although this radiological sign was first identified with susceptibility-weighted images at 7T, the central vein sign can also be investigated with imaging protocols at lower field strength.

The increased cortical lesion detection is of high interest because cortical lesions, specifically the subpial subtype, are not seen in other CNS diseases. Their presence could improve the MS diagnostic sensitivity, and therefore, the most recent revision of the MS diagnostic criteria now includes cortical lesion assessment as an extension of juxtacortical lesion detection in the MRI criteria for dissemination in space.

30.5.2 Role in disease management and therapeutic response

In addition to increasing the diagnostic accuracy in MS, better cortical lesion detection may improve the stratification of relapsing-remitting MS patients at risk for conversion to progressive MS as extensive cortical damage at onset predisposes to faster conversion. Also, an increase in cortical lesion occurrence rate could draw attention to a possible conversion to a progressive state since the dynamic of lesion formation within the cortex at 7T is different across MS phenotypes (Treaba et al., 2019).

While lower and ultrahigh-field strength results have linked cortical lesion load to cognitive and motor impairment, 7T imaging has shown that cortical lesion subtypes might also have different clinical relevance. Specifically, leukocortical lesions contribute to cognitive decline, particularly information processing speed (Nielsen et al., 2013; Harrison et al., 2015), while subpial lesions relate more to physical and neurological disability (Mainero et al., 2009; Nielsen et al., 2013).

As chronic active rim lesions also prevail in patients with a higher disability (Absinta et al., 2016, 2019), they are potentially helpful for patient stratification and disease monitoring. The detection of the rim and cortical lesions may further improve the ability to identify MS patients at risk of progressing disability (Treaba et al., 2021). However, one should keep in mind that while chronic active rim lesions are present only in a subset of MS patients, cortical lesions are frequently encountered (Harrison et al., 2015; Treaba et al., 2019), even in the earliest disease stages (Granberg et al., 2017).

Furthermore, lesion accumulation occurs more rapidly for cortical than chronic active lesions, so tracking cortical lesion development and evolution would be particularly useful in treatment surveys.

30.6 Technical limitations

Disadvantages of clinical use of the 7T MRI include more image distortion (movement, metal-, or air-induced artifacts) and temperature effects than those generated by lower field strengths. Also, the safety precautions are increased at 7T and could potentially prohibit scanning patients who would not otherwise have contraindications for scanning at a lower magnetic field. Finally, at 7T, there is a severe inhomogeneity in the radiofrequency field that could cause specific absorption rate constraints.

30.7 Future directions

High-quality 7T MRI imaging of the brain and the cervical cord is now feasible and available for clinical use in both the United States and Europe.

At the ultra-high field, both conventional and quantitative MRI techniques might improve, through MS-specific neuroimaging markers (e.g., central vein sign, phase hypointense rim lesions, and cortical lesion differentiation), not only the accuracy of an early MS diagnosis but also our understanding of MS-associated microstructural changes within the CNS. Moreover, assessment of cortical lesion load and quantitative approaches to monitor in vivo cortical demyelination and remyelination could be targeted along with more traditional markers of disease activity to predict disease progression and as a foundation for developing new treatments.

However, to achieve reproducible, comparable data and consistent performance and interpretation of the MS studies at 7T worldwide, there is a need for developing and validating standardized neuroimaging protocols. The protocols should include guidelines for a standardized safety screening, MR setup, and instructions for patient positioning in the scanner along with MS-dedicated brain and spine acquisitions within appropriate durations for clinical use.

References

Absinta, M., Vuolo, L., Rao, A., et al., 2015. Gadolinium-based MRI characterization of leptomeningeal inflammation in multiple sclerosis. Neurology 85 (1), 18–28. https://doi.org/10.1212/WNL.0000000000001587.

Absinta, M., Sati, P., Schindler, M., et al., 2016. Persistent 7-Tesla phase rim predicts poor outcome in new multiple sclerosis patient lesions. J. Clin. Invest. 126 (7), 2597–2609. https://doi.org/10.1172/JCI86198.

Absinta, M., Sati, P., Masuzzo, F., et al., 2019. Association of chronic active multiple sclerosis lesions with disability in vivo. JAMA Neurol. 76 (12), 1474–1483. https://doi.org/10.1001/jamaneurol.2019.2399.

Bagnato, F., Hametner, S., Yao, B., et al., 2011. Tracking iron in multiple sclerosis: a combined imaging and histopathological study at 7 Tesla. Brain 134 (Pt 12), 3602–3615. https://doi.org/10.1093/brain/awr278.

Bagnato, F., Hametner, S., Franco, G., et al., 2018. Selective inversion recovery quantitative magnetization transfer brain MRI at 7T: clinical and postmortem validation in multiple sclerosis. J. Neuroimaging 28 (4), 380–388. https://doi.org/10.1111/jon.12511.

Barletta, V., Herranz, E., Treaba, C.A., et al., 2021. Quantitative 7-Tesla imaging of cortical myelin changes in early multiple sclerosis. Front. Neurol. 12, 714820. https://doi.org/10.3389/fneur.2021.714820.

Beck, E.S., Sati, P., Sethi, V., et al., 2018. Improved visualization of cortical lesions in multiple sclerosis using 7T MP2RAGE. AJNR Am. J. Neuroradiol. 39 (3), 459–466. https://doi.org/10.3174/ajnr.A5534.

Cohen-Adad, J., Benner, T., Greve, D., et al., 2011. In vivo evidence of disseminated subpial T2* signal changes in multiple sclerosis at 7T: a surface-based analysis. NeuroImage 57 (1), 55–62. pii:S1053-8119(11)00387-9. https://doi.org/10.1016/j.neuroimage.2011.04.009.

Dal-Bianco, A., Grabner, G., Kronnerwetter, C., et al., 2017. Slow expansion of multiple sclerosis iron rim lesions: pathology and 7 T magnetic resonance imaging. Acta Neuropathol. 133 (1), 25–42. https://doi.org/10.1007/s00401-016-1636-z.

Dula, A.N., Pawate, S., Dortch, R.D., et al., 2016. Magnetic resonance imaging of the cervical spinal cord in multiple sclerosis at 7T. Mult. Scler. 22 (3), 320–328. https://doi.org/10.1177/1352458515591070.

Eden, D., Gros, C., Badji, A., et al., 2019. Spatial distribution of multiple sclerosis lesions in the cervical spinal cord. Brain 142 (3), 633–646. https://doi.org/10.1093/brain/awy352.

Fartaria, M.J., O'Brien, K., Sorega, A., et al., 2017. An ultra-high field study of cerebellar pathology in early relapsing-remitting multiple sclerosis using MP2RAGE. Investig. Radiol. 52 (5), 265–273. https://doi.org/10.1097/RLI.0000000000000338.

Galbusera, R., Parmar, K., Boillat, Y., et al., 2020. Laminar analysis of the cerebellar cortex shows widespread damage in early MS patients: a pilot study at 7T MRI. Mult. Scler. J. Exp. Transl. Clin. 6 (4). https://doi.org/10.1177/2055217320961409. 2055217320961409.

Granberg, T., Fan, Q., Treaba, C.A., et al., 2017. In vivo characterization of cortical and white matter neuroaxonal pathology in early multiple sclerosis. Brain 140 (11), 2912–2926. https://doi.org/10.1093/brain/awx247.

Hammond, K.E., Metcalf, M., Carvajal, L., et al., 2008. Quantitative in vivo magnetic resonance imaging of multiple sclerosis at 7 Tesla with sensitivity to iron. Ann. Neurol. 64 (6), 707–713. https://doi.org/10.1002/ana.21582.

Harrison, D.M., Roy, S., Oh, J., et al., 2015. Association of cortical lesion burden on 7-T magnetic resonance imaging with cognition and disability in multiple sclerosis. JAMA Neurol. 72 (9), 1004–1012. https://doi.org/10.1001/jamaneurol.2015.1241.

Harrison, D.M., Wang, K.Y., Fiol, J., et al., 2017. Leptomeningeal enhancement at 7T in multiple sclerosis: frequency, morphology, and relationship to cortical volume. J. Neuroimaging 27 (5), 461–468. https://doi.org/10.1111/jon.12444.

Herranz, E., Gianni, C., Louapre, C., et al., 2016. Neuroinflammatory component of gray matter pathology in multiple sclerosis. Ann. Neurol. 80 (5), 776–790. https://doi.org/10.1002/ana.24791.

Kaunzner, U.W., Kang, Y., Zhang, S., et al., 2019. Quantitative susceptibility mapping identifies inflammation in a subset of chronic multiple sclerosis lesions. Brain 142 (1), 133–145. https://doi.org/10.1093/brain/awy296.

Kilsdonk, I.D., Jonkman, L.E., Klaver, R., et al., 2016. Increased cortical grey matter lesion detection in multiple sclerosis with 7 T MRI: a post-mortem verification study. Brain 139 (Pt 5), 1472–1481. https://doi.org/10.1093/brain/aww037.

Kolb, H., Absinta, M., Beck, E.S., et al., 2021. 7T MRI differentiates Remyelinated from demyelinated multiple sclerosis lesions. Ann. Neurol. 90 (4), 612–626. https://doi.org/10.1002/ana.26194.

Kolber, P., Droby, A., Roebroeck, A., et al., 2017. A "kissing lesion": in-vivo 7T evidence of meningeal inflammation in early multiple sclerosis. Mult. Scler. 23 (8), 1167–1169. https://doi.org/10.1177/1352458516683267.

Louapre, C., Govindarajan, S.T., Gianni, C., et al., 2015. Beyond focal cortical lesions in MS: an in vivo quantitative and spatial imaging study at 7T. Neurology 85 (19), 1702–1709. https://doi.org/10.1212/WNL.0000000000002106.

Louapre, C., Govindarajan, S.T., Gianni, C., et al., 2018. Heterogeneous pathological processes account for thalamic degeneration in multiple sclerosis: insights from 7 T imaging. Mult. Scler. 24 (11), 1433–1444. https://doi.org/10.1177/1352458517726382.

Maggi, P., Sati, P., Nair, G., et al., 2020. Paramagnetic rim lesions are specific to multiple sclerosis: an international multicenter 3T MRI study. Ann. Neurol. 88 (5), 1034–1042. https://doi.org/10.1002/ana.25877.

Mainero, C., Benner, T., Radding, A., et al., 2009. In vivo imaging of cortical pathology in multiple sclerosis using ultra-high field MRI. Neurology 73 (12), 941–948. pii:WNL.0b013e3181b64bf7. https://doi.org/10.1212/WNL.0b013e3181b64bf7.

Mainero, C., Louapre, C., Govindarajan, S.T., et al., 2015. A gradient in cortical pathology in multiple sclerosis by in vivo quantitative 7 T imaging. Brain J. Neurol. 138 (Pt 4), 932–945. https://doi.org/10.1093/brain/awv011.

Mehndiratta, A., Treaba, C.A., Barletta, V., et al., 2021. Characterization of thalamic lesions and their correlates in multiple sclerosis by ultra-high-field MRI. Mult. Scler. 27 (5), 674–683. https://doi.org/10.1177/1352458520932804.

Mistry, N., Tallantyre, E.C., Dixon, J.E., et al., 2011. Focal multiple sclerosis lesions abound in 'normal appearing white matter'. Mult. Scler. 17 (11), 1313–1323. https://doi.org/10.1177/1352458511415305.

Mottershead, J.P., Schmierer, K., Clemence, M., et al., 2003. High field MRI correlates of myelin content and axonal density in multiple sclerosis—a post-mortem study of the spinal cord. J. Neurol. 250 (11), 1293–1301. https://doi.org/10.1007/s00415-003-0192-3.

Nielsen, A.S., Kinkel, R.P., Madigan, N., Tinelli, E., Benner, T., Mainero, C., 2013. Contribution of cortical lesion subtypes at 7T MRI to physical and cognitive performance in MS. Neurology 81 (7), 641–649. https://doi.org/10.1212/WNL.0b013e3182a08ce8.

Ouellette, R., Treaba, C.A., Granberg, T., et al., 2020. 7 T imaging reveals a gradient in spinal cord lesion distribution in multiple sclerosis. Brain 143 (10), 2973–2987. https://doi.org/10.1093/brain/awaa249.

Pitt, D., Boster, A., Pei, W., et al., 2010. Imaging cortical lesions in multiple sclerosis with ultra-high-field magnetic resonance imaging. Arch. Neurol. 67 (7), 812–818. piii:67/7/812. https://doi.org/10.1001/archneurol.2010.148.

Sati, P., Oh, J., Constable, R.T., et al., 2016. The central vein sign and its clinical evaluation for the diagnosis of multiple sclerosis: a consensus statement from the North American Imaging in Multiple Sclerosis Cooperative. Nat. Rev. Neurol. 12 (12), 714–722. https://doi.org/10.1038/nrneurol.2016.166.

Srinivasan, R., Ratiney, H., Hammond-Rosenbluth, K.E., Pelletier, D., Nelson, S.J., 2010. MR spectroscopic imaging of glutathione in the white and gray matter at 7 T with an application to multiple sclerosis. Magn. Reson. Imaging 28 (2), 163–170. https://doi.org/10.1016/j.mri.2009.06.008.

Strik, M., Shanahan, C.J., van der Walt, A., et al., 2021. Functional correlates of motor control impairments in multiple sclerosis: a 7 Tesla task functional MRI study. Hum. Brain Mapp. 42 (8), 2569–2582. https://doi.org/10.1002/hbm.25389.

Tallantyre, E.C., Morgan, P.S., Dixon, J.E., et al., 2009. A comparison of 3T and 7T in the detection of small parenchymal veins within MS lesions. Investig. Radiol. 44 (9), 491–494. https://doi.org/10.1097/RLI.0b013e3181b4c144.

Treaba, C.A., Granberg, T.E., Sormani, M.P., et al., 2019. Longitudinal characterization of cortical lesion development and evolution in multiple sclerosis with 7.0-T MRI. Radiology 291 (3), 740–749. https://doi.org/10.1148/radiol.2019181719.

Treaba, C.A., Conti, A., Klawiter, E.C., et al., 2021. Cortical and phase rim lesions on 7 T MRI as markers of multiple sclerosis disease progression. Brain Commun. 3 (3), fcab134. https://doi.org/10.1093/braincomms/fcab134.

Wuerfel, J., Sinnecker, T., Ringelstein, E.B., et al., 2012. Lesion morphology at 7 Tesla MRI differentiates Susac syndrome from multiple sclerosis. Mult. Scler. 18 (11), 1592–1599. https://doi.org/10.1177/1352458512441270.

Neurovascular disease

Zihao Zhang[a,b], **Anja Gwendolyn van der Kolk**[c], **Mahmud Mossa-Basha**[d], **and Chengcheng Zhu**[d]

[a]*State Key Laboratory of Brain and Cognitive Science, Institute of Biophysics, Chinese Academy of Sciences, Beijing, China* [b]*Institute of Artificial Intelligence, Hefei Comprehensive National Science Center, Hefei, China* [c]*Department of Medical Imaging, Radboudumc Nijmegen, Nijmegen, The Netherlands* [d]*Department of Radiology, University of Washington, Seattle, United States*

Highlights

- 7T MRI provides a superior contrast-to-noise ratio and spatial resolution compared with 3T, allowing the visualization of small cerebral vessels and brain structures and improving the evaluation of intracranial atherosclerotic plaques and aneurysms.
- Future developments in coils and image acceleration methods will further unleash the imaging power of 7T MRI.
- To establish 7T as a new clinical tool in an era of increasing 7T accessibility, standardization of imaging techniques across different imaging systems is essential. Multicenter clinical trials are necessary to evaluate the true added value in clinical practice compared to lower field strengths.

31.1 Introduction

Neurovascular diseases are disorders in which some part of the brain is affected by bleeding or restricted blood flow. They are associated with physical and cognitive disabilities and are one of the major causes of death. Magnetic resonance imaging (MRI) has become an indispensable tool in the diagnosis, treatment planning, and follow-up of cerebrovascular diseases. Compared with computed tomography (CT) and digital subtraction angiography (DSA), the advantages of using MRI to diagnose cerebrovascular diseases include its superior soft tissue contrast, the visualization of blood vessels without the use of contrast agents, and the absence of ionizing radiation.

Recently, ultra-high field (UHF) MRI at 7 Tesla (7T) has been proven effective in diagnosing various cerebrovascular pathologies. Since the signal-to-noise ratio (SNR) of MRI is roughly proportional to the field strength, 7T MRI provides an intrinsic SNR of about 2.3 times that of 3T and 4.7 times that of 1.5T (Harteveld et al., 2016). The higher SNR supports acquisitions with higher spatial resolution, thus allowing the visualization of smaller cerebral blood vessels and brain structures. On the other hand, the relaxation times change as field strength increases (T_1 is prolonged while T_2 is shortened), which can be used to achieve a higher contrast-to-noise ratio (CNR) with angiographic techniques due to enhanced flow-related enhancement. In addition, sequences sensitive to susceptibility effects—like T_2^*-weighted imaging and quantitative susceptibility mapping (QSM)—benefit from the increased magnetic susceptibility at 7T, enabling better visualization of small veins and microbleeds.

Advances in Magnetic Resonance Technology and Applications. Volume 10. ISSN 2666-9099. https://doi.org/10.1016/B978-0-323-99898-7.00008-0
499

These advantages of UHF MRI can be exploited to provide specific neuroimaging features for cerebrovascular diseases, including intracranial atherosclerosis (ICAS), intracranial aneurysm, and cerebral small vessel disease.

31.2 Intracranial atherosclerosis

ICAS is the most common cause of ischemic stroke worldwide and has a high risk of recurrent ischemic events. Conventional diagnosis of ICAS has mostly been limited to detecting stenosis on lumenography, for instance, CT angiography or time-of-flight magnetic resonance angiography (TOF-MRA). However, ICAS and vessel wall pathology—in general—may exist without luminal narrowing due to arterial wall remodeling. Due to this shortcoming of luminal imaging, intracranial vessel wall imaging (VWI) is required to detect and assess vessel wall lesions and correlate these lesions with cerebral infarction.

31.2.1 Technical development and validation

The first VWI sequence at 7T was proposed by van der Kolk et al. (2011) and consisted of a 3D turbo spin echo (TSE) sequence with an inversion recovery (IR) pulse to suppress cerebrospinal fluid (CSF) and magnetization preparation (MP) to improve SNR of stationary tissues. Although clearly visualizing the intracranial vessel wall and finding more vessel wall abnormalities than 3T sequences, the IR pulses used in this technique to suppress CSF led to a long TR, resulting in low scan efficiency and a spatial resolution of 0.8 mm isotropic, which was surpassed in subsequent years by more efficient 3T VWI sequences. In 2016, Zhu et al. developed T1w SPACE (sampling perfection with application optimized contrast using different flip angle evolution) sequence at 7T with 0.5 mm isotropic spatial resolution, compared it with the T1w SPACE protocol at 3T with similar resolution, and again confirmed that 7T had a higher image quality and sharpness than 3T (Fig. 31.1) (Zhu et al., 2016). While recent technical developments at 3T have significantly improved CSF suppression and achieved shorter acquisition times using compressed sensing and CAIPIRINHA (controlled aliasing in parallel imaging results in higher acceleration) (Sannananja et al., 2022), no comparison study has yet been performed with these new sequences to assess their quality in delineating the intracranial vessel wall compared with 7T sequences.

Taking advantage of the increased SNR and CNR, VWI at 7T has often been used for ex vivo high-resolution imaging studies of vessel specimens. Van der Kolk et al. demonstrated the ability of 7T VWI with different contrast weightings to distinguish intraplaque components using histology as the reference standard (van der Kolk et al., 2015). The vessel wall thickness of major arteries in the circle of Willis (CoW) specimens was measured by Harteveld et al., using 7T VWI with up to 0.11 mm isotropic resolution (Harteveld et al., 2018). They reported average wall thicknesses ranging from 0.45 to 0.66 mm, with a minimum of 0.31 mm and a maximum of 0.86 mm. Excellent consistency was found between MRI measurements and histology. These ex vivo studies laid a solid foundation for the noninvasive assessment of intracranial atherosclerosis using 7T VWI.

31.2.2 Clinical applications

The main populations included in in vivo studies are patients with ischemic stroke or transient ischemic attack (TIA). The SMART-MR (second manifestations of arterial disease-magnetic resonance) study added VWI as part of a standard 7T MRI protocol during the second follow-up period for vessel wall

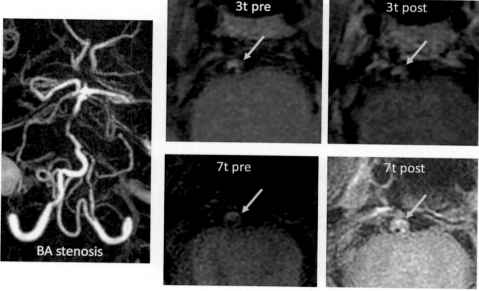

FIG. 31.1

Images of a basilar artery atherosclerotic plaque at both 3T and 7T. The 7T images show better image quality of the vessel wall and sharper delineation of the plaque.

lesion examination. A total of 130 patients with a history of vascular disease were included. The prevalence of vessel wall lesions (8.5 ± 5.7 per person) was higher than previously seen on 3T VWI, which was partially attributed to the higher CNR provided by 7T VWI that increased the certainty of lesion presence. The association between ICAS burden and cognitive function was investigated (Zwartbol et al., 2020). The results reported cognitive decline associated with ICAS, possibly due to ICAS involvement of the posterior and anterior cerebral artery territories, which were upstream from important brain regions for cognition. Regarding cardiovascular risk factors, increasing age, hypertension, diabetes mellitus, and a higher vascular risk score were found to be associated with a higher ICAS burden (Lindenholz et al., 2020). To investigate whether manifestations of small vessel disease (SVD) were affected by large arterial lesions, cerebral parenchymal changes were assessed (Lindenholz et al., 2021). Regression analyses showed that a higher ICAS burden was associated with small subcortical infarcts, lacunes of presumed vascular origin, deep gray matter infarcts, and moderate-to-severe periventricular white matter hyperintensities. These findings suggested that ICAS may eventually result in manifestations of SVD by occluding the orifices of perforating arteries or simultaneously involving both large and small arteries.

Apart from ICAS, 7T VWI can of course also be used to detect vessel wall pathology of other etiologies, like vasculitis. However, no studies using 7T VWI for these diseases have yet been published.

31.3 Intracranial aneurysm

Intracranial aneurysm (IA) occurs in 1%–2% of the general population. Historically, aneurysm size, location, and patient demographics were important factors to formulate optimal management; however, with the advancement of several MRI techniques described below, various new imaging biomarkers can be added to further inform decision-making.

31.3.1 MR angiography

At 7T, benefiting from the stronger flow-related enhancement, both MPRAGE (magnetization-prepared rapid gradient echo) and TOF-MRA can be used to visualize flow in IAs and their parent arteries. Using cardiac-gated 3D GRE with 0.6 mm isotropic resolution, Kleinloog et al. tried to quantify aneurysm volume pulsation in 10 unruptured IAs (Kleinloog et al., 2018). They found that volume pulsations observed on 7T MRI were of the same magnitude as those measured with digital phantom simulations. However, the clinical significance of volume pulsation of aneurysms still needs to be validated against other imaging modalities (e.g., high-resolution cardiac-gated CT angiography) and clarified in future research.

31.3.2 Vessel wall imaging

VWI using 3D TSE sequences with variable refocusing flip angles has been widely used for high-resolution imaging of the aneurysm wall. Like their use in intracranial atherosclerosis, the higher SNR of these 7T sequences can be used for higher spatial resolution and/or greater CSF suppression compared with 3T (Fig. 31.2) (Liu et al., 2022). The presence of wall enhancement on postcontrast VWI is a potential biomarker of wall inflammation and instability (Feng et al., 2022). Superior visualization and higher sharpness of IA wall by VWI at 7T compared with 3T were found (Gottwald et al., 2020). The study showed that thicker aneurysm walls were commonly observed in larger aneurysms and correlated with stronger enhancement (Hadad et al., 2021). VWI has also helped increase insight into the pathogenesis of IAs, showing wall enhancement of parent arteries in regions near the

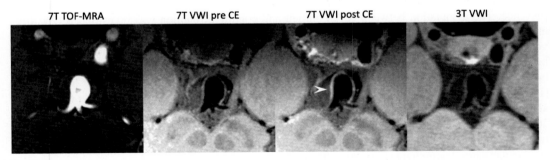

| 7T TOF-MRA | 7T VWI pre CE | 7T VWI post CE | 3T VWI |

FIG. 31.2

Images of an intracranial aneurysm at the top of the basilar artery. VWI at 7T suppresses the flow signal inside the aneurysm and visualizes the aneurysmal wall with a sharper profile than at 3T. The *arrowhead* points to the enhancing part of the aneurysmal wall. *CE*, contrast enhancement; *TOF*, time-of-flight; *VWI*, vessel wall imaging.

aneurysm, suggesting a localized inflammatory process possibly preceding aneurysm formation (Samaniego et al., 2020). Next to aneurysm wall enhancement, a recent histopathologic study showed the potential of VWI in detecting hypointense areas within IA walls that correspond with iron deposition and could be an imaging biomarker for IA instability (Rodemerk et al., 2020). In summary, improved image quality at 7T helps elucidate IA pathophysiology and allows quantification of wall signal intensity, thickness, and contrast enhancement of IAs. These metrics can serve as risk factors for rupture in future prospective studies.

31.3.3 Flow imaging

Flow dynamics measured by 4D flow MRI may be useful in assessing the rupture risk of IAs. With the advances in undersampling trajectory and reconstruction algorithms, high spatiotemporal resolution (0.50 mm isotropic, ~30 ms) within clinically acceptable acquisition times (~10 min) are feasible for 4D flow imaging of IAs (von Morze et al., 2007). Hemodynamic information can be further analyzed in combination with wall thickness and CE provided by VWI; in this way, for instance, low wall shear stress (WSS) was found to occur more often in enhancing regions of aneurysm walls (Cho et al., 2013).

31.4 Cerebral small vessel disease

Cerebral small vessel disease (SVD) is the most common cerebrovascular process in the elderly. It is a chronic, progressive disease affecting the small vessels (arterioles, capillaries, and venules) of the brain and is common in association with acute ischemic and hemorrhagic stroke, as well as chronic cognitive decline and dementia. MRI is widely used to clinically diagnose and study SVD; however, neuroimaging features obtained by conventional MRI are limited to late manifestations such as white matter hyperintensities (WMH) and microinfarcts and oftentimes do not match the clinical symptoms of patients. The lower achievable spatial resolution (within reasonable acquisition time) at 3T and lower field strengths inhibit visualization of the small cerebral vessels that are directly involved with SVD and also hinder the detection of small lesions such as cortical microinfarcts. Using the techniques discussed below, 7T MRI can directly visualize small vessels in the brain, evaluate their hemodynamic functions, and discover subtle parenchymal lesions caused by SVD.

31.4.1 Flow by time-of-flight MRA

Von Morze et al. in 2007 were one of the first research groups that showed a significantly (83%) higher CNR obtained by 7T TOF-MRA compared with 3T (Kang et al., 2009). The smaller cerebral arteries, such as lenticulostriate arteries (LSAs), vessels that contribute to SVD, in particular benefited from the improvement in CNR. The possibility to visualize small cerebral vessels like LSAs with 7T TOF-MRA has opened up new avenues for studying SVD in vivo in a more direct manner compared with lower-field MRI. Kang et al. investigated the morphological changes of LSAs in patients with hypertension (Ling et al., 2019a) and found that while mean curvature and tortuosity of LSAs were comparable to healthy controls, the average number of LSA stems and branches was significantly lower in patients. Patients with chronic stroke and CADASIL (cerebral autosomal dominant arteriopathy with subcortical

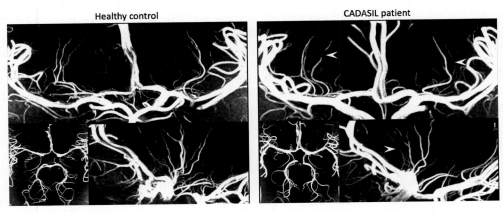

FIG. 31.3

Maximal intensity projection images of 7T TOF-MRA of a healthy control and a CADASIL patient ($0.23 \times 0.23 \times 0.36\ mm^3$, acquisition time 7 min 34 s). Flow deficits in the LSAs are indicated by the *arrowheads*.

infarcts and leukoencephalopathy) showed similar changes in LSA numbers (Fig. 31.3), as well as an increased proportion of LSAs with the discontinuous flow in CADASIL (Schneiders et al., 2012; Kang et al., 2016). These studies show that 7T TOF-MRA is an effective and noninvasive method to evaluate small vessels like perforating arteries as potential culprit vascular structures in SVD.

31.4.2 Velocity by phase-contrast MRA

Time-resolved phase-contrast (PC)-MRI is a common technique to measure blood flow velocity in the body, including the aorta, carotid arteries, and CoW (Sun et al., 2022). Considering the already small size of the CoW, at 3T, velocity measurements of even smaller cerebral vessels—those affected by SVD—become hampered by partial volume effects causing velocity underestimation and flow-direction confounding. The higher SNR and better flow-related enhancement at 7T solve this problem, making it possible to measure the flow velocity of intracranial perforating arteries. Two strategies have been used: (1) pursuing a high spatial resolution and (2) using a high temporal resolution with single-slice coverage. Kang et al., using PC-MRA with a velocity-encoding value of 15 cm/s, successfully acquired the maximum flow velocity and direction in small arteries like the LSAs, posterior communicating artery, and anterior choroidal artery (Bouvy et al., 2016a). Sun et al. found a decrease in average flow velocity in the proximal segments of LSAs in patients with progressive CADASIL (Fig. 31.4), which correlated with aging, functional dependence, cognitive impairment, and mood disturbance (Geurts et al., 2018). Bouvy et al. used 7T PC-MRI with 156 ms/frame acquisition and an in-plane spatial resolution of $0.3\ mm^2$ to measure flow velocity in LSAs at the level of the basal ganglia (BG) and centrum semiovale (CSO) (van den Brink et al., 2021), and the same group subsequently improved the temporal resolution to 57 ms to analyze the pulsatility index (PI) of LSAs with high reproducibility. Their results showed that the PI of LSAs increased in both BG and CSO of patients with SVD-related ischemic stroke, and they are currently enrolling patients with CADASIL and sporadic SVD in a prospective observational cohort study named ZOOM@SVDs, to assess reactivity, flow,

CADASIL patient $v_{LSA} = 8.39$ cm/s

Healthy control $v_{LSA} = 11.15$ cm/s

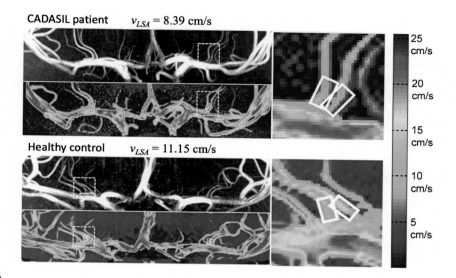

FIG. 31.4

Flow velocities in the LSAs measured by 7T PC-MRA ($0.35 \times 0.35 \times 0.40$ mm^3, acquisition time 7 min 18 s). The velocity decreased with the progression of SVD.

and pulsatility of cerebral small vessels (Bouvy et al., 2017). Overall, these studies confirmed the high reproducibility and reliability of 7T PC-MRI in noninvasive quantification of flow velocity in cerebral small vessels.

31.4.3 Susceptibility-weighted and quantitative imaging

Due to the increased magnetic susceptibility effects at higher field strengths, 7T MRI is ideally suited for susceptibility imaging methods, like susceptibility-weighted imaging (SWI) and quantitative susceptibility mapping (QSM) (Ugurbil, 2014). Iron in the body—specifically in deoxyhemoglobin, hemosiderin, and ferritin—is known for its high magnetic susceptibility, and these susceptibility-sensitive MRI sequences can be used to image venous blood, cerebral microbleeds (CMBs), and subcortical nuclei, respectively.

Recently, there has been an increasing interest in the role of cerebral venous circulation in the pathophysiology and progression of SVD. Bouvy et al. used SWI to assess the morphology of the deep medullary veins (DMVs) in patients with early Alzheimer's disease (AD), amnesic mild cognitive impairment, and healthy controls (Bouvy et al., 2017) and showed that while the number and density of DMVs were similar, the patient group displayed more tortuous DMVs. In CADASIL patients, T_2^*-weighted images showed a significantly reduced number of DMVs in the CSO, while a 7T SWI study in sporadic SVD reported that curved DMVs (defined as inflection angle >30 degrees) were found more frequently (42%) than straight ones (Shaaban et al., 2017). Next to this qualitative use of susceptibility effects to visualize venous structures, 7T MRI can also be used for the objective quantitative assessment using QSM. Ling et al. showed increased susceptibility of superficial veins in

CADASIL, which suggests a hypoperfusion state and was associated with conventional neuroimaging features of SVD like WMHs, lacunar infarctions (LI), and CMBs. It also correlated with disease progression and was related to the clinical phenotype of SVD (Ling et al., 2019b). In this same patient group, increased, abnormal iron deposition in the deep gray matter was associated with clinical characteristics and may be a potential biomarker for disease severity (Sun et al., 2020). Finally, susceptibility imaging methods can be used to detect CMBs, which are one of the imaging biomarkers of SVD (Fig. 31.5), although the high detection rate at 7T necessitates accurate and efficient automated postprocessing tools. The discussed studies show the potential of 7T susceptibility imaging to identify biomarkers that can be used to diagnose SVD at an early stage.

31.4.4 Perivascular spaces by T_2-weighted imaging

The perivascular space (PVS) is the fluid-filled space surrounding small arterioles, capillaries, and venules in the brain parenchyma. Enlarged PVS are associated with older age and are currently seen as one of the MRI hallmarks of SVD, being associated with lacunar infarcts and WMHs. Due to the increased CNR and spatial resolution, T_2-weighted images at 7T can visualize not only the enlarged PVS but also the physiological PVS in normal states (Fig. 31.6A) (Barisano et al., 2021). Bouvy et al. showed that PVS were spatially correlated with LSAs in BG and CSO but not with veins (Bouvy et al., 2014), while Zong et al. suggested an association between vasodilation and PVS based on their observation that inhalation of carbon dioxide significantly increased the volume fraction of PVS in BG and white matter. A subsequent study by Bouvy et al. showed that the number of enlarged PVS correlated with the presence of CMBs (Bouvy et al., 2016b). Advanced postprocessing methods enable improved visualization and quantification of PVS based on neural networks (Jung et al., 2019). In summary, PVS assessment may help elucidate the pathophysiology of SVD, while enlargement of these spaces could become an imaging biomarker, for instance, to reflect disease progression. However, the discrimination between physiological and pathological PVS must be answered by cohort studies in larger populations.

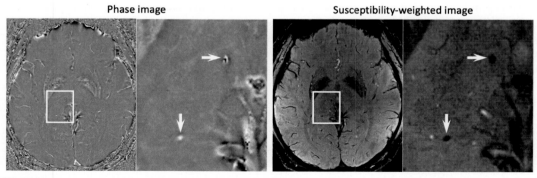

FIG. 31.5

CMBs on the phase and susceptibility-weighted images ($0.30 \times 0.30 \times 1.20$ mm^3, acquisition time 5 min 40 s) of a CADASIL patient. The CMBs within the thalamus are highlighted using *arrows*.

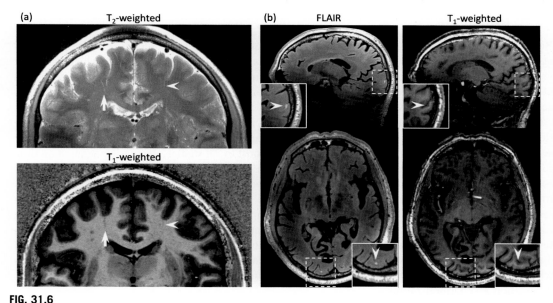

FIG. 31.6

The demonstration of (A) perivascular spaces (PVS) and (B) cortical microinfarct (CMI) in patients with sporadic cSVD. (A) Although some larger PVS can be observed on both T_2-weighted and T_1-weighted images *(arrows)*, the majority of PVS are only visible on T_2-weighted images *(arrowheads)*. (B) The CMI is characterized by hyperintensity in FLAIR and hypointensity in T_1-weighted images.

31.4.5 Cortical microinfarcts by 3D high-resolution imaging

Cerebral cortical microinfarcts (CMIs) are a novel MRI marker of vascular brain injury (Fig. 31.6B). Due to their small size, 3D T_1-weighted and 3D fluid-attenuated inversion recovery (FLAIR) or T_2-weighted sequences with isotropic voxels less than 1 mm^3 should be used to avoid missing lesions, preferably with additional susceptibility-sensitive sequences to exclude confounding features such as CMBs. As an example, CMIs larger than 1–2 mm in the cortical gray matter can be readily visualized by 7T FLAIR with 0.80 mm isotropic resolution, as was shown in a histopathologic study by van Veluw et al. (2016), while another study from this group showed that the detection rate of CMI when using 3T was only 2% of that of 7T (van Veluw et al., 2015). Of note, CMIs are principally only located in the cortex and not the subcortical white matter because of the difficulty in distinguishing microinfarcts from other lesions (like WMH, lacunar infarcts, or PVS) in subcortical regions; when in the subcortical white matter, they should be accompanied by diffusion restriction on diffusion-weighted images (van Veluw et al., 2017). While there is a high detection rate of CMIs at 7T, controversy still exists on the prevalence of CMIs due to the small sample size of existing studies. For instance, while one study showed a higher number of CMIs in patients with AD compared to healthy controls (van Rooden et al., 2014), another study reported no such difference (van Veluw et al., 2014). Larger (multicenter) clinical trials in patients with a definitive diagnosis of SVD might provide more convincing results on the incidence, etiology, and role of CMIs in SVD.

31.5 Prospects

Both hardware (e.g., multichannel coils, x nuclei) and software (e.g., novel sequences, accelerated imaging) of 7T MRI platforms continuously improve. The field inhomogeneity at 7T, which for many years has been a drawback for clinical imaging, has been significantly improved with the introduction of parallel transmitter coils, with the added advantage of allowing simultaneous multiple slice (SMS) acquisition. While most sites still work with head coils, the development of new receiving head-neck coils will enable simultaneous assessment of the intra- and extracranial vasculature, providing more flexibility both in research and clinical settings. Compressed sensing/machine learning and other acceleration techniques are expected to give a further boost to 7T studies, decreasing acquisition time for similar spatial resolutions and making 7T MRI examinations more patient-friendly. The latter has become particularly important since the approval by the FDA and CE of several new 7T MRI platforms, which has resulted in more and more of these platforms being installed each year in both research centers and hospitals worldwide and is accompanied by increasing demand from the clinic for 7T MRI examinations suitable for a variety of patient groups. Nevertheless, there are only a few studies available that have focused on the added value of 7T over lower field strengths in clinical diagnosis, including cerebrovascular diseases; large-scale multicenter studies are required to assess when and how 7T MRI should be used in clinical practice, preceded by technique and protocol standardization and harmonization.

31.6 Conclusion

This chapter reviewed the emerging role of 7T MRI in cerebrovascular diseases for clinical and investigational applications. Several biomarkers of cerebrovascular disease, like aneurysm wall enhancement and enlarged PVS, have been enhanced using the increased SNR and CNR that ultra-high field imaging can achieve. While several limitations of UHF platforms still exist, these may be overcome in time by continuous technical developments within this field, permitting use for research into the pathogenesis of brain diseases and clinical implementation. However, notwithstanding the promising results described in this chapter, future studies will likely show the true clinical added value of 7T MRI for cerebrovascular diseases compared with lower field strengths.

References

Barisano, G., Law, M., Custer, R.M., Toga, A.W., Sepehrband, F., 2021. Perivascular space imaging at ultrahigh field MR imaging. Magn. Reson. Imaging Clin. N. Am. 29, 67–75. https://doi.org/10.1016/j.mric.2020.09.005.

Bouvy, W.H., et al., 2014. Visualization of perivascular spaces and perforating arteries with 7 T magnetic resonance imaging. Investig. Radiol. 49, 307–313. https://doi.org/10.1097/RLI.0000000000000027.

Bouvy, W.H., et al., 2016a. Assessment of blood flow velocity and pulsatility in cerebral perforating arteries with 7-T quantitative flow MRI. NMR Biomed. 29, 1295–1304. https://doi.org/10.1002/nbm.3306.

Bouvy, W.H., et al., 2016b. Perivascular spaces on 7 Tesla brain MRI are related to markers of small vessel disease but not to age or cardiovascular risk factors. J. Cereb. Blood Flow Metab. 36, 1708–1717. https://doi.org/10.1177/0271678X16648970.

Bouvy, W.H., et al., 2017. Abnormalities of cerebral deep medullary veins on 7 Tesla MRI in amnestic mild cognitive impairment and early Alzheimer's disease: a pilot study. J. Alzheimers Dis. 57, 705–710. https://doi.org/10.3233/JAD-160952.

Cho, Z.H., et al., 2013. Microvascular imaging of asymptomatic MCA steno-occlusive patients using ultra-high-field 7T MRI. J. Neurol. 260, 144–150. https://doi.org/10.1007/s00415-012-6604-5.

Feng, J., et al., 2022. Comparison of 7T and 3T vessel wall MRI for the evaluation of intracranial aneurysm wall. Eur. Radiol. 32, 2384–2392. https://doi.org/10.1007/s00330-021-08331-9.

Geurts, L.J., Zwanenburg, J.J.M., Klijn, C.J.M., Luijten, P.R., Biessels, G.J., 2018. Higher pulsatility in cerebral perforating arteries in patients with small vessel disease related stroke, a 7T MRI study. Stroke 50, STROKEAHA118022516. https://doi.org/10.1161/STROKEAHA.118.022516.

Gottwald, L.M., et al., 2020. High spatiotemporal resolution 4D flow MRI of intracranial aneurysms at 7T in 10 minutes. AJNR Am. J. Neuroradiol. 41, 1201–1208. https://doi.org/10.3174/ajnr.A6603.

Hadad, S., et al., 2021. Regional aneurysm wall enhancement is affected by local hemodynamics: A 7T MRI study. AJNR Am. J. Neuroradiol. 42, 464–470. https://doi.org/10.3174/ajnr.A6927.

Harteveld, A.A., van der Kolk, A.G., Zwanenburg, J.J., Luijten, P.R., Hendrikse, J., 2016. 7-T MRI in cerebrovascular diseases: challenges to overcome and initial results. Top. Magn. Reson. Imaging 25, 89–100. https://doi.org/10.1097/RMR.0000000000000080.

Harteveld, A.A., et al., 2018. Ex vivo vessel wall thickness measurements of the human circle of Willis using 7T MRI. Atherosclerosis 273, 106–114. https://doi.org/10.1016/j.atherosclerosis.2018.04.023.

Jung, E., et al., 2019. Enhancement of perivascular spaces using densely connected deep convolutional neural network. IEEE Access 7, 18382–18391. https://doi.org/10.1109/ACCESS.2019.2896911.

Kang, C.K., et al., 2009. Hypertension correlates with lenticulostriate arteries visualized by 7T magnetic resonance angiography. Hypertension 54, 1050–1056. https://doi.org/10.1161/HYPERTENSIONAHA.109.140350.

Kang, C.K., et al., 2016. Velocity measurement of microvessels using phase-contrast magnetic resonance angiography at 7 Tesla MRI. Magn. Reson. Med. 75, 1640–1646. https://doi.org/10.1002/mrm.25600.

Kleinloog, R., et al., 2018. Quantification of intracranial aneurysm volume pulsation with 7T MRI. AJNR Am. J. Neuroradiol. 39, 713–719. https://doi.org/10.3174/ajnr.A5546.

Lindenholz, A., et al., 2020. Intracranial atherosclerosis assessed with 7-T MRI: evaluation of patients with ischemic stroke or transient ischemic attack. Radiology 295, 162–170. https://doi.org/10.1148/radiol.2020190643.

Lindenholz, A., et al., 2021. Intracranial atherosclerotic burden and cerebral parenchymal changes at 7T MRI in patients with transient ischemic attack or ischemic stroke. Front. Neurol. 12, 637556. https://doi.org/10.3389/fneur.2021.637556.

Ling, C., et al., 2019a. Lenticulostriate arteries and basal ganglia changes in cerebral autosomal dominant arteriopathy with subcortical infarcts and leukoencephalopathy, a high-field MRI study. Front. Neurol. 10, 870. https://doi.org/10.3389/fneur.2019.00870.

Ling, C., et al., 2019b. Reduced venous oxygen saturation associates with increased dependence of patients with cerebral autosomal dominant arteriopathy with subcortical infarcts and leukoencephalopathy: a 7.0-T magnetic resonance imaging study. Stroke 50, 3128–3134. https://doi.org/10.1161/STROKEAHA.119.026376.

Liu, X., et al., 2022. Quantitative analysis of unruptured intracranial aneurysm wall thickness and enhancement using 7T high resolution, black blood magnetic resonance imaging. J. Neurointerv. Surg. 14, 723–728. https://doi.org/10.1136/neurintsurg-2021-017688.

Rodemerk, J., et al., 2020. Pathophysiology of intracranial aneurysms: COX-2 expression, iron deposition in aneurysm wall, and correlation with magnetic resonance imaging. Stroke 51, 2505–2513. https://doi.org/10.1161/STROKEAHA.120.030590.

Samaniego, E.A., et al., 2020. Increased contrast enhancement of the parent vessel of unruptured intracranial aneurysms in 7T MR imaging. J. Neurointerv. Surg. 12, 1018–1022. https://doi.org/10.1136/neurintsurg-2020-015915.

Sannananja, B., et al., 2022. Image-quality assessment of 3D intracranial vessel wall MRI using DANTE or DANTE-CAIPI for blood suppression and imaging acceleration. AJNR Am. J. Neuroradiol. 43, 837–843. https://doi.org/10.3174/ajnr.A7531.

Schneiders, J.J., et al., 2012. Comparison of phase-contrast MR imaging and endovascular sonography for intracranial blood flow velocity measurements. AJNR Am. J. Neuroradiol. 33, 1786–1790. https://doi.org/10.3174/ajnr.A3142.

Shaaban, C.E., et al., 2017. In vivo imaging of venous side cerebral small-vessel disease in older adults: an MRI method at 7T. AJNR Am. J. Neuroradiol. 38, 1923–1928. https://doi.org/10.3174/ajnr.A5327.

Sun, C., et al., 2020. Deep Gray matter iron deposition and its relationship to clinical features in cerebral autosomal dominant arteriopathy with subcortical infarcts and leukoencephalopathy patients: A 7.0-T magnetic resonance imaging study. Stroke 51, 1750–1757. https://doi.org/10.1161/STROKEAHA.119.028812.

Sun, C., et al., 2022. Reduced blood flow velocity in lenticulostriate arteries of patients with CADASIL assessed by PC-MRA at 7T. J. Neurol. Neurosurg. Psychiatry 93, 451–452. https://doi.org/10.1136/jnnp-2021-326258.

Ugurbil, K., 2014. Magnetic resonance imaging at ultrahigh fields. IEEE Trans. Biomed. Eng. 61, 1364–1379. https://doi.org/10.1109/TBME.2014.2313619.

van den Brink, H., et al., 2021. Zooming in on cerebral small vessel function in small vessel diseases with 7T MRI: rationale and design of the "ZOOM@SVDs" study. Cereb. Circ. Cogn. Behav. 2, 100013. https://doi.org/10.1016/j.cccb.2021.100013.

van der Kolk, A.G., et al., 2011. Intracranial vessel wall imaging at 7.0-T MRI. Stroke 42, 2478–2484. https://doi.org/10.1161/STROKEAHA.111.620443.

van der Kolk, A.G., et al., 2015. Imaging the intracranial atherosclerotic vessel wall using 7T MRI: initial comparison with histopathology. AJNR Am. J. Neuroradiol. 36, 694–701. https://doi.org/10.3174/ajnr.A4178.

van Rooden, S., et al., 2014. Increased number of microinfarcts in Alzheimer disease at 7-T MR imaging. Radiology 270, 205–211. https://doi.org/10.1148/radiol.13130743.

van Veluw, S.J., et al., 2014. Cerebral cortical microinfarcts at 7Tesla MRI in patients with early Alzheimer's disease. J. Alzheimers Dis. 39, 163–167. https://doi.org/10.3233/JAD-131040.

van Veluw, S.J., et al., 2015. Cortical microinfarcts on 3T MRI: clinical correlates in memory-clinic patients. Alzheimers Dement. 11, 1500–1509. https://doi.org/10.1016/j.jalz.2014.12.010.

van Veluw, S.J., et al., 2016. Microbleed and microinfarct detection in amyloid angiopathy: a high-resolution MRI-histopathology study. Brain 139, 3151–3162. https://doi.org/10.1093/brain/aww229.

van Veluw, S.J., et al., 2017. Detection, risk factors, and functional consequences of cerebral microinfarcts. Lancet Neurol. 16, 730–740. https://doi.org/10.1016/S1474-4422(17)30196-5.

von Morze, C., et al., 2007. Intracranial time-of-flight MR angiography at 7T with comparison to 3T. J. Magn. Reson. Imaging 26, 900–904. https://doi.org/10.1002/jmri.21097.

Zhu, C., et al., 2016. High resolution imaging of the intracranial vessel wall at 3 and 7T using 3D fast spin echo MRI. MAGMA 29, 559–570. https://doi.org/10.1007/s10334-016-0531-x.

Zwartbol, M.H.T., et al., 2020. Intracranial atherosclerosis on 7T MRI and cognitive functioning: the SMART-MR study. Neurology 95, e1351–e1361. https://doi.org/10.1212/WNL.0000000000010199.

Motor neuron diseases and frontotemporal dementia

Mirco Cosottini[a] **and Graziella Donatelli**[b,c]

[a]*Department of Translational Research and New Technologies in Medicine and Surgery, University of Pisa, Pisa, Italy*
[b]*Department of Diagnostics and Imaging, Azienda Ospedaliero Universitaria Pisana, Pisa, Italy* [c]*Imago7 Research Foundation, Pisa, Italy*

Highlights

- Ultra-high field MRI improves the detection of cortical and subcortical alterations in patients with motor neuron diseases.
- Some brain alterations could be useful in the differential diagnosis among different motor neuron disorders.
- In the spectrum of motor neuron disorders, imaging biomarkers at ultra-high magnetic field strengths might be the in vivo surrogate of pathological hallmarks.

32.1 Introduction

Amyotrophic lateral sclerosis (ALS) is a fatal progressive neurological disease with unknown etiology, resulting in muscle atrophy, weakness and spasticity, and leading to respiratory failure. The diagnosis of ALS is mainly based on clinical grounds and requires signs of degeneration of both upper (UMN) and lower motor neurons (LMN), but detecting the contribution of each of them to clinical picture can be difficult. The disease is classified into different phenotypes based on onset (bulbar/pseudobulbar or limb onset), presence of impaired cognition, body segments involved (spinal or bulbar), age of onset, rate of progression, and familial and genetic contribution (Ravits and La Spada, 2009). However, the clinical variability at onset and the different trajectories of progression point out a disease heterogeneity that hampers an exhaustive phenotypic classification (Al-Chalabi et al., 2016). The level of motor neuron involvement (UMNs in the cortex and/or LMNs in brainstem or spinal cord) is one of the key elements in the disease classification. ALS, indeed, is included in the spectrum of motor neuron diseases (MNDs), which encompasses clinical conditions ranging from the early and predominant UMN involvement, which characterizes primary lateral sclerosis (PLS), to the predominant LMN involvement, typical of progressive muscular atrophy (PMA).

From a clinical point of view, it would be desirable to have a robust diagnostic and prognostic biomarker able to go beyond the usual clinical criteria and objectively classify patients. The grouping of patients based on biomarkers, indeed, could enable the development of personalized medicine, as they would be useful for screening patients for clinical trials and monitoring the effectiveness of eventual therapies.

Clinical phenotypes of MNDs can be explored with neuroimaging, and in pioneering studies, some of them have been investigated with magnetic resonance imaging (MRI) at ultra-high field (UHF) searching for a correlation between MRI and pathology.

32.2 The role of magnetic resonance imaging at 7T in the search for biomarkers of upper motor neuron impairment

The main advantages of UHF MRI are the high signal-to-noise ratio that can be exploited to increase the spatial resolution of images and the increased sensitivity to susceptibility phenomena related to tissue composition. Susceptibility-weighted imaging enhances small differences of susceptibility within tissues that are homogenous at lower field strengths, thus providing images with high resolution (in the order of hundreds of microns) and extraordinary anatomical details. Hence, 7T MRI could be proposed as a sort of in vivo microscope to reduce the gap between the point of view of the radiologist (macroscopic) and that of the pathologist (microscopic) (Absinta et al., 2016).

The main neuropathological features of ALS are the loss of LMNs in the brainstem and anterior horns of the spinal cord (Hughes, 1982) and the loss of Betz cells in the primary motor cortex (M1) (Kawamata et al., 1992). The latter is associated with the degeneration of the corticospinal tract (CST) in its full length from the subcortical white matter of the precentral gyrus to the lateral columns of the spinal cord. Moreover, microglial cells infiltrate M1 and spinal cord in the areas of neuronal degeneration (Kawamata et al., 1992).

The detection of LMN degeneration relies on the neurological examination and, mainly, on electromyography and is not currently a main goal for neuroimaging. Recently, the combined use of UHF MR scanners and coils optimized for the imaging of the cervical spinal cord seems promising in evaluating the atrophy of the anterior horns as a possible surrogate marker of LMN degeneration. Indeed, UHF MRI can reveal anatomical details in the cervical spinal cord that are comparable with those shown in histological reports (Sigmund et al., 2012), and the atrophy of the anterior horns was recently reported in a patient with LMN-predominant ALS (Callot et al., 2021).

Pathological hallmarks of UMN involvement in ALS, instead, have been extensively studied with neuroimaging since electrophysiology is a less robust method in a clinical context. The loss of Betz cells has been investigated with many MR techniques including conventional imaging, cortical morphometry, magnetization transfer imaging, and functional MRI, whereas the CST degeneration has been studied using conventional sequences, magnetization transfer ratio (MTR), and, mainly, diffusion tensor imaging (DTI). All these studies have been performed with magnets operating at 1.5T or 3T.

Studies that focused on M1 attempted mainly to reveal the cortical atrophy as the counterpart of the loss of Betz cells. In PLS, the widening of the central sulcus, an indirect sign of M1 atrophy, was described using conventional imaging, while in ALS, the atrophy is less pronounced and was detected using voxel-based morphometry analysis (Agosta et al., 2007). Similarly, cortical thickness was used in ALS as a potential biomarker of UMN involvement and disease progression (Nitert et al., 2022). Microstructural changes in M1 were reported in ALS using measures on magnetization transfer imaging; these alterations were detected also in cortical areas without atrophy (Cosottini et al., 2013), indicating that the neurodegenerative process precedes the loss of tissue. Functional MRI studies in ALS aimed to assess the functional changes in the motor areas by using motor or motor imagery tasks (Konrad et al., 2006). Changes in BOLD activity were found in M1 but also in the frontoparietal motor circuit, which takes on a compensatory role (Cosottini et al., 2012) after the cortical degeneration.

As regards degeneration of the UMN axons, signal hyperintensity was found along the CST, from subcortical precentral white matter to the brainstem, using proton density, FLAIR T_2-weighted sequences, and magnetization transfer imaging. Further insight into CST degeneration came by using MTR and, mainly, DTI (Agosta et al., 2010). The reduced MTR, together with the reduced fractional anisotropy and increased radial diffusivity, has been considered surrogates of axonopathy, myelin breakdown, and Wallerian degeneration that characterize myelin pallor and degeneration of the CST.

As shown, many MR techniques at clinical magnetic field strengths are able to provide information on the UMN involvement, but they have been mainly employed at the group level. Reliable MR biomarkers of UMN dysfunction are not yet available for individual patient evaluation, but 7T MRI may bridge this gap.

Combining the unprecedented spatial resolution of images and the sensitivity to susceptibility phenomena, the iron-sensitive imaging at 7T allows going beyond the homogeneous signal intensity that characterizes the cerebral cortex at 1.5T to depict the normal radiological anatomy of the cortex and to detect indirect signs of UMN pathology. In ALS patients, brain imaging acquisition at UHF is based on comparative studies that investigated the association between MRI signal changes and pathological hallmarks of the disease (Pallebage-Gamarallage et al., 2018).

Cortical layers differ in susceptibility, and differences in signal intensity between superficial and deep layers can be revealed using appropriate sequences. The cortical myeloarchitecture at 7T (Turner, 2013) allows one to classify M1 as an astriate cortex that has a typical MR appearance characterized by a thin superficial hyperintense strip that lies just above a thicker and slightly hypointense band. In ALS, the superficial layers of M1 are preserved while the deeper band is thinner and more hypointense than normal, with a track appearance (Cosottini et al., 2016; Fig. 32.1). In a comparative study with pathology, the rim of signal hypointensity was shown to correspond to iron accumulation in microglial cells (Kwan et al., 2012; Fig. 32.2).

Cortical thinning and hypointensity have been proposed as signs of UMN degeneration because their presence correlates with the UMN impairment measured with appropriate clinical scales (Cosottini et al., 2016). They might be used as diagnostic biomarkers of ALS, but their accuracy depends on the clinical UMN burden in the selected population. Since imaging features are biomarkers of UMN degeneration, they can more properly represent biomarkers of ALS phenotype with predominant UMN involvement (Fig. 32.3A) or PLS. According to this hypothesis, M1 is markedly atrophic and hypointense in patients with PLS (Cosottini et al., 2022) while it has a normal appearance in patients with predominant LMN impairment or PMA (Fig. 32.3B).

The signal hypointensity detectable with iron-sensitive sequences has been further investigated using quantitative techniques such as quantitative susceptibility mapping. Although the magnetic susceptibility of the cerebral cortex is influenced by several components including the oxygenation status of hemoglobin and the myelination of cortical layers, iron content is a major source of magnetic susceptibility and its expected concentration has been proven to correlate with magnetic susceptibility measurements (Costagli et al., 2016). Susceptibility values in M1 of ALS patients are positively correlated with ferritin estimates from histology and with the clinical UMN impairment (Costagli et al., 2016), confirming the role of 7T MR as a microscopic probe in ALS phenotypes with prevalent UMN pathology.

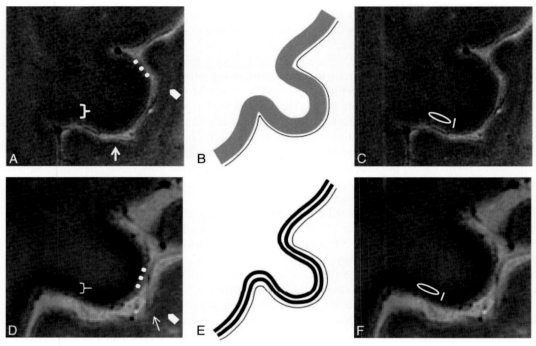

FIG. 32.1

In vivo representation of the primary motor cortex at 7T. The high sensitivity to susceptibility phenomenon of the UHF MRI allows to reveal different layers into the cortical mantle. Within the unaffected primary motor cortex (A–C), the more superficial hyperintense layers (dots) are distinguishable from the deeper astriate components (graph bracket). In ALS with loss of Betz cells, iron-sensitive MR sequences at 7T MRI demonstrates the thinning and signal hypointensity of the deeper portion of the primary motor cortex (D–F). *Reproduced with permission from Cosottini et al. (2016).*

The experience obtained at UHF has been transferred to clinical settings (3T MR systems), confirming the capability of iron-sensitive sequences to evaluate the UMN burden, although with lower sensitivity compared with 7T (Donatelli et al., 2018). Thickness and signal intensity of the deep layers of M1 were assessed visually and measured using a semiautomated algorithm, and the signal hypointensity-to-thickness ratio in each functional region of M1 was found to correlate positively and significantly with the clinical UMN burden of the corresponding limb.

In ALS, the metabolic profile of M1 was investigated at 7T using single-voxel MR spectroscopy with a focus on N-acetylaspartate (NAA) and myo-inositol (mI), which are respectively markers of anatomic and functional integrity of neurons and glial reaction. In the precentral gyrus of patients, NAA was found significantly decreased and mI significantly increased compared with controls (Atassi et al., 2017; Cheong et al., 2017), confirming previous results obtained with 3T MR scanners,

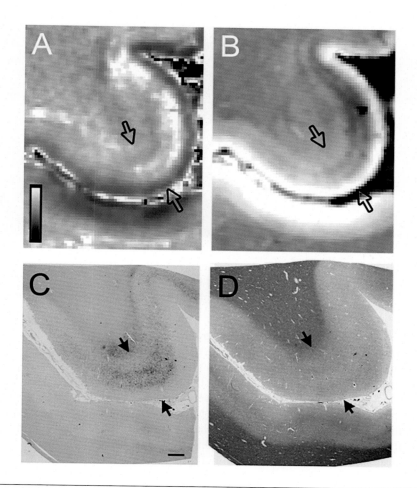

FIG. 32.2

Ex vivo imaging of the primary motor cortex in ALS shows that the signal hypointensity of the deep layers (B) is related to the microglia infiltration of the affected cortex. The microglial cells are rich in iron that is histologically visualized with the Perls' staining (C). (A) and (D) show, respectively, the R2* map and the Luxol fast blue stain of the precentral motor cortex. *Reproduced with permission from Kwan et al. (2012).*

and mI/tNAA was found to correlate with the UMN impairment (Atassi et al., 2017). It would be of interest to evaluate levels of low-concentrated neurotransmitters involved in the pathological process, namely glutamate (Glu) and gamma-aminobutyric acid (GABA). However, the precision of GABA quantification is still matter of debate even at 7T (Cheong et al., 2017), and the interpretation of data on Glu concentration is hampered by its distribution in both the intracellular and extracellular spaces. While GABA concentration seems unchanged in patients (Atassi et al., 2017), the few studies

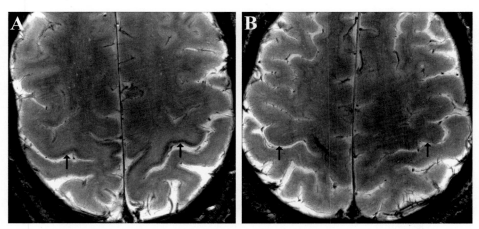

FIG. 32.3

Seven Tesla T_2^*-weighted images of the primary motor cortex in ALS patients. The signal intensity in the deep layers of the primary motor cortex is usually markedly reduced in patients with moderate-to-severe UMN impairment (arrows in A) and normal or slightly reduced in ALS patients with low UMN impairment (arrows in B).

concerning Glu in ALS are conflicting, reporting significantly reduced levels in the precentral gyrus in one study (Atassi et al., 2017) but not in the other (Cheong et al., 2017).

At 7T, degeneration of the UMN axons has been investigated in the entire CST using conventional and advanced imaging techniques. At the brain level, the significant increase in radial diffusivity and decrease in fractional anisotropy and MTR values were confirmed (Verstraete et al., 2014). In the spinal cord, degeneration of the axonal projections of UMNs is visible in vivo as a signal hyperintensity in the lateral columns in FSE T_2-weighted images (Cohen-Adad et al., 2013). The signal alteration is associated with marked myelin loss, microglial inflammatory response, reduced fractional anisotropy, and increased mean diffusivity, as documented in an ex vivo sample (Pallebage-Gamarallage et al., 2018). Changes in these diffusivity indexes have also been recently reported at UHF in the spinal cord of presymptomatic ALS animal models (Gatto et al., 2018).

32.3 Magnetic resonance imaging at 7T to investigate the topography of motor system involvement

Classification of ALS cases in specific clinical phenotypes is based mainly on the topography of motor system involvement and pattern of onset.

In the bulbar palsy, the face-throat region is the first to be affected, with the impairment of muscles involved in speech, chewing, and swallowing. The bulbar onset is reported in 25% of patients and constitutes a negative prognostic factor: the overall median survival from symptom onset is 2–3 years for bulbar onset cases and 3–5 years for limb onset cases. The term pseudobulbar palsy should be used when bulbar symptoms are caused mainly by UMN degeneration. It is manifested by spastic dysarthria, tongue spasticity, brisk gag and jaw jerk reflexes, and palmomental reflex, whereas bulbar palsy due to

LMN degeneration results in flaccid dysarthria and wasting, weakness and fasciculation of the tongue. To distinguish between the contribution of UMN and LMN degeneration to signs and symptoms is difficult for the bulbar forms as well as for the spinal forms of ALS.

The clinical UMN burden can differ from one body region to another and the magnitude of signal hypointensity along M1 might be not uniform in the same patient. The possible uneven distribution of the UMN pathology in the cortex can be detected using iron-sensitive imaging, and there is a somatotopic association between hypointense M1 areas and body regions affected. In ALS patients, the relationship between the degree of T_2^* hypointensity or magnetic susceptibility of M1 and the clinical UMN burden of the corresponding body regions has been demonstrated at UHF for the spinal form (Cosottini et al., 2016; Costagli et al., 2016) and, more recently, in the pseudobulbar palsy at 3T (Donatelli et al., 2019; Fig. 32.4).

The capability of susceptibility-weighted imaging at 7T to detect thin and hypointense M1 areas and the somatotopic relationship between cortical and body regions affected may represent the prerequisites to investigate cortical patterns of disease spread, monitoring the distribution of signal hypointensity over time. The clinical onset of ALS is typically focal, and the disease evolves to affect contiguous and, less frequently, noncontiguous somatic areas. Patterns of disease spread can be investigated based on clinical progression but the unpredictable, not homogeneous and simultaneous involvement of UMNs and LMNs hampered the understanding of pattern of disease diffusion at the spinal and cortical level. Longitudinal MRI studies are not still available, but in a cross-sectional study (Donatelli et al., 2022), the highest frequencies of T_2^* hypointensity were found in M1 regions functionally associated with the body sites of symptom onset. Moreover, the signal hypointensity often affects symmetrically the left and right M1, suggesting the interhemispheric corticomotoneuronal connections as a major path for the spread of UMN pathology.

32.4 Magnetic resonance imaging at 7T in the quest for biomarkers of frontotemporal dementia in amyotrophic lateral sclerosis

Besides motor symptoms, a subset of ALS patients develops cognitive disturbances or even frontotemporal dementia (FTD), indicating that ALS can affect extra-motor brain regions.

The involvement of extra-motor functions in MNDs includes frontotemporal, oculomotor, cerebellar, and sensory systems and characterizes different ALS phenotypes (McCluskey et al., 2014). Up to about 50% of patients with ALS have cognitive or behavioral disturbances, and frontotemporal dementia is diagnosed in about 25% of these cases. The dysfunction of executive capabilities is associated with rapid disease progression and reduced survival (Phukan et al., 2012). Therefore, the identification of biomarkers of extra-motor structures involvement might have prognostic implications, but so far most neuroimaging studies investigating extra-motor brain areas in patients were conducted at the group level.

Clinical, immunohistochemical, pathological, and neuroimaging (Lillo et al., 2012) data support the connection between ALS and FTD as a clinicopathological spectrum linked to proteinopathy TDP-43 (Neumann et al., 2006). Also, neuroimaging studies support the involvement of extra-motor brain areas in ALS: cortical atrophy, cortical dysfunction (Cosottini et al., 2012), and reduced fractional anisotropy in extra-motor areas confirmed the idea that ALS is a multisystem disease beyond motor system involvement (Li et al., 2012).

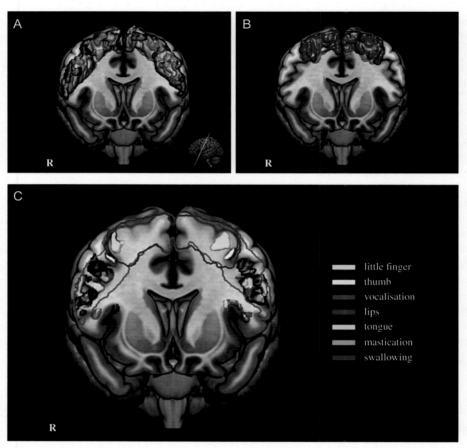

FIG. 32.4

Distribution of the signal hypointensity along the primary motor cortex in ALS patients with (A) and without (B) bulbar signs and symptoms. Thanks to the high spatial resolution, 7T functional MRI allows to separately map each motor function that is somatotopically displayed with different colors along the primary motor cortex (C). ALS patients with pseudobulbar palsy have M1 signal hypointensity extended to the ventral part of M1 *(in orange)*, overlaying the activated areas corresponding to the bulbar motor functions. *Reproduced with permission from Donatelli et al. (2019).*

FTD includes clinical syndromes characterized by behavioral and language deficits and atrophy of the frontal and temporal lobes. Different patterns of frontal and temporal atrophy have been described by employing magnets at conventional magnetic field strengths (Whitwell and Josephs, 2012). The behavioral variant of FTD showed the most severe DTI changes in the anterior portions of the corpus callosum and in the superior and inferior longitudinal fasciculi; these alterations match with the severe atrophy of the anterior portions of the frontal and temporal lobes. The primary progressive aphasia, another FTD variant, is characterized by isolated language deficits persisting for the first 2 years of the disease and includes semantic dementia and progressive non fluent aphasia (Gorno-Tempini et al., 2011). While in semantic dementia the atrophy involves mainly the left anterior and inferior temporal lobe, in progressive nonfluent aphasia the frontal lobes (premotor cortex and Broca's area) are the preferential sites to be affected.

The role of 7T MR in studying ALS-FTD and FTD is still largely unexplored, and specific studies in vivo have not yet been performed. A subclinical cognitive impairment is often present in ALS, but most ALS patients studied at 7T were not affected by FTD and UHF MR changes in extra-motor areas have never been mentioned. However, postmortem 7T MR studies provided interesting results. Findings observed with conventional sequences, DTI, and relaxation maps seem to correspond to specific neuroanatomical signatures associated with different patterns of FTD pathology that have been described based on the potential spreading of pTDP-43 (Brettschneider et al., 2014). Moreover, the small vessel pathology and lacunar infarcts that lead to Wallerian degeneration have been reported in ex vivo samples of FTD cases in association with a severe prefrontal and frontal cortical atrophy (De Reuck et al., 2017).

With these premises, one can suppose that in vivo brain imaging at 7T could provide interesting information in properly designed studies on FTD. As well as in Alzheimer's disease, the refinement of 3D acquisitions with submillimeter (400/650 μm) isotropic resolution (Düzel et al., 2019) would allow to improve brain atrophy estimation and to investigate its relationship with cognitive impairment. Moreover, iron-sensitive sequences could be employed to reveal temporal and prefrontal microgliosis in different FTD phenotypes.

So far, the involvement of extra-motor brain areas has been evaluated in vivo at 7T only with a pilot fMRI study that explored the functional connectivity in a group of 12 ALS patients. This exploratory whole-brain analysis revealed a disruption of functional connectivity between the superior sensorimotor cortex (in the precentral gyrus) and both the left and right cerebellar lobules VI (Barry et al., 2021).

32.5 **Genetic findings**

About 10% of ALS cases are inherited and associated with autosomal dominant mutations. Several genetic cases are familial, but an uninformative family history does not exclude a genetic basis for ALS. The most frequent pathogenetic variants in familial cases are in the gene encoding Cu/Zn superoxide dismutase (SOD1), and some of them are associated with more aggressive forms of the disease. A clear genotype-phenotype correlation in ALS has not been univocally stated: phenotypical heterogeneity can be found in families carrying the same gene mutation as well as different gene mutations can be associated with the same clinical phenotype.

Gene testing plays an important role in the differential diagnosis among MNDs. Examples are the UMN syndromes with clinical onset in the lower limbs of adult patients. In particular, HSP is a genetic disorder characterized by progressive spastic weakness of the lower limbs, but this clinical picture can characterize also the onset of PLS and ALS (Fink, 2001). For this reason, although some clinical features are helpful, the differential diagnosis between these three MNDs could be challenging. Recently, iron-sensitive MR sequences proved their usefulness in classifying HSP, PLS, and ALS patients with onset of UMN symptoms in the lower limbs. Indeed, most HSP patients had normal signal intensity in M1 (86%), whereas all the PLS and the majority of ALS patients (75%) had marked M1 thinning and hypointensity (Cosottini et al., 2022; Fig. 32.5). The normal radiological appearance of M1 in HSP

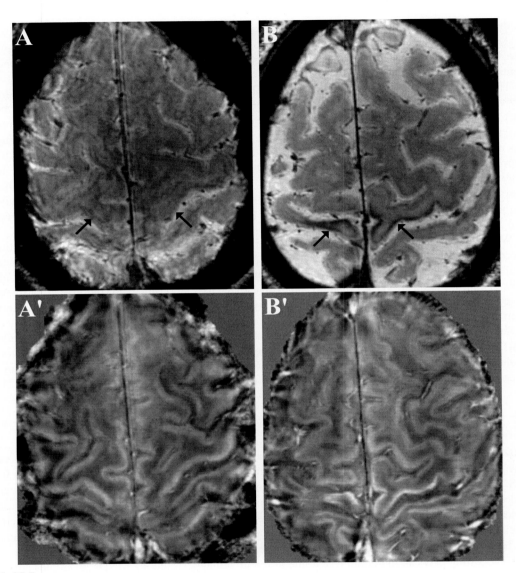

FIG. 32.5

Seven Tesla T_2^*-weighted images (A and B) and quantitative susceptibility maps (A′ and B′) at the level of paracentral lobules in an HSP patient (A and A′) and an ALS patient with lower limb onset (B and B′). The deep layers of the primary motor cortex are markedly hypointense in many ALS patients (arrows in B) because of the increased iron content (high susceptibility values), whereas it has normal signal intensity in most HSP patients (arrows in A).

patients is explained by pathology: HSP is primarily an axonopathy affecting mainly the long descending tracts, while the loss of Betz cells and the microglial infiltration in the cortex are not consistent pathological hallmarks. This is an example of how 7T MRI could be useful in detecting surrogate markers of pathology to be used in the differential diagnosis among MNDs with a similar clinical phenotype.

32.6 Conclusions

ALS phenotypes can be so different among them that seem to have specific underlying pathophysiological mechanisms. Nevertheless, all the phenotypes share the same pathological hallmarks, even though with peculiar distributions across the central nervous system. Whether ALS is a single disorder or a spectrum of diseases, and whether ALS, PLS, and HSP are distinct clinical entities or represent a continuum in the spectrum of MNDs, are still unsolved questions.

The main limitation of pathological studies is the small number of MND cases assessed with necroscopy. This prevents us from establishing a firm association between specific phenotypes or genotypes and histological or immunohistochemical markers and from using this knowledge to classify patients. Imaging biomarkers at 7T try to identify in vivo the pathological changes revealed by necroscopy with the advantage of being employed in a large number of patients and encompassing many clinical phenotypes.

With these premises, 7T MR imaging can be tested at the single subject level in large cohorts of patients to identify diagnostic and prognostic biomarkers of disease that go beyond clinical features and genetic variants and may be used as criteria for a new kind of disease classification.

References

Absinta, M., Sati, P., Reich, D.S., 2016. Advanced MRI and staging of multiple sclerosis lesions. Nat. Rev. Neurol. 12 (6), 358–368.

Agosta, F., Pagani, E., Rocca, M.A., et al., 2007. Voxel-based morphometry study of brain volumetry and diffusivity in amyotrophic lateral sclerosis patients with mild disability. Hum. Brain Mapp. 28 (12), 1430–1438.

Agosta, F., Chiò, A., Cosottini, M., et al., 2010. The present and the future of neuroimaging in amyotrophic lateral sclerosis. AJNR Am. J. Neuroradiol. 31 (10), 1769–1777.

Al-Chalabi, A., Hardiman, O., Kiernan, M.C., Chiò, A., Rix-Brooks, B., van den Berg, L.H., 2016. Amyotrophic lateral sclerosis: moving towards a new classification system. Lancet Neurol. 15 (11), 1182–1194.

Atassi, N., Xu, M., Triantafyllou, C., et al., 2017. Ultra high-field (7 Tesla) magnetic resonance spectroscopy in amyotrophic lateral sclerosis. PLoS One 12 (5), e0177680. https://doi.org/10.1371/journal.pone.0177680.

Barry, R.L., Babu, S., Anteraper, S.A., et al., 2021. Ultra-high field (7T) functional magnetic resonance imaging in amyotrophic lateral sclerosis: a pilot study. NeuroImage Clin. 30, 102648. https://doi.org/10.1016/j.nicl.2021.102648.

Brettschneider, J., Del Tredici, K., Irwin, D.J., et al., 2014. Sequential distribution of pTDP-43 pathology in behavioral variant frontotemporal dementia (bvFTD). Acta Neuropathol. 127 (3), 423–439.

Callot, V., Massire, A., Guye, M., Attarian, S., Verschueren, A., 2021. Visualization of gray matter atrophy and anterior corticospinal tract signal hyperintensity in amyotrophic lateral sclerosis using 7T MRI. Neurology 96 (23), 1094–1095.

Cheong, I., Marjańska, M., Deelchand, D.K., Eberly, L.E., Walk, D., Öz, G., 2017. Ultra-high field proton MR spectroscopy in early-stage amyotrophic lateral sclerosis. Neurochem. Res. 42 (6), 1833–1844.

Cohen-Adad, J., Zhao, W., Keil, B., et al., 2013. 7-T MRI of the spinal cord can detect lateral corticospinal tract abnormality in amyotrophic lateral sclerosis. Muscle Nerve 47 (5), 760–762.

Cosottini, M., Pesaresi, I., Piazza, S., et al., 2012. Structural and functional evaluation of cortical motor areas in amyotrophic lateral sclerosis. Exp. Neurol. 234 (1), 169–180.

Cosottini, M., Cecchi, P., Piazza, S., et al., 2013. Mapping cortical degeneration in ALS with magnetization transfer ratio and voxel-based morphometry. PLoS One 8 (7), e68279. https://doi.org/10.1371/journal.pone.0068279.

Cosottini, M., Donatelli, G., Costagli, M., et al., 2016. High-resolution 7T MR imaging of the motor cortex in amyotrophic lateral sclerosis. AJNR Am. J. Neuroradiol. 37 (3), 455–461.

Cosottini, M., Donatelli, G., Ricca, I., et al., 2022. Iron-sensitive MR imaging of the primary motor cortex to differentiate hereditary spastic paraplegia from other motor neuron diseases. Eur. Radiol. https://doi.org/10.1007/s00330-022-08865-6.

Costagli, M., Donatelli, G., Biagi, L., et al., 2016. Magnetic susceptibility in the deep layers of the primary motor cortex in amyotrophic lateral sclerosis. NeuroImage Clin. 12, 965–969.

De Reuck, J., Devos, D., Moreau, C., et al., 2017. Topographic distribution of brain iron deposition and small cerebrovascular lesions in amyotrophic lateral sclerosis and in frontotemporal lobar degeneration: a postmortem 7.0-Tesla magnetic resonance imaging study with neuropathological correlates. Acta Neurol. Belg. 117 (4), 873–878.

Donatelli, G., Retico, A., Caldarazzo Ienco, E., et al., 2018. Semiautomated evaluation of the primary motor cortex in patients with amyotrophic lateral sclerosis at 3T. AJNR Am. J. Neuroradiol. 39 (1), 63–69.

Donatelli, G., Caldarazzo Ienco, E., Costagli, M., et al., 2019. MRI cortical feature of bulbar impairment in patients with amyotrophic lateral sclerosis. NeuroImage Clin. 24, 101934. https://doi.org/10.1016/j.nicl.2019.101934.

Donatelli, G., Costagli, M., Cecchi, P., et al., 2022. Motor cortical patterns of upper motor neuron pathology in amyotrophic lateral sclerosis: a 3 T MRI study with iron-sensitive sequences. NeuroImage Clin. 35, 103138. https://doi.org/10.1016/j.nicl.2022.103138.

Düzel, E., Acosta-Cabronero, J., Berron, D., et al., 2019. European ultrahigh-field imaging network for neurodegenerative diseases (EUFIND). Alzheimers Dement. 11, 538–549.

Fink, J.K., 2001. Progressive spastic paraparesis: hereditary spastic paraplegia and its relation to primary and amyotrophic lateral sclerosis. Semin. Neurol. 21 (2), 199–207.

Gatto, R.G., Amin, M.Y., Deyoung, D., Hey, M., Mareci, T.H., Magin, R.L., 2018. Ultra-high field diffusion MRI reveals early axonal pathology in spinal cord of ALS mice. Transl. Neurodegener. 7, 20. https://doi.org/10.1186/s40035-018-0122-z.

Gorno-Tempini, M.L., Hillis, A.E., Weintraub, S., et al., 2011. Classification of primary progressive aphasia and its variants. Neurology 76 (11), 1006–1014.

Hughes, J.T., 1982. Pathology of amyotrophic lateral sclerosis. Adv. Neurol. 36, 61–74.

Kawamata, T., Akiyama, H., Yamada, T., McGeer, P.L., 1992. Immunologic reactions in amyotrophic lateral sclerosis brain and spinal cord tissue. Am. J. Pathol. 140 (3), 691–707.

Konrad, C., Jansen, A., Henningsen, H., et al., 2006. Subcortical reorganization in amyotrophic lateral sclerosis. Exp. Brain Res. 172 (3), 361–369.

Kwan, J.Y., Jeong, S.Y., Van Gelderen, P., et al., 2012. Iron accumulation in deep cortical layers accounts for MRI signal abnormalities in ALS: correlating 7 Tesla MRI and pathology. PLoS One 7 (4), e35241. https://doi.org/10.1371/journal.pone.0035241.

Li, J., Pan, P., Song, W., Huang, R., Chen, K., Shang, H., 2012. A meta-analysis of diffusion tensor imaging studies in amyotrophic lateral sclerosis. Neurobiol. Aging 33 (8), 1833–1838.

Lillo, P., Mioshi, E., Burrell, J.R., Kiernan, M.C., Hodges, J.R., Hornberger, M., 2012. Grey and white matter changes across the amyotrophic lateral sclerosis-frontotemporal dementia continuum. PLoS One 7 (8), e43993. https://doi.org/10.1371/journal.pone.0043993.

McCluskey, L., Vandriel, S., Elman, L., et al., 2014. ALS-plus syndrome: non-pyramidal features in a large ALS cohort. J. Neurol. Sci. 345 (1–2), 118–124.

Neumann, M., Sampathu, D.M., Kwong, L.K., et al., 2006. Ubiquitinated TDP-43 in frontotemporal lobar degeneration and amyotrophic lateral sclerosis. Science 314, 130–133.

Nitert, A.D., Tan, H.H., Walhout, R., et al., 2022. Sensitivity of brain MRI and neurological examination for detection of upper motor neurone degeneration in amyotrophic lateral sclerosis. J. Neurol. Neurosurg. Psychiatry 93 (1), 82–92.

Pallebage-Gamarallage, M., Foxley, S., Menke, R.A.L., et al., 2018. Dissecting the pathobiology of altered MRI signal in amyotrophic lateral sclerosis: a post mortem whole brain sampling strategy for the integration of ultra-high-field MRI and quantitative neuropathology. BMC Neurosci. 19 (1), 11. https://doi.org/10.1186/s12868-018-0416-1.

Phukan, J., Elamin, M., Bede, P., et al., 2012. The syndrome of cognitive impairment in amyotrophic lateral sclerosis: a population-based study. J. Neurol. Neurosurg. Psychiatry 83 (1), 102–108.

Ravits, J.M., La Spada, A.R., 2009. ALS motor phenotype heterogeneity, focality, and spread: deconstructing motor neuron degeneration. Neurology 73 (10), 805–811.

Sigmund, E.E., Suero, G.A., Hu, C., et al., 2012. High-resolution human cervical spinal cord imaging at 7 T. NMR Biomed. 25 (7), 891–899.

Turner, R., 2013. MRI methods for in-vivo cortical parcellation. In: Geyer, S., Turner, R. (Eds.), Microstructural Parcellation of the Human Cerebral Cortex: From Brodmann's Post-Mortem Map to In Vivo Mapping With High-Field Magnetic Resonance Imaging. Springer-Verlag, Berlin, pp. 197–220.

Verstraete, E., Polders, D.L., Mandl, R.C., et al., 2014. Multimodal tract-based analysis in ALS patients at 7T: a specific white matter profile? Amyotroph. Lateral Scler. Frontotemporal Degener. 15 (1–2), 84–92.

Whitwell, J.L., Josephs, K.A., 2012. Recent advances in the imaging of frontotemporal dementia. Curr. Neurol. Neurosci. Rep. 12 (6), 715–723.

Parkinson's disease and atypical parkinsonism

33

Stéphane Lehéricy[a,b,c]

[a]*Paris Brain Institute, Center for NeuroImaging Research—CENIR, Paris, France* [b]*Sorbonne University, UMR S 1127, CNRS UMR 7225, ICM Team Movement, Investigations and Therapeutics (MOVIT), Paris, France* [c]*Neuroradiology Department, Pitie-Salpetriere hospital, Assistance Publique—Hôpitaux de Paris, Paris, France*

Highlights

- 7T MRI detects increased iron deposition in the substantia nigra in PD in areas corresponding to nigrosomes and reduced neuromelanin contrast.
- 7T MRI improves visualization of the subthalamic nucleus allowing better targeting for deep brain stimulation and small brainstem nuclei.
- New contrasts including chemical shift imaging and sodium imaging may provide new information on the pathophysiology of parkinsonism.
- Improved spectral resolution for magnetic resonance spectroscopy makes it possible to study compounds such as glutathione and cerebral neurotransmitters more easily.

Over the last decade or so, MRI studies in Parkinson's disease (PD) and atypical parkinsonism have used two main advantages of 7T over lower field strength: the increased SNR, which allowed increasing the spatial resolution of the images, and the increased tissue contrast, which allowed better visualization of small deep brain nuclei. In PD, these two properties were first used to improve imaging of the substantia nigra (SN), detect PD-related pathological changes, study the subthalamic nucleus (STN), and improve deep brain stimulation targeting. In the SN, studies mostly focused on iron imaging and the detection of the dorsal nigral hyperintensity sign. More recently, imaging of other deep nuclei and of patients with atypical parkinsonism was reported. Improved magnetic resonance spectroscopy (MRS) abilities were also used to study brain metabolites and energy metabolism in PD.

33.1 Substantia nigra imaging

33.1.1 The normal substantia nigra

33.1.1.1 Anatomy of the substantia nigra

The SN is subdivided into the pars reticulata (SNr), located ventrally and composed of GABAergic neurons, and the pars compacta (SNc), located dorsally and composed of dopaminergic neurons. The SNr is an output nucleus of the basal ganglia and projects to the thalamus. The SNc provides

Advances in Magnetic Resonance Technology and Applications. Volume 10. **ISSN 2666-9099. https://doi.org/10.1016/B978-0-323-99898-7.00004-3**

the dopaminergic innervation of the striatum. The dopaminergic neurons in the midbrain are located in the retrorubral area (A8), the SNc (A9), and the ventral tegmental area or VTA (A10). The boundaries between these cell groups are poorly individualized, and the contours of the SNc are therefore difficult to draw.

Distinct compartments of the SN have been observed using calbindin D_{28k} immunoreactivity of striatal terminals in the SN. In primates, calbindin-positive fibers are present throughout the SNr and most of the SNc, because dopaminergic neurons of the SNc form cell clusters that penetrate deep into the SNr (Haber et al., 2000). The SN contains calbindin-rich zones called matrix and five calbindin-poor zones called nigrosomes 1 to 5 (Fig. 33.1A). The matrix comprises 60% and the nigrosomes 40% of nigral dopaminergic neurons. Nigrosome 1 is the largest one and is located in the dorsal part of the SN, at intermediate and caudal levels.

The SN has also been subdivided into three tiers: dorsal, ventral, and SNr (Haber et al., 2000). The dorsal tier contains loosely spaced dopaminergic neurons of the VTA, the retrorubral area, and the A9 pars dorsalis (Sulzer et al., 2018). The ventral tier contains densely packed dopaminergic cells of the SNc that penetrate into the SNr. Dopaminergic neurons in A9 project to the associative and motor parts of the caudate nucleus and putamen. Dopaminergic neurons in A10 and A8 mainly project to the ventral striatum. Dopaminergic neurons in the dorsal tier also innervate the cortex.

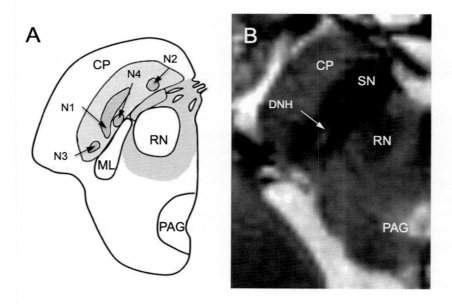

FIG. 33.1

SN normal anatomy and dopamine cell loss in PD. (A) Diagram of the midbrain in the axial plane showing the nigrosomes 1. (B) Corresponding three-dimensional T_2^*-weighted 7T image 0.5-mm isotropic voxel size. The nigrosomes 1 to 4 are indicated by N1 to N4 in the histological image. The dorsal nigral hyperintensity (DNH) area roughly matching N1 is shown by the *arrow* in the MRI image. Abbreviations: *CP*, cerebral peduncle; *ML*, medial lemniscus; *N*, nigrosome; *PAG*, periaqueductal gray matter; *RN*, red nucleus; *SN*, substantia nigra.

33.1.1.2 Neuromelanin and iron in the substantia nigra

Nigral dopaminergic neurons contain neuromelanin, a dark brown intraneuronal pigment. Neuromelanin is synthetized via oxidization of excess dopamine (or other catecholamines) and is regarded as a protective antioxidant mechanism (Sulzer et al., 2018). Neuromelanin is stored in neuromelanin autophagic lysosome organelles where it interacts with metal ions and particularly iron. In the SN, neuromelanin is found from the age of around 3 years and accumulates during aging. Close physical association of neuromelanin and alpha-synuclein in dopaminergic neurons were reported suggesting a link between neuromelanin and PD pathophysiology. Due to their insolubility, neuromelanin deposits were also found in the extracellular space in the region containing intact dopaminergic neurons in normal aging people and patients with Parkinson's disease (Sulzer et al., 2018).

Iron accumulates in the SN. In normal subjects, high level of iron is found in the striato-pallido-nigral pathway including the SN, the globus pallidus, and the subthalamic nucleus, as well as the red nucleus. Iron concentrations are higher in the SNr than in the SNc. Iron content in the SN increases with age. Iron is stored in ferritin, which binds to ferric iron Fe^{3+} and in neuromelanin-containing compounds (Sulzer et al., 2018).

33.1.1.3 MRI of the normal SN at 7T

Two of the most studied MRI sequences for the SN are neuromelanin-sensitive MRI and iron imaging using T_2^* and susceptibility-weighted images. Diffusion imaging also provides interesting information.

Neuromelanin imaging. The neuromelanin-iron complex is paramagnetic, which makes it visible on MRI (Sulzer et al., 2018). Using specific MRI sequences, neuromelanin appears bright and allows a good delineation of the SNc as shown in histological-MRI comparative studies (Blazejewska et al., 2013). At 3T, neuromelanin-sensitive imaging is commonly performed using 2D T_1-weighted fast or turbo spin echo MRI sequence (Gaurav et al., 2021) or 3D T_1-weighted gradient echo sequences with magnetization transfer (O'Callaghan et al., 2021). Many studies have used neuromelanin-sensitive MRI sequences to study the human SN at 3T but not yet at 7T. However, several studies have used 7T MRI to study the locus coeruleus, a small catecholaminergic brainstem nucleus obtaining good results with higher spatial resolution than at 3T using a 3D turbo Flash sequence with magnetization transfer (O'Callaghan et al., 2021). MRI could help improve SNc versus SNr delineation thanks to a better spatial resolution and provide more accurate volume calculation by reducing partial voluming.

Iron imaging. At 7T, spatial resolution of 0.5 mm isotropic for three-dimensional (3D) images (versus 0.8–1 mm at 3T) is easily obtained for T_2^*- and susceptibility-weighted images. Increased spatial resolution allowed improved definition of SN contours and thus the first description of an SN region corresponding to nigrosome 1 using 3D T_2^*-weighted imaging at 7T (Kwon et al., 2012; Blazejewska et al., 2013; Cosottini et al., 2014). This region was visible at the dorsal mid- and inferior levels of the SN and was subsequently called the dorsal nigral hyperintensity (DNH) sign or the swallow tail sign, because of its shape reminiscent of a swallow tail (Schwarz et al., 2014) (Figs. 33.1B and 33.2). The term nigrosome 1 should be reserved to the histological region. On T_2^*- and susceptibility-weighted images at caudal level below the red nucleus, the DNH appears as an oblique band of high signal intensity with low iron levels surrounded by two layers of low signal intensity with high iron levels located in the dorsolateral part of the SN (Kwon et al., 2012; Blazejewska et al., 2013; Cosottini et al., 2014). More rostrally at the inferior level of the red nucleus, the DNH appears as a pocket of high intensity indenting the posteromedial border of the SN (Kwon et al., 2012; Blazejewska et al., 2013; Cosottini et al., 2014) (Fig. 33.2A–C).

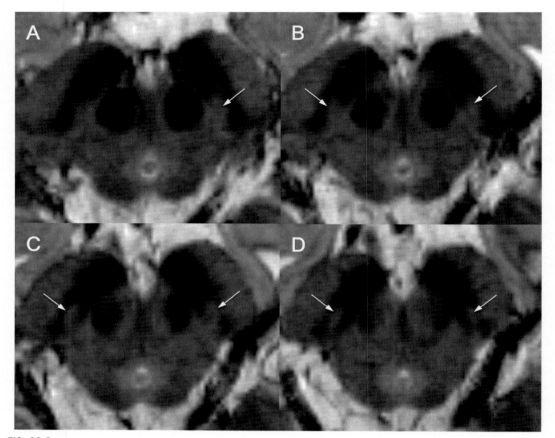

FIG. 33.2

Normal anatomy of the SN at 7T. (A–D) Three-dimensional T_2^*-weighted 7T image 0.5-mm isotropic voxel size at four different levels of the SN from upper (A) to lower levels (D). The dorsal nigral hyperintensity area corresponding to N1 is shown by the *arrows* in each image.

The overlap between nigrosome 1 and this high signal region of the SN was confirmed in histological studies (Blazejewska et al., 2013; Brammerloh et al., 2022). In control subjects, detection accuracy of this sign varied according to readers (77% to 100% in three readers) with variable interrater reliability (typically 0.80 to 0.84) and intrarater reliability (0.62 to 1) (Pyatigorskaya et al., 2018). The other nigrosomes N2–5 were also identified at 7T although less well and less confidently than nigrosome 1 area (Schwarz et al., 2018). Overall, visual assessment of the SN for nigrosomes 1 to 5 revealed normal range visibility scores in 14 of 15 controls in this study. Following the 7T results, improved 3T acquisition techniques using high contrast 3D susceptibility-weighted images and increased high spatial resolution (0.43–0.55 mm in plane resolution with 0.7–0.75 mm slice thickness) also allowed successful detection of nigrosome 1 in healthy control subjects (Schwarz et al., 2014).

Postmortem studies suggested that 7T MRI could distinguish the neuromelanin-iron complex and ferric iron (Fe^{3+}) thanks to their different magnetic properties (Lee et al., 2018). Regions with high ferric iron deposits had low T_2 and T_2^* values, while regions with high neuromelanin content had low T_2^* but not necessarily T_2 values. Based on these results, the authors suggested that regions with high ferric iron could be distinguished from regions with high neuromelanin-iron complex using this mismatch between T_2 and T_2^*, ferric iron being better seen using T_2 map and neuromelanin-iron using T_2^*/T_2 map (or T_2^*/T_2^2 map) (Lee et al., 2018).

7T MRI could also help better understand the complex relationship between dopamine, iron, and neuromelanin in the pathophysiology of PD. Iron is involved in the dopaminergic metabolic pathway leading to neuromelanin organelles and is also present in activated microglia and perivascular macrophage contents (Sulzer et al., 2018). Previous studies at 3T have suggested that the changes in the nigrostriatal dopaminergic system are temporally ordered in PD patients (Biondetti et al., 2021). In these studies, changes started with striatal dopaminergic dysfunction, followed by SNc iron accumulation preceding neuromelanin loss.

33.1.2 Pathological changes in the substantia nigra in PD

A fundamental characteristic of PD is the loss of dopaminergic neurons of the SN. Degeneration of dopaminergic neurons is first detected in the striatum long before the occurrence of motor symptoms with reduced striatal dopaminergic function as shown by PET and I^{123}-ioflupane imaging studies (Stoessl et al., 2014). The presymptomatic phase in the striatum would last for about a decade or even longer in younger patients, reflecting the known earlier degeneration of striatal terminals in Parkinson's disease. Cell loss appears to occur later in the SN, around 5 years before the onset of clinical parkinsonism as estimated in histology studies (Fearnley and Lees, 1991) and neuromelanin sensitive MRI studies (Biondetti et al., 2021). Neurodegeneration of the nigrostriatal system in PD is faster in the early stages than the later stages of the disease probably following negative monoexponential decay, as shown in histological studies using melanized cell counting in the SN (Fearnley and Lees, 1991), studies using neuromelanin-sensitive MRI, Ioflupane (^{123}I) dopamine transporter single-photon emission computed tomography (DaTSCAN) for the assessment of striatal presynaptic dopamine neuronal function, and PET for the assessment of dopamine content in the striatal terminals (Stoessl et al., 2014). The loss of SN dopaminergic neurons at diagnosis was estimated at 30%–50% using histological neuronal counts (Fearnley and Lees, 1991) in line with neuromelanin-sensitive MRI volume measurements of the SN that reported a 23%–53% volume reduction of the SN in the early stages of the disease depending on the method used (Gaurav et al., 2021). Neuromelanin-based SN volume and signal intensity decreased with disease progression (Gaurav et al., 2021). Striatal DaT loss correlated with SNc neuromelanin loss in PD using imaging (Martin-Bastida et al., 2019). Changes in striatal dopaminergic function followed a specific pattern, progressively involving the sensorimotor, associative and limbic regions of the striatum (Biondetti et al., 2021) and the SN (Sulzer et al., 2018). These regions correlated specifically with motor, cognitive, and behavioral deficits.

Although no study used 7T neuromelanin-sensitive imaging in PD patients, several postmortem studies suggested that this technique might provide new and interesting results. For instance, the area of T_2 and T_2^* mismatch, which may help distinguish the neuromelanin-iron complex and ferric iron, could serve as a new biomarker of SN neurodegeneration. This area was significantly reduced in the postmortem brain of PD patients paralleling the reduction in neuromelanin content (Lee et al., 2018).

A second fundamental characteristic of the SN in PD is the increase in iron deposition. This increase is particularly visible and clinically relevant in the DNH area. Patients with PD experience loss of DNH

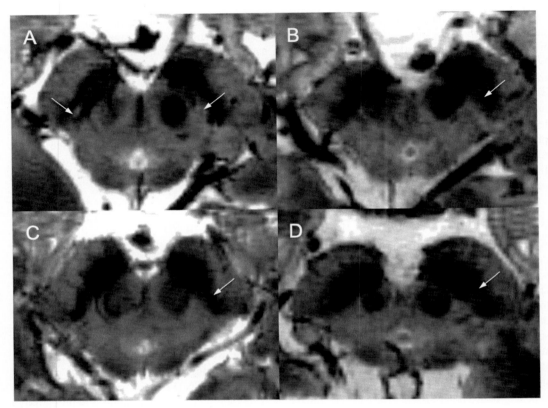

FIG. 33.3

Comparison of 7T anatomy of the SN in healthy volunteer, PD, and PSP patients. (A) Three-dimensional T_2^*-weighted axial image at 0.5-mm isotropic voxel size showing the DNH in a healthy volunteer *(arrows)*. (B, C) The DNH is no longer visible *(arrows)* in the PD patients (B, C) and the PSP patient (D).

as a result of the increase in iron load in nigrosome 1 (Fig. 33.3). This sign was first described at 7T (Kwon et al., 2012). Several subsequent 7T studies reported that the loss of DNH accurately distinguished PD patients from control subjects with 86%–100% sensitivity, 93%–100% specificity, and 91%–98% accuracy (Schwarz et al., 2018; Cosottini et al., 2014; Pyatigorskaya et al., 2018; Blazejewska et al., 2013). Loss of DNH was subsequently detected at 3T with a high diagnostic performance, and the added value of 7T MRI over 3T MRI is not yet clear. Previous study also confirmed that the SNr and SNc could be distinguished on the basis of MRI signal (hypointense in T_2w images in the SNr and hyperintense in T_1w images in the SNc) (Blazejewska et al., 2013). Regions with high neuromelanin content were mostly distinct from regions with high iron content.

Changes in nigrosomes 2 to 5 in PD were detected at 7T although less reliably than in nigrosome 1. PD patients showed larger signal reduction in all nigrosomes than in the iron-rich SN, with 37.2%

reduction in nigrosome 1, which inversely correlated with motor disorder severity assessed using the Unified Parkinson's Disease Rating Scale (Schwarz et al., 2018).

7T MRI could also improve the precision of volumetric measurements of the SN allowing better correlation with clinical scores. In mild-to-moderate PD, SN volume measured using 7T MRI and quantitative susceptibility mapping related to motor manifestations (disease duration, motor score, bradykinesia-rigidity subscore, but not tremor or postural instability/gait difficulty subscores) and laterality-dependent manner (Poston et al., 2020).

Abnormal contours of the SN using T_2^*-weighted 7T MRI (Kwon et al., 2012) and volume changes were also reported in PD but with discordant results including increase (Kwon et al., 2012) or decrease in SN volumes (Pyatigorskaya et al., 2018).

33.2 Other deep brain nuclei

33.2.1 The subthalamic nucleus

The subthalamic nucleus (STN) has also been extensively studied, especially because of its importance for the neurosurgical treatment of PD.

Compared with 1.5T and 3T, 7T MRI improved visualization of the STN with marked improvements in spatial resolution, tissue contrast, and signal-to-noise ratio, suggesting superiority of 7T MRI for visualizing target structures for deep brain stimulation in PD (van Laar et al., 2016). QSM provided better contrast-to-noise ratio than T_2^*-weighted images and improved visualization of the

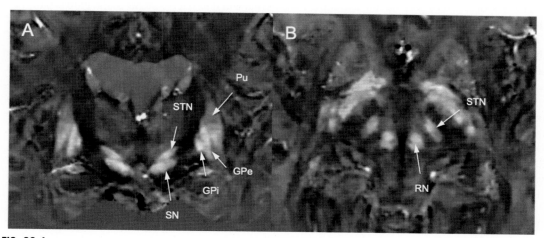

FIG. 33.4

Anatomy of the subthalamic nucleus at 7T using quantitative susceptibility mapping. (A) Quantitative susceptibility map in the coronal (A) and axial (B) planes at 0.6-mm isotropic voxel size showing the subthalamic nucleus in a healthy volunteer *(arrows)*. Abbreviations: *GPe*, external segment of the globus pallidus; *GPi*, internal segment of the globus pallidus; *Pu*, putamen; *RN*, red nucleus; *SN*, substantia nigra; *STN*, subthalamic nucleus. *Image courtesy of Mathieu Santin, Emilie Poirion, Alexandre Vignaud.*

STN (Alkemade et al., 2017) (Fig. 33.4). 7T-derived atlases of the STN have been elaborated that can improve STN localization in individuals imaged at 3T (Husch et al., 2018).

For DBS, it is not certain that the improvement brought by the better visualization of the STN in the DBS procedure (van Laar et al., 2016) or for the planning of the target (Bot et al., 2019) is significant and this aspect is still debated. In another study, the test-retest reliability of neurosurgeons was not influenced by MRI field strength, contrast or targeting session between 3T and 7T (Isaacs et al., 2021). Study of the correspondence between microelectrodes positioning and STN visualization at 7T suggested that the STN representation at 7T did not provide an exact representation of the microelectrode recordings activity location in the dorsal STN (Bot et al., 2019). The dorsal border of the STN on 7T MRI was located more dorsal in the majority of cases than with microelectrode recordings. Compared with 3T, the actual selected location of the electrode was more dorsal when using the 7T scans (Isaacs et al., 2021).

7T MRI also improved visualization of STN connections and neighboring fiber tracts. The STN could be parcellated using diffusion-based tractography into posterolateral sensorimotor, central associative, and anteromedial limbic compartments in patients with Parkinson's disease with 7T MRI (Plantinga et al., 2018). Although, the ideal site for lead positioning within the STN remains controversial, 7T parcellation of the STN could help reduce behavioral side effects observed after placement of a DBS lead in the limbic/associative STN territory and improve lead positioning (Schrock et al., 2021). 7T MRI detected fMRI activation in the STN and other basal ganglia structures in a stop-signal reaction task where 3T did not (de Hollander et al., 2017).

33.2.2 Other deep nuclei and small structures

Segmentation of other deep nuclei, including the external and internal segments of the globus pallidus, the putamen and the thalamus, was also improved at 7T either using atlas derived from 7T images (Tourdias et al., 2014) or more recently using deep learning-based fully automatic segmentation of the globus pallidus (Solomon et al., 2021). White matter null MPRAGE-derived images allowed visualization of thalamic nuclei, including the ventral intermediate nucleus, which is a DBS target in essential tremor (Tourdias et al., 2014).

Fiber tracts adjacent to the pedunculopontine nucleus (PPN) were used in a parkinsonian rhesus macaque to investigate the underlying therapy and side effects of PPN DBS (Zitella et al., 2015). These tracts included the oculomotor nerve, the central tegmental tract, and the superior cerebellar peduncles. Diffusion-based tractography allowed to delineate brainstem nuclei such as the PPN (Bianciardi et al., 2018) and neighboring mesopontine tegmental nuclei (Bianciardi et al., 2018), with histological validation showing reasonable overlap between histological and DTI-based masks of the PPN (Henssen et al., 2019).

7T MRI allowed better precision to detect activation in the cerebral area of the olfactory network (Donoshita et al., 2021). In this study, the piriform cortex was mainly associated with subjective odor intensity, whereas the posterior orbitofrontal cortex were involved in the discrimination of the subjective hedonic tone of the odorant.

The locus coeruleus and subcoeruleus are two small brainstem nuclei that are involved in cognition and the control of muscle tone during rapid eye movement (REM) sleep, respectively. Imaging of the coeruleus/subcoeruleus complex at 7T provided improved spatial resolution and lower partial voluming (O'Callaghan et al., 2021). More recently, 7T MRI using neuromelanin-sensitive imaging was used to study the role of the locus coeruleus in response inhibition in PD (O'Callaghan et al., 2021). The authors tested the relationship between the integrity of the locus coeruleus and the effect of atomoxetine on response inhibition performance, an inhibitor of the presynaptic noradrenaline transporter. Atomoxetine improved stop-signal reaction times in patients with lower contrast-to-noise ratio in the locus coeruleus suggesting that the locus coeruleus is involved in response inhibition in PD patients.

33.3 Magnetic resonance spectroscopy

Increased field strength provides a number of advantages for MRS including increased signal-to-noise ratio, increased in peak height of metabolites and better peak separation. A larger number of metabolites are detected with reduced scanning time.

In PD, changes in the neurotransmitter γ-aminobutyric acid (GABA) were found in the brain, with elevated concentrations in the pons and putamen (Emir et al., 2012). MRS was used to study neurotransmitter changes during response inhibition in patients with frontotemporal lobar degeneration including subtypes of progressive supranuclear palsy (PSP). Deficits in GABA and glutamate were found in these patients in the right inferior frontal gyrus that correlated with impaired response inhibition (Murley et al., 2020).

Glutathione (GSH) can be better quantified at 7T while it is more difficult at 3T because of lower SNR. GSH is a molecule that provides antioxidant and electrophile defenses and acts as a redox buffer. Although PD is associated with oxidative stress and decreased nigral GSH, a pilot study failed to show significant changes in brain GSH following intravenous administration of a high dose of N-acetylcysteine, a well-known antioxidant and GSH precursor (Coles et al., 2018).

Energy metabolism was studied using ^{31}P-MRS. Lower brain adenosine triphosphate (ATP) levels, intracellular pH, and nicotinamide adenine dinucleotide contents were found in the occipital lobe of PD, suggesting subtle defects in energy metabolism and mitochondrial function (Zhu et al., 2021).

GBA1 mutations are important risk factor for PD. Lower levels of N-acetyl-aspartate, GABA, glutamate, and glutamate-to-glutamine ratio were found in the posterior cingulate cortex of patients with Gaucher disease, an autosomal recessive metabolic disorder caused by mutations in GBA1 gene (Kartha et al., 2020).

33.4 Application in atypical parkinsonism

There are few studies on atypical parkinsonism using 7T MRI. In the SN, loss of DNH was observed in almost all patients with PSP and multiple system atrophy most often bilaterally while patients with corticobasal degeneration frequently presented normal DNH aspect (Kim et al., 2016) (Fig. 33.3D). In a postmortem study, nigrosomes were no more visible at 9.4T in PSP, and SN volumes were reduced (Massey et al., 2017).

7T studies in atypical parkinsonism focused on small structures that were not usually imaged or less well at 3T. In PSP, decreased volume of the STN was found using 7T 3D T_2^*-weighted imaging at 0.5-mm isotropic voxel size along with the globus pallidus, putamen, and caudate nucleus (Pyatigorskaya et al., 2020). In contrast, no STN size difference was found in PD (Alkemade et al., 2017; Pyatigorskaya et al., 2020). Using R_2^* values and QSM, increased iron deposition along the myelinated fibers at the anterior SN and third cranial nerve (oculomotor nerve) verified by histological measurements of iron concentrations

(Lee et al., 2021). These results show the level of detail that can be achieved at 7T in analyzing the brains of patients with neurodegenerative lesions in the brain.

To date to our knowledge, there was no study on multisystem atrophy.

7T MRI was used to evaluate vascular pathology in parkinsonism. In a postmortem study in patients with Lewy body dementia (LBD), cortical microbleeds predominated in the frontal regions and were not related to the frequently associated Alzheimer's disease and cerebral amyloid angiopathy, suggesting that they were related to the pathophysiology of LBD (De Reuck et al., 2015).

33.5 Conclusion and future directions

7T MRI has allowed better delineation of SNc and SNr changes, possible distinction between ferritin-iron and neuromelanin-iron using multimodal quantitative parametric mapping, provided more accurate volume calculation with less partial voluming particularly useful for small nuclei such as the STN, better DBS targeting, better evaluation of connectivity changes, and the assessment of energy failure using ^{1}H-glutathione and ^{31}P spectroscopy.

Future studies will investigate structural changes in preclinical PD such as patients with idiopathic rapid eye movement sleep behavior disorders (RBD) and autonomic dysfunction or subjects at-risk of PD subjects such as asymptomatic PD-related mutation carriers. 7T MRI could also provide significant improvement for the study of small deep brain structures in PD and atypical parkinsonism, such as brainstem nuclei, including the pedunculopontine nucleus, raphe nuclei, periaqueductal gray matter, and small nuclei in the medulla oblongata, as well as small white matter tracts such as the medial longitudinal fasciculus.

New contrasts, including chemical shift imaging or sodium imaging, may provide interesting new information of the pathophysiology of parkinsonism. Pilot studies on brain neurotransmitters and energy metabolism have shown the potential of MRS to study PD pathophysiology.

Acknowledgments

The work was supported by Agence Nationale de la Recherche, "Investissements d'avenir" [grant number ANR-10-IAIHU-06, ANR-11-INBS-0006] and Neuratris [ANR-11-INBS-0011].

References

Alkemade, A., de Hollander, G., Keuken, M.C., et al., 2017. Comparison of T2*-weighted and QSM contrasts in Parkinson's disease to visualize the STN with MRI. PLoS One 12, e0176130.

Bianciardi, M., Strong, C., Toschi, N., et al., 2018. A probabilistic template of human mesopontine tegmental nuclei from in vivo 7T MRI. NeuroImage 170, 222–230.

Biondetti, E., Santin, M.D., Valabregue, R., et al., 2021. The spatiotemporal changes in dopamine, neuromelanin and iron characterizing Parkinson's disease. Brain 144, 3114–3125.

Blazejewska, A.I., Schwarz, S.T., Pitiot, A., et al., 2013. Visualization of nigrosome 1 and its loss in PD: pathoanatomical correlation and in vivo 7 T MRI. Neurology 81, 534–540.

Bot, M., Verhagen, O., Caan, M., et al., 2019. Defining the dorsal STN border using 7.0-T MRI: a comparison to microelectrode recordings and lower field strength MRI. Stereotact. Funct. Neurosurg. 97, 153–159.

Brammerloh, M., Kirilina, E., Alkemade, A., et al., 2022. Swallow tail sign: Revisited. Radiology. 305, 674–677.

Coles, L.D., Tuite, P.J., Oz, G., et al., 2018. Repeated-dose oral N-acetylcysteine in Parkinson's disease: pharmacokinetics and effect on brain glutathione and oxidative stress. J. Clin. Pharmacol. 58, 158–167.

Cosottini, M., Frosini, D., Pesaresi, I., et al., 2014. MR imaging of the substantia Nigra at 7 T enables diagnosis of Parkinson disease. Radiology, 131448.

de Hollander, G., Keuken, M.C., van der Zwaag, W., Forstmann, B.U., Trampel, R., 2017. Comparing functional MRI protocols for small, iron-rich basal ganglia nuclei such as the subthalamic nucleus at 7 T and 3 T. Hum. Brain Mapp. 38, 3226–3248.

De Reuck, J.L., Auger, F., Durieux, N., et al., 2015. Detection of cortical microbleeds in postmortem brains of patients with Lewy body dementia: a 7.0-tesla magnetic resonance imaging study with neuropathological correlates. Eur. Neurol. 74, 158–161.

Donoshita, Y., Choi, U.S., Ban, H., Kida, I., 2021. Assessment of olfactory information in the human brain using 7-tesla functional magnetic resonance imaging. NeuroImage 236, 118212.

Emir, U.E., Tuite, P.J., Oz, G., 2012. Elevated pontine and putamenal GABA levels in mild-moderate Parkinson disease detected by 7 tesla proton MRS. PLoS One 7, e30918.

Fearnley, J.M., Lees, A.J., 1991. Ageing and Parkinson's disease: substantia nigra regional selectivity. Brain 114, 2283–2301.

Gaurav, R., Yahia-Cherif, L., Pyatigorskaya, N., et al., 2021. Longitudinal changes in Neuromelanin MRI signal in Parkinson's disease: a progression marker. Mov. Disord. 36, 1592–1602.

Haber, S.N., Fudge, J.L., McFarland, N.R., 2000. Striatonigrostriatal pathways in primates form an ascending spiral from the shell to the dorsolateral striatum. J. Neurosci. 20, 2369–2382.

Henssen, D., Kuppens, D., Meijer, F.J.A., van Cappellen van Walsum, A.M., Temel, Y., Kurt, E., 2019. Identification of the pedunculopontine nucleus and surrounding white matter tracts on 7T diffusion tensor imaging, combined with histological validation. Surg. Radiol. Anat. 41, 187–196.

Husch, A., Petersen, M.V., Gemmar, P., Goncalves, J., Sunde, N., Hertel, F., 2018. Post-operative deep brain stimulation assessment: automatic data integration and report generation. Brain Stimul. 11, 863–866.

Isaacs, B.R., Heijmans, M., Kuijf, M.L., et al., 2021. Variability in subthalamic nucleus targeting for deep brain stimulation with 3 and 7 tesla magnetic resonance imaging. NeuroImage Clin. 32, 102829.

Kartha, R.V., Joers, J., Terluk, M.R., et al., 2020. Neurochemical abnormalities in patients with type 1 Gaucher disease on standard of care therapy. J. Inherit. Metab. Dis. 43, 564–573.

Kim, J.M., Jeong, H.J., Bae, Y.J., et al., 2016. Loss of substantia nigra hyperintensity on 7 tesla MRI of Parkinson's disease, multiple system atrophy, and progressive supranuclear palsy. Parkinsonism Relat. Disord. 26, 47–54.

Kwon, D.H., Kim, J.M., Oh, S.H., et al., 2012. Seven-tesla magnetic resonance images of the substantia nigra in Parkinson disease. Ann. Neurol. 71, 267–277.

Lee, H., Baek, S.Y., Chun, S.Y., Lee, J.H., Cho, H., 2018. Specific visualization of neuromelanin-iron complex and ferric iron in the human post-mortem substantia nigra using MR relaxometry at 7T. NeuroImage 172, 874–885.

Lee, H., Lee, M.J., Kim, E.J., Huh, G.Y., Lee, J.H., Cho, H., 2021. Iron accumulation in the oculomotor nerve of the progressive supranuclear palsy brain. Sci. Rep. 11, 2950.

Martin-Bastida, A., Lao-Kaim, N.P., Roussakis, A.A., et al., 2019. Relationship between neuromelanin and dopamine terminals within the Parkinson's nigrostriatal system. Brain 142, 2023–2036.

Massey, L.A., Miranda, M.A., Al-Helli, O., et al., 2017. 9.4 T MR microscopy of the substantia nigra with pathological validation in controls and disease. NeuroImage Clin. 13, 154–163.

Murley, A.G., Rouse, M.A., Jones, P.S., et al., 2020. GABA and glutamate deficits from frontotemporal lobar degeneration are associated with disinhibition. Brain 143, 3449–3462.

O'Callaghan, C., Hezemans, F.H., Ye, R., et al., 2021. Locus coeruleus integrity and the effect of atomoxetine on response inhibition in Parkinson's disease. Brain 144, 2513–2526.

Plantinga, B.R., Temel, Y., Duchin, Y., et al., 2018. Individualized parcellation of the subthalamic nucleus in patients with Parkinson's disease with 7T MRI. NeuroImage 168, 403–411.

Poston, K.L., Ua Cruadhlaoich, M.A.I., Santoso, L.F., et al., 2020. Substantia Nigra volume dissociates bradykinesia and rigidity from tremor in Parkinson's disease: a 7 tesla imaging study. J. Parkinsons Dis. 10, 591–604.

Pyatigorskaya, N., Magnin, B., Mongin, M., et al., 2018. Comparative study of MRI biomarkers in the substantia Nigra to discriminate idiopathic Parkinson disease. AJNR Am. J. Neuroradiol. 39, 1460–1467.

Pyatigorskaya, N., Yahia-Cherif, L., Gaurav, R., et al., 2020. Multimodal magnetic resonance imaging quantification of brain changes in progressive supranuclear palsy. Mov. Disord. 35, 161–170.

Schrock, L.E., Patriat, R., Goftari, M., et al., 2021. 7T MRI and computational modeling supports a critical role of lead location in determining outcomes for deep brain stimulation: a case report. Front. Hum. Neurosci. 15, 631778.

Schwarz, S.T., Afzal, M., Morgan, P.S., Bajaj, N., Gowland, P.A., Auer, D.P., 2014. The 'Swallow Tail' appearance of the healthy nigrosome - a new accurate test of Parkinson's disease: a case-control and retrospective cross-sectional MRI study at 3T. PLoS One 9, e93814.

Schwarz, S.T., Mougin, O., Xing, Y., et al., 2018. Parkinson's disease related signal change in the nigrosomes 1-5 and the substantia nigra using T2* weighted 7T MRI. NeuroImage Clin. 19, 683–689.

Solomon, O., Palnitkar, T., Patriat, R., et al., 2021. Deep-learning based fully automatic segmentation of the globus pallidus interna and externa using ultra-high 7 tesla MRI. Hum. Brain Mapp. 42, 2862–2879.

Stoessl, A.J., Lehericy, S., Strafella, A.P., 2014. Imaging insights into basal ganglia function, Parkinson's disease, and dystonia. Lancet 384, 532–544.

Sulzer, D., Cassidy, C., Horga, G., et al., 2018. Neuromelanin detection by magnetic resonance imaging (MRI) and its promise as a biomarker for Parkinson's disease. npj Parkinson's Dis. 4, 11.

Tourdias, T., Saranathan, M., Levesque, I.R., Su, J., Rutt, B.K., 2014. Visualization of intra-thalamic nuclei with optimized white-matter-nulled MPRAGE at 7T. NeuroImage 84, 534–545.

van Laar, P.J., Oterdoom, D.L., Ter Horst, G.J., et al., 2016. Surgical accuracy of 3-tesla versus 7-tesla magnetic resonance imaging in deep brain stimulation for Parkinson disease. World Neurosurg. 93, 410–412.

Zhu, X.H., Lee, B.Y., Tuite, P., et al., 2021. Quantitative assessment of occipital metabolic and energetic changes in Parkinson's patients, using in vivo (31)P MRS-based metabolic imaging at 7T. Metabolites 11, 145.

Zitella, L.M., Xiao, Y., Teplitzky, B.A., et al., 2015. In vivo 7T MRI of the non-human primate brainstem. PLoS One 10, e0127049.

Healthy aging and Alzheimer's disease

Matthew J. Betts[a,b,c], **Valentina Perosa**[b,d], **Dorothea Hämmerer**[a,b,c,e], **and Emrah Düzel**[a,b,c,e]

[a]*Institute of Cognitive Neurology and Dementia Research, Otto-von-Guericke University Magdeburg, Magdeburg, Germany* [b]*German Center for Neurodegenerative Diseases (DZNE), Magdeburg, Germany* [c]*Center for Behavioral Brain Sciences, University of Magdeburg, Magdeburg, Germany* [d]*J. Philip Kistler Stroke Research Center, Department of Neurology, Massachusetts General Hospital, Harvard Medical School, Boston, MA, United States* [e]*Institute of Cognitive Neuroscience, University College London, London, United Kingdom*

Highlights

- Ultra-high field MRI permits high-resolution assessment of neurodegenerative processes affecting the brainstem and medial temporal lobe subregions.
- In Alzheimer's disease, 7T MRI enables precise assessment of vascular pathology occurring either as a consequence of AD pathology or as a comorbidity.
- The combination of 7T structural and functional MRI may be particularly powerful for assessing the function of local circuits and relationship to cognitive decline.
- Multi-parametric and longitudinal 7T MRI studies can help identify causal processes occurring in aging and across the AD spectrum.

34.1 Introduction

The use of magnetic resonance imaging (MRI) biomarkers is an important mainstay in the assessment of neurodegeneration in aging and Alzheimer's disease (AD) dementia both in clinical practice and for research. However, there is a pressing need for more sensitive and specific biomarkers of neurodegeneration, and for new approaches to study the influence of AD and its consequences on neuronal dysfunction. MRI at ultra-high field (UHF) strength, i.e., at 7 Tesla (7T), is potentially ideally suited to help address this need as it is safe and can improve sensitivity and specificity compared to conventional 3T MRI. The higher signal-to-noise ratio (SNR) available at 7T permits higher spatial resolution imaging which may provide increased sensitivity for detecting the neural substrates of cognitive decline in aging and AD. Using UHF functional MRI (fMRI), researchers are able to investigate functional activation based on blood oxygenation level-dependent (BOLD) contrast at submillimeter resolution to assess neuronal dysfunction in small brain networks. Moreover, UHF can identify vascular supply patterns using time-of-flight (ToF) imaging to determine the influence of vascular disease on neurodegeneration and progression of clinical symptoms in AD. At UHF, higher SNR together with shorter T_2^* can be exploited to obtain images with unprecedented anatomical detail, for example, using susceptibility-weighted imaging (SWI) and quantitative susceptibility mapping (QSM) to gain new insights into the role of iron deposition and morphological changes in venous vessels in aging and also into the pathophysiology of AD.

AD is typically characterized by long preclinical and prodromal stages with progressive molecular pathology, neurodegeneration, and cognitive impairment. As proposed by the recent ATN (amyloid, tau, neurodegeneration) research framework (Jack et al., 2018), ß-amyloid, tau pathology, and neurodegeneration are considered the hallmarks of clinical diagnosis. While AD pathology, i.e., levels of ß-amyloid and tau pathology, can be determined using molecular imaging, i.e., positron emission tomography (PET) or via cerebrospinal fluid (CSF) and blood plasma, determining the extent of neurodegeneration according to the ATN research framework using UHF imaging may provide a substantial advantage over conventional MRI at 1.5 or 3T. Moreover, by permitting accurate delineation and quantification of neurodegeneration to medial temporal subregions, hippocampal subfields, and brainstem nuclei such as the locus coeruleus, UHF may help to characterize earliest stage neuropathology in AD.

34.2 Assessment of cortical and subcortical neurodegeneration in AD

Assessments of cortical and subcortical gray matter volume or thickness using MRI provide the most direct measures of local neurodegeneration that are currently available. Qualitative assessments of brain structure using either 1.5 or 3T MRI have become a standard tool in the clinical workup of individuals suspected of having AD dementia. Volumetric analysis using structural imaging has also been the principal imaging marker of major cohort studies and clinical trials assessing disease-modifying therapies in predementia stages of AD as recently reviewed by Düzel (2021). However, 1.5T and 3T structural imaging is fundamentally limited by its low resolution (typically about 1 mm) and contrast-to-noise ratio (CNR), which hinder accurate quantification of volumetric changes over short time intervals, i.e., during the duration of a clinical trial or to assess presymptomatic changes at the single-subject level. Accurate delineation of medial temporal subregions such as the entorhinal/ transentorhinal and hippocampal subfield changes that may help characterize early-stage neuropathology is also not possible using 1.5 and 3T structural MRI. Moreover, given that cortical thickness is approximately 2–3 mm, structural MRI at $\leq$3T provides limited sensitivity to detect cortical atrophy.

Recently developed 7T segmentation protocols for the medial temporal lobe (MTL) (Berron et al., 2017), have shown key anatomical landmarks that are difficult to identify at 3T, i.e., necessary to distinguish the dentate gyrus from hippocampal subfield CA3, can be identified reliably using 7T MRI (for more information see Chapter 16). Additional structures for which accurate quantification of volume or thickness is difficult at 3T include subregions of the entorhinal cortex and the transentorhinal cortex, which are affected early on in the pathological cascade of AD (Düzel, 2021). Using 7T MRI, differences in the hippocampal subfield CA1 volume have been observed in individuals with MCI, indicating that volumetric measures of CA1 atrophy may improve diagnostic accuracy at early stages of AD. Additionally, atrophy of the presubiculum and subiculum has been shown to be associated with poorer cognitive performance and may be the earliest marker of hippocampal atrophy in AD (Carlesimo et al., 2015). However, studies assessing the thickness of extrahippocampal subregions such as the transentorhinal region may be more sensitive for differentiating individuals with or without amyloid pathology compared to hippocampal CA1 or whole hippocampal volume atrophy measures

(Wolk et al., 2017). In the future, it will be important to determine whether such effects can be replicated using UHF and whether these observations are dependent on the limited sensitivity and resolution of conventional MRI systems. Moreover, UHF imaging may provide new mechanistic insights into how neurodegeneration in medial temporal subregions progresses by taking advantage of the submillimeter resolution to quantify the structural integrity of different cortical layers. Quantification of laminar thickness and how it is altered in aging but also by AD pathology may reveal microstructural insights into the causal cascade of neurodegeneration owing to the layer-specific organization of neuronal connectivity loops (Düzel, 2021).

An emerging area of advanced structural imaging at 7T that is relevant to both aging and AD is imaging of the locus coeruleus (LC). The LC is the major source of noradrenaline in the brain and one of the first sites to develop neurofibrillary tangles that likely starts to occur in early adulthood (for a review, see Betts et al., 2019a). Studies using 3T MRI have shown that LC MRI contrast correlates with cognitive decline (Hämmerer et al., 2018), is reduced in AD dementia consistent with cell loss, and is associated with both amyloid (Betts et al., 2019b) and tau (Jacobs et al., 2021) pathology. The small size of the LC has also motivated efforts toward imaging its structural and functional integrity in vivo using 7T MRI (Betts et al., 2019a) for instance by using optimized magnetization transfer (MT)-weighted imaging approaches (Priovoulos et al., 2017). Moreover, postmortem imaging of the LC using UHF is also desired for determining how LC MRI contrast is related to its tissue microstructure, i.e., with respect to myelin, iron, and neuromelanin, and also local tau pathology that cannot be visualized due to the insufficient resolution of molecular imaging techniques (Fig. 34.1).

34.3 Toward understanding the role of vascular dysfunction in aging and AD

The importance of vascular health, in particular that of cerebral small vessels, in maintaining cognitive function throughout the lifespan is being increasingly recognized (Xu et al., 2015). Promising avenues are opening up to pinpoint how aging of cerebral vessels affects brain aging. For example, ToF angiography can be acquired with sufficient SNR and resolution, to investigate the morphology of smaller cerebral arteries such as the perforating cortical and deep arteries, allowing to investigate structural changes associated with vascular risk factors (e.g., stenosis, occlusions, and increase in tortuosity) (Bollmann et al., 2021). Furthermore, cerebral blood perfusion can be measured, without contrast agents, using arterial spin labeling (ASL), achieving a better differentiation of brain regions at 7T (Ivanov et al., 2017). Direct assessment of blood flow characteristics (i.e., velocity, pulsatility index) is possible with phase-contrast MRI at UHF, even in small cerebral arteries, and has already uncovered changes related to small-vessel pathology (Geurts et al., 2019).

Brain lesions attributed to small-vessel pathology (microbleeds on SWI and QSM, microinfarcts, and MRI-visible perivascular spaces [PVS] on T_2-weighted images) can be detected with better sensitivity using UHF MRI compared to conventional 3T MRI (see Fig. 34.2). Most importantly, the combination of different MRI sequences can shed more light into the pathophysiological mechanisms behind their development (Rotta et al., 2021). Furthermore, different vascular supply patterns of the

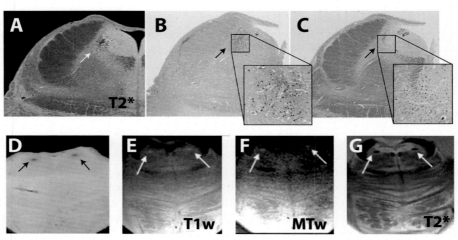

FIG. 34.1

Ultra-high field imaging of the locus coeruleus (LC) in postmortem tissue. Example images include (A) 7T T_2^*-weighted (50 mm resolution) FLASH MRI image; (B) TH staining for LC neurons (*dark*); (C) Luxol fast blue to stain for myelinated fibers surrounding the LC in the same slice (*green*); (D) Block face image after celloidin embedding (LC neurons; *dark*); (E) 7T T_1-weighted (0.2 × 0.2 × 2 mm) TSE image; (F) 7T MT-weighted FLASH MRI image and (G) 7T T_2^*-weighted FLASH image. *Figure adapted from Betts et al. (2019a).*

hippocampus have been studied for the first time in vivo using 7T ToF (Spallazzi et al., 2019) and have been suggested to modulate cognitive reserve in healthy elderly individuals (Perosa et al., 2020) establishing new links between the vasculature and cognition, which need to be further studied in light of AD pathology.

Recent evidence has shown that cerebrovascular disease, in particular cerebral small-vessel disease (CSVD), is also strictly linked to AD (Snyder et al., 2016). Not only are vascular risk factors such as smoking, hypertension, diabetes, and hyperlipidemia epidemiologically associated with AD, but also CSVD-related lesions (microinfarcts, microbleeds, MRI-visible PVS) are found more often in AD than in elderly healthy controls (Cordonnier and van der Flier, 2011). Due to the small dimension of these lesions, the use of UHF MRI is crucial to better pinpoint their prevalence and distribution, whereas a combination of several sequences can shed more light on the mechanisms underlying their development. For example, MRI-visible PVS most likely represent enlarged perivascular compartments, which are a marker of brain clearance dysfunction. The combination of MRI sequences at submillimeter resolution has further the potential to characterize which vessels the PVS relate to (arteries, veins, origin of the vessels) and provide valuable information on the brain's clearance routes (Wardlaw et al., 2020). Since failure in clearance of β-amyloid and other toxic proteins could represent the link between vascular dysfunction and AD, a better understanding of these mechanisms is crucial and may lead to novel therapeutic strategies. The high resolution obtained at UHF has also facilitated ex vivo MRI studies, which aim to pinpoint histopathological correlates of neuroimaging markers of CSVD and possibly establish new ones, which can ultimately be applied in vivo.

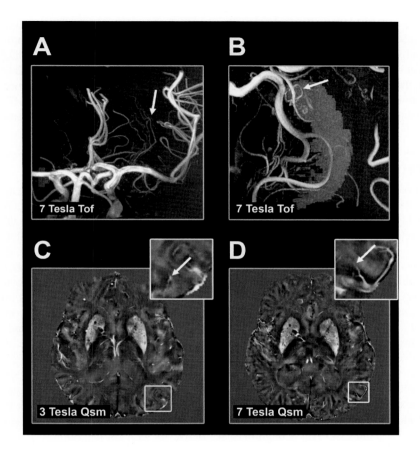

FIG. 34.2

Example time-of-flight angiography (ToF) images acquired using 7T MRI (0.3 mm isotropic resolution), which is able to identify small arteries such as the deep perforating lenticulostriate arteries (*arrow* in A) and hippocampal arteries (*arrow* in B). In (C), small cortical veins can be seen using quantitative susceptibility mapping (QSM), which also demonstrates superior contract at 7T MRI (D) compared to 3T MRI, as can be observed from the direct head-to-head comparison (C and D).

34.4 Iron mapping in aging and AD

Iron dysregulation has shown to be altered in aging and may play a significant role in the pathogenesis of AD. Due to the paramagnetic properties of iron, MRI permits the assessment of iron levels in vivo using novel MRI techniques such as QSM or the T_2^* transverse relaxation time. Previous studies have shown that iron levels and its rate of accumulation are differentially altered in aging and AD (Betts et al., 2016; Spotorno et al., 2020) and correlate with cognitive impairment and AD pathology (Rodrigue et al., 2020; Spotorno et al., 2020). A 7T QSM and resting-state study combined with amyloid PET demonstrated that cerebral iron levels were found to be associated with altered fronto-temporal brain connectivity, increased β-amyloid plaque load, and APOE-e4 carrier status in mild cognitive impairment (MCI) individuals (van Bergen et al., 2016). Similarly, increased hippocampal quantitative susceptibility mapping levels, consistent with higher iron accumulation, in individuals with amyloid pathology has been shown to predict accelerated cognitive decline which could indicate that brain iron might combine with β-amyloid pathology to accelerate the clinical progression of AD (Ayton et al., 2017). While the exact mechanisms linking iron dysregulation and AD pathology remain unclear, the increased sensitivity to detect in vivo gray matter iron levels and inherently better SNR at UHF may help to further understand the relationship between iron deposition, AD pathophysiology, and cognitive decline.

34.5 Determining potential of UHF fMRI in aging and AD

A significant advantage of UHF functional magnetic resonance imaging (fMRI) in aging and AD is the ability to assess functional scans with higher blood oxygenation level-dependent (BOLD) contrast as compared to 3T (Uğurbil, 2021). The related increase in SNR at UHF allows for functional imaging at the submillimeter scale and therefore puts the investigation of functional changes in smaller brain structures such as the locus coeruleus and dorsal raphe nucleus, within reach. Interestingly, despite these brain structures being the first to demonstrate pretangle tau in AD (Grinberg et al., 2009), these nuclei appear to be able to survive the presence of pathological tau for several years (for the locus coeruleus see: Theofilas et al., 2017). However, tau pretangles and tangles in the locus coeruleus might impact dendritic and axonal neurites which support intraneuronal communication (Theofilas et al., 2017). Thus, a decline in locus coeruleus function might precede locus coeruleus cell loss and adds to the relevance of using noninvasive functional imaging methods for exploring the influence of tau pathology on neuronal function in the early stages of AD.

The higher spatial resolution of UHF functional imaging can also be used to investigate altered functional responses in hippocampal subfields in aging and AD which is not possible using conventional functional imaging at 3T (Lee et al., 2020). Recent postmortem work shows that hippocampal subfields differ systematically in the extent of synuclein, tau, and amyloid burden in Lewy body dementia (LBD), AD, and LBD-AD (Coughlin et al., 2020). As with tau pathologies, β-amyloid oligomers likely result in altered functional responses in hippocampal subfields, as they have been shown to cause synaptic dysfunction and reduced long-term potentials (LTPs) (Mroczko et al., 2018). However, few studies so far have exploited the possibility to assess altered function in such anatomically precise regions using UHF in aging or AD. Yet, many interesting research questions await answering. For instance, Jacobsen et al. (2015) used multivariate fMRI analyses in a sample of Alzheimer's patients and healthy elderly controls to localize a "musical memory map" to address in the context of known spatial patterns of amyloid pathology, brain atrophy, and hypometabolism why musical memory appears to be comparatively preserved in AD.

Being able to measure small brain structures with high SNR is also particularly relevant for investigating changes in functional connectivity between small structures such as hippocampal subfields or the neuromodulatory nuclei in the brainstem and target structures across the brain. In younger adults, UHF imaging has for instance been able to provide layer-specific connectivity profiles within hippocampal subfields which are meaningfully related to subprocesses of episodic memory formation (Koster et al., 2018). Finally, fMRI with submillimeter resolution also offers the possibility to investigate functional activations in cortical structures with layer-specific resolution (Weldon and Olman, 2021), which has to date been largely unexplored in aging and AD research.

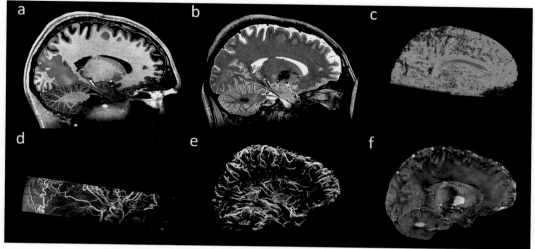

FIG. 34.3

Multiparametric 7T MRI has the potential to provide new insights into age-related physiology and pathophysiology of AD at its earliest stages. Example images include (A) 250 μm T_1-weighted MPRAGE overlaid by 1.8 mm 1-h resting-state fMRI, (B) 450 μm T_2-weighted SPACE, (C) 800 μm DTI in 12 directions with a b-value of 750 s/mm², (D) 150 μm ToF angiography, (E) 330 μm venogram, and in (F) 330 μm quantitative susceptibility mapping (QSM) image (Lüsebrink et al., 2021).

Taken together, the combination of ultra-high-resolution structural and functional imaging may be particularly powerful for assessing the function of local circuits that are affected early in the pathogenesis of AD and may provide more precise measures of neurodegeneration. Since no single imaging modality can quantify the numerous cascades of events from initial presentation of pathology to clinical symptoms, multiparametric and longitudinal 7T MRI studies may help to identify causal processes occurring in aging and across the AD spectrum (see Fig. 34.3).

34.6 The road ahead for UHF imaging in aging and AD

In aging and in the preclinical course of AD, tau pathology may initially manifest in brainstem nuclei and perirhinal/entorhinal subregions before spreading to hippocampal subfields, amygdala, and subsequent neocortex. Thus, the use of 7T MRI to assess the detailed functional connectivity profile of brainstem nuclei and the hippocampus, its subfields, and of the perirhinal and subregions of the entorhinal cortices in aging and preclinical AD is expected to be highly valuable. Combined with molecular imaging, e.g., measures of tau and amyloid pathology, 7T fMRI can improve understanding into how AD pathology impacts brain function particularly at early stages and may also help confirm the efficacy of both pharmacological and nonpharmacological interventions in clinical trials (see Fig. 34.4).

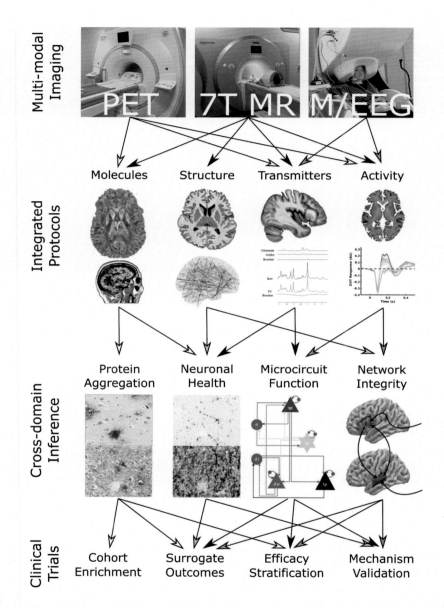

FIG. 34.4

Using multimodal, longitudinal UHF imaging combined with molecular and functional imaging to provide an holistic overview of disease progression in Alzheimer's disease (AD). 7T fMRI combined with positron emission tomography (PET) can improve understanding into how AD pathology impacts brain function particularly at early stages and may complement additional measures of neuronal connectivity such as diffusion tensor imaging (DTI) and magnetoencephalography (MEG) or electroencephalography (EEG). 7T MRI may also be used to identify the contribution of small-vessel-related vascular risk factors to neurodegeneration and neuronal dysfunction in aging and AD. High-resolution iron mapping at 7T may be a future potential alternative or complement to molecular imaging to quantify amyloid pathology. Ultra-high resolution of medial temporal subregions or brainstem nuclei using 7T MRI may help stratify individuals into therapeutic trials. *Figure adapted from Cope et al. (2021), with permission from BMJ Publishing Group Ltd.*

Additionally, high-resolution angiography at 7T may aid the detection of disease comorbidities such as vascular pathology and iron mapping may be a future potential alternative or complement to molecular imaging to quantify amyloid pathology. It is anticipated that high-resolution structural imaging using 7T MRI may also be ideally suited to complement molecular imaging to provide a more holistic overview of disease staging as outlined by the recent framework for AD (Jack et al., 2018). This may be in the form of disease modeling, for example, by taking advantage of the superior spatial resolution of 7T MRI whereby longitudinal multiparametric high-resolution imaging may better inform mathematical models of disease progression but may also help stratify individuals at risk of developing AD-related dementia, into intervention studies (Cope et al., 2021).

An important question to address in the near term is to systematically determine the added benefit of 7T MRI in a direct comparison with conventional 3T MRI for improving research and clinically relevant outcome measures. For example, it will be important to determine if UHF MRI, i.e., at 7T provides additional benefits to current 3T imaging in a head-to-head comparison of brain structure, function, and vasculature for early assessment and prevention of AD. To address this will require identifying the added sensitivity of UHF structural imaging at 7T for detecting and quantifying progressive neurodegeneration in aging and preclinical/prodromal AD as compared with conventional protocols currently available at 3T. It will also be important to determine whether UHF measures of brain atrophy are more closely related to cognitive decline and the clinical manifestations of AD compared to conventional 3T MRI. The use of UHF MRI to understand how neuronal dysfunction in small brain networks is affected in early AD (i.e., in subregions of the entorhinal cortex, locus coeruleus, and additional brainstem nuclei) and how they are related to cognitive decline and neurodegeneration is still in its infancy, and considerable progress is anticipated in the coming years. For example, recent efforts such as the EUFIND (European ultra-high field imaging network for neurodegenerative diseases) consortium are underway to harness the superior resolution of 7T to conduct multicenter studies in AD aiming to address such questions (Düzel et al., 2019). Finally, it will also be important to determine how UHF MRI can help to identify the contribution of small-vessel-related vascular risk factors to neurodegeneration and neuronal dysfunction in aging and AD.

34.7 Conclusion

UHF MRI may be more sensitive for detecting early neurodegeneration, i.e., at prodromal/preclinical stages of AD compared to PET imaging and cerebrospinal fluid biomarkers and may be a highly sensitive tool for the detection of neuronal dysfunction in brain networks affected in normal aging and early AD. Moreover, UHF MRI provides a novel means to assess for vascular pathology occurring either as a consequence of AD or as a comorbidity, for dysfunction in discrete neural networks, and for assessing molecular pathology. With the recent approval of 7T MRI for clinical use, considerable progress is anticipated in the coming years for determining the additional benefit of UHF imaging for characterizing brain structure, function, and vasculature in aging and for the early assessment and prevention of AD.

References

Ayton, S., Fazlollahi, A., Bourgeat, P., et al., 2017. Cerebral quantitative susceptibility mapping predicts amyloid-β-related cognitive decline. Brain 140 (8), 2112–2119. https://doi.org/10.1093/brain/awx137.

Berron, D., Vieweg, P., Hochkeppler, A., et al., 2017. A protocol for manual segmentation of medial temporal lobe subregions in 7 Tesla MRI. NeuroImage Clin. 15, 466–482. https://doi.org/10.1016/j.nicl.2017.05.022.

Betts, M.J., Acosta-Cabronero, J., Cardenas-Blanco, A., Nestor, P.J., Düzel, E., 2016. High-resolution characterisation of the aging brain using simultaneous quantitative susceptibility mapping (QSM) and R2* measurements at 7T. NeuroImage 138, 43–63. https://doi.org/10.1016/j.neuroimage.2016.05.024.

Betts, M.J., Kirilina, E., Otaduy, M.C.G., et al., 2019a. Locus coeruleus imaging as a biomarker for noradrenergic dysfunction in neurodegenerative diseases. Brain 142, 2558–2571. https://doi.org/10.1093/brain/awz193.

Betts, M.J., Cardenas-Blanco, A., Kanowski, M., et al., 2019b. Locus coeruleus MRI contrast is reduced in Alzheimer's disease dementia and correlates with CSF Aβ levels. Alzheimers Dement. Diagn. Assess. Dis. Monit. 11, 281–285. https://doi.org/10.1016/j.dadm.2019.02.001.

Bollmann, S., Mattern, H., Bernier, M., et al., 2021. Imaging of the pial arterial vasculature of the human brain *in vivo* using high-resolution 7T time-of-flight angiography (preprint). Neuroscience. https://doi.org/10.1101/2021.06.09.447807.

Carlesimo, G.A., Piras, F., Orfei, M.D., Iorio, M., Caltagirone, C., Spalletta, G., 2015. Atrophy of presubiculum and subiculum is the earliest hippocampal anatomical marker of Alzheimer's disease. Alzheimers Dement. Diagn. Assess. Dis. Monit. 1, 24–32. https://doi.org/10.1016/j.dadm.2014.12.001.

Cope, T.E., Weil, R.S., Düzel, E., Dickerson, B.C., Rowe, J.B., 2021. Advances in neuroimaging to support translational medicine in dementia. J. Neurol. Neurosurg. Psychiatry, jnnp-2019-322402. https://doi.org/10.1136/jnnp-2019-322402.

Cordonnier, C., van der Flier, W.M., 2011. Brain microbleeds and Alzheimer's disease: innocent observation or key player? Brain 134, 335–344. https://doi.org/10.1093/brain/awq321.

Coughlin, D.G., Ittyerah, R., Peterson, C., et al., 2020. Hippocampal subfield pathologic burden in Lewy body diseases vs. Alzheimer's disease. Neuropathol. Appl. Neurobiol. 46, 707–721. https://doi.org/10.1111/nan.12659.

Düzel, E., 2021. Studying Alzheimer disease, Parkinson disease, and amyotrophic lateral sclerosis with 7-T magnetic resonance. Eur. Radiol. Exp. 5, 36. https://doi.org/10.1186/s41747-021-00221-5.

Düzel, E., Acosta-Cabronero, J., Berron, D., et al., 2019. European ultrahigh-field imaging network for neurodegenerative diseases (EUFIND). Alzheimers Dement. Diagn. Assess. Dis. Monit. 11, 538–549. https://doi.org/10.1016/j.dadm.2019.04.010.

Geurts, L.J., Zwanenburg, J.J.M., Klijn, C.J.M., Luijten, P.R., Biessels, G.J., 2019. Higher Pulsatility in cerebral perforating arteries in patients with small vessel disease related stroke, a 7T MRI study. Stroke 50, 62–68. https://doi.org/10.1161/STROKEAHA.118.022516.

Grinberg, L.T., Rüb, U., Ferretti, R.E.L., et al., 2009. The dorsal raphe nucleus shows phospho-tau neurofibrillary changes before the transentorhinal region in Alzheimer's disease. A precocious onset? Neuropathol. Appl. Neurobiol. 35, 406–416. https://doi.org/10.1111/j.1365-2990.2008.00997.x.

Hämmerer, D., Callaghan, M.F., Hopkins, A., et al., 2018. Locus coeruleus integrity in old age is selectively related to memories linked with salient negative events. Proc. Natl. Acad. Sci. 201712268. https://doi.org/10.1073/pnas.1712268115.

Ivanov, D., Gardumi, A., Haast, R.A.M., Pfeuffer, J., Poser, B.A., Uludağ, K., 2017. Comparison of 3 T and 7 T ASL techniques for concurrent functional perfusion and BOLD studies. NeuroImage 156, 363–376. https://doi.org/10.1016/j.neuroimage.2017.05.038.

Jack, C.R., Bennett, D.A., Blennow, K., et al., 2018. NIA-AA research framework: toward a biological definition of Alzheimer's disease. Alzheimers Dement. 14, 535–562. https://doi.org/10.1016/j.jalz.2018.02.018.

Jacobs, H.I.L., Becker, J.A., Kwong, K., et al., 2021. In vivo and neuropathology data support locus coeruleus integrity as indicator of Alzheimer's disease pathology and cognitive decline. Sci. Transl. Med. 13, eabj2511. https://doi.org/10.1126/scitranslmed.abj2511.

Jacobsen, J.-H., Stelzer, J., Fritz, T.H., Chételat, G., La Joie, R., Turner, R., 2015. Why musical memory can be preserved in advanced Alzheimer's disease. Brain 138, 2438–2450. https://doi.org/10.1093/brain/awv135.

Koster, R., Chadwick, M.J., Chen, Y., et al., 2018. Big-loop recurrence within the hippocampal system supports integration of information across episodes. Neuron 99, 1342–1354.e6. https://doi.org/10.1016/j.neuron.2018.08.009.

Lee, H., Stirnberg, R., Wu, S., et al., 2020. Genetic Alzheimer's disease risk affects the neural mechanisms of pattern separation in hippocampal subfields. Curr. Biol. 30, 4201–4212.e3. https://doi.org/10.1016/j.cub.2020.08.042.

Lüsebrink, F., Mattern, H., Yakupov, R., et al., 2021. Comprehensive ultrahigh resolution whole brain in vivo MRI dataset as a human phantom. Sci. Data 8, 138. https://doi.org/10.1038/s41597-021-00923-w.

Mroczko, B., Groblewska, M., Litman-Zawadzka, A., Kornhuber, J., Lewczuk, P., 2018. Amyloid β oligomers (AβOs) in Alzheimer's disease. J. Neural Transm. 1996 (125), 177–191. https://doi.org/10.1007/s00702-017-1820-x.

Perosa, V., Priester, A., Ziegler, G., et al., 2020. Hippocampal vascular reserve associated with cognitive performance and hippocampal volume. Brain 143, 622–634. https://doi.org/10.1093/brain/awz383.

Priovoulos, N., Jacobs, H.I.L., Ivanov, D., Uludag, K., Verhey, F.R.J., Poser, B.A., 2017. High-resolution in vivo imaging of human locus coeruleus by magnetization transfer MRI at 3T and 7T. NeuroImage. https://doi.org/10.1016/j.neuroimage.2017.07.045.

Rodrigue, K.M., Daugherty, A.M., Foster, C.M., Kennedy, K.M., 2020. Striatal iron content is linked to reduced fronto-striatal brain function under working memory load. NeuroImage 210, 116544. https://doi.org/10.1016/j.neuroimage.2020.116544.

Rotta, J., Perosa, V., Yakupov, R., et al., 2021. Detection of cerebral microbleeds with venous connection at 7-tesla MRI. Neurology 96, e2048–e2057. https://doi.org/10.1212/WNL.0000000000011790.

Snyder, H.M., Asthana, S., Bain, L., et al., 2016. Sex biology contributions to vulnerability to Alzheimer's disease: a think tank convened by the Women's Alzheimer's research initiative. Alzheimers Dement. 12, 1186–1196. https://doi.org/10.1016/j.jalz.2016.08.004.

Spallazzi, M., Dobisch, L., Becke, A., et al., 2019. Hippocampal vascularization patterns: a high-resolution 7 Tesla time-of-flight magnetic resonance angiography study. NeuroImage Clin. 21, 101609. https://doi.org/10.1016/j.nicl.2018.11.019.

Spotorno, N., Acosta-Cabronero, J., Stomrud, E., et al., 2020. Relationship between cortical iron and tau aggregation in Alzheimer's disease. Brain, awaa089. https://doi.org/10.1093/brain/awaa089.

Theofilas, P., Ehrenberg, A.J., Dunlop, S., et al., 2017. Locus coeruleus volume and cell population changes during Alzheimer's disease progression: a stereological study in human postmortem brains with potential implication for early-stage biomarker discovery. Alzheimers Dement. 13, 236–246.

Uğurbil, K., 2021. Ultrahigh field and ultrahigh resolution fMRI. Curr. Opin. Biomed. Eng. 18, 100288. https://doi.org/10.1016/j.cobme.2021.100288.

van Bergen, J.M.G., Li, X., Hua, J., et al., 2016. Colocalization of cerebral iron with amyloid beta in mild cognitive impairment. Sci. Rep. 6, 35514. https://doi.org/10.1038/srep35514.

Wardlaw, J.M., Benveniste, H., Nedergaard, M., et al., 2020. Perivascular spaces in the brain: anatomy, physiology and pathology. Nat. Rev. Neurol. 16, 137–153. https://doi.org/10.1038/s41582-020-0312-z.

Weldon, K.B., Olman, C.A., 2021. Forging a path to mesoscopic imaging success with ultra-high field functional magnetic resonance imaging. Philos. Trans. R. Soc. B Biol. Sci. 376, 20200040. https://doi.org/10.1098/rstb.2020.0040.

Wolk, D.A., Das, S.R., Mueller, S.G., Weiner, M.W., Yushkevich, P.A., 2017. Medial temporal lobe subregional morphometry using high resolution MRI in Alzheimer's disease. Neurobiol. Aging 49, 204–213. https://doi.org/10.1016/j.neurobiolaging.2016.09.011.

Xu, X., Hilal, S., Collinson, S.L., et al., 2015. Association of Magnetic Resonance Imaging Markers of cerebrovascular disease burden and cognition. Stroke 46, 2808–2814. https://doi.org/10.1161/STROKEAHA.115.010700.

Ultra-high field neuro-MRI: Oncological applications

Christian Neelsen[a,b] and Daniel Paech[a,c]

[a]*Division of Radiology, German Cancer Research Center (DKFZ), Heidelberg, Germany* [b]*Department of Radiology, Charité-Universitätsmedizin, Berlin, Germany* [c]*Clinic for Neuroradiology, University Hospital Bonn, Bonn, Germany*

Highlights

- Increased signal-to-noise-ratio (SNR) at ultra-high field (UHF) MRI enables high-resolution anatomic imaging, which could aid tumor diagnostics and clinical decision-making.
- Novel metabolic imaging approaches at UHF, such as x-nuclei MRI and MR spectroscopy with increased spectral resolution, are of great promise for in vivo tumor characterization with links to molecular and genomic features.
- A major challenge remains the translation from the experimental setup into clinical routine that will necessitate new hardware and acquisition techniques.

35.1 Proton MRI/MRS at ultra-high fields (UHF)

35.1.1 High-resolution proton imaging at ultra-high fields

The equilibrium spin polarization increases linearly with the B_0 magnetic field strength. This leads to an at least linear increase in signal-to-noise (SNR) enabling higher spatial resolution and increased contrast-to-noise ratio (CNR).

MR neuroimaging at field strengths of at least 1.5T, preferably 3T, is the current clinical gold standard of diagnosis, treatment planning, and response assessment for both primary brain tumors and metastasis. The most frequent primary brain tumors are gliomas. High-grade gliomas exhibit aggressive and diffuse infiltration, which entails their dismal prognosis. Current imaging techniques do not allow to delineate tumor infiltration margins from healthy brain tissue. Maximal tumor resection while maintaining neurological function followed by radiotherapy is the mainstay of therapy. The increased spatial resolution at higher field strength can help refine target volume for neurosurgery and radiotherapy. This could help to better visualize white matter tracts, which are the preferred infiltration routes of glioblastomas, as well as eloquent brain regions (Fig. 35.1) (Regnery et al., 2019). Increased contrast enhancement on gadolinium-enhanced images may further increase visibility and allow for dose reduction of contrast media (Noebauer-Huhmann et al., 2015). Thus, the detection of small tumors or metastasis may also be improved.

Oligodendrogliomas (ODG) are infiltrative gliomas characterized by 1p/19q codeletion. This is associated with an improved prognosis and response to radiochemotherapy. Characteristic calcifications of ODG are a good imaging marker, commonly assessed with CT. Quantitative susceptibility mapping

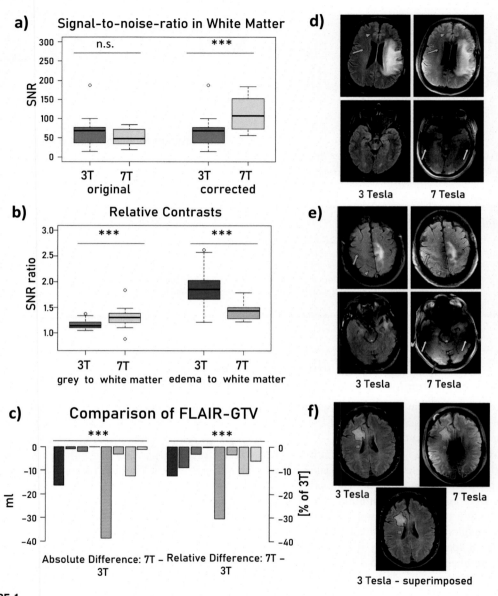

FIG. 35.1

See figure legend on opposite page.

(QSM) enables differentiation of tumoral calcifications and from hemorrhage due to differences in susceptibility (Deistung et al., 2013).

Higher spatial resolution and better background suppression (due to increased T_1) of nonenhanced time-of-flight angiography (TOF) enable characterization of intratumoral vascular architecture, which differs significantly in comparison with normal brain tissue. This method may therefore represent a future marker to monitor antiangiogenic therapies (Radbruch et al., 2014). Improved susceptibility-weighted images also allow visualization of microvasculature, as well as microbleeds associated either with vascular proliferation or with long-term side effects of radiotherapy in the surrounding normal brain tissue (Lupo et al., 2012).

Diffusion-weighted imaging (DWI) is a valuable tool for the evaluation of various brain diseases, particularly stroke. Diffusion is physiologically restricted in biological systems. Diffusivity typically further decreases in neoplasms compared to healthy tissue because of increased cellularity in tumors. Along linear structures, i.e., axons, diffusion is relatively free while in the orthogonal direction diffusion is highly restricted. This can be used in applications as neurite orientation dispersion and density imaging (NODDI). SNR on multiband imaging depends on the spatial differences of coil sensitivities. This leads to a smaller geometry factor or spatially amplified noise at higher field strength. In the work by Wen et al., the effects of shorter T_2 as well as increased B_0 and B_1 inhomogeneity at 7T outweighed the effects of the increased static field strength on DWI. With multiband imaging ($R=3$), however, the larger reduction of SNR at 3T compared to 7T balanced these effects and they achieved similar SNR for NODDI mapping in patients with glioma at 3T and 7T (Wen et al., 2015).

Ultra-high field MRI has also been helpful in the investigation of benign brain tumors. Cushing's disease is an endocrine disorder due to a hormone-producing tumor of the pituitary. A study by De Rotte et al. reported a higher detection rate of pituitary adenoma on 7T MRI compared to 1.5T MRI in patients with biochemical Cushing's disease (De Rotte et al., 2016). In another case report, a pituitary microadenoma could only be visualized on 7T MRI and not even on 3 Tesla (Law et al., 2018). Yao et al. were able to infer tumor consistency from T_2w signal intensity of pituitary adenoma on preoperative 7T examinations. Softer tumors are removed more easily and show lower rates of recurrence. Therefore, preoperative evaluation may improve surgical management and risk stratification (Yao et al., 2020). Rutland et al. performed 7T imaging with DTI tractography showing a reduction in fractional anisotropy of optic tracts and radiations as well as thinning of the primary visual

FIG. 35.1

Comparison of signal-to-noise-ratio (SNR) (A), SNR ratios (B), and gross tumor volume (GTV) (C) between the two different field strengths (***=statistically significant with $P \leq .05$, n.s.=not statistically significant). (A) The corrected SNR is significantly increased at 7T. (B) The relative contrast between white matter (WM) and gray matter (GM) is significantly higher at 7T. But the relative contrast between WM and peritumoral edema (PE) was significantly decreased at 7T. (C) GTVs were smaller at 7T in all observed patients (corresponding patients are shown in the same shade of *gray*). (D) and (E) Exemplary high-resolution FLAIR MRI at 7T with corresponding clinical MRI at 3T in two patients. The visibility of major WM tracts *(green arrows)* and boundaries between GM and WM *(green arrowheads)* is enhanced in the 7T FLAIR. Near the skull base, artifacts due to signal loss *(yellow arrows)* and brightening *(red arrow)* decrease SNR and contrast of the 7T MRI. (F) Exemplary delineation of FLAIR-GTVs at 3T *(blue)* and 7T *(red)* with superimposition of the corresponding volumes on the clinical 3T MR image. *Figure reused with permission from Regnery et al. (2019).*

cortex. MRI at clinical field strength might not be capable of visualizing these microstructural white matter affections. Therefore, 7T imaging may help to assess secondary white matter injury more accurately (Rutland et al., 2019).

35.1.2 Proton MRS

Analysis of the chemical composition with magnetic resonance spectroscopy (MRS) dates back to the beginnings of MRI. Several pathologies have been shown to be associated with specific molecular signatures (Table 35.1). However, the fact that MRS is technically challenging and also clinical time constraints often limit routine use. MRS profits from increased spectral resolution at ultra-high fields. The approximately linear increase in SNR and chemical shift with higher field strength markedly improve resolution of acquired spectra (Weinberg et al., 2021), thereby enabling accelerated and more accurate mapping of metabolites at 7T compared to 3T (Gruber et al., 2017).

MRS may help to differentiate primary brain tumors from metastasis or other processes like abscesses or lymphoma (Weinberg et al., 2021). Initially in 2014 and recently in 2021, the changes in the WHO classification system of brain tumors marked a paradigm shift from histology alone to the incorporation of genetic markers. Genetic subtypes in tumor biology are known to differently alter cell metabolism. MR spectroscopy can quantify various cell metabolites, thereby aiding tumor subtyping and stage stratification. In addition, tumor heterogeneity and malignant transformation over time are of increased concern. Tumor heterogeneity may yield local differences in tumor aggressiveness within one lesion. High-resolution metabolic mapping employing MRS imaging (MRSI) can identify intralesional alterations that may correspond to areas of different tumor aggressiveness. This information could help to guide biopsies or to assist dose painting in radiotherapy. In the follow-up scenario, MRS has been shown to reveal differences between benign, therapy-related changes namely radiation necrosis or pseudoprogression, and disease progression or tumor recurrence, with implications for patient management and therapeutic strategies (Weinberg et al., 2021).

Mutations of isocitrate dehydrogenases (IDHs) are an important prognostic marker. In 2016, the IDH mutation status has been incorporated in the WHO-staging system for glioma. IDH mutations lead to the accumulation of the oncometabolite 2-hydroxyglutarate (2-HG) which alters DNA methylation. An et al. used echo-planar spectroscopic imaging (EPSI) with dual-readout alternated gradients in glioma patients at 7T to map multiple metabolites including 2-HG. This allowed accurate IDH prediction in four patients with glioma confirmed by tissue biopsy (An et al., 2018). Berrington et al. directly compared 2-HG mapping at 3T and 7T. While SNR proved similar, the detection of 2-HG was improved through higher spectral and spatial resolution at 7T (Berrington et al., 2018).

Hangel et al. achieved fast (15 min), whole-brain, high-resolution (0.039 cm^3) MRSI at 7T with the quantification of 10 metabolites (Fig. 35.2).

Higher resolution reduces partial-volume effects and intravoxel B_0 inhomogeneity. A problem in spectroscopy is the splitting of resonances through J-coupling. At higher field strength, the separation of overlapping multiplets of J-coupled spin systems is improved. Several studies have for instance shown successful differentiation of glutamine/glutamate in spectra acquired at 7T. Among others, the study of Hangel et al. showed an increase of glutamine in gliomas, possibly corresponding to altered metabolic pathways. Glutamine could gain further interest with the advent of glutamine-targeting therapies (Hangel et al., 2020). A summary of frequently encountered metabolites in neurooncology is provided in Table 35.1.

Table 35.1 Significance of frequently encountered metabolites in neurooncologic diseases detected via ¹H-magnetic resonance spectroscopy.

Metabolite	Biological and clinical significance in brain tumor imaging	Elevated in	Decreased in
Choline	Precursor of acetylcholine—a component of cell membranes, therefore a marker of cell proliferation – Grading gliomas – Distinction between metastases and glioblastomas because in the latter surrounding edema contains infiltrating cells – Differentiating tumor progression versus pseudo-progression/ radionecrosis	– Neoplasms especially lymphoma or glioma – Inflammation – Gliosis	Necrosis
Lipids	Component of cell membranes – Distinction between metastases and high-grade gliomas – Grading of gliomas	Unspecific marker for high cell turnover – Tends to be higher in metastasis than in glioblastoma – Lymphoma – Metastases – Abscess – Infarction	
2-Hydroxy-glutarate	Oncometabolite only present in tumors with IDH mutation	IDH-1-positive tumors	
Myo-inositol	Precursor of phosphatidylinositol for intracellular signaling pathways – Distinction between lymphoma and gliomas – Grading of gliomas	– Low-grade gliomas – Alzheimer's dementia – Progressive multifocal encephalopathy	– High-grade gliomas – Lymphoma
Lactate	Hypoxia with anaerobic metabolism – Detection of necrosis – Grading of gliomas	Necrotic tissue in abscesses or Glioblastoma	Not present in normal brain tissue due to the exclusive aerobic metabolism
N-Acetyl aspartate	Neuronal mitochondria therefore a marker of neuronal viability – Grading of gliomas – Distinction between gliomas from metastases		Destruction or replacement of neurons: – High-grade gliomas – Radiation necrosis – Lymphoma or metastases – Lymphoma – High-grade gliomas – Necrosis
Creatine	Internal energy transfer: Creatine is relatively maintained across different pathologies and can therefore be used as an internal control for ratio calculations		

Adapted from Weinberg et al. (2021) with permission from Elsevier.

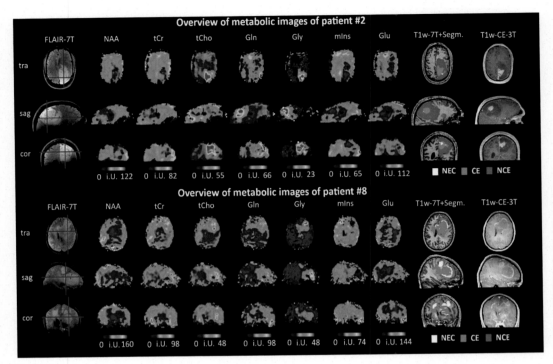

FIG. 35.2

Images of the most reliable metabolites of all primary orientations acquired in patients #2 (glioblastoma) and #8 (anaplastic astrocytoma) from Ref. Hangel et al. (2020). Next to the well-researched marker tCho, Gln and Gly also appear to coincide with tumor activity. The *red reference lines* indicate the positions of the displayed MRSI slices. *Figure reused with permission from Hangel et al. (2020). Elsevier B.V.*

35.1.3 Chemical exchange-sensitive MRI

Chemical exchange saturation transfer (CEST) MRI has recently gained attention as novel technique to measure low-concentration metabolites in vivo. CEST has higher sensitivity compared to conventional MRS because it utilizes the magnetization transfer via exchangeable protons from solutes to the much more abundant water pool. This indirect approach yields large signal amplification. Exchangeable protons bound to solutes have different resonance frequencies in reference to free water protons due to chemical shift. As discussed earlier, chemical shift increases linearly with the B_0 field strength, which yields improved spectral resolution. The most commonly studied CEST effect is the amide proton transfer (APT) (Zhou et al., 2003). Other magnetization transfer effects can interfere with APT-w CEST. In this context, the conventional semisolid magnetization transfer and the relayed nuclear Overhauser effect (rNOE) represent prominent resonances in the so-called "Z-spectrum," the commonly used method to analyze CEST data. Quantification of these effects, e.g., by using multi-Lorentzian fits, can provide additional contrasts. In patients with newly diagnosed glioma, several studies showed a correlation between APT and rNOE signals with tumor grade (Togao et al., 2014). In high-grade glioma at 7T, a correlation between baseline APT signal and overall survival as well as progression-free survival was found (Paech et al., 2019). APT-w signals have additionally been shown to be associated with the IDH status (Paech et al., 2018; Shanshan et al., 2017). At 7T, a more isolated APT signal, i.e., the downfield NOE-suppressed APT (dnsAPT) was found to be the best predictor of the IDH status (Paech et al., 2018).

In the treatment follow-up setting, several studies at 3T found significantly higher APT signals in patients with progressive disease compared to patients with treatment-related changes or residual tumors classified as stable disease (Park et al., 2016). At 7T, rNOE and dnsAPT imaging were found to be an early predictor of stable versus progressive disease at the end of treatment (Meissner et al., 2019). CEST signals are also modulated by pH because of its direct influence on the proton exchange rate. Amine CEST at high B_1 power has been reported to enable noninvasive measurement of tissue pH in vivo. In glioblastoma patients at 3T, lower tissue pH correlated with earlier tumor progression during subsequent radiochemotherapy (Harris et al., 2015).

35.1.4 Dynamic glucose-enhanced (DGE) MRI

Besides detection of endogenous metabolites, chemical exchange-sensitive MRI has been demonstrated to enable detection of exogenously administered agents carrying exchangeable protons, i.e., natural D-glucose. Following intravenous injection, dynamic glucose-enhanced (DGE) MRI allowed time-resolved measurement of changes in local glucose concentrations using either the classical CEST approach (i.e., GlucoCEST (Xu et al., 2015) or chemical exchange-sensitive spin-lock (GlucoCESL) in the human brain) (Schuenke et al., 2017; Paech et al., 2017). Generally, findings reported using the two approaches were similar in patients with high-grade brain tumors. Both studies described partial overlap of gadolinium enhancement with areas of increased glucose concentrations in areas showing disrupted blood-brain barrier (Fig. 35.3) (Schuenke et al., 2017; Xu et al., 2015).

35.2 X-nuclei imaging

Apart from hydrogen, also all other nuclei with a magnetic moment (due to an uneven number of either protons or neutrons) demonstrate potentially measurable magnetization with MRI. Generally, these are referred to as x-nuclei (Table 35.2). The differences in Larmor frequency (corresponding to different gyromagnetic ratios) make x-nuclei highly specific but also require dedicated coils. Due to comparably low concentrations and consequently limited resolution, anatomic sequences for correlation are desirable. Thus, x-nuclei imaging generally necessitates simultaneous or sequential ^{1}H-MRI. This further increases hardware demands and measurement duration.

35.2.1 Sodium-23 (^{23}Na) MRI

After hydrogen, sodium is the second most abundant measurable nucleus in the human body. Several studies have shown increased sodium concentrations in malignancies probably mainly due to an increase of intracellular sodium. Different techniques exist to differentiate between total and

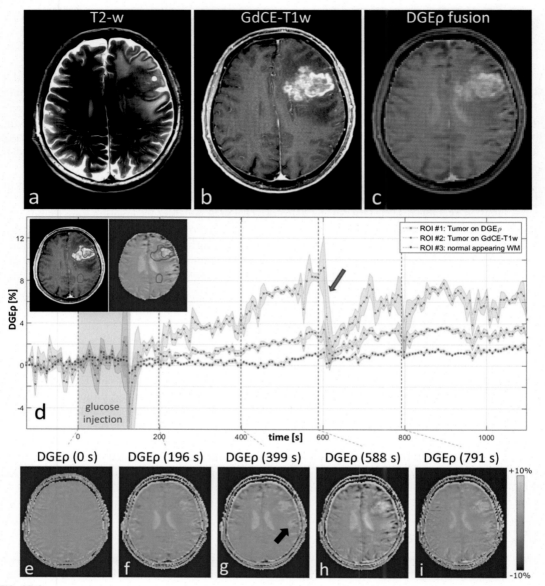

FIG. 35.3

Dynamic glucose-enhanced (DGE) MR imaging in a patient with previously untreated left-frontal glioblastoma using the CESL-based DGE MR imaging technique. (A) T_2-weighted (T_2-w), (B) gadolinium-enhanced T_1-w (GdCE-T_1-w), and (C) glucose-enhanced MR imaging based on $T_{1\rho}$-weighted CESL imaging (DGEr). Increased glucose-enhanced signal can be observed in the tumor region and in the (para-) ventricular area. Note an additional hyperintense region located dorsal of the tumor area *(black arrow)* (G), not discernible in the GdCE-T_1-w image (B). (D) *DGEρ* time curves with a temporal resolution of 7 s shown in the tumor region (ROI #1) and normal-appearing white matter (ROI #2). Continuously increasing *DGEρ* values can be observed in the tumor ROI following glucose injection. The *red arrow* marks an abrupt signal drop induced by patient motion. (E–I) *DGEρ* images (average of five consecutive images) at different time points after glucose injection. *ROI*, region of interest. *Reused with permission from Schuenke et al. (2017). Springer Nature.*

Table 35.2 X-nuclei imaging at ultra-high magnetic fields.

Nucleus	I [$\hbar$]	γ [MHz/T]	α [%]	Relative sensitivity [%]	Typical in vivo concentration c [mol/L] of the isotope
^{1}H	1/2	42.6	99.99	100	79
^{2}H	1	6.54	0.015	0.0001	0.01
^{17}O	5/2	−5.8	0.04	0.0011	0.015
^{19}F	1/2	40.1	100	83.3	≈0.001
^{23}Na	3/2	11.3	100	9.25	0.041
^{31}P	1/2	17.2	100	6.63	0.003
^{35}Cl	3/2	4.2	75.78	0.356	0.027
^{39}K	3/2	2.0	93.26	0.0473	0.108

Values from the literatures, as for instance provided in Platt et al. (2021).

intracellular sodium concentrations allowing for functional assessment of the sodium-potassium pump and Na$^+$ channels. For example, in more viscous environments, e.g., intracellularly, sodium seems to exhibit faster (biexponential) T_2 decay (Hagiwara et al., 2021). Fast relaxing sodium signal (NaR) was specifically increased in glioblastomas (WHO grade IV) compared to WHO grade I-III gliomas and correlated with MIB-1 proliferation rate of tumor cells (Fig. 35.4) (Nagel et al., 2011). Tissue sodium concentration (TSC) has also been shown to correlate with the IDH status (Biller et al., 2016; Regnery et al., 2020) and was found to be an independent and superior predictor of progression-free survival in patients with treatment-naïve gliomas (Biller et al., 2016). TSC also shows treatment-related changes; however, neither ^{23}Na-MRI at 3T nor at 7T yielded a clear association with patient outcome (Paech et al., 2021; Thulborn et al., 2019). Future studies with histopathologic correlations could help to further elucidate the underlying origin of signal alterations in patients with brain tumors.

35.2.2 More exotic x-nuclei
35.2.2.1 Oxygen-17 (^{17}O) MRI

About 99.8% of natural oxygen are oxygen-16 (^{16}O). Oxygen-17 (^{16}O) is a stable nonzero spin isotope of oxygen, however, with very low natural abundance (<0.1% compared to ^{1}H). Therefore, ^{17}O-MRI in humans requires ultra-high magnetic fields, dedicated coil systems, and additional inhalation of ^{17}O$_2$-enriched gas in order to achieve reasonable SNR. Since hemoglobin-bound ^{17}O exhibits very fast relaxation, ^{17}O only becomes detectable in its water-bound form after mitochondrial metabolization. Therefore, ^{17}O-MRI provides a direct window into oxygen-dependent brain metabolism. In concordance with the Warburg theorem, which predicts a shift toward nonoxygen-dependent metabolism in malignancies (i.e., lactate fermentation), gliomas have been shown to exhibit lower oxygen consumption than normal brain tissue (Paech et al., 2020). The method bares high potential also in other neurological diseases, such as neurodegeneration and neuroinflammation. However, ultra-high field scanners are still not widely available and ^{17}O$_2$-enriched gas is relatively costly, which currently limits its broader clinical investigation.

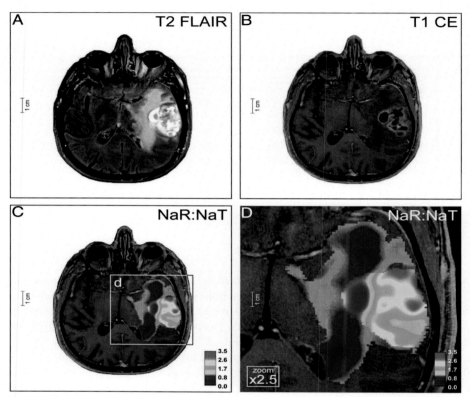

FIG. 35.4

Ganglioglioma. The neoplasia of a 49-year-old patient affects the left thalamus, pallidum, and putamen and is characterized by a largely homogeneous elevated T_2-FLAIR signal (A) and somewhat rim-like contrast enhancement (B). Based on ^{1}H-MR imaging, differential diagnostic considerations included low-grade tumors such as GG and PA but also malignant neoplasias such as GB and cerebral metastasis. Na-MR imaging reveals a mean NaR:NaT of 1.39 (whole tumor VOI) and 1.26 (CE tumor VOI) (C and D) compatible with a low-grade tumor. Thus, the differential diagnoses of GB and M could be ruled out. This result was confirmed by histopathology. Na images are overlaid on T_1-weighted postcontrast images; *color mesh grid*: whole tumor VOI, *solid color*: CE tumor VOI. *Figure reused with permission from Biller et al. (2016). American Society of Neuroradiology.*

35.2.2.2 Deuterium (^{2}H) MRSI

Deuterium (^{2}H) consists of one proton and one neutron and possesses a much lower gyromagnetic ratio than protium (^{1}H). Therefore, the Larmor frequency is much lower. On the other hand, chemical shift is identical to protium. Metabolization of deuterium-labeled substrates (e.g., glucose) leads to a change of the chemical shift, which is detectable in the deuterium MR spectrum. De Feyter et al. applied this method in two patients with glioblastoma. There was little difference in the uptake of ^{2}H-labeled glucose between tumor tissue and normal appearing brain tissue (De Feyter et al., 2018). However, glioblastomas showed increased lactate peaks in the ^{2}H spectrum due to anaerobic metabolism compared to normal appearing brain tissue that produced more glutamine. Although this study was performed at 4T, the authors reported better spectral and spatial resolution at higher field strength in rodents (De Feyter et al., 2018).

35.2.2.3 Phosphorus-31 (^{31}P) MRSI

The chemical shift of phosphates depends on their state of ionization, which is pH-dependent. Therefore, changes in pH alter phosphorus spectra. pH is an important factor for tumor cell differentiation as well as drug penetration. Korzowski et al. were able to demonstrate improved intra- and extracellular pH mapping at 7 Tesla with significantly higher pH in tumor tissue of three glioma patients (Korzowski et al., 2020). In glioblastoma patients treated with Bevacizumab, changes of pH measured by ^{31}P-MRSI at 3T preceded visible tumor progression on anatomic sequences (Wenger et al., 2017). Apart from inorganic phosphate for pH measurement, also other phosphorous metabolites can be assessed with ^{31}P-MRSI.

35.3 Outlook: Future of oncological neuroimaging at UHF

Different field strengths are beneficial for different sequences and applications. At higher field strength, increased signal- and contrast-to-noise ratio yields higher spatial resolution which may aid diagnostic neurooncology, for instance for margin delineation of tumors or differentiation between different tumor entities. Ultra-high field scanners have additionally promoted the translation of novel metabolic NMR techniques into in vivo imaging in humans. In this context, particularly proton MRS, x-nuclei imaging (e.g., ^{23}Na, ^{31}P, ^{17}O), as well as CEST imaging of endogenous and exogenous metabolites, have gained considerable attention in oncologic applications over the last two decades. Yet applications at ultra-high field generally lack validation in larger cohorts. This could, however, be remedied with the advent of an increasing number of ultra-high field scanners and the recently obtained FDA and CE clearance for its clinical use.

Generally, higher field strength does not always hold advantages. Difficulties in clinical routine care come along with ultra-high field systems, e.g., stricter limitations regarding metal implants or concerns about physiologic side effects on the vestibular system with nausea or higher energy deposition with tissue heating. Many but not all oncological applications profit from ultra-high fields. Particularly, in body or lung imaging, lower field strengths are preferred, usually 1.5T or 3.0T, for lung imaging even lower B_0. For instance, for diffusion-weighted imaging, rather the gradients are of major importance. Therefore, in the future, there might not be one scanner for all patients and every application.

Even though strong efforts are being made to translate diagnostic approaches from ultra-high to lower field strength ($\leq$3.0T), this might not be possible without significant penalty on image quality and clinical validity. Also, hardware developments such as dedicated coil systems and novel technical developments, such as parallel transmit (pTx), will further improve 7T MRI approaches and clinical applicability. This might herald the transition of UHF scanners from being a mere research tool to becoming a component of clinical diagnostics.

References

An, Z., Tiwari, V., Ganji, S.K., et al., 2018. Echo-planar spectroscopic imaging with dual-readout alternated gradients (DRAG-EPSI) at 7 T: application for 2-hydroxyglutarate imaging in glioma patients. Magn. Reson. Med. 79, 1851–1861.

Berrington, A., Voets, N.L., Larkin, S.J., et al., 2018. A comparison of 2-hydroxyglutarate detection at 3 and 7 T with long-TE semi-LASER. NMR Biomed. 31, e3886.

Biller, A., Badde, S., Nagel, A., et al., 2016. Improved brain tumor classification by sodium MR imaging: prediction of IDH mutation status and tumor progression. Am. J. Neuroradiol. 37, 66–73.

De Feyter, H.M., Behar, K.L., Corbin, Z.A., et al., 2018. Deuterium metabolic imaging (DMI) for MRI-based 3D mapping of metabolism in vivo. Sci. Adv. 4, eaat7314.

De Rotte, A.A., Groenewegen, A., Rutgers, D.R., et al., 2016. High resolution pituitary gland MRI at 7.0 tesla: a clinical evaluation in Cushing's disease. Eur. Radiol. 26, 271–277.

Deistung, A., Schweser, F., Wiestler, B., et al., 2013. Quantitative susceptibility mapping differentiates between blood depositions and calcifications in patients with glioblastoma. PLoS One 8, e57924.

Gruber, S., Heckova, E., Strasser, B., et al., 2017. Mapping an extended neurochemical profile at 3 and 7 T using accelerated high-resolution proton magnetic resonance spectroscopic imaging. Investig. Radiol. 52, 631–639.

Hagiwara, A., Bydder, M., Oughourlian, T.C., et al., 2021. Sodium MR neuroimaging. AJNR Am. J. Neuroradiol. 42, 1920–1926.

Hangel, G., Cadrien, C., Lazen, P., et al., 2020. High-resolution metabolic imaging of high-grade gliomas using 7T-CRT-FID-MRSI. NeuroImage Clin. 28, 102433.

Harris, R.J., Cloughesy, T.F., Liau, L.M., et al., 2015. pH-weighted molecular imaging of gliomas using amine chemical exchange saturation transfer MRI. Neuro-Oncology 17, 1514–1524.

Korzowski, A., Weinfurtner, N., Mueller, S., et al., 2020. Volumetric mapping of intra- and extracellular pH in the human brain using (31) P MRSI at 7T. Magn. Reson. Med. 84, 1707–1723.

Law, M., Wang, R., Liu, C.J., et al., 2018. Value of pituitary gland MRI at 7 T in Cushing's disease and relationship to inferior petrosal sinus sampling: case report. J. Neurosurg. 130 (2), 1–5.

Lupo, J.M., Chuang, C.F., Chang, S.M., et al., 2012. 7-tesla susceptibility-weighted imaging to assess the effects of radiotherapy on normal-appearing brain in patients with glioma. Int. J. Radiat. Oncol. Biol. Phys. 82, e493–e500.

Meissner, J.E., Korzowski, A., Regnery, S., et al., 2019. Early response assessment of glioma patients to definitive chemoradiotherapy using chemical exchange saturation transfer imaging at 7 T. J. Magn. Reson. Imaging 50, 1268–1277.

Nagel, A.M., Bock, M., Hartmann, C., et al., 2011. The potential of relaxation-weighted sodium magnetic resonance imaging as demonstrated on brain tumors. Investig. Radiol. 46, 539–547.

Noebauer-Huhmann, I.-M., Szomolanyi, P., Kronnerwetter, C., et al., 2015. Brain tumours at 7T MRI compared to 3T—Contrast effect after half and full standard contrast agent dose: initial results. Eur. Radiol. 25, 106–112.

Paech, D., Schuenke, P., Koehler, C., et al., 2017. T1ρ-weighted dynamic glucose-enhanced MR imaging in the human brain. Radiology 285, 914–922.

Paech, D., Windschuh, J., Oberhollenzer, J., et al., 2018. Assessing the predictability of IDH mutation and MGMT methylation status in glioma patients using relaxation-compensated multi-pool CEST MRI at 7.0 tesla. Neuro-Oncology 20, 1661–1671.

Paech, D., Dreher, C., Regnery, S., et al., 2019. Relaxation-compensated amide proton transfer (APT) MRI signal intensity is associated with survival and progression in high-grade glioma patients. Eur. Radiol. 29, 4957–4967.

Paech, D., Nagel, A.M., Schultheiss, M.N., et al., 2020. Quantitative dynamic oxygen 17 MRI at 7.0 T for the cerebral oxygen metabolism in glioma. Radiology 295, 181–189.

Paech, D., Regnery, S., Platt, T., et al., 2021. Assessment of sodium MRI at 7 tesla as predictor of therapy response and survival in glioblastoma patients. Front. Neurosci. 15, 782516.

Park, J.E., Kim, H.S., Park, K.J., Kim, S.J., Kim, J.H., Smith, S.A., 2016. Pre- and posttreatment glioma: comparison of amide proton transfer imaging with MR spectroscopy for biomarkers of tumor proliferation. Radiology 278, 514–523.

Platt, T., Ladd, M.E., Paech, D., 2021. 7 tesla and beyond: advanced methods and clinical applications in magnetic resonance imaging. Investig. Radiol. 56, 705–725.

Radbruch, A., Eidel, O., Wiestler, B., et al., 2014. Quantification of tumor vessels in glioblastoma patients using time-of-flight angiography at 7 tesla: a feasibility study. PLoS One 9, e110727.

Regnery, S., Knowles, B.R., Paech, D., et al., 2019. High-resolution FLAIR MRI at 7 tesla for treatment planning in glioblastoma patients. Radiother. Oncol. 130, 180–184.

Regnery, S., Behl, N.G.R., Platt, T., et al., 2020. Ultra-high-field sodium MRI as biomarker for tumor extent, grade and IDH mutation status in glioma patients. NeuroImage Clin. 28, 102427.

Rutland, J.W., Padormo, F., Yim, C.K., et al., 2019. Quantitative assessment of secondary white matter injury in the visual pathway by pituitary adenomas: a multimodal study at 7-tesla MRI. J. Neurosurg. 132, 333–342.

Schuenke, P., Paech, D., Koehler, C., et al., 2017. Fast and quantitative T1ρ-weighted dynamic glucose enhanced MRI. Sci. Rep. 7, 42093.

Shanshan, J., Tianyu, Z., Eberhart, C.G., et al., 2017. Predicting IDH mutation status in grade II gliomas using amide proton transfer-weighted (APTw) MRI. Magn. Reson. Med. 78, 1100–1109.

Thulborn, K.R., Lu, A., Atkinson, I.C., et al., 2019. Residual tumor volume, cell volume fraction, and tumor cell kill during fractionated chemoradiation therapy of human glioblastoma using quantitative sodium MR imaging. Clin. Cancer Res. 25, 1226–1232.

Togao, O., Yoshiura, T., Keupp, J., et al., 2014. Amide proton transfer imaging of adult diffuse gliomas: correlation with histopathological grades. Neuro-Oncology 16, 441–448.

Weinberg, B.D., Kuruva, M., Shim, H., Mullins, M.E., 2021. Clinical applications of magnetic resonance spectroscopy in brain tumors: from diagnosis to treatment. Radiol. Clin. N. Am. 59, 349–362.

Wen, Q., Kelley, D.A., Banerjee, S., et al., 2015. Clinically feasible NODDI characterization of glioma using multiband EPI at 7 T. NeuroImage Clin. 9, 291–299.

Wenger, K.J., Hattingen, E., Franz, K., Steinbach, J.P., Bähr, O., Pilatus, U., 2017. Intracellular pH measured by (31) P-MR-spectroscopy might predict site of progression in recurrent glioblastoma under antiangiogenic therapy. J. Magn. Reson. Imaging 46, 1200–1208.

Xu, X., Yadav, N.N., Knutsson, L., et al., 2015. Dynamic glucose-enhanced (DGE) MRI: translation to human scanning and first results in glioma patients. Tomography 1, 105–114.

Yao, A., Rutland, J.W., Verma, G., et al., 2020. Pituitary adenoma consistency: direct correlation of ultrahigh field 7T MRI with histopathological analysis. Eur. J. Radiol. 126, 108931.

Zhou, J., Lal, B., Wilson, D.A., Laterra, J., Van Zijl, P.C.M., 2003. Amide proton transfer (APT) contrast for imaging of brain tumors. Magn. Reson. Med. 50, 1120–1126.

Psychiatric applications of ultra-high field MR neuroimaging

36

Lena Palaniyappan[a,b,c,d], Kesavi Kanagasabai[c], and Katie M. Lavigne[a,d,e]

[a]*Douglas Mental Health University Institute, McGill University, Montreal, QC, Canada* [b]*Robarts Research Institute, Western University, London, ON, Canada* [c]*Department of Medical Biophysics, Western University, London, ON, Canada* [d]*Department of Psychiatry, McGill University, Montreal, QC, Canada* [e]*Montreal Neurological Institute-Hospital, McGill University, Montreal, QC, Canada*

Highlights

- Technical advances offered by UHF MRI can improve detection of subtle neurobiological alterations underlying psychiatric disorders.
- To date, research has focused on schizophrenia and affective disorders.
- UHF MRI shows potential for elucidating neurochemical pathways, improving classification, and detailing response to treatment.
- Large-scale collaborations and open sharing of data and techniques will be necessary before UHF MRI can inform diagnostics and treatment selection.

36.1 Introduction

A significant portion of our collective lives are spent living with disabilities; nearly one-third of all those years lived with disabilities are attributable to mental illnesses (Vigo et al., 2016). This disproportionately large contribution to disability stems from two important features of most severe mental illnesses: (1) they start at a very young age, mostly around adolescence, and (2) they have a chronic relapsing nature, with no curative treatments discovered to date. These aspects of psychiatric disorders make their mechanism scrutable only by tracking live subjects over long time periods, with animal or postmortem brain studies being critical but insufficient. In this context, the ability to noninvasively study the structural, functional, and chemical properties of the constituent microscopic units of the living brain assumes paramount importance. Ultra-high field magnetic resonance imaging (UHF MRI) offers high sensitivity and resolution to achieve this goal and has already begun contributing to our current understanding of psychiatric disorders. While many challenges remain to be overcome, in this chapter, we summarize the progress made to date through UHF MRI in major psychiatric disorders, especially schizophrenia and depression. We focus specifically on the distinct insights and the incremental value gleaned to date from the use of UHF in magnetic resonance spectroscopy (MRS), and structural and functional MRI studies of these disorders. While we restrict this chapter to clinical studies from patient samples, the overall utility of UHF in psychiatric disorders is best understood in the context of broader nonclinical applications of UHF MRI discussed elsewhere in this volume.

Advances in Magnetic Resonance Technology and Applications. Volume 10. ISSN 2666-9099. https://doi.org/10.1016/B978-0-323-99898-7.00021-3

36.1.1 **The need for UHF MRI in psychiatry**

Clinical applications for radiology are limited in psychiatry. None of the major psychiatric disorders require MRI imaging for diagnosis or treatment selection. As a result, 1.5T and 3T scanners have so far not found mainstream clinical use in psychiatric practice. In part, this relates to the nature of psychiatric illnesses wherein profound functional changes occur in the presence of structurally subtle disruptions involving distributed neurochemical pathways. But the accurate characterization of these changes is still lacking. Several "imaging needs" are relevant in this regard. First, superior spatiotemporal resolution for functional imaging is required for mechanistic studies that map brain to abnormal behavior. Second, better spectral resolution for neurochemical components is needed for targeted molecular imaging and in vivo pharmacological investigations. Third, in the absence of gross "qualitative" structural changes in psychiatric disorders, precise quantification of structural properties is particularly valuable for early diagnosis and longitudinal tracking of illness-related changes. In this context, as several neurochemical pathways of interest to psychiatric disorders originate in the subcortex, the ability to study the human subcortex at a granular level is an important imaging need in psychiatry. Finally, in many psychiatric disorders, brain changes are subtle, not limited to a single brain region, and are of both primary and compensatory natures; this necessitates a systems approach to brain imaging involving the whole, rather than parts, for person-level predictions and causal inferences. Several improvements offered by technical advances that accompany UHF imaging are of critical incremental value for psychiatry, as discussed with examples in the following sections.

36.2 **Psychiatric applications of UHF MRS**

Schizophrenia, a chronic psychotic disorder, has been the most studied psychiatric illness using UHF to date. Most available treatments for schizophrenia focus on the neurotransmitter dopamine. In the last three decades, neurotransmitter glutamate has gained much interest, based on postmortem findings implicating cortical microcircuit dysfunction. In vivo measurement of glutamate is challenging due to its low concentration and spectral overlap with glutamine. Interestingly, glutamine concentration may represent the more dynamic "shuttled" portion of glutamate, reflecting synaptic turnover (Duarte and Xin, 2019). At lower field strengths, optimal spectral dispersion and separation of the highly coupled spins to quantify metabolites with low in vivo concentrations have been a challenge. As a result, most 3T ^{1}H MRS studies provide a measure of "Glx," a quantity representing glutamate, glutamine, and other overlapping metabolites. Due to this lack of precision, changes in Glx cannot be mapped onto specific metabolic processes relevant to psychiatric disorders such as schizophrenia.

A specific advantage offered by UHF, especially 7T over 3T, is the ability to resolve the neurometabolic spectrum of glutamate from other overlapping metabolites. The lower error rates in quantifying these molecules also translate to a reduced need for large sample sizes to observe the effect of interest, if it is present in a sample. This has been exploited in several 7T ^{1}H-MRS studies to date, with emerging insights firmly supporting the presence of reduced glutamate levels early in the illness in the medial prefrontal cortex (Sydnor and Roalf, 2020). Existing data from 7T MRS have clarified that glutamate, rather than glutamine, is the most affected molecule, and its reductions in the medial prefrontal cortex begin at very early stages of psychosis, in relation to cognitive deficits (Table 36.1). Interestingly, such changes are not seen in depression (Godlewska et al., 2018; Smith et al., 2021). UHF MRS has also allowed investigations into drugs that act on glutamate synthetic pathways, such as ebselen (Masaki et al., 2016), boosting the pharmacoimaging capabilities focused on the glutamatergic system.

Table 36.1 Selected UHF MRS imaging studies in patients with psychiatric disorders.

Study	Patient diagnosis	N Patient: control	Region(s) and voxel size	Pulse sequence	Acquisition parameters (ms)	Major findings
Dempster et al. (2020)	FEP	26:26	dACC: 20 mm iso	Semi-LASER	TE: 100 TR: 7500	– **dACC GSH and GLU SZ > HC** – High dACC GSH, less symptoms upon antipsychotic treatment – High dACC GLU, high functional impairment
Evans et al. (2018)	MDD	20:17	ACC: 20 mm iso	PRESS	TE1: 69 TE2: 37 TR: 2500	– **ACC GLU postketamine infusion MDD > HC**
Godlewska et al. (2018)	MDD	55:50	ACC and OCC: 20 mm iso PUT: 10 × 16 × 20 mm	Semi-LASER	TE: 32 TR: 5000	– **PUT Gln MDD > HC**
Jeon et al. (2021)	CHR	13:30	dACC: 20 mm iso	Semi-LASER	TE: 100 TR: 7500	– **dACC GSH CHR > HC** – Positive association between functioning and ACC GSH
Limongi et al. (2020)	FEP	19:20	dACC: 20 mm iso	Semi-LASER	TE: 100 TR: 7500	– **dACC GSH FEP > HC** – High GSH, high inhibitory activity in dACC – High GLU, lower inhibitory activity in dACC
Pan et al. (2021)	FEP	40:25	dACC: 20 mm iso	Semi-LASER	TE: 100 TR: 7500	– **dACC GSH SZ with high conceptual disorganization > HC**
Roalf et al. (2017)	CHR + SZ	19:17	Subcortex, frontal, parietal and occipital lobes FOV: 220 × 200 Matrix size: 192 × 192	GLU-CEST	TE: 3 GRE readout TR: 6.2 TR: 10500	– GluCEST levels in the **frontal lobe** correlated with **negative symptoms**, while the **parietal lobe** correlated with **positive symptoms**
Smith et al. (2021)	LLD	9:9	ACC and PCC: 28 × 20 × 16 mm	STEAM	TR: 3000 TE: 14 (ACC) TE: 15 (PCC)	– **PCC NAA and GLU HC > MDD** – Higher ACC GSH fewer depressive symptoms
Vingerhoets et al. (2020)	22q11.2DS	17:20	ACC: 25 × 20 × 17 mm striatum: 20 mm iso	STEAM	TE: 6 TM: 10 TR: 5	– Riluzole led to decreased ACC GLU and GABA in all subjects

Note: 22q11.2DS, 22q11.2 deletion syndrome; CHR, clinical high risk; d/ACC, (dorsal) anterior cingulate cortex; FEP, first-episode psychosis; FOV, field-of-view; GABA, gamma-amino butyric acid; GLU, glutamate; GluCEST, glutamate chemical exchange saturation transfer; Gln, glutamine; GSH, glutathione; HC, healthy control; LLD, late-life depression; MDD, major depressive disorder; NAA, N-acetyl aspartate; OCC, occipital cortex; PCC, posterior cingulate cortex; PUT, putamen; SZ, schizophrenia; TE, echo time; TM, mixing time; TR, repetition time.

To fully appreciate how changes in a single neurometabolite relate to a phenotype, it is necessary to study its relationship with other key players within the neurochemical pathway of interest. In particular, the glutamate system has been variously linked to oxidative stress pathways in schizophrenia; the ability to concurrently quantify glutamate (Glu) and glutathione (GSH) will help clarify its role in schizophrenia. While short echo time (TE) sequences are commonly used for neurometabolite measurements by ^{1}H MRS to minimize the effects of long TE on J evolution and T_2 relaxation, Wong and colleagues demonstrated that robust glutamate measurement with minimal macromolecule contribution and reduced scan time is achieved when using long TE (105 ms) with semi-LASER at 7T (Wong et al., 2018). This sequence also yields precise estimates of glutathione, the cardinal antioxidant in the brain. Early studies utilizing the concomitant GSH-Glu measurements in schizophrenia have provided new insights on how GSH may counteract some of the functional effects of aberrations in glutamate levels (Limongi et al., 2020) and contribute to treatment responsiveness (Dempster et al., 2020).

An important gain with psychiatric applications of UHF MRS is the ability to reduce scanning time for single voxel spectroscopy without compromising on the power to detect an effect of interest. This has translated into more robust multimodal acquisitions in the same scanning session as MRS, providing novel insights relating glutamate and glutathione to the white matter structure, myelin content, and functional connectivity (Gawne et al., 2020; Jeon et al., 2021; Limongi et al., 2020; Pan et al., 2021). The shortening of acquisition time, as well as the reduced need for large samples to detect a group-level difference, has made UHF MRS more accessible for acutely symptomatic, untreated patients with schizophrenia, who were routinely left out of prior studies.

UHF MRS is particularly valuable in pharmacological challenge studies with drugs that manipulate glutamate release. Ketamine (Evans et al., 2018) and riluzole (Vingerhoets et al., 2020) challenge studies have leveraged the advantage offered by UHF MRS in this regard, although the lack of whole brain coverage limits interpretation of these studies. UHF also enables implementing multinuclear imaging, thus allowing the quantification of nuclei less abundant than ^{1}H in humans. Thus, lithium (Li), a commonly prescribed drug for depression and bipolar disorder with a narrow therapeutic safety window, can be directly quantified in the brain using Li MRS with higher precision than at 3T. Using an ultra-short echo time steady-state free-precession sequence, whole brain ^{7}Li MRS maps have been successfully obtained (Stout et al., 2020). With the signal-to-noise ratio (SNR) offered by 7T, brain lithium levels have been quantified with a sensitivity close to 0.05 mmol/L (therapeutic plasma concentration being 0.3 to 1.0 mmol/L).

36.2.1 Other forms of UHF neurochemical imaging in psychiatry

Chemical exchange saturation transfer (CEST) is a contrast enhancement approach that depends on the exchange of free protons between solutes and water (solvent). A radiofrequency pulse saturates solute protons in a frequency-selective manner; the rate of exchange of these saturated solute protons with the unsaturated water protons is determined by the solute concentration. For CEST to be effective, the difference in frequency between the solute protons and water protons must be significantly higher than the exchange rate. As this frequency difference increases with static field strength, the CEST effect is higher at UHF even for molecules with high exchange rates. In the absence of UHF, it is difficult to resolve the contrast among glutamate, glutamine, GABA, creatine, and macromolecules as these metabolites are strongly coupled and the chemical exchange rate is higher than the frequency separation. With optimized radiofrequency saturation to amplify contrast and reduction in field inhomogeneity, the gain in the SNR for CEST is sizeable at UHF. This not only increases the number of solutes that can be studied but also enhances the amplitude of the CEST effect, making their peaks more detectable (Ladd et al., 2018).

Proton exchange-based CEST imaging has the potential to provide a whole brain map of specific molecules, with glutamate-CEST effects being particularly relevant to psychiatry. The remarkable gain in the chemical exchange saturation effect for glutamate at UHF also enables the separation of glutamate from glutamine, an important "imaging need" in psychiatry, as discussed earlier. While the CEST-based glutamate measurement is not completely free of contributions from GABA and creatine, employing glutamate-CEST in very early stages of psychosis, Roalf and colleagues demonstrated a frontoparietal reduction in glutamate CEST contrast, which correlated with symptom burden (Roalf et al., 2017). Several other molecules that are critical for energy homeostasis can be studied by tapping CEST effect in UHF (e.g., glucose, lactate, and glycogen), but there are no studies focusing on these approaches in psychiatric patient samples to date.

The developments in UHF MRS and CEST are encouraging in the study of schizophrenia and other psychiatric disorders, but there remain certain methodological issues to ensure the quantitative accuracy of these techniques across brain regions and populations. Specifically, careful adjustments (shimming) of both the main magnetic field (B_0) and radiofrequency (RF) transmit field (B_1^+) are crucial to minimize measurement inhomogeneities and ensure spatial and temporal accuracy. Glutamatergic dysfunction is intrinsically related to gamma-amino butyric acid (GABA) transmission; concurrent quantification of GABA, glutamine, and glutamate from the same voxel at the same time will provide a more complete picture of the excitation-inhibition imbalance in psychiatric disorders. In the case of using 7T for GABA quantification, a potential loss of the SNR may be observed due to a combination of an increased T_2 decay rate and longer echo times required to execute complex RF (Hong et al., 2019). Unlike positron emission tomography studies that offer receptor occupancy profiles, MRS and CEST do not provide means to directly infer the synaptic activity or functional deployment of a neurotransmitter. Functional MRS, which captures task-induced changes in glutamate and GABA, is promising in this regard (Stanley and Raz, 2018), but further clinical studies are required to demonstrate its utility in psychiatric disorders.

For most neurological applications, neurochemical estimates are obtained from a qualitatively pathological lesion; this is not the case when studying psychiatric disorders. The clinical use neurochemical imaging in psychiatry requires a normative approach that quantifies the degree of deviation of an individual from an expected healthy distribution. For most neurometabolites of interest, despite the precision offered by UHF, healthy distribution ranges for neurometabolites have not yet been estimated. Standardization in the employment of pulse sequences and acquisition protocols to isolate and suppress signal, spectral fitting, tissue correction, water suppression techniques, consensus-driven voxel placements, and reporting of reference metabolites could move us closer to the goal of normative estimations. Large-scale 7T studies involving multiple recruiting sites will be required to establish this in the near future. This will be especially crucial for the study of psychiatric disorders such as schizophrenia and depression, where neurobiological heterogeneity is a prime suspect in the lack of therapeutic progress.

36.3 Psychiatric applications of UHF structural MRI

While gross anatomical changes are not a feature of most psychiatric disorders, subtle developmental aberrations in the functional architecture are suspected to contribute to the apparent neural inefficiency, cognitive deficits, and symptoms such as hallucinations in many disorders. The improved spatial resolution of UHF MRI mitigates the partial volume effect (Vu et al., 2017), improving the precision of quantitative structural imaging. The improvement in visualization of the subcortex with UHF has enabled more precise delineation of anatomical subregions. A prime example relevant to psychiatric applications is the hippocampus, its subfields, and adjacent white matter output regions, which are strongly implicated in schizophrenia (Kirov et al., 2013; Park et al., 2021) and affective disorders (Cattarinussi et al., 2021). Similarly, several studies have also utilized myelin contrast to automatically parcellate hard-to-detect structures such as habenula (Cho et al., 2021; Lim et al., 2021), locus coeruleus (Morris et al., 2020), and leverage submillimeter voxel resolution to study subnuclei of the amygdala in depression and bipolar disorder (Brown et al., 2019). Pinpointing the hyperconnectivity patterns specific to subcortical tracts is critical, especially in the case of treatment-resistant depression, where focused neuromodulation might provide symptom relief (Scangos et al., 2021).

For many psychiatric disorders, given the lack of identifiable lesions, intraindividual change trajectories of quantifiable image characteristics hold more clinical value than qualitative changes in any single structure. In this context, quantitative approaches at UHF that exploit changes in relaxation properties are able to capture microstructural features like myelin or iron content using quantitative susceptibility mapping (QSM) and tissue perfusion using techniques such as arterial spin labeling (ASL) and are especially valuable. These quantitative methods, when obtained before and after an intervention, provide means to assess the biological efficacy of the intervention. For example, the concomitant use of structural and diffusion-weighted imaging and ASL in UHF has clarified that electroconvulsive therapy, a treatment reserved for hard-to-treat depression, may be neuroplastic without inducing any vasogenic edema in the hippocampus (Nuninga et al., 2020a,b). Quantitative high-resolution neurovascular imaging, using susceptibility-weighted imaging (SWI), has become a distinct possibility with UHF (Hua et al., 2017), providing an important means to study the vascular and inflammatory hypotheses of many psychiatric disorders, especially schizophrenia and depression.

The superior demarcation of the gray-white matter boundary with UHF neuroimaging also improves tissue segmentation and the accuracy of cortical morphometry; this, in turn, translates to increased experimental power when building multivariate prediction models. In one of the first psychiatric applications of 7T, Iwabuchi and colleagues collected 3T and 7T structural scans on the same day from a cohort of patients with schizophrenia and healthy control subjects and quantified the outperformance of 7T-MRI-based classifiers when identifying patients (Iwabuchi et al., 2013). The diagnostic odds ratio when using 7T was three times higher than that when using 3T for gray matter-based classification, while the number needed to predict (and thus the sample size requirement for future studies) was 50% lower when using 7T than when using 3T (Iwabuchi et al., 2013). See Table 36.2 for structural studies in psychiatric samples in UHF.

36.4 Psychiatric applications of UHF functional MRI

Functional MRI (fMRI) has been the workhorse for making brain-to-behavior inferences in psychiatric research. The hyperlinear increase in the SNR with magnetic field along with an increased sensitivity in the blood oxygenation level-dependent (BOLD) mechanism, particularly in smaller vessels, provides two major advantages to the underlying fMRI contrast. First, higher signal sensitivity at UHF allows for shortened acquisition time and increased temporal resolution and therefore offers the opportunity to study highly resolved event transitions during cognitive tasks (Lewis et al., 2016). Second, with the

Table 36.2 Selected UHF structural imaging studies in patients with psychiatric disorders.

Study	Patient diagnosis	N Patient:control	Structural measure	Acquisition	Voxel size	Duration	Coverage	Main findings
Hua et al. (2017)	SSD	12:12	CBV	iVASO TFE	$3.5 \times 3.5 \times 5$ mm		Whole brain	Distributed decreases and increases in SZ
Iwabuchi et al. (2013)	SZ	19:20	GM and WM intensity	3T: MPRAGE 7T: IR-TFE	3T: 1 mm iso 7T: 0.6 mm iso (1 mm resliced)	12 min	Whole brain	Patient classification − 7T>3T − GM>WM
Kirov et al. (2013)	SZ	16:15	Radiologist-rated intensity	MPRAGE-guided 2D GRE	$232 \times 232 \times 1500\,\mu m$	17 min	Hippocampus DG cell layer	DG intensity SZ<HC
Pan et al. (2021)	FEP	31:25	FA and fiber tract volume	2D spin echo EPI	2 mm iso	12 min	Whole brain	Disorganized thinking in SZ associated with lower cingulum FA
Park et al. (2021)	FEP	41:28	Volume and shape	MP2RAGE	0.8 mm iso	9 min	Volume: whole brain Shape: hippocampus	Hippocampal volume (especially CA4) FEP<HC
Brown et al. (2019)	MDD	24:20	Volume	MP2RAGE T_2-TSE	0.7 mm iso $0.4 \times 0.4 \times 2$ mm		Amygdala nuclei and hippocampal subfields	− MDD=HC − Depressive symptoms related to decreased regional volumes
Cho et al. (2010)	MDD	16:16	Quantitative T_2^* and volume	Dual echo flash	Pixel-wise	11 min	Hippocampal subfields	T_2^* relaxation (right CA1 and subiculum) recurrent MDD>initial MDD>controls
Nuninga et al. (2020a)	MDD BP	22:8	Volume	T_1-TFE T_2-TSE	1 mm iso $0.3 \times 0.3 \times 2$ mm	2 min 8 min	Hippocampal subfields	− DG volume post>pre ECT − Associated with symptom improvement
Nuninga et al. (2020b)	MDD BP	20:8	Perfusion, mean diffusivity	IVIM ASL	1.5 mm iso $1.8 \times 1.8 \times 3$ mm		Hippocampus	− Mean diffusivity, perfusion fraction post<pre ECT − ASL post=pre ECT
Morris et al. (2020)	PTSD GAD PD SAD	15:14	Volume	MT-TFE MP2RAGE	$0.4 \times 0.4 \times 0.5$ mm	7 min 5 min	Locus coeruleus	− Volume patient>HC − Associated with poorer attentional and inhibitory control, higher distress and arousal

Note: BP, bipolar disorder; CBV, cerebral blood volume; DG, dentate gyrus; ECT, electroconvulsive therapy; FA, fractional anisotropy; FEP, first-episode psychosis; GAD, generalized anxiety disorder; GM, gray matter; HC, healthy control; MDD, major depressive disorder; MTR, magnetization transfer ratio; PD, panic disorder; PTSD, posttraumatic stress disorder; SAD, seasonal affective disorder; SSD, schizophrenia-spectrum disorder; SZ, schizophrenia; WM, white matter.

ability to reduce the voxel volume, the spatial fidelity of inferences is much improved. For functional MRI studies, individual differences in effort-making and engagement are minimized in the absence of task constraints; as a result, psychiatric neuroimaging has embraced connectivity-based modeling based on resting state functional MRI. With improved spatial and temporal resolution on offer at UHF, uncovering temporal correlations that underwrite functional network configurations has greatly improved.

As discussed earlier, higher image resolution and reduced partial volume effect with UHF MRI enable smaller voxel sizes in structural studies. This not only increases the reliability of spatial local-ization but also provides unprecedented granularity for mapping functional anatomy. Exploiting this advantage, Doucet and colleagues studied tonotopy, the ordered organization of sound frequency in the auditory cortex that is established in early postnatal life (Doucet et al., 2019). During a passive listening task with limited fMRI spatial smoothing (4.5 mm kernel), they observed abnormally increased activation and altered tonotopic organization of the auditory cortex for a range of tone frequencies. The functional data for this study were mapped with very high 500 μm isotropic resolution anatomical reference acquired with T_1-weighted contrast.

Smaller voxel sizes improve the precision of connectivity estimates from small regions of interest in the subcortex, such as the ventral tegmental area (Morris et al., 2019). This translates to substantial information gain when dynamic causal modeling (Tak et al., 2018), a critical tool for computational psychiatry (Limongi et al., 2020), is employed. In particular, the improved contrast-to-noise ratio obviates the need for extensive spatial smoothing when mapping function to structure. Most psychiatric applications of UHF fMRI to date have exploited the reduction in scanning time with SNR gains, with very few, if any, taking advantage of the improved spatial and temporal resolution (for example, Weidacker et al., 2021). Psychiatric imaging studies in UHF predominantly use >2 mm isotropic voxels for echo-planar imaging (EPI; usually along with submillimeter structural acquisitions) and > 1 s repetition time (TR) for fMRI connectivity analyses. Reducing voxel volume but still achiev-ing whole brain coverage is increasingly becoming feasible with dedicated acquisition protocols (Vu et al., 2017) and is required for many discovery-oriented psychiatric research applications. Post-processing steps enable removal of artifacts and improve temporal and thus functional contrast.

36.5 Future of psychiatric UHF imaging

Our ability to tap into unique biophysical mechanism and/or biomarkers of with UHF, especially 7T, has opened the possibility of its use in psychiatric research. The demonstration of unique capabilities, especially the gain in spectral resolution that enhances the number and accuracy of neurometabolite detection, the gain in the SNR that reduces scanning time, and sample size required for certain exper-iments, has expanded studies that involve patients with varying illness severity and repeated sampling (Table 36.3 and Fig. 36.1). Nevertheless, given the paucity of the need for diagnostic imaging per se in psychiatry, UHF has not yet entered clinical use.

As 7T UHF systems become more commonly available in hospital settings, their application to psychiatric practice has become more accessible. Several challenges remain in utilizing their potential in full. A number of these challenges are technical and are not specific to psychiatric applications per se. Several recent advances are directly addressing these issues now as discussed in prior chapters of this volume. Nevertheless, these technical advances are not uniformly accessible to UHF units engaged

Table 36.3 Psychiatric applications of UHF MRI.

Condition	Demonstrated added value	Further potential use
Schizophrenia	Refined examination of the glutamate hypothesis; increasing accessibility due to reduced scan time; enhancing techniques for pharmacological applications due to high SNR; parsing the role of antioxidant GSH on multimodal brain features; testing nuanced aspects of the vascular hypothesis; reduced sample size requirements for machine learning using anatomical features; improved classification; unprecedented in vivo laminar visualization, delineating changes in tonotopic maps of the auditory cortex; reduced partial volume effects	Functional MRS or CEST to parse the dynamic glutamate pool; fMRI-fMRS or steady state MRS; multi-voxel MRS; examination of oxidative stress effects (e.g., neuromelanin), microstructure of white matter, and energy handling (lactate, ^{31}P molecules such as ATP); and biological effects of pharmaceutical and nonpharmaceutical treatments
Bipolar disorder	Sensitive assessment of brain lithium levels; glutamate-focused pharmacoimaging studies of ebselen (lithium mimetic); parsing the role of subcortical structures in vivo; parsing the biological effects of ECT	Neurochemical and anatomical granular studies in line with schizophrenia; examination of myelin and white matter hyperintensities; granular studies in line with schizophrenia; individual classification and prediction; comparison between UHF and lower field strengths
Depression/ OCD	Resolved assessment of the effect of the rapid antidepressant ketamine on the glutamate system; granular examination hippocampal subfields, habenula, and amygdala; parsing the biological effects of ECT; quantitative high-resolution neurovascular imaging for vascular and inflammatory hypotheses	Neurocircuitry delineation for subcortical neuromodulation and surgical applications in treatment resistance; stratified clinical trials for ketamine and other novel agents affecting the glutamate system; anatomical granular studies in line with schizophrenia; and individual classification and prediction

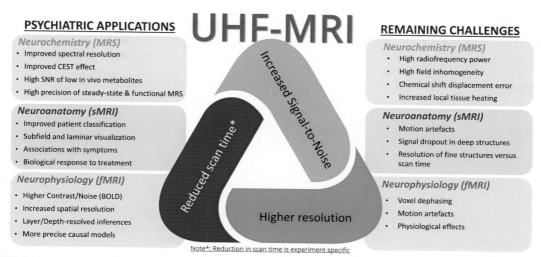

FIG. 36.1

Advantages and challenges of ultra-high field (UHF) magnetic resonance imaging (MRI).

in psychiatric research, reducing the pace of independent replications of exciting early observations of translational promise. Second, psychiatric imaging has firmly entered the era of big data; enabling data pooling is of critical importance to parse some of the neurobiological heterogeneity that is inherent to many psychiatric syndromes. Considerable effort has gone into calibrating and harmonizing 3T MRI (and, to some extent, MRS) sequences in this regard, but such efforts for standardized acquisitions are still at early stages for UHF. Furthermore, the cost of capital, siting, and maintenance of UHF MRI systems is still prohibitive for its widespread use. Overcoming some of the cost barriers will accelerate translational work on UHF in psychiatry, enabling larger clinical sampling.

Further growth of psychiatric UHF imaging is not only contingent upon technical developments but also on the organization of large-scale, combined clinical research efforts. To this end, formation of method sharing networks with focused application-derived goals will be crucial. Openly accessible clinical imaging data will accelerate analytical work as well as building further capacity for UHF imaging in psychiatry. Site-specific differences in scanner profiles at UHF could be a roadblock, but this is not insurmountable, as shown with lower field imaging networks, such as the Enhancing Neuro Imaging Genetics Through Meta-Analysis (ENIGMA) Consortium. Given the promise of neurochemical imaging in psychiatry, and the value of UHF for neurochemistry, the natural next step in psychiatric UHF imaging could be in this direction.

Acknowledgments

The authors want to thank Dr. Joe Gati and Dr. Rob Bartha of the Centre for Functional and Metabolic Mapping (CFMM), Robarts Research Institute, Western University, for their advice on technical aspects of this chapter. We are also grateful to Dr. Jean Theberge for his critical inputs.

References

Brown, S.S.G., Rutland, J.W., Verma, G., et al., 2019. Structural MRI at 7T reveals amygdala nuclei and hippocampal subfield volumetric association with major depressive disorder symptom severity. Sci. Rep. 9, 10166. https://doi.org/10.1038/s41598-019-46687-7.

Cattarinussi, G., Delvecchio, G., Maggioni, E., Bressi, C., Brambilla, P., 2021. Ultra-high field imaging in major depressive disorder: a review of structural and functional studies. J. Affect. Disord. 290, 65–73. https://doi.org/10.1016/j.jad.2021.04.056.

Cho, Z.H., Kim, Y.B., Han, J.Y., Kim, N.B., Hwang, S.I., Kim, S.J., Cho, S.J., 2010. Altered T2* relaxation time of the hippocampus in major depressive disorder: implications of ultra-high field magnetic resonance imaging. J. Psychiatr. Res. 44 (14), 881–886.

Cho, S.-E., Park, C.-A., Na, K.-S., et al., 2021. Left-right asymmetric and smaller right habenula volume in major depressive disorder on high-resolution 7-T magnetic resonance imaging. PLoS One 16, e0255459. https://doi.org/10.1371/journal.pone.0255459.

Dempster, K., Jeon, P., MacKinley, M., Williamson, P., Théberge, J., Palaniyappan, L., 2020. Early treatment response in first episode psychosis: a 7-T magnetic resonance spectroscopic study of glutathione and glutamate. Mol. Psychiatry 25, 1640–1650. https://doi.org/10.1038/s41380-020-0704-x.

Doucet, G.E., Luber, M.J., Balchandani, P., Sommer, I.E., Frangou, S., 2019. Abnormal auditory tonotopy in patients with schizophrenia. NPJ Schizophr. 5, 16. https://doi.org/10.1038/s41537-019-0084-x.

Duarte, J.M.N., Xin, L., 2019. Magnetic resonance spectroscopy in schizophrenia: evidence for glutamatergic dysfunction and impaired energy metabolism. Neurochem. Res. 44, 102–116. https://doi.org/10.1007/s11064-018-2521-z.

Evans, J.W., Lally, N., An, L., et al., 2018. 7T 1 H-MRS in major depressive disorder: a ketamine treatment study. Neuropsychopharmacology 43, 1908–1914. https://doi.org/10.1038/s41386-018-0057-1.

Gawne, T.J., Overbeek, G.J., Killen, J.F., et al., 2020. A multimodal magnetoencephalography 7 T fMRI and 7 T proton MR spectroscopy study in first episode psychosis. NPJ Schizophr. 6, 23. https://doi.org/10.1038/s41537-020-00113-4.

Godlewska, B.R., Masaki, C., Sharpley, A.L., Cowen, P.J., Emir, U.E., 2018. Brain glutamate in medication-free depressed patients: a proton MRS study at 7 tesla. Psychol. Med. 48, 1731–1737. https://doi.org/10.1017/S0033291717003373.

Hong, D., Rankouhi, S.R., Thielen, J.-W., van Asten, J.J.A., Norris, D.G., 2019. A comparison of sLASER and MEGA-sLASER using simultaneous interleaved acquisition for measuring GABA in the human brain at 7T. PLoS One 14, e0223702. https://doi.org/10.1371/journal.pone.0223702.

Hua, J., Brandt, A.S., Lee, S., et al., 2017. Abnormal grey matter arteriolar cerebral blood volume in schizophrenia measured with 3D inflow-based vascular-space-occupancy MRI at 7T. Schizophr. Bull. 43, 620–632. https://doi.org/10.1093/schbul/sbw109.

Iwabuchi, S., Liddle, P.F., Palaniyappan, L., 2013. Clinical utility of machine learning approaches in schizophrenia: improving diagnostic confidence for translational neuroimaging. Front. Psychiatry 4, 95. https://doi.org/10.3389/fpsyt.2013.00095.

Jeon, P., Limongi, R., Ford, S.D., et al., 2021. Progressive changes in glutamate concentration in early stages of schizophrenia: a longitudinal 7-tesla MRS study. Schizophr. Bull. Open 2. https://doi.org/10.1093/schizbullopen/sgaa072.

Kirov, I.I., Hardy, C.J., Matsuda, K., et al., 2013. In vivo 7 tesla imaging of the dentate granule cell layer in schizophrenia. Schizophr. Res. 147, 362–367. https://doi.org/10.1016/j.schres.2013.04.020.

Ladd, M.E., Bachert, P., Meyerspeer, M., et al., 2018. Pros and cons of ultra-high-field MRI/MRS for human application. Prog. Nucl. Magn. Reson. Spectrosc. 109, 1–50. https://doi.org/10.1016/j.pnmrs.2018.06.001.

Lewis, L.D., Setsompop, K., Rosen, B.R., Polimeni, J.R., 2016. Fast fMRI can detect oscillatory neural activity in humans. Proc. Natl. Acad. Sci. 113, E6679–E6685. https://doi.org/10.1073/pnas.1608117113.

Lim, S.-H., Yoon, J., Kim, Y.J., et al., 2021. Reproducibility of automated habenula segmentation via deep learning in major depressive disorder and normal controls with 7 tesla MRI. Sci. Rep. 11, 13445. https://doi.org/10.1038/s41598-021-92952-z.

Limongi, R., Jeon, P., Mackinley, M., et al., 2020. Glutamate and dysconnection in the salience network: neurochemical, effective connectivity, and computational evidence in schizophrenia. Biol. Psychiatry 88, 273–281. https://doi.org/10.1016/j.biopsych.2020.01.021.

Masaki, C., Sharpley, A.L., Godlewska, B.R., et al., 2016. Effects of the potential lithium-mimetic, ebselen, on brain neurochemistry: a magnetic resonance spectroscopy study at 7 tesla. Psychopharmacology 233, 1097–1104. https://doi.org/10.1007/s00213-015-4189-2.

Morris, L.S., Kundu, P., Costi, S., et al., 2019. Ultra-high field MRI reveals mood-related circuit disturbances in depression: a comparison between 3-tesla and 7-tesla. Transl. Psychiatry 9, 1–11. https://doi.org/10.1038/s41398-019-0425-6.

Morris, L.S., Tan, A., Smith, D.A., et al., 2020. Sub-millimeter variation in human locus coeruleus is associated with dimensional measures of psychopathology: an in vivo ultra-high field 7-tesla MRI study. NeuroImage Clin. 25, 102148. https://doi.org/10.1016/j.nicl.2019.102148.

Nuninga, J.O., Mandl, R.C.W., Boks, M.P., et al., 2020a. Volume increase in the dentate gyrus after electroconvulsive therapy in depressed patients as measured with 7T. Mol. Psychiatry 25, 1559–1568. https://doi.org/10.1038/s41380-019-0392-6.

Nuninga, J.O., Mandl, R.C.W., Froeling, M., et al., 2020b. Vasogenic edema versus neuroplasticity as neural correlates of hippocampal volume increase following electroconvulsive therapy. Brain Stimul. 13, 1080–1086. https://doi.org/10.1016/j.brs.2020.04.017.

Pan, Y., Dempster, K., Jeon, P., Théberge, J., Khan, A.R., Palaniyappan, L., 2021. Acute conceptual disorganization in untreated first-episode psychosis: a combined magnetic resonance spectroscopy and diffusion imaging study of the cingulum. J. Psychiatry Neurosci. 46, E337–E346. https://doi.org/10.1503/jpn.200167.

Park, M.T.M., Jeon, P., Khan, A.R., et al., 2021. Hippocampal neuroanatomy in first episode psychosis: a putative role for glutamate and serotonin receptors. Prog. Neuro-Psychopharmacol. Biol. Psychiatry 110, 110297. https://doi.org/10.1016/j.pnpbp.2021.110297.

Roalf, D.R., Nanga, R.P.R., Rupert, P.E., et al., 2017. Glutamate imaging (GluCEST) reveals lower brain GluCEST contrast in patients on the psychosis spectrum. Mol. Psychiatry. https://doi.org/10.1038/mp.2016.258.

Scangos, K.W., Khambhati, A.N., Daly, P.M., et al., 2021. Closed-loop neuromodulation in an individual with treatment-resistant depression. Nat. Med. 27, 1696–1700. https://doi.org/10.1038/s41591-021-01480-w.

Smith, G.S., Oeltzschner, G., Gould, N.F., et al., 2021. Neurotransmitters and neurometabolites in late-life depression: a preliminary magnetic resonance spectroscopy study at 7T. J. Affect. Disord. 279, 417–425. https://doi.org/10.1016/j.jad.2020.10.011.

Stanley, J.A., Raz, N., 2018. Functional magnetic resonance spectroscopy: the "new" MRS for cognitive neuroscience and psychiatry research. Front. Psychiatry 9, 76. https://doi.org/10.3389/fpsyt.2018.00076.

Stout, J., Hozer, F., Coste, A., et al., 2020. Accumulation of lithium in the hippocampus of patients with bipolar disorder: a lithium-7 magnetic resonance imaging study at 7 tesla. Biol. Psychiatry 88, 426–433. https://doi.org/10.1016/j.biopsych.2020.02.1181.

Sydnor, V.J., Roalf, D.R., 2020. A meta-analysis of ultra-high field glutamate, glutamine, GABA and glutathione 1HMRS in psychosis: implications for studies of psychosis risk. Schizophr. Res. 226, 61–69. https://doi.org/10.1016/j.schres.2020.06.028.

Tak, S., Noh, J., Cheong, C., et al., 2018. A validation of dynamic causal modelling for 7T fMRI. J. Neurosci. Methods 305, 36–45. https://doi.org/10.1016/j.jneumeth.2018.05.002.

Vigo, D., Thornicroft, G., Atun, R., 2016. Estimating the true global burden of mental illness. Lancet Psychiatry 3, 171–178. https://doi.org/10.1016/S2215-0366(15)00505-2.

Vingerhoets, C., Tse, D.H., van Oudenaren, M., et al., 2020. Glutamatergic and GABAergic reactivity and cognition in 22q11.2 deletion syndrome and healthy volunteers: a randomized double-blind 7-tesla pharmacological MRS study. J. Psychopharmacol. 34, 856–863. https://doi.org/10.1177/0269881120922977.

Vu, A.T., Jamison, K., Glasser, M.F., et al., 2017. Tradeoffs in pushing the spatial resolution of fMRI for the 7 T human connectome project. NeuroImage 154, 23–32. https://doi.org/10.1016/j.neuroimage.2016.11.049.

Weidacker, K., Kim, S.-G., Nord, C.L., Rua, C., Rodgers, C.T., Voon, V., 2021. Avoiding monetary loss: a human habenula functional MRI ultra-high field study. Cortex 142, 62–73. https://doi.org/10.1016/j.cortex.2021.05.013.

Wong, D., Schranz, A.L., Bartha, R., 2018. Optimized in vivo brain glutamate measurement using long-echo-time semi-LASER at 7 T. NMR Biomed. 31, e4002. https://doi.org/10.1002/nbm.4002.

New horizons

New horizons: Human MRI at extremely high field strengths

David G. Norris[a,b] and Mark E. Ladd[b,c,d,e]

[a]*Donders Institute for Brain, Cognition and Behaviour, Radboud University Nijmegen, Nijmegen, The Netherlands* [b]*Erwin L. Hahn Institute for MRI, University Duisburg-Essen, Essen, Germany* [c]*Medical Physics in Radiology, German Cancer Research Center (DKFZ), Heidelberg, Germany* [d]*Faculty of Medicine, Heidelberg University, Heidelberg, Germany* [e]*Faculty of Physics and Astronomy, Heidelberg University, Heidelberg, Germany*

Highlights

- Field strengths above 10T offer considerable sensitivity gains even compared to 7T systems.
- Considerable technical challenges will need to be overcome to realize these benefits, especially the design and construction of a stable magnet.
- The combination of high-spatial-resolution structural and functional imaging will offer unprecedented insight into structure-function relationships at the individual level.
- Studies in selected cohorts will help unravel important unanswered questions about healthy physiology, pathological processes, brain function, and aging.

37.1 Introduction

The primary motivation for moving to ever higher static magnetic field strengths is the associated increase in sensitivity. The signal-to-noise ratio (SNR) is now believed to scale according to B_0 to the power of 1.65 (Pohmann et al., 2016), an experimental result that is shown in Fig. 37.1. A recent work comparing SNR gain in a spherical phantom at 3, 7, 9.4, 10.5, and 11.7T shows SNR growing even more rapidly: $B_0^{1.94 \pm 0.16}$ (Le Ster et al., 2022). For spectroscopy, there are the additional benefits of reduced spectral complexity and increased chemical shift dispersion. As the static magnetic field strength increases so does T_1, whereas both T_2 and T_2^* decrease. The expected relaxation times for gray matter, white matter, and blood are shown in Table 37.1. From these values, it can be concluded that T_1 contrast will increase with static field strength. The reduction in T_2 and T_2^* values is less beneficial as this will force shorter TE values, and in the case of shorter T_2^* values will also restrict the duration of any echo-planar imaging (EPI) readout. The T_2 of venous blood shortens dramatically, and its signal will be difficult to detect at the highest field strengths considered.

There are considerable technical challenges associated with static field strengths above 10T. These include the increased radiofrequency (RF) power deposition, poorer transmit field homogeneity, and worsened absolute homogeneity of the static field that were already encountered when moving to 7T. In addition to these, there is the additional challenge of designing and constructing the magnet. Finally, and of the utmost importance, are considerations of safety and comfort. In this chapter, we shall first

Advances in Magnetic Resonance Technology and Applications. Volume 10. ISSN 2666-9099. https://doi.org/10.1016/B978-0-323-99898-7.00023-7

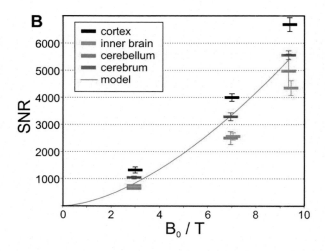

FIG. 37.1

SNR measured for selected brain regions at different static field strengths (3, 7, 9.4T). The red line shows the curve $SNR = B_0^{1.65}$. *Taken by permission from Fig. 5 in Pohmann et al. (2016).*

Table 37.1 Variation of relaxation times in the brain with static field strength.

Static field (T)	Gray matter			White matter			Blood	
	T_1 (s)	T_2 (ms)	T_2^* (ms)	T_1 (s)	T_2 (ms)	T_2^* (ms)	T_1 (s)	T_2 venous (ms)
3	1.3	67	48	0.9	78	49	1.6	51
7	1.8	49	28	1.2	57	27	2.1	20
9.4	2	43	22	1.4	49	21	2.4	12
10.5	2.1	40	20	1.4	46	19	2.6	10
11.7	2.2	38	19	1.5	43	17	2.8	8
14	2.3	34	16	1.6	38	15	3	6
20	2.6	27	12	1.8	30	11	3.9	3

The static field strengths considered correspond to those currently available (3–11.7T) and those considered as next steps by the community. The values are calculated/measured according to the following literature: gray and white matter T_1 (Rooney et al., 2007); gray and white matter T_2 (Bartha et al., 2002); gray matter T_2^* (Uludağ et al., 2009); white matter T_2^* (Peters et al., 2007); blood T_1 (Zhang et al., 2013); venous blood T_2 (Krishnamurthy et al., 2014).

tackle the unique technical and safety challenges posed by static field strengths above 10T before moving on to examine the potential for studying the human brain. In general, we shall confine ourselves to describing general principles of design and measurement rather than describing specific applications. At present, it would appear that the cost of any system above 10T would be so high as to prohibit its widespread clinical use. Hence, such instruments can be expected to be used for gaining fundamental knowledge (which may be transferable to lower field systems) rather than developing techniques for the clinic.

37.2 **Magnet design**

Superconducting magnets are a prerequisite for attaining ultra-high static magnetic fields. In order to remain superconducting, the superconducting filament has to operate below the critical temperature and current density corresponding to the static magnetic field strength. As the static magnetic field strength increases, both critical values fall. This has the consequence of making the magnet larger and less stable. There is then an increased danger that interactions between the gradients and the cryostat induce a quench. For niobium titanium filament, which is used as the standard for field strengths of below 10T, the maximum attainable field is around 12T.

It has proven possible to construct several NbTi magnets with field strengths of 11.7T, although at the time of writing none are yet being used for human imaging. Above this field strength, other superconducting materials need to be considered. Human magnets with field strength at or above 7T are generally classified as ultra-high field (UHF). Given the necessity to switch superconducting technologies at field strengths at and above 12T, it seems appropriate to introduce a new classification, and we therefore indicate this new range of human MRI systems as extremely high field (EHF).

There are two potential candidates for constructing EHF magnets: niobium tin (Nb_3Sn), which, similar to NbTi, is designated a low-temperature superconductor (LTS), and high-temperature superconductors (HTSs) (Parizh et al., 2017; Xu et al., 2021). Although a number of HTS materials exist, for the purpose of this chapter, they shall be treated generically. Up to a field strength of about 17T, Nb_3Sn filament has the advantage of a higher critical current density (c.f. Fig. 4 (Budinger and Bird, 2018)); beyond 20T, HTSs are the only viable solution. In the range of field strengths 11.7 to ~17T, both Nb_3Sn and HTS magnets offer the possibility of more compact magnet design than NbTi magnets at 11.7T (Li and Roell, 2021). At field strengths below 11.7T, most superconducting MRI magnets are nearly perfectly superconducting with minimum downward drift in the current and magnetic field, since any joints in the superconducting wire have almost no resistance. These magnets are called "persistent." LTS and HTS magnets at higher field strengths have to be run in driven mode, i.e., permanently attached to a power supply, as it is technically not possible to form superconducting joints to allow for persistent mode operation. This requires a high performance of the power source to ensure sufficient stability of the field over time. For magnets where the critical temperature is well above 4 K, the possibility exists of refrigerating the magnet with conductive cooling rather than bathing it in liquid helium, which drastically reduces the amount of helium required.

Most clinical MRI magnets at field strengths below 7T are composed of a discrete set of coils. The peak magnetic field in the coils of such a design is much higher than the nominal field strength of the magnet and, at higher field strengths, can exceed the performance of the superconductor. The first generation of 7T magnets thus utilized a compensated solenoid geometry. An alternative geometry is to form the magnet from a series of double pancakes, the positions of which are optimized to ensure homogeneity (Li and Roell, 2021). As with a compensated solenoid, the peak field is not much higher than the central field of the magnet.

The MRI scanner with the highest operating field approved for human studies at the time of writing is a whole-body 10.5T system (88 cm warm bore) at the University of Minnesota. Initial results have been shown in the torso (Uğurbil et al., 2021) and brain. The magnet is wound with NbTi, weighs 110 tons, and relies on passive shielding. The 11.7T Iseult magnet at NeuroSpin in France (Vedrine et al., 2015) achieved first images in September 2021, and at the time of writing is still restricted to

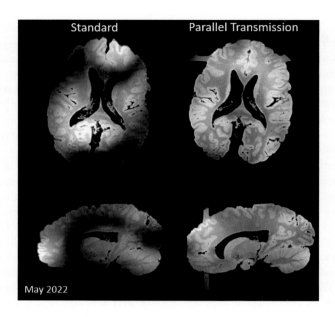

FIG. 37.2

Images acquired in an ex vivo brain at 11.7T. Resolution is 0.7 mm isotropic (3D GRE, TR = 30 ms, TE = 4.7 ms, iPAT = 2 x2, nominal flip angle = 10 degrees, TA = 5 min 30 s). Images were acquired with a 32-channel home-made head coil using phase shimming only (left column) and full parallel transmission (kT-points, right column) to reduce excitation nonuniformities. *Images courtesy of NeuroSpin, CEA, Paris-Saclay, France.*

ex vivo and phantom acquisitions (Fig. 37.2). The magnet has a warm bore of 90 cm, weighs 132 tons, and is actively shielded. The superconductor is NbTi operated at 1.8 K to achieve superfluid conditions. Two further 11.7T head-only magnets (68 and 70-cm warm bore) have been manufactured for NIH in Bethesda, USA, and NRI at Gachon University in South Korea. These magnets have similar configurations, each weighing roughly 60 tons, and are operated at 2.3 K. The Iseult magnet is unique in that it is the only example of the aforementioned magnets that is not operated in persistent mode; instead, it is driven with two redundant power supplies. It is also the only magnet composed of double pancakes (170 in total in the main coil); the other magnets are compensated solenoids.

37.3 Safety considerations

MRI is considered to be a very safe, noninvasive imaging technique because it uses nonionizing radiation. Nevertheless, a number of safety-relevant precautions must be complied with to ensure the safety of both the persons being examined and the personnel operating the systems. The underlying limits for tissue heating, nerve stimulation, and acoustic noise do not vary with field strength according to the IEC 60601-2-33 standard for MRI equipment safety, though at higher magnetic fields, it becomes more challenging to comply with some of these aspects. Since MRI systems with magnetic fields >10T are unlikely to be utilized for clinical diagnosis in individuals, any risks for subjects or personnel need to be weighed against societal benefit and not against individual medical benefit as would be the case for patients.

The electric field of the RF excitation can lead to tissue heating, and wavelength effects can lead to localized hot spots in the tissue. Therefore, local specific absorption rate (SAR) limits play a much more significant role than global SAR limits at high frequencies. Numerical simulations are currently the only reliable method to predict and quantify such hot spots, since in vivo measurement of tissue heating remains challenging. Parallel transmission (pTx) can be utilized to manage SAR concerns (cf. Radiofrequency Fields and Coil Requirements). For a detailed discussion of RF-related safety considerations, the reader is referred to Chapter 4.

Gradient performance is largely unchanged at higher magnetic fields, although it is highly likely that such magnets will be coupled with the highest performance gradients available. Interactions between the gradient switching and the static magnetic field increase the forces and torques on the gradient coil, and can lead to more intense acoustic exposure. Recent work, however, indicates that the acoustic noise levels increase less rapidly with magnetic field strength than previously expected due to opposing eddy currents in the gradient coil inductors being induced by vibrations of the coil conductor in the magnetic field. This effect, which has been termed "Lorentz damping" (Winkler et al., 2017), conforms with experimental observations.

The most obvious change in UHF and ELF MRI systems is the static magnetic field itself. The IEC 60601-2-33 standard currently defines the "normal operating mode" to include field strengths ≤3T, the first-level controlled mode for field strengths ≤8T, and the second-level controlled mode for >8T. Thus, examinations on all systems above 8T are subject to country-specific regulation such as IRB approval, although the boundary between first- and second-level controlled modes may change as more data become available. A number of transitory effects have been reported for high magnetic fields, some of which are related to motion through the magnetic field, which can lead to induction of electric currents in the conductive body tissue. These effects include vertigo, nausea, metallic taste, and light flashes. Reports on cognitive effects are inconsistent and may be related to indirect consequences of interactions with the vestibular system, e.g., hand-eye coordination. Due to the magnetohydrodynamic effect, electrocardiograms are distorted, particularly around the T-wave, impeding correct triggering of the R-wave. No significant vital sign effects have been observed up to 10.5T, the highest field for which human exposure data are available (Grant et al., 2020). Due to transport of the electrically conducting blood through the magnetic field, it has been speculated that heart rate or blood pressure elevation might be observed at magnetic fields higher than 10.5T, but the threshold field strength is still unclear.

Studies in small rodents like mice and rats have revealed behavioral anomalies such as circling in a preferred direction after exposure to 7T and above, e.g., counterclockwise circling when head-up in the magnet, clockwise when head down. Circling rate was higher after exposure to higher magnetic fields (Houpt et al., 2005). These effects and others such as nystagmus observed in human patients when lying stationary in high magnetic fields are attributed to interactions with the vestibular system. Ionic currents flowing in the endolymph of the inner ear generate forces on the cupulae (head rotation sensors) (Ward et al., 2019). Due to anatomical differences, the angle between the currents and the static magnetic field of a solenoidal magnet is smaller in humans than in rodents, so that any effects are likely to be less severe in humans.

Importantly, all of the aforementioned effects disappear either directly after exit from the magnetic field or shortly thereafter. A recent study performed in mice with extensive and repeated exposure to 16.4T revealed that the mice continued to circle even up to weeks after exposure cessation (Tkáč et al., 2021). A separate cohort in the study exposed to 10.5T did not show these effects. Further studies are required to verify and reveal the underlying mechanism of the observed behavior, which might be related to long-term impairment of the vestibular system. If such effects occur in humans and even if such effects resolve with time, they could have far-reaching impact on recommendations to individuals exposed to high magnetic fields, such as avoidance of driving after exposure or postponement of activities requiring fine-motor coordination. Ultimately, even transient physiological side effects may place a limit on the highest magnetic field to which subjects are willing to expose themselves.

Peak magnetic field exposure to personnel working with high-field systems will generally be less than for subjects undergoing examination in the center of the magnet. Nevertheless, maintenance procedures or cleaning of the bore may require special consideration, especially since exposure could be chronic.

A more detailed discussion of bioeffects, patience experience, and occupational safety can be found in Chapter 5.

37.4 Radiofrequency fields and coil requirements

As the main magnetic field strength of an MRI system is increased, the resonant frequency of the precessing nuclei increases in direct proportion. This implies that the wavelength decreases with field strength. Due to the high relative dielectric constant of human tissue, the wavelength in the human body is approximately 11–14 cm at 7T (Fiedler et al., 2018), where the resonant proton frequency is roughly 300 MHz. Up to 1.5T, the quasistatic approximation, i.e., no electric displacement currents in Maxwell's equations, can be utilized when performing analyses. This approximation starts to break down already at 3T and is no longer valid at 7T and higher. A consequence is that wave effects including constructive and destructive interferences have to be considered at fields $\geq$7T. The transition out of the near field is also the underlying reason why the SNR increases more than linearly with field strength (Le Ster et al., 2022; Pohmann et al., 2016). Moreover, SAR is expected to increase less than quadratically.

Numerical simulations reflecting the full Maxwell's equations demonstrate the excitation nonuniformities in the brain that can be expected as field strength increases if standard quadrature excitation is applied (Fig. 37.3) (Cao et al., 2015). Several approaches have been applied to address these issues including adiabatic RF pulses, but the most universal solution can be achieved through multichannel transmit RF coils. In the most straightforward application, the amplitudes and phases of each channel are adjusted relative to one another, termed static B_1^+ shimming (Padormo et al., 2016), which is akin to phased-array radar or beam steering in ultrasound imaging. In full parallel transmission (dynamic pTx), the RF pulses played out on each channel are independent of one another (Padormo et al., 2016). It should be noted that the spatial distribution of the associated RF E-field can also be adjusted to avoid or shift SAR hot spots. This capability is particularly attractive if subjects with conductive implants are to be examined. For a review of these techniques (see, e.g., Ladd et al., 2018; Padormo et al., 2016). Chapter 7 also provides a full discussion of B_1 inhomogeneity and its mitigation by RF pulse design and parallel RF transmission.

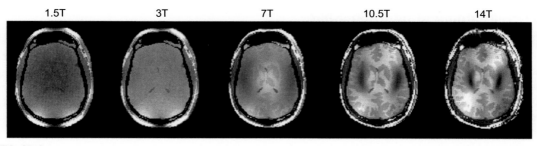

FIG. 37.3

Simulated MR images with quadrature excitation and reception for different field strengths. Constant TE of 3 ms and TR of 500 ms here lead to stronger T_1 weighting at higher field strengths, while decreasing wavelengths decrease both the size of regions of destructive interference and the distance between them. *Reproduced with permission Cao et al. (2015).*

As the Larmor resonant frequency goes up or the object to be imaged becomes larger, the greater the need for pTx, since the object size relative to the wavelength increases. At 7T, single-channel excitation in the brain has been moderately successful, whereas in the body, multichannel is definitely required for general imaging; in small animals, pTx is not required at all. At 14T, pTx will be requisite for high-quality imaging in the brain. In addition, one of the most convincing motivations for going to higher magnetic fields is the emergence of metabolic and physiological imaging with nuclei other than hydrogen. Aside from ^{19}F, whose resonance frequency is close to ^1H, all other nuclei can be imaged without pTx at 7T. However, at 14T, nuclei such as ^7Li and ^{31}P will also benefit from pTx (resonant frequencies of 232 and 241 MHz, respectively). Thus, any pTx hardware should support multiple frequencies in addition to protons to support X-nuclei work.

With additional independent transmit channels, additional degrees of freedom are added that facilitate tailoring the RF fields and promote uniformity or other desired properties. Currently at 7T, most vendors offer 8-channel pTx systems for research purposes. Also, 16-channel prototypes are available from major system vendors. Self-built systems with 32 channels have been constructed at some research sites, and it has been shown that the higher channel count provides advantages for whole-body imaging at 7T (Fiedler et al., 2021). Extrapolating this experience to 14T or higher, it can be expected that at least 16 transmit channels should be available for brain imaging. On the receive side, higher channel counts facilitate parallel imaging acceleration, and there is an inherent synergy between higher magnetic field strength and parallel imaging (Wiesinger et al., 2006). Receive arrays with up to 256 elements have been explored for brain imaging at 7T. It is important to maintain dominance of body tissue noise over coil noise, however, which becomes more and more difficult as the coil elements decrease in size, placing an upper limit on the channel count that provides practical advantages. High field strengths shift this relation in favor of smaller and smaller elements and thus higher receive channel counts. For a detailed discussion of RF coils and parallel imaging, the reader is referred to Chapters 8 and 9, respectively.

37.5 Anatomical neuroimaging

The tissue relaxation times as a function of B_0, documented in the Introduction, combined with the enhanced sensitivity, indicate a range of potential applications, but also some areas where little or no benefit is to be expected from EHF strengths. From the perspective of pulse sequence implementation, spin echo sequences will be the most challenging because of their high SAR and their sensitivity to inhomogeneity in B_1. Nevertheless, spin echo sequences have been applied at 21.1T in small animals, demonstrating the SNR increase achievable (Fig. 37.4).

Both inversion-recovery-based sequences and gradient echo sequences should be readily implemented, and hence applications based on T_1 or T_2^* contrasts are of greatest interest. In terms of contrast mechanisms, the most spectacular gains can be expected from substances in soft tissue that perturb the static magnetic field. These are best and easiest to investigate with T_2^*-weighted sequences, but there is also the effect on T_2 contrast caused by dynamic averaging due to motion in the local magnetic field gradients (Bartha et al., 2002). This effect causes the measured T_2 value to decrease. For DWI, the shortened T_2 values work against the sensitivity gain of higher field strengths, and it will require the application of very strong gradients to achieve increased sensitivity at field strengths above 10T. The following paragraphs will concentrate on those areas where realizable gains can be expected, namely T_1- and T_2^*-based techniques.

Even when moving from 1.5 to 4T, there were fears that the lengthening of T_1 values would reduce the efficacy of anatomical imaging based on T_1. Although pulse sequences based on short-TR, high-flip-angle acquisitions are indeed rarely used at UHF strength due to the longer T_1 values, T_1-weighted methods such as MPRAGE and MP2RAGE (Marques et al., 2010) benefit from the slower recovery after an inversion pulse, and the improvements obtained in going from 3 to 7T indicate that the increase in sensitivity more than compensates for any reduction in contrast. A target spatial resolution of 200 μm

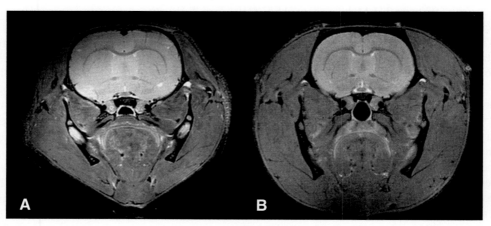

FIG. 37.4

In vivo proton MRI of rat head at 21.1T (A) and 9.4T (B). Both MR images were acquired using a spin echo pulse sequence and the same imaging parameters. The resolution of the images was $0.137 \times 0.137 \times 0.410 \, mm^3$. *Reproduced with permission from Schepkin et al. (2010).*

or better would appear to be eminently achievable at 14T without the need to average data over multiple sessions as has been done at 7T (Lüsebrink et al., 2021). At this level of resolution, there is a considerable potential for obtaining fundamental new insights. As T_1 contrast in the brain is closely associated with myelin concentration, the highly myelinated structures within the isocortex should now be easier to visualize. The stripes of Gennari in the primary visual cortex can already be detected at 3T, but imaging the thinner stripes of Baillarger, which can serve to delineate histologically different regions, has proven possible but challenging at 7T (Fracasso et al., 2016). Imaging of subcortical gray matter should also be greatly improved, including better segmentation of nuclei within structures such as the thalamus, hippocampus, and amygdala as well as the identification of nuclei that have hitherto proven difficult or impossible to identify.

No discussion of T_1-weighted imaging would be complete without mentioning time-of-flight angiography and arterial spin labeling. Both methods can be expected to benefit from increasing static field strength due to the prolonged T_1 of blood, which should increase the sensitivity of angiography, and reduce the transit time dependence and label decay in perfusion. In practice, the experience at 7T with these techniques has been somewhat divergent as it has been possible to generate fantastic angiograms with extremely high spatial resolution (Lüsebrink et al., 2021), whereas ASL (see Chapters 21 and 23) has been particularly challenging, mainly due to inhomogeneities in B_0 and B_1 as well as instabilities in the precession frequency at the preferred labeling position.

One of the biggest success stories of 7T is the contribution made by T_2^*-weighted imaging in its many manifestations (Wang and Liu, 2015). The basic gradient echo sequence is one of the simplest to implement, and its inherently low SAR facilitates the transposition to higher static field strengths. The main technical challenge will probably be the effect of physiological noise and motion, which will increase with TE. Dynamic B_0 shimming should be used in this context to correct for respiration- and motion-induced artifacts. There will clearly be a broad range of applications based on both high-resolution magnitude and phase data acquired at a single TE, and multiecho acquisitions. The reduction in T_2^* values will allow high contrast data to be acquired at shorter TEs, and for fewer echoes to be needed in a multiecho acquisition to accurately compute T_2^*. T_2^* contrast can inform on iron and myelin content as well as deoxyhemoglobin. In the isocortex, it can be used to identify laminar structures in a similar and complementary fashion to T_1-weighted imaging (Fukunaga et al., 2010). In subcortical gray matter, a particularly strong contrast will be obtained from nuclei with a high iron content (caudate, putamen, globus pallidus, substantia nigra, red nucleus). Using quantitative susceptibility mapping (QSM), it will be possible to distinguish para- (iron) and dia- (myelin) magnetic perturbers. Exciting preliminary data obtained from the human head at 10.5T are shown in Fig. 37.5.

Taken together, T_1-weighted imaging/R_1 mapping and T_2^*-weighted imaging/R_2^*, QSM mapping offer new perspectives for individually charting neuroanatomy and relating it to brain activation patterns. By improving the delineation of subcortical nuclei, and identifying hitherto obscured nuclei, we shall be able to better understand the role of these nuclei in brain function.

37.6 Functional neuroimaging

The use of blood oxygen level-dependent (BOLD) contrast to measure brain activation will benefit from both increased sensitivity and spatial specificity as the static field increases. As the optimum TE for measuring extravascular signal changes is matched to the T_2^* of gray matter, the efficiency will

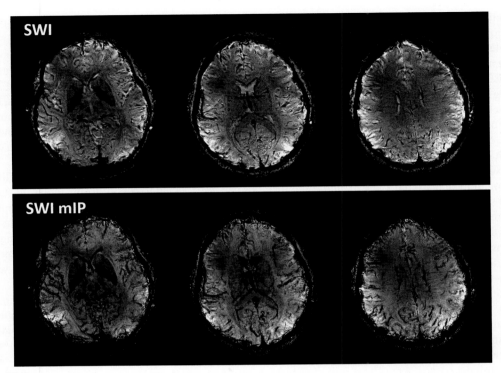

FIG. 37.5

Preliminary susceptibility-weighted imaging (SWI) data obtained at 10.5T and corresponding minimum intensity projections (SWI mIP). Results from three representative slices are shown. Projection thickness is 10.4 mm. Data were acquired at 0.21-mm isotropic in-plane resolution with 1.3-mm slice thickness from a 62.4-mm slab. A 16-channel transmit, 32-channel receive custom-built coil was used. *Data kindly provided by Kamil Uğurbil, CMRR, University of Minnesota Wu et al., 2022.*

also increase as T_2^* shortens. The disadvantage of the shorter T_2^* values and the associated increase in the strength of susceptibility gradients is that stronger shims and better shim correction will be needed. If it is possible to use spin echo fMRI within the constraints of SAR and B_1^+ inhomogeneity, then extravascular signal arising from the vicinity of the capillaries should become increasingly dominant (cf. Fig. 3 in Uludağ et al. (2009)). Another technique that has become increasingly popular in recent years, particularly for high spatial resolution imaging, is vascular space occupancy (VASO) (Huber et al., 2018), which in its simplest form utilizes an inversion-recovery experiment to null out the blood signal. At TE=0, the increase in cerebral blood volume (CBV) upon activation will cause a signal reduction. CBV changes are believed to be better localized to the arterioles and capillaries and should hence be better localized than BOLD, which essentially has a downstream activation profile. The lengthening of T_1 will reduce the efficiency of VASO, but the increase in the difference between the T_1 of blood and that of gray matter will increase the sensitivity, and hence a strong increase in sensitivity with increasing B_0 is theoretically possible.

Whichever imaging technique is chosen, there are a number of reasons why it only makes sense to perform functional neuroimaging at the highest possible spatial resolution. The first is simply economic: Why image at a resolution achievable at lower B_0? For both BOLD and VASO, there is also the question of the physiological noise level, as once the physiological noise regime has been reached, then there is no sensitivity benefit at higher field strength (Huber et al., 2018; Triantafyllou et al., 2016).

At present, there is a considerable growth in laminar fMRI performed both with gradient echo BOLD and VASO at 7T (Huber et al., 2018; Polimeni et al., 2010). At this field strength, it is possible to loosely parcel activation in the isocortex into granular, supra-, and infra-granular layers. This currently allows for relatively unsophisticated interrogation of feed-forward and feedback interactions between brain regions (Sharoh et al., 2019). The availability of still higher field strengths offers the possibility of identifying the six histological layers and thereby performing more detailed investigations of inter-laminar interactions both within and between regions. Columnar fMRI does not benefit from signal averaging across cortical depth, as does laminar fMRI, and this may explain why its growth has been less spectacular. It remains to be determined whether increased sensitivity alone will give an extra impetus to columnar imaging or whether further advances in stimulus paradigms will be necessary to generate applications outside of the primary cortices.

The expected improvements in anatomical neuroimaging will also benefit fMRI, mainly by enabling a closer examination of the relationship between structure and function. In the isocortex, the improved ability to histologically define regions will enable a better understanding of activation patterns and will allow averaging of activation across subjects in the same anatomically defined region, rather than the current situation of averaging via an anatomical atlas. Similarly, the improved identification of subcortical nuclei combined with increased functional sensitivity will make it possible to identify and study them at far greater detail. If all of these improvements are taken together, then it will be possible to perform whole-brain examinations at laminar resolution for both isocortex and larger subcortical regions allowing us to explore the feed-forward and feedback interactions within networks during task and rest.

A final word should be devoted to the potential application of proton spectroscopic imaging. The increased chemical shift dispersion should make it possible to measure the gamma-aminobutyric acid GABA signal without the need for spectral editing techniques. This will enable spectroscopic imaging of the major excitatory (glutamate) and inhibitory (GABA) neurotransmitters at 3–4 mm isotropic resolution with a whole-brain volume TR of the order of minutes. This will make it possible to examine the neurotransmitter distribution in health and disease and to interrogate the balance of excitation/inhibition as a function of cognitive state.

37.7 **Metabolic and physiological imaging**

A key promise of the MRI technique is its ability to deliver information beyond structural details and alterations. Metabolic and physiological changes will almost certainly manifest themselves before structural changes, enabling earlier disease detection, more precise choice of therapy, and direct monitoring of therapy response. Structure/microstructure is generally revealed by examining water or fat molecules in the body, which have very high abundance. Metabolic or physiological information, on the other hand, is often gathered through measurement of hydrogen in other molecules through MRI spectroscopy or spectroscopic imaging (MRS/I), or by the depiction of other nuclei, such as ^{31}P, ^{13}C, or

^{17}O (Ladd et al., 2018; Platt et al., 2021). Another opportunity is provided by ^{2}H: Because of its low natural abundance, it can be used to observe various processes by following the uptake of deuterated substrates such as glucose or water. Further important physiological information can be gained by assessment of ionic concentrations, e.g., of ^{23}Na, ^{39}K, or ^{35}Cl. The prerequisite is that the isotope to be captured has a nonzero spin. These MRI-active nuclei beyond ^{1}H are referred to as X-nuclei. Unfortunately, the potential of MRI to capture such information has not been fully achieved because of limited sensitivity: either the concentration of the target molecules is too low (much lower than water), the MRI-active isotope is not the dominant naturally occurring isotope of the target element, or the inherent sensitivity is lower than ^{1}H because of the lower gamma, often all three.

In the case of ^{1}H, an alternative to MRS/I is being explored based on transferring the signal from diluted biomolecules to the water pool: chemical exchange saturation transfer (CEST). In this technique, ^{1}H atoms attached to the target molecule are saturated with RF energy. If these atoms are in exchange with the hydrogen of water, the water signal is indirectly saturated over time. By subtracting the saturated water image from a water image before saturation, the concentration of the target molecule is revealed. This technique profits significantly from the enhanced sensitivity of higher magnetic fields as well as the greater spectral separation (Fig. 37.6), allowing confounding effects to be resolved at ultra-high magnetic fields. It also benefits from the longer T_1 relaxation times at higher magnetic fields, since more saturated water can be accumulated, increasing the CEST signal. The larger frequency separation from the water proton resonance is especially beneficial for CEST resonances close to water like amine, guanidyl, or hydroxyl groups, which often cannot be resolved with sufficient SNR at lower fields. CEST has thus far been predominantly applied to measuring protein concentration changes related to brain tumors, where it might prove useful in differentiating radiation necrosis from progression of brain metastases, in noninvasive histopathological grading of gliomas, or for predicting isocitrate dehydrogenase (IDH) mutation status. It has also been used to study stroke, epilepsy, and other neurological diseases and traumas (Ladd et al., 2018; Platt et al., 2021).

Beyond ^{1}H, the potential for X-nuclei imaging and spectroscopy is enormous. For instance, Na$^+$, K$^+$, and Cl$^-$ regulate excitation and inhibition of cells, and the concentration gradients between the intra- and extracellular compartments are maintained by the sodium-potassium pump (Na$^+$/K$^+$-ATPase pump). Any disease process that might disrupt ionic homeostasis is thus a candidate for ion imaging. Sodium imaging has, for example, been investigated in brain tumors, multiple sclerosis, stroke, epilepsy, Alzheimer's dementia, Parkinson's disease, Huntington's disease, and traumatic brain injury. It has also been utilized to investigate age-related dependencies in health. Phosphorus is important in studying energy metabolism, cell proliferation, and pH, and ^{17}O enables the direct visualization and quantitation of the cerebral metabolic rate of oxygen ($CMRO_2$).

For a more extensive overview of potential ^{1}H MRI/S and CEST as well as X-nuclei applications at high magnetic fields, see for example Platt et al. (2021). Ultra-high magnetic fields bring these applications closer to practical implementation through higher sensitivity and/or greater spectral separation between individual spectral peaks. Whereas single-voxel spectroscopy is often pursued at lower field strengths, there is a distinct emergence of spectroscopic imaging at higher magnetic fields. For spectroscopic techniques in general, the metabolic profile can be extended through detection and differentiation of additional resonances, providing higher specificity. Another important advantage is the reduction of partial voluming effects through reduced voxel sizes that can contaminate and dilute the signal of interest. Even higher magnetic fields make such techniques more feasible within reasonable measurement times. If the SNR at 14 vs. 7T increases as predicted for ^{1}H, voxel volumes can be

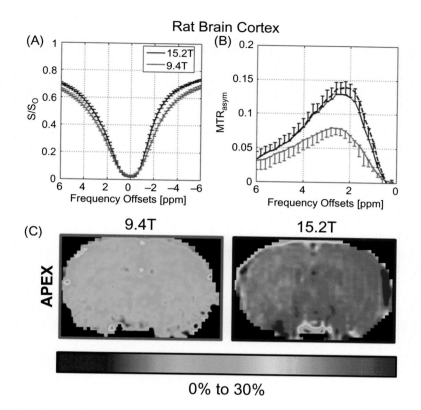

FIG. 37.6

In vivo Z-spectra (A) and MTR asymmetry curve of the rat brain cortex (B), and APEX maps (C), at high power ($\omega_1 = 500$ Hz, $T_{SL} = 0.15$ s) measured at 9.4 and 15.2T. Dashed blue line in (B) indicates 15.2T data compensated for differences in relaxation parameters between the two fields. APEX was determined from the MTR asymmetry at 2.5 ppm. Clearly, a significant increase in MTR_{asym} was observed at 15.2T. APEX=amine-water proton exchange; ω_1=Rabi frequency; T_{SL}=spin-lock time; MTR=magnetization transfer ratio; MTR_{asym}=asymmetric magnetization transfer ratio. *Reproduced with permission from Chung et al. (2017).*

reduced by a factor of three or acquisition times can be cut by a factor of 9, assuming other effects such as changes in relaxation times and SAR are ignored. Note, though, that for lower-gamma nuclei, the quasistatic approximation may still hold, leading to only a linear or slightly better increase in SNR.

37.8 Human MRI systems >11.7T

There are currently projects in China, Europe, and the USA exploring the possibility of going to an even higher magnetic field than 11.7T for human application (Budinger and Bird, 2018; Wu et al., 2020; Xu et al., 2021), all at different stages of realization. The most likely field choice for the next step after

11.7T is 14T, i.e., 600 MHz proton resonant frequency. As mentioned in the Magnet Design section, such systems will necessitate at least partial use of Nb_3Sn or HTS. In addition to the activities of government-funded research organizations like the French Alternative Energies and Atomic Energy Commission (CEA), the Chinese Academy of Sciences (CAS), or the United States National High Magnetic Field Laboratory (NHMFL), at least two commercial vendors have proposed 14T designs based on Nb_3Sn, but no details of these designs are available in the public domain. A third vendor recently published a design based on HTS Bi2223 wire (Li and Roell, 2021), which would be operated in driven mode. This design is interesting since it pursues a double pancake geometry and relies completely on conduction cooling (no liquid helium), leading to a very compact magnet with coil dimensions excluding cryostat of 1.9 m long × 1.3 m outer diameter. The weight of the superconducting wire would be 8.5 tons, but the total magnet weight including formers, structural components, superconducting shim coils, and cryostat would be on the order of 15 tons. In early 2023, funding was announced in the Netherlands for a 14T project based on this magnet design.

Even if existing systems >10T and these proposed magnets >11.7T do not enter into clinical use for diagnosis of individual patients for economic reasons, these systems harbor enormous potential to expand our fundamental knowledge of brain physiology in both disease and health, reveal novel information on brain aging, and provide noninvasive insights into cognitive brain function.

References

Bartha, R., Michaeli, S., Merkle, H., et al., 2002. In vivo ^1H_2O T_2^+ measurement in the human occipital lobe at 4T and 7T by Carr-Purcell MRI: detection of microscopic susceptibility contrast. Magn. Reson. Med. 47, 742–750.

Budinger, T.F., Bird, M.D., 2018. MRI and MRS of the human brain at magnetic fields of 14T to 20T: technical feasibility, safety, and neuroscience horizons. NeuroImage 168, 509–531.

Cao, Z., Park, J., Cho, Z.-H., Collins, C.M., 2015. Numerical evaluation of image homogeneity, signal-to-noise ratio, and specific absorption rate for human brain imaging at 1.5, 3, 7, 10.5, and 14T in an 8-channel transmit/receive array. J. Magn. Reson. Imaging 41, 1432–1439.

Chung, J.J., Choi, W., Jin, T., Lee, J.H., Kim, S.-G., 2017. Chemical-exchange-sensitive MRI of amide, amine and NOE at 9.4 T versus 15.2 T. NMR Biomed. 30, e3740.

Fiedler, T.M., Ladd, M.E., Bitz, A.K., 2018. SAR simulations & safety. NeuroImage 168, 33–58.

Fiedler, T.M., Orzada, S., Flöser, M., et al., 2021. Performance analysis of integrated RF microstrip transmit antenna arrays with high channel count for body imaging at 7 T. NMR Biomed. 34, e4515.

Fracasso, A., van Veluw, S.J., Visser, F., et al., 2016. Myelin contrast across lamina at 7T, ex-vivo and in-vivo dataset. Data Brief 8, 990–1003.

Fukunaga, M., Li, T.-Q., van Gelderen, P., et al., 2010. Layer-specific variation of iron content in cerebral cortex as a source of MRI contrast. Proc. Natl. Acad. Sci. U. S. A. 107, 3834–3839.

Grant, A., Metzger, G.J., Van de Moortele, P.-F., et al., 2020. 10.5 T MRI static field effects on human cognitive, vestibular, and physiological function. Magn. Reson. Imaging 73, 163–176.

Houpt, T.A., Pittman, D.W., Riccardi, C., et al., 2005. Behavioral effects on rats of high strength magnetic fields generated by a resistive electromagnet. Physiol. Behav. 86, 379–389.

Huber, L., Ivanov, D., Handwerker, D.A., et al., 2018. Techniques for blood volume fMRI with VASO: from low-resolution mapping towards sub-millimeter layer-dependent applications. NeuroImage 164, 131–143.

Krishnamurthy, L.C., Liu, P., Xu, F., Uh, J., Dimitrov, I., Lu, H., 2014. Dependence of blood T(2) on oxygenation at 7 T: in vitro calibration and in vivo application. Magn. Reson. Med. 71, 2035–2042.

Ladd, M.E., Bachert, P., Meyerspeer, M., et al., 2018. Pros and cons of ultra-high-field MRI/MRS for human application. Prog. Nucl. Magn. Reson. Spectrosc. 109, 1–50.

Le Ster, C., Grant, A., Van de Moortele, P.-F., et al., 2022. Magnetic field strength dependent SNR gain at the center of a spherical phantom and up to 11.7T. Magn. Reson. Med. 88, 2131–2138.

Li, Y., Roell, S., 2021. Key designs of a short-bore and cryogen-free high temperature superconducting magnet system for 14 T whole-body MRI. Supercond. Sci. Technol. 34, 125005.

Lüsebrink, F., Mattern, H., Yakupov, R., et al., 2021. Comprehensive ultrahigh resolution whole brain in vivo MRI dataset as a human phantom. Sci. Data 8, 138.

Marques, J.P., Kober, T., Krueger, G., van der Zwaag, W., Van de Moortele, P.-F., Gruetter, R., 2010. MP2RAGE, a self-bias field corrected sequence for improved segmentation and T_1-mapping at high field. NeuroImage 49, 1271–1281.

Padormo, F., Beqiri, A., Hajnal, J.V., Malik, S.J., 2016. Parallel transmission for ultrahigh-field imaging. NMR Biomed. 29, 1145–1161.

Parizh, M., Lvovsky, Y., Sumption, M., 2017. Conductors for commercial MRI magnets beyond NbTi: requirements and challenges. Supercond. Sci. Technol. 30, 014007.

Peters, A.M., Brookes, M.J., Hoogenraad, F.G., et al., 2007. T_2^* measurements in human brain at 1.5, 3 and 7 T. Magn. Reson. Imaging 25, 748–753.

Platt, T., Ladd, M.E., Paech, D., 2021. 7 tesla and beyond: advanced methods and clinical applications in magnetic resonance imaging. Investig. Radiol. 56, 705–725.

Pohmann, R., Speck, O., Scheffler, K., 2016. Signal-to-noise ratio and MR tissue parameters in human brain imaging at 3, 7, and 9.4 tesla using current receive coil arrays. Magn. Reson. Med. 75, 801–809.

Polimeni, J.R., Fischl, B., Greve, D.N., Wald, L.L., 2010. Laminar analysis of 7T BOLD using an imposed spatial activation pattern in human V1. NeuroImage 52, 1334–1346.

Rooney, W.D., Johnson, G., Li, X., et al., 2007. Magnetic field and tissue dependencies of human brain longitudinal ^1H_2O relaxation in vivo. Magn. Reson. Med. 57, 308–318.

Schepkin, V.D., Brey, W.W., Gor'kov, P.L., Grant, S.C., 2010. Initial in vivo rodent sodium and proton MR imaging at 21.1 T. Magn. Reson. Imaging 28, 400–407.

Sharoh, D., van Mourik, T., Bains, L.J., et al., 2019. Laminar specific fMRI reveals directed interactions in distributed networks during language processing. Proc. Natl. Acad. Sci. U. S. A. 116, 21185–21190.

Tkáč, I., Benneyworth, M.A., Nichols-Meade, T., et al., 2021. Long-term behavioral effects observed in mice chronically exposed to static ultra-high magnetic fields. Magn. Reson. Med. 86, 1544–1559.

Triantafyllou, C., Polimeni, J.R., Keil, B., Wald, L.L., 2016. Coil-to-coil physiological noise correlations and their impact on functional MRI time-series signal-to-noise ratio. Magn. Reson. Med. 76, 1708–1719.

Uğurbil, K., Van de Moortele, P.-F., Grant, A., et al., 2021. Progress in imaging the human torso at the ultrahigh fields of 7 and 10.5 T. Magn. Reson. Imaging Clin. N. Am. 29, e1–e19.

Uludağ, K., Müller-Bierl, B., Uğurbil, K., 2009. An integrative model for neuronal activity-induced signal changes for gradient and spin echo functional imaging. NeuroImage 48, 150–165.

Vedrine, P., Gilgrass, G., Aubert, G., et al., 2015. Iseult/INUMAC whole body 11.7 T MRI magnet. IEEE Trans. Appl. Supercond. 25, 1–4.

Wang, Y., Liu, T., 2015. Quantitative susceptibility mapping (QSM): decoding MRI data for a tissue magnetic biomarker. Magn. Reson. Med. 73, 82–101.

Ward, B.K., Roberts, D.C., Otero-Millan, J., Zee, D.S., 2019. A decade of magnetic vestibular stimulation: from serendipity to physics to the clinic. J. Neurophysiol. 121, 2013–2019.

Wiesinger, F., Van de Moortele, P.-F., Adriany, G., De Zanche, N., Ugurbil, K., Pruessmann, K.P., 2006. Potential and feasibility of parallel MRI at high field. NMR Biomed. 19, 368–378.

Winkler, S.A., Alejski, A., Wade, T., McKenzie, C.A., Rutt, B.K., 2017. On the accurate analysis of vibroacoustics in head insert gradient coils. Magn. Reson. Med. 78, 1635–1645.

Wu, K., Wu, J., Wu, Y., et al., 2020. An optimized design approach for 14 T actively shielded MRI magnets. IEEE Trans. Appl. Supercond. 30, 1–4.

Wu, X., Grant, A., Ma, X., Auerbach, E., Ladder, J., Sadeghi-Tarakameh, A., Eryaman, Y., Lagore, R., Tavaf, N., Van de Moortele, P.-F., Adriany, G., Ugurbil, K., 2022. Susceptibility-weighted imaging and quantitative susceptibility mapping of the human brain at 10.5 tesla: an initial experience. In: Proceeding of the International Society for Magnetic Resonance in Medicine. Presented at the Joint Annual Meeting ISMRM-ESMRMB, 0647.

Xu, A., Zhu, Y., Wang, J., et al., 2021. Experimental research of the new developed high-Jc Nb3Sn superconducting strand for 14 T MRI magnet. IEEE Trans. Appl. Supercond. 31, 1–4.

Zhang, X., Petersen, E.T., Ghariq, E., et al., 2013. In vivo blood T(1) measurements at 1.5 T, 3 T, and 7 T. Magn. Reson. Med. 70, 1082–1086.

Index

Note: Page numbers followed by "*f*" indicate figures, "*t*" indicate tables, and "*b*" indicate boxes.

Printed in the United States
by Baker & Taylor Publisher Services